Public Record Office Handbook No. 19

TRACING YOUR ANCESTORS IN THE PUBLIC RECORD OFFICE

Amanda Bevan

Sixth edition

PUBLIC RECORD OFFICE

Sixth edition first published in 2002 by

Public Record Office
Richmond
Surrey
TW9 4DU

www.pro.gov.uk/

First published in 1981 by HMSO (0 11440 114 4)
Second edition 1982 (0 11440 180 2)
Third edition 1984 (0 11440 186 1)
Fouth edition 1990 (0 11440 222 1)
Fifth edition published in 1999 by PRO (1 873162 61 8)

A catalogue record for this book is available from the British Library

ISBN 1 903365 34 1

Cover photographs: (front cover) Samuel Coleridge-Taylor, 1901 (PRO, COPY 1/451);
Tom Mann, 1897 (photographer: James Prescott Tildesley; PRO, COPY 1/432);
Oliver George Robert Fox, First World War soldier, taken from the 'PRO Scrapbook'
(PRO, PRO 8/55); Frances Harvey, 1905 (photographer: Alfred Cooper; PRO,
COPY 1/490) (back cover) Thomas Edmund Wooderson, 1887 (PRO, COPY 1/382)

Printed in Great Britain by Antony Rowe, Chippenham, Wiltshire

TRACING YOUR ANCESTORS
IN THE
PUBLIC RECORD OFFICE

Contents

Preface

◆ ◆ ◆

This is the sixth edition of *Tracing Your Ancestors*, and the third that I have largely or wholly written. The task does not get any easier. This edition covers the opening of the 1901 census, and the transfer of personnel records from the First World War – both of which will introduce many more people to the joys of historical research. In addition, the extraordinary growth of computer and Internet resources has made the pace of change much greater. The range of documents and material now available is so large that it is almost beyond the comprehension of any one person. As usual, I have had to rely on my excellent and knowledgeable colleagues on the enquiry desks. This book could not exist without them.

Particular thanks are due to Helen Watt and Mark Forrest of the E 179 Project, who revised Chapters 5, 41 and 43 for this edition, and to Ruth Paley whose Chapters 38–40 and 47a remain largely unchanged. I would also like to thank Dave Annal, Mandy Banton, Keith Bartlett, Alan Bowgen, Paul Carter, Stella Colwell, Bruno Derrick, Alistair Hanson, Liz Hore, Hilary Jones, Roger Kershaw, Sue Lumas, Ann Morton, Stephen O'Connor, Brian Oldham, Lee Oliver, Bruno Pappalardo, William Spencer and Chris Watts for their help and encouragement, and for their patience with my lengthy interrogations of their superior knowledge of the subject under discussion. Thanks are also due to Alan Moore of the Decree Absolute Section, Principal Registry of the Family Division, for helping me to investigate the records in his care. I also owe much gratitude to Deborah Pownall, whose picture research has added immeasurably to the book, and to Kathryn Sleight, for seeing it so unflappably through the press.

My greatest thanks, however, are owed to Tom, Anna, Edmund and Miles Brass, whose family life has suffered through the last year – and whose support and encouragement have been unstinting. As they are not even interested in the subject (yet), what a credit they are to the power of family affection!

February 2002

1

Introduction

◆ ◆ ◆

1.1 About this book

This book is not about how to conduct family history research, or any other kind of historical research. Instead, it is a detailed subject guide to using the documents kept at the Public Record Office (PRO) and the Family Records Centre (FRC) to discover as much as possible of the lives of individual people in the past. The collections discussed here are 'public records', produced in the course of government and the dispensing of justice. Although its main users are people undertaking historical research for the love of it, professional historians or biographers should also find this book a useful guide to records outside their own areas of expert knowledge.

This version is now the sixth edition, and my third. I have to say the task gets bigger every time. This edition in particular is informed by my experience on the enquiry desks over the last four years, learning from my colleagues and from you, the researchers. I have also spent a lot of time working with colleagues on the material that marks many people's earliest contact with the Public Record Office. I have learned so much from all of this that I have had to conduct a major revision of much of the book, in the hope of making things clearer. Some of the longer chapters have been subdivided into **a**, **b** and **c** and so on to create sub-chapters. I hope the whole thing is a little easier to use, but the records are complicated, the finding aids are complicated – history is complicated. It's hardly surprising if this book is complicated too.

In addition, this edition incorporates three of the great changes absorbed by the PRO since the 1999 edition. The first is the enormous interest generated by the opening of the service records of the First World War. So many families were affected by the War that the demand for these records is phenomenal. These documents have shot up to become the most popular records after the census. The second is the opening of the 1901 census, in its wholly new form as a searchable computer record. This has made family history research accessible to many more people. The third change is the release into the public domain not of new records but of old information. The computer version of our catalogue, PROCAT, has shone a spotlight into many a forgotten corner of our historic records, while its availability on the Internet has opened them up to the whole world. Of course, the PRO is not alone in making resources available on the

Internet, and many websites have been added to this edition. However, historical resources on the web are so great in number that very many more have not been mentioned. If you want to explore this route, you are strongly recommended to get hold of Christian's *The Genealogist's Internet* to use alongside this book. Incidentally, if you want to explore the Internet but do not have access to a computer, ask at your local library about provision of Internet access by the council.

Back at the PRO, new accessions are likely to slow down for a while. Second World War personnel records are not likely to hit the PRO until the 2010s, after the 1911 census in 2012. However, we foresee many new developments on the computer front – for example, the latest initiative of putting our pre-1858 wills online should transform family and local history research. At the same time we realize that the computer catalogue itself, good though it is, needs to have more detailed entries to be of maximum use. For the next decade, the major developments are likely to be in improved access to existing holdings, rather than in new accessions. As detailed indexes and document descriptions are entered into PROCAT, we expect underused series to become more popular, and old favourites to gain a new readership. It really has worked a major transformation in making information more accessible.

1.2 Family history research: starting out

The best place to begin family history research is at home, gathering as much factual information, memories and memorabilia as you can from members of your family. You may be surprised at how much you can accumulate. Putting it together will bring out all kinds of queries, as you realise that there are unexplained gaps. Answering those queries may lead to more questions, and so on until you find that you need to start looking outside the family for information. You will find that you probably have to keep going back to revisit family memories as you find out more.

Record Offices are not the place to start family history research, because neither local nor central government has ever had much interest in recording family history. We sometimes get questions from people who expect to find a

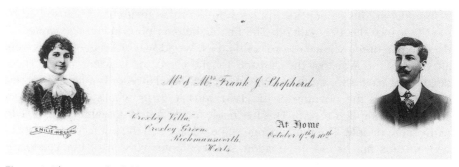

Figure 1 These two look like newly-weds. A search for their marriage certificate (see **3a**) should clear up a few questions – *what year? was she moving to a new area?* – and maybe raise a few more. (PRO, COPY 1/453)

government file kept on their family over the centuries. This was not the case. Records were kept only when people came into contact with government at some point – when their birth, marriage or death was registered; when they completed a census return; when they entered one of the armed services; when they committed a crime; when they were supposed to pay taxes. Because government had no interest in tracking individuals, there are no official indexes to records that will give all the references to John Smith of Little Puddington.

You really do need to have a list of answerable questions, and as much information as you can, before you go to the trouble and expense of visiting a record office. To help you work out what questions you can expect to get answers for, try your local library for books on how to research family history.

There are five books that I find particularly interesting for different reasons. The Reader's Digest book *Explore Your Family's Past* provides a general guide, with illustrations of many different types of documents. Mark Herber's *Ancestral Trails* is an unsurpassed overview of all the records that can be used by family historians, both locally and nationally. Peter Christian's book, *The Genealogist's Internet*, is an invaluable guide to making good use of the huge number of online resources. Stella Colwell's *Family Roots: Discovering the Past in the Public Record Office* uses several in-depth studies to show the wealth of information that can be discovered in the PRO.

David Hey's *Family Names and Family History* is a rather different book. It shows how very many surnames and families remain local to their place of origin, over centuries. Some surnames can even be traced back to individual farmsteads. Hey cites Kevin Schurer's fascinating research on surnames in the 1881 census. Apparently 1,000 surnames covered 60 per cent of the population (my maiden name Bevan being one of them). But there were very many more surnames – 30,000 rare ones (such as my married name Brass) were used by only 10 per cent of the population. If you have a rare name in the family, you are in luck – they are much easier to trace!

The bibliographies in this book contain, besides works for further reading, information on various aids to finding and understanding records. Many of the books cited are available in the PRO. Some can be bought in the shops at the PRO and at the FRC. The PRO bookshop, which runs a mail order service, currently holds about 250 family history titles: for more information check the PRO website (see **1.5**), or contact the PRO. Most of the books recommended can be read in the Guildhall Library (a public library with an excellent genealogical collection), the library of the Society of Genealogists and in good reference libraries. If it is more convenient, you could try inter-library loan, through your local lending library: this is usually available for a very small fee.

Something you should do at some point is to make sure that you are not duplicating research someone else has already done. Try the *Register of One Name Studies,* an alphabetical listing of surnames that have been registered with the Guild of One Name Studies by researchers. Other sources are the *National Genealogical Directory*, produced annually by Burchall, and the *British Isles Genealogical Register*, produced on microfiche by the Federation of Family

History Societies (FFHS). You may also want to check Gibson's guide to *Unpublished Personal Name Indexes.*

A good early step is to contact your local family history society. There is a national network of these throughout the British Isles, most of which publish journals. These organizations can be extremely helpful in providing guidance and contact between family historians. A list of family history societies and like bodies appears in the *Family History News and Digest,* the journal of the FFHS. The address of the FFHS is in **48**. They also publish an excellent series of brief and inexpensive guides to records. You will find among their members people from all walks of life, who have turned their various skills and unvaried enthusiasm and energy into the hunt for their own family history. Many have also turned to the task of making sources for family history known and available. They index records of no direct interest to themselves, on the understanding that someone, somewhere else, is indexing just the set of records they always needed and never knew existed. You will have plugged into a network of interesting and interested people: family historians seem to discover new friends at an even faster rate than 'new' ancestors!

If you have access to the Internet, you will find that a wealth of advice, catalogues and even actual information is available online. Try the family history gateway site www.familyrecords.gov.uk as this leads you on to the official websites for the various United Kingdom national archives you will need to use for family history research. Another UK-based site of great interest is www.genuki.org.uk which covers every county in the UK, and has much information on family history societies amongst many other things. Two excellent US-based sites are www.cyndislist.com with over 65,000 links to other sites, and www.rootsweb.com with over 19,000 mailing lists. To keep up to date, check out Peter Christian's regular 'Internet Section' in *Ancestors*, the PRO's own family history magazine. A word of warning: there are very few original documents online, so most of the information comes from secondary sources. This means that the original (which may be damaged or illegible) has been read by someone and copied out, perhaps several times, before reaching you in a list or index. It may not be accurate, and should not be taken as proof. You must evaluate the information yourself: think about its source, how it fits with what you know, how it fits with what is likely. Try to check original sources whenever you can. Many archives and record offices are able to send you photocopies of the original documents for only a small charge, and you can often use the Internet to order by e-mail.

You may find that you live reasonably near one of the excellent Family History Centres run by the Church of Jesus Christ of Latter-day Saints/The Genealogical Society of Utah (LDS). To find out the nearest centre, write with a stamped addressed envelope to The Genealogical Society of Utah, British Isles Family History Service Centre. Their main UK centre is the Hyde Park Family History Centre (addresses in **48**). The LDS have filmed and indexed vast runs of records vital to the pursuit of family history; and these films can be seen at their local centres, for a small monthly fee. Most have to be ordered from their headquarters in Utah, and take about a month to come. All centres have a copy of the *International Genealogical Index* (see **3b.1**), the index to parish registers, and other sources, and many have the CD-ROM *FamilySearch* (or access to the Internet version), based on the parish registers, which can be a wonderful source for family history before 1837. *FamilySearch* can also be seen at the FRC. The LDS also maintains a Family Registry on microfiche.

Another source for centralized genealogical information is the Society of Genealogists in central London (www.sog.org.uk, address in **48**). They have an incomparable library of published and unpublished source material, including transcripts of many parish registers, listed by county in *Parish Register Copies in the Library of the Society of Genealogists*. You can pay an annual fee to join the Society, or you can pay a daily or hourly charge to use the library.

If you have good reason for believing that your family is entitled to bear a coat of arms, write to the officer-in-waiting at the College of Arms (address in **48**). The College has many pedigrees among its collections and officers will undertake research into these. Scotland and Ireland have their own heraldic authorities.

Once you know what questions you want to ask, and where you can reasonably expect to get them answered, you will need to find out how to get there. You could invest in Gibson and Peskett's inexpensive pamphlet, *Record Offices and How to Find Them* (a typically practical and helpful FFHS guide, which includes maps). The reference work *British Archives*, by Foster and Sheppard lists record offices, other archives, and museums or libraries holding records. As well as giving brief details of their collections, this gives opening times, addresses, phone numbers and conditions of access. *Record Repositories in Great Britain* gives a brief guide to the same type of information (but not the collection details). For information on the whereabouts of private papers and manorial documents, try the Historic Manuscripts Commission (www.hmc. gov.uk). For advice on researching in archives, try www.arts-scheme.co.uk.

1.3 About the Public Record Office

The Public Record Office (PRO) is based at Kew, in the southwest London borough of Richmond. It houses one of the finest, most complete archives in the world. We hold the shared public record created in the course of public administration by the central government of the United Kingdom in its various historic forms. Its odd Victorian name rather conceals the fact that it is effectively the National Archives of the 'United Kingdom'. This means primarily the records of overarching national institutions, such as the Army or the Foreign Office, and of the internal government of England and Wales. These government records run unbroken from Domesday Book in 1086. The respective National Archives of Scotland and Ireland, the Public Record Office of Northern Ireland, and the National Library of Wales hold most of their purely national records of their time as part of the United Kingdom, and of their time as independent states. However, much centrally generated or stored material about all these countries (especially Wales) is held at the PRO. The PRO is also one of the world's major international archives, with vast holdings on the former British colonies, and on foreign relations over eight centuries. It is also one of the greatest map archives of the world.

Until recently, public records were not normally made available for reading until 30 years after the date of the last entry. However, many documents are now being opened at round about 25 years, when they are physically transferred from the department that created them to the PRO. Some documents are closed for much longer: an obvious example is the census, which is closed for 100 years to safeguard personal confidentiality.

All this may sound extremely daunting. I hope you will be pleasantly surprised on visiting the PRO, if you have not been here yet, or for some time. When I look back to my first visit in 1979 to the old Victorian building that was the PRO in Chancery Lane, the whole experience was one of entering a fascinating institution, run according to an arcane system that you had to deduce from the smallest amounts of evidence – with the fear that a question would be met with ridicule. I have to say that this was a false impression: the staff were as kind and friendly as anyone could hope, once I dared to ask them a question. It took me nearly six months of daily attendance to dare ask. (There was a sign saying *Silence* over the enquiry desk and I, and many others, took it literally.) And when I eventually worked out what it was, the system proved to have a rational basis – quite efficient actually, as long as you had a good understanding of the finer points of medieval administration.

I am happy to say that this Dickensian situation no longer applies. Huge efforts have been made by the staff to demystify the place. Recent comments from readers seem to indicate some success:

'As always the staff were extremely helpful. It is a real pleasure coming to the PRO to undertake research.'
'How very impressed I am by the kindness, patience, dedication and knowledge of all your staff.'
'What a wonderful day we have each time we come.'

So please ask if you need to – we are here to (try to) answer your questions. For practical details about the PRO, see **1.9**.

1.4 About the Family Records Centre

The Family Records Centre (FRC) is run jointly by the PRO and the General Register Office of England and Wales. It opened in 1997, on the closure of the Census Rooms at the PRO's former site in Chancery Lane, and of the General Register Office public searchroom at St Catherine's House. Some books and people still use the old names.

At the FRC you can see the main genealogical records held:
- by the PRO
  - censuses (in surrogate form) from 1841–1901
  - the major archive of wills before 1858
  - nonconformist records of births, marriages and deaths before 1837

- Fleet marriage registers before 1754
- by the General Register Office of England and Wales
  - indexes to civil registers of birth, marriage and death, 1837 to date
  - indexes to adoption records 1927 to date.

The other main genealogical sources, held elsewhere, are:

- parish registers of births, marriages and deaths before 1837: held locally, usually in county record offices;
- wills proved in local church courts before 1858: usually in county record offices;
- wills after 1858, held at the Principal Registry of the Family Division's Probate Searchroom, sometimes still referred to as being at its old location in Somerset House (address in **48**).

For practical details about the FRC, see **1.8**.

1.5 The PRO and FRC websites

The PRO has a very popular website at www.pro.gov.uk where you can:

- search the PRO catalogue;
- view online exhibitions about history and the records;
- e-mail an enquiry, advanced order, or photocopy order;
- check out opening times, new accessions, publications, bookshop, independent researchers, etc.

To access the 1901 census, use www.census.pro.gov.uk and to access the wills online, use www.pro-online.pro.gov.uk. The FRC has its own website, at www.familyrecords.gov.uk/frc.htm.

The online catalogue also contains copies of our records information leaflets, which are often more detailed in their instructions than the information given in this book. They are designed to be used in the reading rooms, and can be printed off before coming, or picked up when you arrive.

If you have any queries on the websites, ring the PRO during opening hours for immediate help, or e-mail us for a less quick response.

1.6 Paying for research to be done for you

The staff at the PRO and the FRC can help you with advice and guidance, but we cannot actually do research for you. The PRO and the FRC are open reference institutions ('an amazing palace of reference' in one researcher's description), where people come to the search rooms to conduct their own research. If this is not possible, then you can ask someone to come on your behalf, or you can employ a professional researcher or record agent, who will undertake research for a fee.

The PRO has lists of independent researchers on its website, and can also supply a printed list in response to a phone call or written request. The arrangement between you and the agent will be of a purely private nature. The PRO and FRC can accept no responsibility for any aspect of the arrangements made between record agents and their clients. The Association of Genealogists and Researchers in Archives (see **48**) can also put you in touch with a researcher accredited to the Association.

If you know the exact document reference, photocopies can be ordered by post: there is a minimum charge for this service (£10 at the time of writing). Documents will be copied only if it can be done without causing damage.

1.7 Children at the PRO and FRC

Neither the FRC nor the PRO is a suitable place for young children. The reading rooms are intended to be quiet or silent areas, where records can be consulted without fear of damage. Any children must stay with you at all times, in case of emergency. If they cause a disturbance to other readers, you will have to take them out of the reading rooms. Children are rarely as interested in your research as you might wish, and get bored quickly. Spinning round on chairs attracts cross glances from other readers. The poor child can't even colour in quietly, as only graphite pencils are allowed at the PRO.

From the age of 14 school pupils can get their own ticket for the PRO, if an adult with a reader's ticket accompanies them and vouches for them. If they want to come unaccompanied they have to have a letter on school headed paper signed by the head teacher.

If you need to bribe your way to a day at the PRO or FRC, the shops at both sites sell a range of 'historic' gifts: some of these might appeal to children or to the person looking after them for you!

1.8 Practical details: the FRC

The FRC is open from 10 a.m. on Tuesdays, 9.30 a.m. on Saturdays, and 9 a.m. every other weekday. It closes at 7 p.m. on Tuesday and Thursday, and 5 p.m. on the other days. The FRC is closed on Sundays and public holidays. A reader's ticket is not needed. Pens can be used, and there are power points for laptops in the census and wills searchroom. There is a shop, a cyber-café and an eating area in the building, and several places sell meals and sandwiches nearby. There are lockers if you wish to use them: a £1 coin is needed, but is returned after use.

The FRC has ramp access for wheelchairs and a lift to both floors. It also has three parking spaces reserved for disabled readers, which you have to book in advance by ringing 020 7533 6436. There are some motorized microfilm readers with zoom facilities, for disabled readers, and magnifiers are available for printed sources or copies. If you are totally blind or have limited mobility, try to come with a sighted or more mobile friend. Once in the building, there is still a considerable amount of walking backwards and forwards during the course of a visit.

The Family Records Centre's address is

Post	Family Records Centre, 1 Myddelton Street, London EC1R 1UW
Telephone	Census, will and general enquiries: 020 8392 5300
	Birth, marriage, death, adoption and overseas enquiries: 0151 471 4800
E-mail	Census, will and general enquiries: enquiry@pro.gov.uk
	Birth, marriage, death, adoption and overseas enquiries:
	certificate.services@ons.gov.uk
Fax	020 8392 5307
Minicom	020 8392 9198

Postal enquiries for certificates should be sent to the General Register Office, Smedley Hydro, Trafalgar Road, Southport, Merseyside PR8 2HH. The GRO website is at www.statistics.gov.uk where you can look under 'Services' for information about ordering certificates, as well as finding out about new services.

The FRC is a very busy and popular place. It has an extensive range of leaflets giving you up-to-date guidance on how to use the records and finding aids there, which you will find on your arrival. If you want to be forearmed, or if you are planning several trips, the best thing to do is beg, borrow, steal or even buy a copy of Colwell's *The Family Records Centre: a User's Guide*. It is fully illustrated with examples of the various certificates, census returns and other records that can be seen there, and will give you helpful guidance so that you can carry out your research most effectively.

If you want to take copies, there are self-service reader-printers.

1.9 Practical details: the PRO

The reading rooms at the PRO are open to the public until 5 p.m. Monday to Saturday, with late night opening on Tuesday and Thursday until 7 p.m. They open at 9 a.m. except on Tuesdays (10 a.m.) and Saturdays (9.30 a.m.) Documents cannot be ordered until 9.30 a.m., and this service is currently suspended on Saturdays between 12 and 1.30 p.m. The PRO is closed on Sundays, public holidays and during stocktaking (one week, normally at the beginning of December). There is a restaurant on site, where you can also eat your own food. There is also a bookshop, a cyber-café where you can access the Internet for a small fee, and a museum.

You will need to get a reader's ticket at the PRO in order to see original records. This will be issued at Reception when you arrive, on production of some positive means of identification. We ask for a passport, banker's card, or driving licence or, for foreign nationals, a passport or some other form of national identification document. Children of 14 and over can be issued with a reader's ticket if they come with (and are vouched for by) their parents. If they come without parents, they must bring a letter of recommendation from their school, on headed notepaper and signed by the head teacher.

Large bags and coats are not allowed in the research areas at the PRO. Lockable hangers are provided for coats, and there are lockers for other belongings. These take a £1 coin, which is returned after use. Pens and coloured pencils are not allowed in the reading rooms. Graphite pencils and laptop computers are allowed: power points are available. Supplies of paper, tracing

Figure 2 The entrance to the Public Record Office, at Kew. (Joe Sheehan)

paper and pencils can be bought in the shops, which also sell magnifying sheets. If you want to trace anything, ask for an acetate sheet to put over the document first. To help preserve the documents, please make use of the foam wedges and covered weights that are supplied – instructions for their use are on display.

The PRO welcomes readers with disabilities. There is a lift to all floors, and the facilities are wheelchair-friendly. We have aids to help readers with impaired vision, but the totally blind are advised to come with a sighted friend. Equally, if you have mobility or lifting difficulties, it may be a good idea to come with a friend. Many of the documents are heavy and unwieldy. The PRO is a very large building, and there can be distances to cover between different sources of information. If you contact us in advance, we can provide wheelchair assistance for the 100 metres plus from the car park. You can look at our leaflet on *Physical Access to the Public Record Office and its Services* on our website, or you can contact the PRO to ask for a copy to be sent to you.

The PRO's address is

Post	Public Record Office, Kew, Richmond, Surrey TW9 4DU
Telephone	020 8392 5200
E-mail	enquiry@pro.gov.uk
Fax	020 8878 8905
Minicom	020 8392 9198

If you are walking to the PRO, our pedestrian entrance is off Ruskin Avenue (the nearest station, at Kew Gardens, is about 10 minutes walk). The entry for cars is just to the east of Ruskin Avenue: follow the signposts to the Kew Retail Park. We do have a good-size car park but on busy days it does fill up.

1.10 Finding your way round the PRO

The PRO at Kew is a very large building, with several reading rooms and advice points, and an excellent library (see **1.14**). It can seem a very daunting place. To get round this, we ask all new readers arriving before the early afternoon to take a 20 minute orientation tour. (If you arrive too late, try to take the tour on your second visit!) This investment of time will pay off, as using the PRO is not straightforward.

New readers are often confused by the systems they face at the PRO. We know that they can appear difficult to grasp: if you feel confused, don't take it personally. You are trying to find your way into sets of information compiled in different ways over several centuries by generations of civil servants each skilled in their own little bit of red tape. If we were designing an information system from scratch, it would never look like this weird creation that has grown up over time. Remember, there are staff here to help you.

The first thing to say is that there is no simple way into the records occupying over 167 kilometres of shelving at the Public Record Office. There is, unfortunately, no easy index of personal names to tap into, although there are some publications and records which may be worth checking to start with, and returning to every now and then as you pick up more information. Expect to feel some confusion; be prepared to read and use any leaflets available for your guidance, and be ready to ask if you need to. Even our wonderful online catalogue is only as good as the information it contains – and that is all too often very uninformative.

This book concentrates on the main sources for genealogy in the public records. Nearly all these subjects have, at the PRO, a leaflet that gives detailed and specific instructions on what to do in searching for a particular record. They can also be seen (and printed) from our website. These leaflets are not usually mentioned in each chapter's bibliography, as they are constantly under revision, but please remember to look for and use them.

In addition, the PRO has also produced many specialist guides, for example to records on immigrants, or Tudor taxation records, which will take you deeper into the records than this book can. If you want to use these, they should be available in each room, as well as being for sale in the shop.

Copies of most documents can be bought, depending on the condition of the document.

1.11 The online catalogue PROCAT

From 1997 to 2000, many people at the PRO – and in far-off Mauritius – worked to produce a computer catalogue of the PRO's holdings called PROCAT, based on the paper catalogue created over the centuries. As well as being available on the many terminals at the PRO, PROCAT can also be used online, on the PRO's website at www.pro.gov.uk. If you are accessing it at the PRO, you can buy printouts of any interesting catalogue hits.

PROCAT is not designed to give details about individuals. It gives the overall description of each document, and not a list of its contents. It is at its best (and that is a very exciting best) when pulling together references to subjects or places, when it can do in seconds what would take months of ploughing through paper lists. PROCAT makes searching the whole collection of over 8.5 million records, the work of a moment. You can search by word, date, within all the catalogue or within a part of the catalogue with incredible ease.

It has absolutely transformed subject searching. For example, I had a telephone query from a reader who wanted to know if it was worth a trip to the PRO to look for information about the tapestry works at Mortlake set up by Charles I. In the old days I would have had to say, 'It's possible we have something, but you'll have to come and look. It may take some time, and you will have to read through the paper lists speculatively. As you accumulate information on more and more people involved, you will have to go back over sources you have already checked, to see if those "new" names occurred there, unrecognized.' Instead, I was able to do a subject search on PROCAT using *Mortlake* and *tapestry* as search terms. Within seconds I had five references: one set of accounts, two deeds setting up the works, two surveys of the works, and a probate inventory of one of the tapestry weaver's possessions.

As with most computer systems, the assumption is that everyone will automatically know how to operate it. On the desks we know this is not true. It may be true in twenty years time, but now very many people do not know where to find the letters on the keyboard, let alone how to use a mouse – because they never have to in their daily life. If you recognize this as you, then I hope you will feel encouraged to try out the computer catalogue, because it can be enormously useful, especially when searching for a place, subject or surname. If you are nervous, or worried, remember that the only stupid question is the one that doesn't get asked. If something is unclear, ask about it. If you have never used a computer before, we will talk you through the process.

On the other hand, lots of people are used to using computers, and are just flummoxed by the jargon. We have moved away from the old PRO language of lettercode, class and piece, to the international archival standard terms of department, series, sub-series, piece and item. Many people find these confusing. For example, a standard query now is 'What does department mean? Does it mean the room my seat is in?' No, it doesn't: it means the government department represented by the letters in any PRO reference. (For more on this, see the panel 'PRO terminology'.)

Searching the catalogue

Searching by keyword is easy, and can be very fruitful: many people will not need to go any further into the catalogue than this. To search the catalogue, you need to have at least a search term. This is basically any word.

The best search terms are those which are most likely to crop up in catalogue entries. Place-names are good, as are surnames or occupations. Surnames that come from place-names or occupations can cause problems: searching for Birmingham or Butcher brings up far too many entries.

When it comes to subjects, you may need to do a bit of lateral thinking. If you

---

PRO terminology

department The **department** does not mean which bit of the PRO you are standing in (a common misunderstanding) but instead the code of up to four letters given to the government department or court which produced or collected the records. These can be memorable (e.g. WO for War Office, which administered the Army) or random (e.g. BD for the Welsh Office). This used to be called **lettercode**.

series The **series** is the next level down: the division of all the papers of that department into subject or format series. Since the 1920s, the PRO has given each series a unique code composed of the letters of the department, and a series number. So you can get C 1 for Court of Chancery: Early Proceedings, and CAB 1, for Cabinet Office: Miscellaneous Records. This used to be called **class**.

sub-series Sometimes a series consists of only one kind of record: other times it has one or more **sub-series** in it. These have never been identified by number, but are now identified as a distinct level in PROCAT. A good example would be E 403, the Exchequer of Receipt: Issue Rolls and Registers. If this series had just been catalogued for the first time, it would not be one series but about 20: as it is, these 20 series are identified as sub-series of E 403 in PROCAT.

pieces Each series consists of one or more **pieces**: this is the actual document that you order (or get from a microfilm cabinet) and read. Sometimes the description is helpful, often it is just something on the lines of 1765, March–May Correspondence.

item The **item** is a level of description below the piece: sometimes it is produced as a separate document, more often it is not. Consider, for example, a bound volume of letters. Each letter has been described in the catalogue as a separate item: yet you have to order the whole volume. In other cases, the piece was originally a whole bundle of documents: they have since been flattened, repaired and catalogued and are now produced separately as items.
Complicated? Yes, I'm afraid it is.

---

are interested in early medicine for example, there is no point at all in using a wide category such as *early medicine* or a potentially confusing term such as *doctor* as search terms. It would be far better to use a range of terms such as *apothecary, druggist, physician*. You can indicate phrases such as barber surgeon by enclosing them in quotation marks – *'barber surgeon'*.

You can use more than one search term by using

- AND – King AND Alfred
- NOT – Ham NOT West
- OR – apothecary OR druggist

Other ways you can adapt your search term include restricting it to a range of years, or to a range of departments. If you know you are looking for army records about Aldershot, and that army records are mostly in the WO code (standing for War Office), try restricting the search to WO, and you will not get swamped with records from the education departments, the census, or the Ordnance Survey about Aldershot.

Possible problems
Sometimes you just do not get satisfactory search results from the catalogue.

- This can be because the catalogue entries have been typed in exactly as they are in the paper lists at the PRO on which the catalogue is based. This includes variant and archaic spellings, abbreviations, and punctuation. If you are searching for '*Durham Light Infantry*', the search will not pick up the many references to DLI, or D.L.I., or Durham L.I.
- Another problem is that the original paper catalogue entries are expressed as ranges of surnames or numbers – e.g. Dodds-Drabble. If you are looking for *Dodds* or *Drabble*, you will pick up this reference. If you are searching for *Donaldson*, you will not find it – even though the reference may cover a box full of Donaldsons, with just one Dodds or a single Drabble at either end.
- A common problem is putting in too many search terms. *Malta AND Naval AND hospital* will not pull up all references to the naval hospital at Malta. If for example, a whole series is described as Naval Hospital Records, then the entry for Malta will just read Malta, and this search will not pick it up. The search does not marry up words from series titles (Naval Hospital) with words in the description of individual pieces (Malta).

Working round the problems
A good way to cope with these problems is to use one of the many online leaflets or printed guides to discover which series are likely to be relevant, and then get acquainted with the way that these series are catalogued. You can do this online by browsing the catalogue, or at the PRO by looking at the paper version.

- If the series appears to be searchable online, search it using the type of vocabulary used in that series.
- If it doesn't look searchable online, go into Browse, and find the series description, as this should tell you if a published version exists. For example, the Patent Rolls (one of the longest-lived of all series) are identified only by dates covered in the online catalogue: but they are published from 1201 up to the time of Elizabeth I and have unique 'indexes' at the PRO up to the age of Elizabeth II.
- If you are having real problems, ask for help.

Many of the most popular series are not searchable in the computer catalogue. For example, the registered wills (1383–1858) in PROB 11 are not searchable in PROCAT: the catalogue currently contains brief details about each register, rather

Figure 3 When you have found which document you want to look at, check to see if it is on microfilm. If it is, you can use the self-service system. If not, staff working among the miles of secure storage will collect it for you. (Joe Sheehan)

than listing the contents of each register. The First World War Soldiers Documents in WO 363 are listed by range of surname of the Dodds-Drabble type. War Diaries in WO 95 are notoriously difficult to find online, because of the odd abbreviations of regimental names – should you search for King's Own Yorkshire Light Infantry, or KOYLI or K.O.Y.L.I., or KO Yorks LI, and so on through many more variants.

Some words of warning

Because searching PROCAT is so easy and so productive, it's very easy to assume that it is also comprehensive. In fact, PROCAT can be very deceptive. Because every series list is included, you have technically searched every piece description and it's very easy to assume that you have found everything. The trouble is that piece descriptions vary enormously in quality. PROCAT looks, on the surface, like a broad smooth ocean of data: dive below the surface, and you will see that the data forms underwater mountains, plateaux and chasms. In some places it's easy to catch what you want: in others, impossible as you snag your nets on unseen obstacles.

For example, in the sample search for the Mortlake tapestry works, there is a lot of extra material, not found by the PROCAT search, in both the State Papers Domestic Charles I (SP 16) and in the records of the Crown lands in the LR code. The State Papers are listed as volumes with covering dates only in PROCAT, but have been published in detailed précis in the *Calendar of State Papers Domestic*: the LR records have good manuscript indexes available only at the PRO. I know that these other sources exist and are likely to be fruitful, because it's my job to know it: researchers do not always have this kind of accumulated background knowledge. So always ask, even if you have spent hours on PROCAT.

Another potential problem with PROCAT is the patchy nature of the piece descriptions within even a single series. For example, the series Treasury Correspondence in T 1 is beautifully listed on PROCAT for the years 1746–1794. For this period it provides a highway into subjects of interest to the government. You can search for all kinds of subjects within it, and follow the correspondence back into the departments that actually dealt with that particular subject, whose records are less well listed. But before and after these dates, searching T 1 on PROCAT is no use. Before 1746 you need to look at the wonderful published versions instead (the *Calendars of Treasury Books and Papers*): after 1794, the T 1 list becomes impenetrable without looking at the manuscript registers in T 2 at the PRO.

This kind of 'highway' series exists for several periods. Most of the 'highway' series have received close attention from the PRO in the past, and have been published. The hundreds of PRO published calendars – of state papers (domestic, foreign and colonial), patent rolls, close rolls, treasury papers, inquisitions – are not searchable on PROCAT.

Having said all this, there is still no doubt that PROCAT is a huge advance in making the records at the PRO more easily accessible. It works best where records have been well described at piece level (e.g. for many modern file series) and less well when the piece description is poor. We are aware of this, and have before us the prospect of a long-term programme of catalogue improvements. In the meantime, please ask us for advice if you need help.

1.12 Going behind PROCAT: understanding how the records are arranged and identified

When I was first interviewed for my job at the PRO, I was asked if I knew the difference between a library and an archive. 'Yes', I replied (in rather a foolhardy way) 'a library is arranged for the convenience of its users, and an archive isn't.' It raised a laugh and I still got the job – because the answer was, unfortunately for readers, all too true.

An archive, such as the PRO, does not arrange its holdings by subject, but by the original institutional author – the supposed creator of the records. You need to know that the PRO holdings are divided up according to the government department or court that created them, or to whom they were sent in the course of everyday business. You will soon come to know that ADM means Admiralty, for the Navy, and KB means Court of King's Bench, and so on. To really get the best out of the sources, it's helpful to have some idea of how the government and courts worked, who was responsible for what kinds of affairs, who is likely to have written to whom, what kind of information might have been collected or retained. The staff and publications of the PRO are there to help you find out likely and unlikely places to look.

1.13 Traditional searches: the *PRO Guide* and the lists

The 5,500 page *PRO Guide* gives an overview of the history and content of all the records in its care. It was updated for the final time in 1998, so it is technically out of date. However, very many series are no longer being added to. The *Guide* can still be a very useful aid, particularly when you want to check on or compare several series quickly. At the PRO several printed copies are available so you can sit and browse at leisure. Copies can also be seen at the FRC. You may be able to find a microfiche edition locally. Remember to check on PROCAT as well for new accessions and the most up-to-date information.

The *Guide* occupies several loose-leaf volumes, and is divided into three parts. Part 1 contains the history of government. Part 2 contains series or class descriptions in alphabetical order of department code. Part 3 is the index to the other two parts. The main kinds of finding aid, below the *Guide*, are described in the following panel.

---

list   A list of the pieces comprising a series of records, with dates and simple descriptions (a *descriptive list* gives fuller indications of the contents of each document).

Lists in the Standard Set of lists are filed in A4 binders, in alphabetical order: there are three sets of the full sequence from A to ZSPC – you are welcome to browse among them. However, only the dark green set has been updated since PROCAT became available.

Other lists will be found in the Non-Standard Sets, currently in the Research Enquiries Room and the Map Room. These are often original or older finding aids, or published works. They each bear a small label on the spine saying which series they refer to.

introductory note   An introduction to the contents of a series, explaining why the records were created, and what they contain. These exist for all medieval, early modern and legal series, for most very modern series, and for some other series.

They are usually printed on green paper, and are filed with the lists in what is known as the Standard Set of lists.

calendar   A précis, usually in English, full enough to replace the original documents for most purposes. The documents have been published in date order in many, but not all, calendars.

publications   The PRO publishes readers' guides and handbooks. These are the specialist guides to particular records, referred to in this book.

transcript   A full text, as in the original document.

index   Alphabetically arranged references to people, places or subjects mentioned in the records. Some indexes referred to in this book are actually ***alphabets*** – entry books where all entries are grouped under their first letter, but with no further sorting.

Suppose you want to trace an ancestor who may have nursed at the Royal Greenwich Hospital. First of all, find the multi-volume *Guide to the Contents of the PRO*. Start in Part 3, the index. There are several index entries for Greenwich

Hospital, some followed by a code (e.g. ADM 2), others by a string of numbers. The numbers (e.g. 703/6/3) are references to Part 1, in which each department has its own three figure number, with further sub-divisions for different parts of its organization.

Public Record Office PRO Guide Part 3: Index

GREENWICH HOSPITAL
703/6/3
school ledgers, ADM 72
service records of candidates, ADM 29
staff pensions, ADM 165
staff records, ADM 73

In the Part 1 entry for 703/6/3, you will find a brief history of Greenwich Hospital.

Admiralty   703.6.3

703.6.3   ROYAL GREENWICH HOSPITAL

The Royal Greenwich Hospital was founded by Queen Mary, who in 1694 gave the royal estate at Greenwich for a home for superannuated seamen and marines. The foundation stone was laid in 1696 and the first pensioners were admitted in 1705. In 1716 the forfeited estates of Lord Derwentwater were added to the hospital's endowments (the Northern Estates). In addition to the in-pensioners, the hospital also maintained out-pensioners and provided pensions and allowances for widows and orphans of seamen and marines. It also provided for a limited number of officers. A school for the sons of seamen was attached to the hospital. In 1829 this school absorbed the Royal Naval Asylum for the children of seamen, originally established by the Patriotic Fund of Lloyds, but managed by commissioners since 1805. In 1803 the hospital took over the administration of the Chatham Chest (6.1), which was thereupon renamed the Greenwich Chest. It ceased to house in-pensioners in 1869 and since 1873 the building has become the home of the Royal Naval College (6.4); but the hospital has continued to administer the school, which moved to Holbrook in 1933, and to provide out-pensions and allowances of various kinds.

Records relating to pensioners are in ADM 6, ADM 73, ADM 165, PMG 24, PMG 69–71, WO 22, WO 23; records of widows' and orphans' pensions, etc. are in ADM 73, ADM 162–164, ADM 166. Records relating to staff of the hospital are in ADM 73 and ADM 165. Records of Greenwich Hospital School are in ADM 72, ADM 73, ADM 80, ADM 161. Registers of births, baptisms, marriages and burials for the hospital and school are in RG 4/1669–1679, further registers of baptisms and burials in RG 8/16–18 and burials in ADM 73. See also PRO 30/26.

This provides a description of the Hospital's history, and a very brief guide to its records, with references to the various series involved, but little indication of dates covered.

To find out more, you need to look at Part 2, the series descriptions. In fact, you could have gone there directly from Part 3, where the entries followed by letters and numbers are to series described in Part 2. Neither Part 3 nor Part 1 made any references to nurses at Greenwich Hospital, but both mentioned staff records as being in ADM 73. The description of ADM 73 in Part 2 is more helpful: nurses' records are mentioned at last.

Public Record Office PRO Guide Part 2: Descriptions

ADM 73 Greenwich Hospital Miscellaneous Registers, etc.

1704 to 1981 465 volumes

PRO, Kew

These include the following:

Establishment and muster books, 1704 to 1809. Nurses, labourers, servants, etc. Out-pension pay books, 1781 to 1809. Artificers' wages lists, etc., 1845 to 1866. Burial Registers, 1844 to 1981.

School admission papers, 1728 to 1870. These contain baptismal or birth certificates of the children, with marriage certificates of the parents, fathers' naval services, etc. Arranged under first letters.

School registers, 1728 to 1883. Registers of claims and candidates, admissions, apprenticing, etc., of boys and girls. These generally give full particulars as to the birth of the children, the parents' marriages and circumstances, services, etc., and are mostly indexed.

Registers of freight charges, 1828 to 1914, with an index, 1841 to 1868.

Registers of allowances paid to wives or guardians of children of men in receipt of Naval pensions admitted to public lunatic asylums, 1899 to 1948.

Some pieces open early.

See *PRO Guide Part 1: 703/6/3*

Having identified the series you want to look at, you then have to find the series list to discover which particular document you want to order. You will need to do this when you get references to series from this book, to identify exactly which piece you want.

There may be several lists in one volume, or one list may cover several volumes. Most lists are in rough date order, but some are arranged by subject and others by place. At the front of each list there should be an Introductory Note, which gives more detail about the series than Part 2 of the *PRO Guide*, and often includes instructions on how to order documents.

The Introductory Note for ADM 73 gives a range of piece numbers for staff records, which saves searching through the descriptions of all 465 pieces in this series.

ADM 73 Greenwich Hospital Registers

The majority of these registers is concerned with four distinct classes of person; In-Pensioners, Out-Pensioners, staff and children.

Applications by former warrant officers, ratings and Marines for admission as In-Pensioners, arranged alphabetically, are in pieces 1–35. They consist chiefly of certificates of the applicants' services issued by the Navy Pay Office. Though issued from 1790, these describe services which in some cases go back at least forty years before. Pieces 36–69 are chiefly registers of the In-Pensioners of the Hospital at various dates.

Pay books of out-pensions form pieces 95 to 131. They give only the name of the Out-Pensioner and the amount of his pension. The signatures of those who drew their

---

pensions in cash appear as a receipt; the letter R against others stands in this case for 'Remitted' (to those living at a distance from the Hospital).

Pieces 70 to 88 and 132 to 153 are lists and registers of the staff of the Hospital.

The papers submitted on behalf of children applying for admission to the Greenwich Hospital Schools are arranged alphabetically in pieces 134–389. In almost every case they include certificates of the applicants' fathers' services. Registers of the children admitted are in pieces 390–449.

October 1984

In the list of ADM 73, pieces 83 to 88 look as though they might be useful in this search

Reference ADM 73	ADMIRALTY – GREENWICH HOSPITAL REGISTERS, &c. ADM 73	
	Date	**Description**
82	1865–1869	Muster Book of Servants
83	1704–1864	General Entry Book of Nurses
84	1766–1863	Entry Book of Nurses
85	1783–1863	Register of Nurses
86	1847–1865	Register of Nurses and Servants
87	1704–1772	Alphabetical List of Nurses
88	1772–1864	Ditto
89	1800–1801	Register of Children at Clarence House

The department code **ADM**, the series number **73**, and the piece number **83** are the items of information which will be needed for ordering the first of these documents via the computer.

You may find that you need to operate the two systems of searching together. For example, a keyword search on *Greenwich* and *nurses* in PROCAT turned up an entirely different set of references than the traditional search. It also, and very usefully, brought up a reference to a PRO leaflet on *Royal Navy: Nurses.*

Department	Series	Piece	Item	Scope	Date
ADM	6	329		Register of ratings' widows applying for admission to **Greenwich** Hospital as **nurses**	1817–1831
ADM	6	331		Register of ratings' widows applying for admission to **Greenwich** Hospital as **nurses**	1819–1842
ED	82	70		**Greenwich**, Dreadnought Training School for **Nurses**	1927

1.14 Using the PRO Library

The PRO Library is a specialist history reference library in existence for over 150 years. It has not been open to the public for very long, and it is still a rather underused resource. However, it now has a computer catalogue that we intend to put online, and subject searching has therefore become very much easier. It has excellent sets of periodicals and journals, for all kinds of history. Its holdings of local record society publications are a tremendous resource, and you may even find that the information you are looking for has been printed. (Ask at Library Enquiries Desk for Mullins, *Texts and Calendars*, which is a guide to what each local society has produced: it is continued on the web at www.hmc.gov.uk/main.htm).

The Library holds a very large collection of books relating to the myriad of subjects covered by the records in the PRO. It also has long runs of annual publications, such as the *Army List, Crockford's Clerical Directory*, the *India List*, the *Court and City Register*, the *Imperial Calendar*, the *Annual Register of World Events* (from 1758 to date), *Burke's Landed Gentry*, and collections of local and professional directories.

The Library has the indexes to *The Times* and the Parliamentary Papers (from 1801) on CD-ROM, as well as several other useful CD-ROMs. These can produce extraordinary amounts of information – the Parliamentary Papers in particular are full of details, and using the index on a keyword search can turn up all kinds of published returns of people marginally involved in government, or giving evidence on subjects of social concern. Some of these have been noted in the text (e.g. in **23**), but the field remains wide open for discoveries.

1.15 A starting place? Publications, indexes and pedigrees

You may have arrived at the PRO with a specific query, or with a planned programme of research. At some point, it may be worth taking a side-step, and looking in three or four places to see if any extra information can be picked up quickly.

There are four easy places to check for information in print about a particular person. The first is the *Dictionary of National Biography*, which is in the Library. This contains brief biographies of many thousands of people whose lives were thought to have some national significance. The second is the *British Biographical Archive*. This is a compilation of over 300 other English language biographical dictionaries published between 1601 and 1929, put together on microfiche in a single alphabetical order of surname. It is on open access in the Microfilm Reading Room. It has a printed index called the *British Biographical Index*, available in the PRO Library, which is a useful source in its own right, as it provides a summary of the entries as well as acting as an index to the fiches. The fourth is a CD-ROM, available in the Library, called the *Biography Database 1680–1830*. The current issue contains over 100 directories (national, town and trade); over 1,500 book subscription lists; apprenticeship lists from the Stationers' Company 1701–1800; birth, marriage, death and bankruptcy notices from the *Gentleman's Magazine from 1731–1750* and much more. It contains roughly 900,000 records, and is searchable by name, title, office, occupation and address. It is updated regularly to include more sources.

Indexes to records are not only available at the PRO. Other record offices and libraries obviously have their own indexes, and very many people index records for their own purposes, which they are prepared to search for a fee. It may be that there is an index somewhere, which will save you days of work, or suggest new lines of enquiry. To find out, look at Gibson and Hampson, *Specialist Indexes for Family Historians*, which should be available at every enquiry desk.

Another source which may be worth checking every so often, as you garner more names for your family tree, is the large number of pedigrees that have ended up in the public records, usually in support of some legal claim. Look at the indexes filed with the lists of J 67 and J 68 to start with. Others are in the Chancery Masters Exhibits in C 103–114, and some are scattered in all kinds of series. You can look at the indexes to the *PRO Guide* to identify other series, and then look at the lists, or you can search PROCAT using *pedigree* as a keyword. This will bring up lots of pedigree cattle, but maybe also an entry for a family you are interested in. Most of the pedigrees are listed or indexed only by the 'principal person' – the pivotal person in the legal proof of entitlement to whatever was being claimed. An early work by Wrottesley, *Pedigrees from the Plea Rolls, 1200–1500*, may be worth looking at.

1.16 New skills and knowledge: language, writing, dates and money

As you move backwards from the twentieth century, you will find that you need to acquire new skills and knowledge to understand the documents properly. You will come across odd forms of writing, different methods of dating, archaic measurements, incomprehensible legal phrases and, of course, Latin (in general use for many legal records until 1733). This is all on top of the fact that in very many documents (particularly in registers where a few clerks were entering similar information, year in, year out) there are all kinds of abbreviations which meant something at the time – and which now might as well be in double Dutch.

Words

Reading the writing can often be a skill in itself: classes are the best way to learn this 'palaeographic' skill. Excellent self-help books are also available. However, the problem is that handwriting changes enormously over time – many letterforms are completely different in different centuries. Most courses concentrate on the earlier material. Having done them, I can read most sixteenth-century hands quite fluently, but I do find nineteenth-century clerk's copperplate a real trial. For books to help with understanding the writing, and the Latin, see the bibliography at **5.5**.

The multi-volume *Oxford English Dictionary* can be very helpful when you are satisfied that you have read a word correctly, but you still have no idea what it means. It is especially helpful as it gives dated examples of usage. For legal phrases, and procedures that you don't understand, there are several legal dictionaries at the PRO. For understanding old weights and measurements, try Chapman, *How Heavy, How Much and How Long? Weights, Money and Other Measures Used by Our Ancestors.*

Dates

Dates are an area where you have to learn a few old ideas about dating practices, and then refer to a crib when needed, to help you date documents correctly. Munby's *Dates and Time* is a fascinating account of the subject, but you may still need access to the classic work, Cheney and Jones's *Handbook of Dates.*

For much of the documented past, people in England dated years not by the calendar year (e.g. 1780) but by the regnal year (how long the monarch had been on the throne). A new regnal year began on the anniversary of the monarch's accession to the throne. Thus, 1 Elizabeth I ran from the death of Mary on 17 November 1558 to 16 November 1559; 2 Elizabeth I ran from 17 November 1559 to 16 November 1560; and so on, until 45 Elizabeth I stopped at her death on 24 March 1603, and 1 James I began.

Another problem with years is that, although New Year's Day was celebrated on 1st January, the actual year number did not change until 25th March. This was the Annunciation or Lady Day, nine months to the day before Christmas. This practice did not change officially until 1752, but for some decades beforehand, dates from January to March 24th were expressed as being in 1641/2. You will find that most dates given in PRO lists and publications have been silently amended to the modern form of the year.

The third thing to look out for is Old Style and New Style – the difference between English dates and European dates, from 1582. Pope Gregory XIII reformed the calendar in 1582 by cutting out ten days to return the calendar to the solar year. Other countries followed this lead at different times: broadly speaking, Catholic states adopted the New Style in the sixteenth century, Protestant states in the eighteenth century, and Orthodox states in the twentieth century. People corresponding between countries would date their letters with both dates, as 12/22 December 1635. All kinds of oddities crop up: in 1688 William of Orange left Holland on 11th November, and arrived in England on 5th November.

In the United Kingdom the change took place in 1752, when Wednesday the 2nd September was followed immediately by Thursday the 14th September. This was ignored by the accounting and hiring records, so that the old accounting day of Lady Day (25th March) slipped to 5th April ('old Lady Day'), still the start of the financial year in Britain.

In early modern documents you often find that instead of using the day and month, saint's days and religious feasts are used, so that you could find the phrase 'Tuesday after the Annunciation', or 'in the eve of St Martin'. To translate these, you need to know when the feast day was, and the calendar for that particular year. You can find both of these from the lists and tables in Cheney and Jones's *Handbook of Dates* (available at all the enquiry desks).

The legal system had its own calendar, based around the old agricultural and religious cycles. The legal year began with the Michaelmas term (starting on 6th October), followed by the Hilary, Easter and Trinity terms. Between the terms were the vacations. In the Lent vacation (Hilary to Easter) and the Summer vacation (Trinity to Michaelmas), the judges from the central courts travelled round the country on the assize circuits. Details of the legal terms for each year are given in the latest edition of the *Handbook of Dates*.

You may well find that the patterns of the religious, agricultural and legal calendars are reflected in the records you use: they were certainly reflected in your ancestors' experience of life.

Money

£1 then: how much would it be worth now?

1300	£430.50	1700	£74.87
1320	£344.40	1720	£78.27
1340	£574.00	1740	£82.00
1360	£344.40	1760	£71.75
1380	£430.50	1780	£59.38
1400	£430.50	1800	£30.21
1420	£430.50	1820	£35.14
1440	£430.50	1840	£37.43
1460	£430.50	1860	£44.15
1480	£430.50	1880	£45.32
1500	£430.50	1900	£55.55
1520	£430.50	1920	£19.13
1540	£287.00	1940	£26.09
1560	£287.00	1960	£13.89
1580	£172.20	1980	£2.58
1600	£123.00	2000	£1.00
1620	£90.63		
1640	£82.00		
1660	£71.75		
1680	£78.27		

These figures are taken from the Bank of England's *Equivalent Values of the Pound: a historical series 1270 to 2000*. Try also Munby, *How Much Is That Worth?*

£1 = 20 shillings, or 3 marks, or 240 pennies
1 shilling = 12d (pennies)
1 guinea = £1 1s

£1 in quarters and eighths
1 crown = 5s
1/2 crown = 2s 6d
£1 in thirds
1 noble = 13s 4d
1 mark = 6s 8d

1.17 The Friends of the PRO

The Friends of the PRO receive a newsletter (*Prophile*) and access to events. They also undertake voluntary work in cataloguing records and improving lists and indexes. They have completed work of enormous importance, such as the indexes to wills and administrations, 1701–1749, and the listing of soldiers' discharge papers between 1760 and 1854. If you want to find out more, write to the Friends of the Public Record Office (address in **48**).

1.18 Family history: an introductory bibliography

Many of the works mentioned in this and subsequent bibliographies can be seen in the PRO Library or reading rooms, or bought in the PRO shops at the FRC and the PRO.

General guides to historical sources
M Abbott, *Family Ties: English Families 1540–1920* (London, 1993)
D Hey, *The Oxford Guide to Family History* (Oxford, 1993)
A Macfarlane, *A Guide to English Historical Records* (Cambridge, 1983)
C D Rogers and J H Smith, *Local Family History in England, 1538–1914* (Manchester, 1991)
Society of Genealogists, *Parish Register Copies in the Library of the Society of Genealogists* (Society of Genealogists, 1995)

Biographical dictionaries and specialist indexes
British Biographical Archive (London, 1984 continuing)
Dictionary of National Biography (London, 1909 continuing)
J S W Gibson and E Hampson, *Specialist Indexes for Family Historians* (FFHS, 1998)
G Wrottesley, *Pedigrees from the Plea Rolls, 1200–1500* (London, c.1906)

General guides to dates, etc.
J J Bond, *Handy-Book of Rules and Tables for Verifying Dates* (London, 1869)
C R Chapman, *How Heavy, How Much and How Long? Weights, Money and Other Measures Used by Our Ancestors* (Lochin Publishing, 1996)
C R Cheney and M Jones, *Handbook of Dates for Students of English History* (London, 2000)
L H Munby, *Dates and Time: A Handbook for Local Historians* (British Association for Local History, 1997)
L H Munby, *How Much Is That Worth?* (British Association for Local History, 1996)

General guides to family history research
M J Burchall, *National Genealogical Directory* (annual)
P Christian, *The Genealogist's Internet* (PRO, 2001)
Federation of Family History Societies, *British Isles Genealogical Register* (FFHS, 1997)
T V FitzHugh and S B Lumas, *A Dictionary of Genealogy* (4th edn, 1994)
S Fowler, *The Joys of Family History* (PRO, 2001)
J S W Gibson, *Unpublished Personal Name Indexes* (FFHS, 1987)
R Harvey, *Genealogy for Librarians* (London, 1992): useful for everyone interested in genealogy
M Herber, *Ancestral Trails: The Complete Guide to British Genealogy and Family History* (Society of Genealogists, 2000)
R Pols, *Family Photographs 1860–1945* (PRO, 2002)
S Raymond, *British Genealogical Periodicals: A Bibliography of their Contents* (FFHS, 1991)
S Raymond and J S W Gibson, *English Genealogy: An Introductory Bibliography* (FFHS, 1991)

Reader's Digest *Explore Your Family's Past* (London, 2000)
P Saul, *The Family Historian's Enquire Within* (1997)

Surname studies
Federation of Family History Societies, *Register of One Name Studies* (FFHS, reissued
    regularly)
D Hey, *Family Names and Family History* (London, 2000)

Periodicals
Ancestors, Public Record Office
Family and Community History, the Journal of the Family and Community Historical
    Research Society
Family History, Institute of Heraldic and Genealogical Studies
Family History Monthly
Family Tree Magazine
Family History News and Digest, Federation of Family History Societies
Practical Family History
Prophile, The Friends of the Public Record Office
The Genealogists' Magazine, The Society of Genealogists

General guides to the Public Record Office and the Family Records Centre
British National Archives (Government Publications Sectional List 24, last published
    1984)
S Colwell, *Family Roots: Discovering the Past in the Public Record Office* (London, 1991)
S Colwell, *Dictionary of Genealogical Sources in the Public Record Office* (London, 1992)
S Colwell, *The Family Records Centre: a User's Guide* (PRO, 2002)
J Cox, *The Nation's Memory, A Pictorial Guide to the Public Record Office* (London, 1988)
J Cox, *New to Kew?* (PRO, 1997)
List and Index Society: exact copies of lists as on the PRO shelves at the time of publication.
Public Record Office, *Guide to the Contents of the Public Record Office* (London, 1963, 1968)
Public Record Office, *PRO Guide to the Contents of the Public Record Office* (PRO, 1998
    edition)
Public Record Office, *The Family Records Centre Introduction to Family History* (PRO,
    1999)

Directories of archive institutions
J Foster and J Sheppard, *British Archives: A Guide to Archive Resources in the United
    Kingdom* (London, 1995)
J S W Gibson and P Peskett, *Record Offices and How to Find Them* (FFHS, 1998)
I Mortimer, *Record Repositories in Great Britain* (Royal Commission on Historic
    Manuscripts and PRO, 1999)

2

Censuses of population

◆ ◆ ◆

2.1 Census returns: England, Wales, Isle of Man and Channel Islands, 1801–1901

From 1801 onwards, information about the population of the United Kingdom has been collected every ten years by means of a census. The census (enumeration) returns taken together form the most important and useful modern source for genealogical, local, demographic and other studies in the care of the PRO. The census returns are the nearest we can come to a ten-yearly snapshot of a family's development, and they can record children whose existence might otherwise have gone undetected.

Censuses started in 1801, but until 1841 censuses were simply headcounts, and did not name individuals. The returns from 1841 onwards should in theory give information about all people in England, Wales, the Isle of Man and the Channel Islands on a specific night in the census years. The census recorded everyone present at each specific address overnight on the chosen enumeration date (always a Sunday, and from 1851 in the spring), so an entire family unit, plus collateral relatives, lodgers, employees, servants and friends may be included. Not everyone was at home, of course, and not everyone had a home. There are many institutional entries for barracks, schools, ships, and even prisons and asylums (not all of which give names). However, most searches start and end with the family household. From 1851, the relationship of everyone to the head of the household is given.

The information collected varied from census to census. As the information given to the census enumerator is treated as confidential for 100 years, the 1911 census will not be open to the public until 2012.

One thing you do need to be aware of is that the people themselves supplied the information in the census. There is no guarantee as to its accuracy. We know, for example, that far more people described themselves as naturalized citizens than ever took out naturalization papers. Apparently it is also happens regularly that the number of women describing themselves as between 30 and 40 is always significantly less than the number of the same women who had described themselves as 20–30 ten years before, even allowing for any deaths. Family relations could be entered in ways quite other than the truth – and unless the enumerator who had to help with and collate the census forms happened to know the actual circumstances, who would know any differently?

2.2 Where to read the 1901 census returns

Anywhere – where there is an Internet connection! The 1901 census was released to the public in 2002, online for the first time, with a newly created index database, at www.census.pro.gov.uk. There are also banks of computers at the FRC so you can access the 1901 census online there and then move on to checking the earlier censuses still on microfilm.

The 1901 database has transformed use of the census. All the 32,527,843 people listed in 1901 are now easily accessible. You can search by last name, first name, age, place of birth, place, institution, vessel (ship), address or by its RG 13 reference. People away from home can at last be found with ease, and lost relatives traced without problem.

The database can be checked for free, and a copy of the actual census entry can then be downloaded for a small fee per page, payable by credit/debit card. If you are doubtful about paying over the Internet, you can buy vouchers to use instead, from many local archives and libraries, as well as from the FRC and PRO shops. A list of institutions selling them is on the census website. In fact, all you need to know about using this service is available, along with the 1901 census, at www.census.pro.gov.uk.

If you want to look at the census returns on microfiche, you can do this – but not at the FRC. Instead, the PRO has a full set for England and Wales, the Isle of Man and the Channel Islands, with place indexes, and many local archives have bought the fiches for their own locality. This method of access is very similar to the way previous censuses are currently accessed, and is particularly useful if you are undertaking a local study, or want to set people in their local context.

To set the 1901 census in its wider context, the PRO has an online exhibition on life in 1901 at www.pro.gov.uk/pathways/census.htm and has also published Hey's *How our ancestors lived: a history of life a hundred years ago.*

2.3 What is in the 1901 census?

The 1901 census was taken on 31 March 1901. It records information submitted on full address, name, age last birthday, marital status, relationship to the head of the household, sex, occupation, parish and county of birth, and various medical disabilities. Like the 1891 census, the 1901 returns contain additional information on employment status, and, for Wales, on the language spoken. Individuals were recorded in the households or institutional grouping in which they lived.

2.4 Where to read the 1841–1891 census returns

The Family Records Centre holds microfilm copies of the census returns for all England, Wales, the Isle of Man and the Channel Islands for 1841, 1851, 1861, 1871, 1881 and 1891. Many county record offices and local history libraries also

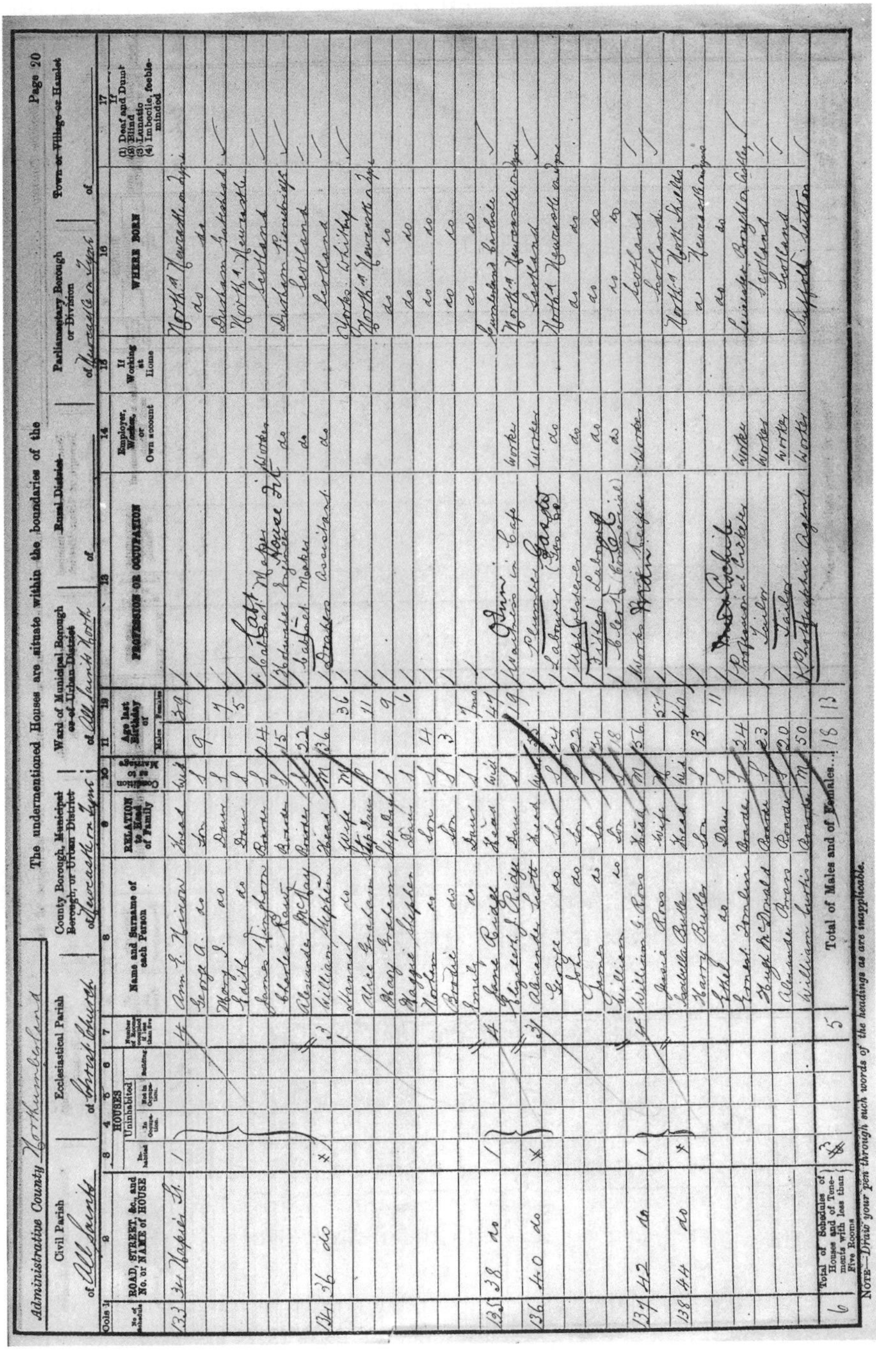
Administrative County Northumberland — The undermentioned Houses are situate within the boundaries of the — Page 20

Civil Parish of All Saints | Ecclesiastical Parish of Christ Church | County Borough, Municipal Borough, or Urban District of Newcastle on Tyne | Ward of Municipal Borough or of Urban District of All Saints North | Rural District of | Parliamentary Borough or Division of Newcastle on Tyne | Town or Village or Hamlet of

Total of Males and of Females

NOTE.—Draw your pen through such words of the headings as are inapplicable.

Figure 4 It took a minute to find Alexander Brass (my husband's grandfather) in the 1901 census online – it would have been impossible by the old methods. Here he is, in a Newcastle boarding house, working his way from Scotland to London. (PRO, RG 13/4785)

hold copies of the census returns (on microfilm or microfiche) for their local area. For more information see Gibson and Hampson, *Census Returns 1841–1891 in Microform: A Directory of Local Holdings.* In some localities, much work has gone into indexing these local copies. At Kingston-upon-Thames, for example, there is a project to put all Victorian data from census, birth, marriage and death registers and other sources into a single searchable database (see http://humansciences.king.ac.uk/humanities/history/local/index.htm). In the USA, copies of all available census returns are held by the Genealogical Society of Utah in Salt Lake City (address in **48**).

However, after releasing the 1901 census online, the PRO is now planning to convert earlier censuses, starting with the 1881 and 1891 censuses. We hope that images of the 1881 census, linked to the existing database will be available online by the end of 2002, at about the same time as the images and new database for the 1891 census.

2.5 What is in the 1851–1891 censuses?

These censuses were taken on 30 March 1851, 7 April 1861, 2 April 1871, 3 April 1881 and 5 April 1891. The entries are written in ink. The full address, name, age last birthday, marital status, relationship to the head of the household, sex, occupation, parish and county of birth are all given for each person who was recorded: there was also a column for various medical disabilities. The 1891 returns contain additional information on employment status, and, for Wales, on the language spoken. Individuals were recorded in the households and houses in which they lived.

The surviving records of the 1851 census for England and Wales, the Channel Islands and the Isle of Man form part of the series HO 107: Census Returns. Those of 1861, 1871, 1881 and 1891 are in RG 9, RG 10, RG 11 and RG 12 respectively.

Don't forget the 1881 index of 26,000,000 names. There are also many indexes for the 1851 census, which can be seen at the FRC or consulted elsewhere. Indexing of other censuses has been more sporadic. See Gibson and Hampson, *Marriage, Census and Other Indexes for Family Historians.*

2.6 What is in the 1841 census?

The names of individuals were first officially included in the census taken on 6 June 1841. The 1841 census is written in pencil, which can make it difficult to read. The information collected for each person included full name, age, sex and occupation. For those under 15, ages were given exactly (if known): for people over 15, ages were rounded down to the nearest five years. For example, someone of 64 would appear as 60, another of 29 as 25. Some information relating to the place of birth was also given, but was restricted to whether or not a person was born in the county of residence (Y for Yes, N for No), and, if not, whether in Scotland (S), Ireland (I), or foreign parts (F). The 1841 census also gives the same kind of information as earlier censuses on housing. It indicates which individuals lived in a particular house, and individual households within that house. The relationships between members of the same household are not recorded, but can often be inferred.

The surviving records of the 1841 census for England and Wales, the Channel Islands and the Isle of Man form part of the series HO 107.

2.7 Finding the right entry, 1841–1891: name indexes and general information

Before starting a search, you need to know where to look. There are some name indexes to the census, but there is no overall index except for 1881. However, much work has been done on census indexing by very many groups and individuals unconnected with the PRO, and it may be that an index exists for the locality you are interested in. The best way to find out is to check Gibson and Hampson, *Marriage, Census and Other Indexes for Family Historians*, which is arranged by county. Individuals, who charge for a search to help cover their costs, hold many of these indexes. The FRC has many additional finding aids such as street indexes to towns with a population over 40,000, and many other name indexes for specific places, produced by family history societies. The 1851 census has the most of these name indexes.

However, if you don't have an exact address but have some clues that far back, the 1881 census is the place to start, as it has an index including about 26,000,000 names. For this, thanks are due to the very many people involved in the 1881 Project, co-ordinated by the British Genealogical Record Users Committee. The 1881 index can be seen at the FRC, at the Family History Centres run by the LDS, at the Society of Genealogists and at many other places as well.

However, apart from the 1881 index, most finding aids are to help you find a known address. You need to have at least an approximate home address, or an idea of where your ancestors might have been on the night of the census. Examples could be on holiday, in an institution such as a prison, barracks or workhouse, working away from home, or on board a ship in port or within territorial waters. Remember that many addresses will have changed over time, as streets lengthened and were renumbered in the expanding cities and towns of Victorian England. There are specialist works available at the FRC to help with this problem for London. The censuses are arranged by place, grouped in the registration districts used for the registration of births, marriages and deaths. Maps of these registration districts can be found in RG 18: facsimiles can be seen at the FRC. They are arranged by year, and can be useful in identifying the registration districts of the smaller places that do not appear in the indexes to the census.

This chapter provides basic information: for a guide to using the census, see *Making Use of the Census,* by Lumas, written from an unrivalled depth of knowledge of the make-up and genealogical use of these records. For the history, original use, structure and complexities of the census records, see *A Clearer Sense of the Census,* by Higgs, which explains the ideas behind the compilation of the censuses, and warns against accepting their contents as literal truth.

Figure 5 Remember not to treat all information in the census as guaranteed truth! (*Punch*, April 20 1861, PRO Library)

There are some pitfalls in using the censuses, and interpreting the evidence is not always as straightforward as it might appear. A good general rule is: the younger the person described, the more accurate the information on age and place of birth.

2.8 How are the census records arranged?

The census returns are arranged in small books covering enumeration districts of usually a few hundred houses. Small towns, parishes and hamlets can readily be searched in their entirety. The returns for large towns and cities fill numerous books, so you have to know the address of an individual before beginning a search for them in the census (except for 1881). There are street indexes to help you find a particular street in a large town on the right film, available at the FRC and at Salt Lake City.

To help you once you are at the FRC, there are leaflets giving specific instructions and up-to-date advice on how to use the various finding aids to each census.

2.9 What was in the 1801–1831 censuses?

The censuses of 10 March 1801, 27 May 1811, 28 May 1821 and 29 May 1831 were confined to the compilation of numerical totals (by parish) of the following: houses habited and uninhabited; families; men and women; occupations (in broad categories); and various statistics of baptisms, marriages and burials. A partial enumeration of age was taken in 1821, and a more extensive investigation into occupations took place in 1831.

People's names were not recorded in the official returns for these years. However, in the course of carrying out the censuses, some local enumerators did compile unofficial listings of named individuals. Those that survive in local record offices are listed by Gibson and Medlycott in *Local Census Listings, 1522–1930*, or in Chapman's *Pre-1841 Census and Population Listings.*

Most of the information in these records was published in Parliamentary Papers: an incomplete set can be seen at the PRO. A reader's ticket is needed to consult them. The original documents were destroyed in 1904, with the exception of the clergymen's returns of numbers of baptisms, marriages and burials by parish, 1821–1830, which survive in HO 71, at the PRO.

2.10 Census returns: other places

Scottish census returns are held by the Registrar General for Scotland, New Register House, Edinburgh EH1 3YT. Those for 1841 to 1901 are open to public inspection. The 1881, 1891 and 1901 Scottish censuses are available online, at www.origins.net/GRO/ on a pay-to-view system.

Census returns for the whole of Ireland are held by the National Archives, Four Courts, Dublin 7, Republic of Ireland. Unfortunately, few nineteenth century Irish census returns have survived but the Irish returns for 1901 and 1911 are fairly complete, and are open to public inspection there.

Colonial census returns, if they survived, will be kept in the appropriate national archives. However, the PRO does hold a few colonial censuses. The best known of these are the censuses of convicts (and some free settlers) in New South Wales and Tasmania, 1788–1859 (HO 10: see **40.4** for further details). In addition, the PRO has a census of 1811 from Surinam, detailing slaves and free black and white inhabitants (CO 278/15–25); a 1715 census of the white population of Barbados (CO 28/16); and a census of the colony of Sierra Leone on 30 June 1831 (CO 267/111).

2.11 Censuses of population: bibliography

W A Armstrong, 'The Interpretation of the Census Enumerators' Books for Victorian Towns', *The Study of Urban History*, ed. H J Dyos (London, 1968)

M W Beresford, 'The unprinted Census returns for 1841, 1851 and 1861 for England and Wales', *Amateur Historian*, vol. V, pp. 260–269

M E Briant Rosier, *Index to Census Registration Districts* (FFHS, 1995)

C Chapman, *Pre-1841 Census and Population Listings* (Dursley, 1994)

S Colwell, *The Family Records Centre: a User's Guide* (PRO, 2002)

J S W Gibson and E Hampson, *Census Returns 1841–1891 on Microform: A Directory to Local Holdings* (FFHS, 1997)

J S W Gibson and E Hampson, *Marriage, Census and Other Indexes for Family Historians* (FFHS, 7th edn, 1998)

J S W Gibson and M Medlycott, *Local Census Listings, 1522–1930, holdings in the British Isles* (FFHS, 1994)

D Hey, *How our ancestors lived: a history of life a hundred years ago* (PRO, 2002)

E Higgs, *A Clearer Sense of the Census: the Manuscript Returns for England and Wales, 1801–1901* (London, 1996)

R Lawton, ed., *The Census and Social Structure, an Interpretative Guide to nineteenth century Censuses, for England and Wales* (London, 1978)

S Lumas, *Making Use of the Census* (PRO, 2002)

M Medlycott, 'Some Georgian "Censuses": The Militia Lists and "Defence" Lists', *Genealogists' Magazine*, vol. XXIII, pp. 55–59

D Mills and C Pearce, *People and Places in the Victorian Census: A Review and Bibliography, 1841–1911* (Historical Geography Research Group, 1989)

M Nissel, *People count: A history of the General Register Office* (London, 1987)

K Schurer and T Arkell, eds, *Surveying the People* (Oxford, 1992)

R Smith, 'Demography in the 19th Century', *Local Historian,* vol. IX (1970–71)

P M Tillot, 'The Analysis of the Census Returns', *Local Historian,* vol. VIII (1968–9)

E A Wrigley, ed., *An Introduction to English Historical Demography* (Cambridge, 1966)

E A Wrigley, ed., *The Study of Nineteenth Century Society* (Cambridge, 1972)

3

All in the family: birth, adoption, marriage, divorce and death in England and Wales

◆ ◆ ◆

3.1 Introduction

The documents concerned with recording the existence of an individual are both easy and complex. They can be easy to find or hard to find, easy to understand or hard to understand. Sometimes they hide more than they reveal, other times they seem to reveal a truth that turns out after years of research not to be true. Remember, to the people concerned these records had a different significance than they do to you. They came with all kinds of baggage – proof of respectability, religious faith (and by inference loyalty), and of legal claim to anything from entitlement to poor relief to inheriting property.

Although not actually intended as such, in a way they represent the church and state view of how life should be conducted, forced upon the teeming variety of actual existence. People were required to comply – but they also tried to put the best face on things, from their own perspective. We do it ourselves – giving our occupation in a way that sounds good, for example. And in many ways the system was not foolproof. The fact of a registration many miles away did not actually prevent a bigamous marriage. In a place where your business was not known, it was quite easy for people to hide the actual facts of their lives while giving every appearance of conforming to the expectations of society.

Many families will have records of these vital events in the collective life of a family among their family papers – notes in a Bible, or a birthday book, or bundles of certificates. If so, you have a head start in your research.

Official certificates of birth, marriage and death, issued at the time, have existed for only about 170 years. The first thing to know is that 1837 is an important date for only these events in England and Wales. After 1st July 1837, certificates of birth, marriage and death were issued at the time by the state, and can also be found in a central register, or from its district registries. So you may be lucky enough to have the original certificates, or to find a later copy elsewhere, or you may have to look for the registered version. The actual registers are still held by the General Register Office of England and Wales (GRO) and are not open for inspection. However, you can access the indexes in many places, and can buy certified copies only (copies which a court will accept as if they were the original) of any certificate that you think looks promising.

Before 1st July 1837, the various churches made a different type of record of these events, which was and is held locally. These are usually records of baptism, marriage and burial, not birth, marriage and death. The information was stored in the church register, and could be copied out in case of need by the cleric in charge, who would certify that it was a true copy. These earlier certificates can therefore take many forms – some were simple letters, others entered onto a pre-printed form. For centuries, certificates of baptism had to be provided by people wishing to take up positions of trust in government (civil or armed servants of the state) to prove that they were members of the state Church of England. You may be able to find one of these copy certificates, but the usual course is to go to the church register or a transcript of it. These records are more difficult to find, as they are scattered, but they are usually open to inspection. If you want to buy a copy, it does not need to be certified and therefore costs less.

The PRO is not the obvious place to look for birth, marriage and death certificates. However, it does have some collections of interest (particularly the major national collection of nonconformist registers, and collections of copy certificates), as well as some regimental registers of births and marriages for Army and Militia regiments in England and Wales (see **18a.1.2**) and for the Royal Marines (see **20.5**). At the PRO, you can also access the indexes for the bulk of records held elsewhere – in the GRO indexes on microfiche, and through the *IGI* or FamilySearch.

This chapter deals first of all with birth, marriage and death after 1837 (**3a**); then with the same events before 1837 (**3b**), and then with illegitimacy, adoption, divorce and burial (**3c**) both before and after 1837.

3a

Civil registration of births, marriages, deaths and adoptions from 1st July 1837

◆ ◆ ◆

3a.1 The central civil register

For many, the Family Records Centre in central London is the most convenient place to look for records of birth, marriage or death for the whole of England and Wales, as it holds the index to the central GRO register. (See **1.8** for the address and other details.) However, if you know that your family stayed in one locality, you may find it more convenient to use the local register office for that area (see **3a.2**).

The FRC holds indexes to births, deaths and marriages registered in England and Wales since civil (non-religious) registration began on 1st July 1837. The indexes are arranged by date of registration, and then alphabetically. There are four sets for each year, covering each quarter, and labelled with the last month in each quarter – March, June, September and December. From 1983, the indexes cover the whole year. The indexes to the Adopted Children Register from 1927 are also here.

The FRC also holds the main collection of records of birth, death and marriage of English and Welsh people at sea or abroad (see **4**), as well as similar records returned by the armed services. For registers and indexes of Scots and Irish births, marriages and deaths (at home, overseas and in the services), kept by the General Register Offices of Scotland, Ireland and Northern Ireland, see **8** and **9**.

The actual registers of birth, marriage and death are not kept at the FRC, but at the GRO's head office at Southport. Applications to buy a certified copy of the register entry (identified from the indexes) are sent by the FRC to Southport, and the certificate is then either posted to you, or returned to the FRC for collection.

Several of the larger record offices and libraries (including the PRO) have copies of the indexes on microfiche: a list of where they are held can be supplied by the FRC. An alternative to looking for a set of the official indexes is to search the FreeBMD Project's database of nearly 20 million index entries, at http://freebmd.rootsweb.com.

If you are able to identify the certificate you want, you can order a copy direct from Southport by post, phone or e-mail. You will need to give the year, volume and page reference. The address of the GRO at Southport is given in **1.8**.

The FRC produces its own guidance in a booklet called *General Register Office: Tracing Records of Births, Marriages and Deaths*. There is also the PRO specialist publication, Colwell, *The Family Records Centre: A User's Guide*, and a pocket guide on *Using Birth, Marriage and Death Records* by Annal. In addition, the subject is covered in all the general genealogical guides, and in several specific ones.

3a.2 Local civil registers

Registration of birth, marriage and death took place locally (as it still does). The local registrars sent in returns every quarter to the Registrar General for copying into the central register, but also kept their own local registers. As a result there are two series of registers, equally valid. The local registers have their own indexes – the index entries from the index to the national register will not work. The local indexes are more accurate than the central index, which was created from copies of copies – errors have naturally crept in. (There is an interesting book by Foster on errors in the marriage register indexes.) And obviously, the local office may be the best place to go if the family is known to have stayed put.

Local civil registers are normally still kept by the local register offices or District Registry. They are usually prepared to help family historians, but this is not their main business – don't ask too much of them. You will still have to buy copy certificates, but you should be able to access the indexes. The level of access varies from office to office.

To find the local register office, try the telephone directory, or the library. If you can access the Internet, look at www.genuki.org.uk which has a list of them, county by county, with details of how to contact them, whether you can make an appointment to search the indexes, and how to order a copy.

If you are interested in finding out more about registration procedures, you may be interested in looking at Lewis's 1888 *Synoptical Index of Regulations*, available in the PRO Library. Files of correspondence about individual cases are in RG 48 at the PRO.

3a.3 Can't find an entry in the indexes?

Failure to find a birth, marriage or death entry in the indexes may be for the following reasons:

- Before 1875 there was no penalty for non-registration and there may be omissions in the birth and death registers. A study by Hughes comparing Liverpool baptismal records with registered births showed a shortfall of almost 33 per cent as late as 1874. You may need to look at parish and non-parochial registers until 1875.
- Before 1927 there was no official adoption procedure and there is no record of the birth of the adopted child under the name by which he or she was known.

Figure 6 The introduction of civil registration in 1837 did not remove the Anglican church's responsibility for recording marriages. The details were sent on to the local civil registrar. (PRO, COPY 1/13)

- There may have been a clerical error when the entry in the local registrar's register was transferred to the central register. The local registers are more accurate.
- Surnames could be spelled differently, especially if the informants were illiterate. The official completing the certificate would use his preferred version of Gardener, Gardiner, Gardner, or Gairdner – and the next time that family registered an event, it might have been a different official with a different preference.
- Some people were known by a forename that was not the first forename on their birth certificate. Euphrosyne Stella may well have chosen to be known as Stella.
- The child may not have been named by the date of registration. Entries under the sex of the infant are given at the end of each surname section.
- In the nineteenth century at least 10 per cent of marriages took place after the birth of the first child.
- Many couples concealed the fact that they were not married by simply adopting the same name: on a birth certificate it would look as though they were married. This would only work in a town large enough to guarantee anonymity, or in a new locality.
- A birth or marriage may have been registered by the Army: see **18a.1**.
- Registers of births on Lundy Island, in the Bristol Channel, were treated as foreign registers, and are in the PRO, in RG 32–35, indexed by the general indexes in RG 43. Some records from the Channel Islands were treated the same way.
- Did the event happen somewhere outside England and Wales? Try the registers of births, marriages and deaths at sea or overseas for people normally resident in England and Wales (see **4**).
- People normally resident in Scotland, Ireland and Northern Ireland will be found in the registers kept there (including registers of births, marriages and deaths at sea or overseas) (see **8** and **9**).

It may be worth checking the Registrar General's correspondence on births, marriages and deaths, from 1874, at the PRO (RG 48). These papers include files on individual cases of difficulty, but some are closed for 50 or 75 years.

Announcements of many births, marriages and deaths may be found in local newspapers held in public libraries and in the British Library Newspaper Library at Colindale (address in **48**). For more details, see Gibson's *Local Newspapers 1751–1920*. It may also be worth looking in professional, trade or trade union journals or magazines, for obituaries or other announcements.

For burial records, it may be worth looking in the *National Burial Index:* see **3b.3**. See also **3c.6** for more burial and cemetery records.

3a.4 Adoptions

Before 1927 there was no official system of adoption and it is usually extremely difficult to trace private arrangements. Some charities, such as Barnardos, arranged adoptions, and may conduct searches for a fee. Certificates of any adoption in England and Wales since 1 January 1927 may be obtained from the FRC. They show the date of the adoption, the name of the child adopted, and the full name and address of the adoptive parents. The FRC has booklets available at the downstairs enquiry desk on *Access to Birth Records, The Adoption Contact Register* and *Information for Adopted People and their Relatives*. See also www.statistics.gov.uk/nsbase/registration/adoptions.asp.

3a.5 Civil registration of births, marriages, deaths and adoptions: bibliography

D Annal, *Using Birth, Marriage and Death Records* (PRO, 2000)

S Colwell, *The Family Records Centre: A User's Guide* (PRO, 2002)

M W Foster, *A 'Comedy of Errors' or the Marriage Records of England and Wales 1837–1899* (New Zealand, 1999. (The review of this by A Camp, in *Family Tree Magazine*, vol. 15, no. 5, gives a useful summary of the problems with marriage indexes)

General Register Office, *Abstract of Arrangements respecting Registration of Births, Marriages and Deaths in the UK and other Countries of the British Commonwealth of Nations, and in the Irish Republic* (London, 1952)

General Register Office, *General Register Office: Tracing Records of Births, Marriages and Deaths* (ONS, 1997)

J S W Gibson, *Local Newspapers 1751–1920* (FFHS, 1987)

D Hughes, 'Liverpool infant mortality rates c.1865–1874: A city much maligned?', in *Lancashire Local Historian*, no. 6, 1991, pp. 32–43

J Lewis, *Synoptical Index of the Regulations for the duties of Superintendent Registrars, Registrars of Births and Deaths, and Registrars of Marriages, and incidentally also of the Statutes relating to the Registration of Births, Marriages and Deaths in England and Wales* (London, 1888)

M Nissel, *People Count, A History of the General Register Office* (London, 1987)

T Wood, *An Introduction to Civil Registration* (FFHS, 1994)

3b

Births, baptisms, marriages, deaths and burials before 1st July 1837

◆ ◆ ◆

3b.1 Births, baptisms and marriages: the *International Genealogical Index*

If you want to trace a baptismal or marriage record from before July 1837, start with the *International Genealogical Index*, known as the *IGI*. This is an index to births, baptisms and marriages worldwide. The indexes to the British Isles cover the period from the beginning of parish registers to about 1885. (Religious registration was required in England and Wales from 1538, in Scotland from 1552, and in Ireland from 1634, but few of the earliest registers survive.) The indexes for England and Wales are mainly to Church of England parish registers held locally and to nearly all the non-parochial registers at the PRO.

The *IGI* covers the British Isles in several separate sequences; one for each English and Scottish traditional county, one each for Ireland, the Channel Islands, and the Isle of Man, and two for Wales, to cover the Welsh system of naming. The *IGI* is available at both the FRC and the PRO, but we cannot provide prints. However, these are available from the sets of the *IGI* kept at the Guildhall Library, the Society of Genealogists and the Genealogical Library of the Church of Jesus Christ of Latter-day Saints. Local libraries and record offices may well have the local county index: see Gibson's book on the *IGI* or check out local holdings on www.familia.org.uk.

The *IGI* is also included in the computer compilation called FamilySearch. This contains millions of entries relevant to family historians, ranging from the *IGI* to information given by individuals researching their own family histories. It is a wonderful resource, and highly addictive – but remember to check the origin of any information, and use the proverbial pinch of salt if things look slightly doubtful. You can access FamilySearch on the Internet at www.familysearch.org and at the FRC and PRO.

There are some drawbacks to the *IGI*. Its coverage is not complete, as some registers have not been included. There is no guarantee that the registers that have been covered are included in full. In addition, useful information that may appear in the register, such as age or father's occupation, is not given in the *IGI*. If you do find a likely ancestor in the *IGI*, you are strongly advised to check the source, or a transcript of it, yourself. If the entry looks as if it comes from a parish register, you can usually discover the present location of the register, and the existence and whereabouts of any transcripts, from *The Phillimore Atlas and Index of Parish Registers,* edited by Humphery-Smith. If the entry refers to a nonconformist chapel, then it is most probably in RG 4, and can be seen on microfilm at the FRC and the PRO. Some of the nonconformist registers contain a lot more information than is included in the *IGI.*

3b.2 Marriages (and London baptisms) before 1837: the Boyd and Pallot Indexes

The Boyd Marriage Index, available at the Society of Genealogists and the Guildhall Library, has a 12 per cent coverage of English marriages between 1538 and 1837. It is being put online by the Society, and you can already access parts of it at www.englishorigins.com. The FRC has odd volumes of the Boyd Index, covering grooms, 1538–1625 and 1726–1800, and brides, 1575–1600 (A–S only), 1601–1625, 1751–1775 (E–R only) and 1776–1800.

For London, try the Pallot Marriage and Baptism Indexes, covering the years c.1781–1837. These index marriages and baptisms from all but two of the City of London parishes, and many more besides, and extracts from nonconformist registers. The Institute of Heraldic and Genealogical Studies hold the actual index, and will search it for a fee (address in **48**). You can also access it on www.ancestry.com as a charged service. If you are a member of the Society of Genealogists, you can access it for free in the Society's library. Some of the entries relate to registers that no longer survive, owing to bomb damage during the Second World War. For anyone looking for a London marriage or baptism this is indispensable.

See Gibson and Hampson, *Marriage and Census Indexes for Family Historians,* for information on these and other marriage indexes.

3b.3 Deaths: the *National Burial Index*

The *IGI* does not include deaths – and deaths can be difficult to trace. The Federation of Family History Societies is tackling the problem, and has currently indexed over 4,000 burial registers in its *National Burial Index.* This can be seen on CD-ROM at both the PRO and the FRC, and in many other places. The first edition indexes over 5.3 million burials in England and Wales, from 1538 to 2000 (although very few twentieth century burials are included). It is currently most useful for deaths between 1800 and 1840.

The information has been extracted from the burial registers kept by parishes, nonconformists, Catholics, and secular cemeteries. Where these details are available, it includes surname and forename, age, date of burial, and county and parish or cemetery of burial. The early material is thin, reflecting as it does the sporadic survival of parish registers from that date. It is not yet a complete index to all burials, but its obvious value reflects the enormous benefit of the voluntary work done in compiling it by the members of the Federation of Family History Societies. Several counties are not yet included at all (e.g. Cornwall, Devon,

Sussex, Nottinghamshire and Cumberland). However, given time (and assistance) the FFHS will have created a wonderful resource.

However, at the moment the *NBI* is an incomplete tool. If you do not find the person you are looking for in it, look at **3c.6** for more suggestions.

3b.4 Parish registers, 1538–1837: the main source

Before 1st July 1837, no national records of birth, marriage or death were kept. An attempt had been made in 1538 to set up such a system when the new Church of England was required to keep parish registers of baptism, marriages and burials. However, after 1538 religious diversity grew extensively, so that not everyone attended the parish church to be included in the parish register.

The parish registers of the Church of England, the main source for tracing births, marriages and deaths before 1837, are not kept at the PRO or the FRC. Instead, they are kept locally, either still in the church or in a local, county or diocesan record office. To discover the present location of the registers of a particular parish, consult *The Phillimore Atlas and Index of Parish Registers*, edited by Humphery-Smith.

The *National Index of Parish Registers* (a multi-volume work with general volumes covering the various types of sources available for Anglican, nonconformist, Catholic and Jewish genealogy, and county volumes listing the availability of parish and other registers) is well worth consulting. You can also discover the existence of copies of parish registers from these two works, which also give their date range and whereabouts.

Figure 7 A baptism into the Church of England, 1820 (Mary Evans Picture Library)

Very few in fact survive from 1538: the average starting date for surviving registers is 1611 for England, and 1708 for Wales.

3b.5 Non-parochial registers before 1837: at the PRO and FRC

The PRO and the FRC have a major source for registered baptisms, marriages and burials in England and Wales – a very large collection of non-parochial religious registers, from outside the parish structure of the Church of England. Some of the registers date from after 1837, but they can still be useful as a complement to the civil registers, as failure to use the civil registration system was not penalised until 1875. They are all seen on microfilm.

The non-parochial registers (RG 4–8) are often referred to as 'nonconformist registers'. However, in addition to several thousand Protestant nonconformist registers, the collection also includes a number of Church of England registers from churches outside the usual parish structure, 27 Catholic registers, and a few registers of foreign churches in England, as well as some cemetery records.

Before 1837, the parish register was the only official place to register baptisms, marriages and burials. Thousands of people refused to comply with the Church of England rites and wished to be baptised and buried by their own church, and to record these events in the registers of their own faith. However, from 1754 to 1837, marriages had to be performed by a beneficed Anglican clergyman in order to be acknowledged in law. An exception was made for Quakers and Jews, because of the detailed way they recorded marriages. Other nonconformists, in order to ensure the legitimacy of their children, and their ability to inherit, had to marry in the Anglican church, and have the event recorded in the parish register. Nonconformist registers between 1754 and 1837 therefore record details of births/baptisms and deaths/burials only. After 1837, they may include marriages as well.

When civil registration was set up in 1837, parliamentary commissioners collected most nonconformist registers and some Anglican non-parochial registers. The registers were deposited in the new General Register Office, where they were used to issue birth certificates that had the status of a legal record (now RG 4–6). Another collection was made in 1857 (now part of RG 8; some were placed in RG 4). On both occasions Catholic and Jewish congregations retained the registers of most of their churches and synagogues. Not all nonconformist registers were surrendered to the General Register Office. Some remained with the congregations (or the minister or priest) and still do so; yet others are in county record offices, or with the archives of the colleges and societies of the various denominations. Look at the *National Index of Parish Registers* for guidance on their known whereabouts.

Both the 1837 and the 1857 collections were transferred to the PRO in 1961, and became widely available for the first time. Other registers were later deposited at the PRO in RG 8 for safe keeping. Many, but not all, of the births and baptisms in the authenticated registers in RG 4 (but not RG 8) have been included in the *International Genealogical Index*.

3b.6 Using nonconformist registers

At the PRO and FRC you can access several thousand nonconformist registers and certificates from England and Wales (RG 4, RG 5, RG 6, RG 8). The main churches represented in the PRO's holdings are the Society of Friends or Quakers (in RG 6), the Presbyterians, the Independents or Congregationalists, the Baptists, the Wesleyan and other Methodists, the Moravians, the Countess of Huntingdon's Connexion, the Bible Christians and the Swedenborgians, as well as various foreign churches. The English Independent congregation of St Petersburg, Russia, also deposited its registers of births, baptisms, and burials, 1818–1840 (RG 4/4605).

With the exception of the Quaker registers (see **3b.8**), nonconformist registers are in RG 4 and RG 8, largely depending on whether they were collected by the 1837 or the 1857 commission. There are certificates from the two central nonconformist registries of births in RG 5. Most of the registers are in RG 4, and have been indexed in the *IGI*; there are many fewer in RG 8, and these are not centrally indexed. However, they are exactly the same kind of registers as in RG 4, and should not be overlooked. The revised lists and the Introductory Notes of RG 4 and RG 8 were republished by the List and Index Society in 1996.

The registers date from 1567 to 1970. The earliest registers belong to the foreign Protestant churches that were granted toleration in England well before any native dissent was made lawful. Registers of English dissenting congregations are very rare before active persecution stopped; the earliest English registers date from the 1640s. The last date, 1970, is something of an oddity, from the dissenting church of Cam, Gloucestershire: it is the last entry in a volume in almost constant use between 1776 and 1970 (RG 8/12C). Most of the registers come from the eighteenth and early nineteenth centuries. After 1754 they do not include marriages, although these do reoccur after 1837 in a few registers in RG 8.

Nonconformist registers often served a far wider area than the traditional Anglican parish, because of the way the various denominations were organized. The paper list of RG 4 includes cross-references from outlying areas, which do not as yet appear on PROCAT. Nonconformity was a very widespread movement in the eighteenth and nineteenth centuries: the 1851 ecclesiastical census showed that a quarter of the population were regular attenders of nonconformist chapels.

Indications that you should investigate the nonconformist registers, and the large amounts of biographical material kept by some of the denominations, might be a long family history of nonconformity; if a post-1837 marriage took place in a nonconformist chapel or in a register office; and if a parish register has a suspiciously high number of marriages and burials of one surname, in proportion to the number of baptisms. On the other hand, known nonconformist ancestors may need to be traced back to the parish registers, for pre-conversion events, occasional conformity, and the records of marriage and burial (if there was no local nonconformist burial ground).

Having discovered a nonconformist ancestor, it is worth digging a little deeper

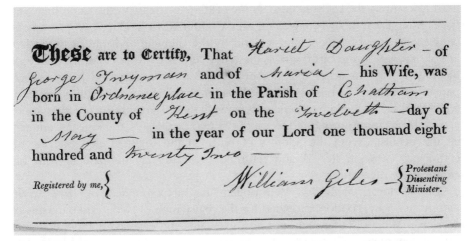

Figure 8 The register of the (Particular Baptist) Providence Chapel, Chatham records births, not baptisms, as Baptists practise adult baptism. (PRO, RG 8/13)

into his or her beliefs, and the organization and discipline of the particular denomination. There is a specialized guide which gives more detailed advice than can be given here. This is Shorney's *Protestant Nonconformity and Roman Catholicism: A Guide to Sources in the Public Record Office*. Steel's *Sources for Nonconformist Genealogy and Family History* covers archive holdings in the PRO and elsewhere. Another useful guide is by Palgrave-Moore, *Understanding the History and Records of Nonconformity*. For a general introduction to the beliefs and regional concentrations of the various nonconformist denominations there is *The Geography of Religion in England*, by Gay.

Less extensive works can also be very useful; for Baptists, try *My Ancestors Were Baptists*, by Breed; for Quakers, *My Ancestors Were Quakers*, by Milligan and Thomas; for Methodists, *My Ancestors Were Methodists*, by Leary and Gandy. These also give indications as to the published works available in denominational libraries such as Dr Williams's Library.

3b.7 Two nonconformist central registries of births, [1716]–1838

There were two nonconformist central registries, set up in an attempt to provide legally acceptable records of births. Many thousands of births were recorded in these registries. The registers and indexes they produced are now in RG 4, and the certificates from which the registers were compiled are in RG 5. You can see them at both the PRO and FRC.

The Protestant Dissenters' Registry at Dr Williams's Library, then in Redcross Street, London, was founded in 1742; it served the congregations of Baptists, Independents and Presbyterians in London and within a 12-mile radius of the capital. However, parents from most parts of the British Isles and even abroad also used the registry. Almost 50,000 births were registered in it. The Register was started in 1742, with retrospective entries going back to 1716, and continued to 1837 (RG 4/4658–4665, with indexes at RG 4/4666–4676). The certificates used to compile the registers also survive (RG 5/1–161, with the same index as the registers). Parents wishing to register a birth had to produce two parchment certificates signed by their minister and by the midwife and one or two other people present at the birth, giving the name and sex of the child, the name of the parents, the name of the mother's father and the date and place (street, parish and county) of birth. After 1828, paper certificates were required instead, which had to be signed by the parents as well; these signatures made them more acceptable as legal proof. On receipt of the two certificates, the registrar entered all the details, except the address of birth, in the register, filed one of the certificates (now in RG 5) and returned the other to the parents with his certificate of registration.

The Wesleyan Methodist Metropolitan Registry, founded in 1818 at 66 Paternoster Row, London, provided for the registration of births and baptisms of Wesleyan Methodists throughout England, Wales and elsewhere, independently of any congregational records. Over 10,000 children were registered here. The registers continued till 1838, with retrospective registration of births going back to 1773 (RG 4/4677–4679, with an index at RG 4/4680). One of two original certificates submitted by the parents was entered in the register and filed (RG 5/162–207, indexed by RG 4/4680), and the other was marked as entered and was returned to the parents. The certificates and the register entry have the name and sex of the child, the name and address of the father, the name of the mother and of both her parents, the date and place of birth, and the name of the Wesleyan circuit, with the signature (or name, in the register) of the parents, the witnesses to the birth, and the baptising minister.

For more information on these, look at the Introductory Notes filed before the lists of RG 4 and RG 5.

3b.8 Quaker registers

The records and registers of the Society of Friends, or Quakers, 1613–1841, are very full, and in excellent order. However, to understand and use them properly, you do need to understand the rather complicated administrative structure of the Society. This is explained in *My Ancestors Were Quakers* by Milligan and Thomas, and also in Steel's *Sources for Nonconformist Genealogy and Family History*; the latter includes a full discussion of Quaker birth, marriage and death registers and practices. You also need to understand the distinctive Quaker dating practices (they used numbers for the names of months and days, as they would not use the common names derived from pagan gods). For an explanation of these, and how they changed significantly over time, see Munby, *Dates and Time*, Appendix 11.

You can see these registers, together with original birth and burial notes, and original marriage certificates and copies, 1656–1834 in RG 6, at both the FRC and the PRO. They are arranged by (county) Quarterly Meeting and by Monthly Meeting. There are also a few registers and other records, 1761–1840, at RG 8/81 and RG 87–89. Most local meetings were under the Quarterly Meeting of their own county, but several are to be found with the records of unexpected quarterly meetings. There is a 'Key to Cross-Border Locations' filed with the paper list, which shows (for example) that the records of the meeting of Ringshall, Buckinghamshire, are to be found in the Quarterly Meeting of Bedfordshire and Hertfordshire.

Quaker birth certificates were signed by any witnesses at the birth, who also had to give their own residence. The marriage certificates were signed by a large number of witnesses, not all of whom were Quakers. Some of the witnesses were identified as relatives. Marriage between two Quakers, conducted according to the Quaker usage, was accepted as legal from 1661, and was exempted from Lord Hardwicke's Marriage Act in 1753.

Outside the PRO, there are indexes to (or rather alphabetical digests of) the registers, made in 1841–1842 and 1857, which are kept at Friends House Library (address in **48**): these can be consulted for a fee. Duplicate digests were also made, and sent to the county-based Quarterly Meetings in place of their registers. For more information on their present location, and on Quaker records in general, consult *My Ancestors Were Quakers*. The Introductory Note to RG 6, filed with the paper list, is well worth reading. The List and Index Society have published both the list and the Introductory Note.

3b.9 Catholic registers

For various reasons, only 27 Catholic churches surrendered their registers to the commissioners in 1837; they are now in RG 4, at the PRO and FRC. Of these, 44 came from Yorkshire, 13 from Durham, 10 from Northumberland, 2 from Lincolnshire and 1 each from Cumberland, Dorset, Hampshire, Lancashire, Nottinghamshire, Oxfordshire, Warwickshire and Westmorland: however, some may have been personal to the priest, and thus cover events in other places as well. Most date from the mid or late eighteenth century, but there are two or three dating from the late seventeenth century.

For the location of other Catholic registers, see the county volumes of the *National Index of Parish Registers,* and *Sources for Roman Catholic and Jewish Genealogy and Family History*, by Steel and Samuel. The latter also discusses the information in the registers.

3b.10 Registers of foreign churches in England

The registers of several foreign churches are in RG 4, listed separately except for those of the Scottish churches, which are included in the county lists; there are also a few in RG 8. Most are Huguenot (French and Walloon Protestant) registers, from the several churches of London, 1599–1840, and from Bristol 1687–1807, Canterbury 1591–1837, Norwich 1595–1752, Plymouth 1692–1807, Southampton 1567–1779 and Thorpe-le-Soken 1684–1726 (in RG 4); Huguenot registers from Dover, 1646–1731, are in RG 8/14. The Huguenot Society has published most of these registers. The other foreign registers are all from London; they are those of the French Chapel Royal 1701–1754, the Dutch Chapel Royal 1689–1754, the German Lutheran Chapel Royal 1712–1836, the German

Lutheran churches 1694–1853, and the Swiss church, 1762–1839, all in RG 4.

Two later French registers came from the French Episcopal Church of the Savoy, in Bloomsbury, London, 1843–1900 (RG 8/34), and from the Reformed French Church in Brighton, 1865–1879 (RG 8/94). The registers and papers of the Russian Orthodox church in London, 1721–1927, which are mostly in Russian are at RG 8/111–304; they include registers of births, marriages and deaths.

These registers can be seen at both the PRO and FRC.

3b.11 Anglican registers in the PRO and FRC

Oddly enough, the PRO does have quite a few Anglican registers – but these are from churches outside the parish system. Any with the code RG can be seen at the FRC and PRO: any with a different code can be seen only at the PRO.

The commissioners for non-parochial registers collected some Anglican registers as well as nonconformist registers, in both 1837 and 1857. Most of these Anglican registers came from the custody of the Consistory Court of London in 1837, and are either from abroad (see **4.3**), or relate to the so-called 'Fleet marriages' (see **3b.13**).

Other Anglican registers came from Mercers' Hall, Cheapside, London (marriages, 1641–1754, and burials, 1641–1833, RG 4/4436) and from the chapels royal at St James's Palace, Whitehall and Windsor Castle, 1647–1709 (RG 8/110). Some of the later registers of the chapels royal, 1755–1880, were deposited directly in the PRO (PRO 30/19/1), but others remain in the custody of the Chapel Royal, St James's Palace. In addition, the PRO has marriage licences for marriages in the Chapel Royal, Whitehall (not royal marriages), 1687–1754 and 1807 (RG 8/76–78). There are also some odd registers elsewhere in the PRO's holdings. Among the PRO's own records are the registers of the Rolls Chapel, Chancery Lane, 1736–1892, with gaps (PRO 30/21/3/1). Another Anglican oddment is the long series of registers from the Dockyard Church of Sheerness, Kent, covering 1688–1960 (ADM 6/429–433 and 438).

However, the bulk of the reputable Anglican registers in the PRO came from the military, naval and charitable hospitals, as non-parochial registers. The birth, marriage and death registers of Greenwich Hospital (including the Royal Naval Asylum and the Royal Hospital Schools) cover 1705–1864 (RG 4/1669–1679 and RG 8/16–18): those of the Army's Chelsea Hospital cover 1691–1856 (RG 4/4330–4332, and 4387). Although Greenwich Hospital and Chelsea Hospital were Navy and Army institutions, these registers appear to include local inhabitants as well. For details of other Army registers in the PRO, see **18a.1.1**. For details of Royal Marine registers, see **20.5**.

One of the PRO's main hospital holdings is the series of records of the British Lying-In (i.e. maternity) Hospital, Holborn, London. This was set up in 1749, and catered for the distressed poor (married women only) with special attention to the wives of soldiers and sailors. Admission was by recommendation: many women appear to have been the wives of servants, recommended by their husbands' employers. The baptismal registers, 1749–1830 (RG 8/62–66) are simply a hospital-composed list of names, parents and dates of birth and baptism until 1814, when proper Anglican baptismal registers appear, and give the parents' address. However, they are supplemented by a fascinating source, the hospital's own record of the admission of the mother and the birth, which gives the names of the parents, the occupation of the father, the age of the mother, place of settlement (place of marriage after 1849), the expected date of delivery, the date of admission, the date of delivery, the name of the child and date of baptism, the date of discharge or death, and the name of the person on whose recommendation the woman was admitted (RG 8/52–61). These hospital records cover 1749–1868, and give details of 42,008 admissions, and about 30,000 baptisms, by no means all of Londoners; one women at least came from the Cape of Good Hope, and others came from Yorkshire, Ireland, the Isle of Wight and Jersey.

Another register from a charitable institution is the marriage register of the chapel of God's House Hospital, Kingston-upon-Hull, 1695–1715 (RG 8/101).

From less charitable institutions, the prisons, there are a few records of births

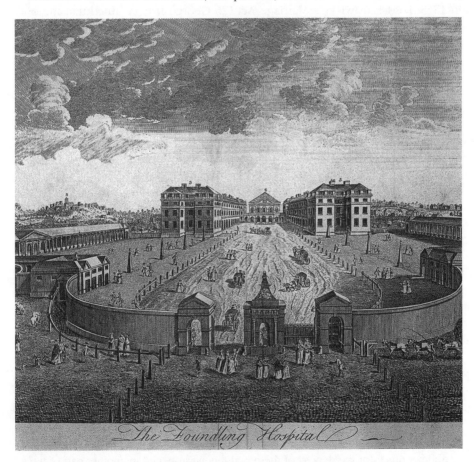

Figure 9 The Foundling Hospital, one of the great eighteenth century charities. Its baptism and burial registers, 1741 to 1838, are in the PRO. See **3c.2** for more details. (Mary Evans Picture Library)

and burials. The Westminster Penitentiary has a register of baptisms, 1816–1871 (PCOM 2/139) and another of burials, 1817–1853 (PCOM 2/140). There is a register of deaths and inquests at the Millbank Penitentiary, 1848–1863 (PCOM 2/165): in this case, most burials were in the Victoria Park cemetery, whose records are discussed in **3c.6**. For other prison records, see **39**, and for other inquests, see **37**.

3b.12 Marriage licences

The PRO has some marriage licences for the Chapel Royal, Whitehall, 1687–1754 and 1807 in RG 8/76–78, but in general the PRO is not the place to look for these documents. See Gibson's *Bishops' Transcripts and Marriage Licences*. For online searching, try www.englishorigins.com.

3b.13 Fleet marriage registers before 1753

In 1753, Lord Hardwicke's Marriage Act (26 George II c.33) ruled that the only lawful marriage was one celebrated by a beneficed Anglican clergyman, in an Anglican church after banns or with a licence. An exception was made for Jews, and also for Quakers, who kept excellent records and who had an elaborate method of validating marriages, including signature of a marriage certificate by many witnesses (see **3b.8**). As a result, nonconformists had to marry in the Anglican church; Catholics generally continued to marry in their own church.

However, Lord Hardwicke's Marriage Act was not aimed directly at preventing nonconformist marriages, but at preventing clandestine Anglican ones. Before it came into effect in 1754, unbeneficed and sometimes unscrupulous clergymen were able to make a living by performing marriages on request, in places exempt from ecclesiastical jurisdiction. One of the most popular of these was the Fleet Prison and its precincts in London; the registers kept by the presiding ministers are known as Fleet registers (RG 7). The report of the 1837 commissioners on non-parochial records on the Fleet marriages is worth quoting at length.

> The generality of them were celebrated by Clergymen of low character, some at the Chapel of the Fleet, others at various taverns and other places within the precincts of the Fleet and King's Bench Prisons, and the Mint in Southwark. These Registers were, in some instances, in the keeping of the Ministers who performed the ceremony, and they were also often kept by the proprietors of the houses or taverns in which the marriages happened to have taken place. After the door was closed against marriages of this description by the operation of the Marriage Act (in 1754), it appears, that a clerk of one of the Fleet Ministers collected a number of them together, and opened an office, where reference might be had to them. Another office for the deposit of these registers was opened in another part of the town; but in 1813 the great bulk of them came into the hands of a private individual, of the name of Cox, from whom the Government purchased them in

1821, and, by the direction of Lord Sidmouth, then Secretary of State for the Home Department, they were deposited in the Registry of the Consistorial Court of London. We apprehend that by far the greater number of the Registers of the Marriages celebrated within the precincts of these several places are comprised in this collection. There are, however, exceptions; for two of the Fleet Registers are known to be in the possession of a professional gentleman in Doctors' Commons, a third has found its way into the Bodleian Library at Oxford. [Now Rawlinson Ms.360.]

The Chapel at May Fair was built about 1730, and Marriages took place there under the same circumstances with those in the places above referred to. Many of the Registers of this Chapel formed a part of the purchase made by the Government in 1821, the remainder are preserved in the church of St George, Hanover Square.

These registers from the Fleet and King's Bench Prisons, the Mint and the May Fair Chapel, 1694–1754, are now in RG 7. In addition, there are two volumes covering 1726–1735 that were brought into court as evidence and are now in PROB 18/50 (these are presumably the two held by the gentleman in Doctors' Commons). The RG 7 registers can be seen at the PRO and FRC: the PROB 18 register can be seen only at the PRO.

The information in the Fleet registers should be treated with extreme caution, as the dates given are unreliable (particularly before 1714), and names or indeed whole entries may be fictitious. The Fleet registers have entries from over the whole country, but with more from London and the Home Counties; about 200,000 marriages are thought to have been celebrated there. The Fleet was frequented for marriages and for some baptisms by craftsmen and sailors in general; professionals and the aristocracy went to the more salubrious May Fair Chapel instead. Such clandestine marriages could result in prosecution, and there are records of many such cases among the Act Books of the Commissary Court of London in the Guildhall Library, and in the records of the Consistory Court of London in the London Metropolitan Archives. For more information see 'The Rise and Fall of the Fleet Marriages' by Brown, or the chapter on clandestine marriages in Steel's *Sources of Births, Marriages and Deaths before 1837 (I)*.

Herber has started producing a series of transcripts of the Fleet registers, called *Clandestine Marriages in the Chapel and Rules of the Fleet Prison 1681–1754*. There is an index to Fleet marriages for Sussex, south-west Kent and south-east Surrey, arranged chronologically within parish of residence of bride and groom; an index cross-referring to the bride's surname is in preparation.

Lord Hardwicke's Act also brought to an end the legal basis of what became known as 'common law marriages', where couples could marry by an informal exchange of vows without any involvement of the church. It did not actually stop people entering into these relationships, but it removed their status as a valid marriage. The main idea was to prevent people of property entering what their families considered ill-advised marriages, but in fact it took away an ancient right most used by the poor. It only goes to show how deeply ingrained that right was in the public mind that so many people still think the law accepts common law marriages, and fail to make adequate legal provision for their partners or children in case of their death.

3b.14 Births, baptisms, marriages, deaths and burials before 1st July 1837: bibliography

T Benton, *Irregular marriage in London before 1754* (Society of Genealogists, 1993)

G R Breed, *My Ancestors Were Baptists* (Society of Genealogists, 1988)

R L Brown, 'The Rise and Fall of the Fleet Marriage', in *Marriage and Society*, ed. R B Outhwaite (London, 1981)

S Colwell, *The Family Records Centre: A User's Guide* (PRO, 2002)

Dr Williams's Trust, *Nonconformist Congregations in Great Britain: A list of histories and other material in Dr Williams's Library* (London, 1973)

J D Gay, *The Geography of Religion in England* (London, 1971)

J S W Gibson, *Bishops' Transcripts and Marriage Licences* (FFHS, 2nd edn, 1985)

J S W Gibson, *Local Newspapers 1751–1920* (FFHS, 1987)

J S W Gibson, *Bishops' Transcripts and Marriage Licences, Bonds and Allegations* (FFHS, 2001)

J S W Gibson and E Hampson, *Marriage and Census Indexes for Family Historians* (FFHS, 7th edn, 1998)

J S W Gibson and M Walcot, *Where to Find the International Genealogical Index* (FFHS, 1985)

M Herber, *Clandestine Marriages in the Chapel and Rules of the Fleet Prison 1681–1754* (2 vols, London, 1998 and 1999)

C R Humphery-Smith, *The Phillimore Atlas and Index of Parish Registers* (Chichester, 1984)

International Genealogical Index, compiled by the Church of Jesus Christ of Latter-Day Saints (also known as LDS and Mormons)

W Leary and M Gandy, *My Ancestors Were Methodists* (Society of Genealogists, 1982)

List and Index Society, *Non-Parochial Registers of Births, Marriages and Deaths (RG 4, 8)* vols 265 and 266 (1996)

List and Index Society, *Society of Friends' Registers (RG 6)* Vol. 267 (1996)

E H Milligan and M J Thomas, *My Ancestors Were Quakers* (Society of Genealogists, 1983)

L H Munby, *Dates and Time: A Handbook for Local Historians* (British Association for Local History, 1997)

National Index of Parish Registers (Society of Genealogists, 1968 continuing). For individual volumes, see the works listed under D J Steel

P Palgrave-Moore, *Understanding the History and Records of Nonconformity* (2nd edn, Norwich, 1989)

Parliament, *Report of the commissioners appointed to inquire into the state, custody, and authenticity of registers or records of births or baptisms, deaths or burials and marriages, in England and Wales other than parochial registers* (London, 1838: parliamentary paper presented to both Houses)

Parliament, *Report of the commissioners appointed to inquire into the state, custody and authenticity of certain non-parochial registers or records of births or baptisms, deaths or burials, and marriages in England and Wales (1857)* (London, 1858: parliamentary paper presented to both Houses)

D J Steel, *Sources for Nonconformist Genealogy and Family History* (National Index of Parish Registers, vol. II, 1973)

D J Steel and E R Samuel, *Sources for Roman Catholic and Jewish Genealogy and Family History* (National Index of Parish Registers, vol. III, 1974)

D J Steel and others, *Sources of Births, Marriages and Deaths before 1837 (I)* (National Index of Parish Registers, vol. I, 1968)

M Walcot, 'English Marriage Indexes', *Genealogists' Magazine*, vol. XIV, pp. 204–208

E Welch, 'Nonconformist Registers', *Journal of the Society of Archivists*, vol. II, pp. 411–417

3c

The loosening of family ties: illegitimacy, foundlings, divorce, and burial

◆ ◆ ◆

3c.1 Illegitimacy

Illegitimacy is not an easy thing to trace – more often it is something discovered by accident. Try Paley, *My Ancestors Were Bastards* for an overview of the sources, most of which are held locally (petty sessions, quarter sessions and Poor Law records).

At the PRO are T 4 and TS 17, about the transmission of property by illegitimate people who died without leaving a will. In these circumstances, any property went to the Crown. TS 17 is searchable by name in PROCAT; T 4 is not, and initially looks unpromising. In fact it includes quite a few eighteenth century petitions from next of kin, asking for letters of administration to be granted to them instead of to the Treasury Solicitor.

3c.2 Foundlings, 1741 to present

For London foundlings (abandoned children), try the records of the Foundling Hospital, London, set up by Thomas Coram in 1741. These are split between the PRO, the GRO, and the London Metropolitan Archives (address in **48**). At the PRO are the registers of baptisms and of all too many burials, for 1741–1838 (RG 4/4396 and 4328). These registers continue from 1853–1948 in the keeping of the GRO (Corrections Branch). An index is available at the FRC and short birth certificates may be bought in the usual way. However, only the Thomas Coram Foundation (address in **48**) will give details of parentage. They also hold a very affecting collection of tokens, left by the mothers with their children. Similar tokens are among the records held by the LMA, which holds the majority of the other records, including petitions from parents for the admission of their child (the system in operation from 1760), apprenticeship registers, minutes, etc.

For registration of foundlings after 1 July 1837, look in the birth indexes, under 'Unknown' (which appears after Z), at the FRC or at the PRO. In 1977 the Abandoned Children Register was introduced: the children are indexed in the usual way under the name given to the child.

3c.3 Putting asunder: divorce, matrimonial disputes and separation before 1858

Before 1858 (except in Scotland) true divorce was rare and expensive, and achieved by private bill in the House of Lords. There was only one divorce bill before 1670. The PRO has a very few of these private acts for divorce, in C 89 and C 204, but they should all be available at the House of Lords Record Office.

The church courts heard matrimonial disputes before 1858. Church court records, which are deposited in diocesan record offices, are largely unindexed and can be extremely difficult to interpret.

The church courts could decree a legal separation, known as divorce *a mensa et thoro* (i.e. from board and bed), but the parties had to undertake not to remarry. Disputes over property rights and settlements after a divorce *a mensa et thoro* appear to have been heard in Chancery: for example, there are decrees from as early as 1538 in C 78. The Privy Council also appears to have had an interest in making sure that separation settlements were adhered to, and there are some entries in its registers in PC 2 about individual cases.

Some private separation agreements, apparently not involving the church courts, have been found enrolled on the Close Rolls in C 54. They appear to have grown in popularity from the Interregnum, when church courts did not operate and private ingenuity filled the gap. Private separations restoring the wife to the status of a *feme sole*, responsible for her own debts, were not recognized by common law or equity, as a married woman was in law treated as a *feme covert*, with her legal personality identical to that of her husband. Attempts to enforce them often led to much litigation in Chancery (see **47b**).

In order to remarry, the marriage had to be declared null from the beginning, on the grounds of want of ability to marry (e.g. a pre-contract to marry another, or want of consent to the marriage: for example, if the parties were under age and therefore incapable of consenting). This total dissolution of a marriage was described as a divorce *a vinculo matrimonii* (from the bond of matrimony). These uncommon procedures were abolished in 1754.

Appeals from ecclesiastical courts in matrimonial cases went to the High Court of Delegates between 1532 and 1832, and to the Judicial Committee of the Privy Council from 1833 until 1858. Copies of the proceedings of the lower, ecclesiastical, courts for 1609–1834 are in DEL 1 (indexed in DEL 11/7), and for 1834–1858 in PCAP 1. The cases as presented to the appeal courts are in DEL 2, DEL 7 and PCAP 3: judgements are included. These records have been relatively little used, but they can be very informative.

3c.4 Putting asunder: divorce, matrimonial disputes and separation from 1858: the background

From 11 January 1858, the new secular Court for Divorce and Matrimonial Causes heard all divorce and matrimonial cases (e.g. restitution of conjugal rights, legitimacy, protection of earnings) until 1875, when it was reformed into the Probate, Divorce and Admiralty Division of the new Supreme Court. All divorce suits took place in London – a fact that served to restrict divorce to better-off couples. London lawyers had to be engaged, the petition had to be filed in the London registry, appearance in court was required – it all needed money and time that most people did not have.

From 1878, a different route was available for poorer women. If her husband had been convicted of aggravated assault against her, the wife could apply to the local magistrate for a separation and maintenance order. By 1886, this route had been opened further: a husband who wilfully refused or neglected to maintain his wife and children, and deserted them, could be ordered to pay maintenance up to £2 a week. By 1895, these various different possibilities had grown into a system to protect virtuous wives and their children from violent, cruel or neglectful husbands. Women seen as immoral were not covered: no husband could be obliged to maintain a wife who had already committed adultery, or who did so after separation. (Many law reformers condemned this kind of separation as a 'living death'.) Women flocked to the magistrates' courts to obtain these orders, partly because required to by some Poor Law authorities. By 1900, over 10,000 orders were being issued each year. These separation orders continued in bulk for many years, until the advent of cheap and relatively easy divorce, when effectively only those with a religious objection to divorce continued to use them. If the orders survive, they will be kept in local record offices.

If a husband or wife wanted a real divorce, with the chance to remarry, a judicial separation was a poor substitute. From 1914, poor petitioners were eligible for financial aid to seek a divorce, under the Poor Persons Rules, which helped a little. The real opening of divorce to all classes took place in the 1920s, with the extension of legal aid, and the provision of some local facilities. This was partly in response to the failure of many marriages during the First World War, and partly because in 1923 women were at last allowed to sue for divorce on the grounds of the husband's adultery alone. (Before this, women had to prove another cause, such as cruelty, in addition to adultery, although men could sue for adultery alone.) In 1922, ten assize towns were named as suitable for the hearing of certain kinds of divorce. From 1927, petitions could be filed in 23 district registries, while the cases could be heard in 18 assize towns. This option proved increasingly popular: within 10 years nearly a quarter of all suits were started at district registries.

The Second World War caused so much dislocation of marriages that the rising torrent of divorce suits became a flood. The summer assizes in one town alone in 1946 had to process 320 divorce cases in 6½ days, with the scenes outside the court being described as like the crowds at a racecourse. The county courts were finally able to hear divorce suits in the late 1960s. Most divorces now take place at county courts.

3c.5 Putting asunder: divorce and matrimonial disputes from 1858: the records

If you are looking for legal proof of a divorce in any court, from 1858 to the present day, contact the Principal Registry of the Family Division, Decree

Figure 10 Appearance in the Divorce Court was an ordeal in itself, and one that, for many years, brought great social shame. (Mary Evans Picture Library)

Absolute Section (address in **48**). For a fee, they will access a union index to the registered court copies of decrees absolute for you, and either provide a copy of the information themselves (if the divorce was granted by the Supreme Court) or arrange for a copy to be sent to you from the relevant county court. If you want the information on the cause of the divorce, you must specifically ask them to include the details from the decree nisi as well. If the divorce took place within the last five years, you can also contact the county court where it took place for a cheaper service. If you can discover the case number from the public access indexes at the PRO or FRC, you can order a copy of the decree at a reduced cost from the Principal Registry.

For each suit, case files were created, identified by year and a number. Surviving ones can be seen at the PRO. These give more detail, including the petition, copies of any relevant certificate, details of whether the plaintiff was suing as a poor person, affidavits – and the decrees nisi and absolute. Most have been stripped of further material, but a selection were kept complete, to show all stages of a suit. If there is a previous or later petition, a cross-reference is given on the front of the file.

The survival rate of these case files is excellent until 1927, not bad until 1937, and then disastrous. From 1938 onwards, only an absolutely minute sample (of full case files) has been kept: so far none after 1954 has been transferred. The surviving case files are in J 77, with indexes in J 78. The indexes can also be seen at the FRC. The dates given in the lists of both J 77 and J 78 are the dates of filing the initial petition, not the date of the divorce itself (which is used by the index at the Principal Registry).

What does all this imply for the chance of finding a divorce case file?

1858–1927	All files should survive in J 77.	Indexed in J 78	A very few are known to be missing.	Missing ones indexed in J 78 and noted as missing in J 77 list.
1928–1937	About 80 per cent of files should survive in J 77.	Indexed in J 78.	District registries divorce suits (about 20 per cent of total) were destroyed on the recommendation of Lord Denning.	District Registry cases not indexed in J 78. Only decrees survive, at the Principal Registry. Index accessed by staff there.
1938–1954	No files survive except approximately 250 chosen as examples of different kinds of suits: in J 77	Principal Registry divorces indexed in J 78	Divorce files destroyed on the recommendation of Lord Denning.	Decrees survive only for these cases, at the Principal Registry. Index to Principal Registry and District Registry divorces accessed by staff there.
1955–	No files survive.			Decrees only survive, at the Principal Registry. Index accessed by staff there.

If there is no case file, you will have to try local newspapers for any further details. You may find this worth doing anyway, particularly before the mid 1920s, as divorce reporting was a staple fare of many newspapers.

Case files do not survive for the local district registries, which could handle divorce suits from 1927 (the first decrees absolute from suits started at district registries were issued in February 1928, by the Supreme Court). The district registries were increasingly popular: in their first three years, 17 per cent of divorce suits were filed in district registries, rising to 23 per cent in 1937. For these suits only the decree is left in official custody, at the Principal Registry. However, it is not easy to tell where a suit was filed. It seems that the only way you can find out if a divorce *granted between 1928 and 1937* will or will not have a case file at the PRO is:

- to buy a copy of the decree absolute from the Principal Registry, specifying in your request that you wish to know if the suit was filed in a District Registry (no case file) or in the Principal Registry (case file);
- to do a speculative search in J 78.

The indexes in J 78

The indexes in J 78 are not in strict alphabetical order. They are more like entry books, with the parties entered in the relevant pages for surnames of the same letter, as the suit was filed. They are available on microfilm, at both the PRO and the FRC, but the files in J 77 can be seen only at the PRO. You will need to get the file number from the index, and match it up in the list of J 77. The index is not very easy to use, as each volume covers more than one year – and some years are in more than one series in J 77. Once you have found the entry, double-check which year it is in – the turn of the year is usually marked within each letter-block, though not always very clearly. The indexes also indicate the kind of petition, abbreviated as shown here:

HD	Petition by husband for decree of divorce
WD	Petition by wife for decree of divorce
HN	Petition by husband for decree of nullity
WN	Petition by wife for decree of nullity
HJS	Petition by husband for decree of judicial separation
WJS	Petition by wife for decree of judicial separation
HRCR	Petition by husband for decree of restitution of conjugal rights
WRCR	Petition by wife for decree of restitution of conjugal rights
Legit	Petition for declaration of legitimacy
Div Ct	Appeal to Divisional Court from Justices
Prot	Application for order for protection of wife's earnings and property

Series	Number of files	File references	Index
1858–1866	2,547 files, listed by letter and number	J 77/1–63	J 78/1
1867–1884	10,000 files, listed by number	J 77/64–332	J 78/1–3
1885–1898	20,045 files, listed by number	J 77/333–657	J 78/3–5
1899–1909	10,000 files, listed by number	J 77/658–988	J 78/5–7
1909–1917	10,000 files, listed by number	J 77/988–1309	J 78/7–9
1917–1920	10,000 files, listed by number	J 77/1309–1611	J 78/9–10
1921–1922	10,000 files, listed by number	J 77/1611–1918	J 78/11–11
1922–1925	10,000 files, listed by number	J 77/1918–2234	J 78/11–12
1925–1928	10,000 files, listed by number	J 77/2235–2572	J 78/12–14
1928–1931	10,000 files, listed by number	J 77/2572–2908	J 78/13–15
1931–1934	10,000 files, listed by number	J 77/2908–3272	J 78/15–16
1934–1936	10,000 files, listed by number	J 77/3273–3546, J 77/3643–3704	J 78/16–17
1936–1938	7670 files, listed by number: 7671–10,000 (for early 1938) destroyed	J 77/3547–3642; J 77/3705–3864	J 78/17–18

1858–1937

For 1858 to 1937 almost all files filed in the Principal Registry survive, in J 77. The 20 per cent or so of divorce suits filed in the District registries from 1927 do not survive. The files were closed for 75 years until recently, but have now all been made available. For 115 cases between 1858 and 1934, representing the full range of disputes heard by the court, all documentation has been preserved. There is a list of these 115 cases in front of the paper list of J 77 – remember that you will have to match up the number given with the relevant block of years in the list.

The files in J 77 are mostly arranged in blocks of 10,000: the series changed when 10,000 was reached, so the series cover odd blocks of time.

If you find that a file from 1858–1882 is missing, try the court books in J 170.

If the court suspected that the divorce was in collusion – by agreement of the parties, which was then illegal – the case was remitted to the King's Proctor for investigation. Try the indexed registers of investigated cases in TS 29, although records dating from less than 75 years ago are still closed.

1938 to date

Unfortunately no case files survive for petitions *filed* in either the Principal or the district registries after 31 December 1937. (If you are looking for a divorce *granted* in 1938, 1939 or even 1940 it may be worth looking for a case file in J 78, because of the time-lag.) Case papers are now destroyed after about 20 years. If you are within the 20 year period, you can appear before a District Judge to request permission to see the case papers: contact the Principal Registry for details.

The sole exception is the sample of 251 full files in J 77. To see if you are lucky enough to have a case file included in this sample, try a search in PROCAT using the name and J 77. Hardly anybody will be lucky. If nothing is found, you will have to depend on the decrees alone, plus any reports in local newspapers.

However, the indexes to suits filed at the Principal Registry before 1 January 1959 still exist at the PRO and FRC, and can at least provide evidence that a divorce or matrimonial suit took place. This index is the only official place to find evidence of the existence of failed suits. (You may be able to find more details on failed suits in local newspapers.) For November 1946–1949, there are no indexes, only divorce receipt books. These have very little to recommend them: you would be far better off ignoring them and going for the Principal Registry material unless you are looking for a failed suit.

3c.6 A last farewell: burial grounds and cemeteries

Many people want to find out where a person is buried, as well as the date of death. Start with the *National Burial Index*, described in **3b.3**, or look for a published obituary or death notice in the local newspaper. If these sources aren't fruitful, you may need to carry out a search in the original parish or cemetery registers. Of course, you have to have a reasonable guess as to where and when the person died. After 1837, the death certificate will provide this information (though not burial details).

Burials after 1853 could take place in either a parish or nonconformist cemetery, or in one of the many local authority or privately-run cemeteries that ringed Victorian cities. If you are looking for a city burial, you may need to consult maps of the area to find out which was the likeliest place of burial. Burial records are generally held and maintained by local authorities: try the local phone book for addresses. For Greater London, consult Webb, *Greater London Cemeteries and Crematoria*. Records of one of these large cemeteries,

Figure 11 Mourners at the graveside of Constance Noble in 1866: what sad story lies behind this picture? (PRO, COPY 1/11)

the Victoria Park Cemetery in Hackney, London, 1853–1876, can be seen at the FRC and the PRO (RG 8/42–51; each volume is arranged in surname letter order).

If the death was before 1854, the most likely place of burial was in the local parish churchyard (and recorded in the parish register) or in the local nonconformist burial ground. Although the nonconformist registers do include details of deaths and burials, burials were usually in the parish churchyard, and noted in the parish register, until nonconformist burial grounds were established. Some of these were small and local, such as the Protestant Dissenters' Burial Ground at Great Dunmow, Essex, 1784–1856 (RG 4/597) or the Dissenters' Ground at Boston, Lincolnshire, 1789–1856 (RG 4/24–25). However, nonconformists also established large burial grounds or cemeteries for dissenters; this practice later spread to all denominations. The main pre-1854 burial records in the PRO and FRC are those of these large cemeteries established in London. These are the:

- Bethnal Green Protestant Dissenters' Burying Ground, or Gibraltar Burying Ground, 1793–1837 (RG 8/305–314); index at FRC
- Bunhill Fields Burial Ground, City Road, 1713–1854 (RG 4/3974–4001, 4288–4291 and 4633
  - with indexes at RG 4/4652–4657
  - other records for this cemetery, at the Guildhall Library, include an alphabetical list of burials, 1827–1854;

- Bunhill Burial Ground or Golden Lane Cemetery, 1833–1853 (RG 8/35–38);
- South London Burial Ground, East Street, Walworth, 1819–1837 (RG 4/4362);
- Southwark New Burial Ground, 1821–1854 (RG 8/73–74);
- Spa Fields, Clerkenwell, 1778–1849 (RG 4/4316–4322, 4366–4367).

In addition, the PRO and FRC have the Anglican registers of burials at the Royal Hospital, Greenwich, 1705–1864 (RG 4/1669–1676, and RG 8 16–18), and of the Royal Hospital, Chelsea, 1692–1856 (RG 4/4330–4332 and 4387).

The PRO and FRC also have the registers of the Necropolis Burial Ground in Everton, Liverpool, for all denominations, 1825–1837 (RG 4/3121).

Also worth consulting are the records of the removal of tombs and gravestones from churchyards, cemeteries and burial grounds of all denominations (including some Jewish ones), in order to develop the land for some other purpose (RG 37). These are modern records of the actual removals and reinterments, but the tombs and gravestones themselves date from 1601 to 1980, with most coming from the later eighteenth and the nineteenth centuries. The files usually include a list of names, where these were discoverable, and frequently contain transcripts of the monumental inscriptions. They also indicate the place of reinterment. The Society of Genealogists has a significant collection of indexes to Monumental Inscriptions recorded from gravestones by many Family History Societies.

3c.7 The loosening of family ties: illegitimacy, foundlings, divorce, and burial: bibliography

W R Cornish and G de N Clark, *Law and Society in England 1751–1950* (London, 1989)
A Horstman, *Victorian Divorce* (London, 1985)
O R McGregor, *Divorce in England* (London, 1957)
H Mellor, *London Cemeteries: Illustrated Guide and Gazetteer* (Godstone, 1985)
R Paley, *My Ancestors Were Bastards* (FFHS, 2002 forthcoming)
C Webb, *Greater London Cemeteries and Crematoria* (Society of Genealogists, 1999)

4

Births, marriages and deaths
of Britons overseas and at sea

◆ ◆ ◆

4.1 General introduction

There are considerable numbers of sources available within Britain for births, marriages and deaths of Britons in other countries and at sea. Civil registration records were kept abroad by British consulates, or at sea by the masters of British ships. From various dates in the nineteenth century, they were obliged to send on the information they had recorded to the separate General Register Offices of England and Wales, Scotland, Ireland (and Northern Ireland, from 1922), or to the Registrar General of Shipping and Seamen, who then forwarded the information to England, Scotland or Ireland. The army also kept its own registers, whether at home or abroad. Regimental registers before 1881 seem to have ended up with the General Register Office of England and Wales (although the PRO has a few, see **18a.1**). Armed service registers, from about 1881, and registers (or indexes) of war deaths may be found in the relevant General Register Office.

The various Register Offices had compiled their own registers and indexes from the information thus returned. These registers are the obvious place to start. See **8** and **9** for the Scottish and Irish registers kept by their General Register Offices. The registers kept by the General Register Office for England and Wales at Southport are not open to public inspection. Certified copies have to be bought in the same way as home certificates (see **3a.1**). The indexes to the various types of register can be consulted at the FRC and also at the PRO: they are listed in **4.14**. In the course of time, many of the original records from which these registers had been created came to the PRO. The consular records are in FO series, and the marine records and registers are in BT series: they are freely available for inspection subject to the normal closure rules.

In addition to the sources discussed above, there are records of religious registration, which date from much earlier. These tend to be split between the PRO and the Guildhall Library, which has a large deposit of the Bishop of London's records. The Bishop of London had a historic jurisdiction over Britons abroad (mostly in Europe), and registers were returned to him. Some also went to the General Register Office of England and Wales, and were later sent on the

PRO: they are in the RG code, and can be seen at both the PRO and FRC. For religious registration, you may well need to go to both the Guildhall and the PRO or FRC, and to consult Yeo, *The British Overseas* (a guide to the sources at the Guildhall) in tandem with **4.15**.

The PRO's overseas holdings as are currently known (but not marine or armed forces registers) are listed by country, in **4.15**.

The subject of overseas and marine registration is quite complicated. In this chapter, look at **4.2–4.6** and **4.14–4.15** for overseas registration records and **4.7–4.11** and **4.14** for marine registers. For armed forces' registers, look at **18a.1** and **20.5**.

4.2 Overseas registers for England and Wales: an introduction

Overviews of the records in the Guildhall and some other places, and in some of the Foreign Office records at the PRO, are included in *The British Overseas*, by Yeo. This lists the sources country by country: but it does *not* include the overseas registers kept by the GRO at Southport, nor other records at the PRO. This present chapter lists *only* the indexes of the GRO registers (**4.14**) and the holdings of the PRO (**4.15**). As a result, you need to consult both *The British Overseas* and this book in order to get full information on what is available for a particular country. A copy of *The British Overseas* can be seen at both the PRO and the FRC.

One general point is that, in the case of British colonies, registration records before independence were and are kept locally, and you will need to enquire in the country concerned. Look at Yeo, *The British Overseas*, to find the addresses for the official holdings. There are microfiche copies of the indexes to the Australian registers, 1790–c.1900, at the Society of Genealogists. After 1949 you may find some entries in the indexes relating to the registers kept by the United Kingdom High Commissions in colonies and ex-colonies. These are kept at the FRC (see **4.5** and **4.14**).

An exception to the rule of colonial records being held in those countries is provided by pre-independence India. Records of British and European baptisms, marriages and burials in the Indian sub-continent, including Burma and Aden (1698–1948, with a partial continuation to 1968), are at the India Office Library and Records (address in **48**). There are also some Indian records in the PRO and at the FRC. Some other exceptions are listed in **4.15**. See also **13.9**.

There are sections of the *International Genealogical Index* that relate to records of births, baptisms and marriages in countries other than Britain (see **3b.1**).

4.3 Religious registers, from the seventeenth century onwards

Religious records of baptisms, marriages and burials in foreign countries are either still held locally (especially if there was a formal church organization), or were returned to the Bishop of London. Most of these Bishop of London registers have since been deposited in the Guildhall Library, where there is a very extensive collection called the Bishop of London's International Memoranda: see

The British Overseas for further details. However, some (originally sent to the Bishop for safe keeping) were later deposited in the General Register Office of England and Wales, and have now been passed on to the PRO. They can now be seen on microfilm (RG 32–36, with indexes at RG 43) at both the PRO and FRC.

4.4 Overseas civil registration from 1849

Statutory civil registration of English and Welsh citizens in foreign (*not* colonial) countries began in 1849, under the Consular Marriages Act, although on a voluntary basis. Civil registration of Scots abroad began in 1860, and of the Irish abroad in 1864. Since then, the Foreign Office has returned registers of births, marriages and deaths, compiled at its embassies and consulates, to the General Register Offices of England, Scotland, Ireland (1864–1921) and Northern Ireland (from 1922); the full addresses are given in **48**. There is a large collection of odd registers collected by the General Register Office at the FRC: some from overseas and some (the regimental registers of births and marriages) partly from this country as well. The other General Register Offices of Scotland and Ireland were also supposed to receive similar information: see **8** and **9**.

The Family Records Centre (and the PRO, on microfiche only), have indexes to the official sets of registers. These contain information returned to the General Register Office of England and Wales by British consuls, British High Commissions, the British armed forces, and the institutions responsible for the registration of births and deaths on ships, aircraft, hovercrafts and offshore installations. Public access is to only the index: you cannot see the register, which is kept at Southport, but have to purchase a copy of the particular certificate you want. The indexes are listed in **4.14**.

4.5 Confusion and duplication: making the best use of the records at the PRO

With so many statutory and non-statutory registers, returns and copies being sent to so many different places, it is not surprising that duplication and confusion exist. In theory, the PRO may contain more information, as the registers kept by British representatives was collected by them once, and then divided and sent to different destinations. In addition, the records at the PRO are open for inspection.

Try using the GRO indexes (also available on microfiche at the PRO) to the registers kept by the GRO at Southport to find the initial information you are looking for. Then check to see if the PRO has a consular or religious version for the right place and date (use **4.15**), or a marine register (see **4.14**). This way, you can browse in the whole register at the PRO, rather than buying a single copy certificate. If you are looking for someone who lived in a close-knit British community abroad, you may find all kinds of clues in the register as to the life they led and the people they knew. You should also find that the consular registers include information not in the GRO registers – that is, information sent to the General Register Offices of Scotland, Ireland and Northern Ireland.

4.6 Foreign registers in the PRO

The holdings of the PRO overlap the registers in the FRC in many respects, although they are not as up-to-date. The PRO has duplicates of many of the consular returns, and also has a number of regimental registers, and records of births, marriages and deaths at sea. There are some unique records as well.

The major unique source is the collection of miscellaneous non-statutory registers and records, 1627–1958, deposited by the General Register Office in the PRO in 1977 (RG 32–36, with indexes in RG 43). They can now be seen at both the PRO and the PRO section of the FRC. They relate to the births, baptisms, marriages, deaths and burials abroad, and on British and foreign ships, of British subjects, nationals of the colonies, of the Commonwealth, or of countries under British jurisdiction. Some foreign nationals are also included. References, by country, are given in **4.15**; however, this includes only the most well represented countries in RG 32–36, and there are many others besides (e.g. Uruguay and Gibraltar). You should check in the indexes in RG 43 even if the country you are interested in does not appear in **4.15**, or if it does with a wrong date-range.

The embassy and consular records of the Foreign Office at the PRO often contain duplicates of the statutory registers sent in to the General Register Office from 1849 onwards, and also contain earlier records. Although they do not cover the whole range of registers at the FRC, there are some Foreign Office registers that appear to be unique. Even when they duplicate the FRC registers they have the considerable advantage that you can browse through them, if they are over 30 (in some cases 50) years old. For details of the various registers, listed by country, see **4.15**.

There is also a 46-volume series of consular correspondence with the Foreign Office on marriages abroad, covering 1814–1905. The series is split between FO 83 and FO 97, with a register and index for 1814–1893 at FO 802/239. It includes information on some individual marriages. Also in FO 83 are covering despatches to certificates of marriages abroad giving the names of the parties, 1846–1890; general correspondence and circulars on consular marriages; and acknowledgements of receipt of certificates by the Bishop of London's Registry.

References to similar correspondence can be traced in the Foreign Office card index for 1906–1919, and in the printed index for 1920–1957; both these indexes are in the Research Enquiries Room at the PRO. However, many of the documents they refer to no longer exist.

As many of these records appear to partly duplicate the records in the Guildhall, it is worth checking *The British Overseas* to find out which place has the more complete collection. The list in **4.15** indicates whether *The British Overseas* gives references to other sources outside the PRO. Records at the Guildhall, as at the PRO, are produced directly to the public, sometimes on microfilm.

Other records of births, marriages and deaths abroad occur elsewhere among the public records; these are included in **4.15**. Two possible sources that are not listed in **4.15** are the Protestant Dissenters' Registry at Dr Williams's Library, and the Wesleyan Methodist Metropolitan Registry. Both of these registered births abroad as well as in the United Kingdom. For more details, see **3b.7**.

4.7 Marine registers: an introduction

An official registration system (initially for deaths only, at sea) was in operation from 1851, and the registers it created are available in the records of the Registrar General of Shipping and Seamen, at the PRO. These should cover all the events relating to British nationals that were later transmitted to the various General Register Offices plus records for other nationalities. Indexes to the GRO registers for England and Wales composed from these returns are available at both the FRC and the PRO. Seamen and passengers were registered differently until 1891. Marriages were legal only if conducted by a clergyman, not by the master of the ship: it appears that the master had to be reminded of this, so perhaps many had been marrying people illegally!

Miscellaneous records of births, marriages and deaths at sea from 1831–1958 are in RG 32, indexed by RG 43.

4.8 Deaths of seamen, 1851–1890

By the Seamen's Fund Winding-up Act 1851, the masters of British (including colonial) ships were required to hand over the wages and effects of any seamen who had died during a voyage. Registers (BT 153) were maintained until 1889–1890 (but 1881–1888 do not survive). They provide useful information: the name, register ticket number, date of engagement, and the place, date and cause of the man's death, with the name and port of his ship, the master's name, the date and place of payment of wages, the amount of wages owed and the date they were sent to the Board of Trade. The indexes to these registers (BT 154, BT 155) are by seamen and by ship, and give simple page references. Associated with the registers are printed monthly lists of dead seamen for 1886–1890 (BT 156) giving name and age, rating, nationality or birthplace, last address, and cause and place of death. There are also nine manuscript registers (BT 157), containing half yearly lists of deaths, classified by cause, for 1882–1890. For deaths after 1890, see **14.10**.

4.9 Births, marriages and deaths of passengers, 1854–1891

Following the Merchant Shipping Act of 1854, registers were compiled from the official logs deposited with the RGSS, of births, marriages and deaths at sea. All three are recorded from 1854 to 1883, births and deaths only from 1883 to 1887, and deaths only from 1888–1890 (BT 158). Masters were further required by the Registration of Births and Deaths Act of 1874 to report births and deaths of British nationals on board ships to the Registrar General of Shipping and Seamen, where they were entered in two separate registers (BT 159, BT 160). Indexes are available.

These are not mere duplicates of the marine registers held by the GRO at Southport (**4.14**), as the BT registers contain much material on people of other nationalities, or on people of any nationality where sufficient proof of death (such as a body) was not found.

Figure 12 Committing a body to the deep: a burial at sea on a passenger steamer, 1879 (Mary Evans Picture Library)

4.10 Passengers and seamen: births, marriages and deaths, 1891–1964

From 1891 a new series of registers (BT 334) begins which combine records of passengers and seamen at sea.

Birth entries (available 1891–1960) record name of ship, official number, port of registry, date of birth, name, sex, name of father, rank or profession or occupation of father, name of mother, maiden surname of mother, father's nationality/birthplace and last place of abode, and mother's nationality/ birthplace and last place of abode.

Marriage entries for 1854–1972 record name of ship, official number, names of both parties, ages, whether single, widow or widower, profession or occupation, fathers' names, and professions or occupations of fathers.

Death entries (available 1891–1964, indexed to 1960) record name of ship, official number, port of registry, date of death, place of death, name of deceased, sex, age, rating (for seamen), rank or profession or occupation (for non-seamen), nationality and birthplace, last place of abode, cause of death, remarks.

The series also contains indexes to births and deaths; these are arranged both by ships' names and individuals' names. It should be noted that, although the Registrar General of Shipping and Seamen was required to report births, marriages and deaths to the appropriate Registrar General of Births, Deaths and Marriages, over 50 per cent of the entries in BT 334 are blank in the column headed 'Which RG has been informed'. In cases where the ship was lost, it seems that the GRO may not have been informed. One register of deaths and births at sea (1892–1918), first reported at Falmouth, has survived in CUST 67/74.

Inquiries into deaths at sea can be found in BT 341, for 1939–1964. It includes passengers and crew of all nationalities but you need to know the name of the ship. For deaths of merchant seamen in the two world wars, use the rolls of honour in BT 339, or the Commonwealth War Graves Commission's Debt of Honour register (www.cwgc.org.uk).

For records after 1964, use the GRO general indexes for British nationals, available at the FRC and the PRO (see **4.14 no. 1**). For others, write to the Registry of Shipping and Seamen (address in **48**).

4.11 Other sources for deaths, etc., at sea

Details of some births and baptisms at sea (potentially from 1831–1931) are also included in RG 32/1–16 (indexed in RG 43/2). There are also registers of marriages aboard naval ships, 1842–1889 (RG 33/156, indexed in RG 43/7). These often appear to be the marriages of people living in places where other methods of obtaining a valid British marriage may have been difficult, such as the Cayman Islands. Deaths of British citizens on board French ships, 1836–1871, are in RG 35/16 (in French); deaths on board Dutch ships, 1839–1871, are in RG 35/17 (in Dutch): both are indexed by RG 43/4.

Registers of the deaths of emigrants at sea, 1847–1869, are in CO 386/169–172.

4.12 Commonwealth War Graves, and other burial grounds

The Commonwealth War Graves Commission has details of servicemen who died overseas and on ships in the two world wars. Try their excellent website, www.cwgc.org.uk which is searchable by name. For details of military graves other than for the two world wars, contact the Ministry of Defence, PS4(CAS)(A). The addresses are in **48**.

The British Association for Cemeteries in South Asia (BACSA) is a voluntary organization which deals with the preservation, conversion and registration of European cemeteries in South Asia (Persian Gulf to Hong Kong), and in particular those that were formerly administered by the East India Company, and the British government in India. It compiles records of both civilians and soldiers, and produces a twice-yearly magazine, *Chowkidar.* For more information, contact the BACSA Secretary: a stamped addressed envelope would be appreciated. The address is in **48**.

4.13 Births, marriages and deaths of Britons overseas and at sea: bibliography and sources

Published works

General Register Office, *Abstract of Arrangements Respecting Registration of Births, Marriages and Deaths in the United Kingdom and the Other Countries of the British Commonwealth of Nations, and in the Irish Republic* (London, 1952)

K Smith, C T Watts and M J Watts, *Records of Merchant Shipping and Seamen* (PRO, 1998)

J Wall, 'The British Association for Cemeteries in South Asia', *Genealogists' Magazine,* XXIV, pp. 1–4

C T Watts and M J Watts, *My Ancestor was a Merchant Seaman* (Society of Genealogists, 2002 forthcoming)

G Yeo, *The British Overseas, A Guide to Records of Their Births, Baptisms, Marriages, Deaths and Burials Available in the United Kingdom* (Guildhall Library, London, 4th edn, 1994)

Unpublished finding aids

RG 43: indexes to most of RG 32–36, and to RG 4/4605, on microfilm. Some entries relate to registers held by the GRO at Southport

4.14 Indexes at the FRC (also available at the PRO) to the Overseas, Marine and Armed Services Registers kept by the General Register Office of England and Wales

General Indexes, from 1966		
1966–date	1	**Registers of Births Abroad; and Marriages Abroad; and Deaths Abroad (Civilian and Armed Forces)** These registers took over from the Air, Consular, Marine, Miscellaneous, and Services series, and apparently from the marriage and death sections of the United Kingdom High Commission series (all below). The birth indexes give name, mother's maiden name, place of registration and date or year of birth. The marriage registers include the spouse's surname. The death registers give age.
Colonial Indexes, 1940–1981		
1940–1981	2	**UKHC Registers of Births Abroad 1950–1965; and Marriages; and Deaths** The United Kingdom High Commissions kept these registers in colonies and ex-colonies. Although the birth registers start in 1950, they do include a few births from the 1940s.
Civilian Indexes, 1837–1965		
1849–1965	3	**Consular Registers of Births; and Marriages; and Deaths** Arranged alphabetically within a range of five or so years; no closer indication of date is given. Deaths were not registered with consuls until 1859. The indexes include name and consul's registration district: from 1906, the spouse's name is given in the marriage index, and the age in the death index. These are the statutory consular registers, kept as a result of the 1849 Act. Among the Foreign Office embassy and consular records at the PRO are the duplicates kept by the consulates. It may be worth using the index at the FRC, and then looking at the duplicate registers at the PRO: this would save the cost of buying the wrong certificate if the index is not sufficiently precise. However, the reference given in the index at the FRC does not apply to the PRO. You will need to match up the place of registration with the right consulate, and then find that consulate's records from **4.15**.
1837–1965	4	**At sea: Marine Registers of Births; and Deaths** These give name and year of English and Welsh births and deaths at sea; after 1875, the name of the ship is given as well. The age is given for deaths. From 1837 to 1874 they relate to events occurring on British merchant and naval ships; from 1875, to other ships carrying passengers to or from the United Kingdom as well.

1947–1965	5	***Air Registers of Births; and Deaths*** The index gives name, age (for deaths), place and year of births and deaths occurring in civil aircraft in flight.
1941–1965	6	***Protectorates of Africa and Asia: Registers of Births*** The registers for 1895–1957, and the indexes up to 1940, are at the PRO.
1956–1965	7	***Miscellaneous Foreign Registers of Births, Marriages and Deaths*** The index gives name, place and year. Most entries appear to be from the Gulf States, Singapore, etc.
1818–1864	8	***Index to Registers of Births, Marriages and Deaths in the Ionian Islands*** The index is to a military register, a civil register, and a chaplain's register. It gives names only. See also **4.15**, under **Greece**.

Armed Forces Indexes, 1761–1965

1761–1924	9	***Regimental Registers of Births*** These record the births of children of serving soldiers in the United Kingdom and abroad (from c.1790). The indexes are arranged alphabetically, giving name, place, year and regiment. There are also marriage registers, but these are not indexed and cannot be inspected: see **18.2** for more information.
1796–1880	10	***[Army] Chaplains' Returns of Births; and Marriages; and Deaths*** These all relate to events abroad. The index gives name, place and a date range of two to three years.
1881–1955	11	***Army [and other Services] Returns of Births; and Marriages; and Deaths*** These all relate to events abroad and include the Navy as well. The indexes give name, station and date. From 1920, entries relating to the Royal Air Force are included.
1956–1965	12	***Service Departments Registers of Births; and Marriages*** These relate to Army, Navy and Air Force births and marriages abroad. The indexes give name, station and year.

Armed Forces: Indexes to War Deaths, 1899–1948

1899–1902	13	*Natal and South Africa Forces*
1914–1921	14	*Army Other Ranks' War Deaths*
1914–1921	15	*Army Officers' War Deaths*
1914–1921	16	*Naval War Deaths*
1914–1921	17	*Indian Services' War Deaths*
1939–1948	18	*Army Other Ranks' War Deaths*

1939–1948	**19**	*Army Officers' War Deaths*
1939–1948	**20**	*Naval Ratings' War Deaths*
1939–1948	**21**	*Naval Officers' War Deaths*
1939–1948	**22**	*RAF All Ranks' War Deaths*
1939–1948	**23**	*Indian Services' War Deaths*

4.15 Table of overseas birth, marriage and death records in the PRO

African Protectorates	births 1911–1946; marriages 1912–1935; deaths 1911–1946	RG 36[2]
Algeria	deaths 1840–1958	RG 35/14–15, 20–24[2]
Angola *Luanda*	births 1865–1906; marriages 1871–1928; deaths 1859–1906	FO 375/1–4
Argentina[1] *Buenos Aires*	marriages 1826–1900	FO 446/3–6, 28–30
Ascension Island[1]	baptisms/births from 1858–1861 and onwards deaths 1858–1920	RG 32[2] RG 35[2]
Austria[1] *Vienna* *Vienna* *Vienna*	deaths c.1831–1920 marriages 1846–1890 marriages 1883–1891 baptisms 1867–1886 and onwards	RG 35/20–44[2] FO 83[3] FO 120/697 RG 32[2]
Belgium[1] (including *Belgian Congo*) *Antwerp* *Antwerp* *Antwerp* *Antwerp* *Brussels* *Brussels* *Ghent*	deaths 1831–1871 deaths 1871–1920 military deaths in hospital, etc., 1914–1920 　(In alphabetical order, but not indexed 　in RG 43. There are no certificates for 　surnames beginning with C, F, P, Q or X.) baptisms and burials 1817–1852; marriages 1820–1849 baptisms and burials 1831–1836, 1841–1842; marriages 1832–1838, 1841–1842 baptisms 1840 and onwards marriages and deaths: correspondence 　1927–1951 marriages 1816–1890 marriages 1846–1890 marriages 1849–1850	RG 35/1–3[2] RG 35/20–44[2] RG 35/45–69 RG 33/1–2[2] RG 33/155[2] RG 32[2] FO 744 RG 33/3–8[2] FO 83[3] RG 33/9[2]
Bermuda[1]	naval dockyard baptisms, marriages and burials 1826–1946	ADM 6/434, 436, 439

1 You may also need to consult Yeo, *The British Overseas*.
2 Entries in RG 32–36 are largely indexed by RG 43: at both PRO and FRC.
3 Indexed in FO 802/239.

Brazil[1]		
Bahia	marriages 1816–1820	RG 33/155[2]
Maranhão	marriages 1844	RG 33/155[2]
Parà	births and deaths 1840–1841	RG 33/155[2]
Rio de Janeiro	marriages 1809–1818	RG 33/155[2]
Rio de Janeiro	births 1850–1859	FO 743/11
Rio de Janeiro	baptisms 1850 and onwards	RG 32[2]
Rio de Janeiro	marriages c.1850 and onwards	RG 34[2]
Rio de Janeiro	burials 1850 and onwards	RG 35/20–44[2]
Rio de Janeiro	marriages 1870–1890	FO 83[3]
São Paulo	births 1932; marriages 1933	FO 863/1–2
Brunei	births 1932–1950	RG 36[2]
Bulgaria[1]		
Plovdiv	births 1880–1922; deaths 1884–1900	FO 868/1–2
Rustchuk	births 1867–1908; deaths 1867–1903	FO 888/1–2
Sofia	births 1934–1940	FO 864/1
Varna	births 1856–1939; deaths 1851–1929	FO 884/1–5
Burma		
Rangoon	marriages 1929–1942	RG 33/10[2]
China[1]	births, marriages and deaths 1869–1876	FO 681/1
Amoy	births 1850–1950; marriages 1850–1949; deaths 1850–1948 (see also **China** FO 681/1)	FO 663/85–95
Canton	births 1864–1865, 1944–1950; marriages 1865, 1943–1949; deaths 1865, 1944–1950 (see also **China** FO 681/1) for a list of British subjects in Canton, 1844–1951, see FO 694	FO 681/2–9
Changsha	births 1905–1941; marriages 1906–1936; deaths 1906–1933	FO 681/10–12
Chefoo	births 1861–1943; marriages 1872–1940; deaths 1861–1942	FO 681/13–22
Chengtu	births 1902–1915; marriages 1904–1924; deaths 1904–1926	FO 664/3–5
Chinanfu (Tsinan)	births and marriages 1906–1935; deaths 1906–1931, 1937	FO 681/23–27
Chinkiang	births 1865–1866, 1899–1926; marriages 1865–1866, 1896–1959; deaths 1865–1866, 1889–1927 (see also **China** FO 681/1)	FO 387/4–5, 7–11
Chungking	births 1888–1951; marriages 1891–1949; deaths 1891–1950	FO 681/28–34
Darien	births and marriages 1907–1940; deaths 1910–1940	FO 681/35–88
Foochow	births 1858–1866, 1905–1944; marriages 1909–1942; deaths 1858–1866, 1921–1945 (see also **China** FO 681/1)	FO 665/3–8
Formosa (Taiwan)	births, marriages and deaths 1866	FO 681/57

1 You may also need to consult Yeo, *The British Overseas.*
2 Entries in RG 32–36 are largely indexed by RG 43: at both PRO and FRC.
3 Indexed in FO 802/239.

Formosa (Taiwan)	deaths 1873–1901 (see also **China** FO 681/1)	FO 721/1
Hankow	births 1863–1951; marriages 1869–1949; deaths 1861–1950 (see also **China** FO 681/1)	FO 666/2–22
Ichang	births 1879–1938; marriages 1881–1937; deaths 1880–1941 (damaged by fire)	FO 667/2–6
Kuikiang	births 1866–1929; marriages 1872–1928; deaths 1863–1929 (see also **China** FO 681/1)	FO 681/39–45
Kunming	births 1949–1951; deaths 1950	FO 668/2–3
Kwelin	births 1942–1944; deaths 1943	FO 681/46–47
Mukden	births and deaths 1949 (date of registration); marriages 1947–1948	FO 681/48–49, 79–80
Nanking	births 1930–1948; marriages 1929–1949; deaths 1930–1947	FO 681/50–53
Newchang	births, marriages and deaths between 1869 and 1876	FO 681/1
Ningpo	births 1858; marriages and deaths 1856–1858 (see also **China** FO 681/1)	FO 670/2–4
Peking	births 1911–1914; deaths 1911–1913 (date of registration) (see also **China** FO 681/1)	FO 564/13–14
Shanghai	births 1856–1864; marriages 1851; deaths 1851–1864	FO 672/1–3
Shanghai	marriages 1852–1951	RG 33/12–20[2]
Shanghai, Union Church	marriages 1869–1951 (see also **China** FO 681/1)	RG 33/21–32[2]
Shantung Province	marriages 1912–1914	RG 33/33[2]
Swatow	births 1864–1865, 1947–1949 (date of registration); marriages 1865; deaths 1864–1865 (see also **China** FO 681/1)	FO 681/54–56
Taku	births 1862–1875; deaths 1871–1875	FO 673/9–10
Tengyueh	births 1904–1941; marriages 1913–1941; deaths 1906–1941	FO 681/60–62
Tientsin	births 1864–1951; marriages 1862–1952; deaths 1863–1952 see also **China** FO 681/1	FO 674/297–327
Tsingtao	births 1911–1950; marriages 1923–1949; deaths 1921–1951	FO 675/7–10
Wei-hai-wei	births 1899–1929; marriages 1905–1940; deaths 1899–1929, 1938–1941	FO 681/63–71
Wei-hai-wei	births, marriages, deaths 1899–1930	RG 33/34[2]
Wei-hai-wei	births, marriages, deaths 1899–1930	RG 36[2]
Wei-hai-wei	index to births, marriages and deaths 1899–1930	RG 43/19[2]
Whampoa	births and deaths 1865 (see also **China** FO 681/1)	FO 681/72–73
Yunanfu	births 1903–1948; marriages 1904–1949; deaths 1903–1950	FO 681/74–78
Colombia[1]	marriages 1824–1827	RG 33/155[2]
	marriages 1846–1890	FO 83[3]

1 You may also need to consult Yeo, *The British Overseas*.
2 Entries in RG 32–36 are largely indexed by RG 43: at both PRO and FRC.
3 Indexed in FO 802/239.

Cartagena	births 1853–1924; deaths 1858–1927	FO 736/2–3
Denmark[1]	deaths 1842–1872	RG 35/4–7[2]
Copenhagen	marriages 1846–1890	FO 83[3]
Copenhagen	marriage affidavits 1853–1870	FO 211/236
Copenhagen	marriages 1853–1874	RG 33/35[2]
Copenhagen	baptisms 1866–1870; marriages and burials 1869–1870 and onwards	RG 32[2]
For Danish colonies, see **West Indies**		
Ecuador		
Guayaquil	births, marriages and deaths 1879–1896	FO 521/2
Estonia see **Russia**		
Falkland Islands[1]	births and baptisms [1853–1951]	RG 32[2]
	marriages [1854–1951]	RG 34[2]
	burials 1854–[1951]	RG 35/20–44[2]
Finland[1]		
Helsinki	births 1914–1924	FO 753/19
Helsinki	deaths 1924	FO 768/5
Kristinestad	deaths 1928	FO 756/1
Raahe (Brahestad)	deaths 1930	FO 755/1
Tampere	births 1906–1923; deaths 1909–1934	FO 769/1–2
Turku (Abo)	births 1928; deaths 1929	FO 754/1–2
Vyborg	births 1924–1931; deaths 1929–1937	FO 751/1–3
France[1]	deaths 1831–1871	RG 35/8–13[2]
	deaths 1871–1920	RG 35/20–44[2]
	military deaths in hospital, etc., 1914–1920 (In alphabetical order, but not indexed in RG 43. There are no certificates for surnames beginning with C, F, P, Q or X.)	RG 35/45–69
Boulogne	baptisms and burials 1815–1896; marriages 1829–1895 (index at RG 33/161)	RG 33/37–48[2]
Brest	births 1842	RG 33/155[2]
Calais and St Omer	baptisms 1817–1878; marriages 1818–1872; burials 1819–1878 (index at RG 33/49)	RG 33/50–55[2]
Dieppe	births 1872–1892; deaths 1871–1894	FO 712/1–3
Le Havre	baptisms, marriages and burials 1817–1863	RG 33/56–57[2]
Le Tréport	births 1917–1926; deaths 1899–1929	FO 713/1–2
Nantes	marriages 1851–1867	FO 384/1
Paris	baptisms, marriages and burials 1784–1789, 1801–1809, 1815–1869; marriages 1869–1890	RG 33/58–77[2]
Paris	deaths 1846–1852	RG 35/11[2]
Paris	marriages 1852–1890	FO 83[3]
Paris	marriages 1935–1937	FO 630/1
Rouen	baptisms 1843–1844	RG 33/78[2]

1 You may also need to consult Yeo, *The British Overseas*.
2 Entries in RG 32–36 are largely indexed by RG 43: at both PRO and FRC.
3 Indexed in FO 802/239.

French colonies (Cochin China, Guadeloupe, Guyana, Haiti, India, Martinique, Mexico, New Caledonia, Réunion, Saigon, Shanghai, Senegal, Society Islands)	deaths 1836–1871	RG 35/14–16[2]
(See also **Algeria, Réunion, Madagascar, Tahiti** and **West Indies**)		
Germany[1]	deaths c.1831–1920	RG 35/20–44[2]
Aachen	deaths 1925	FO 604/7
Bavaria	baptisms, marriages and deaths 1860–1861	FO 151/3
Bavaria	marriages 1860–1861	FO 149/99
Bavaria	marriages 1884–1897 (see also RG 32)	FO 601/2–6
Berlin	marriages 1846–1890	FO 83[3]
Berlin	births 1944–1954; deaths 1944–1945	FO 601/2–6
Bremen	births 1872–1914; marriages 1893–1933	FO 585/1–5
Bremerhaven	births 1872–1893	FO 585/1
Bremerhaven	marriages 1903–1914	FO 586/1
Cologne	births and marriages 1850–1866; deaths 1850–1866 and 1879–1881	FO 155/5–11, 17
Cologne	births 1880; marriages 1920–1934	FO 604/8–10
Darmstadt	births 1869–1898; deaths 1871–1905	FO 716/1–2
Darmstadt	marriages 1870–1890	FO 83[3]
Dresden	births, baptisms and burials 1817–1836	RG 33/79[2]
Dresden	marriages 1846–1890	FO 83[3]
Dresden	births and deaths 1859–1866	RG 33/80[2]
Dresden	births 1901–1907; marriages 1899–1900	FO 292/2, 4–5
Düsseldorf	births 1873–1884; baptisms 1903–1907; marriages 1873–1878, 1893–1898; deaths 1876–1884	FO 604/1–6, 8
Essen	births 1922–1927	FO 604/11
Frankfurt	marriages 1836–1865	FO 208/90
Frankfurt	marriages 1846–1869	FO 83[3]
Hanover	baptisms, marriages, deaths and burials 1839–1859	RG 33/81[2]
Hanover	marriages 1846–1869	FO 83[3]
Hanover	births 1861–1866	FO 717/1
Karlsruhe	births 1860–1864; deaths 1859–1864	FO 718/1–2
Konigsberg	marriages 1864–1885	FO 509/1
Leipzig	marriages 1850–1865; deaths 1850–1860	FO 299/22
Munich	marriages 1846–1890	FO 83[3]
Saxony	marriages 1850–1865; deaths 1850–1869	FO 218/3
Stuttgart	marriages 1847–1890	FO 83[3]
(See also **Poland**)		
Greece[1]	marriages 1846–1890	FO 83[3]
Ionian Islands, Zante	baptisms, marriages, deaths and burials 1849–1859. The registers for 1818–1848 are at Southport: see **4.5**.	RG 33/82[2]

1 You may also need to consult Yeo, *The British Overseas.*
2 Entries in RG 32–36 are largely indexed by RG 43: at both PRO and FRC.
3 Indexed in FO 802/239.

	The index covers both sets, and can be seen at the FRC (ONS) and at Kew: see **4.14 no. 8**.	
Hawaii	births 1848–1893 marriages 1850–1853 registers of British subjects 1895–1944	FO 331/59 RG 33/155[2] FO 331/60–61
Hong Kong	deaths from enemy action in the Far East 1941–1945, indexed in RG 43/14 (see also **Indonesia** RG 33/132)	RG 33/11
Hungary *Budapest*	marriages 1872–1899	FO 114/1–5
Indian States[1] *Bikaner, Eastern Rajputana, Gwalior, Hyderabad, Jaipur, Madras States, Mysore, Punjab States, Travandrum, and other states*	births and deaths 1894–1947 (most from 1930s and 1940s) (indexed in RG 43/15)	RG 33/90–113
Jammu and Kashmir, Kolhapur and Deccan states, Udaipur	births 1917–1947 (indexed in RG 43/15)	RG 33/157–158, 160
Srinagar	deaths 1926–1947 (indexed in RG 43/15)	RG 33/159
Indian Sub-continent[1] *French India*	deaths c.1831–1920 deaths 1836–1871	RG 35/20–44[2] RG 35/16[2]
Indonesia **(Dutch East Indies)**[1] *Borneo* *Borneo and Sarawak* *Java* *Java* *Oleh Leh* *Sumatra*	deaths 1839–1871 deaths 1871–1920 births 1907; deaths 1897–1907 deaths from enemy action 1941–1945 births 1869–1941; baptisms 1906; deaths 1874–1898 and 1912–1940 deaths 1839–1871 births and deaths 1883–1884 births and deaths 1883–1884	RG 35/17[2] RG 35/20–44[2] FO 221/2–3 RG 33/132[2] FO 803/1–3 RG 35/20–44[2] FO 220/12 FO 220/12
Iran (Persia)[1] *Bushire* *Isfahan* *Tabriz*	births 1903–1950; marriages 1895–1950; deaths 1899–1950 births, marriages and deaths 1849–1895 births 1829–1950; marriages 1893–1951; deaths 1892–1943 births 1851–1951; marriages 1850–1950; deaths 1882–1931	FO 923/1–25 FO 560 FO 799/34–37 FO 451/1–9
Iraq (Mesopotamia)[1]	births, marriages and deaths 1915–1931 (with marriage indexes in RG 33/138–139) births, marriages and deaths 1915–1931 (indexed in RG 43/16)	RG 33/133–137[2] RG 36[2]
Israel see **Palestine**		
Italy[1] *Agrigento*	deaths 1871–1920 births 1857–1904; deaths 1857–1885	RG 35/20–44[2] FO 653/2–4

1 You may also need to consult Yeo, *The British Overseas*.
2 Entries in RG 32–36 are largely indexed by RG 43: at both PRO and FRC.
3 Indexed in FO 802/239.

Catania	births 1878–1939; deaths 1878–1904, 1919–1940	FO 653/5–7
Florence	marriages 1840–1855, 1865–1871	RG 33/114–115[2]
Florence	marriages 1856	FO 352/43
Gela	births 1904–1930	FO 653/8
Licata	births and deaths 1871–1900	FO 720/1
Livorno (Leghorn)	births, baptisms, marriages and burials 1797–1824	RG 33/116–117[2]
Marsala	births, 1847–1922; deaths 1847–1919	FO 653/9–11
Mazzara	births 1810–1911	FO 653/12–13
Messina	births and deaths 1854–1957	FO 653/14–17
Milazzo	deaths 1887–1903	FO 653/18
Naples	baptisms, marriages and burials 1817–1822	RG 33/118[2]
Naples	baptisms, marriages and burials 1835–1836	RG 33/155[2]
Palermo	births 1837–1891, 1932–1940; deaths 1850–1919	FO 653/19–21
Porto Empedocle	births 1906	FO 653/22
Rome and Tuscany	baptisms and marriages 1816–1852	FO 170/6
Rome	marriages 1870–1890	FO 83[3]
Rome	marriages 1872–1889	RG 33/119[2]
Sicily	births 1810–1957; deaths 1847–1957	FO 653/2–38 & FO 720/1
Sicily	baptisms 1838	RG 33/155[2]
Syracuse	births 1909–1918; deaths 1912–1919, 1953–1957	FO 653/23–25
Taormina	deaths 1909–1922	FO 653/26
Trapani	births 1871–1906, 1924–1927	FO 653/27–28
Turin	marriages 1847–1869	FO 83[3]
Turin	marriages 1858–1864	RG 33/120[2]
Venice	marriages 1874–1947	RG 33/121[2]
Japan[1]	marriage declarations and certificates 1870–1887	FO 345
Kobe	baptisms and marriages 1874–1941; burials 1902–1941	RG 33/122–126[2]
Nagasaki	births 1864–1940; marriages 1922–1940; deaths 1859–1944	FO 796/236–238
Osaka	marriages 1892–1904	RG 33/127–130[2]
Shimonoseki	births 1903–1921; marriages 1906–1922; deaths 1903–1921	FO 797/48–50
Tokyo	marriages 1870–1890	FO 83[3]
Tokyo	marriages 1875–1887	FO 345/34
Yokohama	marriages 1870–1874	FO 345/34
Jordan *Amman*	births 1946; marriages 1927	RG 36[2]
Kenya (East African Protectorate)	births 1904–1924 (partly indexed by RG 43/18)	RG 36[2]
Latvia see **Russia**		
Lebanon *Beirut*	marriages c.1859–1939	FO 616/5

1 You may also need to consult Yeo, *The British Overseas*.
2 Entries in RG 32–36 are largely indexed by RG 43: at both PRO and FRC.
3 Indexed in FO 802/239.

Libya *Tripoli*	marriages 1916, 1931–1940; deaths 1938–1939	FO 161/4–7
Lithuania see **Russia**		
Madagascar[1] *Diego Suarez* *Tamatave* *Tananarive (Antananarivo)*	births 1907–1921 deaths 1935–1940 births 1865–1868	FO 711/1 FO 714/1 FO 710/1
Malaysia[1] *Borneo* *Borneo and Sarawak* *Johore* *Sarawak*	births 1917–1949 births 1920–1948; deaths 1941–1945 births 1907; deaths 1897–1907 deaths from enemy action 1941–1945 births 1924–1931 births 1910–1948; marriages 1921–1935; deaths 1910–1948	RG 36[2] RG 33/131–132[2] FO 221/2–3 RG 33/132[2] RG 36[2] RG 36[2]
Malta[1]	marriages 1904–1936	FO 161/7
Mauritius see **Réunion**		
Mexico *Mexico City* *Mexico City* *Mexico City* *Vera Cruz*	marriages 1850 and onwards deaths c.1850–1920 burials 1827–1926 marriages 1846–1869 births and deaths 1854–1867 births, deaths and burials 1858–1867	RG 34[2] RG 35/16, 20–44[2] FO 207/58 FO 83[3] FO 723/1–2 RG 33/140[2]

Netherlands[1]
The Hague
 	
The Hague
Rotterdam
	deaths 1839–1871 and 1871–1920
	baptisms 1627–1821; marriages 1627–1889;
	    births 1837–1839, 1859–1894;
	    deaths 1859–1907
	    (These also include some church records;
	    for others, see FO 259.)
	marriages 1846–1890
	baptisms and marriages 1708–1794
		RG 35/17 & 20–44[2]
		RG 33/83–88[2]
		
		FO 83[3]
		RG 33/89[2]

For Dutch colonies, see **Indonesia, Surinam** and **West Indies**		
Norway *Bodo* *Drammen* *Kragero* *Lofoten Islands* *Oslo (Christiania)* *Porsgrund and Skien*	deaths 1831–1920 births 1888–1890; deaths 1895 deaths 1906 deaths 1895 births 1850–1932 births 1850–1932; marriages 1853–1936; deaths 1850–1930 births 1885–1891	RG 35/20–44[2] FO 724/1–2 FO 532/2 FO 725/1 FO 726/1 FO 529/1–14 FO 531/2

1 You may also need to consult Yeo, *The British Overseas*.
2 Entries in RG 32–36 are largely indexed by RG 43: at both PRO and FRC.
3 Indexed in FO 802/239.

Palestine[1]	births and deaths 1920–1935 (indexed in RG 43/17)	RG 33/141[2]
	births 1923–1948; deaths 1941–1945 (partly indexed in RG 43/18)	RG 36[2]
Jaffa	births 1900–1914	FO 734/1
Jerusalem	births 1850–1921; deaths 1851–1914	FO 617/3–5
Jerusalem	military baptisms 1939–1947	WO 156/6
Sarafand	military baptisms 1940–1946; banns of marriage 1944–1947	WO 156/7–8
Paraguay	births 1863 and onwards	RG 32[2]
	deaths 1831–1920	RG 35/20–44[2]
Peru[1]	births and deaths 1837–1841; marriages 1827 and 1836	RG 33/155[2]
Poland[1]		
Breslau (Wroclaw)	births 1929–1938; deaths 1932–1938	FO 715/1–2
Danzig (Gdansk)	births 1851–1910; deaths 1850–1914	FO 634/16–18
Lodz	births 1925–1939	FO 869/1
Stettin	births 1864–1939; deaths 1857–1933	FO 719/1–2
Portugal[1]	deaths 1831–1920	RG 35/20–44[2]
Azores	births, baptisms, marriages, deaths and burials 1807–1866	FO 559/1
Azores	baptisms, marriages and burials 1835–1837	RG 35/155[2]
Azores	baptisms 1850–1857	RG 32[2]
Azores	burials 1850–1857	RG 35/20[2]
Cape Verde Islands	marriages 1894–1922	FO 767/6–7
Lisbon	marriages 1846–1890	FO 83[3]
Lisbon	marriages 1859–1876	FO 173/8
Luanda see **Angola**		
Oporto	baptisms, marriages and burials 1814–1874	RG 33/142[2]
Oporto	baptisms, marriages and burials 1837	RG 33/155[2]
Oporto	baptisms 1835 onwards	RG 32[2]
Oporto	marriages 1835 onwards	RG 34[2]
Oporto	burials 1835–1844	RG 35/20[2]
Réunion (Mauritius)	deaths 1836–1871	RG 35/16[2]
	marriages 1864–1921	FO 322/1–2
Romania[1]		
Braila	births 1922–1930; deaths 1921–1929	FO 727/1–2
Bucharest	births 1851–1931; baptisms 1858–1948: deaths 1854–1929	FO 625/2–4, 6
Bucharest	marriages 1870–1890	FO 83[3]
Constanta (Kustendje)	births 1866–1873	FO 887/1
Galatz	marriages 1891–1939	FO 517/1–2
Lower Danube	baptisms 1869–1907	FO 625/5
Lower Danube	marriages 1868–1914	RG 33/143[2]
Lower Danube	burials 1869–1870	FO 786/120
Sulina	births 1861–1932; deaths 1860–1931	FO 728/1–2 & FO 886/1–2

1 You may also need to consult Yeo, *The British Overseas*.
2 Entries in RG 32–36 are largely indexed by RG 43: at both PRO and FRC.
3 Indexed in FO 802/239.

Russia[1]	births, baptisms, and deaths 1835–1870	RG 35/18–19[2]
	births 1849–1909; marriages 1849–1861; deaths 1849–1915	FO 267/44–46
	deaths 1871–1920	RG 35/20–44[2]
Archangel	births 1849–1909; marriages 1849–1861; deaths 1849–1915	FO 267/44–46
Batum	births 1884–1921; marriages 1891–1920; deaths 1884–1920	FO 397/1–6
Berdiansk (Osipenko)	marriages 1901	FO 399/1
Ekaterinburg (Sverdlovsk)	deaths 1918–1919	FO 399/5
Estonia, Pernau	births 1894–1930; deaths 1894–1930	FO 339/11–12
Estonia, Tallin (Reval)	births 1866–1940; marriages 1921–1939; deaths 1875–1940	FO 514/1–9
Konigsberg (Kaliningrad)	births 1869–1933; marriages 1864–1904; deaths 1857–1932	FO 509/1–4
Latvia, Libau	births 1883–1932; deaths 1871–1932	FO 440/10 & FO 661/4–5
Latvia, Riga	births 1850–1910; deaths 1850–1915	FO 377/3–4
Latvia, Riga	births 1921–1940; marriages 1920–1940; deaths 1921–1940	FO 516/1–9
Latvia, Windau	births 1906–1909	FO 399/19
Lithuania, Kovno and Memel	births 1924–1940; deaths 1922–1940	FO 722/1–4
Moscow	births 1882–1918; marriages 1894–1924; deaths 1881–1918	FO 518/1–4
Nicolaiyev	births 1872–1917; deaths 1874–1915	FO 399/7–8
Novorossisk	births 1911–1920; deaths 1896–1920	FO 399/9–10
Odessa	births 1852–1919; baptisms 1893; marriages 1851–1916; deaths 1852–1919	FO 359/3–12
Poti	births 1871–1906; deaths 1871–1920	FO 399/13–14
Rostov	births 1891–1914; marriages 1904–1918; deaths 1906–1916	FO 398/1–9
St Petersburg (Petrograd, Leningrad)	baptisms 1818–1840; burials 1821–1840. Independent denomination. (Indexed in RG 43)	RG 4/4605[2]
St Petersburg (Petrograd, Leningrad)	births, baptisms, marriages, deaths and burials 1840–1918 (with an index for 1886–1917 in RG 33/16[2])	RG 33/144–152[2]
St Petersburg (Petrograd, Leningrad)	births 1856–1938; marriages 1892–1917; deaths 1897–1927	FO 378/3–9
St Petersburg (Petrograd, Leningrad)	marriages 1870–1890	FO 83[3]
Sebastopol	births 1886–1898; marriages 1910; deaths 1893–1908	FO 393/3, 15–16
Theodosia (Feodosiya)	births 1904–1906; deaths 1907–1918	FO 339/17–18
Vladivostok	births 1911–1927; marriages 1916–1923; deaths 1908–1924	FO 510/1–10
Singapore	births 1922	RG 36[2]

1 You may also need to consult Yeo, *The British Overseas.*
2 Entries in RG 32–36 are largely indexed by RG 43: at both PRO and FRC.
3 Indexed in FO 802/239.

Somaliland (Somalia)	births 1905–1920 (partly indexed by RG 43/18)	RG 36[2]
Spain[1]	deaths 1831–1920	RG 35/20–44[2]
Aguilas	births 1875–1911; deaths 1874–1911	FO 920/1–2
Balearic Islands	births, marriages, deaths (1815–1880)	FO 214/51–53
Bilbao	deaths 1855–1870	FO 729/1
Cartagena	births 1847–1887; marriages 1858–1904; deaths 1855–1871	FO 920/3–6
Garrucha	births 1876–1890; deaths 1883–1905	FO 920/7–8
Madrid	marriages 1846–1890	FO 83[3]
Madrid	registers of British subjects 1835–1895, 1906–1931	FO 445
Pormàn	births 1907; deaths 1911	FO 920/9–10
Seville	births, marriages and deaths 1948	FO 332/14–16
Sudan[1]	births 1916–1950; marriages 1907–1950; deaths 1917–1946 (partly indexed by RG 43/18)	RG 36[2]
Surinam (Dutch Guiana)		
Paramaribo	births 1897–1966; marriages 1922–1929; deaths 1889–1965	FO 907/1–32
Sweden[1]	deaths 1831–1920	RG 35/20–44[2]
Gothenburg	marriages 1845–1891	RG 33/153[2]
Gothenburg	baptisms 1881–1890	FO 818/15
Hudiksvall	deaths 1884	FO 730/1
Oskarshamn	deaths 1887	FO 731/1
Stockholm	marriages 1847–1890	FO 83[3]
Stockholm	births, marriages and deaths 1920–1938	FO 748
Switzerland[1]	marriages 1816–1833	FO 194/1
	deaths 1831–1920	RG 35/20–44[2]
Geneva	births 1850–1934; marriages 1850–1933; deaths 1850–1923	FO 778/13–22
Lausanne	births 1886–1948; marriages 1887–1947; deaths 1887–1948	FO 910/1–20
Montreux	births 1902–1939; marriages 1927–1933; deaths 1903–1941	FO 911/1–3
Syria[1]		
Aleppo	baptisms and burials 1756–1800	SP 110/70
Damascus	births, marriages and deaths 1932–1938	FO 684/16–17
Tahiti		
Papeete	births 1818–1941; marriages 1845–1941; deaths 1845–1936	FO 687/22–23
Raiatea	births, marriages and deaths 1853–1890	FO 687/34, 36–38
Taiwan see **China** *Formosa*		
Tristan da Cunha	marriages 1871–1951; deaths 1892–1949 (Registers of births and baptisms, 1867–1955, were returned to Tristan da Cunha in 1982.)	PRO 30/65

1 You may also need to consult Yeo, *The British Overseas*.
2 Entries in RG 32–36 are largely indexed by RG 43: at both PRO and FRC.
3 Indexed in FO 802/239.

Tunisia		
Bizerta	deaths 1898–1931	FO 870/1
Djerba	deaths 1925	FO 871/1
Gabes	deaths 1925	FO 872/1
Goletta	births 1885–1888	FO 878/1–2
Monastir	deaths 1905–1908	FO 873/1
Sfax	deaths 1896–1931	FO 874/1
Susa (Sousse)	deaths 1894–1931	FO 875/1
Turkey[1]	deaths 1831–1920	RG 35/20–44[2]
Adana	marriages 1913, 1942 and 1946	FO 609/1–3
Adrianople (Edirne)	births 1888–1912; marriages 1887–1914	FO 783/3–7
Ankara and Konieh	births 1895–1909	FO 732/1
Constantinople (Istanbul)	marriages 1885–1958	RG 33/154[2]
Constantinople (Istanbul)	marriages 1895–1924	FO 441/1–35
Dardanelles	births 1900–1914	FO 733/1
Smyrna (Izmir)	baptisms, marriages and burials 1833–1849	RG 33/155[2]
Trebizond	registers of British subjects 1836–1913	FO 526
Uganda[1]	marriages 1904–1910 (partly indexed by RG 43/18)	RG 36[2]
United States of America[1]		
Florida, Pensacola	births 1880–1901; deaths 1879–1905	FO 885/1–2
Hawaii see **Hawaii**		
Louisiana, New Orleans	births 1850–1932; marriages 1850–1881; deaths 1850–1932	FO 581/15–19
Massachusetts, Boston	births 1871–1932; deaths 1902–1930	FO 706/1–3
Michigan, Detroit	births 1910–1969; marriages 1936–1937; deaths 1931–1945, 1949–1968	FO 700/44–53
Minnesota, St Paul	births 1943–1966; deaths 1944	FO 700/71–74
Missouri, Kansas City	births 1904–1922, 1944–1966; marriages 1958–1961; deaths 1920–1926, 1943–1949, 1952–1965	FO 700/54–60
Nebraska, Omaha	births 1906	FO 700/61
Ohio, Cincinnati	births 1929, 1943–1948, 1951–1958; deaths 1947, 1950–1955	FO 700/31–35
Ohio, Cleveland	births 1914–1930, 1944–1969; deaths 1948–1969	FO 700/36–43
Oregon, Portland	births 1880–1926; deaths 1929	FO 707/1–2
Pennsylvania, Pittsburgh	births 1954–1956	FO 700/63
Rhode Island, Providence	births 1902–1930; deaths 1920 (date of registration)	FO 700/8–9
Texas, Dallas	births 1951–1954; deaths 1951	FO 700/24–25
Texas, El Paso	births 1916–1930; deaths 1914–1926	FO 700/26–27
Texas, Galveston	births 1838–1918; deaths 1850–1927	FO 701/23–24
Washington, Aberdeen	births 1916; deaths 1914	FO 700/22–23
Washington, Tacoma	births 1896–1921; deaths 1892–1907	FO 700/20–21
Venezuela[1]	marriages 1836–1838	RG 33/155[2]
West Indies		
Antigua	baptisms and burials 1733–1734, 1738–1745; marriages 1745	CO 152/21, 25

1 You may also need to consult Yeo, *The British Overseas*.
2 Entries in RG 32–36 are largely indexed by RG 43: at both PRO and FRC.
3 Indexed in FO 802/239.

Barbados	baptisms and burials 1678–1679	CO 1/44
Cuba	baptisms 1847–1848; marriages 1842–1849	RG 33/155[2]
Curaçao	births 1897–1966; marriages 1922–1929; deaths 1889–1965	FO 907/1–32
Danish (US) Virgin Islands i.e.-		
St Croix	deaths 1849–1870	RG 35/4[2]
St John	deaths 1849–1872	RG 35/4[2]
St Thomas	deaths 1849–1870	RG 35/4–7[2]
Dominica		
Aux Caves	births 1870–1905	FO 376/1
Aux Caves	deaths 1870–1905	FO 376/2
Dominican Republic	births 1868–1932; marriages 1921–1928; burials 1849–1910; deaths 1874–1889	FO 683/2–6
Guadeloupe	deaths 1836–1871	RG 35/16[2]
Guiana (Dutch) see **Surinam**		
Guyana (French)	deaths 1836–1871	RG 35/16[2]
Haiti	births 1833–1850; marriages 1833–1893; deaths 1833–1850	FO 866/14, 21–22
Haiti	births 1870–1907	FO 376/1–2
Haiti	deaths 1836–1871	RG 35/16[2]
Martinique	deaths 1836–1871	RG 35/16[2]
Montserrat	baptisms and burials 1721–1729; marriages 1721–1729	CO 152/18, 25
Nevis	baptisms and burials 1726–1727, 1733–1734, 1740–1745	CO 152/16, 21, 25
St Kitts	baptisms and burials 1721–1730, 1733–1734, 1738–1745; marriages 1733–1734, 1738–1745	CO 152/18, 21, 25
Zanzibar	births 1916–1918; marriages 1917–1919; deaths 1916–1919	RG 36[2]

1 You may also need to consult Yeo, *The British Overseas.*
2 Entries in RG 32–36 are largely indexed by RG 43: at both PRO and FRC.
3 Indexed in FO 802/239.

5

Medieval and early modern
sources for family history

◆ ◆ ◆

5.1 Problems

Before the parish registers started in 1538, births, marriages and deaths were not officially recorded, although the priest may well have kept notes. However, many series of records of use for family history start well before 1538, and continue long after. In general they contain information about the wealthier members of society, and most ordinary people were very sparsely documented. Information about such people's lives does exist, but it occurs in records created for quite other purposes, such as land transfer or trials.

Medieval records are generally much more difficult to use than those from the sixteenth century and later. They are usually in a highly abbreviated form of Latin. English starts to become more common in informal documents in the late fifteenth century, but Latin was used in formal records until 1733 (except during the Interregnum). The handwriting and letterforms are very different from those of the present day alphabet. The use of surnames was general by about 1300, but there was no consistency in spelling. Surnames were not always used, nor always passed from parent to child. Different surnames could be used in different contexts. Even a fairly distinctive surname may be difficult to trace and may offer little guidance on family relationships.

Two invaluable books for tackling the problems presented by the language, palaeography (handwriting) and diplomatic (the form of documents) of medieval records are *Latin for Local History*, by Gooder and *Latin for Local and Family Historians: A Beginner's Guide*, by Stuart (see **5.5**). Two useful, but inexpensive, guides to working with these records are *Examples of Handwriting 1550–1650* by Buck and *Simple Latin for Family Historians*, by McLaughlin. A useful tip, if you have a Latin document that you cannot understand, is to look at a similar document from the 1650s, when they were all in English. As so much of a formal document is common form, you may be able to use the English version to identify the whereabouts on the parchment of the crucial unique pieces of the Latin text that you need to concentrate on.

One further obstacle exists. Many of the surviving records come from the Exchequer, Chancery and the law courts, or relate to land law: to fully understand them, you do need to be prepared to do some reading. Try *A Guide to English Historical Records*, by Macfarlane; and *English Local Administration in the Middle Ages*, by Jewell.

5.2 Possibilities

Many of the most important medieval records have been published, or have detailed lists and indexes, and it is best to start with these: it is possible to go a long way using published works. Most of these are available in the PRO, either in the Library or the Map Room.

Because so many medieval documents are large, the Map Room has become the best place to use if you are looking at early records. Ask at the desk if you need advice: there should be someone with medieval knowledge available to give you general guidance. They will not be able to translate for you, nor to read documents on your behalf, although they can help with the odd word or two. You would need to employ an independent researcher if you find you cannot cope with the original documents: ask for a list, or look at the PRO website.

Possible sources for genealogical information fall into two kinds: those where information is arranged or has been indexed by name, and those where the arrangement is by place. Where you start depends on what you know already. You may have to look at all kinds of records, as there are none that are obviously genealogical.

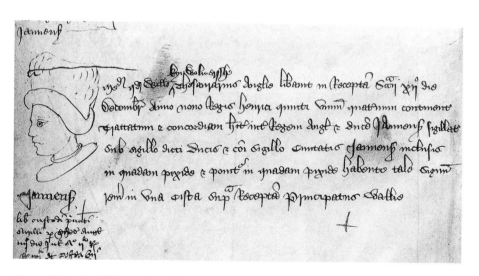

Figure 13 Latin, different letter forms and abbreviations – surmountable problems? This catalogue entry (written by an archivist on 12 December 1421) includes a sketch of a Genoese merchant, identical to the picture on the box where he stored the treaties with Genoa. An early ancestor of our department codes? (PRO, E 36/273)

5.3 Records searchable by name

The advent of PROCAT has transformed searching by name for late medieval people, largely by providing a route via one main series – the Early Chancery Proceedings in C 1, dating from c.1382 to 1558. These lawsuits had a detailed paper list, which has been typed into the online catalogue. Unfortunately, the dates assigned to each bundle were not typed in as well (although we hope to put this right soon). This means that C 1 will not currently turn up if you try to restrict a search by date – instead restrict it to C 1, or to C. You can check the leaflet on *Early Chancery Proceedings: Equity Suits Before 1558* to work out the likely date (do a search on the title to find this leaflet in PROCAT). Remember also that variant spellings were used, so look for alternatives as well. Having given these warnings, there is no doubt that it is far easier to find cases in C 1 than it ever was – and as the records are often very informative, this is now an obvious way in to late medieval family history. Later Chancery proceedings appear in C 2 onwards, but these have not been listed so well: they do crop up with great regularity (as 'Smith v Jones') when doing a name search, giving very few clues, but tantalizing the interest of family historians. Other indexes may exist at the PRO that can give more details. Another very useful (and well-described) series to search online is E 134 – depositions in Exchequer suits. Although this series does not start until the mid sixteenth century, many of the depositions are about events decades earlier.

Records from C 1 and E 134 crop up regularly when doing a name or place search. The records of these lawsuits can be very informative. Chancery, from c.1380, tends to cover disputes over wills, marriage settlements, landed estates and other matters. Exchequer, from c.1558, has a bias towards economic disputes – manorial customs, mills, weirs, common lands, etc. It seems also to have taken over disputes about land sold at the Dissolution of the Monasteries from the Court of Augmentations, which has its own set of fascinating cases. The lists of records of similar courts are not yet searchable online. For 'poor men's causes', try the records of the Court of Requests, from Henry VII–1642. These contain cases concerning the title and ownership of property, dower, and jointure and marriage contracts, allegedly of poor men against mighty suitors. The Court of Star Chamber, Henry VII–1641, was concerned with the enforcement of law and order. There are many cases about the goods of suicides. For more information on using the records of these courts, and of the less informative common law courts, see **47a–d**.

Another source you can find by using the name as a search term online is the collection of inquisitions post mortem, from 1415–1485, and 1509–c.1640. These are another fruitful source for people of some social status, and the actual document will give the name and age of the next heir on the death of a landowner. They are in Latin, but follow a standard form. Inquisitions from 1235–1418 and 1485–1509 have been published in English précis as in the *Calendars of Inquisitions Post Mortem*: see **41.7** and **41.12** for more detail. Many have been published by local record societies as well.

Wills are one of the most useful of the sources accessible by name, often giving considerable family detail. The PRO has medieval and early modern wills proved in the Prerogative Court of Canterbury, from 1383. They are those of wealthy men, unmarried women and widows dying in the south of England or abroad. You will need to use printed indexes to find wills. For more information, see **6**.

Up until the late 1500s, it is easy to check documents issued from, or inspected in, the royal Chancery and recorded on parchment rolls, as most have been published and indexed. Although largely concerned with people of sufficient status to have direct dealings with central government, they do contain many references to other people as well. The most important are the

- Patent Rolls (C 66) which contain, for example, grants of land, licences to alienate property held by tenure in chief, and grants of wardship;
- Close Rolls (C 54) which record, among other things, enrolments of private deeds and other useful information such as writs of livery of seisin;
- Fine Rolls (C 60), which include grants of wardship and marriage and writs of livery of seisin;
- Charter Rolls (C 53) which contain grants of property in the presence of witnesses.

Details of the calendars are given in **5.5**: these series are not searchable online. The Patent and Close Rolls continue into the twentieth century, but after the late and early 1500s, respectively, have not been published.

The registers of the King's (Privy) Council (not all of which are in the PRO) have also been published and indexed. Because it is easy to do, it may be worth checking these if you have a person you wish to know more about. The medieval council registers have been published as *Privy Council Proceedings, 1386–1542*. The registers of the later Privy Council have been published as *Acts of the Privy Council of England, 1542–1631*. They continue after 1631, but have not been published. There is no guarantee that a person came to the attention of the council, but you may find something of interest.

Other possible sources that are easy to use, and may perhaps contain something of interest, start in the early sixteenth century and continue until the mid eighteenth century. From 1509, large numbers of letters and papers survive relating to the government of the country, known as the State Papers, Domestic. These have been published (in brief) as *Letters and Papers . . . of Henry VIII*, and the *Calendar of State Papers, Domestic, 1547–1704*, and are very well indexed. It may be worth checking the indexes on the off-chance that someone you are researching is mentioned. There are similar series for Scotland, Ireland, and for colonial and foreign affairs: see the bibliography. You may also wish to look among the records of the economic life of the nation, in the various series of *Calendars of Treasury Books and Papers, 1557–1745*, which are also well indexed.

Apart from those deeds enrolled on the Close Rolls, the PRO has deeds which came into the Crown's hands when it acquired property through purchase, forfeiture or other forms of escheat, or were produced as evidence in law suits. Some of the PRO's extensive holdings of medieval deeds have been calendared and indexed, and are even searchable online, but there is no cumulative index, and it can be a lengthy job to look through all the lists (see **41.9**).

There are many pedigrees on the Early Plea and Essoin Rolls (KB 26), the *Coram Rege* Rolls (KB 27) and the *De Banco* Rolls (CP 40): see Wrottesley, *Pedigrees from the Plea Rolls*. You may also find useful the copious extracts, mainly from the *De Banco* Rolls and similar legal records, made by General Plantagenet-Harrison in the late nineteenth century. There are several volumes, all handwritten with indexes, which are on the whole reliable (now PRO 66/3). His main interests were in Yorkshire, and in all pedigrees, but you should be cautious in trusting to the accuracy of the latter.

5.4 Records searchable by place

To use the other types of records, those arranged by place, you need to have some idea of where your ancestors lived. If you have this, then it is possible to trace fairly humble people through manorial records. These were the records kept by or on behalf of the lords of manors, who acted both as agrarian landlords and as local judicial and administrative authorities. Manor court rolls recorded, among other things, land transactions within the manor, minor lawsuits between tenants and minor breaches of the peace. It is sometimes possible to trace the inheritance of a peasant back through several generations. Rentals and surveys also name the tenants of the manor and describe their individual holdings. Ministers' and receivers' accounts were the accounts rendered by officials responsible for the revenues of manors and other estates. Like rentals and surveys, they also include the names of tenants. The PRO holds a considerable number of manorial documents, mostly from those manors, which formed part of the Crown lands. For further details about these documents see **41.2**, **41.5** and **41.6**.

Many manorial documents are held in archives outside the PRO: to discover whether there are any surviving records for a particular manor, contact the National Register of Archives (address in **48**).

The feet of fines (CP 25/1–25/2) are the records of fictitious lawsuits entered into to evade conveyancing restrictions, and they run from 1190 to 1833 (see **41.10**). A foot of fine was the bottom copy of a series of three or more copies of a final agreement between two parties. Until the fourteenth century, those made in the central common law courts appear in the records of the Court of Common Pleas and Court of King's Bench. From then on, they were made in the Court of Common Pleas only. Other fines can be found in the palatinate jurisdictions. The fines are arranged by county. Many have been published by local record societies.

Muster rolls can be a valuable source of information, recording the names of able-bodied men liable for service in the militia. They do not list all men, only those between the ages of 16 and 60 years of age. Their principal value lies in the fact that they can establish the parish of a named male. In some cases it is possible from the valuation made of a man's lands and goods, to gain an indication of the status of the family. Unfortunately, there is no separate list of muster rolls that can be found in many different series in the PRO, as well as elsewhere. You will need to look at Gibson and Dell, *Tudor and Stuart Muster Rolls.*

Taxation records can also be useful in tracing rich and poor, although the very poor were usually exempt. The series of Subsidy Rolls (E 179) includes the surviving assessments and returns made for many different taxes from the twelfth to the seventeenth century. The best known are probably the hearth tax returns which cover the years 1662–1674, providing the name of the householder and number of hearths for which he was responsible. There are even exemption certificates for paupers. There are records of many other taxes that can also be extremely useful. The terms of each tax are given in Jurkowski, Smith and Crook, *Lay Taxes in England and Wales, 1188–1688.*

The 1332 subsidy, for example, was the first for which assessments survive on any scale, although its catchment was primarily confined to prosperous householders. The poll tax returns of 1378–1380, which theoretically covered all male adults except the itinerant and the very poor, often give occupations and the relationships between members of the household. The subsidies of 1532–1535 again covered extensively the householders of middling and higher status. The lists are arranged by county, and the description of each document indicates the area covered (often by hundred or wapentake rather than parish or manor) and whether or not the names of assessed individuals are given (see **43**).

Many of the records discussed in **5.3** are equally suitable for place-name searching. Looking for information on the locality can bring you extra information about people who lived there. Maybe they gave evidence in lawsuits, for example. Think about looking at records not directly related to your family, and you may find hidden gold: even if you don't find them by name, you will be visiting disputes and events they probably knew about.

5.5 Medieval and early modern sources for family history: bibliography

Published works: records
Acts of the Privy Council of England, 1542–1631 (London, 1890–1964)
Calendar of Charter Rolls, 1226–1516 (London, 1903–1927)
Calendar of Close Rolls, 1227–1509 (London, 1892–1963)
Calendar of Fine Rolls, 1272–1509 (London, 1911–1963)
Calendar of Patent Rolls, 1216–1509, 1547–1582 (London, 1891–1986) (for 1509–1547, see *Letters and Papers . . . of Henry VIII*). (The series is being continued by the List and Index Society.)
Calendar of Inquisitions Miscellaneous, Henry III to Henry VII (London, 1916–1968)
Calendar of Inquisitions Post Mortem, Henry III to Henry IV, and *Henry VII* (London, 1898–1989)
Calendar of State Papers, Colonial, 1513–1738 (London, 1860–1969)
Calendar of State Papers, Domestic, 1547–1704 (London, 1856–1998)
Calendar of State Papers, Foreign, 1558–1589 (London, 1858–1950)
Calendar of State Papers, Ireland, 1509–1670 (London, 1875–1910)
Calendar of State Papers relating to Scotland, 1547–1603 (London, 1898–1969)
Calendar of Treasury Books, 1660–1718 (London, 1904–1961)
Calendar of Treasury Papers, 1557–1728 (London, 1868–1889)
Calendar of Treasury Books and Papers, 1729–1745 (London, 1898–1903)
Descriptive Catalogue of Ancient Deeds preserved in the Public Record Office (London, 1890–1915)

Inquisitions Post Mortem, Henry V–Richard III (List and Index Society, vols 268–269, 1998)
Journals of the Board of Trade and Plantations, 1704–1782 (London, 1920–1938)
Letters and Papers of Henry VIII (London, 1864–1932)
Privy Council Proceedings, 1386–1542 (London, 1834–1837)

Published works: guides

W S B Buck, *Examples of Handwriting 1550–1650* (Society of Genealogists, 1996)
A J Camp, *My Ancestor came with the Conqueror* (Society of Genealogists, 1988)
M Ellis, *Using Manorial Records* (PRO, 1997)
P Franklin, *Some Medieval Records for Family Historians* (FFHS, 1994)
R E F Garrett, *Chancery and other Legal Proceedings* (Shalfleet Manor, 1968)
J Gibson and A Dell, *Tudor and Stuart Muster Rolls* (FFHS, 1991)
E A Gooder, *Latin for Local History* (London, 2nd edn, 1978)
J Guy, *The Court of Star Chamber and its Records to the reign of Elizabeth I* (PRO, 1985)
R W Hoyle, *Tudor Taxation Records: A Guide for Users* (PRO, 1994)
H M Jewell, *English Local Administration in the Middle Ages* (David & Charles, 1972)
M Jurkowski, C Smith and D Crook, *Lay Taxes in England and Wales, 1188–1688* (PRO, 1998)
A Macfarlane, *A Guide to English Historical Records* (Cambridge, 1983)
E McLaughlin, *Simple Latin for Family Historians* (FFHS, revised edn, 1991)
J Morris, *A Latin Glossary for Family and Local Historians* (FFHS, 1989)
P B Park, *My Ancestors Were Manorial Tenants* (Society of Genealogists, 1994)
J F Preston and L Yeandle, *English Handwriting 1400–1650* (Binghamton, USA, 1992)
D. Stuart, *Latin for Local and Family Historians: A Beginner's Guide* (London, 1995)
J Titford, 'Pre-Parish Register Genealogy: English Sources in the Public Record Office', in eds. K A Johnson and M R Sainty, *Genealogical Research Directory 1998* (Sydney, 1998)
G Wrottesley, *Pedigrees from the Plea Rolls, 1200–1500* (London, c.1906)
M L Zell, 'Fifteenth and Sixteenth Century Wills as Historical Sources', *Archives*, vol. XIV (1979), pp. 75–80

6

Inheritance: death duties, wills, administrations and disputes

◆ ◆ ◆

6.1 Wills as sources for family history

Wills are among the best sources for family history, particularly before the civil registration of births, marriages and deaths started in 1837. Not everybody left a will. Poor people had very little to bequeath. Others may have been sufficiently well off, but not had the control of any property – for example, most wives during the life of their husbands, before 1882. The estates of the more prosperous of those who died intestate (not leaving a valid will) were subject to letters of administration, granted through the same court as would have proved a will: the general information discussed below is the same for wills or administrations.

There is as yet no national union index to wills or administrations, which are to be found in many record offices: the Society of Genealogists are intending to put this right (see www.englishorigins.com). At the same time, the PRO has started to put online its major holding of Prerogative Court of Canterbury (PCC) wills (but *not* administrations) from before 1858, at www.pro-online.pro.gov.uk. On this site you will find actual images of the wills, accessed by keyword searching: using the index this way is free, but you have to buy copies of the images. We are starting at January 1858 and working backwards to 1420 by 2003. For the period c.1820 to 1858, the PCC was moving towards becoming a national probate court, and you should look at the PCC wills online first, before moving on to check other probate courts. Before then, many local probate courts were active and you may need to work out which court you need to investigate: a will or administration may well be held locally.

However, the quality of the information you can gain from a will is often so high that it is well worth the effort of searching. It has been estimated that every will names about ten other people. If you can, try to look for wills of friends or relatives as well. You may find references to your ancestor, to help build up a rounded view of the circle of kinship, friendship and business contacts that made up his or her social world.

When you find and look through a will, you may get the impression that you are reading, in your ancestor's own words, about his faith or his different levels

Figure 14 This Elizabethan will register shows the three Greek fates – Clotho spinning the thread of a life at birth, Atropos weaving it through the years, and Lachesis snipping it at death. This fatalistic belief that life was pre-ordained fitted well with Protestant views on predestination. (PRO, PROB 11/46)

of affection for different members of the family. This may be a false impression. Wills were often written in formulaic language, by clerks or lawyers. Nevertheless, they did express the wishes of the testator (the person leaving the will). For example, any declaration of faith is likely to have been one acceptable to the testator, even if not in his own words.

The evidence found in a will needs to be interpreted with caution. Firstly, we may misunderstand descriptions of family relationships. The words *father*, *brother* and *son, mother, sister* and *daughter* may be used to refer to in-laws as well as blood relatives. The term *cousin* was used for all types of kin. Secondly, the will might make no mention of real estate (land). Certain types of real estate, depending upon the terms of tenure, could be left by will after 1540; from 1660 the only exception to this is land held by copyhold, which was not devisable by will until 1815. Nevertheless, if an eldest son was to inherit the real estate, as his father's heir-at-law, his father's will did not need to mention him or his inheritance. Similarly, married daughters may not be mentioned if they had had property settled upon them at the time of their marriages. The failure to leave a bequest to a near relative does not necessarily mean bad feeling. Be wary: it may be wrong to assume that all legatees would be still alive at the time probate was granted, or that the testator necessarily left sufficient means to cover all bequests.

Before the establishment of the national (English and Welsh) Court of Probate in 1858, wills were proved in church courts, and some other courts with probate jurisdiction, such as manor courts (see **6.22**). The surviving records are now deposited in many different record offices, but the Public Record Office holds the records of the most important, the Prerogative Court of Canterbury, which can be seen at the PRO, the FRC and, increasingly, online. Because wills can be found in so many places, this chapter cannot be a full guide to the subject. For the most recent overview, you could read Herber, *Ancestral Trails*, Chapter 12. This gives an excellent explanation of the varying laws, customs and legal practices governing inheritance, and thus how wills were not an expression of a free choice as to the disposal of property. It also gives guidance on how to find a will and understand what it says. If you have managed to find an early will, you may find it illuminating to read *When Death Us Do Part: Understanding and Interpreting the Probate Records of Early Modern England* (edited by Arkell, Evans and Goose). As with all evidence from the past, the more you know about the context in which a document was made, the less likely you are to misunderstand it.

Once you get to the PRO or FRC, especially if you are looking at medieval or early modern wills, you are strongly advised to read the Introductory Note to the PROB 11 paper list. This gives a clear and brief explanation of the law of property, the restrictions on what could be devised by will, and how people invented different ways of getting round the letter of the law in order to protect their estates from the Crown's feudal rights, or to provide for younger sons, etc. Doing this may give you a completely different understanding of a will. All the Introductory Notes to the other PROB series will also repay reading, if you find yourself using those records.

6.2 Another starting point, 1796–1903: death duty registers for hard data

Death duty registers give different information from the wills (and much better information than administrations). In particular they will show what actually happened to a person's estate after death (rather than what they hoped would happen), and what it was actually worth, excluding debts and expenses. They can also give the date of death, and information about the people who received bequests (beneficiaries), or who were the next of kin, such as the exact relationship to the deceased. Because the registers could be annotated for up to 50 years after the first entry, they can give a wealth of additional information. This can include such data as dates of death of spouse; dates of death or marriage of beneficiaries; births of posthumous children; change of address; references to lawsuits in Chancery delaying the settling of the estate, etc.

They also provide a good first place to look for details of wills and administrations between 1796 and 1858. The indexes in IR 27 will tell you where the will was proved (judged valid) or the administration issued (when there was no valid will). This is a very helpful short cut to finding the actual will or administration, as there were very many probate courts before 1858 (and district registries after 1858). These are not arranged by date of death, but by date of probate or issue of the grant of administration. However, not all wills and administrations appear in the indexes, as not all estates were subject to the death duties.

All the indexes in IR 27 can be seen on microfilm at both the FRC and the PRO, as can the main series of registers in IR 26, for 1796–1857. However, the registers from 1858–1903 are stored off site. They are seen at the PRO, but only on three working days' notice, so you may need to ring in advance with the references. Many of the registers for the 1890s were destroyed by fire. There is no such information available after 1903, as the Inland Revenue switched from using registers to individual files, which were destroyed after 30 years.

From 1796 legacy, estate and succession duty (death duties) were payable on many estates over a certain value, which itself changed over time. As the scope of estate duty was extended throughout the nineteenth century, so more people were included. Before 1805, the registers cover about a quarter of all estates. By 1857, there should be an entry for all estates except those worth less than £20. However, unless the assets were valued at £1,500 or more, the taxes were often not collected, and so the register entry was not filled in with all the details. Britons resident abroad, but with estates in England and Wales, were exempt from the tax. Tax was payable on bequests to people outside a closely defined family circle (whittled down from offspring, spouse, parents and grandparents in 1796, to spouse and parents in 1805, and to spouse only in 1815).

The register entries use a lot of abbreviations: a leaflet is available at the PRO and the FRC that explains them. You may also find what look like references to correspondence: if they date from 1812–1836, try to follow them up in IR 6 where you will get a different view of the matter – that of the executor or administrator, perhaps struggling to prove a generous will by distributing a too-small estate while being harassed by the Inland Revenue.

For more information on death duties, see the Introductory Notes to IR 26 and IR 27. For the procedure involved, see *Ham's Inland Revenue Yearbook*, which gives contemporary instructions. The PRO Library has copies of this annual work (under slightly varying titles) from 1875 to 1930.

At the FRC and PRO there are indexes that cover death duty register entries for probates and administrations, granted 1796–1811 in the consistory courts and lesser courts of the dioceses of Durham, Ely, Exeter, and Oxford. Similar indexes for the dioceses of Bangor, Bath and Wells, Bristol, Canterbury, Carlisle, Chester and Chichester can be seen at the FRC only.

Copy wills were also once among the death duty records: these have largely been destroyed. Those for Cornwall, Devon and Somerset (from the major local probate courts) were sent to the respective record offices, to try to fill some of the gap caused by the loss of local probate records from those counties by enemy action. Those for Somerset have been indexed by Hawkings: the indexes can be seen at the FRC.

6.3 Wills and administrations after 1858

Wills proved from 12 January 1858 to the present day were proved (judged to be an accurate representation of the deceased's lawful intentions) before the Court of Probate. From 1875, this has been part of the Supreme Court, under various titles. Wills may be read (for a small fee) at the Principal Registry of the Family Division's Probate Searchroom (address in **48**) between 10.00am and 4.30pm, Monday to Friday. The same applies to letters of administration, which may be granted if no valid will was made or could be found. Copies of wills and probate and administration grants are obtainable either in person or by post, provided you know the date of death. Postal applications should be addressed to the York Probate Sub-Registry (address in **48**). A handling charge is payable in addition to the copying charge.

However, microfiche copies of the *National Probate Calendar* (which acts as the index to these wills) for 1858–1943, can also be seen at the PRO, the FRC, and the Guildhall. The Society of Genealogists has microfilm copies. The *Calendar* can give quite a lot of information about the testator and executors.

If you want to know more about the actual procedure involved in getting a grant of probate or letters of administration, look at *Ham's Inland Revenue Yearbook*, which gives contemporary instructions. The PRO library has copies of this annual work (under slightly varying titles) from 1875–1930. See also Collins, on using wills after 1858.

6.4 Wills and administrations before 1858: in many record offices

Before 1858, a will was usually proved by one of the many church courts, whose records are usually held locally. The PRO holds the records of only one of them, the Prerogative Court of Canterbury (which was actually located at Doctors' Commons, in London, for most of its history). It can be quite a problem to find out which was the relevant court. For 1796 onwards, the death duty indexes provide this information in many cases: see **6.2**.

If the deceased held property in one archdeaconry the will would be proved (or letters of administration granted, if there was no will) in the archdeacon's court; if in more than one archdeaconry but within one diocese, in the bishop's diocesan court. However, if the deceased held personal property worth over £5 in two distinct dioceses or jurisdictions, then the estate was subject to the archbishop's provincial court, known as the Prerogative Court of York (PCY) or the Prerogative Court of Canterbury (PCC). The province of York covered Yorkshire, Durham, Northumberland, Westmorland, Cumberland, Lancashire, Cheshire, Nottinghamshire and the Isle of Man; Canterbury covered the rest of

England and Wales. If the deceased held property in both provinces, then the will was proved in both the PCY and the PCC.

Records of the Prerogative Court of York are held at the Borthwick Institute (address in **48**). The surviving records of other courts with probate jurisdictions are deposited in local record offices. To find out where they are, use Gibson, *A Simplified Guide to Probate Jurisdictions.* It may be well worth checking the PRO Library to see if the wills, or indexes to the wills, of these more local courts have been published by one of the many record societies. A check in *Will indexes and other probate material in the Library of the Society of Genealogists,* by Newington-Irving, can also save valuable time.

With the English Civil War, the situation grew complicated, as there were two rival PCCs: one with the King at Oxford, and one in London. If you are looking for a will that fell in the PCC's jurisdiction in the 1640s, read the advice in the PROB 11 Introductory Note (filed before the paper list at the PRO and the FRC). Between 1653 and 1660 a single court administered almost all probate jurisdiction for England and Wales. This was the Court for the Proving of Wills and Granting Administrations. Its records are in unbroken series with those of the Prerogative Court of Canterbury, at the PRO: they are very well indexed, by place and occupation as well as by name. However, one may reasonably assume that many people did not prove wills in this period, if it involved going to a court in London.

If someone (subject or foreigner) died overseas leaving property in England and Wales (including Bank of England stock or stock in one of the great companies such as the East India Company), then all the usual rules were ignored, and the will was proved at the PCC. See www.englishorigins.com for an online index to Bank of England will extracts, 1717–1845.

6.5 PCC: whose wills or administrations?

Although the PCC records relate mainly to the testamentary affairs of the wealthier sections of society in the province of Canterbury, the great prestige of the court attracted business to it that strictly speaking belonged to lower courts. As time went on, the declining value of money meant that the £5 barrier became less of a restriction, and in the eighteenth and nineteenth centuries the property of more and more people's estates came within its jurisdiction. From 1810, the Bank of England would not accept probate from any court except the PCC, for holders of Bank of England stock.

Most people affected by the 'dying overseas' rules were poor seamen. This brought into the PCC a large number of wills of seamen of slight value, until 1815, when the affairs of seamen dying with less than £20 wages owing were directed to local church courts. Many Americans continued to hold property in England, and have their wills proved in the PCC: see Coldham's *American Wills and Administrations in the Prerogative Court of Canterbury, 1610–1857.*

However, as in all courts of probate before the Married Women's Property Act of 1882, it is rare to find wills made by married women, as their property was until then deemed to belong to their husbands. Wills by widows and spinsters exist in quantity.

6.6 PCC wills and administrations at the FRC, and at the PRO

The PRO holds the records created or collected by the Prerogative Court of Canterbury, 1383–1858, including the wills of the Court for the Proving of Wills and Granting Administrations, 1653–1660. Administrations issued by the PCC date from 1559 to 1858. Copies of the main series (PROB 11, some of PROB 12, and PROB 6 and PROB 7) can be seen, usually on microfilm, at the FRC as well as at the PRO: all the other series mentioned below have to be seen at the PRO. In some cases, if the registered copy of the will in PROB 11 does not give information about marital status, occupation, or place of residence, it may be found in the probate act books, in PROB 8, at the PRO.

Scott's *Prerogative Court of Canterbury: Wills and Other Probate Records* is a practical introduction to the wealth of the PCC records, and contains fuller information than can be included here. It includes samples of documents, and specific guidance on using particular finding aids.

6.7 Finding a will in the PCC: indexes, etc., 1383–1858

The PRO is currently involved in a major project to get images of all the wills in the PROB 11 series of registered copy wills available for purchase online. As part of this project, an index to the images online is being created, giving name, occupation and place. This online index can be a wonderfully useful tool in finding out that a will exists, and if you just want to get a copy of the will for private research purposes, you need only await its completion (the project is working backwards, very speedily, from 1858). Try it out, at www.pro-online.pro.gov.uk, or on the PRO and FRC public screens. However, although it is a very quick and useful way to find out whether a particular will is in the PCC registers, it does not identify the will sufficiently within the volume if you want to look at it on microfilm, or to cite it in a publication. For these purposes, you will need to go through the old procedure, described below. Another point to note is that the will index online gives the domicile at the time the will was written, whereas the old indexes in (and based on) PROB 12 give the domicile of the testator at the time of death. These may be quite different, as a will could have been written decades before death.

All the wills in the PCC are covered by personal name indexes. However there is no single union index. Instead there is a wide variety of different personal name indexes. Several have one or more supplementary indexes, to place names, occupations and conditions, names of persons other than testators such as executors, and ships' names. Most of them were compiled before the will registers were transferred to the PRO, and therefore do not use PRO references.

To find a will, you need to check one of the many indexes, in different formats for different periods. More detailed practical instructions on using the indexes are available in the reading rooms at the FRC and the PRO. In addition, the lists of PROB 11 and PROB 12 have scholarly Introductory Notes if you want to investigate them in more depth.

Some of the indexes shown in the panel cover both wills and administrations.

Indexes to wills

1383–1700	published indexes, in several date sequences
1701–1749	index compiled by the Friends of the PRO
1750–1800	index compiled by the Society of Genealogists
1801–1852	annual 'calendars' in PROB 12
1853–1858	two alphabetized 'calendars' in PROB 12

Most of these indexes are published works, and may be available locally: see **6.23** to identify the full titles against the date range and volumes covered.

6.8 Understanding and using the will indexes and will registers

Will registers in PROB 11 bear a name before 1841: the same name was also applied to those calendars now in the series PROB 12, PROB 13, and PROB 15 which cover single years, and therefore correspond to specific will registers. The earliest will registers in PROB 11 generally cover several years and consist of only one volume. By the end of the sixteenth century the practice of confining each register to the wills and sentences registered in a single year had been established, and (with the growth in the Court's business) registers came to be made up of more than one volume. With the passage of time the number of volumes in a register increased, and by the mid nineteenth century a single register might consist of 20 volumes.

Many of the indexes at the PRO, and older published sources, give you a reference based on the old register name. For example, looking for John Small in the index for 1649 gives the reference 64 Fairfax. This is composed of the name of the register and an internal quire number. You can convert the register name to a PROB 11 reference by looking at the PROB 11 list. You then have to identify the quire while looking at the register on microfilm.

These will registers each use a traditional numbering system, by quire instead of by page or folio. A quire consists of eight folios (i.e. 16 pages). The quire number is *written* in large roman or arabic numbers on the top left hand corner of the first page of the quire, and can be seen on the microfilm quite easily. An

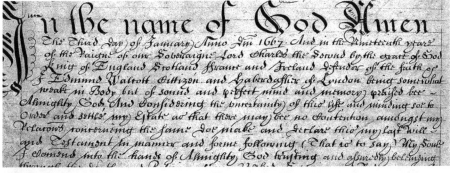

Figure 15 Wills before the nineteenth century usually began like this one of Edmund Walcott, written on 3rd January 1667/1668 (see **1.16**). The handwriting is typical of most registered wills. (PRO, PROB 11/326 folio 204v)

index entry is to the quire, and so may be to any of the 16 pages within that particular quire; you just have to look through, using the details in the margin, to find the right will. When you have found it, take a note of the *stamped* folio number on the top of each right hand page. You will need this when using the self-service copiers. You can use either the quire number or the folio number to cite the document, but the folio number is more precise. Looking for John Small's will meant turning Fairfax into PROB 11/208, and quire 64 into folio 53.

6.9 Proving a will in the PCC

When a will was proved before the PCC, a copy of the will was made. A probate act (a commission, in the name of the archbishop of Canterbury) was issued, and attached by a seal to the copy will. These were then given to the executor as his authority to carry out the distribution of the estate, according to the terms of the will.

The issue of the probate act was recorded in the probate act book (now in PROB 8 and PROB 9). The registry filed the original will, which is now in PROB 10 if it survives. If the executor paid a fee, a copy of the will would also be made in the Court's will registers, with a clause noting the granting of probate entered after the will (now PROB 11). The vast majority of wills proved before the Prerogative Court of Canterbury were registered.

Nuncupative wills (wills which were spoken before witnesses, not written down and signed) are in PROB 11, if registered. They usually start as shown here:

Memorandum that Anne Marshall of Bisham in the Countye of Berks Spinster beinge of good and perfecte mynde and memorie made her last will and Testament nuncupative in theis wordes followinge or the like effect
PROB 11/135, fo. 266v

Nuncupative wills are also identified as nuncupative in their probate clauses, and sometimes in the entries in the calendars of wills in PROB 12, PROB 13, and PROB 15.

The texts of almost all wills proved were copied into large parchment registers, now seen on microfilm (PROB 11). Almost all are in English; by the sixteenth century wills written in Latin are rare. Wills written in other modern European languages (usually Dutch and French) have an authenticated English translation. However the probate clauses appended to the text of the wills, and the texts of sentences (judgements), are in Latin until 1733, with the exception of those in registers for 1651 to 1660 which are in English. They generally follow a standard form, so the example given here should help you to make sense of others:

Probate clause of the will of William Christie
(PROB 11/572, fo.212v*)*

Probatum fuit hujusmodi Testamentum apud London coram Venerabili viro Roberto Wood Legum Doctore Surrogato Venerabilis et Egregij viri Johannis Bettesworth Legum etiam Doctoris Curiae Praerogativae Cantuariensis Magistri Custodis sive Commissarij legitime constituti Vicesimo Secundo die Mensis Februarij Anno Domini Millesimo Septingentesimo Decimo nono Juramento Thomae Willisee Executoris unici in dicto Testamento nominati Cui commissa fuit Administratio omnium et Singulorum bonorum jurium et creditorum dicti defuncti De bene et fideliter administrando eadem ad Sancta Dei Evangelia Jurato. Examinatur.

English translation

This will was proved at London before the worshipful Robert Wood LL.D [Doctor of Laws] surrogate of the worshipful and wise John Bettesworth also LL.D Master Keeper or Commissary of the Prerogative Court of Canterbury lawfully constituted on the twenty-second day of the month of February 1719 [/20] by the oath of Thomas Willisee named sole executor in the said will to whom administration of all and singular the goods rights and credits of the said deceased was granted being sworn on the holy gospels to administer the same well and faithfully. Examined.

6.10 Complications with executors: grants of administration with will annexed

If the executor appointed in the will was unable or unwilling to prove the will, letters of administration with will annexed were issued instead. This is noted in the probate clause, after the text of the will in PROB 11.

If the executor died, or renounced the administration of the estate, before its distribution had been completed, letters of administration with will annexed *de bonis non administratis* (of goods not administered) were issued. This is noted in the margin of the register, alongside the text of the will.

If more than one executor was appointed, and the executors sought probate at different dates, a subsequent grant of probate was made. This is also noted in the margin.

Such marginal annotations can be highly abbreviated; often they are not as informative as the corresponding entries in the probate act books (PROB 8, PROB 9). Probate acts, letters of administration with will annexed, and letters of administration with will annexed *de bonis non administratis* are described in the Introductory Note to the PROB 8 list.

Administration acts with will annexed are entered in the probate act books (PROB 8, PROB 9), and the wills are registered in the will registers (PROB 11). Administrators with will annexed were required to enter into bonds for their proper administration of the estate, and such bonds are in the administration bond series (PROB 51, PROB 54, PROB 46).

Grant of administratio *de bonis non administratis*
(grant of administration of goods unadministered)

PROB 6/96, f 97ᵛ

Elizabetha Carleton	*Decimo Sexto die Em<u>ana</u>v<u>i</u>t Com<u>missi</u>o Johanni*	*ult<u>imus</u> [dies] Nov<u>em</u>bris*
	Heskew Marito <u>legi</u>timo et Adm<u>ini</u>stratori bonor<u>um</u>	
	&c [<u>jurium et creditorum</u>] Eliz<u>abeth</u>ae Heskew dum vixit	
	filiae n<u>atu</u>ralis et <u>legi</u>timae Eliz<u>abeth</u>ae Carleton nup<u>er</u>	
	p<u>aro</u>ch<u>i</u>ae Sanc<u>t</u>ae Mariae Magdalenae Bermondsey in	
	Com<u>itatu</u> Surriae def<u>unc</u>tae h<u>a</u>bentis &c [<u>dum vixit et</u>	
	<u>mortis suae tempore bona jura sive credita in diversis</u>	
	<u>diocesibus sive peculiaribus jurisdictionibus sufficientia</u>	
	<u>ad fundandum jurisdictionem Curiae Praerogativae</u>	
	<u>Cantuariensis</u>] ad Adm<u>ini</u>strandum bona jura et credita	
	di<u>c</u>tae def<u>unc</u>tae p<u>er</u> Eliz<u>abeth</u>am Heskew modo etiam	
	demortuam inadm<u>ini</u>strata De bene &c [<u>et fideliter</u>	
	<u>administrando eadem ad sancta Dei evangelia</u>] jurato	*ult<u>imus</u> [dies] Maij 1721*

Elizabeth Carleton	On the seventeenth day a commission was issued to	last [day] of November
	John Heskew lawful husband and administrator of the	
	goods etc [rights and credits] of Elizabeth Heskew while	
	she lived natural and legitimate daughter of Elizabeth Carleton	
	formerly of the parish of St Mary Magdalen Bermondsey	
	in the county of Surrey deceased having etc [while she	
	lived and at the time of her death goods rights or credits in	
	different dioceses or peculiar jurisdictions sufficient to found	
	the jurisdiction of the Prerogative Court of Canterbury] to	
	administer the goods rights and credits of the said deceased	
	not administered by the said Elizabeth Heskew now also	
	deceased having been sworn [on the holy gospels] to	
	well and [faithfully administer the same]	last [day] of May 1721

- Letters omitted from the original texts on account of abbreviation have been supplied underlined. Words omitted from the original have been supplied underlined in square brackets.
- The first date in the right hand margin is the date by which the administrator was required to return an inventory of the intestate's personal estate. The second date is the date by which the administrator was required to return an account of his or her administration of the estate.

6.11 PCC original and other wills

So-called original wills are in PROB 10, stored off site. They take three days to be produced to the PRO, so you will need to order them in advance. Original wills survive in almost complete sequence from 1620; before 1620, an 'original will' may in fact be a facsimile copy made by the court. There is usually no advantage in looking at the original if there is a registered copy in PROB 11.

Wills of some famous people were extracted from the original wills now in PROB 10, and placed in PROB 1. Some supplementary series of wills, usually copies or rejected wills, may be found in PROB 20–23.

Not all wills were registered in PROB 11. Between 1383 and 1558 unregistered wills (now in PROB 10) are indicated in the index by the letter F. Genuine cases

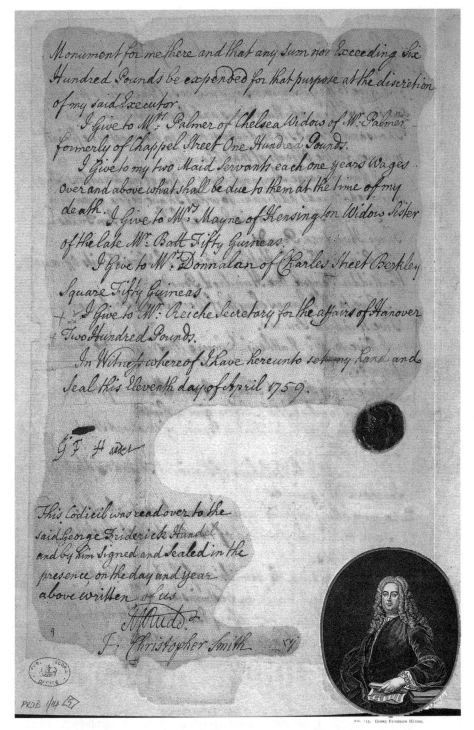

Monument for me there and that any Sum nor exceeding Six
Hundred Pounds be expended for that purpose at the discretion
of my said Executor.
  I Give to Mrs. Palmer of Chelsea Widow of Mr. Palmer
formerly of Chappel Street One Hundred Pounds.
  I Give to my two Maid Servants each one years Wages.
over and above what shall be due to them at the time of my
death. I Give to Mrs. Mayne of Kensington Widow Sister
of the late Mr. Batt Fifty Guineas.
  I Give to Mr. Donnalan of Charles Street Berkley
Square Fifty Guineas.
+ I Give to Mr. Reiche Secretary for the affairs of Hanover
+ Two Hundred Pounds.
  In Witness whereof I have hereunto set my hand and
Seal this Eleventh day of April 1759.

G: F: Handel

This Codicil was read over to the
said George Friderick Handel
and by him Signed and Sealed in the
presence on the day and year
above written of us
          A: Hud:
  J: Christopher Smith

Figure 16 This original will bears Handel's signature. Like many less famous testators,
Handel regularly added codicils to his will, including this one from his deathbed.
(PRO, PROB 1/14 folio 5 and Mary Evans Picture Library)

of unregistered wills, particularly after 1660, are very rare. If a calendar or an index compiled from a calendar does not supply a quire number alongside the name of a testator, it is sometimes assumed that the will was not registered and that therefore there is no copy of the will in PROB 11. However, in the majority of these cases, the registered text of the will can be found in the will register by searching in the quires where the wills of other testators whose surnames began with the same initial letter and whose wills were proved in the same months were registered. In many other cases where no quire number is supplied, the entire entry in the calendar will be found to be a clerical error.

Probate copies of wills, as handed over to the executors, often turn up as evidence in legal disputes. The exhibit series of C 103–114 and J 90 are full of them. The easiest way to find them may be to search in PROCAT, using 'will' or 'probate', and the name, plus the series.

6.12 Abstracts and other finding aids to PCC wills

In addition to the indexes and finding aids discussed above, and listed in detail in the bibliography, a large number of other indexes, finding aids, abstracts and editions of Prerogative Court of Canterbury and other wills and sentences registered in PROB 11 have been compiled. Some of them have been published, others deposited in such places as the Society of Genealogists' library. They have been compiled on varying principles to different types of wills, including those proved in particular periods of time, those relating to holders of certain surnames, those relating to particular counties or other geographical areas, and those of certain professions and occupations. The last two categories can be most useful to local and social historians.

Mention should also be made of four publications, each covering a single year, which abstract and/or index (by personal names, and in some cases by place-names and occupations) all the wills registered in four particular years: 1620, 1630, 1658, and 1750.

PROB 11/135–136	J H Lea, *Abstract of wills in the Prerogative Court of Canterbury: Register Soame 1620* (Boston, Mass., 1904). A copy can be seen at the FRC, but not at the PRO
PROB 11/157–158	J H Morrison, *Prerogative Court of Canterbury: Register Scroope (1630)* (London, 1934). A copy can be seen at the FRC, but not at the PRO.
PROB 11/272–285	William Brigg, *Genealogical abstracts of wills proved in the Prerogative Court of Canterbury: Register Wootton 1658*, 7 volumes (Leeds, 1894–1914). A copy can be seen at the FRC, but not at the PRO.
PROB 11/776–784	George Sherwood, *A list of persons named in the PCC wills proved in the year 1750: Register Greenly (4,382 wills naming 40,320 persons arranged in eight groups topographically)* (London, privately published, 1918). There is a copy in the library of the Society of Genealogists, but not at the FRC or the PRO.

There is no published list of all the different indexes, finding aids, abstracts and editions that have been produced. However, many of them are listed in Gibson's *Probate Jurisdictions: Where to look for wills.*

6.13 Grants of administration: intestates' estates, 1559–1858

Intestacy is the state of dying without leaving a valid will. The PCC would grant letters of administration to persons with a claim on an intestate's estate, where the estate came within the jurisdiction of the Court. Probate courts were required to grant administration of the estate to the deceased's widow or next of kin. Administration of the estate of a married woman was granted to her husband. The estates of illegitimate intestates who died unmarried and without issue were granted to the Crown: the Treasury received many letters from relatives asking if they could have letters of administration instead, and these are now in T 4.

The possessions of intestates with no next of kin reverted to the Crown: see the good list in TS 17.

Grants of administration were registered in the administration act books (PROB 6). These are divided into 'seats' reflecting the clerical organization of the PCC. The system of seats is explained in **6.15**.

The act book ordinarily records only the marital status and place of residence of the intestate, the name of the administrator and his or her relationship to the intestate, and the date of the grant. From 1796, and in many cases before that date, a valuation of the deceased's personal estate is given in the margin. The court was required to grant administration to the deceased's next of kin, and the entry in the administration act book may therefore include the names of relatives who had ignored summonses to appear before the court, or who had renounced their claims to administer the estate. Be wary of assuming that a known relative (closer in blood than the person to whom administration was granted) had died by the time the grant was made, merely because the known relative is not mentioned in the administration act book.

The information that the administration act books usually supply is:

- date of the grant of administration;
- name of the intestate;
- his or her parish of residence;
- name of the administrator;
- his or her relationship to the intestate;
- dates by which an inventory and an account had to be returned.

The administration act books may also give information about the marital status, occupations, and places of death of the intestates. Information about intestates' occupations and places of residence becomes more frequent in later years. By the nineteenth century, administration act books often supply such additional details as the names of the regiment the intestate served in, or the name of the street in which he or she lived at the time of death.

6.14 Finding an administration grant

All the administrations in the PCC are covered by personal name indexes. However there is no single union index. Instead there is a wide variety of different personal name indexes. Because many of these indexes have been compiled from the (sometimes faulty) contemporary 'calendars', these are not guaranteed to be 100 per cent accurate. The majority of them do not use PRO references.

To find an administration, you will need to check one of the many indexes, in different formats for different periods. More detailed practical instructions on using the indexes are available in the reading rooms at the FRC and the PRO. In addition, the list of PROB 6 has a scholarly Introductory Note if you want to investigate the subject in more depth. Some of the indexes shown here cover both administrations and wills.

Indexes to administrations

1559–1660	published indexes, in several date sequences
1661–1662	annual 'calendars' in PROB 12
1663–1664	typescript indexes
1665–1700	annual 'calendars' in PROB 12
1701–1749	index compiled by the Friends of the PRO
1750–1852	annual 'calendars' in PROB 12
	A card index covering 1750–1800 is at the Society of Genealogists: this can be searched for you, for a fee
1853–1858	two alphabetized 'calendars' in PROB 12

Most of these indexes are published works, and may be available locally: see **6.23** to identify the full titles against the date range and volumes covered.

The indexes to administration acts supply the calendar year of grant, the month of the grant, and the place of residence of the deceased. Use the calendar year of the grant to find the right book in the relevant series list for PROB 6, PROB 7, PROB 8, or PROB 9. The month of the grant and the place of residence is usually enough to locate the particular administration or probate act within the act book.

Some of the published indexes supply folio references to the act books: these relate to the handwritten numbers in the volumes, and not to the stamped numbers. If a folio number is not supplied for grants of administration made before 1719, you have to note the month of the grant from the index and then search through the relevant monthly section of the act book. For grants made after 1719, you need to understand the 'seat' system used by the PCC (see **6.15**).

From 1719 to 1743 the act books in PROB 6 and PROB 8 are divided into monthly sections. Each monthly section is sub-divided into a sub-section by seat. The sub-sections are not arranged in a consistent order. From 1744 to 1858 these act books are divided into five sections corresponding to the five seats of the Court. The seat sections usually appear in the following order: registrar's seat, Surrey seat, Welsh seat, Middlesex seat, London seat. Each seat's section is subdivided into 12 monthly sub-sections, and the acts generally appear in alphabetical order by the initial letters of the testators' and intestates' surnames.

6.15 The 'seat' system used in the PCC, 1719–1858

In 1719 the PCC began a new system for organizing the issue of grants of probate and administration. This system lasted until the abolition of the Court in 1858. You need to understand the system in order to locate an administration act in PROB 6 or PROB 7, a probate act in PROB 8 or PROB 9, an administration bond in PROB 46, or a commission to swear executors in PROB 52, during the period 1719 to 1858.

The Court divided the business of granting probate and administration between five 'seats'. Each seat had its own distinct geographical area of responsibility as shown here.

Registrar's seat	Testators or intestates dying overseas or at sea, except in cases where the grant was made to the widow, and she lived in an area within the jurisdiction of one of the other seats, in which case probate or administration passed at that seat.
	Testators or intestates living outside the province of Canterbury.
	Estates which were, might be, or had been subject to litigation within the PCC. (If, however, a subsequent grant of probate or administration was made it would be passed at the seat which would have been responsible had there been no litigation).
Surrey seat	Cornwall, Devon, Dorset, Hampshire, Somerset, Surrey, Sussex, Wiltshire.
Welsh seat	Berkshire, Derbyshire, Gloucestershire, Herefordshire, Leicestershire, Northamptonshire, Oxfordshire, Rutland, Shropshire, Staffordshire, Warwickshire, Worcestershire, Wales.
Middlesex seat	Bedfordshire, Buckinghamshire, Cambridgeshire, Essex, Hertfordshire, Huntingdonshire, Kent, Lincolnshire, Middlesex (except those parishes listed below), Norfolk, Suffolk.
London seat	City of London. Charterhouse; Furnivall's Inn; Glasshouse Yard; Gray's Inn; Holy Trinity Minories; Liberty of the Rolls; Liberty of the Tower of London; Lincoln's Inn; Old Artillery Ground; Precinct of Norton Folgate; Precinct of St Katherine by the Tower; Precinct of the Savoy; St Andrew Holborn; St Anne Soho; St Botolph Aldersgate; St Botolph without Aldgate; St George Bloomsbury; St George the Martyr Holborn (Queen Square); St Giles Cripplegate; St Giles in the Fields; St James Clerkenwell; St James Westminster; St John Clerkenwell; St John the Evangelist Westminster; St John Wapping; St Leonard Shoreditch; St Luke Old Street; St Margaret Westminster; St Mary le Strand; St Mary Matfelon Whitechapel; St Sepulchre.

6.16 Understanding the administration act books

The administration act books in PROB 6 do not ordinarily give the complete texts of individual letters of administration, rather they record the information unique to individual letters. The vast majority of the entries in the administration act books take the form of cursory formulaic summaries of the original grants. Except for the period 1651 to 1660 the act books are in Latin until 1733. From 1651 to 1660, and after 25 March 1733, the act books are in English, although certain technical phrases and abbreviations continued to be used in Latin.

Ordinary grant of administration
PROB 6/96, f 97ᵛ

Joh<u>annes</u> *Bayly*	*Tricesimo die Em<u>ana</u>v<u>it</u> Commiss<u>io</u>* *Elizabethae Bayly viduae Rel<u>ic</u>tae Johannis* *Bayly nu<u>per</u> paro<u>chi</u>ae S<u>an</u>c<u>t</u>ae Mariae* *Rotherhithe in Com<u>itatu</u> Surriae sed in Nave* *Regia Le Dreadnought def<u>unc</u>ti h<u>a</u>bentis &* *c <u>[dum vixit et mortis suae tempore bona jura sive</u>* *<u>credita in diversis diocesibus sive peculiaribus</u>* *<u>jurisdictionibus sufficientia ad fundandum</u>* *<u>jurisdictionem Curiae Praerogativae Cantuariensis]</u>* *ad Adm<u>ini</u>strandum bona jura et credita d<u>ic</u>ti* *def<u>unc</u>ti De bene &c <u>[et fideliter administrando</u>* *<u>eadem ad sancta Dei evangelia]</u> jurat<u>ae</u>*	*ult<u>imus</u> [dies] Nov<u>em</u>bris* *ult<u>imus</u> [dies] Maij 1721*
John Bayly	On the thirtieth day a commission was issued to Elizabeth Bayly widow relict of John Bayly formerly of the parish of St Mary Rotherhithe in the county of Surrey but in HMS *Dreadnought* deceased having etc [while he lived and at the time of his death goods rights or credits in different dioceses or peculiar jurisdictions sufficient to found the jurisdiction of the Prerogative Court of Canterbury] to administer the goods rights and credits of the said deceased having been sworn [on the holy gospels] to well and [faithfully administer the same]	last [day] of November last [day] of May 1721

- Letters omitted from the original texts on account of abbreviations have been supplied underlined. Words omitted from the original have been supplied underlined in square brackets.
- The first date in the right hand margin is the date by which the administrator was required to return an inventory of the intestate's personal estate. The second date is the date by which the administrator was required to return an account of his or her administration of the estate.

In some instances a grant was made limited to a particular part of the deceased's estate, or with special conditions attached. Limited grants of the estates of soldiers and sailors, limited to their wages were commonly made to creditors of the soldiers and sailors who had advanced them money on the security of their wages. Grants limited to Bank of England and East India Company stock held both by foreign nationals whose property was otherwise held in their countries of residence, and by trustees of married women, become increasingly common in the eighteenth and nineteenth centuries. Such grants are indicated in the PROB 12 index, and entered in full in PROB 6 and PROB 7. They may give detailed information about the relationship of the administrator to the deceased, and so can be of great genealogical value. Before 1744 limited and special grants of administration are generally to be found at the front of the section for the month in which they were passed. From 1744 (PROB 6/120) they are entered either in one group at the beginning or end of the different seat sections of the administration act books, or at the beginning of the appropriate monthly sub-sections of the seat in question. Limited and special grants of administration made after 1809 are entered in PROB 7.

6.17 What did administrators do?

Administrators had first to enter into a bond with the court to ensure that they fulfilled their responsibilities. Bonds generally give the names, marital status, occupations and places of residence of the administrator and his or her sureties. Those for 1714–1857 are in PROB 46. The rate of survival before 1714 is poor and at present only a few sixteenth century bonds (PROB 51) can be seen.

Administrators were required to collect the credits owed to the intestate, and to pay the debts of the intestate, and the expenses of the estate (such as medical fees, funeral bills, and fees for the maintenance of dependants). Statute and custom regulated the distribution of the estate after the payment of expenses and debts. One third of the estate was to be distributed to the wife of the intestate, and the remaining part was to be distributed in equal portions among the children of the intestate. Distribution of the estate could not be made until one year after the grant of administration was made. Beneficiaries were required to enter into bonds committing them to refund their portions or parts of their

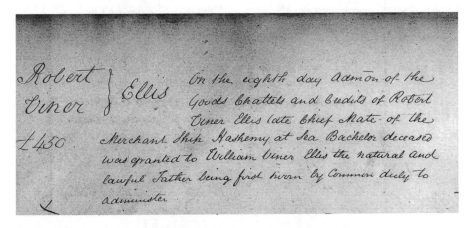

Figure 17 From 1796, administrations include a rough valuation of the estate in the margin, for death duty purposes. See **6.2** for more on death duty registers, which can be detailed. (PRO, PROB 6/216)

portions (should it be necessary for them to do so) if the administrator needed to settle unanticipated debts of the estate. Husbands of intestates received the whole of their wives' personal estates.

A person with a claim to a share in an intestate's estate could seek a judicial distribution of the estate, 12 months after the grant of administration was issued. This meant asking for an order from the court that required the administrator to distribute the estate in accordance with the Statute of Distributions. Such causes can be traced in the litigation series of the Prerogative Court of Canterbury and provide valuable evidence of the distribution of estates. Orders for the distribution of estates are in PROB 16.

The date of death of an intestate, or of a testator whose executors were sworn outside London, can often be found in the warrant for the grant of administration or commission to swear executors (PROB 14).

6.18 Disposing of the estate: inventories and accounts: the PRO

The executors or administrators had to prove to the court that they had carried out their functions properly. To do this, they had to submit inventories of the deceased's moveable property (including debts), and accounts of their expenditure (sometimes including expenditure on children over several years). This kind of probate record is relatively poorly used by family historians, despite there being a series of indexes to the relevant series.

1417–1660	Inventories Series I	PROB 2	index with list
1642–1722	Cause Papers	PROB 28	index to causes, testators or intestates
1653–1721	Exhibits pre-1722	PROB 36	card indexes to causes, testators and intestates
1661–1720	Parchment Inventories	PROB 4	card indexes to names and places
1661–1732	Paper Inventories	PROB 5	index with list
1662–1720	Filed Exhibits with Inventories	PROB 32	index with list
1683–1858	Indexes to Exhibits	PROB 33	original indexes to exhibits in PROB 31 and PROB 37
1702, 1718–1782	Inventories Series II	PROB 3	index with list
1722–1858	Exhibits, Main Series	PROB 31	index of wills; card indexes of names and places to the inventories and other exhibits
1783–1858	Cause Papers, Later Series	PROB 37	indexes to testators and intestates

PROB 31 and PROB 37 are also indexed by place of residence, and include many people resident in the Americas and East Indies.

The rate of survival for these documents is very poor before 1666, and erratic for the later seventeenth century and early eighteenth century. After the mid eighteenth century, they were exhibited only if the estate was subject to litigation, if the administrator or executor renounced his or her responsibilities, or if the beneficiaries of the estate were children. As well as using the indexes to these series, it is a good idea to look at the Introductory Note in front of the relevant series list, as it will give you information about what to expect.

Inventories, listing the deceased's personal property, and accounts, recording executors' and administrators' receipts and expenditure, may provide the most illuminating evidence about the deceased's social status, wealth and business activities. For example, the inventories of the goods, chattels and credits of Richard Tyacke of Godolphin, Cornwall, submitted in 1826, account for a total value of over £25,000. They list leases for term of lives (one worthless as the person on whom the lease depended was on the point of death), shares in pilchard fishing (worthless), tin mines and merchant trade, debts owing, and the farm stock and furniture.

With an inventory, remember that what is listed will be what belonged to the deceased. This may not be the entire furnishings of a house, as other furnishings may have belonged to other people in the household, and so are not listed.

Sometimes you can get a declaration in place of an inventory, when the goods have already been disposed of. These can be quite informative, because they give the details of where the goods went.

Accounts can be particularly valuable, as they may continue for some years and include all kinds of information – payments for the maintenance of dependants, details of funeral or nursing costs, etc.

6.19 Litigation before 1858: the PRO

In many cases, a will was disputed in the PCC. Cox provides a fascinating history of testamentary disputes, in *Hatred pursued beyond the grave*.

There are three main ways to discover if there was a dispute (a 'cause' in PCC language). Remember that before the mid 1700s, causes were known by the name of the plaintiff, and not by the name of the person whose estate was being disputed. The first clue may be from the will register in PROB 11, until about 1800: there may be a sentence (judgement) entered in the margin next to the will, if the victorious party had paid for this to be done. The second, and easiest, way is to check the card index to the initial proceedings (1661–1858) in PROB 18. This is arranged in two parts, by name of cause (e.g. Smith *contra* Jones) and by name of the deceased testator or intestate. Thirdly, if you go to the relevant act book (PROB 6–9) or the PROB 12 calendar, you may find a marginal note saying *by decree* or *by sentence* (sometimes abbreviated). This means that the estate was the subject of a lawsuit or cause.

The stages through which a cause passed are recorded in the acts of court (PROB 29, PROB 30). These records are concerned with procedure and you may find other series of litigation records more fruitful. The main series to check are allegations (the initial complaint, by the plaintiffs) in PROB 18, answers by the defendants in PROB 25, depositions in PROB 24 and PROB 26, cause papers in PROB 28 and PROB 37, and exhibits in PROB 31 and PROB 36. Scott, in *Wills and Other Probate Records,* gives a step by step account of finding records in two testamentary disputes. The basic procedure was very similar to that used by the equity courts (see **47b**).

Annotations of existence of a cause			
1559–1858	Act Books: Administrations	PROB 6	
1810–1858	Act Books: Limited Administrations	PROB 7	
1526–1828	Act Books: Probates	PROB 8	
1781–1858	Act Books: Limited Probates	PROB 9	
1384–1858	Registered Copy Wills	PROB 11	
1383–1858	Register Books	PROB 12	
Proceedings			
1661–1858	Allegations (i.e. the start of the cause)	PROB 18	card indexes to causes, testators and intestates
1664–1854	Answers	PROB 25	
1642–1722	Cause Papers	PROB 28	
1783–1858	Cause Papers, Later Series	PROB 37	index to testators and intestates. List and Index Society 184
Depositions			
1657–1809	Depositions	PROB 24	
1826–1858	Depositions Bound by Suit	PROB 26	indexes to causes, testators and intestates
Exhibits			
1653–1721	Exhibits pre-1722	PROB 36	card indexes to causes, testators and intestates
1662–1720	Filed Exhibits with Inventories	PROB 32	indexed by name. List and Index Society 204

1722–1858	Exhibits, Main Series	PROB 31	index of wills; card indexes of names and places to the inventories and other exhibits
Procedural records			
1536–1819	Acts of Court Book	PROB 29	
1740–1858	Acts of Court	PROB 30	indexes to causes, testators and intestates. List and Index Society 161.

Sentences, the court's final judgements, were registered in PROB 11 if the successful party paid a fee for the registration, until the end of the eighteenth century. They are listed in the calendars in PROB 12 in a separate section which is to be found either adjacent to the section for surnames beginning with the letter *S*, or at the end of the volume. Sentences will give you the name of the deceased testator or intestate, the names of the parties to the cause, and the type of sentence.

Proctors for the opposing parties drafted the sentences. The judge in the cause then promulgated the sentence that accorded with his verdict. The principal types of sentences were:

- *sententia pro concessione administrationis bonorum* — sentence granting letters of administration
- *sententia pro confirmatione administrationis bonorum* — sentence confirming the grant of letters of administration
- *sententia pro revocatione administrationis bonorum* — sentence revoking letters of administration
- *sententia pro valore testamenti* — sentence in favour of the validity of a will
- *sententia pro confirmatione testamenti* — sentence confirming a grant of probate
- *sententia pro revocatione testamenti* — sentence revoking a grant of probate

Other types of sentences related to the jurisdiction of the Prerogative Court of Canterbury, the production of inventories and accounts, and the validity of codicils.

The PCC was only concerned with the validity of wills presented for probate or the claims of persons seeking letters of administration. Cases concerned with the inheritance and devisal of real estate and with trusts were heard in Chancery (see **47b**). A single will may have led to lawsuits in both the PCC and in Chancery at the same time.

6.20 Appeals before 1858: wills from other courts in the PRO

If probate was not granted by the PCC, it may be worth investigating to see if an appeal took place. Appeals from the Prerogative Court of Canterbury, and other church courts, in testamentary causes, went to the Court of Arches (whose surviving records are at Lambeth Palace Library) and to the High Court of Delegates. If either of these two courts granted probate, then the will may be found in their records, as well as in the PCC or the relevant lower court. Proceedings called before the Delegates can be seen at the PRO (DEL 1 and DEL 2, both indexed by DEL 11/7; DEL 7, indexed by IND 1/10323; and DEL 8). Wills and affidavits brought into court, 1636–1857, are in DEL 10. The muniment books (DEL 9) contain transcripts of documents and exhibits in testamentary appeals, 1652–1859. Both are indexed in DEL 11/6 and DEL 11/7. After 1834, appeals lay to the Judicial Committee of the Privy Council until 1858: see PCAP 1 and PCAP 3.

6.21 Litigation after 1858: at the PRO

After 1858, testamentary causes were by the new Court of Probate (later part of the Probate, Divorce and Admiralty Division of the High Court), with appeal to the House of Lords. A seven per cent sample of case files and papers relating to contentious probates of wills, from 1858 onwards, is in J 121. A very small sample of exhibits is in J 165.

6.22 Other probate records at the PRO

Other wills are found throughout the public records: a useful book, *A List of Wills, Administrations, Etc, in the Public Record Office, London, England: 12th–19th century*, lists many of them. A copy can be seen in the Map Room. Because some of them are individually described in the lists, it may be worth trying a keyword search in PROCAT – use the surname plus 'probate' or 'will'. For example, there are many wills in Chancery Masters' Exhibits, C 103–115. There is also a list of wills and related records in E 211.

Some manor court rolls include enrolled wills. An exceptionally good example is the manor of Newcastle-under-Lyme, part of the Duchy of Lancaster. This has a series of enrolment books of deeds and wills, 1810–1934, in DL 30/510/1–510/63, with indexes in DL 30/511/1–511/4. Other Duchy manors, such as Knaresborough, also enrolled wills. It may be worth checking in the PRO's holdings of court rolls if you think that the person you are seeking was a tenant of a Crown manor: see **41.6**.

The Paymaster General kept records of probates and letters of administration granted for Army and Navy personnel (it is not clear if they are for officers only) and their widows, between 1836 and 1915. The registers can give clues to relationships, and the later ones give the address of the deceased (PMG 50). Wills were deposited in the Navy Pay Office by naval ratings, Royal Marine other ranks and some warrant officers: see **19.2.2–19.2.3**. There are also some Royal Marine wills in ADM 96. Wills of some army officers, 1755–1881, may be found in WO 42, and there is an index available at the PRO. Wills and copies of wills may be found, very occasionally, among deceased soldiers' effects in the casualty returns, 1809–1910 (WO 25/1359–2410 and 3251–3471).

The probate records of the British Consular Court at Smyrna, Turkey, 1820–1929, and of the Shanghai Supreme Court, 1857–1941, are in FO 626 and FO 917 respectively. Other wills of some Britons in China, 1837–1951, are in FO 678/2729–2931.

6.23 Wills and administrations: published and unpublished indexes

---

Will indexes

Try the online index at www.pro-online.pro.gov.uk, and on the PRO and FRC public screens. This is really an index to the digitized images available for purchase online. It is *very* useful at telling you whether a particular will is in the PCC registers, but it does not identify the will sufficiently within the volume if you want to look at it on microfilm, or to cite it in a publication.

If you want to look at wills at the PRO or FRC, use the online index to get the date of probate, and then check in the old indexes listed below to get the full reference.

1	1383–1558	PROB 11/1–41	*Index of wills proved in the Prerogative Court of Canterbury*, [vol. I A–J, vol. II K–Z], eds J Challenor and C Smith, Index Library, X–XI (London, British Records Society, 1893–1895).
2	1558–1583	PROB 11/42A–66	*Index of wills proved in the Prerogative Court of Canterbury*, vol. III, eds S A Smith and L L Duncan, Index Library, XVIII (London, British Records Society, 1898).
3	1584–1604	PROB 11/66–104	*Index of wills proved in the Prerogative Court of Canterbury*, vol. IV, eds S A Smith and E A Fry, Index Library, XXV (London, British Records Society, 1901).
4	1605–1619	PROB 11/105–134	*Index of wills proved in the Prerogative Court of Canterbury*, vol. V, ed. E Stokes, Index Library, XLIII (London, British Records Society, 1912).
5	1620	PROB 11/135–136	J H Lea, *Abstract of wills in the Prerogative Court of Canterbury: Register Soame 1620* (Boston, Mass., 1904). Abstracts of all wills registered. A copy can be seen at the FRC, but not at the PRO.
6	1620–1629	PROB 11/135–156	*Index of wills proved in the Prerogative Court of Canterbury*, vol. VI, ed. R H E Hill, Index Library, XLIV (London, British Records Society, 1912). See also 7 below.

7	1620–1624	PROB 11/135–144	*Year book of probates: Abstracts of probates and sentences in the Prerogative Court of Canterbury*, eds J Matthews and G F Matthews (London, 1914). This index contains some references not in 6 above. The abbreviations it uses are explained in 9.1 below, page 5. It does not have a place-name index, but there is one in 6.
8	1630	PROB 11/157–158	J H Morrison, *Prerogative Court of Canterbury: Register Scroope (1630)* (London, 1934) Abstracts of all wills registered. A copy can be seen at the FRC, but not at the PRO.
9			*Year books of probates (from 1630): Abstracts of probate acts in the Prerogative Court of Canterbury*, eds J Matthews and G F Matthews (London, 1902–1927).
9.1	1630–1634	PROB 11/157–166	vol. I (1902)
9.2	1635–1639	PROB 11/167–181	vol. II (1903)
9.3	1630–1639	PROB 11/157–181	*Sentences and complete index nominum (probates and sentences)* extra volume (1907). This volume indexes sentences 1630–1639, and all surnames in it and in 9.1–9.2.
9.4	1640–1644	PROB 11/182–192	vol. III (1905). See also 13 below.
9.5	1645–1649	PROB 11/192–210	vol. IV (1906). See also 13 below. Tracing probate acts and wills 1643–1646 is subject to particular difficulties. Further information is supplied in the appendix to the PROB 10 Introductory Note.
9.6	1650–1651	PROB 11/211–219	vol. V (1909). See also 10 and 13 below.
9.7	1652–1653	PROB 11/220–232	vol. VI (1911). See also 10 and 13 below.
9.8	1654	PROB 11/233–242	vol. VII (1914). See also 10 and 13 below.
9.9	1655	PROB 11/243–251	vol. VIII (1927) [surnames A–Musgrave only]. See also 10 and 13 below. 9.8–9.9 do not have place name indexes, but there is one in 10 which covers the same period.
10	1653–1656	PROB 11/225–260	*Index of wills proved in the Prerogative Court of Canterbury*, vol. VII, eds T M Blagg and J Skeate Moir, Index Library, LIV (London, British Records Society, 1925). See also 13 below.

11	1657–1660	PROB 11/261–302	*Index of wills proved in the Prerogative Court of Canterbury*, vol. VIII, ed. T M Blagg, Index Library, LXI (London, British Records Society, 1936). See also 13 below.
12	1658	PROB 11/272–285	W Brigg, *Genealogical abstracts of wills proved in the Prerogative Court of Canterbury: Register Wootton 1658*, 7 volumes (Leeds, 1894–1914). Abstracts of all wills registered. A copy can be seen at the FRC, but not at the PRO.
13	1640–1660	PROB 11/182–302	Sentences registered in PROB 11/182–302 are indexed in *Index to administrations in the Prerogative Court of Canterbury*, vol. VI, ed. M Fitch, Index Library, C (London, British Records Society, 1986).
14	1661–1670	PROB 11/303–334	*Prerogative Court of Canterbury: Wills, sentences and probate acts*, ed. J H Morrison (London, 1935).
15	1671–1675	PROB 11/335–349	*Index of wills proved in the Prerogative Court of Canterbury*, vol. IX, ed. J Ainsworth, Index Library, LXVII (London, British Records Society, 1942).
16	1676–1685	PROB 11/350–381	*Index of wills proved in the Prerogative Court of Canterbury*, vol. X, ed. C H Ridge, Index Library, LXXI (London, British Records Society, 1948).
17	1686–1693	PROB 11/382–417	*Index of wills proved in the Prerogative Court of Canterbury*, vol. XI, ed. C Ridge, Index Library, LXXVII (London, British Records Society, 1958).
18	1694–1700	PROB 11/418–458	*Index of wills proved in the Prerogative Court of Canterbury*, vol. XII, ed. M Fitch, Index Library, LXXX (London, British Records Society, 1960).
19	1701–1749	PROB 11/459–775	Friends of the Public Record Office, *Index to PCC wills and administrations* (London, 1998. Microfiche). The index has been compiled from PROB 12/71–119. Where entries in PROB 12/71–119 appear to be defective they have been checked against the administration act books (PROB 6), the probate act books (PROB 8), and the registered wills (PROB 11).

20	1750	PROB 11/776–784	G Sherwood, *A list of persons named in the PCC wills proved in the year 1750: Register Greenly* (4,382 wills naming 40,320 persons arranged in eight groups topographically) (London, privately published, 1918). There is a copy in the library of the Society of Genealogists, but not at the FRC or the PRO.
21	1750–1800	PROB 11/776–1351	*An index to wills proved in the Prerogative Court of Canterbury 1750–1800*, ed. A J Camp, 6 vols (London, Society of Genealogists, 1976–1992). Compiled from PROB 13/186–242, checked (not systematically) against PROB 12/120–176.
22	1801–1852	PROB 11/1352–2164	PROB 12/177–271
23	1853–1858	PROB 11/2165–2263	PROB 12/272–288: *Calendar of the grants of probate and letters of administration made in the Prerogative Court of Canterbury, 1853–1857, 1858*, 16 vols (London, nd). (Locations of copies of this index outside the PRO are listed in Gibson, *Probate Jurisdictions: Where to look for wills*. The index has also been published in microfiche by Hampshire Record Office, together with the calendars of grants of probate and administration for the period 1858 to 1935.)

Wills of American testators

| 24 | 1610–1857 | PROB 11/115–2262 | P W Coldham, *American wills proved in London, 1611–1775* (Baltimore, 1992). It can be used to advantage in conjunction with his *American Wills and Administrations in the Prerogative Court of Canterbury, 1610–1857* (Baltimore, 1989). This work supersedes Coldham's earlier works on the same subject. |

Administration indexes

The online index to PCC wills at www.pro-online.pro.gov.uk, does not include administrations. Use the indexes listed below.

| 25 | 1559–1571 | PROB 6/1 | *Administrations in the Prerogative Court of Canterbury*, [vol. I], ed. R M Glencross (Exeter, 1912). |
| 26 | 1572–1580 | PROB 6/2 | *Administrations in the Prerogative Court of Canterbury*, vol. II (Exeter, 1917). |

27	1559–1580	PROB 6/1–2	B Lloyd, Preliminary addenda and corrigenda to Mr R M Glencross's letters of administration granted by the Prerogative Court of Canterbury, 1559–1580 (typescript, 1979).
28	1581–1595	PROB 6/3–5	*Index to administrations in the Prerogative Court of Canterbury*, vol. III, ed. C H Ridge, Index Library, LXXVI (London, BRS, 1954).
29	1596–1608	PROB 6/5–7	*Index to administrations in the Prerogative Court of Canterbury*, vol. IV, ed. M Fitch, Index Library, LXXXI (London, BRS, 1964).
30	1609–1619	PROB 6/7–10	*Index to administrations in the Prerogative Court of Canterbury*, vol. V, ed. M Fitch, Index Library, LXXXIII (London, BRS, 1968).
31	1620–1630	PROB 6/10–13	*Prerogative Court of Canterbury: Letters of administration*, ed. J H Morrison (London, 1935).
32	1631–1648	PROB 6/14A–23	*Index to administrations in the Prerogative Court of Canterbury*, vol. VI, ed. M Fitch, Index Library, C (London, BRS, 1986). (This index also includes sentences registered from 1640 to 1660 in PROB 11/182–302.)
33	1643–1644	PROB 6/234	Grants made by the Prerogative Court of Canterbury at Oxford, were omitted from 32 above. PROB 6/234 contains a contemporary index which has been reproduced and is available on the open shelves. (This reproduction was formerly PROB 12/23B.)
34	1649–1654	PROB 6/24–30	*Index to administrations in the Prerogative Court of Canterbury*, vol. 1, ed. J Ainsworth, Index Library, LXVIII (London, BRS, 1944). For further information on tracing administration acts 1653–1654 see the PROB 6 Introductory Note, appendix 2.
35	1655–1660	PROB 6/31–36	*Index to administrations in the Prerogative Court of Canterbury*, vol. II, ed. C H Ridge, 3 vols, Index Library, LXXII (A–F), LXXIV (G–Q), LXXV (R–Z) (London, BRS, 1949–1953).
36	1661	PROB 6/37	Surnames A – Sweetinge: typescript index.

37	1661	PROB 6/37	Surnames other than those in the sequence A – Sweetinge: PROB 12/38
38	1662	–	The administration act book is not extant for 1662. Use PROB 12/39 (see also PROB 13/96–97, PROB 15/72).
39	1663–1664	PROB 6/38–39	Typescript index
40	1665–1700	PROB 6/40–76	PROB 12/41–69
41	1701–1749	PROB 6/77–125	Friends of the Public Record Office, *Index to PCC wills and administrations* (London, 1998. Microfiche). The index has been compiled from PROB 12/71–119. Where entries in PROB 12/71–119 appear to be defective they have been checked against the administration act books (PROB 6), the probate act books (PROB 8), and the registered wills (PROB 11).
42	1750–1800	PROB 12/126–176	There is a card index to these administrations acts, largely compiled from PROB 13/186–236, at the Society of Genealogists, which the Society will search for a fee.
43	1801–1852	PROB 6/177–228	PROB 12/177–271
44	1853–1858	PROB 6/229–233	PROB 12/272–288: *Calendar of the grants of probate and letters of administration made in the Prerogative Court of Canterbury, 1853–1857, 1858*, 16 vols (London, nd). (Locations of copies of this index outside the PRO are listed in Gibson, *Probate Jurisdictions: Where to look for wills*, 12. The index has also been published in microfiche by Hampshire Record Office, together with the calendars of grants of probate and administration for the period 1858 to 1935.)
Administration acts relating to estates of American intestates			
45	1610–1857	PROB 6/7–233	P W Coldham, *American Wills and Administrations in the Prerogative Court of Canterbury, 1610–1857* (Baltimore, 1989). This work supersedes Coldham's earlier works on the same subject.

6.24 Inheritance: death duties, wills, administrations and disputes: bibliography

T Arkell, N Evans and N Goose, eds, *When Death Us Do Part: Understanding and Interpreting the Probate Records of Early Modern England* (*Local Population Studies*, Supplement, 2000)

A J Camp, 'The Genealogist's Use of Probate Records', eds G H Martin and P Spufford, *Records of the Nation* (British Record Society, 1990), pp. 287–298

E J Carlson 'The historical value of Ely consistory probate records', in *Index of the probate records of the Consistory Court of Ely 1449–1858, part 1: A–E,* eds. E Leedham-Green and R Rodd, Index Library CIII (London, British Record Society, 1994), xvii–lix. Of value for all church courts with probate jurisdiction

P W Coldham, *American Wills and Administrations in the Prerogative Court of Canterbury, 1610–1857* (Baltimore, 1989)

A Collins, *Basic Facts About Using Wills After 1858* (FFHS, 1998)

J Cox, *Affection Defying the Power of Death: Wills, Probate and Death Duty Records* (FFHS, 1993)

J Cox, *Hatred pursued beyond the grave* (HMSO, 1993)

J Cox, *Wills, Inventories and Death Duties* (PRO, 1988)

A L Erickson, 'An Introduction to Probate Accounts', eds. G H Martin and P Spufford, *Records of the Nation* (British Record Society, 1990), pp. 273–286

J S W Gibson, *A Simplified Guide to Probate Jurisdictions: Where to look for wills* (FFHS, 4th edn 1994)

Ham's Inland Revenue Yearbook (annual: PRO library has 1875–1930)

D Hawkings, *Index of Somerset Estate Duty Office Wills and Letters of Administration 1805–1811* (1995)

D Hawkings, *Index of Somerset Estate Duty Office Wills 1812–1857* (2 vols, 1995)

M D Herber, *Ancestral Trails* (Society of Genealogists, 2000)

A List of Wills, Administrations, Etc, in the Public Record Office, London, England: 12th–19th century (1932)

C Marshall, 'In the Name of God? Will Making and Faith in Early Modern England', eds G H Martin and P Spufford, ed., *Records of the Nation* (British Record Society, 1990), pp. 215–249

R Milward, *A Glossary of Household, Farming and Trade Terms From Probate Inventories* (Derbyshire Record Society, *Occasional Paper No 1*, 3rd edn, 1993)

N Newington-Irving, *Will indexes and other probate material in the Library of the Society of Genealogists* (Society of Genealogists, 1996)

M Overton, *A Bibliography of British Probate Inventories* (Newcastle, 1983)

PCC Sentences: a rough list transcribed from the original calendars for the period 1643–1652

M Scott, *Prerogative Court of Canterbury: Wills and Other Probate Records* (PRO, 1997)

'Wills and Administrations in the Court of Delegates', *The Genealogist*, new series 11 [1903], pp. 165–171, 224–227; 12 [1903], pp. 97–101 (Probate records in DEL 9)

7

Welsh genealogy

◆ ◆ ◆

7.1 Welsh genealogy: records elsewhere

Most Welsh family history is traced by exactly the same means as English family history – Wales and England have been one nation since the 1540s. However, the two societies did not grow similar until much later – especially with regard to language. Welsh was the native tongue of most inhabitants of Wales until well into the nineteenth century.

A major difficulty faced by family historians in Wales is caused by the late adoption of fixed surnames, and the relatively small stock of names that evolved from the previous naming practices – Jones, Davies, Pritchard, Price, Williams, Parry, Bevan or Evans, Thomas, etc. For advice on understanding the patronymic system used until the seventeenth or eighteenth century, read Rowlands and Rowlands, *The Surnames of Wales*, or Morgan and Morgan, *Welsh Surnames*.

Parish Registers of Wales (Williams and Watts-Williams) is a useful guide to the whereabouts of original parish registers and copies in Welsh record offices and libraries and in the library of the Society of Genealogists. The National Library of Wales (www.llgc.org.uk) also holds many parish registers and transcripts as well as wills, tithe records, title deeds and personal and estate records. These are described in the *Guide to the Manuscripts and Records, the National Library of Wales*. Wills proved in Welsh consistory courts before 1858 have been indexed by the LDS in *Abstracts and Indexes of Wills*. Most of the Welsh record offices produce their own genealogical leaflets, as does the Welsh Tourist Board. For a very useful directory of what is available where and when, see *Researching Family History in Wales*, by Istance and Cann. A good survey of the available literature, and of where finding aids to records in Wales can be seen in England, is given by Herber, in *Ancestral Trails*. One famous source which used to be in the PRO, the Golden Grove Book of Pedigrees (an early eighteenth century genealogical collection) is now in the care of the Carmarthenshire Archives Service (address in **48**). For Welsh manor court records, held nationally and locally, see Watt's *Welsh Manors and their records*, and also the Manorial Documents Register online at www.hmc.gov.uk/mdr.

The records of Welsh courts before 1830, formerly held in the PRO in the WALE series, have been transferred to the National Library of Wales. Relatively little survives before the introduction of the Courts of Great Sessions (similar to the English assizes) in 1540, but a lot thereafter. For details, see Parry, *A Guide to the Records of Great Sessions in Wales*. Monmouthshire was not included in the Great Sessions circuits, but was added to the English Western assize circuit in 1543.

7.2 Welsh genealogy: records in the PRO and FRC

Most of the records discussed in this book should be as helpful in tracing the history of Welsh families as they are for English families. There are some specific records which, because they relate solely to Wales, or because they are arranged by place, may be particularly helpful. Tax records in E 179 are the most obvious genealogical source, with the hearth taxes of the late seventeenth century being the most useful (see **43**).

For births, marriages and deaths from 1837, go to the FRC (see **3a**). Because of the strong nonconformist tradition in Wales, the nonconformist registers of births, marriages and deaths in RG 4 and RG 8 (for 1700–1858) are a very fruitful source. The list is arranged by county, with a further list available by denomination (see **3b.6–3b.7**). Census returns are also arranged by place (see **2**). The 1891 and 1901 censuses note whether people were Welsh speakers.

For an easy way into sixteenth and seventeenth century disputes in Wales and Monmouthshire, look at the several volumes published by the University of Wales, Board of Celtic Studies. These cover the courts of Star Chamber, Chancery, Augmentations and Exchequer: they are well indexed, and provide an easy way into these records (details given in the bibliography, where the relevant works are marked *). They can be seen in the PRO Library, where there are also many works on Welsh history. The Exchequer equity depositions in E 134 continue to be searchable by county until 1760: they continue listed by date until 1841 (see **47c**).

The assize records for the Chester and North Wales circuit and the South Wales circuit, c.1831 onwards (ASSI 57–67, ASSI 71–77), effectively continue the records of the courts of Great Sessions, now in the National Library of Wales. The records of the Palatinate of Chester (CHES 1–38) also cover Flintshire, and other parts of North Wales (see **38** and **47d**).

There are registers of ex-soldiers and sailors living in Wales who were in receipt of a Chelsea or Greenwich out-pension, 1842–1862 (WO 22/114–117). Some of the entries relate to widows and children. Try also a PROCAT search of WO 97 and WO 121 for soldiers discharged to pension between 1760 and 1854, as these can be searched by county of birth as well as by name.

7.3 Early Welsh records in the PRO

Among the earlier records that stayed in the PRO are the records of some of the marcher lordships and of the principality. Because of the history of its con-quest by the Normans and Plantagenets, medieval Wales was composed of the principality (basically Anglesey, Caernarvon, Merioneth, Cardigan and Carmarthen), run by the Crown, and several quasi-independent marcher

Figure 18 A Welsh archer from the 1280s. A Flemish observer wrote of Welsh soldiers, fighting for Edward I in Flanders around 1300, that *in the very depth of winter they were running about bare-legged. …They could not have been warm. The money they received from the King was spent in milk and butter. They would eat and drink anywhere. I never saw them wearing armour…Their weapons were bows, arrows and swords. They also had javelins…* (Lodowyk van Velthem, *Spiegel Historiaal*) (PRO, E 36/274 folio 32)

lordships, some of which had fallen into the Crown's possession. In the 1530s and 1540s Wales was divided into shires and given a form of local government based on the English model. The marcher lordships were not actually abolished, and some of them continued to provide local courts. For more details, see the *PRO Guide*, part 1, sections 352–355.

The PRO has an unsurpassed collection of records from the marcher lordship of Ruthin or Dyffryn Clwyd, brought in for safe keeping from the leaking Ruthin town hall in the 1840s. They stretch from the thirteenth to the nineteenth centuries, and include court rolls with lists of tenants, views of frankpledge, lists of freeholders and inhabitants, and proceedings in the lordship court, which handled debt cases until the 1820s. The court rolls are in SC 2; the other records are well listed in WALE 15.

There are also records from some other marcher lordships. Most of these are court rolls and surveys, and they are not as extensive as those of Ruthin. Records of marcher lordships held by the Duchy of Lancaster (Kidwelly, Ogmore, Monmouth, Brecon, Caldicot, Iscennen, etc.) are in DL 28–30, DL 41–42 and SC 2. Records of marcher lordships that had fallen into Crown hands are in SC 2, SC 6, SC 11, SC 12, LR 2, LR 9, LR 11 and LR 13.

7.4 Welsh genealogy: bibliography

An * shows that this work is in the University of Wales, Board of Celtic Studies, *History and Law* series.

I Edwards, *A Catalogue of Star Chamber Proceedings Relating to Wales* (Cardiff, 1929) *

G Hamilton Edwards, *In search of Welsh Ancestry* (Chichester, 1986)

M Herber, *Ancestral Trails* (Society of Genealogists, 2000)

J Istance and E E Cann, *Researching Family History in Wales* (FFHS, 1996)

E G Jones, *Exchequer Proceedings (Equity) Concerning Wales. Henry VIII–Elizabeth* (Cardiff, 1939) *

T I Jeffreys Jones, *Exchequer Proceedings Concerning Wales in Tempore James I* (Cardiff, 1955) *

E A Lewis, *An Inventory of the Early Chancery Proceedings Concerning Wales* (Cardiff, 1937) *

E A Lewis and J Conway Davies, *Records of the Court of Augmentations relating to Wales and Monmouthshire* (Cardiff, 1954) *

S Lewis, *Topographical Dictionary of Wales* (London, 1840)

G Morgan, 'Welsh Names in Welsh Wills', *Journal of the Society of Archivists*, vol. XXV (1995), pp. 178–185

T J Morgan and P Morgan, *Welsh Surnames* (Cardiff, 1985)

National Library of Wales, *Guide to Genealogical Sources at the National Library of Wales* (National Library of Wales leaflet)

National Library of Wales, *Guide to the Manuscripts and Records, the National Library of Wales* (National Library of Wales, 1994)

G Parry, *A Guide to the Records of Great Sessions in Wales* (Aberystwyth, 1995)

B Rawlins, *The Parish Churches and Nonconformist Chapels of Wales: their records and where to find them* (LDS, Salt Lake City, 1987)

J Rowlands, *Welsh Family History: A Guide to Research* (Association of Family History Societies for Wales, 1993)

J Rowlands and S Rowlands, *The Surnames of Wales* (FFHS, 1996)

H Watt, *Welsh Manors and their Records* (National Library of Wales, 2000)

C J Williams and J Watts-Williams, *Cofrestri Plwyf Cymru, Parish Registers of Wales* (National Library of Wales and Welsh County Archivists Group, 1986)

8

Scottish genealogy

◆ ◆ ◆

8.1 Scottish genealogy: records in Scotland, and access at the FRC

Civil registration of births, marriages and deaths began in Scotland on 1 January 1855. The records, along with many parish registers (c.1700–1855), minor foreign registers from 1855, and the decennial census returns for 1841–1891, are held by the General Register Office (Scotland), where they can be searched for a fee. The indexes can be searched on the web at www.origins.net but a charge is payable. Certificates have to be ordered from the General Register Office (Scotland). You get access to:

- indexes to the birth, marriage and death registers from 1 January 1855, including adoptions from 1930 and divorces from May 1984
- indexes of all the names in the Scottish Church Registers of births, baptisms, and marriages, 1555–1854 (excluding those church registers held by the National Archives of Scotland).

Deaths and burials are not covered before 1855.

The General Register Office (Scotland), also holds various series of registers of births, deaths and marriages which took place outside Scotland, but which relate to Scots or people normally resident in Scotland. These are similar to the registers for the English and Welsh abroad (see 4). They include births and deaths at sea (from 1855); returns from foreign countries (from 1860); armed services registers (from 1881), war registers (from 1899); and consular returns (from 1914). For more on births, marriages and deaths, see Sinclair, *Jock Tamson's Bairns*.

Scottish censuses for 1891 and 1901 are available online, at www.origins.net/GRO as are the indexes to the 1881 census. Earlier censuses from 1841 are kept at the General Register Office (Scotland).

Wills, judicial records, deeds etc., are in the National Archives of Scotland: see Sinclair's *Tracing Your Scottish Ancestry*, and the *Guide to the National Archives of Scotland*. Wills are gradually being put online: look at www.scan.org.uk for an introduction to Scottish wills, Scottish handwriting and the wills and indexes currently online. The Scottish Genealogy Society, the Scots Ancestry Research

Society and the Association of Scottish Genealogists and Record Agents are available to undertake paid research.

8.2 Scottish genealogy: material elsewhere

The Society of Genealogists has a very extensive collection of Scottish materials. To find out what they have, look at *Sources for Scottish Genealogy in the Library of the Society of Genealogists*.

8.3 Scottish genealogy: records in the PRO

After the union of Scotland and England into the United Kingdom of Great Britain in 1707, Scots appear regularly in the main series of government records. They crop up in the records of the Army, Navy, Treasury, Customs, Excise, Merchant Navy, Foreign Office, Colonial Office, office of the Secretaries of State and so on. The legal systems remained different, so look in Scotland for anything to do with the courts or with legal affairs *within* Scotland.

The PRO has the wills of Scots possessed of property in the form of goods, money and investments in England (see **6**), and also the records of Scottish churches in England (see **3b.10**). The Apprenticeship Books include details of Scottish apprentices (see **28**) and the Scots are well represented in the records of the Merchant Navy (see **26**), the Metropolitan Police (see **24.3–24.5**), and of course, the armed forces.

The records of the Army are particularly fruitful, because of the territorial base of so many regiments and militia regiments (see **18**). Try searching WO 97 and WO 121 in PROCAT for soldiers discharged to pension between 1760 and 1854, as they can be searched by county of birth as well as by name. For ex-soldiers and ex-sailors living in Scotland and in receipt of a Chelsea or Greenwich pension, there are registers arranged by district pay office (e.g. Ayr, Paisley) for 1842–1862 (WO 22/118–140). Some of the entries relate to widows and children.

For Scottish emigrants to North America see **14.6**.

Of course, the Secretaries of State, based in London, conducted a stream of correspondence with Scotland. Much of this is included in the *Calendars of State Papers Domestic*, and in the (indexed) descriptive list of the State Papers, Scotland, 1688–1782 (SP 54). Many individuals are referred to in these papers. SP 54 is searchable online: after 1745, you may find it worthwhile searching T 1 online, until 1800, as the Treasury was deeply involved in Scottish affairs, and this section of its papers are well listed. For the period before 1603, there are the separate *Calendar of Letters and Papers Relating to the Affairs of the Borders of England and Scotland* and *Calendar of State Papers Relating to Scotland and Mary, Queen of Scots, 1547–1603*.

See also the biographical dictionaries mentioned in **1.15**.

8.4 Scottish genealogy: bibliography

Calendar of Letters and Papers Relating to the Affairs of the Borders of England and Scotland (London, 1894–1896)

Calendar of State Papers, Domestic, 1603–1704 (London, 1857–1972)

Calendar of State Papers Relating to Scotland and Mary, Queen of Scots, 1547–1603 (London, 1898–1969)

K B Cory, *Tracing Your Scottish Ancestry* (Edinburgh, 1996)

J P S Ferguson, *Scottish Family Histories* (Edinburgh, 1986)

S Fowler, *Tracing Scottish Ancestors* (PRO, 2001)

G Hamilton Edwards, *In search of Scottish Ancestry* (Chichester, 1986)

M D Herber, *Ancestral Trails* (Society of Genealogists, 2000)

S Lewis, *Topographical Dictionary of Scotland* (London, 1846)

D Moody, *Scottish Family History* (London, 1988)

M Moore, *Sources for Scottish Genealogy in the Library of the Society of Genealogists* (Society of Genealogists, 1996)

Scotland, A Genealogical Research Guide (LDS, Salt Lake City, 1987)

Scottish Record Office, *A Guide to the National Archives of Scotland* (Edinburgh, 1996)

C Sinclair, *Jock Tamson's Bairns* (Edinburgh, 2000)

C Sinclair, *Tracing Your Scottish Ancestry: A Guide to Ancestry Research in the Scottish Record Office* (London, 1997)

D J Steel, ed., *Sources for Scottish Genealogy and Family History* (London, 1970)

9

Irish genealogy

◆ ◆ ◆

9.1 Irish genealogy: records in Ireland

So many Irish records have been lost or destroyed (notably in the burning of the Irish Public Record Office in 1922) that it is well worth making a preliminary approach to the Irish Genealogical Research Society for help: the address is given in **48**. For a detailed recent overview of the surviving records and the availability of finding aids, and for general advice, read Herber, *Ancestral Trails*. Two indispensable works put out by the respective archives of Ireland and Northern Ireland are Grenham, *Tracing Your Ancestors in Ireland*, and Maxwell, *Tracing Your Ancestors in Northern Ireland*.

A population census was taken in Ireland every ten years between 1821 and 1911, and those that survive are in the National Archives in Dublin. The records from 1861–1891 were deliberately destroyed by the government, and only a few of the 1821–1851 censuses survived the fire of 1922. For a list of survivals, and of transcripts or abstracts from lost censuses, see Gibson and Medlycott, *Local Census Listings, 1522–1930, holdings in the British Isles*. Unlike the early English censuses, these Irish censuses include names. Returns for 1901 and 1911 are fairly complete and are open. A census was also taken in the republic in 1926, which is now open to public inspection. Records of applications for old age pensions between 1908 and 1922 may have used census data as a proof of age, for these applicants were born before the introduction of civil registration in 1864. These applications survive at the National Archives in Dublin, and at the Public Record Office of Northern Ireland (PRONI), in Belfast. They have been indexed by name, and a copy of the index can be seen at the Society of Genealogists.

The civil registration of all births, marriages and deaths in Ireland began on 1 January 1864, although the civil registration of marriages other than Roman Catholic had started in 1845. The records for the whole of Ireland until 1921, for the republic of Ireland from 1921 to date, and of non-Roman Catholic marriages from 1 April 1845 are in the General Register Office of Ireland in Dublin. Copy certificates can be bought online, from www.groireland.ie. The records of births, marriages and deaths in Northern Ireland since 1 January 1922 are in the General Register Office in Belfast: an index to them is available at the FRC. Copy certificates can be bought online, from www.groni.gov.uk.

The two General Register Offices also hold various series of registers of births, deaths and marriages that took place outside Ireland, but which relate to people normally resident there. These are similar to the registers for the English and Welsh abroad (see **4**). Those at Dublin include births and deaths at sea (from 1864); consular returns (from 1864), armed services registers (from 1883), and indexes to war registers (from 1899). After partition, the General Register Office of Northern Ireland kept similar series, with marine registers and consular returns from 1922, and armed service registers from 1927.

Irish parish registers have also suffered much destruction. The *International Genealogical Index* includes about 2 million entries. To find out what survives, and where it can be seen, use Mitchell's *A Guide to Irish Parish Registers*. This lists what survives for each parish, and also includes Presbyterian and nonconformist registers. Very usefully, it includes references to copies held by the Society of Genealogists.

- Anglican Church of Ireland parish registers started in 1634, but few survive before the late 1700s. Only a minority of the population used them. About half had been deposited in the Irish Public Record Office for safe keeping: these were destroyed in 1922.
- Roman Catholic parishes (which were usually bigger than Anglican parishes) see Grenham, *Tracing Your Irish Ancestors*.
- Presbyterian registers are either still with the congregations, or with the Presbyterian Historical Society in Belfast. See Falley, *Irish and Scottish-Irish Ancestral Research*.

Wills were proved before church courts until 1858. Virtually all registered Irish probate records before 1904 were destroyed in 1922. Vicars's index to them is now the main clue to what was once there, but there are several attempts to reconstruct the lost data. The PRO Library has a copy of the CD-ROM *Index of Irish Wills 1484–1858*. Many probate copies of wills survived, along with other material. For example, the Society of Genealogists has 18 volumes of abstracts from Irish wills, 1569–1909, and Herber gives details of abstracts of wills surviving in many locations. PRONI has copies and extracts of many Ulster wills, and for a fee, the Ulster Historical Foundation (at the same address), will undertake genealogical searches. Calendars of all wills proved and administrations granted 1858–1922 may be seen in the *National Probate Calendar* at the FRC, PRO, National Archives and PRONI. From 1922, try the National Archives or PRONI.

For records of land holding from 1708, try the Registry of Deeds in Dublin. These can include copies of wills that were used to prove entitlement.

Most of the historic archive was destroyed in 1922: fortunately, some volumes of calendars had been published beforehand (and can be seen in the PRO Library). Particularly useful are the published versions of the *Patent and Close Rolls of Chancery in Ireland, Henry VIII, Edward VI, Mary and Elizabeth, and for the 1st to 8th year of Charles I*. For other such publications, ask in the PRO Library to see HMSO, *Sectional List 24: British National Archives*, to get the full titles.

9.2 Irish genealogy: records in the PRO

Kings of England had claimed the title Lord of Ireland since 1169, although leaving much of the work to governors and viceroys. After the union of Ireland, Scotland and England into the single United Kingdom of Great Britain and Ireland in 1801, Irish people appear regularly in the main series of government records, until the union dissolved in 1922, leaving Northern Ireland as part of the UK. For generations, Irishmen came over as seasonal migrant labour, and went back home with the money earned. Family migration from Ireland did not start until the dreadful famine of the 1840s forced people to leave. Because they were travelling within the same kingdom, there are no records treating the Irish as immigrants: they were internal migrants, within one country.

The Irish crop up in the records of the Army, Navy, Treasury, Customs, Excise, Merchant Navy, Foreign Office, Colonial Office, office of the Secretaries of State and so on. The legal systems were distinct, so look in Ireland for anything to do with the courts or with legal affairs *within* Ireland. For records in the PRO relating to Irish history, and only incidentally to Irish genealogy, see Prochaska's book, *Irish History from 1700: A Guide to Sources in the Public Record Office*.

Of course, thousands of Irishmen served in the Army and the Navy – indeed, by some estimates as many as 40 per cent of privates in the Army were Irish. Some records are obviously Irish, such as the muster rolls of the Irish militia, 1793–1876, in WO 13. Before the Union with the United Kingdom in 1801, Ireland had a separate Army with its own organization and establishment. From 1801, Ireland remained a separate command, and the Irish regiments retained their Irish identity, but the Army was merged with the British Army. Records relating to the Army in Ireland, 1775–1923, are in WO 35. Over 185,000 Irishmen served in the Army during the First World War – 50,000 in the regular Army, and 135,000 as volunteers (there was no conscription in Ireland).

To explore the records of Irish soldiers and sailors, see **18** and **19**.

The Royal Kilmainham Hospital, founded in 1679, acted as a permanent hospital for disabled soldiers (in-pensioners) and also distributed money to out-pensioners: see **18b.4.2** and following sections. Records of the payment of pensions, 1842–1862 and 1882–1883, are in WO 22/141–205 and 209–225, arranged by district: they are useful for tracing changes of residence and dates of death.

The only separate naval records for Irishmen are of nominations to serve in the Irish Coastguard, 1821–1849 (ADM 175/99–100).

The State Papers, Ireland (SP 60–67) contain despatches from the Crown's representative in Ireland – the Lord Deputy or Lord Lieutenant, his council and other officials to the Secretaries of State. They can contain letters sent in by soldiers, officials, and private individuals; drafts and minutes of answers made to such letters; accounts of expenditure or requests for funds; instructions sent out to officials; projects for English colonization or establishing new trades and industries; reports on the state of Ireland, etc. They are full of references to individuals, and are relatively easy to use as they have been published in précis and indexed from 1509–1670 in the *Calendar of State Papers, Ireland*. The first volume in a new and fuller edition has just been published, covering 1571–1575. From 1670 to 1704, they have been included in the *Calendar of State Papers, Domestic*. In fact, the State Papers, Ireland continue up to 1782: for the later period there are brief lists in the PRO and much fuller lists in the Public Record Office of Northern Ireland. The same types of letters and papers continue in various Home Office and Colonial Office classes after 1782, but they are not fully listed, nor indexed, and so are not easy to use. If you want to investigate these, try Prochaska and the *PRO Guide*.

Some of the records discussed more fully elsewhere in this book may be helpful in tracing Irish family history. The Prerogative Court of Canterbury may have proved the wills of Irish people who died with goods in England before 1858 (see **6**). Between 1858 and 1922, details of wills can be found from the *National Probate Calendar*, of which the PRO has a copy.

The records of the Royal Irish Constabulary, 1836–1922, are full and informative: see **24.7**. For Irish Revenue Police, 1830–1857, who tried to prevent illicit distilling, try CUST 111: see also **25.2**. For Customs officers in Ireland, 1682–1826, see CUST 20. After this, try *Ham's Customs Year Book* and *Ham's Inland Revenue Year Book* which the PRO Library has in a run from 1875–1930. These list Customs and Inland Revenue officials (up to 1923 for Ireland), and include a name index. For a general Irish directory to officials and people of status, see *Thom's Irish Almanac and Official Directory*, which the PRO Library has from 1844–1928, with an odd volume for 1944. The Library also has runs of the *Dublin Almanac*, 1836–1849, and the *Dublin Directory*, 1840–1857. See also the biographical dictionaries mentioned in **1.15**.

The records of the Irish Tontines of 1773, 1775 and 1777 (see **44**) cover 1773–1871, and list many people, with addresses.

The records of the Irish Reproductive Loan Fund, in T 91, may be helpful if you are looking for a family in Munster or Connaught in the mid 1800s. The fund provided loans at interest to the industrious poor, who had to provide some form of security for the loan. Records of the local associations, which administered the loans, survive for counties Cork, Clare, Galway, Limerick, Mayo, Roscommon, Sligo and Tipperary. In addition to the notes of security (signed by the debtor and two guarantors), there are loan ledgers, repayment books and defaulters books. They do not give much detail other than place of abode and occupation.

The Irish Sailors' and Soldiers' Land Trust was set up to provide cottages in Ireland, with or without gardens, for ex-servicemen (including airmen) after the First World War. In the 1920s and 1930s over 4,000 cottages were provided. Because of rent strikes in the republic, no further cottages were built there after 1932, but cottages continued to be built by the Trust in Northern Ireland until 1952. Provisions were later made to sell the cottages to the tenants or their widows. You will need to know the location of the cottage to use the records, as there are no name indexes. The tenancy files in AP 7 are the place to start. They are closed for 75 years, but privileged access can be given provided you sign a written undertaking not to publish or reveal the names or other particulars of people named in the tenancy files. Ask in the Research Enquiries Room for a copy of the form to sign.

From 1925, there is a 'census' for the unions of Dunganon, Castledery, Clougher and Omagh, in CAB 61/164–168. This was of political importance: it gave the name of the head of each household, and the number (no other details) of Catholic and non-Catholic persons in each household, in these border areas of Ulster.

Maps of Ireland may be seen in the Map Room. The earliest date from the late 1500s (the Barony Maps in ZMAP 5). The Survey of 1655–1658 (ZOS 7) was the legal basis for the identification of Irish lands. The 1839 six–inch Ordnance Survey maps in ZOS 15 are the most detailed: they have a key sheet near the beginning of each county volume. The one–inch Ordnance Survey maps in ZOS 14 date from 1851–1852. Lewis's *Topographical Dictionary of Ireland* is also useful in identifying places, and filling out their history.

Figure 19 The industrious poor in rural Ireland were able to apply for government loans to improve their situation, from the Irish Reproductive Loan Fund. Surviving records are in T 91. (PRO, COPY 1/446)

9.3 Irish genealogy: bibliography

D Begley, *Handbook on Irish Genealogy* (Dublin, 1976)

D Begley, ed., *Irish Genealogy: a Record Finder* (Dublin, 1982)

B de Breffny, *Bibliography of Irish Family History and Genealogy* (Cork and Dublin, 1974)

A Camp, *Sources for Irish Genealogy in the Library of the Society of Genealogists* (Society of Genealogists, 1990)

B Davis, *An Introduction to Irish Research, Irish Ancestry; a beginner's guide* (FFHS, 1994)

M Falley, *Irish and Scottish-Irish Ancestral Research: A Guide to the Genealogical Records, Methods and Sources in Ireland* (GPC, 1989, reprint of 1962 edition, 2 vols)

S Fowler, *Tracing Irish Ancestors* (PRO, 2001)

J Gibson and M Medlycott, *Local Census Listings, 1522–1930, holdings in the British Isles* (FFHS, 1994)

J Grenham, *Tracing Your Irish Ancestors* (Dublin, 1992)

S Helferty and R Refause, *Directory of Irish Archives* (Dublin, 1993)

M D Herber, *Ancestral Trails* (Society of Genealogists, 2000)

Irish Records Index, *Index of Irish Wills 1484–1858. Vol.1 Records at the National Archives of Ireland* (CD-Rom)

Irish Roots Quarterly

S Lewis, *Topographical Dictionary of Ireland* (London, 1846)

M MacConghail and P Gorry, *Tracing Irish Ancestors* (Glasgow, 1997)

E MacLysaght, *Bibliography of Irish Family History* (2nd edn, 1982)

I Maxwell, *Tracing Your Ancestors in Northern Ireland* (PRONI, 1997)

B Mitchell, *A Guide to Irish Parish Registers* (GPC, 1988)

J Morrin, *Patent and Close Rolls of Chancery in Ireland, Henry VIII, Edward VI, Mary and Elizabeth, and for the 1st to 8th year of Charles I* (London, 1861–1864)

W Nolan, *Tracing the Past. Sources for Local Studies in the Republic of Ireland* (Dublin, 1982)

A Prochaska, *Irish History from 1700: A Guide to Sources in the Public Record Office* (British Records Association and Institute of Historical Research, 1986)

Public Record Office, *Calendar of State Papers Ireland 1509–1670* (London, 1860–1910)

Public Record Office and Irish Manuscripts Commission, *Calendar of State Papers Ireland, Tudor Period, 1571–1575*, ed. M O'Dowd (London, 2000)

A Vicars, ed., *Index to the Prerogative Wills of Ireland, 1536–1810* (Dublin, 1897, reprinted 1989)

10

Isle of Man genealogy

◆ ◆ ◆

10.1 Manx genealogy: records on the Isle of Man

The Isle of Man, although subject to the English Crown, has its own Parliament, laws and courts. For a very useful gateway website for Manx family history, try www.isle-of-man.com/interests/genealogy/index.shtml. See Narasimham, *The Manx Family Tree: A Beginners' Guide to Records in the Isle of Man* for details of all the following records, and their indexes.

The civil registration of births and marriages on the Isle of Man began on a voluntary basis in 1849. It became compulsory for births and deaths in 1878, and for marriages in 1884. The original registers can be seen at the General Registry of the Isle of Man. Microfilm copies of the indexes up to 1964 can be seen at the Society of Genealogists, as can copies of some nineteenth century registers.

Parish registers survive for some parishes from the early 1600s. The *International Genealogical Index* (see **3b.1**) is complete for Manx marriages, and refers to many baptisms. Microfilm copies of all parish registers can be seen at the Manx National Heritage Library, with some available at the Society of Genealogists.

Wills were proved in church courts until 1884, and then in the Manx High Court of Justice. Wills proved since 1911 are at the General Registry. Wills from the early 1600s to 1910 are kept in the Manx Museum. Wills of some wealthy Manx inhabitants may be found in the Prerogative Courts of York and Canterbury, before 1858: see **6**.

The Manx National Heritage Library has other records of interest to family historians, such as the militia records of the Manx Fencibles.

10.2 Manx genealogy: records in the PRO and FRC

The censuses from 1841–1901 cover the Isle of Man, and can be seen at the FRC, with copies at the Manx Museum. The 1851, 1881, 1891 and 1901 censuses have been indexed (see **2**).

Of course, islanders may well turn up in any of the services and other records as described in this book. Topographically arranged records, such as the payments of pensions to ex-soldiers and sailors on the Isle of Man, 1852–1862 in WO 22/207, are particularly useful. Details of soldiers born in the Isle of Man, and discharged to pension between 1760 and 1854, may be found by searching WO 97 and WO 121 in PROCAT using Isle of Man and the surname as keywords. The records of the Customs include staff lists for 1671–1922 and superannuation registers for 1803–1922 in CUST 39. The latter can give widows' pensions and the dates of birth of any children.

The Crown purchased the sovereignty of the Isle of Man from the Duke and Duchess of Athol in 1764. For correspondence between the Isle and the Secretaries of State, 1761–1783, see SP 48. The Privy Council was involved in the administration of the Isle of Man: some of its papers are in SP 48, but most are in PC 1 and PC 8. The Home Office has entry books of correspondence with Man, in HO 99, from 1760–1921. There are lists of charitable bequests, by parish, in HO 99/22, dating from c.1680 to c.1825. An investigation into smuggling in 1791 produced numerous depositions from Manx office-holders and worthies: they are in HO 99/21. Smuggling was a major cause of government worry about Man: a search in T 1 between 1746 and about 1800 will bring up many references to Treasury interest in Manx smugglers.

Because the Crown held extensive estates in Man, it may be well worth checking among the records in the CRES, LRRO and LR series; CRES 40/88–92, for example is a set of volumes containing a detailed valuation of the properties of the Duke of Athol on Man, to be bought by the Crown, and of other Crown properties on Man, made in 1826.

10.3 Manx genealogy: bibliography

J R Dickinson, *The Lordship of Man under the Stanleys: Government and Economy in the Isle of Man, 1580–1704* (Manchester, 1996)

M D Herber, *Ancestral Trails* (Society of Genealogists, 2000)

J Narasimham, N Crowe and P Lewthwaite, *The Manx Family Tree: A Beginners' Guide to Records in the Isle of Man* (Isle of Man, 3rd edn, 2000)

F Wilkins, *2,000 Manx Mariners: an eighteenth century survey* (Kidderminster, 2000)

11

Channel Islands genealogy

◆ ◆ ◆

11.1 Jersey

The portal website for Jersey family history is undoubtedly http://user.itl. net/~glen/: you should check this out for the most up-to-date information.

The Jersey Archive (www.jerseyheritagetrust.org) holds parish registers of baptism, marriage and burial before 1842, as well as much other material such as wills, land transactions and legal records: it has an online catalogue. The Jersey Archive offers a paid research service.

Civil registers of births, marriages and deaths from 1842 are held by the Superintendent Registrar of Jersey and he can undertake fee-paid searches and issue certified extracts from those registers in his custody: these registers are not open to the public. The Superintendent Registrar cannot undertake genealogical research of a general nature.

For general research, try contacting either the Société Jersiaise (www.societe-jersiaise.org) or the Channel Islands Family History Society: one of their members may be prepared to undertake paid research. Addresses are in **48**.

A few records of births, marriages and deaths in Jersey are in the PRO, among the foreign registers in RG 32, indexed by RG 43.

The censuses also cover Jersey (see **2**) and are obviously a main source: copies are available in Jersey. For 1851, 1871 and 1891 there are published name indexes for the whole of Jersey, thanks to the Channel Islands Family History Society, which are an enormous help. There is also, of course, the 1881 name index at the FRC.

The Association Oath Roll for Jersey (C 213/462) appears by its length to contain the signatures, or marks and names, of all the island's men in 1696. It has been published in facsimile, with full transcripts, by Glendinning as *Did Your Ancestors Sign the Jersey Oath of Association Roll of 1696?* There is also a petition of c.1847, to Queen Victoria, not to amend the island's constitution, which is signed by 5567 inhabitants (PC 1/4564), but this is not in any discernible order.

Details of soldiers born in Jersey, and discharged to pension between 1760 and 1854, may be found by searching in WO 97 and WO 121 in PROCAT, using Jersey as the search criterion. Details of ex-soldiers and sailors in receipt of a Chelsea or Greenwich pension, or their widows and orphans, living in Jersey, 1842–1862, may be found in WO 22/205–206. Muster rolls of the Jersey militia,

1843–1852, are in WO 13/1055. Many of the other records described in this book will also include islanders.

11.2 Guernsey, Alderney and Sark

As with Jersey, the portal website for family history in these islands is undoubtedly http://user.itl.net/~glen/. You should check this out for the most up-to-date information.

La Société Guernesiase (www.societe.gov.gg) has indexed many of the major family history records for Guernsey, including the parish registers, the censuses, monumental inscriptions, obituaries etc. They also offer a paid research service covering Guernsey, Sark and Alderney: you need to write (address in **48**) as they cannot accept e-mail enquiries. The website gives access to many other Guernsey family history websites.

The Priaulx Library holds microfilm copies of most of the civil and ecclesiastical registers, and their indexes. Access to the microfilms is free of charge to personal callers: those unable to visit can ask for research to be done for a modest fee (www.gov.gg/priaulx: address in **48**). Civil registration of births, deaths and non-Anglican marriages, began in Guernsey in 1840; in Alderney in 1850; and in Sark, of deaths in 1915. From 1919 all marriages and from 1925 all births and deaths in Guernsey, Alderney and Sark have been registered in Guernsey. The Priaulx Library does not have the civil marriage registers after 1901, although it does have the indexes: for these marriage certificates, and for the most modern events, you will need to contact the Greffe (address in **48**). Copies of the nineteenth century civil registration records for Guernsey can also be seen at the Society of Genealogists, where there are also indexes up to 1966.

Deeds, judicial records and wills may be consulted by searchers in person at the Greffe, Guernsey; all are indexed. Permission to consult wills of personalty from 1664 should be obtained from the Registrar of the Ecclesiastical Court. Microfilm copies of the census returns for Guernsey, Alderney and Sark are also available in Guernsey as well as at the FRC (see also **2**).

Some records of births, marriages and deaths in Guernsey, Alderney and Sark are in the PRO, among the foreign registers in RG 32, indexed by RG 43. Details of soldiers born in Guernsey, and discharged to pension between 1760 and 1854, may be found by searching WO 97 and WO 121 in PROCAT using Guernsey as the search criterion. Details of ex-soldiers and sailors in receipt of a Chelsea or Greenwich pension, or their widows and orphans, living in the Channel Islands, 1842–1852, may be found in WO 22/205. Muster rolls of the Guernsey militia, 1843–1852, are in WO 13/887.

The Association Oath Roll of 1696 for Guernsey (C 213/463) has been published in the *Eye on the Past in Guernsey*, by Glendinning.

11.3 The Channel Islands: general historical sources

The Channel Islands are subject to the Crown of England, but they are not part of the United Kingdom. Many of the records created there are in French, and relate to a different legal system. For Jersey historic records, contact the Jersey Archive (www.jerseyheritagetrust.org); for Guernsey historic (but not genealogical) records, the Island Archive Service (http://user.itl.net/~glen/archgsy.html). The addresses are in **48**.

For medieval records held in the PRO relating to the Channel Islands, try the various accounts in E 101 and the Chancery miscellanea in C 47. For a survey of this material, an account of the medieval government of the islands, and a list of wardens and sub-wardens, see Le Patourel, *The Medieval Administration of the Channel Islands, 1199–1399.*

For later general papers in the PRO relating to the administration and domestic affairs of the Channel Islands, see the series below. The papers do sometimes contain references to individuals, such as the lists of French Protestants living in Jersey in 1750 (in SP 47/4), but they are a historical rather than genealogical source. All may give you a perspective on life in the Channel Islands in the past. For example, the correspondence and papers for Alderney in 1821 included the census return (no names given), explaining that the total decay in trade had caused much emigration to America, France and the other islands. (For Channel Island emigration to North America, see the book by Turk.) Many are in French. Those with a calendar reference have been published and indexed.

Correspondence and papers between the Channel Islands and the Secretaries of State		
1547–1625	SP 15	*Calendar of State Papers, Domestic, Addenda*
1625–1649	SP 16	*Calendar of State Papers, Domestic, Charles I*
1660–1670	SP 29	*Calendar of State Papers, Domestic, Charles II*
1670–1781	SP 47	1670–April 1704 *Calendar of State Papers, Domestic, Charles II–Anne* May 1704–1760 not calendared – use the manuscript précis in SP 130/63–64 1760–1775 *Home Office Papers of the Reign of George III* 1776–1781 not calendared The Introductory Note to SP 47 tells you how to translate any obsolete references you may find in these published works into modern references.
1782–1849	HO 98	
1840–1979	HO 45	
Entry books of the above correspondence		
1748–1760	SP 111	
1760–1921	HO 99	Calendared 1760–1775 in *Home Office Papers of the Reign of George III*
Correspondence and papers between the Channel Islands and the Privy Council		
18th–19th century	PC 1	
1860–1956	PC 8	

For details of French refugees in Jersey, 1793–1796, see FO 95/602–603 and HO 98 (for all the islands). There is a collection of apprentices' indentures, 1846–1886, in CUST 105.

11.4 The Channel Islands in the Second World War

The PRO holds material on the occupation of the Channel Islands by the Germans in the Second World War. For example, WO 208/3741 includes accounts of life in occupied Jersey and Alderney, taken in October 1944. Ask at the Research Enquiries Desk to see the Press Packs 92D and 96F for further references. More information on other occupation records (including registration cards with photographs) is available from the local archives: see **11.3**.

11.5 Channel Islands genealogy: bibliography

M Axton and R Axton, *Calendar and Catalogue of Sark Seigneurie Archives, 1526–1927*, List and Index Society, Special Series vol 26, 1991

M L Backhurst, *Family History in Jersey* (Channel Islands Family History Society, 1991)

L R Burnes, 'Genealogical Research in the Channel Islands', *Genealogists' Magazine*, vol. XIX, pp. 169–172

Channel Islands Family History Society, *The 1851 Census of Jersey: An All-Island Index* (1996)

Channel Islands Family History Society, *The 1871 Census of Jersey: An All-Island Index* (1998)

Channel Islands Family History Society, *The 1891 Census of Jersey: An All-Island Index* (1994)

J Conway Davies, 'The Records of the Royal Courts', La Société Guernesiaise, *Transactions*, vol. XVI, pp. 404–414

A Glendinning, *Did Your Ancestors Sign the Jersey Oath of Association Roll of 1696?* (Channel Islands Family History Society, 1995)

A Glendinning, *Eye on the Past in Guernsey* (Channel Islands Family History Society, 1992)

M D Herber, *Ancestral Trails* (Society of Genealogists, 2000)

J Le Patourel, J H Lenfestey and others, *List of Records in the Greffe, Guernsey* (List and Index Society, Special Series Vols 2 and 11, 1969 and 1978). Additional lists may be consulted in typescript at the Greffe

J H Le Patourel, *The Medieval Administration of the Channel Islands, 1199–1399* (Oxford, 1937)

David W Le Poidevin, *How to Trace your Ancestors in Guernsey* (Taunton, 1978)

M G Turk, *The Quiet Adventurers in North America* (Maryland, 1993)

12

Immigrants, aliens and citizenship

◆ ◆ ◆

12.1 Introduction

Individual immigrants have been coming to Britain for centuries. Migrants from Ireland and the colonies, who were deemed to have a natural loyalty to the Crown, were treated differently from aliens. Aliens (to my sons' disappointment) were people from foreign countries (and not further away), who acknowledged another sovereignty. They were treated as a separate legal species, with fewer rights, because they were under no constraint of loyalty to the Crown. As a result, they are far better documented than migrants from the colonies or Ireland. However, the Crown only took real interest in documenting aliens at times of great political upheaval in Europe – during the French Revolution, during the revolutionary decade of the 1840s, and throughout the twentieth century.

There is a specialist guide to immigration records, *Immigrants and Aliens*, by Kershaw and Pearsall, which you should consult for more detailed advice. It includes a very useful list of relevant collections in local record offices, as well as a preface pointing out other potential sources of information.

The journal *Immigrants and Minorities* may well contain articles of interest on specific immigrant communities not mentioned here (e.g. Lithuanians in Lanarkshire), which may provide further PRO references. Once migrants had arrived and settled, you will find people in the normal ways, through registration of births, marriages and deaths, the census, etc.

12.2 Aliens arriving before 1793

Foreigners coming to settle were treated with some suspicion, as owning allegiance to another state. Medieval aliens had to pay double taxes, and there are separate lists of contributors to the 'alien subsidies' or taxes in E 179 (see **43**). There are also three surveys of aliens living in London, taken in November 1571 (SP 12/82); December 1571 (SP 12/84) and [September] 1618 (SP 14/102). The Huguenot Society has published these. Many French and Germans came to England to escape religious persecution of Protestants on the continent: they were generally welcomed into the Protestant UK (see **34.4**). Many of the German Protestant exiles from the Palatinate, shipped from Holland to England *en route* to the Americas in 1709, chose to stay in

England or Ireland instead: for more details see **14.7**.

References before the eighteenth century may be traceable through the published *Calendars of State Papers, Domestic*, as well as through the main series of Chancery enrolments (see **41.8**). For the later seventeenth and the eighteenth century, try the published calendars of Treasury records, continued in the online catalogue to 1794 in T 1. See Kershaw and Pearsall, *Immigrants and Aliens*, Chapter 8, for more detailed information.

For most of the eighteenth century, passes (for foreigners as well as natives) into and out of the country were issued by the Secretaries of State, and noted in SP 44/386–411 for 1697–1784, and (in an overlapping book) in FO 366/544, for 1748–1794. These are included (and indexed) in the *Calendar of State Papers, Domestic* until 1704, and again in the *Calendar of Home Office Papers* for 1760–1775: for other years there is no index.

12.3 Aliens arriving 1793–1826

The French Revolution produced the next great influx of aliens. A registration system was first set up by the Aliens Act of 1793, and lasted until 1826. On entering England, aliens were required to register with a Justice of the Peace, and to give their name, rank, address and occupation. The JP then sent a certificate into the Aliens Office. These certificates appear to have been destroyed, although an index survives from 1826–1836, in HO 5/25–32. However, the records of the Justices of the Peace may have survived in local record offices: see Kershaw and Pearsall, *Immigrants and Aliens*, Appendix 2, for more details. Some passes issued to aliens are in HO 1, recording name, port of entry, nationality, religion, occupation, place of residence and intended destination. Aliens arriving in English ports, 1810–1811, may be traced in FO 83/21–22.

The arrival of the émigrés provoked much government documentation (HO 69, PC 1, FO 95 and WO 1). In particular, the records of the Treasury's French Refugee Relief Committee, 1792–1828, contain lists of names of those receiving pensions (T 50, T 93). For entry books of correspondence about aliens, see HO 5.

12.4 Aliens arriving 1836–1869

The political situation in Europe was in turmoil in the middle of the 1800s, with revolutions occurring or looking likely in several countries – including the UK. From 1836, a new Aliens Act required incoming aliens to sign certificates of arrival. They survive in HO 2 for aliens arriving in England and Scotland, 1836–1852 only. The certificates give nationality, profession, date of arrival, last country visited and, sometimes, other information as well. They are indexed to 1849 only (HO 5/25–32).

The masters of ships sent lists of alien passengers, 1836–1869, to the Home Office (HO 3). They are bound up in date order, and there is no general index. However, if you are looking for a German, Pole or Prussian between 1847 and 1852, then try the Metzner index in the Research Enquiries Room. This covers both HO 2 and HO 3. For entry books of correspondence about aliens, see HO 5.

The PRO has records of annuities and pensions paid to some refugees for services to the Crown. These include, for example, allowances to Polish refugees, 1828–1856 (PMG 53, and T 1/409) and 1861–1865 (AO 3/1418), and allowances to Spaniards, 1855–1909 (PMG 53, and T 1/4285).

12.5 Aliens and others arriving by sea, 1878–1960: inwards passenger lists

The Inwards Passenger Lists (BT 26) can be a useful source of information for foreigners and others arriving by sea between 1878 and 1960, from places outside Europe and the Mediterranean area. These passenger lists are no good for travel within Europe, unless the ship had stopped at a European port on its inward voyage, when any passengers picked up were included on the list. This cuts out most immigrants from Eastern Europe, but offers more hope for the Mediterranean area.

The Passenger Lists after 1960 have not been preserved centrally, though it may be worth getting in touch with the right shipping line to see if they have kept later ones. There are no passenger lists for arrivals by air.

The passenger lists give name, age, occupation and address (in the United Kingdom), and the date of entry: each ship provided separate lists for British citizens and aliens. Unfortunately, there are no name indexes or even ship indexes. You have to know at least an approximate date of arrival, or the port of entry, or the name of the ship. After 1906 the Registers of Passenger Lists (BT 32) give, under each port, the names of the ships and their dates of arrival. It may be worth checking in *Lloyd's Register* for further clues: a copy is available at the PRO.

12.6 Alien registration, from c.1914

In 1905, worried by the increasing numbers of Jews arriving from Russian Poland, an Aliens Act was passed to make aliens able to enter the UK only at the discretion of the authorities. For entry books of correspondence about aliens, see HO 5. Records do not seem to survive before the First World War.

Registration of aliens was tightened up in 1914 and again in 1919. Aliens had to register with the local police. Surviving registration cards for the London metropolitan area are in MEPO 35 – but only about 1,000 cases survive from the tens of thousands created since 1914. The cards are informative: you can find them by searching on the name in MEPO 35 on PROCAT. Some (but not all) police registration records have survived locally – for example, Bedfordshire Record Office holds 25,000 record cards, from 1919 until the 1980s. For similar locally held collections, check Kershaw and Pearsall, *Immigrants and Aliens*, Appendix 2. See HO 213 for policy files of the Home Office Aliens' Department from 1914 onwards. Registration of aliens became a concern of MI5: some lists and addresses of suspected aliens are in KV 1.

During the First World War the British authorities interned enemy aliens, in internment camps in the United Kingdom. Very few records of individual internees survive. Specimen lists of German subjects interned as prisoners of war

Figure 20 Malvina Brandeis came to the UK in 1914, aged 32; registered as an alien in 1917; had her photograph replaced in 1941, aged 59; and later became a British citizen. (PRO, MEPO 35/20)

in 1915 and 1916 can be found in WO 900/45 and WO 900/46 and a classified list of interned enemy aliens can be found in HO 144/11720/364868. Nominal rolls of male enemy aliens of the age of 45 and upwards, submitted to the Secretary of State by commandants of internment camps, are included among a census of aliens in the United Kingdom from 1915 to 1924 in HO 45/11522/287235. References to individual internees can also be found among the card index to the Foreign Office general correspondence in the Research Enquiries Room.

Home Office records dealing primarily with policy relating to internees and internment camps can be found among the Home Office General Correspondence (HO 45) and Home Office Supplementary Correspondence (HO 144). Both series of records are arranged by subject matter: papers relating to internment and internees may be found under the headings 'Aliens' and 'War'. Other material on enemy internees is in MEPO 2/1796–1799 (1917–1920).

12.7 Refugees, 1914–1945

Several thousand Belgians fled to the UK during the First World War. For these Belgian refugees, 1914–1919, there is a considerable amount of material entered on the 'history cards' in MH 8/39–93. Each card relates to a whole family, unless the refugee was single with no known relatives. The details given are names, ages, relationships, wife's maiden name, allowances and the address for payment. Some hostel lists of refugees in 1917 are in MH 8/10.

For Jewish refugees of the 1930s and 1940s, see **36.5**.

Records of the Czechoslovak Refugee Trust are in HO 294: they relate not only to Czechoslovak refugees, but also to German and Austrian refugees. The series includes some specimen personal files on families: these are closed for 50 years (some for 75 years) from the last date on the file.

A large collection of aliens' personal files opened between 1934 and 1948, with some earlier papers attached, has been selected for permanent preservation as HO 405. However, it will take very many years to process and release them, and they may not be released in full for 100 years: applications to see particular files will be considered by the Home Office if they are still closed. Although it is a very large collection, it is estimated that only 40 per cent of these files survive. The personal files of famous aliens are in HO 382.

12.8 Aliens during the Second World War

Remember that aliens had to register with the police as a matter of course: only a small sample of registration records for London are in the PRO, in MEPO 35. Many (but not all) police registration records have survived locally – for example, Bedfordshire Record Office holds 25,000 record cards, from 1919 until the 1980s. See Kershaw and Pearsall, *Immigrants and Aliens*, Appendix 2, for details.

The PRO holds records to do with internment of aliens during the war. The main records are indexes that cover both aliens considered for internment but still at liberty in the UK, and those actually interned. Some pieces are closed for 85 years but many give family history details such as date of birth, address, occupation and details of employers. The index cards are in HO 396, and cover 1939–1947. Only a very small sample of personal case files of internees survives. These records, in HO 214, are particularly useful in depicting the life of an internee. The files were created whenever the Home Office became involved in a personal case for whatever reason. However, the aliens personal files, 1934–1948, in HO 405 also include internment papers: see **12.7**.

Internees primarily consisted of enemy aliens, but during the first two years of the Second World War other aliens were also interned, including refugees who had fled Nazi Germany to escape persecution. By the end of 1942, most internees had been released. Of those that remained, many were repatriated from 1943 onwards. It was not, however, until late 1945 that the last internees were finally released.

Fears of invasion led to a general feeling of hostility towards all enemy aliens. After the outbreak of war in September 1939, known Nazi sympathizers were rounded up. This was the start of a campaign that lasted to mid 1940. By then 8,000 internees had been gathered into camps, to be deported to the colonies and the dominions. Passenger lists survive for merchant vessels leaving British ports for ports outside Europe and the Mediterranean Sea in the series of records BT 26. These records are arranged by date and port of departure and are not indexed by surname. You need to know the name of the ship and preferably port of departure in order to avoid a very time consuming and speculative search. Registers of passenger lists in BT 32 give, under the different ports, the names of ships and the month of departure.

Many ships carrying internees were lost at sea by enemy torpedoes. Survivors' reports of lost vessels can be found among the Admiralty war history cases and papers in ADM 1. A card index, arranged by name of vessel, is located in the Research Enquiries Room. Similarly, official inquiries into such losses may be found among the War Cabinet Memoranda series in CAB 66. The sinking of the SS *Arandora Star* (with the loss of 800 internees) by a German U-boat in July 1940 led to vigorous protests about the British internment policy, which was changed in 1942 to internment of *enemy* aliens in camps in Britain only. There is a memorandum on the loss of the *Arandora Star*, at the Research Enquiries desk.

Internment camp records can be found in HO 215. This contains lists of internees, giving name, date of birth and (if applicable) date of release. Unfortunately, these are arranged by name of internment camp. HO 215 also contains general files relating to internment, conditions in camps, visits to camps, classification and segregation of internees, and the movement of internees abroad. HO 213 also contains a selection of files relating to internment camps during the Second World War, as do the series HO 45 and HO 144 under the subject headings 'Aliens' and 'War'. For further information on defence regulation 18B and the internment of fascists ask at the PRO for Source Sheet No. 25, 'Fascism and anti-Fascism in the United Kingdom'. There is a memorandum on Isle of Man Internment Camps during the Second World War at the Research Enquiries Desk.

References to individual internees and internment camps may be found in the printed indexes of the general correspondence of the Foreign Office, available in the Research Enquiries Room. Surviving papers referred to in these indexes may be found in FO 371 but, before ordering any documents, you need to convert the old Foreign Office reference recorded in the printed index to a modern PRO reference: guidance is available on how to do this. Other Foreign Office records on enemy aliens interned by the British are in FO 916. The series consists of general files relating to reports on internment camps and a number of lists of alien internees, arranged by location, name and number of camp.

12.9 Poles in and after the Second World War

For details of war service in the Polish Free Forces, write to the Ministry of Defence, Polish Section (address in **48**). The records of the Polish Resettlement Corps, set up in 1946 to ease their transition to civilian life in Britain and abroad, are in WO 315. Other records relating to Polish resettlement are in AST 18, with some in AST 7, AST 11, AST 1/23 and ED 128. Many of these records are in Polish, and some are closed for 75 years. There are also some files on World War Two Polish pensions in PIN 15/2905–2917.

12.10 Deportations, 1906–1963

The power to expel aliens who had become paupers or criminals was given by the Aliens Act of 1904 (although monarchs had been expelling their own citizens and others for centuries – from the Jews expelled by Edward I in 1290, to the gypsies that the Tudors made efforts to expel). The registers of deportees, 1906–1963, are in HO 372. These tend to give name, nationality, date of conviction and offence, as well as whether (and when) the deportation order was revoked. Related files are in HO 382 and HO 384.

12.11 Aliens into subjects: denization and naturalization, before 1880

Foreigners resident in England, wishing to regularize their position, had two options: they could apply for denization (which made them almost equivalent to denizens or native-born, and granted them most of a free subject's rights and the protection of the king's laws), or naturalization (which granted them all rights, and made them a subject of the Crown). However, most foreign settlers did not bother to go through these legal formalities, and so do not appear in these records. In general, applications were only considered from people who had lived here for five years within the previous eight. The process itself was expensive, and until the First World War did not bring many advantages. We get a surprising number of enquiries about people who had described themselves in the census as naturalized – when they had left no trace among the naturalization processes. They obviously thought it was a good thing to claim to be.

Denization took place when an alien was made a denizen by letters patent from the Crown. As a denizen, he could purchase land, but could not inherit it. Any children born after the parents' denization appear to have been subjects: those born before could only be denizens. Denizens had the additional burden of paying a higher rate of tax, and were ineligible for government posts. Letters patent of denization were enrolled on the Patent Rolls (C 66) and the Supplementary Patent Rolls (C 67). Denizations before 1509 can be traced through the indexes to the *Calendar of Patent Rolls:* in the early volumes individual names are not given in the index, and it is necessary to look under 'Denizations' or *'Indigenae'*. For the period 1509 to 1800, indexes to denizations have been published by the Huguenot Society. A copy of these, together with a typescript index to denizations between 1801 and 1873, is attached to the list of HO 1 at the PRO. The indexes are not absolutely complete. Denizations of Protestant refugees, 1678–1688, are entered in SP 44/67. Some draft bills for denization, 1830–1880, are in C 197/29.

Naturalization was more expensive than denization. It originally required a private act of Parliament, as well as the swearing of oaths of allegiance and supremacy, and taking Holy Communion according to the Anglican rite, effectively disbarring Roman Catholics and Jews. It made the foreigner into the king's subject, able to inherit land, and affected the children born before naturalization as well. Indexes to naturalization by private act of Parliament up to 1900 are attached to the HO 1 list at the PRO. The acts themselves may be seen at the House of Lords Record Office. Between 1708 and 1711, all foreign Protestants who took the oaths of allegiance and supremacy in open court were deemed to have been naturalized (KB 24, E 169/86; see **15.1**). The information from these oath rolls has been published by the Huguenot Society. Between 1740 and 1773, foreign Protestants in the Americas were naturalized by the same process: see **14.7**. Many Spanish Jews in Jamaica were also granted naturalization, which was easier for a Jew to get in the West Indies than in England.

12.12 New British citizens: naturalization since 1844

In 1844, naturalization procedure was simplified, and the Home Office began granting certificates of naturalization. You may be lucky enough to have a naturalization certificate in your family papers. If not, it is worth looking for the official copy at the PRO. You should also find correspondence giving the background to the application. Records survive in several series, most with a joint index.

Copies of naturalization certificates		Correspondence on individual naturalizations	
1844–1873	C 54	1844–1871	HO 1/17–176
1870–1987	HO 334	1872–1878	HO 45
		1879–1934	HO 144. Check the PRO catalogue: if not already open, contact the Home Office.
		1934–1948	HO 405: all files will be initially closed for 100 years. The Home Office will review the closure period on request. Once opened, they remain open.
1987–	Contact the Immigration and Nationality Department	1948–	Contact the Home Office

There is a joint index, attached to the HO 1 list: it is not searchable online. The index gives name, country of origin, date of the certificate, place of residence, from 1879 (e.g. Liverpool), and the reference to the copy of the certificate and to any related papers. Unfortunately, you need to go through a keying up process to find the modern reference. Ask for help if necessary. For C 54 it is a double process: use the indexes C 275/126–140 on the open shelves in the Map Room: the entry in them will read something like 'Hoffmeyer, Otto: certificate'. Ask the staff for help in converting the reference once you have found it.

The joint index goes up to 1936: from 1937 to 1980 you need to look at the annual reports available in the research enquiries room. Up until 1961, these were presented to Parliament, and were printed as parliamentary papers. Parliamentary papers are available on microfiche in the microfilm reading room. After 1980, the PRO has no name indexes, although we are expecting the index for 1981–1987 in 2002. If you are looking for a certificate issue after 1980, and do not already have the certificate number, you need to write to the Immigration and Nationality Department and ask for it: see **48** for the address.

Although the intention is to preserve all naturalization records, we know that it is *not* a complete collection. If you cannot find a file by the usual methods but have solid reason to believe one existed, you could try a name search on PROCAT in HO 144, in case the file turned up belatedly and was added to that series with a full description. You could even ask the Home Office to check whether the old file has been linked to a post-1935 file that hasn't yet been transferred into HO 382 or HO 405 (address in **48**). These are both exceedingly remote possibilities, especially where the person was naturalized before 1939. If nothing turns up, we have to assume that the file doesn't exist any longer. But do remember the initial warning: many people before 1914 simply described themselves as being naturalized, or never bothered with naturalization in any form.

The naturalization certificates are covered by the 30-year rule. Enquiries about naturalizations within the last 31 years should be sent to the Home Office: see **48** for the address.

12.13 Registering British citizenship, from 1949

Under the British Nationality Act of 1948, people could register as British citizens if they were citizens of the United Kingdom or Republic of Ireland, of the Channel Islands, of the Isle of Man, or of British colonies, protectorates or Trust Territories. The Home Office kept a copy of the certificate (known as an R certificate) that was issued. These are in HO 334, from 1949. These certificates are subject to the 30–year rule. If you are looking for the copy of a certificate issued less than 31 years ago, write to the Home Office: see **48** for the address.

The PRO has no name indexes for these certificates. If you do not already have the registration certificate number, you need to write to the Immigration and Nationality Department and ask for it: see **48** for the address.

12.14 Renouncing British citizenship

The Naturalization Act of 1870 allowed for the renunciation of British nationality by people born in the United Kingdom of foreign parentage. These 'declarations of alienage' can be found in HO 45 and HO 144: most date from the first half of the twentieth century. The introduction of conscription in the First World War may well have caused an upsurge in these declarations. They are easily searched online, as the name is included in the catalogue entry. Some give proof of the entitlement to British citizenship.

12.15 Immigrants, aliens and citizenship: bibliography

Published works

Huguenot Society, *Returns of Aliens Dwelling in the City and Suburbs of London* (Publications of the Huguenot Society, vol. X)

Immigrants and Minorities (Frank Cass, 1982 onwards). Each volume generally includes a bibliography of recent published and unpublished works. Unfortunately, this journal is not available in the PRO library.

R Kershaw and M Pearsall, *Immigrants and Aliens* (PRO, 2000)

R E G Kirk, *Returns of Aliens in London, 1523–1603* (Huguenot Society, vol. X, London, 1900–1908)

W Page, *Denization and Naturalization of Aliens in England, 1509–1603* (Huguenot Society, vol. VIII, Lymington, 1893)

Public Record Office, *Calendar of Close Rolls, 1227–1509* (London, 1892–1963)

Public Record Office, *Calendar of Home Office Papers 1760–1775* (London, 1878–1899)

Public Record Office, *Calendar of Patent Rolls, 1216–1509, 1547–1582* (London, 1894–1986)

Public Record Office, *Calendar of State Papers, Domestic Series, 1547–1704* (London, 1856–1972)

Public Record Office, *Calendar of Treasury Papers, 1557–1728* (London, 1868–1889)

Registers of Churches, of Huguenots in London and elsewhere (Huguenot Society, London, 1887–1956)

Rotuli Parliamentorum, Edward I to Henry VII (London, 1783, Index, London, 1832)

W A Shaw, *Letters of Denization and Acts of Naturalisation for Aliens in England, 1603–1800* (Huguenot Society, Lymington, 1911, Manchester, 1923 and London, 1932)

Unpublished finding aids

Index to Denizations, 1801–1873, and to Acts of Naturalization, 1801–1935, attached to HO 1 list

Indexes to 'Foreign' Churches in RG 4

Index of Memorials for Denizations and Naturalizations, 1835–1844

B Lloyd, 'List and Registers of Dutch Chapel Royal, 1689–1825'

Metzner index to German, Polish and Prussian aliens, 1847–1852, in HO 2 and HO 3

13

Britons abroad: in foreign
countries and in the Empire

◆ ◆ ◆

13.1 Foreign countries and British lands abroad

Many of us looking back now find it quite hard to really believe that for several centuries the British had homes from home across the globe. From the reign of James VI and I, Britons conquered and colonized large areas across the world. Now we look at them and see foreign countries: then the distinction between foreign and colonial was quite distinct. And in the colonies, a Briton was at home. This distinction really only began breaking down in the later half of the twentieth century, as the United Kingdom shrank back in itself, and began to cut old ties with its colonies.

For more detail on Britons abroad, you may like to look at the specialist guide by Kershaw, *Emigrants and Expats*.

13.2 Going to foreign parts: licences, passports and passenger lists

For the late sixteenth and early seventeenth centuries, there are registers of people applying for licences before going overseas, in E 157. The earliest dates from 1572–1578. There are lists of soldiers taking the oath of allegiance before going to the wars in the Low Countries, 1613–1624, and licences to go abroad, mostly to Holland, 1624–1632. For passes to go abroad between March 1650 and February 1653, see SP 25/111.

For most of the eighteenth century, passes (for natives as well as foreigners) into and out of the country were issued by the Secretaries of State, and noted in SP 44/386–411 for 1697–1784, and (in an overlapping book) in FO 366/544, for 1748–1794. These are included (and indexed) in the *Calendar of State Papers, Domestic* until 1704, and again in the *Calendar of Home Office Papers* for 1760–1775: for other years there is no index. The weekly emigration returns kept between 1773 and 1776 include Britons travelling for business or pleasure, as well as emigrants: see the card index to TS 47/9–11 at the PRO.

From 1794, the issue of passports (or safe conducts) was regulated, but they were not a requirement for people leaving the country. It was rare for someone travelling abroad to apply for one: most holders of passports were merchants or diplomats. Until 1858, UK passports could be granted to people who were not British, but who requested the protection of the UK while travelling. These passports were simple pieces of paper, requesting that foreign powers should allow the holder to travel without hindrance. During the First World War, many European countries used passports to prove national identity: Britain made them mandatory for British travellers in 1914. The first hard-cover passports were introduced in 1915.

If you have passports in the family, they should contain useful material. Unfortunately, the records of the *issue* of passports are disappointing, as they contain little information.

The registers of passports issued, 1795–1948, are in FO 610: for March to May 1915, the register is in FO 613/2. The entries, in date order, show merely the date, the number of the passport issued, and the name of the applicant. There are indexes for 1851–1862 and 1874–1916, but they give no more information (FO 611). A very miscellaneous collection of over 2,000 British and foreign passports, 1802–1961, is in FO 655; they are listed haphazardly, by date and place of issue. A small selection of case papers, 1916–1983, is in FO 737. For more detail, it may be worth checking in the correspondence of the Passport Office, 1815–1905 (FO 612/21–71). Records of British passports issued in foreign countries and British colonies may sometimes be found in consular and colonial records.

Passenger lists do not survive before 1890. From 1890 to 1960 they are in BT 27 for passengers travelling *beyond* Europe and the Mediterranean. See **14.2** for more details.

13.3 Britons in foreign countries: records in the PRO

For births, marriages and deaths of Britons in foreign countries, see **4**. These records, taken as a historical source, can establish the existence of an expatriate community: the large number of burials in Oporto, for example, may lead you on to finding out more about the British community there.

Under the Naturalization Act of 1870, Britons born abroad (but not in the colonies) could petition for a certificate of British nationality. This was needed only if their birth had not been registered at a British consulate. They submitted evidence to the nearest consulate, including their father's birth certificate, their parents' marriage certificate, and their own birth certificate. The consul then forwarded the petition and documents to the Home Office, with the request that the documents were returned to their owner. However, some of the files do contain a brief précis of this information, which can be very useful. Others, alas, do not. Look in HO 45, trying as a keyword search 'origin AND [surname]'. You may then find it worthwhile going back to the correspondence of the relevant consulate, in the FO code.

For the early modern period, you will need to explore the State Papers Foreign. After 1782, the embassy and consular archives of the Foreign Office should be fruitful terrains to explore: there are very many series involved. Use Atherton's *'Never Complain, Never Explain'* for advice on finding your way round the enormous quantity of information accumulated by the Foreign Office. The Foreign Office Index at the PRO is well worth checking, as would be the many series of Foreign Office correspondence arranged by country. There are leaflets available at the PRO and on the PRO website to help you. You may not find a direct reference to your ancestors, but you will find much about the institutions and events of where they were living.

For wills proved in British probate courts in Turkey and China, see **6.22**. For the repatriation of some distressed Britons abroad, see FO 83. FO 83/423–425 covers pauper lunatics, 1865–1873, and FO 83/759 covers Britons wounded in war, 1868–1870. For the repatriation of mentally ill Britons from China, 1908–1932 see C 211/70–75.

For people working for the Foreign Office, look at the *Imperial Calendar*, or the *Foreign Office List* for information on postings.

13.4 British subjects interned by enemies

For Britons interned by the French during the revolutionary and Napoleonic wars, there are lists and accounts of prisoners of war in France and elsewhere, in ADM 103 and ADM 30/63/12–17. The agent in charge of each prison transmitted these, and recorded, in a numbered sequence, the names, origins and eventual disposal of all the prisoners under his charge. They include naval prisoners of war as well as civilian internees.

For records relating to British subjects interned in enemy countries in the First and Second World Wars, look in FO 371, using the indexes. For the Second World War, look in FO 916 as well. This series consists of general files relating to reports on internment camps and a number of lists of British internees, arranged by location, name and number of camp. For civilian (including British) internees in enemy and enemy occupied colonies look in CO 980. See **22** for prisoners of war.

13.5 Britons in the Empire: records in the PRO

Most colonial records are still where they were created – in the old colony or dominion – except for India (see **13.9**). This applies particularly to records of birth, marriage and death. However, there was a huge central administration of colonial and dominion affairs, which received regular despatches, petitions, reports and publications from or about the colonies. These records are now in the codes CO, DO or FCO, for various periods.

Early records have been published in précis in the *Calendar of State Papers, Colonial*. The volumes of this that cover America and the West Indies have recently been republished on CD-ROM: this can be seen in the PRO Library. They are now very easily searched. Other volumes, covering other parts of the world, still have to be seen in hard copy, but they do have reasonable indexes.

Records after 1740 are not well catalogued, and you will need to use the original registers of correspondence at the PRO to find your way around them.

Figure 21 Many Britons experienced long voyages on a regular basis – not always as pleasant as this return to Bombay. Families suffered extended separations from relatives, and often from their older children, sent back to school 'at home'. (PRO, CO 956/692)

See the guides to these records by Pugh and by Thurston. The many series of colonial Original Correspondence are well worth exploring. There are leaflets available at the PRO and on the PRO website to help you use the various indexes to these records. You may not find a direct reference to your ancestors, but you will find much about the institutions and events of where they were living.

For Army pensioners in Canada and South Africa between 1772 and 1899, taken from WO 120/35, 69 and 70, see Crowder, *British Army Pensioners Abroad, 1772–1899.*

The colonies had their own legal systems, and most disputes were settled locally. However, there are many records of disputes from the colonies in the PRO. Most involve shipping, and are to be found in the High Court of Admiralty records in HCA and PCAP. Some came as appeals from common law courts, and ended up before the Judicial Committee of the Privy Council. The Privy Council has kept the records of these colonial appeals and you will need to make an appointment to see them: see **48** for the address. Similarly, many disputes were actually litigated in England, particularly in Chancery or in the Prerogative Court of Canterbury. In some cases, the evidence brought into court as an exhibit was left behind. These exhibits are now in C 103–115, E 140 and J 90; and in PROB 31, PROB 32 and PROB 36. These exhibits can contain letters and accounts from the colonies.

13.6 Colonial Office and Dominions Office lists

The annual *Colonial Office List* or the *Dominions Office,* available at the PRO, give a country by country guide, and a staff list. If you are looking for someone who was involved in colonial administration, this is the first place to try. The staff lists give brief career details. You could also try all the usual sources such as *Who's Who,* and *Who Was Who,* as well as the biographical dictionaries mentioned in **1.15**, which are available in the PRO Library.

13.7 Government gazettes from the colonies and dominions

The government of each British colony or dominion published its own newspapers, known as government gazettes (or official or royal gazettes), for most of the nineteenth and twentieth centuries. They can provide valuable information for family historians, because the PRO does not (with a few minor exceptions) hold the internal records of colonial governments. Government gazettes usually have an index at the beginning of each volume.

Gazettes frequently list or refer to named individuals. Some of the more common entries in which individuals appear in gazettes are lists of immigrants and emigrants, voters rolls, and notifications of appointments to positions in official bodies and the police and military services. Other items about individuals include notices concerning deaths and estates of the deceased, divorce, insolvency, and legal disputes and criminal cases. Frequently, the gazette will give valuable information about the person in question, including his or her address.

If you are looking for individuals working for colonial governments, you *may* also find them listed in the Blue Books. These were books in which (mainly statistical) information on each colony was reported. They are usually arranged in the CO and DO 'miscellanea' series, but occasionally they can be found in the supplements to the gazettes. In addition, there are series entitled 'public service lists' in several series for Australia (1902–1927), Canada (1887–1910), Iraq (1919–1920), New Zealand (1916–1920). To find these records, consult the CO and DO indexes, or PROCAT.

The majority of people named in the gazettes were settlers. However, members of colonized populations do appear in the records. This is especially true in countries where local people, at certain points, played a role in the workings of government – as policemen or clerks, for instance. Where people were legally property they might also appear in the records. Gazettes from the Caribbean, for example, carry advertisements for the return of slaves who had escaped. Some gazettes – depending on time and place – contain lists of Indian indentured labourers or of people applying for British citizenship. The records are also more likely to name male rather than female ancestors, but, since women did, for instance, own property, get divorced, leave wills and vote, their names do appear from time to time.

To find a particular person in the gazettes, you will need to know the colony and the period you are looking for. It will also help to have an idea of the kind of transaction the person may have been involved in. The names of individuals often appear in the annual indexes of the gazettes, but usually they are listed in sub-sections. For instance, those appointed to positions in the colony will probably be listed in the 'appointments' category of the index.

13.8 Newspapers from the colonies and dominions

The PRO also holds a small selection of newspapers published in the colonies, mostly covering the period c.1830–c.1860, although there are a few eighteenth century examples. These are listed in the 'newspapers' section of the CO index, which also provides references for a few government gazettes (see above). However, the British Library Newspaper Library (address in **48**) has much more extensive holdings of colonial newspapers. You can search their catalogue by place as well as title, at www.bl.uk/catalogues/newpapers.

13.9 The British in India

The PRO is not the place to trace Britons and Anglo-Indians in India. The central government body involved was not the Colonial Office but the India Office, whose records are now held at the British Library. The India Office Records include the archives of the East India Company (1600–1858), of the Board of Control or Board of Commissioners for the Affairs of India (1784–1858), of the India Office (1858–1947), of the Burma Office (1937–1948), and of a number of related British agencies overseas. More detailed information is available in Baxter, *India Office Library and Records: A Brief Guide to Biographical Sources.*

The India Office Records hold collections that cover the pre-independence history of present-day India, Pakistan, Bangladesh and Burma, on the neighbouring countries of South and South-East Asia, and on St Helena, South Africa, the Gulf States, Malaysia, Singapore, Indonesia, China and Japan. They are rich in biographical information on East India Company servants, civil servants and Indian Army personnel, and on Europeans resident in pre-1947 India.

They have a biographical card index, which is being compiled from a variety of sources. It currently contains 295,000 entries for civil and military servants and their families, and for non-official Europeans living in India. In addition, there are copy registers of births/baptisms, marriages and burials of European and Eurasian Christians in India, Burma and territories controlled from India, as well as wills, grants of probate and administration; inventories; and pension material. In addition, they hold the records of the Indian Army, the various naval forces, the Indian railway companies and the Civil Service.

For an overview of what relevant records the PRO holds, ask at the Enquiry Desk for Husainy's 'Records Relating to the East India Company and India in the PRO'. The PRO Library holds a run of the annual *East India Register*, continued by the *India List* (under various titles) from 1791–1947, as well as the separate *Indian Army List*. These are all very informative and well worth a look. For Army pensioners in India between 1772 and 1899, taken from WO 120/35, 69 and 70, see Crowder, *British Army Pensioners Abroad, 1772–1899.*

For an overview of the problems of and sources for tracing Anglo-Indian families, see Charles, 'Anglo-Indian Ancestry'. See also *Sources for Anglo-Indian Genealogy in the Library of the Society of Genealogists.* The National Army Museum also has useful material (see **18d.7**). Have a look at the website for family history in British India, www.ozemail.com.au/~clday/. There is also the Families in British India Society, with a website at www.links.org/FIBIS/ and its own journal, as well as *The Indiaman Magazine*, with a website at www.indiaman.com. For the Anglo-Indian home page, see elecpress.monash. edu.au/ijais/otherais.htm. The British Association for Cemeteries in South Asia is also worth contacting, and you may be interested in the British in India Museum. The addresses are given in **48**.

13.10 Britons abroad: bibliography

L Atherton, *'Never Complain, Never Explain': Records of the Foreign Office and State Paper Office, 1500–c.1960* (PRO, 1994)

I A Baxter, *India Office Library and Records: A Brief Guide to Biographical Sources* (London, 1990)

British Library, *India Office Records, Sources for Family History Research* (London, 1988)

J A Bryden, 'Genealogical Research in Gibraltar', *Genealogists' Magazine*, vol. XXIV, pp. 289–293

Calendar of State Papers, Colonial 1574–1738 (London, 1860–1970)

G Charles, 'Anglo-Indian Ancestry', *Genealogists' Magazine*, vol. 27, no. 3, pp. 104–110 (Sept. 2001)

N K Crowder, *British Army Pensioners Abroad, 1772–1899* (Baltimore, 1995)

East India Register (various titles)

I V Fitzhugh, *Tracing Your West Indian Ancestors* (PRO, 1995)

G Grannum, 'East India Company Ancestry', *Genealogists' Magazine*, vol. XXI, pp. 150–154

A Husainy, 'Records Relating to the East India Company and India in the PRO: A Guide' (2002, available at the PRO Research Enquiries Desk)

India [Office and Burma Office] List, 1791–1947

The Indiaman Magazine

Indian Army List, 1901–1939

R Kershaw, *Emigrants and Expats: A guide to sources on UK emigration and residents overseas* (PRO, 2002)

M Moir, *A General Guide to the India Office Records* (London, 1988)

Public Record Office, *The Records of the Foreign Office 1782–1939* (London, 1969)

R B Pugh, *The Records of the Colonial and Dominions Office* (London, 1964)

N C Taylor, *Sources for Anglo-Indian Genealogy in the Library of the Society of Genealogists* (Society of Genealogists, 1990)

A Thurston, *Records of the Colonial Office, Dominions Office, Commonwealth Relations Office and Commonwealth Office* (London, 1995)

14

Voluntary emigrants

◆ ◆ ◆

14.1 Emigrants: general points

Large-scale emigration from Britain took place to the American colonies, the West Indies, Canada (British North America), the United States of America, Australia, New Zealand and southern Africa. For a fuller treatment of the subject (which, as you can see, is complicated!) see Kershaw, *Emigrants and Expats*.

The PRO has many records relating to emigration but, because of the nature and limited scope of many of them, there can be no certainty of finding information on any particular individual. Involuntary emigrants are easier to trace: see **40**, on the transportation of convicts. For records of births, marriages and deaths of Britons abroad, see **4** and **13.9**.

If you are trying to trace ancestors back *into* the United Kingdom, there is little likelihood of finding a family before the central registration of births, marriages and deaths (1837 in England and Wales, 1855 in Scotland) *unless* their place of origin is known. You will have to do some research among published works and in the archives of the emigrant's place of destination before starting the search in the Public Record Office. Much of the more easily accessible information about emigrants to America and Australia has been published over the years: the most useful items are listed in the bibliographies at **14.12** and **40.5**.

14.2 Outwards Passenger Lists

The PRO has Outwards Passenger Lists for 1890–1960 (BT 27). These are lists of passengers leaving the United Kingdom by sea for destinations outside Europe and the Mediterranean area. They give the name, age, occupation and some sort of address of the passengers, but they are arranged by year and port of departure, and there are no name indexes. The Registers of Passenger Lists, 1906–1951 (BT 32) list the ships leaving each port, which can be a useful way of finding the right record in BT 27.

For passenger lists before 1890, you will need to look outside the PRO's records. The records of the countries receiving the travellers do tend to be fuller – and earlier in date – than those of the UK in bidding them goodbye. Many of them have been published, or are available on the Internet. For an overview of what is available, and links to other sites, look at the gateway site

Figure 22 The earliest emigrants had to survive appalling conditions. Public outrage, government intervention and the advent of steamships eventually improved matters, although long voyages were still considerable ordeals. (PRO, CO 384/93)

http://home.att.net/~wee-monster/onlinelists.html. Other works or sites you may need to use are:

- for the Americas: consult the massive index published by Filby and Meyer, which is available at the PRO. This *Passenger and Immigration Lists Index* gives the names of nearly 2.5 million immigrants to the American colonies, the USA and Canada, from the sixteenth to mid twentieth centuries.
- for the USA: http://www.ellisislandrecords.org/ for New York passenger arrivals, 1892–1924
- www.theshipslist.com
- http://istg.rootsweb.com the site of the Immigrant Ships Transcribers Guild

14.3 Emigrants: general sources for most destinations, 1814–1896

The records of the Colonial Office include much material relating to emigrants. Many letters from settlers or people intending to settle in British North America, Australia, the West Indies and other places can be found in Emigration Original Correspondence, 1817–1896 (CO 384). There are separate registers for British North America for 1850–1863 (CO 327) and 1864–1868 (CO 328).

The Land and Emigration Commission was established in 1833 to promote emigration by providing free passage and land grants: ask at the Research Enquiries Desk for the memorandum on it, if you want more information. The

Emigration Entry Books, 1814–1871 (CO 385) and the Land and Emigration Commission Papers, 1833–1894 (CO 386) give names of emigrants.

Many poor emigrants were provided with assistance for the passage by their parish, under the provisions of the 1834 Poor Law Amendment Act. You may be able to find parish lists of emigrants, giving their occupation and destination. These are in MH 12, among much other Poor Law material, and are unindexed. You need to know the likely Poor Law Union the emigrants came from before starting this quest (see **31**). Other records relating to parish-organized emigration will be found locally: see the article by Burchall, listed in the bibliography under North America and West Indies.

14.4 Emigrants: possible sources for ex-soldiers and sailors, 1817–1903

Many ex-soldiers settled in the colonies. The awards of pensions to soldiers in British regiments stationed abroad, and in native or colonial regiments, 1817–1903, are in WO 23/147–160. These registers are arranged by the date of the board that granted admission to pension, but entries relating to a particular place (e.g. Canada, the West Indies, or the Cape) are fairly easy to find. These registers can provide a birthplace and details of service. Many of the entries relate to British soldiers who left the army while their regiment was abroad, and who appear to have settled there.

Another potentially useful source for tracing people in receipt of a pension payable by the War Office (usually ex-soldiers and sailors, but also members of the East India Services) may be the registers of pension payments, 1842–1883, in WO 22, which are arranged by place of payment. There are separate registers for places like Canada, New South Wales and New Zealand, but also composite registers for miscellaneous colonies and for 'consuls' – who presumably had the responsibility for administering payments in foreign countries rather than colonies. The pensions were sometimes to widows or dependent children.

A long search in the following sample of records may be successful. The Admiralty records include, for instance, medical journals from emigrant ships (ADM 101), and registers of troops (ADM 108, MT 23) shipped to various parts of the world. The Audit Office accounts have references to pensions paid to colonists (AO 1–3), and the Patent Rolls (C 66) contain entries relating to grants of offices and lands in America and elsewhere.

14.5 Emigrants to North America and the West Indies: material elsewhere

If you are tracing an ancestor back into Britain from North America, try to do some research locally before coming to the Public Record Office. In particular, try to get some idea of the port and date of entry into the new country, and the county or smaller area in the United Kingdom that your ancestor came from.

Records of immigration to the USA are held in the National Archives in Washington, along with service records, land records and census returns. Proper censuses began in the USA in 1790, and are available on microfilm. The individual state archives hold registers of births, marriages and deaths. The National Archives of Canada has census returns on microfilm going back to the earliest French-Canadian census of 1666 and 1667. The French-Canadian records at Quebec are particularly full.

Photocopies, microfilms and transcripts of much of the PRO's North American material can be consulted at the Library of Congress, some state libraries, and the National Archives of Canada. The Genealogical Society of Utah has copies of the census returns for England and Wales, and a huge index containing a great deal of information from British sources.

There are several genealogical societies in North America, which it may prove useful to contact. The main ones are the National Genealogical Society, for the USA, and the International Society for British Genealogy and Family History, based in North America. See also *Genealogical sources in the United States of America*, by MacSorley, which is intended for those wishing to undertake research from the UK.

14.6 Emigrants to North America and the West Indies: British emigrants

The PRO has a lot of material relating to early emigration to the West Indian and American colonies. Much of this has been printed in some form. Most of it is administrative in character, but it can include useful genealogical material. Main published sources include the records of the Privy Council (PC 1, PC 2 and PC 5), printed as *Acts of the Privy Council of England, Colonial Series*. Various useful classes of Treasury papers have been described and indexed in the *Calendar of Treasury Papers, 1557 to 1728* and the *Calendar of Treasury Books and Papers, 1729 to 1745*. The major early collection of papers relating to the West Indies and the American colonies (CO 1) has been described and indexed in the *Calendar of State Papers, Colonial, America and West Indies*, which includes references to the many other succeeding classes as well. Records relating to the West Indies are described in Grannum's *Tracing Your West Indian Ancestors*.

For unfree emigrants, see **40**.

Registers of passengers bound for New England, Barbados, Maryland, Virginia and other colonies survive for 1634–1639, and for 1677 (E 157): the information in them, together with similar information (from CO 1) has been printed in Hotten, with more added by Brandow. For a further listing of passengers to America, 1618–1688, taken from the port books in E 190, see the typescript index available (by 'AMDG') at the PRO (filed in the Map Room as 'refers to E 190 vol 3'). Port books (E 190) list the names of passengers who were transporting dutiable goods, but you need to have some idea of the port of departure or else be prepared for a very lengthy search after 1688. If you are researching an early emigrant, you may be interested in Games' study of 5,000 travellers to America and the West Indies in 1635, *Migration and the Origins of the English Atlantic World*: this was based on the 1635 London port book.

There is a considerable amount of information on the inhabitants of Barbados, 1678–1680, including lists of property owners, their wives, children, servants and slaves, some parish registers, and lists of the militia (CO 1/44 no. 47 i–xxxvii,

CO 29/9 pp. 1–3). There is a descriptive list of the various records (with no names) in the *Calendar of State Papers, Colonial America and West Indies, 1677–1680*, no. 1236 i–xxxvii, which you should look at first. The white inhabitants of Barbados were listed in a census in 1715 (CO 28/16).

A useful, though unfortunately short-lived, register (T 47/9–12) was kept of emigrants going from England, Wales, and Scotland to the New World between 1773 and 1776. The information for England and Wales has been summarized in a card index, available at the PRO, which gives name, age, occupation, reason for leaving the country, last place of residence, date of departure, and destination. For 1815 only, there are details of 757 settlers enrolling for emigration to Canada, at Edinburgh. Most came from Scotland, but some were from Ireland and England (AO 3/144).

Some information on colonists is contained in the correspondence and papers of the Colonial Office, which cover the West Indies as well as the continent of America, and start in 1574: see the printed calendars listed in **14.12**. The Chancery Town Depositions (C 24) contain interesting information about life in early colonial America, including much genealogical data, but they are not well listed: see the article by Currer-Briggs for reference to an index.

Details on tracts of land in West and East New Jersey, Pennsylvania, New England and elsewhere are in the records of the West New Jersey Society (TS 12), a company formed in 1691 for the division of the land. There are many names in the correspondence, minute books, share transfers, deeds and claims. For the settlement of East Florida in 1763, and compensation for its handing back to Spain in 1783, see the records in T 77, and the article by Foot. For employees and settlers of the Hudson's Bay Company, see BH 1, and the article by Douglas.

In 1696, the mayor, recorder and commonalty of New York City swore the oath of association in support of William III: the resulting oath roll contains the signatures and marks of much of the male population of the city (C 213/470: see **15.1**).

Records relating to slave owners in the West Indies, 1812–1846, are among Treasury, Audit Office and National Debt Office papers (T 71, AO 14, NDO 4). The surveys in T 71 may give the names of owners, plantations and even sometimes the slaves. Among the Chancery Masters' Exhibits, in C 103–114, are many private papers from West Indies plantations.

During and after the American War of Independence, many people suffered losses on account of their loyalty to the British crown, and many subsequently migrated to Canada (British North America). They were entitled to claim compensation under the Treaty of Peace in 1783 and a new Treaty of Amity between Great Britain and the United States of America in 1794. The Treasury records contain the reports of commissioners investigating individual claims, and some compensation and pension lists, 1780–1835 (T 50, T 79). Commissioners were also appointed in 1802, and their papers contain lists of claimants of pensions, and papers supporting their claims (AO 12, AO 13). The Declared Accounts of the Audit Office (AO 1) contain the accounts of payments and pensions made. Similar claims for compensation to loyalists were made when

East Florida was ceded to Spain in 1783, and they are now among the Treasury records (T 77).

Musters of Canadian militia and volunteers, 1837–1850, are in WO 13/3673–3717.

Americans who died with goods in England and Wales had their wills proved and inventories presented in the Prerogative Court of Canterbury (see **6**). These wills and administrations, 1600–1858, have been indexed by Coldham. For the inventories, see **6.18**.

For nineteenth century and later emigrants, see **14.2** and **14.3**.

The muster rolls for Canadian militia and volunteers, 1837–1843, may be worth checking (WO 13/3673–3717): earlier records are in Canada. For ex-soldiers and sailors (or their widows and orphans) in receipt of a Chelsea or Greenwich pension, who had settled in Canada, the registers of payment of the pension may be useful. There are separate volumes for Canada, 1845–1862 (WO 22/239–242) and for Nova Scotia, 1858–1880 (WO 22/294–296). The composite volumes for several colonies, 1845–1875, may also be useful (WO 22/248–257).

For Dominions Office correspondence on post-war assisted passages, see DO 35/3366–3443.

14.7 Emigrants to North America and the West Indies: foreign emigrants coming via Britain in the eighteenth century

Emigrants from other countries to the American colonies can sometimes be traced through records in the PRO. Lists of the names of Palatine subjects, who emigrated to America by way of Holland and England in 1709, occur in several classes: the easiest way to discover them is to use the published works by Knittle, MacWethy and the *New York Genealogical and Biographical Review*. (See also **12.2**.)

Between 1740 and 1772, foreign Protestants living in the Americas could become naturalized British citizens by the act 13 George II c.7. This required seven years' residence, the swearing of oaths of allegiance (making an affirmation for Quakers), and taking the sacrament according to the Anglican rite (the last requirement was waived for Quakers and Jews). Every year lists of those naturalized (now in CO 5) had to be sent to the Commissioners for Trade and Plantations in London, where they were copied into entry books (CO 324/55–56). These provisions covered the West Indies as well as the American continent, but in fact only Jamaica (1740–1750), Maryland (1743–1753), Massachusetts (1743), New York (1740–1770), Pennsylvania (1740–1772), South Carolina (1741–1748), and Virginia (1743–1746) returned the lists to London. Over 7,000 foreign Protestants took advantage of this act: Giuseppi has printed their names in the Huguenot Society volume XXIV.

Another method of naturalization, used by hundreds rather than thousands, was by the expensive process of obtaining an act of the colonial assembly (CO 5). To trace one of these naturalizations it will usually be necessary to have a good idea of the date and also the colony of residence.

14.8 Emigrants to Australia and New Zealand

European settlement of Australia began with the penal colony of New South Wales in 1788. In the PRO, there are few records relating to voluntary emigrants to Australia and New Zealand until the Passenger Lists (BT 27) begin in 1890: see **14.2**. In Australia, however, there is material relating to British settlers who received assisted passages there. In the PRO, there is far more extensive documentation of the transportation of convicts to Australia (see **40**). However, to some extent the records of convict transportation also cover free emigrants, as, in some cases, a convict's family would accompany him as voluntary emigrants, and can be traced through some of the same records.

Censuses of convicts were conducted at intervals between 1788 and 1859 in New South Wales and Tasmania (HO 10): although primarily concerned with the unfree population, they do contain the names of those members of the convicts' families who 'came free' or who were 'born in the colony'. The fullest is that of 1828: see the edition by Sainty and Johnson, *New South Wales: Census... November 1828.* The other editions by Baxter are also very useful: that for 1823–1825 gives a lot of background detail.

New South Wales Original Correspondence (CO 201) starts in 1784, and

Figure 23 Emigrants needed a powerful dream to lure them away from home and family and far across the world. For these men, the Australian gold rush of the 1890s proved unmissable. (PRO, COPY 1/450)

contains lists of settlers (and convicts), 1801–1821. The correspondence of 1823 to 1833 has also been indexed. The papers of the Land and Emigration Commission (CO 386) also contain correspondence and entry books of the South Australian Commission.

New Zealand was not used as a penal colony. Details of emigrants may be found in the New Zealand Company records, which contain registers of cabin passengers emigrating, 1839–1850, applications for free passage, 1839–1850, lists of German emigrants, and lists of maintained emigrants (CO 208). For lists of ships going to New Zealand from 1840 to 1885, see Brett, *White Wings*.

Between 1846 and 1851, Army pensioners were encouraged to settle in New South Wales and New Zealand, although many of them failed as settlers. References to the settlement of ex-soldiers in Australia and New Zealand will be found in the PRO's *Alphabetical Guide to Certain War Office and Other Military Records*, under *Australia and New Zealand*. There are also lists of ex-soldier emigrants, 1830–1848, to Australia (WO 43/542) and New Zealand (WO 43/543). Pensions from the Army and Navy were payable at district offices: records survive for offices in New South Wales, 1849–1880 (WO 22/272–275); in South Australia, Queensland, Tasmania and Victoria, 1876–1880 (WO 22/227, 297, 298 and 300); and in New Zealand, 1845–1854 and 1875–1880 (WO 22/276–293). Others deserted to settle: see *The Deserters* by Sexton.

For Dominions Office correspondence on post-war assisted passages, see DO 35/3366–3443.

Microfilms of many PRO documents were filmed by the Australian Joint Copying Project and are available in Australia at the National Library in Canberra (www.nla.gov.au), and at the Mitchell Library in Sydney. Try accessing the National Archives website at www.naa.gov.au. For New Zealand, try www.archives.govt.nz, and the Dictionary of New Zealand Biography database at www.cultureandheritage.govt.nz/History/DNZB.

14.9 Emigrants to South Africa

Registers of payments to Army and Navy pensioners (including some widows and orphans) at the Cape of Good Hope and elsewhere in South Africa, 1849–1858 and 1876–1880, are in WO 22/243–244. The muster rolls of the Cape Levies, 1851–1853, may prove useful (WO 13/3718–3725).

Military records as a whole may be worth exploring for troops in South Africa (see **18**). For example, there are records of claims by civilians for compensation for property requisitioned during the Boer War, which are indexed (WO 148).

The Genealogical Society of South Africa will give advice: see also Lombard's article.

14.10 Welsh emigration to Patagonia

Between 1865 and the First World War, about 3,000 Welsh people emigrated to Patagonia in a conscious attempt to found a new Wales. Many of later generations migrated again, to Canada, South Africa and Australia, but a significant Welsh speaking community remains. For an overview of this community emigration, see Derrick, 'Welsh Emigration to Patagonia'. This gives references to passenger lists and many other documents in the PRO. To find Parliamentary Papers, try a search on the CD-ROM index (available in the PRO Library) using 'Welsh' and 'colony' or 'Welsh' and 'settlement' as search terms. For a Welsh Patagonian genealogy and oral history site, visit www.welsh-patagonia.com. For a full bibliography compiled by the National Library of Wales, try www.llgc.org.uk/lp/lp0066.htm.

14.11 Children's emigration

Schemes to promote the emigration of poor children and orphans date back to the early seventeenth century. In the nineteenth century, it was encouraged by Poor Law legislation, and by the activities of charities such as Dr Barnardo's. Most of the surviving papers at the PRO on child emigration in the late nineteenth and the twentieth centuries are policy papers. MH 102 contains records on child migration after the Second World War: some of the records are closed for 75 years, but others, seen by the Child Migrants Trust (address in **48**), are now open after 30 years.

See Bean and Melville's *Lost Children of the Empire* for a useful overview of the subject. For child emigration to Australia, see *Good British Stock: Child and Youth Emigration to Australia*, by the National Archives of Australia: this lists relevant PRO series. For Canada, see the website (at www.archives.ca) of the National Archives of Canada.

14.12 Emigrants: bibliography

General

Acts of the Privy Council of England, Colonial Series, 1613–1783 (London, 1908–1912)

L Atherton, *'Never Complain, Never Explain': Records of the Foreign Office and State Paper Office, 1500–c.1960* (PRO, 1994)

P Bean and J Melville, *Lost Children of the Empire* (1989)

Calendar of State Papers, Colonial, America and West Indies, 1574–1738 (London, 1860–1969)

Calendar of Treasury Books, 1660–1718 (London, 1904–1962)

Calendar of Treasury Papers, 1557–1728 (London, 1868–1889)

Calendar of Treasury Books and Papers, 1729–1745 (London, 1898–1903)

J S W Gibson, 'Assisted Pauper Emigration, 1834–1837', *Genealogists' Magazine,* vol. XX, pp. 374–375

Journals of the Board of Trade and Plantations, 1704–1782 (London, 1920–1938)

R C Kershaw, *Emigrants and Expats: A guide to sources on UK emigration and residents overseas* (PRO, 2002)

Public Record Office, *Alphabetical Guide to Certain War Office and other Military Records preserved in the Public Record Office,* Lists and Indexes, vol. LIII (London, 1931)

Public Record Office, *List of Colonial Office Records,* Lists and Indexes, vol. XXXVI (London, 1911)

Public Record Office, *List of Records of the Treasury, Paymaster General's Office, Exchequer and Audit Department and Board of Trade, prior to 1837,* Lists and Indexes, vol. XLVI (London, 1922)

Public Record Office, *List of State Papers, Domestic, 1547–1792, and Home Office Records, 1782–1837*, Lists and Indexes, vol. XLIII (London, 1914)

R B Pugh, *The Records of the Colonial and Dominions Office* (London, 1964)

A Thurston, *Records of the Colonial Office, Dominions Office, Commonwealth Relations Office and Commonwealth Office* (London, 1995)

North America and the West Indies

'AMDG', 'Ships, Merchants and Passengers to the American Colonies 1618–1688' (unpublished MS, dated Purley 1982). [Taken from the Port Books in E 190.]

C M Andrews, *Guide to the Materials for American History to 1783 in the Public Record Office of Great Britain* (Washington, 1912 and 1914)

C E Banks and E E Brownell, *Topographical Dictionary of 2885 English Emigrants to New England, 1620–1650* (New York, 1963, 1976)

C Boyer ed., *Ships' Passenger Lists: The South* (1538–1825); *National and New England* (1600–1825); *New York and New Jersey* (1600–1825); *Pennsylvania and Delaware* (1641–1825) (4 vols, Newhall, California, 1980)

J C Brandow, *Omitted Chapters from Hotten . . . Census Returns, Parish Registers and Militia Rolls from the Barbados Census of 1679/80* (Baltimore, 1983)

M J Burchall, 'Parish-Organised Emigration to America', *Genealogists' Magazine*, vol. XVIII, pp. 336–342

P W Coldham, *American Loyalist Claims* (Washington, 1980) (Indexes AO 13/1–35, 37, which contain claims for compensation from American loyalists who escaped to Canada, 1774–1793.)

P W Coldham, *Bonded Passengers to America, 1615–1775* (Baltimore, 1983)

P W Coldham, *The Bristol Registers of Servants Sent to Foreign Plantations 1654–1686* (Baltimore, 1988)

P W Coldham, *The Complete Book of Emigrants, 1607–1776* (4 vols, Baltimore, 1987–1993)

P W Coldham, *Emigrants from England to the American Colonies, 1773–1776* (Baltimore, 1988)

P W Coldham, *English Adventurers and Emigrants, 1609–1660 Abstracts of Examinations in the High Court of Admiralty, with Reference to Colonial America* (Baltimore, 1984)

P W Coldham, *English Estates of American Colonists: American Wills and Administrations in the Prerogative Court of Canterbury, 1610–1699 and 1700–1799* (Baltimore, 1980)

P W Coldham, *English Estates of American Settlers: American Wills and Administrations in the Prerogative Court of Canterbury, 1800–1858* (Baltimore, 1981)

P W Coldham, *Lord Mayor's Court of London, Depositions relating to America, 1641–1736*, National Genealogical Society (Washington, 1980)

N Currer-Briggs, 'American Colonial Gleanings from Town Depositions', *Genealogists' Magazine*, vol. XVIII, pp. 288–294

D Dobson, *The Original Scots Colonists of Early America 1612–1783* (Baltimore, 1989)

D Dobson, *Scottish Emigration to Colonial America 1607–1785* (Georgia, 1994)

A Douglas, 'Genealogical Research in Canada', *Genealogists' Magazine*, vol. XXIII, pp. 217–221

A Douglas, 'Gentlemen Adventurers and Remittance Men' [Hudson's Bay Company], *Genealogists' Magazine*, vol. XXIV, pp. 55–59

R H Ellis, 'Records of the American Loyalists' Claims in the Public Record Office', *Genealogists' Magazine*, vol. XII, pp. 375–378, 407–410, 433–435

P W Filby, *American and British Genealogy and Heraldry* (Chicago, 2nd edn, 1975)

P W Filby ed., *Passenger and Immigration Lists Bibliography 1538–1900* (Michigan, 1981)

P W Filby and M K Meyer eds, *Passenger and Immigration Lists Index,* 13 volumes (Michigan, 1981–1995.) (Lists about 2,410,000 names of immigrants to USA and Canada, from the sixteenth to mid twentieth centuries.)

W Foot, '"That most precious Jewel" – East Florida 1763–83', *Genealogists' Magazine,* vol. XXIV, pp. 144–148

G Fothergill, *A List of Emigrant Ministers to Australia 1690–1811* (London, 1904)

A Games, *Migration and the Origins of the English Atlantic World* (Cambridge, Mass., 1999)

M S Giuseppi, *Naturalizations of Foreign Protestants in the American and West Indian colonies,* Huguenot Society, vol. XXIV, 1921

I A Glazier and M Tepper, *The Famine Immigrants: Lists of Irish Immigrants Arriving at the Port of New York, 1846–1851* (Baltimore, 1983)

G Grannum, *Tracing Your West Indian Ancestors* (PRO, 1995; new ed. forthcoming, 2002)

A C Hollis Hallett, *Early Bermuda Records 1619–1826* (Bermuda, 1991)

J C Hotten, *Original Lists of Persons emigrating to America, 1600–1700* (London, 1874) [see also Brandow]

C B Jewson, *Transcript of Three Registers of Passengers from Great Yarmouth to Holland and New England, 1637–1639,* Norfolk Record Society, vol. XXV (1954)

J and M Kaminkow, *A List of Emigrants from England to America, 1718–1759* (Baltimore, 1964)

W A Knittle, *Early Eighteenth Century Palatine Emigration* (Philadelphia, 1937)

A Kulikoff, *From British Peasants to Colonial American Farmers* (Chapel Hill, 2000)

A H Lancour, *A Bibliography of Ships' Passenger Lists, 1538–1825* (New York, 1963)

M E MacSorley, *Genealogical sources in the United States of America* (Basingstoke, 1995)

L D MacWethy, *The Book of Names especially relating to the Early Palatines and the First Settlers in the Mohawk Valley* (New York, 1932)

G E McCracken, 'State and Federal Sources for American Genealogy', *Genealogists' Magazine,* vol. XIX, pp. 138–140

B Merriman, 'Genealogy in Canada', *Genealogists' Magazine,* vol. XIX, pp. 306–311

National Archives and Record Service, *A Guide to Genealogical Research in the National Archives* (Washington, 1982)

New York Genealogical and Biographical Records, vols. XL and LXI (New York, 1909 and 1910) (for Palatine emigrants)

L St Louis-Harrison and M Munk, *Tracing your ancestors in Canada* (National Archives of Canada, 1998)

G Sherwood, *American Colonists in English Records* (2 vols., London, 1932, 1933) Lists passengers not mentioned in Hotten.)

C J Stanford, 'Genealogical Sources in Barbados', *Genealogists' Magazine,* vol. XVII, pp. 489–498

M Tepper ed., *New World Immigrants,* (Baltimore, 1980) (a consolidation of passenger lists)

M Tepper, *Passengers to America: A Consolidation of Ship Passenger Lists from the New England Genealogical Register* (Baltimore, 1988)

M Tepper, *American Passengers Arrival Records* (Baltimore, 1993)

D Whyte, *A Dictionary of Scottish Emigrants to the USA* (Baltimore, 1972)

Australia and New Zealand

C J Baxter, *Musters and Lists New South Wales and Norfolk Island, 1800–1802* (Sydney, 1988)

C J Baxter, *Musters New South Wales, Norfolk Island and Van Diemen's Land, 1811* (Sydney, 1987)

C J Baxter, *General Muster and Land and Stock Muster of New South Wales, 1822* (Sydney, 1988)

C J Baxter, *General Muster of New South Wales, 1823, 1824, 1825* (Sydney, 1999)

H Brett, *White Wings. Vol 1 Fifty years of sail in the New Zealand trade 1850–1900. Vol 2 Founding of the provinces and old time shipping: passenger ships from 1840 to 1885* (Auckland, 1924 and 1928, reprinted 1976)

A Bromell, *Tracing Family History in New Zealand* (Wellington, 1991)

P Burns and H Richardson, *Fatal Success: A History of the New Zealand Company* (Auckland, 1989)

M Chambers, *Finding Families: The Guide to the National Archives of Australia for Genealogists* (Canberra, 1998)

Fitzmaurice, *Army Deserters from HM Service* (Forest Hill, Victoria, 1988 continuing)

M Flynn, *The Second Fleet* (1993)

M Gillen, *The Founders of Australia, A Biographical Dictionary of the First Fleet* (Sydney, 1989)

D T Hawkings, *Bound for Australia* (Guildford, 1987)

H and L Hughes, *Discharged in New Zealand – Soldiers of the Imperial Foot Regiments who took their discharge in New Zealand 1840–1870* (Auckland, 1988)

L Marshall and V Mossong, 'Genealogical Research in New Zealand', *Genealogists' Magazine,* vol. XX, pp. 45–49.

J Melton, *Ship's Deserters 1852–1900* (Sydney, 1986)

A G Peake, *Bibliography of Australian Family History* (Dulwich, South Australia, 1988)

A G Peake, *National Register of Shipping Arrivals: Australia and New Zealand* (Sydney, 1992)

M R Sainty and K A Johnson eds, *New South Wales: Census . . . November 1828 . . .* (Sydney, 1980)

R Sexton *The Deserters: Military and Naval Deserters as settlers in Australia and New Zealand 1800–1865* (1998)

N Vine Hall, *Tracing your Family History in Australia – A Guide to Sources* (London, 1985)

H Woolcock, *Rights of Passage: Emigration to Australia in the 19th Century* (London, 1986)

South Africa

E Bull, *Aided Immigration to South Africa, 1857–1867* (Pretoria, 1991)

R J Lombard, 'Genealogical Research in South Africa', *Genealogists' Magazine,* vol. XIX, pp. 274–276

E Mosse Jones, *Rolls of the British Settlers in South Africa* (Capetown, 1971)

P Philip, *British Residents at the Cape 1795–1819* (Capetown, 1981)

Patagonia

B Derrick, 'Welsh Emigration to Patagonia', *Ancestors* (forthcoming)

15

Oaths of allegiance, and loyal addresses

◆ ◆ ◆

15.1 Oath rolls

Between the sixteenth and nineteenth centuries, people were required on various occasions to swear oaths in support of the Crown and the Anglican church. Some of these oaths were sworn by those taking up or holding official positions and by lawyers on being admitted to the courts. Others were sworn by aliens, in the process of becoming naturalized British subjects. Still others were taken by people to signify their loyalty to the Crown in times of political upheaval. Not all such oaths are recorded in the Oath Rolls held by the PRO. The most notable exception is an oath in support of Crown, Parliament and the Protestant Religion, intended to be taken by all men over the age of 18 in 1641. These Protestation returns were sent into Parliament, and are now in the House of Lords Record Office (address in **48**): they are listed by Gibson and Dell.

Anyone taking up any civil or military office was required by the Corporations Act of 1661 and the Test Act of 1672 to take the oaths of allegiance and supremacy. They also had to deliver a certificate into court stating that they had received the sacrament of the Lord's Supper according to the rites of the Church of England. These acts were not repealed until 1828. The Sacrament Certificates, signed by the minister and churchwardens of the parish, survive from 1672 to 1828, but are not always easy to use (C 224, CHES 4, E 196, KB 22).

The oath rolls are found in different places, depending on the occupation and place of residence of the person taking the oath. Oaths could be sworn before Justices of the Peace at Quarter Sessions or, if one resided within 30 miles of Westminster, at one of the central courts of law in Westminster Hall. As a result, oath rolls may be found either in local record offices or in the PRO. Oath rolls, including classes devoted to the oaths of lawyers (see **29**), survive in the records of Chancery (C 193/9, C 184, C 214, C 215), Common Pleas (CP 10), Exchequer (E 169, E 200, E 3), and King's Bench (KB 24, KB 113). Oath rolls of attorneys in the courts of Chester and Durham also exist (CHES 36/3, DURH 3/217). Oaths of clergy (1789–1836) and of Roman Catholics after the conditions were relaxed (1778–1829) are in CP 37.

Between 1708 and 1711, all foreign Protestants who took the oaths of allegiance and supremacy in court, and who produced a sacrament certificate, were deemed to have been naturalized (KB 24, E 169/86). The Huguenot

Society, in its volumes XXVII and XXV, has indexed the rolls in the PRO: other rolls, of oaths taken before the Quarter Sessions, may survive in county record offices. See **14.7** for oaths of allegiance on naturalization, in North America and the West Indies.

The Association Oath Rolls (C 213 and C 214) contain the signatures or marks and names of people subscribing to the 'Solemn Association' of 1696, in support of William III after an attempt had been made, by Jacobites, to assassinate him. The oath of association was taken by everyone in a position of any authority – all members of Parliament, all military, naval and civil office-holders of the Crown, the clergy and the gentry, freemen of the city companies, and others besides. In some places, such as Jersey, Westminster and Suffolk, almost every adult male appears to have subscribed, and the returns approximate to a census of adult men: the Jersey and Guernsey rolls have been published in full by Glendinning. Transcripts are also appearing for other counties, such as Surrey and Wiltshire. C 213 also includes rolls from certain colonies and overseas settlements, such as Holland, Malaga, Geneva, Jamestown and New York.

15.2 Loyal addresses

Loyal addresses to the Crown were often subscribed with many names and published. For example, the editions of the *London Gazette* between September 1775 and March 1776 contain 150 loyal addresses supporting the war against America. The *London Gazette* can be seen at the PRO in ZJ 1.

15.3 Oaths of allegiance and loyal addresses: bibliography

J Gibson, *The Hearth Tax, Other Later Stuart Tax Lists, and the Association Oath Rolls* (FFHS, 1996)

J Gibson and A Dell, *The Protestation Returns 1641–42 and other contemporary listings: collection in aid of distressed Protestants in Ireland, subsidies, poll tax, assessments or grants, vow and covenant, solemn league and covenant* (FFHS, 1995)

A Glendinning, *Did Your Ancestor Sign the Jersey Oath of Allegiance Roll of 1696?* (Channel Islands Family History Society, 1995)

A Glendinning, *Eye on the Past in Guernsey* (Channel Islands Family History Society, 1992)

C R Webb, 'The Association Oath Rolls of 1695', *Genealogists' Magazine*, vol. XXI, pp. 120–23

W A Shaw ed., *Letters of Denization and Acts of Naturalization for Aliens in England and Ireland 1701–1800* (Huguenot Society, vol. XXVII, Manchester, 1923)

A Supplement to Dr W Shaw's Letters of Denization and Acts of Naturalization (Huguenot Society, vol. XXXV, Frome, 1932)

16

Electoral registration

◆ ◆ ◆

16.1 Poll books

Poll books are locally compiled lists of men who were entitled to vote (and sometimes of who they voted for) dating from the seventeenth to the nineteenth century. Until the late nineteenth century, only a minority of the male population (and none of the female) was normally entitled to vote in parliamentary elections. In the counties, the traditional qualification was ownership of freehold land worth at least 40 shillings a year, although in some boroughs all householders might have the right to vote. Electoral records need to be used with some knowledge as to the local qualification. The franchise was extended in 1832, 1867 and 1884 to cover most male householders, but not until 1921 did it cover all males over 21 normally resident in a constituency. Women over 30 who were householders or married to householders were also given the vote in 1921. Women did not receive voting rights equal to those of men until 1928.

There are large collections of poll books in the British Library, the Guildhall Library and the library of the Society of Genealogists. County record offices and local libraries have collections relating to their own areas. For a guide to their use and whereabouts, see Gibson and Rogers, *Poll Books c.1696–1872.*

16.2 Electoral registers

After the 1832 Reform Act an annual register of persons (still mostly male property-holders) entitled to vote was kept. These registers were compiled every year (except for 1916–1917 and 1940–1944) and were deposited with the clerk of the peace. Most historic ones are now in local record offices or libraries, as well as the British Library. For a useful guide, see Gibson and Rogers, *Electoral Registers since 1832 and Burgers Rolls.*

Those few electoral registers that the PRO has are listed here, and may be seen in the PRO Library. Most come from the early 1870s, but there are some for Norfolk from 1832–1833.

Current electoral registers for the locality can be seen in local public libraries: a national set is kept at the British Library.

16.3 Electoral registers in the PRO Library

England

Bedfordshire	1874
Berkshire	1874; Wallingford 1874
Bristol City	1874
Buckinghamshire	1874; Aylesbury 1874; Buckingham 1874
Cambridgeshire	1872; Isle of Ely 1874
Cheshire	East 1874; Mid 1874; West 1874
Cumberland	East 1874; West 1874; Carlisle City 1875; Cockermouth 1874; Whitehaven 1875
Cornwall	1872–1875; East 1874; West 1874; Bodmin 1874; Helston 1874; Launceston 1874; Liskeard 1872, 1873; St Ives 1875
Derbyshire	East 1868–69, 1870; North 1870; South 1870
Devon	1875; East 1874; North 1874; South 1874; Barnstaple 1874
Dorset	1872, 1874; Poole 1870; Shaftesbury 1872; Wareham 1871
Durham	North 1874; South 1874; Hartlepool 1874; Stockton 1875
Essex	East 1875; South 1875; West 1875; Colchester 1874
Gloucestershire	1872, 1874; Cirencester 1872; Stroud 1873; Tewkesbury 1874
Hampshire	1874; North 1874; South 1874; Andover 1874; Petersfield 1874
Herefordshire	1874
Hertfordshire	1875
Huntingdonshire	1874; Huntingdon 1874
Kent	East 1874; Mid 1874; West 1874; Canterbury 1873
Lancashire	North 1874; North East 1874; South East 1874; South West 1874; Oldham 1873
Leicestershire	South 1874
Lincolnshire	Mid Lincs, Kesteven 1874; Mid Lincs, Lindsey 1874; North Lincs, Lindsey 1874; South Lincs, Kesteven 1874; Grantham 1874
Middlesex	1874
Monmouthshire	1874
Norfolk	East 1832–33; North 1874; South 1874; West 1832–33, 1874
Northamptonshire	North 1874; South 1874; Peterborough 1874
Northumberland	North 1874; South 1874; Berwick-upon-Tweed 1875
Nottinghamshire	North 1874; South 1874; East Retford 1872, 1874; Newark 1873
Oxfordshire	1874; New Woodstock 1873–74
Rutland	1874
Shropshire	North 1874; South 1874; Shrewsbury 1874; Wenlock 1874
Somerset	East 1874
Staffordshire	East 1874; North 1874; West 1874;

	Newcastle-under-Lyme 1873; Stafford 1874; Stoke-on-Trent 1871–72; Tamworth 1871–72; Walsall 1874; Wednesbury 1874; Wolverhampton 1874
Suffolk	East 1873, 1874, 1875; West 1874; Eye 1875
Surrey	East 1872; Mid 1872; West 1872; Guildford 1873
Sussex	1871, 1873; East 1874; West 1874; Chichester 1874; Horsham 1872; Midhurst 1871; New Shoreham 1871; Rye 1874
Warwickshire	North 1873, 1875; South 1874; Coventry City 1874
Westmorland	1872
Wiltshire	1872, 1874, 1875; South 1874; Calne 1874; Chippenham 1871; Cricklade 1873; Malmesbury 1871; Westbury 1874; Wilton 1874
Worcestershire	East 1874; West 1874
Yorkshire	East Riding 1874; North Riding 1874; West Riding, North 1874; West Riding, South 1874; Dewsbury 1874; Huddersfield 1875; Leeds 1874; Wakefield 1874; York City 1873

Wales

Anglesey	1873, 1874, 1875; Beaumaris 1870, 1874
Brecon	1871
Cardigan	1871–72, 1874; Aberystwyth, Cardigan and Lampeter 1871; Adpar 1871; Lampeter-Pontstephen 1871
Carmarthen	1872; Carmarthen Borough 1871
Caernarvon	1873, 1874, 1875; Caernarvon Borough 1873
Denbigh	1874, 1875
Flint	1874; Flint Borough 1875
Glamorgan	1873, 1874, 1875; Loughor and Neath 1874
Merioneth	1874
Montgomery	1872, 1874; Montgomery Borough 1874
Pembroke	1871–72; Pembroke Borough 1875
Radnor	1875; New Radnor 1873

16.4 The Absent Voters' Register, 1918 and 1919

The 1918 Representation of the People Act allowed members of the armed forces and others connected with the war effort to have a postal or proxy vote in their home constituency. The registers of absent voters can be seen at the British Library: local copies may be held in local record offices. If you have a name and a home address for a First World War soldier, sailor or airman, but no idea as to regiment or service details, they can provide a useful route to finding out more as they give brief service details. Men applying had to be over 19 (younger than other electors) and, obviously, to have survived up to 1918.

16.5 Electoral registration: bibliography

N Connell, 'Absent Voters' Registers', *Family Tree Magazine*, December 1998, p. 5

J S W Gibson and C Rogers, *Electoral Registers since 1832 and Burgers Rolls* (FFHS, 1990)

J S W Gibson and C Rogers, *Poll Books c.1696–1872* (FFHS, 1994)

N Newington-Irving, *Directories and Poll Books, including almanacs and electoral rolls, in the Library of the Society of Genealogists* (Society of Genealogists, 1995)

17

Changes of name

◆ ◆ ◆

17.1 Changes of name

It is perfectly legal for anyone to simply change his or her name without drawing any attention to the change, unless there is an intention to defraud. Many people who changed their name did not wish to draw attention to the fact. For example, in an age when it was almost impossible to divorce, some people simply took their new partner's name to give the appearance of marriage, and any children the appearance of legitimacy.

There were several ways to record the change of name, such as a statutory declaration before a JP or Commissioner for Oaths (which could not be enrolled), or an advertisement in the newspapers, may have been used instead. (It may be possible to check local newspapers at the British Library Newspaper Library: address in **48**.)

An alternative was just to assume an alias – with intention to defraud. For an index to habitual criminals and their aliases, from 1869, see **39.4**.

17.2 Changes of name by deed poll, 1851 onwards

For most people a deed poll means a change of name. Actually, a deed poll is the technical term for a deed involving only one party (poll meaning the parchment was smooth-cut, whereas an indenture or indented deed between two or more parties was cut in a zigzag way so each could be matched up with the other parts).

Changes of name by deed poll were (and are) made before a solicitor who could enrol them, for safe keeping. Relatively few changes of name were enrolled, as it was not a legal obligation and extra fees were payable. Most people who come to the PRO looking for an enrolled change of name are disappointed. The original deed poll will have been given to the person who changed their name. Although the solicitor who prepared the deed poll may have kept a copy on file, it is unlikely to be a certified copy, nor is the file likely to have been kept for more than five years.

From 1851 the indexes to the Close Rolls (C 54) include references to changes of name by deed poll that had been enrolled. In 1903, this function was taken over by the Supreme Court of Judicature Enrolment Books (J 18), with indexes also in J 18. The indexes vary from time to time: until 1903 only the former name is given, but since then both are present, either as a note or a cross-reference. These records and indexes are seen in the Map Room. For a change of name in the last five years, apply to the Royal Courts of Justice, Room 81 (address in **48**).

17.3 The *London Gazette*

From 1914, all deeds poll enrolled in the Supreme Court had first to be advertised in the *London Gazette* – but again, this does not mean all changes of name. However, for the duration of the Second World War, British subjects could only change their name if 21 days before doing so they had published in the *London Gazette*, the *Edinburgh Gazette* or the *Belfast Gazette* a notice giving details of the proposed change.

A supplementary index to both old and new names exists in the quarterly indexes to the *London Gazette* for 1938–1964: copies of the relevant pages are shelved by the J 18 indexes in the Map Room. The *London Gazette* itself may be seen in the PRO under ZJ 1.

17.4 Changes of name by foreigners in the UK, 1916–1971

Enemy aliens resident in Britain had been forbidden to change their names in 1916: the ban was extended to all foreigners in Britain in 1919. The only exceptions made were when a new name was assumed by royal licence; or by special permission of the Home Secretary; or when a woman took her husband's name on marriage. In the first two of these cases, the change had to be advertised in the *Gazettes* (see above). These restrictions were removed in 1971, and anyone can now change their name.

17.5 Royal licences and private acts of Parliament: c.1700 onwards

Royal licences to change a name appear very infrequently among the records from the late seventeenth century. The change is usually in response to a bequest conditional upon adopting the deceased's name, or a marriage settlement requiring the husband to adopt the wife's name, or when a change to the coat of arms was also required. Warrants for such changes of name were entered into the current series of entry books; before 1782 in SP 44; from 1782 to February 1868 in HO 38; and from February 1868 in HO 142. These usually have internal indexes in each volume. Records of such changes of name were often advertised in the *London Gazette*. It may be worth also checking the records of the College of Arms (address in **48**).

Private acts of Parliament were also used in the same kinds of instance (although only once since the 1880s): the originals are in the House of Lords Record Office (address in **48**).

17.6 The Phillimore *Index to Change of Name, 1760–1901*

This is a composite index from several sources, and does not claim to be an index to all changes of name. Its full details are *An Index to Change of Name Under Authority of Act of Parliament or Royal Licence and including Irregular Changes from 1 George III to 64 Victoria, 1760 to 1901.* A copy is shelved with the C 54 finding aids in the Map Room.

The sources covered are: private acts of Parliament; royal licences published in the *London* and *Dublin Gazettes*; notices of changes of name published in *The Times* after 1861; a few notices from other newspapers; the registers of the Lord Lyon [king of arms], where Scottish changes of name were commonly recorded; records in the office of the Ulster King at Arms; and some private information.

It thus omits changes by royal licence not advertised in the *London Gazette*, and changes by deed poll enrolled in the Close Rolls but not advertised in *The Times*.

17.7 Changes of name: bibliography

H Mead, *Change of Name* (London, 1995)
W P W Phillimore and E A Fry, *An Index to Change of Names, 1760–1901* (London, 1905)

18

The Army: an overview

◆ ◆ ◆

18.1 Introduction

Army records are among our most popular records with family historians. For many people, tracing a father, grandfather, or great-grandfather who fought in the First World War is their first step into researching their family history. Others come to Army research after finding a census entry, or a certificate, describing a man as a soldier in a particular regiment, or as an Army pensioner. For some researchers, the organization of the Army is something familiar to them from their own experience in it: to others, it is all new and strange. Some people want to know as much as they can about a soldier's time in the Army: others want to concentrate on the family tree.

Researching in Army records is not always easy, but can be very rewarding. One of the things that often surprises people is how much time soldiers spent abroad: the British Army was involved in colonial defence and conquest since the time of Charles II, even when not fighting wars in Europe.

As you can tell from the length of this chapter, researching among Army records can cover an enormous number of sources. The main chapter is basically divided into five sub-chapters:

18	background information on the Army
18a	records of most use for the family tree
18b	service records, up to 1914
18c	service records, from 1914 onwards
18d	linked services.

You may have to follow cross-references from one to another. I apologise if this is confusing: it is a big subject – or rather a series of interrelating subjects. You may find that turning back to the Contents list at the start of the book is the best way to navigate it.

Service records tend to be those papers that document the soldier's professional life rather than his personal one. There is some overlap, however, particularly as soldiers' families gradually became entitled to more long-term consideration from the state (in the form of pensions), and so next of kin were recorded. One thing to remember is that very many series of military papers simply no longer exist: we know for example that soldiers' wives could be sent back to their husbands' parish of origin, but finding any military paperwork on this is very unlikely.

The service records have been split into two sections, before and after 1914. This is because 1914 saw the beginning of the great twentieth-century militarization of the British people. Because so many men (and more women) served after 1914, Army service records were in many ways simplified, and in other ways made more complex. Before 1914, you may have to look in a lot of places, with no guarantee of finding a record because the Army was not particularly interested in the individual soldier's family situation. From 1914, information was carefully recorded – but may no longer survive for 1914–1918, because of enemy bombing in 1940. However, what survives does provide information on a giant cross-section of the men of the United Kingdom, and a smaller one of women. Service records *after* the First World War are not yet at the PRO, but are already of interest to huge numbers of families.

Within both sections, the next division is between officers and other ranks. Non-commissioned officers are other ranks. Officers tend to have fuller records, and pensions provided for their families from a much earlier date: they were wealthier and socially more important. This does not mean that you cannot find out quite a lot about an ordinary British soldier. If you are prepared to trawl through some of the less popular series mentioned here, you may be able to find out detailed information on particular individuals.

18.2 Background information on the Army

Some understanding of the organization of the Army is helpful. Garrisons and barracks (after an initial period of quartering troops on local people) were established for the quartering of troops throughout the country. In times of war, when the garrison troops were needed elsewhere, special battalions of veterans (ex-soldiers given a pension to be subject to recall) were raised to take their place, in order to safeguard order in Britain itself.

The basic unit of the Army was the regiment, under the command of a colonel. The regiments were of various types: cavalry, infantry, artillery and engineers. In peacetime, a regiment usually consisted of two battalions, each split into 10 companies (troops in the cavalry) of about a 100 men each. One battalion was usually posted abroad, to guard the Empire or to take part in whatever war was going on. The other battalion was based at home – that is, anywhere in the British Isles or Ireland – and was responsible for recruiting and training, as well as home defence. From about 1870, each regiment had a permanent regimental depot (at a third location); before then, the depot was wherever the home battalion happened to be. Before 1870, recruitment was to the regiment, and was usually from the locality where the home battalion happened to be posted at the time (they moved about quite a lot). However, recruiting parties did range quite widely. After 1870, regiments could still recruit directly, but a man had the option of joining 'the Army' and being assigned to any regiment.

More battalions were created in times of need, particularly during the two world wars, when one regiment might easily have 10 battalions or even more. The Middlesex Regiment had over 40 between 1914 and 1918. The First World War was really the first period of mass enlistment into local battalions, like the famous 'Pals' battalions. Before then, each regiment had men from across the United Kingdom.

The Army was manned by commissioned officers (usually wealthy men: commissions were generally purchased before 1871), and other ranks (drawn from the poorer classes). Until 1914 there was voluntary enlistment into the other ranks. Conscription was used in 1916–1918, and again in 1939–1961: the First World War considerably improved the social status of soldiers, as more families became personally involved.

As well as the Regular Army, each county had its own militia regiments from 1757. These were a conscripted part-time force: in wartime, they acted as full-time soldiers. Other ranks in militia regiments had a better public reputation – were more respectable – than the common soldiery of the regular army. From 1881, each militia regiment was attached to a regular Army regiment, as its third battalion. Volunteer forces were raised in the Napoleonic wars, and again from 1859. In 1908, they were formed into the Territorial Force, which provided much of the manpower of the First World War, before conscription in 1916. It was renamed the Territorial Army in 1920.

18.3 Regimental changes and *Army Lists*

Each basic unit of the British Army, the regiment, formed its own social family. Regimental museums are the place to find out about this world: many have collections of paintings and photographs as well as records (see Wise's *Guide*). A regiment is likely to have had several name changes and amalgamations over its history. These can make it complicated to match up the regiment you know a soldier belonged to, with a list of records arranged by a completely different regimental name. A quick way round this is to ask at the enquiry desk for Swinson, *A Register of the Regiments and Corps of the British Army*. The site www.regiments.org covers not just British land forces, but also Empire, Indian and Commonwealth ones too. For the First World War, try www.1914–1918.net, which has good information on units. You could also try WO 389/17, which is a register of the formations, amalgamations, disbandments and changes of title of infantry regiments, 1914–1919.

Another cause of confusion can be 'regimental order of precedence'. Each regiment had its own known place in the hierarchy. This was something all members of the Army would have known about, and it often made sense to the War Office to order their records in this way, even during the Second World War. For example, an entry book of payments to officers' widows might have all the surnames beginning with A entered together – but within the A's, the widows would not be entered in alphabetical order, but in the order of the regiment's place in the hierarchy. To find out where your regiment sat in the order of precedence, look at the Introductory Note to the paper list of WO 106 at the PRO, or in any *Army List*.

The *Army List* defined the regimental order of precedence. For 300 years, the

No. CLXXIII.
2nd January, 1882.

PUBLISHED QUARTERLY.
Price 10s. 6d.

THE

NEW ARMY LIST,

MILITIA LIST,

YEOMANRY CAVALRY LIST,

AND

INDIAN CIVIL SERVICE LIST;

EXHIBITING THE

RANK, STANDING, AND A SUMMARY OF THE WAR SERVICES

OF EVERY REGIMENTAL OFFICER IN THE ARMY

SERVING ON FULL PAY,

INCLUDING

THE ROYAL MARINES

THE

INDIAN STAFF CORPS AND LOCAL INDIAN FORCES

DISTINGUISHING THOSE

WHO HAVE SERVED IN THE PENINSULA,

WHO WERE AT WATERLOO,

WHO HAVE RECEIVED MEDALS AND OTHER DISTINCTIONS,

AND

WHO HAVE BEEN WOUNDED, AND IN WHAT ACTIONS;

WITH THE PERIOD OF SERVICE BOTH ON FULL AND HALF PAY.

GIVING ALSO

THE DATES OF EVERY OFFICER'S COMMISSIONS

AND

DISTINGUISHING THOSE OBTAINED BY PURCHASE

WITH AN INDEX.

BY THE LATE

LIEUTENANT GENERAL H. G. HART.

EDITED BY HIS SON.

LONDON:

JOHN MURRAY, ALBEMARLE STREET.

1882.

Figure 24 The *Army List* and *Hart's Army Lists* contain a wealth of information, on officers and on regiments, but not on individuals from the ranks. (*Hart's Army List* for 1882, PRO Library)

Army has produced regular editions of the *Army List*. Although we talk about 'the' *Army List*, there are in fact several series with that name. The first official *Army List* was published in 1740. For each year between 1798 and 1951, there are two (and sometimes three) series of *Army List* available, which can be seen in the PRO. The different series vary in format and content: some are just lists of officers: others (the monthly lists) contain a lot of detail about the organization of regiments. For more information, see the leaflet on *Army Lists* available at the PRO (and on the PRO website).

The Monthly *Army Lists*, 1798–June 1940, cover the officers of the Regular Army *plus* those of the Militia, Territorial and Colonial forces. These are arranged by regiment, and give some idea of where the regiment was. This can be very useful if you want to find out more, or if you have little information – for example, a man described on a certificate as a soldier but with no other details. You may be able to work out what regiments were in that area from looking at the relevant monthly *Army List*. However, you can also use records of where regiments were stationed in WO 379 and WO 380.

18.4 Printed works, websites and other places

Each sub-chapter on the Army has its own brief bibliography. If you have any odd moments in the PRO, it would be a good idea to spend them exploring the PRO Library holdings, and noting books to order from your own library. The PRO Library has several general histories of the British Army, and of specific wars or campaigns, which can help you to make sense of the military world in which your ancestor lived. It also holds an excellent collection of regimental histories, which can often be the easiest way to find out more about where a soldier was likely to have served. You may also want to spend some time in the PRO bookshop, looking at its excellent range of military history books.

This book can indicate only the most generally useful records: for more information, see *Army Records for Family Historians*, by Fowler and Spencer. Most of the series you will be using will be from the War Office, in the WO code. If you want to explore further in the War Office, among the records that relate to warfare and Army administration, and not to individuals, you will need to use Roper's *The records of the War Office and related departments, 1660–1964*. These records *may* (sometimes) be of interest in discovering more about a soldier's life.

There are a growing number of websites for military history. See Christian, *The Genealogist's Internet,* for a good guide. The two previously mentioned, www.regiments.org and www.1914–1918.net are good starting places. For Scotland, look at www-saw.arts.ed.ac.uk/army.

There are also many other places to look for information about soldiers. The most obvious are the Imperial War Museum, the National Army Museum and the various regimental museums: these specialize in the life of the Army, and you should be able to discover some general idea of how your ancestor lived as a soldier. Most regiments have their own museums, some of which also have archival collections. Ask at the Research Enquiry Desk to see a copy of Wise's *A Guide to Military Museums*. If private papers exist, they may be traceable through the National Register of Archives (www.hmc.gov.uk/nra). Addresses are given in **48**.

18.5 The Army: an overview: bibliography and sources

Army List (London, annually from 1754)
D Ascoli, *A Companion to the British Army, 1660–1983* (London, 1983)
P Christian, *The Genealogist's Internet* (PRO, 2001)

S Fowler and W Spencer, *Army Records for Family Historians* (PRO, 1998)

M Roper, *The records of the War Office and related departments, 1660–1964* (PRO, 1998)

A Swinson, ed., *A Register of the Regiments and Corps of the British Army: the Ancestry of the Regiments and Corps of the Regular Establishments of the Army* (London, 1975)

A S White, *A Bibliography of the Regiments and Corps of the British Army* (London, 1965)

T Wise, *A Guide to Military Museums* (1999)

18a

The Army: sources for family history

◆ ◆ ◆

Most War Office (Army) records do not give details of parentage, marriage or children. However there are some (not all in the PRO) that do. They can cover both officers and men, although, as with so much of Army life, officers and men were treated differently when it came to marriage and family.

The Army was not very interested in other ranks' wives and children until the Crimean War – which attracted on-the-spot journalists and also many tourists. The presence of these amazed and concerned onlookers, and extensive press coverage, drew attention not merely to the low standards of medical care, but also to the problems of other ranks' families. Reform was not immediate, but when it came it set the tone for the Army's continued concern for the wives and children of its men.

18a.1 Army registers of births, marriages and deaths, 1761–1987

There are three main series of Army registers of birth, marriage and death. Most are not in the PRO. The General Register Office holds the largest number, but some regiments apparently still hold copies. As they have never been analysed as a series (and most are not available for public inspection), we do not know what percentage of Army marriages and births are covered. The PRO is currently undertaking a survey of all holdings of Army registers, so perhaps the situation will be clarified soon.

18a.1.1 Army registers of births, marriages and burials at the GRO

All these series of Army registers are kept in the General Register Office of England and Wales. Although you cannot see them, you can buy certificates of the events they include. The registers do sometimes contain extra information, which is not included in the certificates as supplied.

At the moment, only the indexes are freely available to the public, at the FRC and at the PRO. However, even the indexes can be helpful.

- Regimental registers of births/baptisms and marriages, covering both at home (from 1761) and abroad (from c.1790) to 1924.
  - There is an index to the births (giving name, place, year and regiment), that can be seen at the FRC and the PRO.

- There is no index to the marriages in the regimental registers. To find out details of a marriage, you have to know the husband's regiment and a rough date. At the FRC is a list of the marriage registers, arranged by regiment: if your regiment is there, with entries for the right period, ask at the enquiry desk in the FRC to be put in touch with the Overseas Section, which may conduct a search for you.

- Religious registers. Army chaplains' registers of births, baptisms, marriages, deaths and burials abroad, 1796–1880.
  - These are indexed. Unfortunately, the indexes do not give the regiment, simply name, place and date range.
  - The indexes can be seen at the FRC and PRO.

- Civil registers from 1881.
  - From 1881 the religious registers appear to be continued by the Armed Forces returns, 1881–1955, of births, marriages and deaths overseas.
  - From 1956–1965, there are combined service department registers of births and marriages overseas.
  - From 1965, separate service registers were abandoned, and entries were made in the general series of overseas registers.
  - Indexes can be seen at the FRC and PRO.

The indexes can be used to cross refer to each other, and to the usual civil registers: there are often duplicate entries, and sometimes unexplained absences. Thus:

- Alice Abbott, born Bangalore 1885 appears in both the Chaplains' index *and* the Regimental index. The latter gives her father's regiment – the Royal Artillery.
- Mabel Louisa Abbott, born Jersey 1883, appears in the Chaplains' index but not in the Regimental index.
- Amelia Aaron, born Aldershot 1859, appears in the Regimental index (father's regiment, 12th Foot) and also in the civil index – September quarter, registration district Farnham.

Finding a soldier's service record between 1855 and 1882 can be difficult if you do not know his regiment. Even if you already have a birth certificate of your soldier's child from the civil registers, it is worth checking the regimental indexes to see if there is another certificate. You may be able to find the regiment without ordering another copy – although if the duplicate is in the chaplains' registers (and successors) you will need to buy the copy.

Similar armed services registers (from 1881), and war registers (from 1899) exist in the keeping of the General Register Offices of Scotland, Ireland, and Northern Ireland (from 1927). These contain returns for people who were born, or who were normally resident, in Scotland, Ireland and Northern Ireland. We think that these people would also appear in the records of the GRO for England and Wales. See **48** for addresses.

Records for the military while on the Ionian Islands appear to have been kept separately. The General Register Office has registers of births, marriages and deaths, 1818–1864: the index is to a military register, a civil register, and a chaplain's register. It gives names only, and can be seen at the FRC and PRO. See also **4.15**, under Greece.

18a.1.2 Army registers of births, marriages and burials at the PRO

The PRO has a small number of regimental registers of births, baptisms, marriages and burials, of the kind kept by the General Register Office. Some of these are annotated with information on discharge: others have the baptismal entries of the children entered on the same page as the marriage certificate of the parents. The PRO has baptism and marriage registers as listed here.

	Former militia name		
King's Own Yorkshire Light Infantry, 3rd battalion	1st West Yorkshire Militia	1865–1904	WO 68/499
Rifle Brigade, 6th battalion	114th West Meath Militia	1834–1904	WO 68/439
Royal Horse Artillery		1817–1827, 1859–1883 (most are 1860–1877)	WO 69/63–73, WO 69/551–582
Somerset Light Infantry, 3rd and 4th battalions	Somerset Militia	1836–1887, 1892–1903	WO 68/441
West Norfolk Regiment		1863–1908	WO 68/497
West Yorkshire Rifles, 3rd battalion	2nd West Yorkshire Militia	1832–1877	WO 68/499

In addition, there are Army registers of baptisms for Dover castle, 1865–1916 and 1929–1940; Shorncliffe and Hythe, 1878–1939; Buttervant, 1917–1922; and Fermoy, 1920–1921 (WO 156). This series also includes burial registers for the Canterbury garrison, 1808–1811, 1859–1884 and 1957–1958, and baptisms and banns of marriage for Army personnel in Palestine, 1939–1947. The PRO does not currently know the whereabouts of the registers of other garrison churches: we would be glad to hear of any.

The baptism, marriage and burial registers of the Royal Chelsea Hospital, for 1691–1856, are in RG 4/4330–4332, and 4387.

18a.2 Military wills

Officers' wills are likely to be found by following the advice given in **6**. For registers of powers of attorney, see **18a.3.1**.

If a soldier died abroad before 1858 and left assets over a certain amount, grants of probate or administration were issued in the Prerogative Court of Canterbury: see **6**. (Between 1800 and 1858, they are usually indexed in a separate section at the end of each letter in the indexes in PROB 12.)

However, military wills of smaller estates did not have to be proved in court, so there is no record of these unless they have survived among casualty returns in the War Office records: see **18b.4.4** for more details.

18a.3 Army officers: sources for family history

Officers were not supposed to marry before the age of 30, and then only with their colonel's permission. Reports by officers of their marriage were made between 1830 and 1882: some of the marriages date from about 1799. Of course, if the officer or his wife did not survive until 1830, there will be no report.

These reports are in WO 25/3239–3245. They are indexed up to 1851 by maiden name of *wife*, giving place and date of birth and marriage, and witnesses (Miss Fairbrother's index). Miss Fairbrother also indexed the 1829 return of serving officers by wife's maiden name, giving as well date and place of birth, marriage, children's birth, and sometimes death. The 1829 return, in WO 25/780–806, is discussed in **18b.3.2**. There are also certificates of marriage and birth of children, 1755–1908, in WO 42, which is indexed. The various military registers of births, marriages and burials (see **18a.1**) may include references to officers' families, if they followed the regiment.

After 1882, information about the wife should be found in the officer's service record: see **18b.3.3**.

Provision of an authentic baptism certificate was required for commissioned officers, as membership of the established church implied loyalty to the Crown. As a result there are many baptism certificates for Army officers in the War Office records. There are two main caches, for the regular Army, 1755–1908, in WO 42, and for militia officers, 1777–1868, in WO 32/8903–8920 (code 21A). There are indexes to both.

Many officers, when applying for a commission, would give some statement as to their family background. See the Commander-in-Chief's memoranda in WO 31, discussed in more detail at **18b.3.2**.

18a.3.1 Army officers: letters of attorney

Registers of letters of attorney for Army officers exist in several series. Many of these letters were made in favour of the wife or other close relative, or were granted by the probate courts to the widow as executrix.

1755–1783	Registers of letters of attorney	WO 30/1
1756–1827	Registers of letters of attorney	PMG 14/142–164
1759–1816	Entry books of powers of attorney, apparently arranged by date	PMG 14/104–125

1802–1821	Registers of letters of attorney granted by officers' widows	PMG 14/165–167
1811–1814	Alphabetical entry books	PMG 14/126–137
1836–1899	Registers of letters of attorney: includes Ordnance officers from 1858	PMG 51

There is also a series of indexed registers of letters of attorney, 1699–1857, relating to Ordnance (Royal Artillery and Royal Engineers) officers, civilian staff and creditors who expected to receive payments of any kind from the Ordnance Office (WO 54/494–510).

18a.3.2 Pensions to officers' widows and dependants

Other than this, more information is only likely to be found in military records if the officer died leaving his family in want. From 1708 pensions existed for the widows of officers killed on active service; from 1720, pensions were also paid to the children and dependent relatives (usually indigent mothers over 50) in similar cases, out of the Compassionate Fund and the Royal Bounty. These pensions were not an automatic right, and applicants had to prove their need.

Officers' widows' pensions 1713–1920
(See **18a.3.3** for First World War widows' pensions.)

These records can be useful for finding out where the family was settled, as they give place of payment. This may be through the Post Office, with no location. In many cases, it is through a government office in a particular place, such as the I.R. (Inland Revenue) at Athlone, the Comm[t] (Commissariat) at Toronto, the Cust[oms] at Bristol. You should be able to find the officer's death date – the date when the warrant *started*, not when it was granted. You can also find the date of the widow's death.

1808–1920	Ledgers of payments of widows' pensions: these give name, address, other details and where paid.	PMG 11
1755–1908	Application papers for widows' pensions and dependants' allowances: these can include proofs of birth, marriage, death, and wills, etc.	WO 42
1815–1895	Registers of payments.	WO 23/105–123
1815–1892	Lists of widows receiving pensions.	WO 23/88–92
1713–1829	Lists of widows receiving pensions.	WO 24/804–883
1808–1825	Abstracts of applications: there is an index in the Research Enquiries Room	WO 25/3073–3089

1760–1818?	Application papers, as above, of uncertain date, arranged alphabetically.	WO 25/3089–3197
1764–1816	Correspondence relating to widows' pensions: the volumes are internally indexed, and contain details on many widows.	WO 4/1023–1030
1735–1811	Registers of payments.	WO 25/3020–3058
1748–1811	Indexes to pensions.	WO 25/3120–3123

Selected correspondence on widows' pensions is also in WO 43. There is a card index in the Research Enquiries Room, and an online search in PROCAT in WO 43 may identify interesting material for some widows – for example, the widow of army surgeon, Daniel Davies, 18th Foot, who was left to support five deaf and dumb children in the 1850s (WO 43/913).

Compassionate allowances, 1773–1915

These can be detailed, giving the names and birth dates of children.

1812–1915	Ledgers of payments.	PMG 10
1805–1895	Summary of those placed on the Compassionate List.	WO 23/120–123
1858–1894	Registers of those placed on the Compassionate List.	WO 23/114–119
1822–1885	Ledgers of pension payments for the widows of foreign officers.	PMG 6 and PMG 7
1803–1860	Correspondence relating to the Compassionate Fund.	WO 4/521–590
1812–1813	About 2,000 'compassionate papers' – affidavits by the widows and children, in receipt of a compassionate pension, that they received no other government income. In rough alphabetical order. Give details of the officer, often the age of the children, and sometimes the name of the guardian, as well as some indication of county or country of residence (they were sworn before local justices).	WO 25/3110–3114
1773–1812	Registers of compassionate allowances awarded to dependants.	WO 25/3124–3125
1779–1812	Ledgers of payments.	WO 24/771–803

Registers of pensions to the widows of Royal Artillery and Royal Engineers officers, 1833–1837, are in WO 54/195–196, with ledgers of payments, 1836–1875, in PMG 12. For pensions and compassionate allowances to the widows and dependants of commissariat officers, 1814–1834, see WO 61/96–98.

18a.3.3 First World War: pensions to dependants of deceased officers, all services

Widows of men who served in the First World War were able to claim even if their husbands had died many years after 1918. This section covers all armed services: it is placed here because the Army had by far the most casualties.

Pension, etc.	Date	Reference	Information
deceased officers: pensions paid to relatives	1916 April–1920 March	PMG 44/1–7	Name and address of the claimant, rank and name of officer, date of birth and date of payment. Some volumes indexed.
missing officers: pensions to relatives	1915 March–1920 March	PMG 47/1–3	Name and address of relative receiving pension, relationship to missing officer and name and rank of officer, dates of payment.
officers' children: allowances	1916–1920	PMG 46/1–4	Child/children's names; name, rank and regiment of father; record of payments and who collected the money.
officers' widows' pensions	1917 September–1919 July	PMG 45/1–6	Name and address of widow, officer's name, rank and date of birth, date of payments.
officers' widows and dependants: special grants and supplementary allowances	1916–1920	PMG 43/2	Name and address of claimant, rank and name of officer, date of birth, and payment: indexed.
all services, all ranks	1920–1989	PIN 26	See **18c.1.6**.

An eight per cent sample of widows' and dependants' pension case files, for all services, is in PIN 82. It is arranged in alphabetical order of serviceman's name, with his regiment or ship, and cause of death: it is most easily searched on PROCAT.

18a.4 Army other ranks: sources for family history

Before the reforms of the 1850s, other ranks could marry at 26. If their wives were allowed 'on the strength' of the regiment as part of the married establishment, they could live in barracks among the soldiers, and were entitled to draw half-rations free, and quarter-rations for children. Wives married without permission lived in lodgings or in the various shanties that grew up around garrison towns.

When regiments were ordered abroad, only four or six wives per company (of 100 men) were allowed to travel with their men – to act as nurses, cooks and washerwomen for the regiment. The wives were chosen by ballot (practically on the quayside), drawing papers marked 'to go' or 'not to go'. Practically no evidence remains of this.

The Army did not provide for those left behind. If they had no means of subsistence, they had to go back to the soldier's parish of origin, to draw poor relief there. (This is one reason why the Army was interested in the soldier's parish of origin, recorded in the description books: see **18b.4.6**.) You may find some trace of them in the overseers' accounts for the parish, kept in local record offices. With a great deal of hard work you may even be able to track them through the accounts of the parishes they passed through on the way (see **31** on Poor Law records.) Of course, rules were made to be bent, and these ones were: other wives were smuggled aboard ship. Local women were married – or not – and camp followers formed an integral part of the Army's progress. To avoid becoming a camp follower, a soldier's widow would marry another soldier fast.

After the reforms of the late 1850s, married quarters began to be built, and were allotted to the families 'on the strength'. Staff sergeants were now all permitted to marry, as were 50 per cent of other sergeants. Up to 40% of other ranks were allowed to marry, but permission was only granted after seven years' service, two good conduct badges, and savings of £5. Women did not follow the Army on campaign, although they could go if a regiment was ordered to the colonies – to the West Indies, or India. From 1868–1883 marriage rolls, containing information of those wives and children who were on the regimental books, were often included with the muster books in WO 12 and WO 16: it is always worth looking to see if these survive with the musters. (see **18b.4.6**).

There are sometimes references to next-of-kin in the casualty returns and registers of effects (see **18b.4.4**).

18a.4.1. Army other ranks: widows and orphans

Sufficient public concern was raised by the Crimean War for a government supported charity, the Royal Patriotic Fund, to become involved in supporting Army and Navy widows, orphans and other dependants. The Fund presented two reports to Parliament, in 1860 and 1871, listing respectively all the dependants it had helped by removing children from the care of their mother and those whose pleas were rejected (because the man's death had not been caused by the Crimean War). These reports can be seen at the PRO as *Parliamentary Paper* microfiche 66.322–323, and 77.362–363: indexes are available at the PRO. They give the names of wife and children, date of marriage, date of birth of children, place of wife's residence, and what happened to the children.

Other, fuller, records are still held by the Royal Patriotic Fund (address in **48**). These may be transferred to the PRO: check this on PROCAT using 'Royal Patriotic Fund' as the search term.

THE SOLDIER'S DREAM.

Oʜ sad was my heart as for marching we mustered,
  For I thought of the wife I was leaving behind,
And the six hungry mouths round their mother that clustered,
  With bread at high price, and with work hard to find.
On my watch aboard ship, standing sentry ashore,
  By the bivouac fire, still that thought would pursue;
Till I dreamed a glad dream—and was sorry no more—
  'Twas the time of the night when they say dreams are true.

I dreamed that I saw the poor babes I'd forsaken,
  And her whom too soon a sad mother I'd made,
Looking still, as she looked, when that last leave was taken,
  Not knowing from whom to seek counsel or aid.
I heard their shrill cry as they asked her for bread,
  Heard her answer—"The bread of the parish or none!"
Saw them shivering for cold on a blanketless bed,
  And crouched round a hearth whence the last spark was gone.

When sudden, with look like an angel of grace,
  And hands that bore raiment and firing and food,
I saw a kind lady come into the place
  To cheer my sad wife and her clamorous brood.
"Take, eat, and be warm; 'tis the offering of friends,"
  She said; "not the dole on the pauper bestowed;
It comes from the country your husband defends,
  Which to you pays a debt that to him it feels owed.

"His heart will be stouter, his arm will be stronger,
  When he knows that his children are clothed, taught, and fed;
That his wife lives in dread of the workhouse no longer,
  To the shame of the country for which he has bled."
Then I cried in my sleep, "Take the soldier's thanksgiving!"
  When lo! the *réveillé* proclaimed break of day;
And I stood to my arms with a heart free from grieving,
  All fears for my wife and my babes chased away.

Figure 25 Soldiers' families easily became destitute when the Army took no responsibility for them. Private charity grew into a national charity (the Royal Patriotic Fund), and eventually into a state responsibility. (*Punch*, 1854, PRO Library)

There is a selection of over 1,000 personal files on the widows of Army other ranks and naval ratings whose service was between about 1880 and 1914, in PIN 71. This series is searchable online in PROCAT by name (but it does not say whether the man was Army or Navy). It only includes some Boer War widows. However, it is well worth looking in, and really needs some further investigation. The dates given in the list are the date of the man's enlistment and the date the widow's pension stopped. There are also over 5,000 disablement pension files of the same period in PIN 71, arranged the same way.

Another source for the families of British and colonial armed forces who died in the South African War is the 1901 report to Parliament by the Royal Patriotic Fund of widows, children and close dependents supported by the Fund up to 14 February 1901. This can be seen at the PRO in *Parliamentary Paper* microfiche 107.348–349: an indexed hard copy is also available. This report does not give details of service: see **18b.10** to discover more.

18a.4.2 Army other ranks: schools for orphans and other children

The Royal Hibernian Military School was founded in Dublin in 1769, for the children of soldiers on the Irish establishment: in 1924 it merged with the Duke of York's Military School. Unfortunately, enemy bombing in 1940 destroyed most of its records: what survives is a boys' index book (WO 143/27), drawn up in 1863 with retrospective entries from c.1835, and with annotations up to c.1919. This gives name, class, references to petitions and registers now lost, corps, and remarks (e.g. volunteered 16th Foot 5 August 59). A further index, from 1910, is in WO 143/26.

The Royal Military Asylum was founded at Chelsea in 1801, as a boarding school for children of serving or dead soldiers. There was a branch at Southampton, which seems to have existed between 1825 and 1840 (WO 143/61–63). Girls were admitted to the female branch until 1840: this was abolished in 1846. The Royal Military Asylum was renamed the Duke of York's Royal Military School in 1892, and moved to Dover in 1909.

At first, many of the children were not orphans, but most later entrants appear to have lost at least their father and quite frequently both parents. Children appear to have been admitted between the ages of 2 and 10, and were discharged in their mid-teens. Most of the girls not claimed by their parents were apprenticed, often as servants: the boys went into the Army, or were apprenticed if they were not fit for military service.

The boys' admission and discharge registers, 1803–1956, are very informative, although unfortunately they are arranged only by date of admission (WO 143/17–23 and 70). One of the boys' registers, for 1804–1820, is in letter order. The information for the girls (in WO 143/24–25) is fuller. It includes number, name, age, date of admission, from what regiment, rank of father (P, T, S, etc., for private, trooper, sergeant), parents' names and if living, their parish of settlement, when dismissed, and how disposed of (e.g. died, retained by parents while on pass, apprenticed). The boys' admission register gives the same information except parents' names. The discharge registers give more information on apprenticeship, regiment or other fate.

If you find a child at the Royal Military Asylum, try going beyond the admission and discharge registers to see if you can find out more. For example, there are registers of boys' offences, 1852–1879 in WO 143/53–58; an apprenticeship book, 1806–1848 (WO 143/52); correspondence, reports and memoranda from 1805–1917 (WO 143/37–45, with a subject index in WO 143/46); and records of the Normal School, 1847–1872 (WO 143/47–51).

Many other military orphanages were built during the nineteenth century, such as the Royal Victoria Patriotic Asylum, or the Royal Caledonian Asylum. Their records are not in the PRO. However, the Royal Patriotic Fund supported many children through these and other schools or orphanages. For a list of children of Crimean War soldiers and sailors who were supported in this and other ways, see the Royal Patriotic Fund 1860 report to Parliament (*Parliamentary Paper* microfilm 66.322–323: an index exists at the PRO).

18a.5 The Army: sources for family history: bibliography

V Bamfield, *On the Strength: the story of the British Army Wife* (London, 1974)

S Fowler and W Spencer, *Army Records for Family Historians* (PRO, 1998)

N T St John Williams, *Judy O'Grady and the Colonel's Lady: The Army Wife and Camp Follower Since 1660* (Oxford, 1988)

18b

The Army: service records before 1914

◆ ◆ ◆

18b.1 Soldiering before 1660

Before the Civil War, there was no regular standing army in Britain. Although some records of soldiers do exist before 1660, it is extremely unlikely that they will provide any useful genealogical material on individuals.

The most useful are not Army but Militia (local forces) records. Able-bodied men aged between 16 and 60 were liable to perform military service within their counties, and occasionally outside them, in times of need. From the 1540s, the records of musters of this militia were returned to the secretaries of state, and many of these, with some earlier ones from 1522 onwards, are scattered among various series in the PRO. The deputy lieutenants of the counties, however, retained some muster books, and these are now in private collections or county record offices. See Gibson and Dell's *Tudor and Stuart Muster Rolls* for a county-organized analysis and directory of surviving muster rolls.

From the sixteenth century, regiments were raised to meet special requirements and were usually known by the names of colonels who commanded them: there was no central administration. Such few references as there are to individual soldiers should be sought among the State Papers Domestic, State Papers Foreign, and the Exchequer and Audit Office Accounts (AO 1–3): the regimental index in the PRO's *Alphabetical Guide to War Office Records* is a good place to start. Other places to look are:

- for the payment of military wages – Exchequer Issues (E 403) and Exchequer Accounts (E 101);
- for officers' commissions and widows' pensions – the *Calendars of State Papers, Domestic*;
- for oaths of allegiance taken by soldiers going to the Low Countries, 1613–1624 – the licences to pass beyond the seas (E 157).

The establishment of the Army is given in 1640 in SP 41/1. All officers serving in the Civil War and Commonwealth period are listed in Peacock's book *The Army List of Roundheads and Cavaliers*. The Commonwealth did keep a standing army, and there is much documentation about this army in the Commonwealth Exchequer Papers (SP 28).

Individual parliamentary soldiers who were owed arrears of pay after 1649 might be given certificates known as debentures. These certified what they were owed and, secured on property confiscated by Parliament, could be used to purchase such properties, which could then, in turn, be sold to pay off their debts. The Certificates for the Sale of Crown Lands, in E 121, contain thousands of names of officers and men who had served in the parliamentary forces. However, this series is arranged by the county in which the confiscated Crown lands were situated and is not indexed, either by name or regiment; moreover, a particular regiment might be assigned several properties, in more than one county. It only covers England and Wales.

Similar debentures were issued to parliamentary soldiers who had served in Ireland where confiscated lands were to be divided by lot. Fewer than 12,000 were subsequently returned for certificates of possession. Most soldiers did not settle but probably sold them on to their officers. About 7,500 grants were confirmed after 1660. Unfortunately, these debentures, which were held in Dublin, have not survived. Calendars of some grants that were confirmed after 1660, indexed by personal name, are in the *Fifteenth Report* of the Irish Record Commission (1825). The Books of Survey and Distribution, held by the National Archives in Dublin (some counties in print) record the final land settlement. References to troops serving in Ireland (mainly to officers) can also be found in the *Calendars of State Papers, Ireland*.

Records of the Committee for Indemnity (SP 24) which was set up to indemnify parliamentary soldiers and officials from legal liability for acts committed during the civil war, contain many references to individual soldiers. Cases are arranged alphabetically.

Muster rolls for the Scots Army in England in January 1646, unindexed but arranged by regiment and company, are in SP 41/2.

18b.2 The Army, 1660–1914

Before 1914, the Army was a relatively small, professional organization, composed disproportionately of Scots and Irish. (According to the Friends of the PRO, their listing of discharge papers from 1760–1854 has shown relatively few Welshmen.)

The PRO has few personnel records for the late seventeenth century Army, but very large amounts for the Army over the next three centuries. The eighteenth century Army that founded the British Empire changed over time: the Peninsular and Crimean Wars also brought many changes, culminating in the Army reforms of the 1870s and 1880s. The growth of the Empire saw the Army fighting, living and dying on every continent. (There are registers covering the embarkation of troops for foreign service, the roster of regiments serving in Ireland, and regiments stationed in the colonies, in WO 379/13–14, for 1859 to 1914.)

In long wars, a revived militia was called up to afforce the Regular Army (see **18b.5** for more on the militia). On occasion, volunteers swelled the professional troops, particularly during the Napoleonic Wars when invasion was likely, the mid nineteenth century when revolution was feared, and the South African (Boer) War.

18b.3 Army officers before 1914

In this book, 'officer' means a commissioned officer, who held his rank by virtue of a royal commission. The other kind of officer, a non-commissioned officer, held his rank by a warrant instead, and is a senior member of the 'other ranks'.

There are four sorts of commissioned officer. General officers and regimental officers were sometimes called Field Officers – that is, able to take command on a field of battle.

general officers	these coordinated the efforts of the whole army: field marshal, general, lieutenant-general, major-general.
regimental officers	colonel (in command of a regiment), lieutenant-colonel, major.
company officers	captain (in command of a company) and his subalterns, lieutenant, cornet (cavalry), ensign (infantry). In 1871 cornets and ensigns became second lieutenants.
others	paymaster, adjutant, quartermaster, surgeon and chaplain.

There were also many other ranks, such as brigadier-general, colonel-commandant, brigade-major, etc. Officers were graded by seniority, which ruled promotion within the regiment: if an officer was promoted out of sequence, he was given brevet rank, e.g., as a brevet-major. Some officers held two ranks at the same time, the regimental rank, which was higher, and was usually a special appointment, and the army rank, which was the actual rank of his commission.

18b.3.1 Army officers: *Army Lists* and biographical dictionaries

Brief biographies of eminent soldiers may be found in the *Dictionary of National Biography*, and the *British Biographical Archive* (see **1.15**). Hart's unofficial *Hart's Army List* (1839–1915) includes many professional biographical details of eminent and less eminent officers, giving far more information than the official *Army Lists*. It covers both the British Army and the Indian Army. Although the first volume dates from 1839, it contains details of (living) officers' services going back many decades before then. An incomplete set covering 1840–1915 is on open access at the PRO: a full set is included in WO 211. (See Fig. 24, on p. 184.)

Hart's working papers are in the PRO. They include many letters from Army officers between 1838 and 1873, giving details of their service history, correcting errors, and adding to entries. Some include extra material such as extracts from military journals, or from newspapers. These are also in WO 211.

Hart was compiling a biographical dictionary of Army officers when he died: the text of the entries for many officers of senior rank is also in WO 211. Most of the officers covered are great names from the wars with France.

The official *Army Lists* can be used to trace the broad outline of an officer's career. It includes British Army officers and some Indian Army officers. The first official *Army List* was published in 1740; since 1754 they have been published regularly. There are complete record sets, with manuscript amendments, of the annual lists (1754–1879) and the quarterly lists (1879–1900) in WO 65 and WO 66: incomplete sets are on open access. Large reference libraries may also have a set. Manuscript lists of Army officers were kept from 1702–1752 (WO 64); there is an index in the Research Enquiries Room at the PRO.

The *Army List* was arranged in order of regiment, with a name index from 1766 (Engineers and Artillery officers were included in the index only from 1803). From 1879 it included a gradation list of officers – i.e. a list in order of seniority, giving dates of birth and promotions, and, from April 1881, details of service. For later *Army Lists*, see Fowler and Spencer, *Army Records for Family Historians*. The *Army List* did not include militia officers before the mid nineteenth century. For more information on other printed sources for militia officers, see Spencer, *Militia and Volunteer Forces 1757–1945*.

Details of officers granted commissions before 1727 can most easily be traced in Dalton's *English Army Lists and Commission Registers, 1661–1714*, in his *Irish Army Lists, 1661–1685*, and in his *George I's Army, 1714–1727*, all available at the PRO. The *Royal Military Kalendar* has details of officers of field rank (major) upwards. It was compiled in 1820, of officers then alive, so that the service covered goes back well into the eighteenth century.

Announcements of all commissions were made in the *London Gazette* (ZJ 1).

Officers of the Honourable East India Company army, the Indian Army and of British regiments stationed in India are given in the *India List* and the *Indian Army List*: the PRO Library has incomplete sets of these.

18b.3.2 Army officers before 1871

There are many regimental publications of officers' services: it may be worth checking the PRO Library. At first only the regiments kept officers' service records, although the War Office undertook sporadic surveys from 1809. There are joint indexes covering both series (WO 76 and WO 25): one is to names, and the other to regiments.

The main place to look for an officer's service record is in the regimental records of officers' services, in WO 76. These start in 1755, and continue until 1914. Not all regiments are represented, and the records of some were lost. The information kept by the regiments varies a great deal, but it usually gives the ranks held, service details, and some personal particulars – sometimes including names of wives and children.

The War Office conducted five surveys between 1809 and 1872. Officers were supposed to return various pieces of information – but of course not all did.

1809–1810	1st	Arranged alphabetically. Details of military service only.	WO 25/744–748
1828	2nd	Arranged alphabetically. Covers only officers retired or on half pay (and therefore refers to service completed some years before). Age at commission, date of marriage and date of children's birth.	WO 25/749–779
1829	3rd	Arranged by regiment. Covers only serving officers. Age at commission, date of marriage and date of children's birth. *Wives* indexed separately, by maiden name, giving date and place of birth, marriage, children's birth, and sometimes death (Miss Fairbrother's index).	WO 25/780–805
1847	4th	As the 2nd.	WO 25/808–823
1870–1872	5th	Arranged by year of return and then by regiment. Personal details.	WO 25/824–870

Remember, if you cannot find an officer in the index to WO 25 and WO 76, it may be because he slipped through the net: the regimental records may be incomplete, or he may have missed the War Office survey years. Try looking at Hart's papers in WO 211, particularly for officers who served between 1838 and 1875.

Until 1871, most cavalry and infantry officers purchased their commissions: a number of commissions were also granted without purchase. Cadets could attend the Royal Military College (at Great Marlow from 1802, and at Sandhurst from 1812), but attendance at the RMC was not compulsory. Commissions in the Engineers and Artillery were not bought, but granted on merit: cadets had to be trained at the Royal Military Academy at Woolwich: see **18b.3.4**.

Most of the information in commission purchase records is formal, and can be got from the *Army List* or the *London Gazette*. *Hart's Army List* is especially useful as it notes purchased commissions with a small P. There is a more detailed leaflet on sources at the PRO, or on the PRO website. For more information about the purchase system, see the books by Spiers and Bruce. The most fruitful sources are given here.

1704–1858	Indexed Letter Books: correspondence about the purchase and sale of commissions. A good source for details of fees paid. Later volumes can include addresses of officers – either where the regiment was stationed or their own private address.	WO 4/513–520
1780–1874	Original commissions: a small collection only.	WO 43/1059
1793–1870	Commander-in-Chief's Memoranda: applications to purchase and sell commissions. Arranged (usually in monthly bundles) by the date of commission as announced in the *London Gazette* (this date is given in the *Army Lists*). They often contain statements of service, certificates of baptism, and letters of recommendation.	WO 31

In 1871, the old system of purchasing commissions was replaced by promotion based on selection and professional qualification. The holders of commissions at this time were eligible for compensation on their retirement. Registers were drawn up of all officers holding a commission on 1 November 1871, with the dates and estimated value of their commission: later annotations show the date of retirement and the sum granted in compensation. These registers (in WO 74/177–182) do not give personal details.

18b.3.3 Army officers from 1871

The regimental records of service in WO 76 continue until about 1914, and are the first place to look for an officer's service record. (The records of the Royal Garrison Regiment, 1901–1905, are in WO 19.) There are some oddments in WO 25, for officers whose service ended before 1914. Look in the card indexes to WO 25/WO 76. We know that this index is not complete, so if there is no entry in it, you should go on to identify the regiment's records in WO 76 and look anyway. If you do find an unindexed officer, please let us know. If you do not know the regiment, check the *Army List* index first.

For officers who retired before 1914, but who came back to serve in the First World War, look in WO 374. For officers commissioned after 1901, look also in WO 339 and WO 374 as well as WO 76. Unfortunately, the records in WO 76 do not survive for officers who served *after* 1914, as enemy bombing in 1940 destroyed those records.

At the same time, the War Office introduced a new system of keeping personal records, as promotion was now to be by merit. A confidential report on each officer's ability was completed each year by the Commanding Officer of the unit and sent to the Military Secretary, but these were destroyed in the bombing of 1940.

From 1877, examination for a cadetship at the Royal Military College, Sandhurst (by now incorporating the India Military Seminary previously at Addiscombe), or the Royal Military Academy, Woolwich, became the normal route of entry. Details of examination results are in CSC 10. If the exam was failed, another route in would be to get a commission in the Militia, and then sit the Civil Service Exam: the exam results for this are also in CSC 10. The papers

1871–1891	Original applications for compensation (for abolition of sale of commissions) from officers of the British and Indian establishment, with certificates of service attached, related correspondence, and memoranda as to sums awarded.	WO 74/1–176 Indexed (by regiment) in WO 74/177–182
1803–1914	Original submissions and entry books of submissions to the Sovereign of recommendations for staff and senior appointments, rewards for meritorious service, and for commissions and appointments. Block submissions only after c.1900.	WO 103

Figure 26 Officers missing from the records: Frederick Guthrie Tait's photograph was chosen from those registered for copyright, as that of a typical officer of the Boer War period. His name did not appear in the WO 25/WO 76 index – a common problem with Boer War officers, but one which can be surmounted by using other sources.

The *Army List* gives Tait as a lieutenant in the 2nd battalion Black Watch from 1894, having transferred from the Leinster Regiment, which he joined from the Royal Military College in 1890. He was seconded to the Army Staff to be Superintendent of Gymnasia in Scotland. In 1900, he disappeared from the *Army List*.

The GRO Index to Boer War deaths (**4.14**) shows he was killed on 7th February 1900. The *Last Post* (**18b.10**) gave much extra information. It reported

that Tait survived a severe wound at Magersfontein, only to be wounded at Koodoosberg, uttering the last words *They have got me this time*. He was described as a famous amateur golfer, and the son of P G Tait – who had been named on the photograph copyright form as Professor of Natural Philosophy at Edinburgh.

An internet search revealed that his father is still famous, as well as the touching details that the two used to play golf at St Andrews, and that Peter Guthrie Tait (who looked like a typical absent-minded professor) wrote the classic paper on the trajectory of golf balls, while the more obviously athletic Freddy became Amateur Champion.

Freddy's photograph was registered for copyright after his death, perhaps as part of an appeal to raise money for a ward at the St Andrews Cottage Hospital. *The Times* reported that his father, much affected by Freddy's death, died 18 months later, and also that a memorial ward was opened in 1902, with money from 145 golf clubs and a large circle of friends. (Local papers would give much more detail.)

I then recalled that the WO 25/WO 76 index is known to be incomplete. I looked in the WO 76 list for the 2nd battalion, Black Watch – but the only register for the right date was for the 1st battalion. I looked at it just in case – and there he was! There were a few more pieces of information – height, birth date, army qualifications in gymnastics, musketry and range finding, father's address, and marital status – single. The personal material was not mentioned at all.

Frederick Guthrie Tait is now named in the WO 25/WO 76 index. And if your officer is not, try looking in WO 76 anyway. (PRO, COPY 1/446) in CSC 10 are more interesting than they sound: they often give details of what a likely career would be. The two other sources that might be worth investigating are shown in the table on p. 203.

18b.3.4 Officers of the Royal Engineers and Royal Artillery

Commissions in the Royal Engineers and Royal Artillery were granted to those men who had been selected to attend (and successfully passed) a course of instruction at the Royal Military Academy at Woolwich. Royal Artillery and Royal Engineers officers were the responsibility of the Board of Ordnance until 1855, when they were transferred to the War Office: before 1855, there are separate and extensive records for them. Only the most obvious have been described here: have a look through the WO 54 list for others. After 1855, look in the various series for commissioned officers described above.

1670–1855	RA	RE	Original warrants and patents of appointment	WO 54/939–945
1743–1852 with gaps	RA	RE	Commission books	WO 54/237–247
1727–1751	RA	–	Artillery officers' service records	WO 54/684
1751–1771	RA	–	Artillery officers' service records: these seem to be missing	
1771–1914	RA	–	Artillery officers' service records	WO 76
1786–1850	–	RE	Returns of Engineers officers	WO 54/248–259
1796–1922	–	RE	Engineers officers' service records	WO 25/3913–3920

For Royal Artillery officers, check the *List of Officers of the Royal Regiment of Artillery, 1716–June 1914.* Hart's personal copy of John Kane's *List of Officers of the Royal Regiment of Artillery as they stood in 1763, with a continuation to the present time [1805]* has his own annotations up to 1839: it is in WO 211/69. You could also try a speculative search in WO 18, for an officer serving between (or before) 1770 and 1820. This series consists of bound volumes of original warrants for payments on various accounts (cadets, pensions, recruiting, hospitals and effects of deceased men), together with the original receipts, certificates of existence, letters petitioning for allowance, etc., from the individuals concerned. They are arranged only by year, but if you have time a trawl may be profitable.

For Royal Engineers officers, consult the *Roll of Officers of the Corps of Royal Engineers from 1660 to 1898.*

A search in WO 54 should turn up many items of interest, such as the Royal Artillery Married Society register of officers and widows, 1788–1816 (WO 54/312).

18b.3.5 Non-regimental Army officers

Not all officers were regimental officers. For other officers see:

Staff	1792–1830	pay index	WO 25/695–699
	1802–1870	lists of staff officers, some with addresses	WO 25/700–702
	1782–1854	general returns of staff in British and foreign stations	WO 25/703–743
Commissariat	1798–1842	general returns of service	WO 61/1–2
Commissariat and Transport	1843–1889	register	WO 61/5–6
War Office		senior staff	*Army Lists*
	1809–1819	Registry of officers, clerks etc of the War Office	WO 381/4
	1852–1857	War Office establishments	WO 381/10

18b.3.6 Officers: half-pay and pension records before 1914

Before 1871 there was no general entitlement to a retirement pension; an officer would either move off the active list onto half pay, or would sell his commission. Half-pay officers are included in the *Army List*, but sometimes do not appear in the index. Records of half pay do not contain much genealogical information. The most useful are probably the ledgers of payment, 1737–1921, in PMG 4. These give date of death or date of sale of the commission (which ended entitlement to half pay): from 1837 they also give addresses. Later ledgers give date of birth as well. From 1737 to 1841, the ledgers are arranged by regiment and are unindexed: from 1841 they are in one alphabetical sequence of names.

Pensions were available for wounded officers from 1812. Registers of such pensioners, 1812–1892, are in WO 23/83–92; correspondence on such claims, 1812–1855, can be found in WO 4/469–493. Further correspondence, 1809–1857, can be found in WO 43: there is a card index to this. Actual records of payments are in PMG 9 (including First World War payments) and PMG 12.

18b.4 Army other ranks before 1914

In the Army, the 'other ranks' were the privates (infantry) and troopers (cavalry), trumpeters and drummers, supervised by corporals and sergeants who were non-commissioned officers promoted from the ranks: specialist regiments and corps used different names.

The information kept on each soldier reappears in different permutations in many different types of document (even so, this is only a fraction of the original documentation). This basic personal information you may be able to piece together includes name, age, trade on enlistment, place of enlistment, place of birth, physical description, state of health and date of death or discharge. Some records contain information on wife, children or other next of kin. Parents are not recorded as a matter of course, unless as next of kin.

Surviving Army records on other ranks before 1914 are of four kinds:

Becoming a soldier	• Joining up (attestation) papers – surviving ones are filed with discharge papers. Many do not survive.	**18b.4.2.1–2**
	• Description books (includes place of birth)	**18b.4.6**
Being a soldier	• Regimental muster books and regimental pay lists – these only survive until 1897. – These provide a fairly complete guide to a soldier's Army career from enlistment, through movements with the regiment throughout the world, to discharge. – Each muster book and pay list covers a short space of time. It can take a long time to collect information. Try discharge papers unless you know your soldier died in service or deserted.	**18b.4.6**
Leaving the Army	• Discharge papers, for soldiers who survived their service. – This is the place we recommend to start your search, unless you know your soldier died in service or deserted.	**18b.4.2.1–2**
	• Casualty returns, for soldiers who died or deserted.	**18b.4.4**
Drawing a pension	• Pension records. • Payment registers.	**18b.4.2.1–4** **18b.4.2.4**

We usually recommend researchers to start looking for discharge to pension papers (if they know their soldier survived), as this can be the quickest way to find accumulated information. The discharge papers have been the focus of enormously valuable indexing projects by the Friends of the PRO, which have added greatly to our knowledge of Army pensions.

If, however, you are looking for a trooper or NCO of the Household Cavalry (Royal Horse Guards and Life Guards) between 1799 and 1920, look first at the full service records in WO 400 (due into the PRO by late 2002). If you are looking for a sapper or miner before 1856, go to **18b.4.8**. Similar records for the five Foot Guards regiments are still kept at the Guards Regimental HQ (address in **48**).

18b.4.1 An overview of Army pensions for other ranks, to 1913

Before 1806, enlistment was technically for life – but only the soldier made this commitment. The Army authorities could discharge him at any point. Many fit soldiers were discharged from their regiments at the end of a war, and sent to serve in the 'invalid' or garrison battalions, before being eventually discharged as 'worn out'. Other soldiers were discharged direct from the line regiments of the 'fighting' army as 'worn out' (and therefore entitled to a pension). These worn-out pensioners could be recalled at any time to serve, usually in an invalid or garrison battalion – but even in a line regiment if they were fit enough. If medical evidence was not produced as to why they could not serve, the pension was stopped. The pension rate was 5d a day. Sergeants who had over 20 years' service and a good record qualified for 1s a day: to receive this they had to have a letter from the king (and were thus known as 'lettermen'). You may find records of both discharges (from the line regiment and later from the garrison/invalid force) in WO 97.

Invalid and garrison battalions have muster books and pay lists in the usual series: see **18b.4.6**. The garrisons tended to be at coastal forts or in Ireland or the Channel Islands. The 'invalids' were subject to recall into the fighting Army at any time (subject to a medical examination). Invalid battalions were sent to Australia to police the convicts and guard the colony. Soldiers could continue to serve in invalid or garrison forces for up to another 20 or 30 years before they were actually discharged to pension as 'worn out', to make way for a new tranche of 'invalids' at the end of another war.

Soldiers who enlisted under the liberal 1806 regulations were entitled to discharge after 21 years' service (25 years for Cavalry), with a pension of 1s a day plus an extra ½d a day for each year's service after that. After 1817, soldiers could also take a reduced pension at or after 14 years' service. Soldiers wounded or maimed in the course of duty also qualified for pension. Relatively few served their full term of 21 years, and even fewer continued on for the further five years needed to claim the pension equivalent to full pay.

However, according to a War Office report by Charles Babbage in 1832, very many men were still being discharged as 'worn out' before completing their 21 years' service. Babbage presented two opposing explanations for this: either, the severity of Colonial Service rendered soldiers useless, or, commanding officers thought younger men made a regiment look smarter (WO 43/610, f. 90). Babbage thought it was the latter.

For most of the nineteenth century, most soldiers who did not die through disease, accident, or war, were discharged before or by the age of 41. Many of these received a pension. In the 1840s, according to the War Office, there were about 73,000 Army pensioners living in the UK, nearly half of them under 55 and now recovered from the illness or disability that had earned them the pension.

What does all this mean for anyone researching a soldier?

- It is well worth looking among the records of men discharged to pension. Although only a minority earned the full pension after 21 years or more service, many soldiers received a smaller pension.

- If you find an Army pensioner in the censuses, with his age, you can make a rough estimate as to his likely years of service. Most soldiers were recruited between the ages of 18 and 25, with a very few enlisting up to the age of 30: the average age of men completing 21 years' service was 41. With likely start and end dates, you can try the muster lists and pay books.
- If you know the rate of pension, you can make an estimate as to the length of service that earned it.
- Service at Waterloo counted as two years' service.
- Two years' service in the East and West Indies counted as three years for soldiers enlisted between 1806 and 1818 (but not after).
- You may need to look later than you expected, for a final discharge from a garrison regiment or invalid battalion, or from the reserve.

The pension system was revised slightly by the Miller report of 1875. After 1883, soldiers discharged after completing one of the new limited engagements, or who had bought their discharge, were also eligible for a pension. A further round of reforms took place in 1900–1905. A snapshot of the situation in the late 1870s is given here.

Permanent pensions (as at late 1870s)		
	European: daily rates	**Black (native soldiers in the colonies): daily rates**
After 21 years' service	8d–1s	6d
NCOs received extra, for every year of service as an NCO. Aggregated pensions not to exceed	3s	1s 4d
On reduction of the Army Soldiers discharged after 14 years' service.	As above: deduct ½d for each year short of 21 years.	As above: deduct ½d for each year short of 21 years.
On premature discharge Soldiers discharged after 18 years' service (on regiment being posted abroad, or if considered to be comparatively inefficient).	As above: deduct ½d for each year short of 21 years.	As above: deduct ½d for each year short of 21 years.
Wounds or injuries* Totally incapable of earning livelihood. Incapable of service. Blindness – total. Blindness – 1 eye – allowance added to discharge pension. * Could be applied for retrospectively.	1s 6d–3s 6d 6d–3s 1s–2s 6d 6d	9d–1s 6d–10d 9d–1s 6d

Temporary pensions		
	European: daily rates	**Black: daily rates**
Unfitness caused in or by Army service Less than 7 years' service. 7–18 years' service. If still disabled at the end of the period, the pension could be extended or made permanent. In some cases, a gratuity of £30 could be made instead: it was only to be paid when the soldier was settled in his intended place of residence.	6d, for no more than 18 months. An extra 3 months pension for each year of service.	1½d, for no more than 2 years. An extra 4 months pension for each year of service.
Good conduct and Royal Bounty payments		
Good conduct pay	The amount of good conduct pay received daily at the time of discharge (or at the time of promotion to NCO) could be added to the pension. Not added to pensions for wounds, injuries or blindness.	
Royal Bounty For gallant conduct. For extreme suffering from wounds.	European: 6d n/a	Black: 3d 3d

Men who did not have the requisite number of years or wounds to qualify for a pension could apply to the monarch via the War Office for a pension: these letters are in WO 246.

Pensions could be forfeited for:

● felony, gross fraud or gross misconduct;
● failing to serve in a regiment of the line or in support of the civil power when called upon.

Pensioners who also received poor relief had their pension paid to the parish: see **31**.

18b.4.2 Army other ranks: Chelsea and Kilmainham pensions

Before (and after) the founding of the Royal Hospitals, disabled ex-soldiers were often granted places as almsmen in royal church foundations: petitions for such places, often giving details of service and wounds, for 1660 to 1751, are in SO 5/31.

The main system of Army pensions to other ranks was operated by the Royal Hospital Chelsea (London, founded 1681) and the Royal Hospital, Kilmainham (near Dublin, founded 1679). Chelsea and Kilmainham supported both in-pensioners, who lived in the hospitals, and a much larger number of out-pensioners. The out-pensioners remained under military discipline to some extent: they formed a reserve pool to be called on in case of wartime emergency or domestic crisis.

Soldiers in the British Army on what was called the British Army Establishment received pension payments from the Royal Hospital Chelsea. Some British regiments were on the Irish Establishment (this means paid for by money from the Irish Exchequer, *not* Irish regiments) and received pensions from the Royal Hospital Kilmainham before 1823. The distinction between the two is confusing, as regiments moved on and off the Irish Establishment. After 1823, Chelsea paid all pensions, but Kilmainham continued to provide the medical examinations for soldiers discharged in Ireland.

If you cannot find a soldier in the pension records, you really do need to know which regiment he served in, as most records before 1873 are arranged in order of regiment. If you do not know the regiment, turn to **18b.4.7**. Pension records, by their very nature, refer to service often begun many years before the date of the pension award. Do remember this when looking at the covering dates given below – they do *not* refer to the dates of service, but to date of *discharge*.

See also **18b.4.2.4**, for records relating to the actual payment of the pension to your soldier, which can provide information on his life after leaving the Army.

18b.4.2.1 Army other ranks: records of discharge to Chelsea pension, 1760–1913, and other discharges

The PRO holds an enormous number of Chelsea records. Current advice (if you are looking for a soldier who you know survived his service) is to start with WO 97. If you have no luck, and you are looking for

- a soldier who joined about 1880, try a surname search in PIN 71 on PROCAT;
- a soldier discharged between 1823 and 1913, try trawling through WO 117;
- a soldier discharged before 1823, try the Kilmainham pensions in WO 118 and WO 119;
- a soldier discharged between 1787 and 1813, try a surname search in WO 121 on PROCAT.

If you still cannot find anything, then it may be worth trying the hinterland of Chelsea records described in the table on p. 214.

Start with the Royal Hospital Chelsea Soldiers' Documents in WO 97, dated 1760–1913. These comprise the attestation and/or discharge papers of soldiers discharged to pension (and of some who were rejected for pension).

From 1883 to 1913, this series also includes the discharge papers of men discharged after the new short service of seven years in the regular Army, followed by five years in the reserve. The discharge documents will appear after the five years in the reserve: there will not be any if the men died in that period.

Figure 27 Thomas Roberts was discharged in 1802 because of a reduction in the size of his regiment – the war with France was (temporarily) over. Although this certificate is not in very good condition, it does give enough clues to carry on research in other sources. (PRO, WO 97/204)

Similarly, if they were called up in 1914 while in the reserve, their papers will have been moved into WO 364, where they may not survive (see **18c.1.5**). However, it's fair to say that after 1883 most soldiers are in WO 97, *if they survived their service.* Some have even been found for men who died in service.

The Soldiers' Documents in WO 97 give age, birthplace, trade or occupation on enlistment, a record of service including any decorations, the reason for discharge to pension, and, in some cases, place of residence after discharge and date of death. From 1883, they also contain details of next of kin, marriage and children.

They are arranged as shown here.

Date of discharge	Arrangement	
1760–1854	By regiment: searchable online in PROCAT. You can search by name, regiment, and birthplace. The dates given are either of enlistment, or of discharge, or of both: you will need to check the document itself to find out which. *Does not include regiments 'on the Irish establishment' before 1823.*	WO 97/1–1271
1855–1872	By regiment. Not searchable online by name. If you do not know the regiment, there is a privately-owned index, which you can pay to have consulted. Ask at the Microfilm Reading Room desk for Gibson and Hampson, *Specialist Indexes for Family Historians* for details.	WO 97/1272–1721
1873–1882	By cavalry, artillery, infantry or corps. Not searchable online by name.	WO 97/1722–2171
1843–1899	By name: misfiled papers. Not searchable online by name, as description is by range of surnames. See below for more detail.	WO 97/6355–6383
1883–1900	By name. Not searchable online by name, as description is by range of surnames.	WO 97/2172–4231
1900–1913	By name. Not searchable online by name, as description is by range of surnames.	WO 97/4232–6322
1900–1913	By name: misfiled papers. Not searchable online by name, as description is by range of surnames.	WO 97/6323–6354

The misfiled papers for 1843–1899 in WO 97/6355–6383 are not all misfiles, but the papers of soldiers who joined up under an assumed name, and later admitted to their real name. Their records were altered to give the real name, which is what they are now filed by. Some are misfiles, however, as are the later ones from 1900–1913.

There are other, similar, records, which may be worth checking if you find nothing in WO 97 – or even if you do find material there!

- For soldiers who joined up about 1880 onwards, try a *surname* search on PROCAT in PIN 71, which includes over 6,000 detailed disability pension and widows' pension files. The list of this series has its quirks, but if you find something you will find a lot – including the papers not in WO 97. Don't be put off if you find a suitable one but it is for a widow, and you know the soldier was discharged: the widow could be applying years after her husband left the Army for the continuation of her now-dead husband's disability pension. The widows' pensions are listed by widow's name only, with no indication as to husband's name or service (naval ratings are also included). The date range given against each description runs from date of enlistment to the date the pension ceased.
- For 1823–1913, try the registers of pensions paid for length of service in WO 117 for 1823–1913. They are in date order, and then by Chelsea number (given in WO 97): even without the number, you can make a guess as to date of discharge, and then trawl through the registers. From 1857 they give regiment, rank, age, years of service, rate of pension, details of foreign service, regimental surgeon's report, character reference, cause of any disability, place of birth, trade, height and physical description. From 1874 you may also find intended place of residence, date of discharge and number of good conduct badges. From 1903 you will also find date of enlistment, and from 1905, details of medals.
- For Kilmainham pensions before 1823, see **18b.4.2.2**.
- For 1787–1813, try the Discharge Documents of Pensioners 1787–1813 in WO 121/1–136: these are searchable online by name in PROCAT. There are approximately 20,000 certificates of soldiers awarded pensions. (The Friends of the PRO estimate that over half are also in WO 97: and that these papers are more informative.)

Further material, shown here, also exists.

1782–1833	Discharge documents, mostly of men previously discharged to pension, who have come back for garrison duty, and are being discharged again. Also includes petitions of men whose pensions have been stopped, asking successfully for restoration of pension.	WO 121/137–222
1735–1868	Correspondence on out-pensions.	WO 246/97–101
1816–1817	Discharge Documents of Pensioners, Foreigners' Regiments.	WO 122
1838–1896	Deferred pension records.	WO 131

1715–1882	Disability pensions, arranged by date of admission to pension.	WO 116/1–124, 252
1882–1913	Disability pensions, arranged by date of admission to pension.	WO 116/186–251
1877–1914	Personal files on over 5,000 disabled soldiers and naval ratings, who served between 1877 and 1914 and received disability pensions; this is searchable on PROCAT by name (but it does not say whether the man was Army or Navy). The dates given are the date of the man's enlistment and the date the pension stopped. Includes medical records, accounts of how injuries were incurred, and the man's own account of the incident, and conduct sheets. These conduct sheets give place of birth, age, names of parents and siblings, religion, physical attributes, marital and parental status.	PIN 71

Disability pension records exist from 1715 to 1914 (shown here), although only those of the last 50 years are easy to find.

You could also try the Chelsea Regimental Registers, 1715–1857, in WO 120, although these are really about ex-soldiers, in receipt of a pension, who were liable to be called back to serve. They give a brief description, age, place of birth, particulars of service and reason of discharge, for the period c.1715–1843. For 1843 to 1857, they give only the date of award, rate of pension and the district pay office where the pension was paid. From about 1812 the dates of death have been added, the last in 1877. There is a partial index for 1806–1838, available on request in the Microfilm Reading Room.

There are other possibilities as well. From 1810 soldiers were able to purchase their discharge: this gave good men the chance to leave, as well as those the regiment wished to be rid of. Men with good conduct awards (medals or pay) were entitled to discounts on the purchase of their discharge. These discharges were as shown here.

1817–1829	By purchase	WO 25/3845–3847
1830–1838	By own request	WO 25/3848–3849
1830–1856	With modified pension	WO 25/3850
1838–1855	Free or free deferred pension	WO 25/3851–3858
1856–1861	Free permanent pension	WO 25/3859–3861
1861–1870	Free permanent pension, modified/deferred pension, or purchase	WO 25/3863–3868
1852–1870	First period, incorrigible, ignominy, penal servitude, or 21 years with militia	WO 25/3869–3878

1856–1857	Regiment under reduction	WO 25/3879–3882
1866–1870	Limited service act	WO 25/3883–3893
1863–1878	On return from India (at the Royal Victoria Hospital, Netley)	WO 12/13077–13105
1871–1884	General register	WO 121/223–238
1882–1883	Gosport discharge depot musters: men returning from overseas	WO 16/2284
1883–1888	Gosport discharge depot musters: men returning from overseas Index available	WO 16/2888–2916
1884–1887	Without pension (Gives address to which discharged)	WO 121/239–257

18b.4.2.2 Army other ranks: records of discharge to Kilmainham pension, 1706–1822, and at Kilmainham, 1823–1863

The Royal Hospital Kilmainham dealt with pensions for regiments on the Irish Army Establishment from 1679 until 1800, when the British and Irish Army Establishments were united in principle, if not in practice. Regiments seem to have been placed on the Irish Establishment when they were sent to Ireland: some of them seem to have remained on it even if they were then sent off to America or elsewhere. The Irish Establishment also included many Irish regular and militia regiments. Kilmainham continued to issue and pay pensions until 24 December 1822, when all payments of pensions were taken over by Chelsea (by the statute 7 George IV c. 16). However, after 1822 soldiers discharged in Ireland had to be examined at Kilmainham until at least 1863, and any recommendation (including refusals of pension) was forwarded to Chelsea. The related discharge certificates of soldiers who were granted or refused pensions were also sent, and are filed in WO 97.

The earliest record of Kilmainham pensions is a survey conducted in 1744 of all pensioners thought to be still alive (some are marked as dead): the earliest grant seems to be about 1706 (WO 118/45). All the men in this register seem to be from or settled in Ireland, but the regiments are from across the British Isles. Later registers show that many of the men are neither from nor settled in Ireland, but were discharged while serving in Ireland.

You need to access these records by using the indexes, which cross-refer to three series: the brief admission books (by page); the admission registers (by number) and the certificates (by the same number). The indexes are actually alphabets, grouping soldiers by first letter of surname.

		In	Indexed by
Admission Books (brief details only)	1759–1809 1809–1816 1816–1819	WO 118/36 WO 118/46 WO 118/38	WO 118/39 WO 118/40 WO 118/41
Admission Registers (fuller data)	Series A 1807–1819 Series B 1819–1822	WO 118/2–12 WO 118/42–43	WO 118/39–41 WO 118/44
Certificates (other data)	Series A Series B Series GB	WO 119/7–55 WO 119/56–66 WO 119/67–69	WO 118/39–41 WO 118/44

Each type of document can give different information, so it is worth checking all of them. Other registers record alterations to pensions in 1807, when Kilmainham pension rates were made equivalent to Chelsea rates in 1806. It seems that this was done in two tranches. Pensioners apparently resident in Ireland in 1807 are recorded in WO 118/1 and 2 (up to entry 2127), with the original A certificates in WO 119/1–8. Pensioners resident in Great Britain (not Ireland) are recorded in WO 118/35, with the related original GB certificates in WO 119/67–69.

For soldiers with Kilmainham pensions, but living in British colonies, who were transferred to Chelsea between 1819 and 1822, see WO 118/13 and WO 119/70.

Soldiers discharged in Ireland after 1822 continued to have entry to pension administered by the Kilmainham board. Medical examinations took place there every month, and certificates recording the Kilmainham decision on acceptance or rejection of the claim to pension were sent on to Chelsea, where they will be found in WO 97. These examinations are recorded for 1823–1863 in WO 118/15–34: it is not clear if they stopped then, or if the paperwork no longer survives. Existing pensioners were re-examined in 1822. The information given includes name, regiment, residence, service details, birthplace, trade, description and conduct, as well as fairly detailed medical notes.

18b.4.2.3 Army other ranks: Chelsea and Kilmainham in-pensioners

In-pensioners had to give up claims to out-pension rates, and take a more modest pension plus accommodation at Chelsea or Kilmainham. If they wished, they could move out of the hospital and back onto the out-pension. Out-pension records tend to be more detailed, so you need to look at both.

Kilmainham records are rather sparse: there are two registers of in-pensioners covering 1839–1922 in WO 118/47–48, and giving details of previous admission to out-pension. Pensioners were transferred from Kilmainham to Chelsea in 1929. Chelsea records are much fuller. The main collection of muster rolls (1702–1865), and admission books and rolls (1778–1917) are in WO 23, with separate indexes of admissions for 1837–1872 and for 1858–1933 in WO 23/146 and 173 respectively. The report of the 1894 Belper Committee into Chelsea and

Kilmainham contains minutes of evidence from in-pensioners and a list of inmates. The evidence is very interesting, showing how men were forced to part from their wives, often leaving them destitute. In addition, there are the burial, marriage and baptism registers of the Chelsea Hospital for 1691–1856 in RG 4/4330–5332 and 4387. For later records, see **18c.2**.

18b.4.2.4 Army other ranks: records of Army pensioners

Army pensioners formed a significant proportion of the population. In 1894, there were just over 74,000 Army pensioners in the UK, with another 8,000 living abroad: over half of them were under 55. This is remarkably similar to the number in the 1840s, when there were about 73,000 Army pensioners living in the UK, nearly half of them under 55 and now recovered from the illness or disability that had earned them the pension. However, the greatest number of pensioners occurred in the late 1820s and 1830s, when men who had fought in the (first) Great War – against France – were coming out of the Army and into the pension lists. The needs of Empire kept the figures high after that.

	No. of out-pensioners in the UK
1782	11,907
1806	21,689
1816	39,217
1828	85,515
1840s	73,000
1894	74,000

Much encouragement was given to Army pensioners to emigrate to the colonies in the early part of the nineteenth century: this applied especially to those discharged in that or a relatively close colony. Pensioners were not awarded land after 1831, but they were able to receive their commuted (lump-sum) pension in the colony, and got part of it in advance to kit out themselves and their families for the journey. (See WO 247/79 for more information directed at would-be emigrants: this includes at the back a list of commuted pensioners residing in Canada in 1839, to whom Chelsea had agreed to give some extra assistance.)

Before 1842, pensioners who lived more than 25 miles from London, but still in England, Scotland and Wales, received their pension from the local excise man, from locally raised excise duties. In Ireland, the postmaster paid out the pensions. Pensioners living within 25 miles of Chelsea were paid at Chelsea. Records of the excise and postmaster payments from before 1842 do not seem to have survived. (For details of the payment system, see WO 26/40, pp. 157–179.)

For 1842 to 1883, out-pensions were paid through district pension offices, including many overseas offices. These records are arranged by place of the pension office, which can be very useful if you know only the area or country in which the man, or his dependents, resided, and not his regiment (WO 22, and PMG 8 for payments made in Hanover). There are separate registers of men admitted to pension from colonial regiments, 1817–1903, who did not have to appear in person. In many of these cases, details of service and birthplace are given (WO 23/147–160). Some of these entries relate to men from the British Army who retired while their regiment was overseas, and who were given permission to receive their pension there. After this, pensions were paid through the Post Office.

The main series of service records of those soldiers who were discharged to pension are described in **18b.4.2.1**. There are many other records from Chelsea Hospital, which can be very useful. In particular, the Chelsea registers etc., 1702–1917 (WO 23), contain a vast amount of information. The series includes:

- pension claims from soldiers in colonial regiments, 1836–1903;
- East India Company Army pensioners, 1814–1875;
- Chelsea registers, 1805–1895, of pensioners by regiment (as in WO 120);
- pensions for the Victoria Cross, wounds or other merit.

18b.4.3 Army war dead, before 1914

Nominal rolls of the dead were kept for many of the campaigns fought during the second half of the nineteenth century.

China	1857–1858	WO 32/8221, 8224, 8227
	1860	WO 32/8230, 8233, 8234
New Zealand	1860	WO 32/8255
	1863–1864	WO 32/8263–8268, 8271, 8276–8280
South Africa	1878–1881	WO 25/3474, 7770, 7706–7708, 7727, 7819
Egypt	1882,1884	WO 25/3473
Sudan	1884–1885	WO 25/3473, 6123, 6125–6126, 8382
Burma	1888	WO 25/3473
Sierra Leone	1898	WO 32/7630–7631
South Africa	1899–1902	WO 108/89–91, 338
China	1915	WO 32/4996B

Some of these have been published: check the bibliography. These rolls do not include the normal occurrences of death in peacetime or outside the war zone.

18b.4.4 Army other ranks before 1914: soldiers who died

Each regiment made regular returns of its casualties, where the usual round of one or two deaths from sickness is suddenly broken by long lists of men killed in action. If you know your soldier's regiment, try the casualty returns. The main collection of monthly and quarterly regimental casualty returns covers 1809–c.1875, with a few entries and annotations in the indexes continuing up to 1910 (WO 25/1359–2410, 3251–3260, indexed in WO 25/2411–2755, 3261–3471). There is also a series of entry books of casualties, 1797–1817, from the Muster Master General's Office (WO 25/1196–1358).

These can provide quite a lot of personal information. Despite their title, the casualty returns refer to absences, desertions and discharges, not just to the dead and wounded. The information given is name, rank, place of birth, trade at enlistment, the date, place and nature of the casualty, any debts or credits, and the next of kin or legatee. Wills, inventories of effects, letters from relatives, and accounts have also been found, but *very* infrequently.

If a soldier died in service, it will also be recorded in the regimental muster books and pay lists. It can be difficult to find records of soldiers who died in service after 1898, when the muster books and pay lists no longer survive. For married men after 1898, it may be easiest to look at the over 1,000 widows' pension records in PIN 71, as widows' pensions became available to all other ranks' widows on the married roll in 1903. However, before this widows and children were apparently dealt with by the Royal Patriotic Fund. This body presented Parliament with three detailed reports on aid given to widows and orphans of the Crimean War, and of the South African War: see **18a.4.1**. Records of *some* dead soldiers have been found in WO 97, so it may be worth looking there on the off-chance.

If you do not know the regiment, try the records relating to payments to next of kin of dead soldiers. There are long gaps in these records but they are arranged alphabetically and are easy to use.

1810–1822	Registers of authorities to deal with the effects (possessions) of dead soldiers. Give name, regiment, period of death, amount of effects and credits, date of order to agent, agent's name, and name and address of person applying (usually next of kin).	WO 25/2966–2971
1830	Index of deceased soldiers' effects: gives the regiment.	WO 25/2974
1830–1844	Register of deceased soldiers' effects and credits: gives the regiment.	WO 25/2975
1862–1881	Record books of deceased soldiers' effects.	WO 25/3476–3490, indexed by WO 25/3491–3501

1882–1899	Do not appear to survive.	
1900–1913	Records of deceased soldiers' effects.	National Army Museum

18b.4.5 Army other ranks before 1914: deserters

If a soldier deserted, it will be recorded in the regimental muster books and pay lists: see **18b.4.6**. It can be difficult to find records of soldiers who died in service after 1898, when the muster books and pay lists no longer survive. However, information on deserters was forwarded to the Army authorities by means of the casualty returns, 1809–1910 (see **18b.4.4**).

Deserting		
1811–1852	Registers of deserters, giving descriptions, date and place of enlistment and desertion, and outcome. • 1811–1827 by cavalry, infantry and militia (militia 1811–1820). • 1827–1852 by regiment.	WO 25/2906 –2934
1828–1845	Details of deserters, giving name, parish and county of birth, regiment, date and place of desertion, a physical description and other relevant information, were published in the police newspapers *Hue and Cry* and the *Police Gazette*.	HO 75/1 –18
Capture/surrender		
1689–1830	An incomplete card index (by deserters, county of capture and regiment) to captured deserters. Compiled from bounty certificates of rewards (paid out of locally-collected taxes) to the informant. • Rewards paid out in Bedfordshire, Berkshire, Buckinghamshire, Cambridgeshire and Cheshire. • Rewards paid out in London and Middlesex. (You will get one or more large boxes of tax documents, with no obvious clue as to where the bounty certificates will be. Look for a bundle wrapped up in a stiff brown paper. If there is not one, look for a bundle of paper, not parchment.)	E 182/2 –114 E 182/594 –673
1803–1815	Deserters who surrendered themselves under proclamation.	WO 25/2955
1813–1848	Registers of captured deserters, giving name, regiment, date of capture and place of confine-ment, whether discharged the Army, or returned to his regiment, and to whom the reward (if any) was paid. • Indexes 1813–1833 in WO 25/2952–2954.	WO 25/ 2935 –2951
Punishment		
1799–1823	Unindexed registers for the *Savoy* hulk, in which some deserters were sentenced to imprisonment	WO 25/2956 –2961

You may be able to find correspondence on individual deserters, 1744–1813 and 1848–1858, in WO 4/591–654. These are indexed by the deserter's name.

For deserters in Australia (HO 75), consult Fitzmaurice, *Army Deserters from HM Service*.

18b.4.6 Army other ranks before 1914: regimental records: muster books, pay lists, description books

The basic regimental service records were the muster books, pay lists and description books: these were used for the day-to-day administration of the regiment.

1732–1878	Main series of muster books and pay lists	WO 12
1710–1878	Artillery	WO 10
1816–1878	Engineers	WO 11
1780–1878	Militia and volunteers	WO 13
1877–1898	Main series, artillery, engineers: coverage is incomplete, and information given is very limited	WO 16

In general, each muster book and pay list occupies one volume per year, and you may therefore have to search through several volumes. The first entry for a recruit in the muster generally gives his age, place of enlistment and trade, but does not give birthplace. Remember, recruitment is not usually into the 1st (the overseas) battalion, so look in the records of the 2nd battalion, or the regimental depot, for this first entry.

If the soldier died in service, or was discharged, you should find an entry to that effect in one of the quarterly lists of men becoming non-effective: however, these lists are not always present. Where one does exist, it should give the birthplace of the man discharged or dead, his trade and his date of enlistment.

From about 1868 to about 1883, the musters also contain marriage rolls, which sometimes give information about children as well as wives, if they occupied married quarters.

Description books

There are two main series of description books: the depot rolls, or description books, and the regimental description books.

The depot rolls or description books, 1768–1908 (WO 67), are usually the fuller of the two series. Men were usually allotted a number (this number does not appear on any forms until the 1830s). Depot rolls, however, do not list soldiers who enlisted where the regiment was stationed. Neither do they list soldiers who transferred from one regiment straight into another.

The regimental description books in WO 25 can contain these details, but they

Figure 28 Troopers of the Royal Horse Guards, in their London barracks, just before embarkation for the South African War. Full service records of all Household Cavalry other ranks, 1799–1920, are expected into the PRO (as WO 400) in late 2002. (PRO, COPY 1/445)

are not books containing details of every man in the regiment who served between the covering dates. They were started in 1825, or slightly earlier, after an investigation into the fraudulent claims of service. Regiments had to write down the services of every man in the regiment who was still serving at that time, and to list them in chronological order of enlistment (or alphabetically). Consequently, the further back one goes, the fewer the men from that period. Most books would appear to have between 1,000 and 1,500 names (some have a lot more), but considering that regimental strength was 1,000 and the regiments had been through 22 years of war and wastage, this is a small percentage of the total number.

1768–1908	Depot description books. Compiled as recruits were assembled at the regimental depot. Give a description of each soldier, his age, place of birth and trade.	WO 67
1778–1878	Regimental description and succession books. Give a description of each soldier, his age, place of birth and trade and successive service details. • Not all start in 1778 or go to 1878. • Only a small percentage of all soldiers are included. • Some are arranged alphabetically, others by date of enlistment.	WO 25/266–688

18b.4.7 Army other ranks before 1914: how to find the regiment

If you do not know the soldier's regiment, and have been unable to find him in WO 97, there are still some possible ways to find it out. Unfortunately, you cannot assume that he would have joined the regiment that by its name appears to have been local. Before 1870, each regiment recruited its own soldiers, usually from the locality where the home battalion happened to be posted at the time (they moved about quite a lot). However, recruiting parties did range quite widely. After 1870, regiments could still recruit directly, but a man had the option of joining 'the Army' and being assigned to a regiment.

If you have a photograph, you could try to identify the uniform: see the article by Barnes on this subject.

The regimental registers of births, 1761–1924, kept by the General Register Office are indexed, and the indexes can be seen at the FRC and the PRO. The index gives the regiment and place of birth of children born to the wives of serving soldiers, if they were attached to the regiment. If you have some knowledge of offspring or areas of service, this can be an easy way to narrow the field. To actually identify the correct child, parent and regiment, you may have to buy more than one certificate (see **18a.1.1**).

If you know the county or country in which your soldier was living between 1842 and 1862 for England and Scotland, or between 1842 and 1882 for Ireland and abroad, you may be able to find the regiment fairly easily. Between these dates there are records of payment of pensions, arranged by the district pay offices, which name the regiment served in (WO 22, and PMG 8 for payments in Hanover). For nearly 9,000 pensioners in India, Canada and South Africa between 1772 and 1899, taken from WO 120/35, 69 and 70, see Crowder, *British Army Pensioners Abroad, 1772–1899.*

Another possibility, if the soldier died in service, would be to check the records of deceased soldiers' effects: see **18b.4.4**. These are arranged by initial letter of surname and give the regiment, which opens up the regimental records to you. However, if the soldier died owing money to the Army, instead of vice versa, you are unlikely to find a reference to him here.

If you have any information on place of service, you may be able to identify the regiment from Kitzmiller's *In Search of the 'Forlorn Hope'.*

There are also two series of early nineteenth century Army-wide returns of service of non-commissioned officers and men, arranged by regiment, and then alphabetically. One contains statements of periods of service and of liability to serve abroad, as on 24 June 1806 (WO 25/871–1120). The other contains returns of the service of non-commissioned officers and men not known to be dead or totally disqualified for service, who had been discharged between 1783 and 1810 (WO 25/1121–1131). Looking through these without knowing the regiment would be a long shot, but possible.

18b.4.8 Army other ranks before 1914: Artillery and Engineers (Sapper and Miner) service records

Because the Royal Artillery, the Royal Engineers, and the Royal Corps of Sappers and Miners were the responsibility of the Ordnance Office (and not of the War Office) until 1855, they have a different set of records. Until 1772, the Royal Engineers were officers only, using casual labour for the physical work: after this a Corps of Royal Military Artificers, composed of other ranks only, was raised. In 1811, it became the Royal Corps of Sappers and Miners, with both officers and other ranks. This was amalgamated with the Royal Engineers after the abolition of the Ordnance Office in 1856.

However, many documents relating to Sappers and Miners are described in the lists as relating to Royal Engineers. Description books for 1793–1833 are in WO 54/313–316. Entry books of discharges, casualties, and transfers of Artillery and Engineer (Sapper and Miner) soldiers, 1740–1859, are in WO 54/317–337. A register of deceased Sappers and Miners, 1824–1858, gives date and cause of death and to whom any effects went (WO 25/2972). Service records of the Royal Artillery, 1791–1855, and for the Royal Horse Artillery, 1803–1863, are in WO 69. These include attestation papers, and show name, age, description, place of birth, trade, and dates of service, of promotion, of marriage, of discharge and of death. They are arranged under the unit in which the soldier last served: to find this, use the indexes and posting books (WO 69/779–782 and WO 69/801–839). This series also contains records of Royal Horse Artillery births and marriages (see **18a.1.2**). Laws's guide to the location of Artillery batteries may be useful if you know only the area of service. After 1856 (RA) or 1863 (RHA) look in WO 97 for discharge papers (see **18b.4.2.1**).

There is a miscellaneous collection of records of service for soldiers in the Artillery, Sappers and Miners, etc., and for civilian subordinates of the Board of Ordnance, arranged alphabetically in the Ordnance Office In-Letters (WO 44/695–700). Also for the Artillery from before 1770 to 1820, try WO 18. This consists of bound volumes of original warrants for payments on various accounts (pensions, recruiting, hospitals, deceased soldiers' effects, etc.), together with the original receipts, certificates of existence, letters petitioning for allowance, etc., of the individual concerned. Unfortunately, the list is only by year: you may have to spend a long time looking.

Registers of Artillery and Sapper and Miner pensioners, compiled in 1834 but dating back to the Napoleonic wars, are in WO 23/141–145; they include descriptions. Royal Artillery registers of pensions for long service and disability, 1833–1913, are in WO 116/125–185. There is an incomplete series of registers recording the deaths of soldiers in the Artillery, 1821–1873, in WO 69/583–597. Papers relating to Artillery and Engineers (Sapper and Miner) deaths and personal effects, 1824–1859, are in WO 25/2972–2973 and 2976–2978.

Musters and pay lists for the Royal Artillery, 1708–1878, are in WO 10; for the Royal Sappers and Miners, and the Engineers, 1816–1878, they are in WO 11. Musters for both Artillery and Engineers, 1878–1898, are in WO 16.

18b.5 Militia regiments, volunteers and the Territorial Force

For an in-depth study, see Spencer, *Militia and Volunteer Forces 1757–1945.*

By the 1757 Militia Act, militia regiments were reorganized in all counties of England and Wales. A form of conscription was used: each year, the parish was supposed to draw up lists of adult males, and to hold a ballot to choose those who had to serve in the militia. The militia lists (of all men) and the militia enrolment lists (of men chosen to serve) should in theory provide complete and annual censuses of all men aged between 18 and 45 from 1758 to 1831. The surviving lists, held locally, can be very informative, giving details about individual men and their family circumstances. However, the coverage of the country, for various reasons, is not complete. For more information see the article by Medlycott or the book by Gibson and Medlycott. Records of the militia once formed are also usually in county record offices. Other locally-held sources are the Poor Law records, which can include orders for the maintenance of the children of militia men.

There are some major records relating to the militia in the PRO. Muster rolls (in WO 13) are the main source, although they were only kept when the militia was 'embodied' (this means serving in a military capacity, and not in aid to the civil power). The sergeants (often ex-regular soldiers) and drummers were the only full-time staff of the militia, so information can usually be found on them (discharges are in WO 121). The muster rolls cover militia regiments for 1780–1783; for 1793–1814; and intermittently in the 1830s, 1840s and 1850s. In most cases, these muster rolls do not indicate place of origin. These muster rolls in WO 13 also include those of the supplementary militia, 1798–1816, and local militia, 1808–1816, together with those of other volunteer forces such as the fencibles, the yeomanry and the volunteers.

More useful for family history are the Militia Attestation Papers, 1806–1915 (WO 96), which were filled in at recruitment, and, in most cases, were annotated to the date of discharge to form a record of service. They include the date and place of birth. Most date from the mid-nineteenth century. These attestation papers are arranged in the order of precedence of the regular army unit to which the militia regiments were attached after the reorganization of the Army in 1881. The list of WO 96 gives the name of the regular unit as at 1881, not the earlier militia unit. The way round this problem is to consult the *Army List* of 1882 or after, and to find out from there which militia regiments were attached to which regiment.

The Militia Records, 1759–1925 (WO 68), include records of some militia regiments in Great Britain and Ireland, and consist of enrolment books, description books, pay lists, returns of officers' services, casualty books, regimental histories, etc., and also registers of marriages, births and baptisms (see **18a.1.2**). The Military Correspondence, 1782–1840 (HO 50), and the Military Entry books, 1758–1855 (HO 51) contain much material on the militia.

A few militia soldiers qualified for pensions as a result of service in the French Revolutionary and Napoleonic wars, and their discharge certificates among the ordinary Soldiers' Documents (WO 97) give their place of birth and age on enlistment: see **18b.4.2.1**. Many Irish militia soldiers qualified for pension: see **18b.4.2.2**. Other details of militia pensioners, admitted to pension between 1821 and 1829, may be found in a peculiar register drawn up in 1858, and arranged first by year of admission, and then by age on admission (WO 23/25).

The PRO has some sources for local payments of subsistence from the Land Tax to families of conscripted soldiers (and other militia payments), in E 182 (arranged by county where the payment was made). They can be difficult to find, as the records include many other things, and there are no indexes.

In 1908 the militia was restyled. Volunteer units of infantry, yeomanry (cavalry) and artillery, etc., were formed into the Territorial Force, which was renamed the Territorial Army in 1920. Most of the records are held locally: the muster rolls of some London and Middlesex Volunteer and Territorial regiments (1860–1912) are in the PRO (WO 70). Very many of the men who served in the First World War served as Territorials, and their records are described in **18c.1.5**.

18b.6　Military medals before 1914

There are a considerable number of records relating to the creation and award of military medals, but they generally only give the barest details about the recipient. Because medal records contain little genealogical information, they are not discussed at length here. See instead, Spencer, *Using Medal Records*. If you are interested in tracing the history of a medal's creation and design, consult the records of the Royal Mint, particularly MINT 16. This series also contains a little correspondence from a few recipients of medals.

There were three main types of military medal: for a particular campaign; for gallantry and meritorious service; and for long service and good conduct.

Campaign medals began with the Waterloo Medal. There was a medal for earlier service, mostly in the Peninsular War and America, 1793–1814, called the Military General Service Medal, but in fact this was not issued until 1847, and then only to men who had survived until that date: see the books by Mullen and Challis.

The Waterloo Medal Book records the corps and regiments engaged in the battle, giving the name and rank of officers and men (MINT 16/112). Wellington's despatch of 29 June 1815, listing the officers killed and wounded, was printed as a supplement to the *London Gazette* of 1 July 1815: copies can be found in ZJ 1 and also in MINT 16/111. After Waterloo, medals were awarded for most major campaigns – for example, the Indian Mutiny Medal of 1857. Clasps were often awarded for particular battles within a campaign, such as a Sebastopol clasp for a Crimea Medal. The medal rolls for campaign medals, 1793–1913, are in WO 100 (seen on microfilm): they are arranged by regiment. Correspondence and papers relating to some of the actual medals are in MINT 16. The India Office Library and Records hold the medal rolls for some campaigns that took place in India.

Gallantry medals were first awarded during the Crimean War. All gallantry awards bestowed upon members of the British army were announced in the *London Gazette* (ZJ 1). Awards announced in the New Year or Birthday Honours (January and June) were not accompanied by citations. There is a leaflet on gallantry medals available at the PRO or on the PRO website (www.pro.gov.uk).

Records of Long Service and Good Conduct Medals, for other ranks who had served at least 18 years, run from 1831 (WO 102). The records of the Meritorious Service Medal, for non-commissioned officers, run from 1846 (WO 101). The records include details of candidates for, as well as recipients of, these awards. A register of annuities paid to recipients of the meritorious or long service awards, 1846–1879, is in WO 23/84.

18b.7 American War of Independence, 1776–1783

Beyond the general run of records already discussed, you may find these sources useful for soldiers engaged in this conflict.

The muster books and pay lists of many regiments involved in this war may be found (see **18b.4.6**), but the certificates of men discharged in North America, which should give the age and place of birth, can seldom be traced. It is unlikely that you will find anything but a man's name, rank and date of discharge in the musters. There are some pay lists and account books for Hessian troops, but they provide few personal details. Muster rolls of the Hessian troops in British pay in North America are held in West Germany: there is an index available at the Research Enquiries Desk. Some Audit Office accounts (AO 3) may be useful for loyalist troops. The Loyalist Regiment Rolls for provincial troops are in the National Archives of Canada.

18b.8 The Wars with France 1793–1815

The wars with France were known, before 1914, as the Great War. It has been calculated that as many as 10 per cent of the eligible male population were involved in the fighting. Unfortunately, there is no simple way of finding the soldiers of this period. You need to use the normal procedure of regimental registers in WO 75 for officers, and a combination of the pension papers (in WO 97, WO 121, WO 118 and WO 119) and the musters in WO 12 for other ranks. However, there are a couple of shortcuts.

For officers, try Hart's papers in WO 211. The first part of this contains Hart's biographies of senior officers of the Peninsular War. Later pieces contain re-ports by officers who survived into the late 1830s of their time in the French wars. Try also the *Biographical Dictionary of British Officers Killed and*

Wounded, 1808–1814 in Hall's *History of the Peninsular War*, vol. 8.

For other ranks, try the 1806 regimental service returns in WO 25/871–1120.

For soldiers in general, you could try the prize registers in WO 164. Soldiers were eligible for prize money, from the proceeds of their victories: if they had died, their dependants could claim it. The Royal Chelsea Hospital was given the right to administer the unclaimed prize monies in 1809, but the records of claims go back to actions well before then. The registers in WO 164 are divided by action, and by which regiments had a claim: they were annotated for several years afterwards with details of who had claimed the money, and who did not. For some of the major actions of the Peninsular War, and the battle of Waterloo, the lists of original payments are included.

A sample entry would be that for the prize money of John *Hainsley*, gunner in the Royal Artillery, who was due prize money for action on Martinique, St Lucia and Guadeloupe in 1794. The prize money was claimed by his widow, Janet *Ainslie*, on a certificate by Captain Colebrooke, in 1799, and again in 1800 (WO 164/57, p. 22 and WO 164/71, p. 22).

The series also includes the Peninsula letter books (WO 169/1–16) and the Waterloo letter books (WO 169/17–19), of claimants who believed they were entitled to prize money: many of these were the parents, widows, uncles and so on of the soldier. They are indexed by both claimant *and* soldier. The dates of the letters range from 1816 to 1831: obviously, many of the soldiers were dead, if relatives were making the claim. For example, Catherine Graham, of Blackwater Town, County Tyrone, was awarded £7 17s 7d Peninsular Prize money due her late brother Sergeant John Cooper of the 3rd Foot, in 1829 (WO 164/16, p. 138).

The Waterloo Medal Book records the corps and regiments engaged in the battle, giving the name and rank of officers and men (MINT 16/112). Wellington's despatch of 29 June 1815, listing the officers killed and wounded, was printed as a supplement to the *London Gazette* of 1 July 1815: copies can be found in ZJ 1 and also in MINT 16/111.

18b.9 Crimean War, 1854–1856

Beyond the general run of records already discussed, you may find these sources useful for soldiers engaged in this conflict. For the Crimea, there are two series of special muster rolls:

1854–1856	the troops at the Scutari depot	WO 14
1854–1856	British, German and Swiss legions	WO 15

The reports of the Royal Patriotic Fund of aid given to some of the widows and orphans of soldiers who served in the Crimea, and of similar petitions rejected, are very interesting: the rejected petitions include details of the soldier's service after the Crimea. See **18a.4.1** for more details.

18b.10 South African (Boer) War, 1899–1902

Beyond the general run of records already discussed, you may find these sources useful for soldiers engaged in this conflict. See Fig. 26, p. 204, for an example.

Death registers of British soldiers who died in South Africa, 1899–1902, are kept by the General Register Office: indexes can be seen at the FRC and PRO (see **4.14**). See also the *South Africa Field Force Casualty List, 1899–1902*, available at the PRO. This is a published version of the casualty returns in WO 108/89–91 and 338. There is also Watt's *In Memoriam: Roll of Honour, Imperial Forces, Anglo-Boer War 1899–1902*. For officers, use Dooner's *Last Post*, which gives brief biographies of naval, military and colonial officers who died or were killed.

Figure 29 These three Suffolk Volunteers were photographed before leaving for the Boer War. Many families will have similar photographs, especially from the First World War. (PRO, COPY 1/450 (i))

Officers' service records may or may not survive, depending on how long they served. Unfortunately, records of many officers commissioned about 1901 no longer survive, thanks to weeding of supplementary files in the 1930s, and enemy bombing of the main series of records in 1940. Read **18c.1.4** for more details. (See **18b.3.3** for officers' service records.)

The service records of British regular soldiers (as at the time of discharge to pension or death) are in WO 97, in alphabetical order. There are two sequences for this date, so make sure you order the right box of both: see **18b.4.2.1.** If they re-enlisted for the First World War, their earlier records *may* have been added to their later records: you may need to check both (see **18c.1.5**).

Very many men volunteered for the Boer War, and served in the volunteer force, the Imperial Yeomanry. Volunteers' records are not kept with those of the regular Army. The soldiers' documents of the Imperial Yeomanry, 1899–1902, are in WO 128. The easiest way into these records is to use the published index, Asplin's *Roll*, which is available at the PRO. Further details about the records of the Imperial Yeomanry can be found in Spencer, *Militia and Volunteer Forces 1757–1945*. Other forces were raised locally in South Africa: enrolment forms and nominal rolls of these local armed forces, 1899–1902, are in WO 126 and WO 127. Some records of the City Imperial Volunteers are at the Guildhall Library.

The Medal Rolls for the Queen's and King's South African Medals (in WO 100) may sometimes contain a few personal details, such as the date of discharge or death, and the home address.

Personal files on over 5,000 disabled soldiers and naval ratings, who served between 1877 and 1914 and received disability pensions, are in PIN 71; many will be Boer War soldiers. This series is searchable on PROCAT by name (but it does not say whether the man was Army or Navy). The dates given are the date of the man's enlistment and the date the pension stopped. The information contained includes medical records, accounts of how injuries were incurred, and the men's own accounts of the incidents, and conduct sheets. These conduct sheets give place of birth, age, names of parents and siblings, religion, physical attributes, marital and parental status. There are also over 1,000 personal files on the widows of Army other ranks and naval ratings whose service was between about 1880 and 1914, in PIN 71. This series is searchable online the same way.

The reports of the Royal Patriotic Fund of aid given to the widows and orphans of the British and colonial forces are very interesting. See **18a.4.1** for more details.

18b.11　Army service records before 1914: bibliography

Army Lists, etc., of personnel
Army List (London, annually from 1754)

K J Asplin, *The roll of the Imperial Yeomanry, Scottish Horse & Lovats Scouts: 2nd Boer War, 1899–1902; being an alphabetical list of 39,800 men of these volunteer forces who enlisted for the 2nd Boer War. Listing regimental details, clasps to Queen's South Africa Medal and casualty status* (2 vols, Salisbury, 2000)

British Biographical Archive (London, 1984 continuing)

L S Challis, *Peninsula Roll Call* (London, 1948)

F and A Cook, *The Casualty Roll for the Crimea* (London, 1976)

C Dalton, *English Army Lists and Commission Registers, 1661–1714* (London, 1892–1904)

C Dalton, *George I's Army, 1714–1727* (London, 1910–1912)

C Dalton, *Irish Army Lists, 1661–1685* (London, 1907)

C Dalton, *Waterloo Roll* (London, 2nd edn, 1904)

Dictionary of National Biography (London, 1909 continuing)

M G Dooner, *The 'Last Post': being a Roll of all Officers (Naval, Military or Colonial) who gave their lives in the South African War, 1899–1902* (1903, reprinted 1980)

E Dwelly, *Waterloo Muster Rolls: Cavalry* (Fleet, 1934)

H G Hart, *Army List* (London, 1839–1915)

List of Officers of the Royal Regiment of Artillery, 1716–June 1914 (London, 1914)

A L T Mullen, *Military General Service Medal, 1793–1814* (London, 1990)

A L T Mullen, *Military General Service Roll, 1793–1814* (London, 1990)

E Peacock, *The Army List of Roundheads and Cavaliers* (London, 2nd edn, 1874)

A Peterkin, W Johnston and R Drew, *Commissioned Officers in the Medical Services of the British Army* (London, 1968)

Roll of Officers of the Corps of Royal Engineers from 1660 to 1898 (London, 1898)

Royal Military Kalendar (London, 1820)

South Africa Field Force Casualty List, 1899–1902 (1972)

S Watt, *In Memoriam: Roll of Honour, Imperial Forces, Anglo-Boer War 1899–1902* (University of Natal, 2000)

General works

D J Barnes, 'Identification and Dating: Military Uniforms', in *Family History Focus*, eds, D J Steel and L Taylor (Guildford, 1984)

A Bruce, *An Annotated Bibliography of the British Army, 1660–1714* (London, 1975)

A Bruce, *The Purchase System in the British Army, 1660–1871* (Royal Historical Society, London, 1980)

Calendar of State Papers, Domestic (London, 1856–1972)

Calendars of State Papers, Ireland (London, 1860–1912)

N K Crowder, *British Army Pensioners Abroad, 1772–1899* (Baltimore, 1995)

C Firth and G Davis, *The Regimental History of Cromwell's Army* (Oxford, 1940)

Y Fitzmaurice, *Army Deserters from HM Service* (Forest Hill, Victoria, 1988)

S Fowler and W Spencer, *Army Records for Family Historians* (PRO, 1998)

J S W Gibson and A Dell, *Tudor and Stuart Muster Rolls* (FFHS, 1991)

J S W Gibson and E Hampson, *Specialist Indexes for Family Historians* (FFHS, 1998)

J S W Gibson and M Medlycott, *Militia Lists and Musters, 1757–1876* (FFHS, 1989)

J Hall, *The History of the Peninsular War, vol. 8: The Biographical Dictionary of British Officers Killed and Wounded, 1808–1814* (London, 1998)

J M Kitzmiller, *In Search of the 'Forlorn Hope': a Comprehensive Guide to Locating British Regiments and their Records* (Salt Lake City, 1988)

M E S Laws, *Battery Records of the Royal Artillery, 1716–1877* (Woolwich, 1952–1970)

W Lenz, *Manuscript Sources for the History of Germany since 1500 in Great Britain* (German Historical Institute in London, *Publications*, vol. 1) This has many references to German troops in British service in the eighteenth and nineteenth centuries

M Medlycott, 'Some Georgian "Censuses": the Militia Lists and "Defence" Lists', *Genealogists' Magazine*, vol. XXIII, pp. 55–59

Public Record Office, *Alphabetical Guide to certain War Office and other Military Records preserved in the Public Record Office* (Lists and Indexes, vol. LIII)

Public Record Office, *Lists of War Office Records* (Lists and Indexes, vol. XXVIII and Supplementary vol. VIII)

E E Rich, 'The Population of Elizabethan England', *Economic History Review,* 2nd series., vol. II, pp. 247–265. (Discusses the Elizabethan muster rolls)

W Spencer, *Records of the Militia and Volunteer Forces 1757–1945* (PRO, 1997)

W Spencer, *Using Medal Records* (PRO, forthcoming 2002)

E M Spiers, *The Army and Society 1815–1914,* (Longman, 1980)

A Swinson, ed., *A Register of the Regiments and Corps of the British Army: the Ancestry of the Regiments and Corps of the Regular Establishments of the Army* (London, 1975)

18c

The Army: service records, from 1914 onwards

◆ ◆ ◆

For the 50 years after 1914, most British families had a direct experience of military life among at least some of their members, in a way that was entirely new. Millions served in the First and Second World Wars, and national service continued until 1961. So many men and women served, so many died, and so many carried mental and physical wounds for the rest of their lives, that these two wars made a huge mark on the British people. In many ways, this experience combined with universal suffrage to produce a new personal and political perception that Britons were not subjects, but citizens, with all the rights of citizens to a better life. Both the national provision of decent housing in the 1920s and the health and education reforms of the 1940s owe much to this feeling that 'we all fought – we all deserve better'.

18c.1 The First World War

The First World War saw mass mobilization of soldiers for the first time in the United Kingdom. Conscription started in 1916. We don't know exact figures, but historians think that about 7.2 million men served in the army between 1914 and 1919.

With so many men serving, it can be quite difficult to track a particular man down, especially as so many of the service records were burned when the War Office record store caught fire as a result of enemy action in 1940. However, it is still worth looking at the PRO: even if you cannot find a service record, you may be able to piece together quite a lot of information from other sources.

A lot of people come in to the PRO with a man's army number: unfortunately, this does not help in finding the records. It does help if you know which regiment and battalion a man served in, especially if he had a common name. If you don't already know this, there are three ways to proceed. If the man survived until 1918, and was then 19 or over, try checking the Absent Voters' Register discussed in **16.4**. This is arranged by home address, and gives brief service details. If you know the man died, look at the Commonwealth War Graves database (see **18c.1.1**). If he survived, or if you don't know what happened to him, look at the medal roll index and the medal roll itself (see **18c.1.2**). If you find several likely people, you will have to follow them all and do some detective work on the results.

For a fuller explanation of all the records relating to service in the Army during the First World War, see Spencer, *Army Service Records of the First World War.*

18c.1.1 First World War: the war dead

Information on men who died in the war is often much easier to trace than information on men who survived. For a start, there is the Debt of Honour Register on the website of the Commonwealth War Graves Commission (www.cwgc.org). This is accessible from the PRO. You can find here a record of all Army personnel who died in the First War, with date of death, place of burial, regiment and sometimes a mention of parents or wife. If you are looking for a really common name, you may have some problems, as quite often only an initial is given instead of a forename. However, you can combine it with a search of the CD-ROM of *Soldiers [and Officers] Died in the Great War*, in the PRO Library. This covers both soldiers and officers, and lists all the men who died

Figure 30 'The Cenotaph – that mass of national emotion frozen in stone.' (H V Morton, *The Heart of London*, 1925) (PRO, WORK 20/139)

between 1914 and 1919. It is a computerization of an 81-volume publication. To use the books you had to know the regiment: now you can search by any of the following categories of information:

- surname
- forename
- initials
- date of death
- place of birth (town)
- place of birth (county)
- place of enlistment (town)
- place of enlistment (county)

- died
- died of wounds
- killed in action
- theatre of war of death
- rank
- regiment
- battalion
- regimental number

Gallantry medals which may have been won are also listed.

There are also published obituaries, apparently written by relatives, in De Ruvigny's *Roll of Honour*, which can be seen at the PRO. Many other obituaries will have been published in local newspapers, professional journals, staff magazines and school magazines: these can be well worth seeking out.

You should be able to order a death certificate from the ONS: there are indexes to the death registers for Army war dead, 1914–1921, at both the FRC and the PRO (see **4.14**). At the PRO, there are many French and Belgian certificates for the deaths of British soldiers who died in hospitals or elsewhere outside the immediate war zone, 1914–1920, arranged by first letter of surname (RG 35/45–69): certificates for surnames beginning C, F, P, Q and X are missing.

The National Army Museum has the records of deceased soldiers' effects for the First World War, but these are not yet available for research.

18c.1.2 First World War: the medal rolls – an alphabetical index to the Army

The index to the medal rolls at the PRO is the nearest thing we have to an index to the Army in this period. Soldiers who served abroad during the Great War were awarded one or more campaign medals – all too often after their death. The medal rolls are in 3,273 volumes, arranged by regiment in WO 329. They record awards of the following medals to officers and other ranks of the Army and Royal Flying Corps – also to many civilians who saw service overseas:

- 1914 Star
- 1914–1915 Star
- British War Medal

- Victory Medal
- Territorial Force War Medal
- Silver War Badge

The index contains almost all the information to be found on the actual rolls. However, cards for regular army soldiers tend not show the battalion (a subdivision of a regiment) in which they served, though cards for men in the

Territorial Force often do give the battalion. If the battalion is not shown on the card, you can pick this up from the medal roll. You will need to know the battalion for further research.

The medal roll is also marked to show whether the medal had actually been received or not. If there is a tick against the name, the medal had been received by the soldier or next of kin, by registered post. If there was a cross, either the delivery had failed, or the medal had been deliberately returned. After ten years, these medals were melted down. Some people look at the medal roll in the hope of asking for the medal to be issued now. However, the Army Medal Office cannot now issue First World War medals, as the medals are no longer produced. Instead they will tell you to look for a private source, such as a military tailor or a medal dealer. For more detail see Spencer, *Using Medal Records.*

18c.1.3 First World War: using the medal rolls index

The index is seen on microfiche. Each fiche contains up to 360 index cards. The index cards are arranged in alphabetical order of surname, and then by alphabetical order of forename *initials.* Men with only one initial are placed before men with two. (For example, Buckland P[hilip] is filed before Buckland P[ercy] C[lifford].) If you are researching a common name, or several names, you may find that a long and time consuming search is needed. Very often there are several men of the same name.

If you have any family tradition as to regiment, note this – it may help you identify your Brown G among the many others. You may need to do some investigation here, as family tradition and official records often express the same information in different ways. For instance, my grandfather Percy Buckland always told me that he had served in the Queen's Westminsters. There was no index card giving this as a regiment. A search in the sources given in **18c.1.10** showed that the Queen's Westminsters was also known as 16th (County of London) Battalion of the London Regiment, Queen's Westminster Rifles, a Territorial Force battalion – and there was a card for him giving the 16/London Regiment. It would be an awful lot quicker to have checked the known regimental details first.

Hyphenated surnames were filed in the card index in two different ways, and you may have to check both possibilities. Most such names are indexed, and were originally filed, by the second part of the name. Thus, 'Frederick A Browning-Smith' would have been indexed under '-SMITH, Frederick A Browning'. His card may still be found at the appropriate point among the Smiths. However, some index cards for hyphenated surnames were refiled by the Army Medal Office under the first part of the name, at the end of the sequence for that element on its own. For example, 'Frederick A Browning-Smith' might appear after 'BROWNING, Z G', although his card would still read '-SMITH, Frederick A Browning'. (Incidentally, if you have a 'problem' surname that could conceivably be spelled a different way, you can assume that the Army used the spelling given in the medal index, or in the *Army List.*)

When you have identified on the fiche the index card for the name you are researching, you should have in front of you a card like the one shown here.

Name	Corps	Rank	Reg^d No.
	*16/London R	*Pte*	*4069*
BUCKLAND	—--—		*551406*
Percy C			

MEDAL	ROLL	Page	Remarks
VICTORY	*TP 16/101/B/2*	*139*	
BRITISH	— do —	*do*	*Disemb.*
15 **STAR**	*TP /20A*	*2*	
Theatre of War first sent to	*(1) France*		
Date of entry therein	*2.9.15*		

Remember, the medal roll index contains almost all the information to be found on the actual medal rolls themselves – except sometimes the battalion a man served in. If you don't already know which battalion you are looking for, make sure you go beyond the index to look at the medal roll itself. You need to note down the old reference on the card (e.g. TP 16/101/B/2 page 139), and convert it to a modern WO 329 reference, so you can order the actual medal roll. Pick up the *How to* leaflet at the PRO to find out how to do this.

18c.1.4 First World War: officers' service records

Service records as originally maintained by the Army do not survive for officers whose service ended after 1914, as they were destroyed by enemy bombing in 1940. However, in addition to the main service record, there was a correspondence file, which, depending on length of service, could become very bulky. These did survive the bombing, and are now the main source for officers who fought in the First World War, and who left the service between 1914 and

1922. These correspondence files are arranged in two series WO 339 (mostly regular Army and emergency reserve) and WO 374 (mostly Territorial Force). In total some 217,000 individual files can be found in these two series. There are also a few files of notable individuals in WO 138 – mostly top brass, but also Wilfred Owen.

These files can contain medical records, reports made by repatriated prisoners of war, details relating to pensions, and in fact almost anything not necessarily about his ability. Unfortunately many correspondence files of regular Army officers who obtained their commissions before 1901 were weeded or destroyed in the 1930s. You may therefore find a lot of information, or you may find very little.

WO 374 is arranged in alphabetical order, and can be searched on PROCAT.

The quickest way to access WO 339 is to search it online in PROCAT, using the surname. If this turns up several people of the same name, you will need to go to WO 338, the index to WO 339, which gives more detail to help you identify the right person. WO 338 also contains references to officers who served after 1922 (see **18c.2**), as well as to those officers whose correspondence files were weeded, and for whom no service papers therefore survive. WO 338 gives the 'long number' used by the Army registry system: if you are unfortunate enough to be looking for an officer whose papers were weeded to extinction, it may be worth using the long number to check in the original register for the correspondence files in WO 340.

You may find many Indian Army officers in WO 338 (with IA instead of regiment), WO 339 and WO 374. These were officers on leave or retired, who became officers in short-staffed regular Army or new Territorial Force regiments.

Records of British Army other ranks commissioned into the Indian Army have been added to WO 339 (as WO 339/139092–139906): you will need to use these pre-commission records with the post-commission records kept at the India Office Library and Records (address in **48**).

For more detailed information, see Spencer's *Army Service Records of the First World War.*

Brief details of an officer's career can also be found in the *Army List*: see **18.3**.

18c.1.5 First World War: other ranks' service records

Surviving service records for soldiers discharged after 1913 are in three series, not searchable in PROCAT. You cannot tell if a record exists without looking through the documents.

WO 364	For about 750,000 men medically discharged as a result of sickness or wounds,.contracted or received 1914–1919.	In alphabetical order on 4,915 reels of microfilm.	The *unburnt documents* – a complete set.
WO 363	For about 2,000,000 of the men who died or who were demobilized at the end of the War, up to 1920 – both regular soldiers and 'duration of the war servicemen only'.	In alphabetical order on about 20,000 reels of microfilm.	The *burnt documents*
WO 400	Household Cavalry, up to 1920	Not in the PRO until late 2002	Original records – a complete set
–	Foot Guard regiments	At the Guards Regimental HQ (see **48**)	Original records – complete set

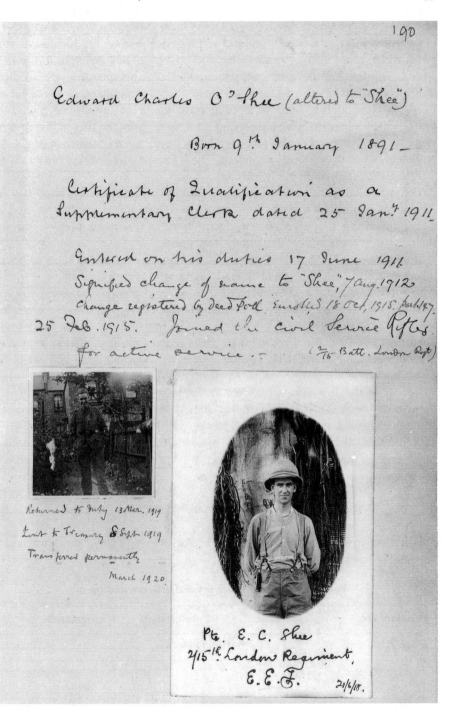

190

Edward Charles O'Shee (altered to "Shee")

Born 9th January 1891 –

Certificate of Qualification as a Supplementary Clerk dated 25 Jan.y 1911

Entered on his duties 17 June 1911
Signified change of name to "Shee", 7 Aug. 1912
Change registered by deed poll. Enrolled 18 Oct, 1915. Part 147.
25 Feb. 1915.   Joined the Civil Service Rifles
for active service. –   (2/15 Batt. London Regt.)

Returned to duty 13 Mar. 1919
Lent to Treasury 8 Sept 1919
Transferred permanently
           March 1920

Pte. E. C. Shee
2/15th London Regiment,
E. E. J.   21/6/18.

Figure 31 It is worth looking for soldiers among the records of their peacetime lives. The PRO's own records produced a scrapbook of staff who served in the Great War. Many other institutions may have similar records. (PRO, PRO 8/55)

The surviving records of service in WO 363 were those that were damaged, but not destroyed, as a result of bombing in 1940. At the time, the records of other ranks were stored in regimental order: the infantry regiments were in the main path of the fire and bore the worst casualties. This means that you are quite likely to find service records for a soldier in a cavalry regiment, or in the Labour Corps, but less likely to find one in an infantry regiment. Unfortunately, we don't know which regiments took a direct hit, as it were, from the fire, although work done to date shows that the records of the Royal Sussex Regiment, the Essex Regiment, the West Kent Regiment, the Warwickshire Regiment and the Wiltshire Regiment were badly affected.

The condition of the surviving records can be very good or very bad: they can sometimes be difficult to read. They were sorted into alphabetical order, and are being filmed. Their preservation in microfilm form was made possible through financial support from the Heritage Lottery Fund.

Here in WO 363 (if you are lucky), you can find the records of men who were killed in action or who died of wounds, men who were prisoners of war, men who survived the war and even men executed for desertion. However, you may well find that you are unlucky. Unfortunately there is no index to these records: the only way to find out if a service record survives is to check the relevant microfilm. You may also want to check the register of misfiled records, kept at the Microfilm Reading Room desk: several men have been found out of alphabetical order, and these are going to be refilmed right at the end of the project.

Not all of the survivors are as yet available, as the process of microfilming them takes time. This series is being filmed in blocks, by first letter of the surname. The letters *not* in the PRO at the time of writing are G and H: these should be available by the end of August 2002. Any files that have been discovered in the wrong alphabetical sequence are being refilmed afterwards, to go in a separate section of misfiles.

18c.1.6 First World War: disability and other pensions

This section covers all armed services: it is placed here because the Army had by far the most casualties.

Pensions to disabled or invalid officers and men

Pension, etc.	Date	Reference	Information
officers: half pay	up to 1921	PMG 4	
disabled officers and men		PMG 9, PMG 42	Registers of payments of pension
invalid officers: temporary retired pay and gratuities	1917 April–1919 February	PMG 42/1–2	Rank, name, address, date of warrant, amount paid
all services, all ranks	1920–1989	PIN 26	See below

Pension case files are in PIN 26. This series contains 22,756 personal files on people awarded (or refused) pensions, from all services. Although large, this represents only two per cent of the pensions awarded. The series list is arranged by type of pensioner, and then alphabetically, so that it may be worth checking on the off-chance: PIN 26 is easily searched by surname on PROCAT. Unfortunately, it is not at all clear what all the various sub-series mean, so you may have to check in more than one sequence. The series is open, even if documents in it are not yet 30 years old. Earlier documents than 1920 exist in the files. The files can contain fascinating material, some medical, some social, and can cover many years, with claims being raised a good four decades or more after the end of the war.

Pension case files, all services

PIN 26	Type of pensioner (all searchable by surname in PROCAT)
1–203	All services, all ranks. Not in alphabetical order.
204–16374	[Army: other ranks], disability.
16375–16683	[Army: other ranks], disability (with some out of alphabetical order at the end).
16684–17178	Navy, disability.
17179–19523	Widows (by name of husband). (See also PIN 82.)
19524–19720	Alternative widows' pensions (by name of husband). (See also PIN 82.)
19721–19820	Mercantile Marine, death and disability.
19821–19853	Dependants (by own name).
19854–19923	Men (DM series).
19924–19954	Officers (DO series).
19955–19984	Alternative disabled pensions.
19985–20286, 22744	Nurses, disability.
20287–21065	Overseas, death and disability.
21066–22756	Officers, death and disability.

For soldiers who served before 1914, were discharged to a disability pension and then re-enlisted during the First World War, try a surname search in PIN 71.

For soldiers admitted to the Royal Hospital Chelsea as in-pensioners before 1933, see **18b.4.2.3**. In addition, you should check the selection of personal files of deceased pensioners, 1923–1980 in WO 324: these are searchable in PROCAT by surname. Some will still be closed.

18c.1.7 First World War: gallantry medals

All gallantry awards bestowed upon members of the British Army were announced in the *London Gazette* (ZJ 1). The indexes of the *London Gazette* for the First World War are available on the open shelves in the Microfilm Reading Room. Citations (the reason why) for all awards granted for gallantry during the First World War can also be found in the *London Gazette*. Awards announced in the New Year or Birthday Honours (January and June) were not accompanied by citations.

Name indexes of recipients of the Distinguished Conduct Medal (DCM) and Military Medal (MM) awarded for gallant service in the First World War are available on microfiche. No citations were published for the Military Medal. A further register of the DCM can be found in WO 391. A name index for the Military Cross (MC) awarded during the First World War can be found in WO 389. The register of Distinguished Service Order (DSO) can be found in WO 390.

Records of Long Service and Good Conduct Medals, for other ranks who had served 18 years, are in WO 102. The records of the Meritorious Service Medal, for non-commissioned officers, run from 1846 to 1919 (WO 101). The records include details of candidates for, as well as recipients of, these awards.

For more detailed advice, see Spencer, *Using Medal Records*.

18c.1.8 First World War: courts martial

Death sentences were passed by the British Army in courts martial between 1914 and 1924, for offences such as sleeping on duty, cowardice, desertion, murder, mutiny and treason, on over 3,000 British soldiers, on members of Dominion, Colonial and foreign forces, and on several British and foreign civilians. Over 90 per cent of these sentences were later changed to other punishments – hard labour or penal servitude.

For all offences except mutiny, start with Oram and Putkowski, *Death Sentences passed by the Military Courts of the British Army, 1914–1924*. This gives a list by surname and a list by date. Each entry gives a reference number. Add WO to the front of this number, and you have the full PRO reference. Most records of courts martial are in WO 213, WO 92 or WO 90.

Over 2,000 men were charged with mutiny between 1914 and 1922. Start with Putkowski, *British Army Mutineers, 1914–1922*. This gives a list by surname; a list by unit; a list by date for mutinies at home, and a list by date for mutinies abroad. Each entry gives a full PRO reference, including the internal page number. When ordering one of these documents, leave out the page number. Most records of courts martial of mutineers are in WO 86, WO 90, WO 92 and WO 213.

For courts martial that did not pass a death sentence, you need to track down the records of the court in the PRO or perhaps in the regimental museum.

18c.1.9 First World War: war diaries

Many people, having found what battalion their man served in, go on to look for the war diary of that battalion. A war diary is a daily record of operations, intelligence reports and other events, kept for each battalion by an appointed junior officer. It is *not* a personal diary (try the Imperial War Museum for a collection of those). Specialist units, such as military hospitals, also kept war diaries. One copy was sent into the War Office, and is now in the PRO. Other copies were kept by the unit, and may now be with the regimental records. Copies of the war diaries for Dominion, Indian and Colonial forces are also kept at the PRO.

Some war diaries may be difficult to read. Many were scribbled hastily in pencil. Others are the second carbon copy of the original. Some use obscure abbreviations. Some diaries will record little more than daily losses, map references, etc.: others will be much more descriptive. It is unusual for diaries to mention the names of ordinary soldiers. You can *sometimes* find details in the diaries about awards of the Military Medal and the Meritorious Service Medal.

Regimental museums *may* hold copies of their war diaries, but you will probably find it easier to look at the PRO. The PRO holds the duplicates sent into the War Office: most are now in WO 95. War diaries containing confidential information (often concerning courts martial) were kept back for years by the Ministry of Defence. These are now in WO 154, and can be read. A large number of maps were extracted for safe keeping, and are in WO 153. Some war diaries of the Royal Flying Corps are in AIR 1. Royal Naval Division war diaries are in ADM 137 until 1916, and then in WO 95.

There are several ways to find a war diary in WO 95. Using the online catalogue, you can do a keyword search in WO 95, giving (part of) the unit name and battalion number (15 *not* 15th) as keywords. If this is not successful, try a variant of the name. If this is not successful, try browsing the list of WO 95 to see what kinds of terms are used. You can always use the paper catalogue at the PRO, which is arranged in order of battle, with several indexes. If it is not in WO 95, try WO 154.

War diaries of smaller units, such as medical, engineer and service units, can be difficult to find. Keyword searches can be helpful – try several variants (see **5**). Try the list of Royal Artillery, Army Service Corps, Machine Gun Corps and Medical Units, giving the Division, Corps or Army they fought with, in WO 95/5494. You can also consult the *Orders of Battle*, which list month by month the location of each unit, and the Division or Army to which it was attached. Ask, at the Reference Desk at the PRO, for the set of the *Orders of Battle* for Belgium, France and Germany, arranged by Division (not by unit).

There are also some related sources you may wish to look at:

- Correspondence and Papers of Military Headquarters, WO 158
- Miscellaneous Unregistered Papers, WO 161
- Intelligence Summaries, WO 157
- Gallipoli, Palestine, and Italian Campaigns: Photographs, WO 317, WO 319, WO 323
- Campaign Maps, WO 153, WO 297, WO 298, WO 300, WO 301, WO 302, WO 303

Figure 32 After the Great War, the Army needed to advertise the advantages of being a soldier. (PRO, ADM 1/8331)

At the PRO you can see the official *History of the Great War.* This multi-volume, multi-author work was written from official documents (still then closed to the public) directly after the war.

18c.1.10 First World War: identification and embarkation of regiments

The easiest way to identify units is to use www.1914–1918.net or James, *British Regiments, 1914–1918.* A slower way would be to consult WO 380/17 for a register of the formations, amalgamations, disbandments and changes in title of infantry regiments, 1914–1919. For cavalry regiments, ask at the enquiry desk for Swinson, *A Register of the Regiments or Corps of the British Army.* For details of changes of uniform and colours, try the various registers in WO 380, indexed by WO 380/11. For the dates of embarkation of units going overseas, 1914–1918, see WO 379/16.

18c.2 Soldiers' records: between the World Wars

The service records of officers who served after 1922, and of other ranks who were discharged after 1920, are still held by the Ministry of Defence (for whom they are still an active set of records). They are not open to public inspection, but next of kin can request a précis of the service record, and this will be provided for a fee. Write to the Ministry of Defence, Army Personnel Records (see **48**).

Records of soldiers admitted to the Royal Chelsea Hospital as Chelsea Pensioners after 1933 are still kept by the Hospital: the address is in **48**. For those admitted before 1933, see **18b.4.2.3**. In addition, you should check the selection of personal files of deceased pensioners, 1923–1980, in WO 324: these are searchable in PROCAT by surname. Some will still be closed.

At the National Army Museum you can see the records of deceased soldiers' effects for soldiers who died in service (or who were discharged insane), after 31 March 1921. These give details of money owing, and to whom it was paid: contact the National Army Museum to arrange access (see **48**).

18c.3 Second World War: soldiers' records

Service records for the Second World War are still held by the Ministry of Defence (for whom they are still an active set of records). They are not open to public inspection, but the individual concerned can request a précis of the service record, which will be provided for a fee. The only other people who can do this are anyone to who has been given the living individual's written consent, or (if the individual has died) the official next of kin. Write to the Ministry of Defence, Army Personnel Records (see **48**).

In the PRO Library you can see the new computer version of the Army Roll of Honour for the Second World War. The Roll of Honour contains details of men who were killed or died while in the Army between 1st September 1939 and 31st December 1946. This includes men who died from natural causes, but excludes those who died 'dishonourable deaths' – by execution for a capital crime while in the Army, for example. The Roll of Honour was originally compiled in 1944–1949, on coded punch cards, and has been in the PRO for some years. However, the new CD-ROM has decoded the information, and it can now be easily searched. The information given is:

- Surname and forenames
- Army service number
- Date of death
- Rank
- First unit served in
- Unit serving in at time of death
- Place of birth
- Place of domicile
- Place of death
- Decorations

You can find out about burials from the Commonwealth War Graves Commission database, the Debt of Honour register (which can be accessed on their website at www.cwgc.org). This register can also supply personal details, such as the names and addresses of parents or wives. The indexes to the registered death certificates for the Army war dead, 1939–1948, can be seen at both the PRO and the FRC: see **4.14**. You have to buy the certificates from the ONS, and these should give cause of death. There are also retrospective registers of deaths from enemy action in the Far East 1941–1945 (RG 33/11 and 132, indexed in RG 43/14). At the National Army Museum you can see the records of deceased soldiers' effects for soldiers who died in service (or who were discharged insane), during the Second World War. These give details of money owing, and to whom it was paid: contact the National Army Museum to arrange access (see **48**).

At the PRO you can see the official *History of the Second World War.* This multi-volume, multi-author work was written from official documents (still then closed to the public) directly after the war. Some copies are marked up with document references, so you can go back to the sources easily.

For records of Long Service and Good Conduct Medals (for other ranks who had served 18 years), see WO 102.

Recommendations for awards for gallantry or meritorious service made during the Second World War are in the series WO 373. This series, which is available on microfilm, is arranged by operational theatre (where the award was won) and then in *London Gazette* date order. You have to know the type of award, the operational theatre and the date the award was announced. WO 373 also contains recommendation for most awards made to members of the Army up to 1967, including Korea and Malaya. See Spencer, *Using Medal Records.*

If you know details of the battalion or unit in which your man served, you may want to look for the war diary, to see what that battalion or unit was actually up to. A war diary is a daily record of events, often with appendices of signals and orders. For the Second World War, the war diaries are in several series, so you need to know in what areas of the world the battalion served.

- British Expeditionary Force, WO 167
- British North Africa Forces, WO 175
- Central Mediterranean Forces, WO 170
- Dominion Forces, WO 179
- GHQ Liaison Regiment, WO 215
- Home Forces, WO 166
- Madagascar, WO 174
- Medical services, WO 177
- Middle East Forces, WO 169
- Military Missions, WO 178
- North-West Europe, WO 171
- North-West Expeditionary Force, WO 168
- Ships Signals Sections, WO 257
- South-East Asia Command, WO 172
- Special Services, WO 218
- Various smaller theatres, WO 176
- War Office Directorates, WO 165
- West Africa Forces, WO 173

Records of soldiers admitted to the Royal Chelsea Hospital as Chelsea Pensioners after 1933 are still kept by the Hospital: the address is in **48.** In addition, you should check the selection of personal files of deceased pensioners, 1923–1980, in WO 324: these are searchable in PROCAT by surname. Some will still be closed.

The *Home Guard List,* 1939–1945, arranged by Command (area) and including name indexes, is available in the PRO Library.

18c.4 Soldiers' records: after the Second World War

Service records are still held by the Ministry of Defence (for whom they are still an active set of records). They are not open to public inspection, but next of kin can request a précis of the service record, and this will be provided for a fee. Write to the Ministry of Defence, Army Personnel Records (see **48**).

Recommendations for most gallantry or meritorious service awards made to members of the Army up to 1967, including Korea and Malaya, are in WO 373. This series, which is available on microfilm, is arranged by operational theatre (where the award was won) and then in *London Gazette* date order. You therefore have to know the type of award, the operational theatre and the date the award was announced, unless you are prepared to spend some time looking.

You can, however, find operational records of later wars in the PRO: a leaflet is available at the PRO or on the PRO website.

Records of soldiers admitted as Chelsea Pensioners to the Royal Chelsea Hospital after 1933 are still kept by the Hospital: the address is in **48**. In addition, you should check the selection of personal files of deceased pensioners, 1923–1980, in WO 324: these are searchable in PROCAT by surname. Some will still be closed.

At the National Army Museum you can see the records of deceased soldiers' effects for soldiers who died in service (or who were discharged insane), up to 1960. These give details of money owing, and to whom it was paid: contact the National Army Museum to arrange access (see **48**).

18c.5 The Army: service records, from 1914: bibliography

Army Lists, etc., of personnel
Army List (London, annually)
British Biographical Archive (London, 1984 continuing)
Dictionary of National Biography (London, 1909 continuing)
H G Hart, *Army List* (London, 1839–1915)

General works
P Dennis, *The Territorial Army 1907–1940* (Royal Historical Society, 1987)
History of the Great War (HMSO)
History of the Second World War (HMSO)
E A James, *British Regiments, 1914–1918* (Heathfield, 1998)
Marquis de Ruvigny's *Roll of Honour* (London, n.d.)
G Oram and J Putkowski, *Death Sentences passed by the Military Courts of the British Army, 1914–1924* (London, 1998)
J Putkowski, *British Army Mutineers, 1914–1922* (London, 1998).
W Spencer, *Army Service Records of the First World War* (PRO, 2001)
W Spencer, *Records of the Militia and Volunteer Forces 1757–1945* (PRO, 1997)
W Spencer, *Using Medal Records* (PRO, forthcoming 2002)
A Swinson, ed., *A Register of the Regiments and Corps of the British Army: the Ancestry of the Regiments and Corps of the Regular Establishments of the Army* (London, 1975)

18d

The Army: 'support' services

◆ ◆ ◆

18d.1 The Yeomen of the Guard

The Yeomen of the Guard have been protecting the monarch since 1485. Many of them were ex-Army. The PRO has muster rolls from 1690–1887 in WO 94/37–39; and pay records from 1715 to 1911 (with a gap for 1834–1874) in WO 94/24–35. Pension records, dating from 1873–1941, are in PMG 35/1–16.

18d.2 Army chaplains

Until the end of the eighteenth century, chaplains were employed on a regimental basis, but after 1796 one chaplain served three or four regiments. The first Presbyterian chaplains were appointed in 1827; Catholic chaplains in 1836; Wesleyans in 1881, and Jewish chaplains in 1892. As chaplains were commissioned officers, they will be found in the *Army List* and through the normal routes for finding officers.

In addition, there are certificates of service, 1817–1843, in WO 25/256–258. Records of payment, 1805–1842, are in WO 25/233–251. The registers of retired pay, 1806–1837 (WO 25/252–253), give details of chaplains who saw service in the eighteenth century. Letters from chaplains, 1808–1836, are in the Chaplain General's Letter Books (in WO 7).

18d.3 The Royal Military Police

The Royal Military Police became a separate organization from the middle of the nineteenth century, and enquiries about military policemen should be sent direct to them (address in **48**). They have an incomplete run of personnel records. Their archive includes the Corps Order books for the First World War – the equivalent of the Army's daily war diaries. For background, try Sheffield, *The Redcaps: a history of the Royal Military Police*.

18d.4 Royal Army Medical Corps

The archives of the Royal Army Medical College and several collections of private papers of officers and men of the RAMC are kept by the Wellcome

Figure 33 1915: Army casualties in France, after a German gas attack. (PRO, CN 4/40)

Library. The Army Medical Services Museum has collections showing life in the various medical services. Addresses are in **48**.

The easiest way to start looking for officers is to consult *Commissioned Officers in the Medical Services of the British Army,* by Peterkin and others. There is a series of records of service of officers of the Medical Department, 1800–1840, in WO 25/3896–3912, which includes details of the professional education of surgeons. These records are indexed. There is a certain amount of information for 1811–1818 in WO 25/259–263: for 1809–1852, there are casualty returns of medical staff (WO 25/265, 2384–2385, and 2395–2407). For 1825–1867, there are registers of the qualifications of candidates for commissions in the Medical Department (WO 25/3923–3944). The Royal Army Medical Corps has a medal book, 1879–1896, which may be worth a look (WO 25/3992).

Records of regular RAMC officers who served before and in the First World War will be found in WO 339 or WO 374: there is a separate index in WO 338/23, covering 1871–1921. Records of the many doctors recruited into the RAMC for the duration of the First World War, and given temporary commissions (identified as RAMC(T)), have unfortunately been destroyed.

18d.5 The Army nursing services

Testimonials of women wishing to nurse in the Crimea, c.1851–c.1856, may be found in WO 25/264. A few women nursed at Netley Hospital and on campaign after then. The much larger Army Nursing Service was established in 1884, and renamed Queen Alexandra's Imperial Military Nursing Service (QAIMNS) in 1902. Two reserve military nursing services were also established. In 1894 Princess Christian's Nursing Reserve was set up, to be renamed Queen Alexandra's Imperial Military Nursing Service Reserve (QAIMNS(R)) in 1908. The

Territorial Force Nursing Service (TFNS), established in 1908, became in 1921 the Territorial Army Nursing Service.

The records of professional qualifications and recommendations for appointment of staff nurses in QAIMNS, 1903–1926, are in WO 25/3956. There are some pension records, but few nurses served long enough to qualify for a pension. Pension records for nurses appointed before 1905 are in WO 23/93–95 and 181; pensions for QAIMNS nurses, 1909–1928, are in PMG 34/1–5. There are some service records for National Aid Society Nursing Sisters, 1869–1891 in WO 25/3955.

First World War service records of 15,792 nurses are in WO 399, in two series: one for the QAIMNS and the QAIMNS(R) and one for the TFNS. They are arranged alphabetically by name, and are searchable on PROCAT. If a nurse married, her record may be under her married name. Although dated 1914–1922 in the catalogue, they actually cover the careers of nurses whose service finished before 1939. Registers of First World War disability pensions for nurses are in PMG 42/1–12, with a selection of case files in PIN 26/19985–20826 (searchable on PROCAT). Records of the volunteer nursing services, the First Aid Nursing Yeomanry Corps (FANYs) and the Voluntary Aid Detachments (VADs) are held by the British Red Cross (address in **48**). There is a detailed history of the FANYs in HO 322/451.

The Royal Red Cross medal was instituted especially for military nurses in 1883 (WO 145). Nurses were also awarded medals for service in Egypt, 1882, and South Africa, 1899–1902 (WO 100) and the First World War (WO 329); the latter has a separate name index for nurses on microfiche. Details relating to some awards granted to members of the QAIMNS can be found in WO 162/652.

See **18d.8** for published histories.

18d.6 The Women's Auxiliary Army Corps

The Women's Auxiliary Army Corps was established in 1917. No officers' service records are known to survive, but those of other ranks are in WO 398 for 1917 to 1920. Details relating to some awards granted to members of the WAAC can be found in WO 162/652.

18d.7 The Indian Army and the British Army in India

There was an army in India that was maintained by the East India Company until 1859. This army consisted of separate divisions of European and Indian troops, which were both officered by Europeans. After 1859 the Company's Indian troops became the Indian (Imperial) Army. The European Regiments became Regiments of the Line, and the Company's Artillery and Engineers became part of the Royal Artillery and Royal Engineers: these formed the British Army in India. Details of regiments and of officers of the Honourable East India Company army, the Indian Army and of British regiments stationed in India are given in the *India List* and the *Indian Army List*: the PRO Library has incomplete sets of these. Officers from the various Indian armies are given in *Hart's Army List*, with some officers in the *Army List* as well.

The service records of the British Army in India will be found with the other army records in the PRO. There are musters of regiments in India from 1883 to 1889 (in WO 16). When a soldier was discharged on his return home, this was recorded in the depot musters of his regiment (WO 67), in the musters of the Victoria Hospital, Netley, 1863–1878 (WO 12/13077–13105), or in the musters of the Discharge Depot, Gosport, 1875–1889 (in WO 16).

British officers after 1859 were trained at Sandhurst (cavalry and infantry) before beginning their careers in India. Their records of service are with the India Office Library and Records. These can be consulted up to 1947.

The service records of European officers and soldiers of the Honourable East India Company's service, and of the Indian (Imperial) Army are mainly preserved at the India Office Library and Records, but there are some records in the PRO. Lists of officers of the European Regiments, 1796–1841, are in WO 25/3215–3219. Compensation for the sale of Indian Army commissions, 1758–1897, is recorded in WO 74. Alphabetical lists of East India Company Army pensioners (other ranks) for 1814–1866 are in WO 23/21–23, and there are more detailed registers for 1849–1868 in WO 23/17–20, and for 1824–1856 in WO 25/3137.

Registers of the death of officers in all the Indian services for the Second World War are at the General Register Office, FRC (see **4.14**). The National Army Museum has Hodson's Index, a very large secondary source card index of British officers in the Indian (Imperial) Army, the Bengal Army and the East India Company Army (but not the British Army in India). Many of the entries go beyond bare facts to include colourful stories of life. Civilians and government staff are included if they had seen Army service. The cards from this index relating to the Bombay Marine, the East India Company's Navy, are to be passed to the National Maritime Museum: the main deposit of Bombay Marine records is in the India Office Library and Records.

See also **13.9** and **18c.1.4**.

18d.8 Army 'support' services: bibliography

Army Lists, etc., of personnel
Army List (London, annually from 1754)
British Biographical Archive (London, 1984 continuing)
Dictionary of National Biography (London, 1909 continuing)
H G Hart, *Army List* (London, 1839–1915)

General works
A Peterkin, W Johnston and R Drew, *Commissioned Officers in the Medical Services of the British Army* (London, 1968)
J Piggott, *Queen Alexandra's Royal Army Nursing Corps* (London, 1990)
H Popham, *F.A.N.Y.: the story of the Women's Transport Service, 1907–1984* (London 1984)
G D Sheffield, *The Redcaps: a history of the Royal Military Police* (London, 1994)
A Summers, *Angels and Citizens: British Women as Military Nurses, 1854–1914* (London, 1988)
I R Whitehead, *Doctors in the Great War* (1999)

19

The Royal Navy

◆ ◆ ◆

19.1 Naval records: introduction

Naval records can appear complex, given the large numbers of different ranks (reflecting the specialist ranks of so many of the men in the Navy). However, in many ways they are simpler than Army records: the Navy kept good in-service records from the 1840s/1850s, so pension records are not as important. Also, the First World War records were not affected by later destruction to anything like the same extent as the Army records.

The PRO publishes two detailed guides to naval records. Pappalardo's *Tracing Your Naval Ancestors* is the most up to date, while Rodger's *Naval Records for Genealogists* concentrates on the earlier naval archive. It is quite a complex book to use, but it has a comprehensive index. The information given here is only a small selection of the immense range of records that Rodger and Pappalardo list. However, even Rodger and Pappalardo cannot cover the entire wealth of naval records, and there is much to discover among correspondence classes, for example (see **19.15**).

Of course, there are other places to discover more about life in the Navy, notably the National Maritime Museum at Greenwich, which has a huge collection of naval artefacts, records, etc., the Royal Naval Museum (see the

Figure 34 Many Admiralty records include lovely engravings: this one dates from 1747 (PRO, ADM 7/202)

article by Trotman), and the museum ships, HMS *Victory* and HMS *Belfast*. Addresses are given in **48**.

19.2 Sources for naval families

Later service records tend to give brief family details (see **19.5.1** for officers and **19.7.3** for ratings). Pension records are a prime source (see **19.6.1** for officers and **19.8.4** for ratings). Officers' passing certificates may include details of parents: see **19.3.3**. See also the indexes to the registers of naval births, marriages and deaths abroad, 1881–1965, available at the FRC and PRO mentioned in **4.14**. Certificates have to be bought in the usual way.

The following sources are not as widely known as they should be. You may need to do quite a lot of work before knowing that you need to use some of them (to discover, for example, that your seaman was killed in action). However, the naval wills discussed in **19.2.2** could act as a starting point for anyone trying to trace a seaman before 1853. See **19.16** for more records on naval dead and casualties, 1742–1948.

19.2.1 Naval officers and ratings killed in action, 1675–1832: the Royal Bounty to families

The widows, dependent children, or indigent widowed mothers aged over 50, of officers and ratings killed in action were entitled to a lump sum of one year's wages, known as the Royal Bounty, paid by the Navy Pay Office. Many people applied for the Bounty. They were not all successful: the Navy Pay Office was very concerned to find out whether the death was actually caused by wounds received in action, or whether the widowed mother was of the right age or sufficiently indigent. Many mothers applied who were not widowed, for example. It seems that the public perception of the Royal Bounty was more generous than that of the Navy Pay Office.

Proofs had to be sent in to support applications for the Bounty: these consisted mainly of marriage and death certificates, with other documents attesting the age, relationship or poverty of the applicants. There is a broken series of these very useful papers (both those accepted and those rejected) running from 1675–1822 (ADM 106/3021–3034), with a manuscript index at the PRO.

For those who were successful in their claim, there are pay lists of the Royal Bounty, 1739–1787 and 1793–1832, which give the name, address and relationship of the dependant, the name, rank and ship of the dead man, and the amount paid (ADM 106/3018–3020 and ADM 30/20). Unfortunately these are not indexed.

Applications for bounty, 1798–1821, are in ADM 106/3021–3022, with particulars for bounty, 1806–1817, in ADM 106/3033.

19.2.2 Naval wills, 1784–1861

From 1786, the depositing of wills in the Navy Pay Office was strongly encouraged, as part of a fight against fraudulent claims for back pay and prize money (26 George III, c. 63). Not all men did so, but enough did to make this a very useful source both for family history, and for finding a man's ship before 1853 (see **19.7.1** on why you need to know this). They are not simply of use for men who died in service, as claims could also be made after the death of pensioners. Also, many men deposited wills but never had call to use them: maybe they had no further claim on the Navy Pay Office.

Wills of ratings, Royal Marine other ranks and some warrant officers, generally written on pre-printed forms, and witnessed by the captain and officers as required, were sent into the Navy Pay Office either as a matter of practical forethought or, in some less provident cases, straight after being written on the deathbed. Most are very simple, and bequeath any pay or prize money owing (usually to a parent, wife or sibling, but sometimes to a friend) and appoint an executor. The parish at least is usually given – a piece of information that can help enormously with research on dry land! Wills from 1786 to 1861 are in ADM 48/1–105, with registers that can act as indexes in ADM 142/1–14. There is also a card index that currently indexes surnames A–H.

The registers in ADM 142/1–14 are worth consulting, even with an A–H name, as you can sometimes deduce the rough date of death from them. (See below for a tip on using them.) The registers give name, date of will ('executed' here simply means 'made' – not the execution of the will, but the making of the will), the ship, the man's number in the ship's muster, current residence, and the name, address and relationship or occupation of the executor. When the will was registered, a cheque (i.e. a certificate) was sent to the executor, to be produced back to the Navy Pay Office when the time came to prove the will. If a note was made that the cheque was then sent on to Doctors' Commons, or to a probate court, this means that the man was dead and probate procedure had started. Comparing the various dates should give you an idea of date of death.

The Navy Pay Office kept notes on applications from executors and next of kin after death, which may (sometimes) have attached to them wills, birth, marriage or burial certificates and other documents (ADM 44 and ADM 45). The actual applications do not seem to survive. Because applications were often some time after the date of death (and the Navy Pay Office's investigations often took several years after the application), you may end up with a date of death far earlier, or an application far later, than you expected.

1800–1860	Ratings and Marine other ranks who died in service	ADM 44	ADM 141: gives ship, date of claim, date of death [DD = discharged dead] and date of order to pay [Cas = cashier]
1830–1860	Naval officers, dockyard employees and pensioners (ratings)	ADM 45	Card index

Before you try to access these, you need to know that the registers in ADM 141 and ADM 142/1–14 use an odd system of alphabetization. Take the first letter of the surname you are looking for: add to it the next vowel (Y is treated as a vowel), and then the first consonant, whether that appears before or after the vowel. You should end up with three letters that will appear at the top of the page in ADM 141, but are just used to order the names without any warning in ADM 142. For example, Pritchard would be found under PIR, Evans under EAV, Whyte under WYH. Cross-references are given for variant spellings (e.g. Towel/Tole). In ADM 141, you need to pick up the initial letter and the number given in the relevant entry, to make a letter/number sequence to pick up in the ADM 44 list. The notes on the applications in ADM 44 are more difficult to read than the register entries, so note as much as you can from the register.

Until 1815, seamen who died with over £20 of back wages owing to them (a frequent occurrence) had their wills proved (or administration granted, if they died intestate) in the Prerogative Court of Canterbury, whose records are in the PRO (see **6.5** and **6.13**). Seamen with less money owing to them had their wills proved in the relevant local probate court and are not so easy to find (see **6.4**). After 1815, they were all proved in the relevant local court until 1858. From 1858, look in the National Probate Calendar (available on microfiche at the PRO and FRC: see **6.3**).

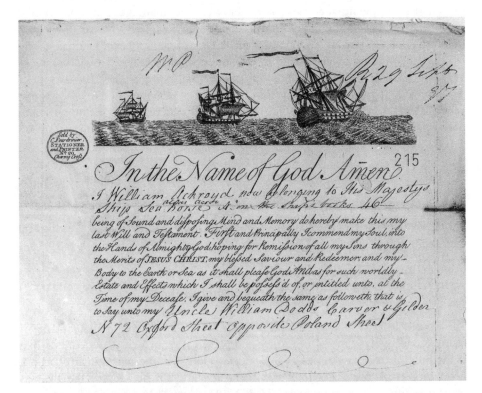

Figure 35 Naval wills were usually written on a variety of printed forms, often illustrated with the dangers of a life at sea. (PRO, ADM 48/1)

There is also a register of wills made at the naval hospital, Gibraltar 1809–1815 (ADM 105/40). Other wills of naval seamen, to c.1750, may be found in the records of the Commissary Court of London (London division) at the Guildhall Library.

19.2.3 Naval wills, 1862–1901

In 1862 a new series of naval wills started, this time apparently filed after death. Very few actual wills survive (but they should be found in the National Probate Calendar, see **6.3**). There is a remnant from 1862 to 1882 in ADM 48/106–107. However, the registers for this series survive from 1862 to 1901 in ADM 142/15–19, and these give name, ship, date of registering the will, and date of death. ADM 154, registers of men discharged dead, 1859–1878, may also be worth a look.

19.2.4 Royal Hospital School, Greenwich

The school, attached to the Royal Greenwich Hospital, was established for the sons of seamen shortly after the hospital was founded in 1694. In 1805 it was joined by a similar school for younger orphans (boys and girls), the Royal Naval Asylum. Orphans of officers and ratings killed in action or who had died in service had the prior claim for admittance, but entry was not restricted to them. The school admission papers, 1728–1870, include certificates of birth or baptisms for the children applying for entry, together with the marriage certificate of the parents, and details of the father's naval service (ADM 73/154–389: see also **19.8.2** for entry books). They are arranged by initial letter of the applicant's surname. The registers of applications, which are mostly indexed, include the same information, 1728–1883 (ADM 73/390–449). Registers of later claims are in ADM 161–163.

There are apprenticeship registers for children leaving the Royal Hospital School, 1808–1838, in ADM 73/421–448. The church registers, including many burials, for the Royal Hospital School and the Royal Naval Asylum are in RG 4/1669–1679, and RG 8/16–19.

19.2.5 Royal Greenwich Hospital: employment of ratings' widows, 1704–1863

The Royal Greenwich Hospital offered help to some widows of naval ratings by employing them as nurses. The records can include family details: see **19.13.3** and **1.13**.

19.2.6 The Royal Patriotic Fund

The Royal Patriotic Fund presented two reports to Parliament, in 1860 and 1871, listing respectively some of the Army and Navy Crimean War dependants it had helped and those whose pleas were rejected (because the man's death had not been caused by the Crimean War). These reports can be seen at the PRO as *Parliamentary Paper* microfiche 66.322–323 and 77.362–363: indexed hard copies are also available at the PRO. They give the names of wife and children, date of marriage, date of birth of children, place of wife's residence, and what happened to the children. Further records of the Royal Patriotic Fund (up to about 1917) can be seen on application (address in **48**).

19.3 Naval officers

There are some sources that cover the whole of this period, which are described first, although they are not necessarily the best place to start research. Otherwise, there is a general spilt in the mid nineteenth century, when the Navy began to keep systematic records on individual officers.

The fighting officers of the Royal Navy held office by virtue of a royal commission: they were, in descending order of rank, admiral of the fleet, admiral, vice-admiral, rear-admiral, commodore, captain, commander, lieutenant-commander, lieutenant and sub-lieutenant. Midshipmen and masters' mates were technically ratings, but were not treated as such. The initial promotion to the commissioned rank of lieutenant from midshipman or master's mate was by examination: however, passing the examination did not guarantee getting a commission. Subsequent promotions were by merit and luck as far as the rank of captain, and by seniority above that. The names of the ranks changed their meanings somewhat over time, and in particular 'captain' was often used as the title for the officer in command of a vessel, whether he was a captain or a lieutenant.

The senior warrant officers were the master, purser, boatswain, gunner, carpenter and surgeon (see **19.13.1** for surgeons): engineers were added later. These were all experts in their own field, who held their authority by a warrant, and who were examined by and answerable to other authorities. For example, masters were examined by Trinity House and returned their accounts to the Navy Board. However, masters became commissioned officers from 1808, as did pursers and surgeons in 1843, and engineers in 1847. Many more warrant officers were able to rise to commissioned rank in the late nineteenth and twentieth centuries.

Junior warrant officers (i.e. those who did not have to keep accounts) were the armourer, chaplain, cook, master at arms, sailmaker and schoolmaster. Rodger gives much more detail, particularly of the expansion of the warrant officers from three branches in 1867 to 24 in 1945, of which all but one could proceed to commissioned rank. His book contains many references to scattered sources relating to the junior warrant officers, which are not given here.

Chaplains can be traced through succession books (see **19.4.3**), but it is easier to use Kealy's *Chaplains of the Royal Navy, 1626–1903*. More recent records are still held by the Chaplain of the Fleet (address in **48**).

As well as the records described below, there are in the PRO many other possible sources of information on an officer's career. Examples are records of candidates for promotion and registers of officers unfit for service. These records are numerous and have become scattered among many different PRO series. The easiest way to locate them is to use the reconstructions of the original series in Rodger's *Naval Records for Genealogists*.

Sometimes commissioned and warrant officers can be found in the same sources, other times they appear in different series. A reference here to 'Naval officers' or 'officers' means that both are covered, otherwise 'commissioned officers' or 'warrant officers' will be specified.

19.3.1 Naval officers: published sources

There are no systematic records listing men serving in the Navy before the Restoration (1660). The various seventeenth-century State Paper series can contain much information on the Navy, particularly during the Interregnum: these have been printed in brief in the *Calendar of State Papers, Domestic*, and are therefore fairly easy to use.

From the end of the eighteenth century, it is fairly easy to trace the outlines of a commissioned officer's career in the Royal Navy. Start with the printed *Navy Lists*, which began as *Steel's Navy List* in 1782 and were updated quarterly from 1814. These contain seniority lists of officers, from lieutenant upwards, which are keyed to disposition lists of ships of the Navy with the officers appointed to them. Warrant officers appear in the *Navy Lists* at varying later dates. The *Navy Lists* are available on open shelves at the PRO, including the wartime confidential editions of 1914–1918 and 1939–1945 in ADM 177.

The *New Navy List*, compiled by Haultain, covers February 1841–February 1856. It contains similar information to the *Navy List*, but with the addition of details of war service, going back even to the 1780s. This too can be seen at the PRO.

Other printed sources are also available. From 1660, the main printed source is Syrett and DiNardo's *The Commissioned Sea Officers of the Royal Navy 1660–1815*. O'Byrne's *Naval Biographical Dictionary* gives the services of all commissioned officers alive in 1846. Admirals' and captains' services may be described in Charnock's *Biographia Navalis* (up to 1798), Campbell and Stevenson's *Lives of the British Admirals* (up to 1816), Marshall's *Royal Naval Biography* (up to 1835), and in the *Dictionary of National Biography*. See also the *British Biographical Archive* (see **1.15**).

The PRO does not hold the officers' newspaper, the *Naval Chronicle*, which should be available at the British Library Newspaper Library. However, the PRO Library does have Tracy's abridged version for 1793–1798, and also Hurst's *Naval Chronicle, 1799–1818: Index to Births, Marriages and Deaths.*

19.3.2 Naval officers: full pay and half pay registers, 1668–1920

These full and half pay registers were used for the issue of certificates of service, needed as a passing qualification for a commission, or to establish entitlement to a pension. Kept by the Navy Pay Office, they were the authoritative record of an officer's service. However, they are not necessarily the best place to start, as the information included is not very full.

1795–1830	Full pay. Separate indexed registers for each rank (including surgeons and chaplains): gives name, rank and successive appointments.	ADM 24/1–92
1830–1872	Full pay. General register of officers: gives name, rank and successive appointments. Separate registers for surgeons continue until 1858. Separate indexes.	ADM 24/93–170
1847–1874	Full pay: warrant officers and engineers.	ADM 22/444–474

The Registers of Officers' Half Pay (a retainer for the services of unemployed officers, also used as a kind of pension for 'retired' officers) can provide addresses and other information over a much longer period.

1668–1689	Half pay. In Bill Books, entered in no particular order with many other entries as well.	ADM 18/44–67	Not indexed
1693–1836	Half pay.	ADM 25/1–255	In seniority order
1836–1920	Half pay and retired pay. Also Royal Marine officers (1859–1873).	PMG 15	With indexes or in alphabetical order
1867–1900	Half pay.	ADM 23/33–140	

For 1837, there is an address book for commissioned officers, mates, masters, surgeons, pursers and chaplains on half pay (PMG 73/2).

19.3.3 Naval officers' passing certificates, 1660–1902

The Navy was a service that needed high professional skills. As a result, entry into the early stages of the profession was regulated by examination from the 1660s. There are several series of passing certificates for the different ranks: they often include certificates of previous service, and sometimes baptismal certificates.

Lieutenants' passing certificates, 1691–1902
The passing certificates of masters' mates and midshipmen qualifying as lieutenants often include certificates of service to date, and sometimes include baptismal certificates. The easiest way to access these is to use Pappalardo, *Royal Naval Lieutenants: Passing Certificates 1691–1902*, which acts as an index to the records shown.

Figure 36 Two pursers and a captain's clerk, c.1830 – included in memory of the writers of so many of the ship-based records now in the PRO (Lithograph from *Costume of the Royal Navy and Marines*, Private Collection/Stapleton Collection/ Bridgeman Art Library)

1691–1832	Passing certificates and supporting documents	ADM 107/1–63
1854–1902	Passing certificates	ADM 13/88–101 and 207–236
1744–1819	Original passing certificates (an incomplete collection)	ADM 6/86–116
1788–1818	Passing certificates issued abroad	ADM 6/117–118

There are some records relating to the examinations not in Pappalardo's index. These include registers of the examination of prospective lieutenants, 1795–1832, which give name, age, qualifying service and remarks for each candidate (ADM 107/64–70). Registers of certificates of service of prospective candidates, 1802–1848, are in ADM 107/71–75. There are even records of young gentlemen failing to pass for lieutenant (sometimes with the reasons given) for 1801–1810 (ADM 30/31).

In theory, every commissioned officer above the rank of lieutenant should have qualified for his initial lieutenancy by serving the requisite sea time and by passing the lieutenancy exam. However, some officers achieved the promotion through acts of bravery, others through patronage. In these cases there will be no passing certificate.

Masters' passing certificates, 1660–1850
Masters were supreme professionals in the knowledge of their ship, and in their seamanship. They tended to stay longer with a ship than the fighting officers, and

were re-examined if they moved on to a different type of ship. Passing certificates for qualifications in seamanship date from c.1660–1830 (ADM 106/2908–2950); they may include certificates of baptism and service. One master may have had several certificates, as promotion to a different rate of ship required a different qualification. The certificates are arranged alphabetically.

There is also an unusual series of service records for masters, compiled in the 1830s and 1840s, but covering the period 1800–1850 (ADM 6/135–168). Records were kept in individual files, containing passing certificates, certificates of service and a variety of other certificates and correspondence: the files are in alphabetical order by surname.

Gunners' passing certificates

1731–1812 (with gaps)	Passing certificates	ADM 6/123–129
1856–1863	Passing certificates	ADM 13/86–87
1864–1867	Passing certificates	ADM 13/249–250

Pursers' and paymasters' passing certificates

Pursers, later renamed paymasters, oversaw the supply and issue of the ship's stores, and also of the seamen's pay: they had to be men of some financial substance to be appointed. Pursers became commissioned officers from 1843.

1803–1804	Notes on candidates for promotion	ADM 6/121
1813–1820	Passing certificates	ADM 6/120
1847–1854	Notes on candidates for promotion	ADM 11/88
1851–1867	Passing certificates	ADM 13/79–82
1868–1889	Passing certificates	ADM 13/247–248

Boatswains' passing certificates

1810–1813	Passing certificates	ADM 6/122
1851–1855	Passing certificates	ADM 13/83
1856–1859	Passing certificates	ADM 13/85
1860–1887	Passing certificates	ADM 13/193–4

Examination results from the Royal Naval College, Greenwich, 1876–1957, are in ADM 203.

19.3.4 Naval officers: certificates of eighteenth-
and nineteenth-century service

Certificates of previous service had to be produced to prove qualification for commissions, warrants or pensions. The dates of service always predate the certificate, often by very many years. Some will be found with the passing certificates (see **19.3.3**), others with records relating to entitlement to pension (see **19.7.2**). Still others were bound up to form the first service registers (see **19.5.1**). Outside these areas, there are many other sub-series, mostly in ADM 29. See Rodger for more details.

19.4 Naval officers: service records before c.1840

Genuine service records do not start until the mid nineteenth century. Instead, information has to be pieced together from a variety of sources, including the passing certificates described above.

19.4.1 Naval officers: surveys, 1816–1861

The series of surveys conducted between 1816 and 1861 are the most convenient records of officers' service, but they do not cover all officers and are not always to be trusted.

The end of the Napoleonic wars in 1815 meant that the Navy shrank in operational strength from 145,000 to 19,000 men. Because there was no means of retiring officers, there were ten times as many as were required. In order to discover which officers had the best claims to be employed, the Admiralty sent out circular letters to officers, asking them to provide dates of birth or details of service. The replies were bound up and used for reference by the Admiralty. However, the coverage is by no means complete, as it depended on the officer receiving and replying to the letter. Many replies were lost, and the accuracy of some of them is doubtful. The exercise was repeated on several occasions.

Survey date	Coverage	References	Indexes
1816–1818	General returns	ADM 9/2–17; strays at ADM 6/66	ADM 10/2–5 Also printed indexes at the PRO
1816–1818	Boatswains, gunners and carpenters	ADM 11/35–37	
1822	Commissioned officers including masters: age	ADM 6/73–83	

1828	Admirals	ADM 9/1, strays at ADM 6/66	ADM 10/1
1831	Commissioned officers including masters: age	ADM 6/84–85	
1833–1835	Masters	ADM 11/2–3	
1846	Commissioned officers: age, address and previous service	ADM 9/18–61	ADM 10/6–7 Also printed indexes at the PRO
1851	Masters: age, address and previous service	ADM 11/7–8	ADM 10/6–7
1852, 1859	Pursers	ADM 11/42–44	
1855, 1861	Masters	ADM 11/9	

19.4.2 Naval officers: various lists, 1651–1837

There are various versions of an early list of all admirals, captains and commanders, with notes of their service, death or fate. The easiest to use are probably the alphabetical lists, 1660–1685 (ADM 10/15), 1660–1688 (ADM 10/10, which continues to 1746 arranged by seniority) and 1651–1737 (ADM 7/549). The first two also include lieutenants. There are black books of commissioned officers not to be employed for future service 1759–1815 (ADM 12/27B-27E), and another of warrant officers 1741–1814 (ADM 11/39).

19.4.3 Naval officers: succession books, 1673–1849

Succession books were a type of officers' service record arranged by ship, not by individual officer. However, most are indexed by name as well as ship, so they can provide a fairly easy way of tracing a commissioned or warrant officer from ship to ship. In the usual form, a page was devoted to each ship, and the successive appointments to each position in the ship were listed.

Boatswains and carpenters could and did transfer between sea service and dockyard work: records relating to dockyard employees are discussed in **19.11**.

| 1673–1688 | Commissioned and warrant officers. | ADM 6/425–426 |
| 1688–1725 | Admirals, captains and commanders only. | ADM 7/655 |

1699–1824	Junior officers appointed by Admiralty warrant or order, e.g. midshipmen, volunteers per order, chaplains, masters at arms, schoolmasters and scholars of the Royal Naval Academy.	ADM 6/427 and 185
1733–1763, 1771–1807	Masters, surgeons, surgeons' mates, sailmakers and some others.	ADM 106/2896–2901
1764–1831	Pursers, gunners, boatswains, carpenters and some dockyard officers.	ADM 106/2898 and 2902–2906
1780–1849	Captains, commanders and lieutenants.	ADM 11/65–72
1800–1839	Pursers, gunners, boatswains, carpenters and some dockyard officers.	ADM 6/192 and ADM 11/31–33

19.5 Naval officers: service records from c.1840–c.1930

In the mid nineteenth century, the Navy began to create a central record-keeping system for officers. In the earliest registers, information was added about previous service, so that the data can go back many years. Finding service records is relatively straightforward.

19.5.1 Naval officers: service registers from c.1840–1917/1931

For c.1840 to May 1917 (for commissioned officers) and up to 1931 (for warrant officers) there are registers of service, mostly in ADM 196, with indexes on open access at the PRO. For officers serving when the new system was introduced, these registers contain much earlier data. The dates given in the list are of entry: data was added to these registers up to the death or pension, and so can continue for many years beyond 1917 or 1931 – in some cases, until the 1950s.

In these registers, each officer has a page to cover his entire career, on which was noted dates of birth, marriage and death, home address, names of parents and wives (but almost never of children), names of ships served on, details of pay and pension, and assessments of character and ability. Several different departments kept these registers, and an officer's career may be entered in three or four almost identical registers. This can be useful, as there are frequent gaps in the various series.

Engineers were the first officers to whom this system of record keeping was applied, from 1837 (see ADM 196/71 followed by ADM 29/105–111 for engineers entering 1837–1879).

Records of officers in the Royal Naval Air Service, 1914–1918, are in ADM 273: see **21.2** for more details.

19.5.2 Naval officers: confidential reports 1884–1943

For 1884–1943, there are several series of confidential reports on officers, giving their commanding officer's (often brutally candid) view of suitability for promotion. These are also in ADM 196. You may need to get the officer's date of entry or promotion from the *Navy List* to access these easily.

Date of Promotion	Confidential reports on	Reference	Indexes
1884–1939	Assistant Clerks, Paymaster Cadets and Paymasters	ADM 196/171	Includes index
1885–1928	Lieutenants and Sub-Lieutenants	ADM 196/141–151	Indexed by ADM 196/138–139
1893–1943	Captains and Admirals	ADM 196/86–94	Include indexes
1900–1912	Gunners	ADM 196/166	Includes index
1908–1931	Commanders	ADM 196/125–128	Include indexes. Union index in ADM 196/129
1913–1930	Acting Mates and Mates promoted to Lieutenant, and recording service as far as Lieutenant Commander	ADM 196/154 –155	Include indexes

19.5.3 Naval officers: entrants after 1917/1931

The service records of commissioned officers who received their first commission after May 1917, and of warrant officers who received their first warrant after 1931, are still maintained by the Ministry of Defence, Royal Naval Records (address in **48**).

19.6 Naval officers: pensions

Until well into the nineteenth century, provision of pensions within the Navy was haphazard. There was no general entitlement to a pension for long service, although half pay was used to provide a kind of pension for officers, eventually merging into retirement pay. At various dates from 1836, officers became eligible for a retirement pension, or superannuation, either automatically on reaching a certain age, or upon application. See **19.3.2** for half pay and retirement pay up to 1920.

Extra pensions were available for particularly deserving cases, and there is usually a certain amount of personal information recorded in support of claims to these pensions. Pension records for officers are extensive, and are fully listed by Rodger. A few commissioned officers received Greenwich Hospital out-pensions: there are registers covering 1814 (ADM 22/254–261), 1815–1842 (ADM 22/47–48) and 1846–1921 (PMG 71). Warrant officers, and the civil establishment of the Navy, were paid pensions out of the Navy estimates. There are registers for 1694–1832 (ADM 7/809–822, indexed by ADM 7/823). See also **19.8.1** for pensions for wounds paid out of the Chatham Chest, 1653–1799.

19.6.1 Naval officers: pensions to widows, etc.

The pension records described here are only the most important of those available: all are listed in detail in Rodger's book.

The Charity for the Relief of Officers' Widows paid pensions to the poor widows of commissioned and warrant officers. Pay books, 1734–1835, are in ADM 22/56–237; for 1836–1929 they are in PMG 19/1–94. The papers submitted by widows applying for pensions between 1797 and 1829 include many marriage and death certificates (ADM 6/335–384): there is an index at the PRO. Similar papers for 1808–1830, referred for further consideration in doubtful cases, are in ADM 6/385–402. Entry books of sworn statements in place of marriage certificates, 1801–1818, are in ADM 30/57.

From 1809, the Admiralty administered the Compassionate Fund, voted by Parliament. It dealt with pensions and grants to orphans and other dependants of commissioned officers killed in action or who had died in service, not otherwise eligible for assistance. The registers of applications for relief give the officer's rank, date of death, length of service and ship, date and place of marriage, the applicant's age, address and relationship to the dead officer, and other circumstances: they run from 1809 to 1836 (ADM 6/323–328). Pay books for the Compassionate List run from 1809 to 1921, giving the names and ages of recipients, and their relationship to the dead officer: from 1885 warrant officers' next of kin were eligible. For 1809–1836, use ADM 22/239–250: for 1837–1921, use PMG 18.

The Admiralty's own pensions included pensions to the widows and orphans of commissioned officers and masters, dating from 1673, and of other warrant officers from 1830. There is an application book for widows' pensions, 1809–1820, in ADM 22/238.

1673–1781	ADM 18/53–118
1694–1832	ADM 7/809–822, indexed by ADM 7/823
1708–1818	ADM 181/1–27

1734–1835	ADM 22/56–237
1830–1932	ADM 23
1836–1870	PMG 16
1836–1929	PMG 19
1870–1919	PMG 20

Widows of warrant officers killed in action or on service were also eligible for pensions paid by the Chatham Chest: the registers of payment 1653–1799, were shared with the pensions to wounded men (ADM 82, described in **19.8.1**). Greenwich Hospital also provided a school for children of officers and men, to which orphans had priority of admission (see **19.2.4**).

For First World War pensions to dependants, see **18a.3.3**.

19.7 Naval ratings

There are some sources that cover the whole of this period. Otherwise, there is a general spilt in 1853, when the Navy decided it needed to retain an increasingly specialized set of men, and so began to offer better terms and conditions of service, with a central registry of ratings.

19.7.1 Naval ratings before 1853: musters and pay books

There was no centralized record of ratings' services until the introduction of continuous service in 1853. Before then, the main sources for tracing a seaman are the individual ship's muster book and pay book. To use these, you need to know at least one of the ships on which he served, and when. With this information, you should be able to work your way slowly from muster to muster, and from ship to ship.

If you are fortunate enough to research a seaman who was in receipt of a Chatham or Greenwich pension, for which there are indexed registers, you ought to be able to discover the ships he worked in quite easily (see **19.8.3**). In case the sailor died in service, or even if he did not, try the wills and relatives' applications for back pay described in **19.2.2**, as these provide an index for many seamen, 1786–1861. This may give you the name and date of at least one ship served on. If you are still unlucky, you will need luck and hard work. It may be worth doing an exploratory search in the certificates of service which were issued for some ratings (see **19.7.2**).

Musters, or lists of the ship's company, are available from 1667 to 1878 (ADM 36–40, ADM 41, ADM 115 and ADM 117). After 1878 the few surviving ships' ledgers are in ADM 117, but these muster-like records were mostly destroyed by enemy action in 1941. The musters can be found very easily by doing a search in PROCAT using the ship's name and the date range you want (this will also bring up ships' logs). If you are unsuccessful, try checking variant spellings of a ship's name as the catalogue is not always consistent – you may find references to both the HMS *Weasel* and the HMS *Weazle*, for example. Look in the *Navy List* of a suitable date for variant spellings.

The musters followed a standard format, described by both Rodger and Pappalardo, who give the various abbreviations used. There were general musters, held annually, and eight-weekly or monthly musters, which contain extra information on various deductions from pay, such as for treatment of venereal disease.

Within each muster, there were separate sections: the ship's company, the Marines, supernumeraries for wages and victuals, and supernumeraries for victuals only. In the latter case, these were men actually on the ship, but who technically belonged to (and were paid on) another ship. To find out if a man was actually present onboard or not, look at the columns 'mustered' and 'chequed'; if there is an entry in the latter, then the man was absent with leave – perhaps on another ship for victuals only! If you are trying to track a man from ship to ship, take care to look right through these categories, as men recently turned over are likely to be found among the supernumeraries.

Information on each member of the ship's company was entered into the following columns in both general and monthly musters:

- Number
- Entry & Year
- Appearance [i.e. arrival on board]
- Whence & Whether Prest [pressed] or not (This is where you may find the name of the previous ship)
- Age [from 1764: it means age at first entry to the ship, not at the time of the muster]
- Place & Country of Birth [from 1764]
- No. and Letter of Ticket [for wages]
- Men's Names
- Qualities [Rank or rating]
- D DD or R [discharged, discharged dead or run; also DS, discharged to sick quarters]
- Time of Discharge & Year
- Whither or for What Reason (this is where you may find the name of the ship to which he was turned over)

From about 1800, description books may (rarely) be included with the musters. These give age, height, complexion, scars and tattoos.

The pay books, 1691–1856 (ADM 31–35), which duplicate much of the information of the musters, have one big advantage; they contain 'alphabets' (indexes of surnames in alphabetical order of first letter only) from about 1765, some 50 years before the musters had them. It may be worth checking through the alphabets in the pay lists before going on to look at the musters, 1667–1878 (ADM 36–41). The pay books were copied from the musters, and may contain more errors: in some cases, they may also include information about next of kin to whom remitted wages were paid.

When tracing men from ship to ship, it may be useful to consult the hospital musters, particularly if the name was marked DS (discharged to sick quarters): see **19.13.4**.

19.7.2 Naval ratings, 1790–1894: certificates of (earlier) service

The standard way of tracing a naval seaman or rating, before the introduction of continuous service in 1853, is to use the muster books and pay books (see **19.7.1**). However, this can take so long and is so dependent on getting the right ship, that it is sensible to investigate easier sources: if you are lucky, you will save yourself considerable time. The best way is to look for a certificate of service, which ratings needed to support a claim for a pension, a gratuity or a medal.

Thus there are certificates of service issued by the Navy Pay Office, 1790–1865, among the papers of ratings and marines applying for entry to Greenwich Hospital as *in-pensioners*. Although the certificates were issued from 1790, the services recorded go back at least 40 years before then (ADM 73/1–35, arranged alphabetically).

There are also entry books of certificates of service of warrant officers and ratings, sent to Greenwich Hospital between 1836 and 1894. These were for the assessment of the claims of their children to be admitted to the Hospital Schools. These are scattered, in ADM 29/17, 19, 25, 34, 43, 50, 59, 70 and 80–96, and are indexed by ADM 29/97–104. As orphans had priority, many of the certificates are of the service of men already dead, and, as always, the service predates the certificate by many years.

The original certificates of service to which these entry books refer are in ADM 73/154–389, together with supporting documentation such as baptismal and marriage certificates.

| 1853–1872 | Arranged by continuous service number: use the alphabetical indexes | ADM 139 |
| 1873–1923 | Arranged by service number: use the alphabetical indexes | ADM 188 |

19.7.3 Naval ratings, 1853–1923: service records

The first centralized registration of ratings began in 1853, with the introduction of 'continuous service', instead of the previous uncertain length (i.e. discharged when no longer needed). As ratings entered the Navy, they signed up for 10 years' service if they were 18 or over: existing ratings could sign up for seven years' service. It took some time before most existing ratings were on the new system. Both (and boys under 18) were given a continuous service number. Their details were entered in a register – date and place of birth, and physical characteristics on entry. (For those who entered as boys, there is a form giving parental consent.) Further details were added throughout their career, to form a summary of their service.

The registers between 1853 and 1872 are in ADM 139: there are separate indexes, also in ADM 139. Be careful to note from the index whether the service

Figure 37 George Pusey, a signal boy, photographed in 1902 with his Royal Humane Society Medal awarded for trying to save a drowning sailor. He joined up at 15 in 1901 and served until 1920, becoming a Yeoman of Signals (ADM 188/375 no 214121). (PRO, COPY 1/456)

number has an A or B at the end, or no letter at all. Make sure you look at the top of the page, as this often says Series A or Series B. When you go to the list of ADM 139 to match up the number, take care to look for the right series – plain, A or B – or you may get the wrong document.

The system was modified for entrants from 1873 onwards, when a different numbering system was started. Between 1873 and 1894 service numbers were issued to new entrants on a next man, next number basis. Men were transferred from the old registers to the new ones, along with new entrants. The new registers from 1873–1923 are in ADM 188, in service number order. There are separate indexes, also in ADM 188, to give you the service number. The registers give date and place of birth, physical characteristics on entry, and a summary of service, compiled over the years. Some entries have a cross-reference to a 'new register': these will be the continuation books in ADM 188/83–90. These are again in service number order – just look for the number you already have.

The last entrants in this system were ratings entering the Navy in 1923: their entries have been annotated beyond 1923. They record service up until 1928, and then you will find a stamped entry saying something like 'Records transferred to card'. This refers to the next registration system, started in 1928, when the Navy switched to using an index card for each man. These records are not yet in the PRO.

As the Royal Navy became a more complex service, it was decided to group service numbers together to identify which branch of the service a man served

DISTINGUISHING BADGES OF PETTY OFFICERS,
MEN AND BOYS IN THE ROYAL NAVY.

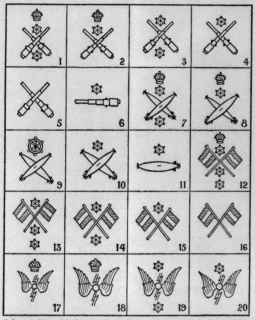

1) Gunner's Mate and Gunlayer, 1st Class. (2) Gunner's Mate. (3) Gunlayer, 1st Class.
(4) Gunlayer, 2nd Class. (5) Gunlayer, 3rd Class. (6) Seaman Gunner and P.O. (G) (Not
Gunlayer or Gunner's Mate). (7) Torpedo Gunner's Mate, Higher Standard. (8) Torpedo
Gunner's Mate. (9) Torpedo Coxswain. (10) Leading Torpedo Man. (11) Seaman Torpedo
Man and P.O. (T). (12) Chief Yeoman of Signals. (13) Yeoman of Signals. (14) Leading
Signalman. (15) Signalman. (16) Ordinary Signalman and Signal Boy. (17) Chief Petty Officer
Telegraphist. (18) Petty Officer Telegraphist. (19) Leading Telegraphist. (20) Telegraphist

Figure 38 This 1913 badge chart is useful in identifying rank from photographs. It also shows the growth of expert trades among naval ratings. (PRO, ADM 1/8331)

in. Between 1894 and 1907 blocks of service numbers were issued to the branches, to be allocated as a new man joined that branch. It is therefore possible to find two men who joined the service on the same day, having wildly differing service numbers. Between 1873 and 1907 service numbers between 40,000 and 366,000 were issued.

In 1908 the service number system was changed again. Rather than have a plain numeric service number, alphabetical prefixes denoting the branch of the service were used: J for Seamen, K for Stokers, L for Domestics and M for Miscellaneous. Between 1908 when the system was started and 1923, the date of the last available record of service, the numbers available for each prefix are; J 115433, K 63500, L 15101 and M 38000.

In 1903 the Royal Navy started a short service (SS) system. The SS papers are also in ADM 188. Those men with SS numbers 1–12000 served as seamen, and those with numbers 100001–126000 served as stokers.

If you find a service number starting with a Y, this is of a man who enrolled under the deferred scheme – the Royal Naval Volunteer Reserve. Unless he has another number as well, he will not have been called on to serve, and there will be no service record. If he does have another number, trace him through that in ADM 188 as usual.

When the Royal Naval Air Service (RNAS) was formed in July 1914, ratings serving in it were given a service number prefix F, and their papers are in ADM

188 with those of other ratings. The F prefix used by the RNAS was issued to 55,000 men between July 1914 and 31 March 1918. Men of the RNAS who became members of the RAF on formation had the F prefix removed and a 2 added to the front of their service numbers (see **21.2**).

19.7.4 Naval ratings, after 1923

These service records are not yet in the PRO. Write to the following (address in **48**). You will need to prove entitlement to buy a précis of the record – you must either be the rating, or next of kin, or have written permission from the rating or next of kin.

Entry after 1923	Ministry of Defence, Royal Naval Records
Service after 1928	Ministry of Defence, Royal Naval Records
Service after 1938	Ministry of Defence, HMS *Centurion*

19.8 Naval ratings' pensions

Until the late nineteenth century, there were three principal bodies responsible for a varied collection of naval pensions to ratings. These were the Chatham Chest, the Royal Greenwich Hosptial, and the Navy Pay Office. Records of all these are in ADM. It may also be worth checking for petitions for a pension in SP, SO and PC. For example, disabled seamen were often petitioners to the Crown for places as almsmen in the royal church foundations: there is a register of such petitions, 1660–1751, in SO 5/31.

From the late nineteenth century, other departments became involved, such as the Paymaster General (PMG) and the Ministry of Pensions (PIN).

19.8.1 Naval ratings' pensions: the Chatham Chest, 1653–1799

The Chatham Chest, set up about 1590, and funded by a deduction from seamen's wages, paid pensions to wounded warrant officers (including midshipmen and surgeons), ratings and dockyard workers killed in action or on service. The earliest payments are in the account books, 1653–1657. There are registers of payments to pensioners, 1675–1799, with alphabetical lists of the pensioners at Lady Day in each year. The indexes of pensions, 1744–1797, give names, amount of pension, particulars as to wounds, names of ships in which they served, and other information. All these records are in ADM 82.

19.8.2 Naval ratings' pensions: Royal Greenwich Hospital, from 1694

The Royal Greenwich Hospital was founded in 1694 as a home for infirm naval seamen and Royal Marines: in-pensioners lived there until 1869. There are entry books of these in-pensioners, 1704–1869, which give very full particulars, and are mostly indexed. Admission papers, although dating from 1790–1865, relate to service going back to at least 1750; they give descriptions, with details of service and the nature of disablement. Both entry books and admission papers are in ADM 73. Papers of candidates for admission, 1737–1859 are in ADM 6/223–266, with a card index covering 1737–1840 (ADM 6/223–247). The church registers of the hospital, 1705–1864 (RG 4/1669–1679 and RG 8/16–18) can be interesting: most entries relating to in-pensioners are of deaths, and occasionally include some comment as to manner of death.

However, most Greenwich pensioners were out-pensioners, who lived elsewhere. They received the out-pension as a form of superannuation, but were often still in full employment elsewhere. If pensioners re-entered the Navy, their pension would lapse until their discharge.

Registers of candidates for out-pensions, 1789–1859 (with gaps), are in ADM 6/267–320. Pay books of out-pensions, 1781–1809, are in ADM 73/95–131. For 1814–1846 they are in ADM 22/254–443, arranged alphabetically. From 1842–1883 they were paid by the War Office, through district pension offices, including many abroad: these records are arranged by place (WO 22). After this they were paid by the Paymaster General through the Post Office. Payments to seamen and Marines living abroad 1879–1921 are in PMG 71/5–13.

Other pensions were available for wounds, or for meritorious service, or for medals and honours. Records of these are in ADM 23 and PMG 16.

19.8.3 Naval ratings' pensions after 1853

In 1853 continuous service for ratings was introduced, with the aim of rewarding long service with a pension after 20 years. Seaman who achieved and kept the character marking 'very good' were entitled to a higher pension. The majority of ratings entered as boys, signed their first continuous service engagement at 18, and therefore retired at 38 (many retired at 43, after signing on for a further five years). This left a man with much of his working life remaining. The Navy employed pensioners in many duties in dockyards and naval establishments: see **19.11**.

Few records of pensions to continuous service ratings survive. Payments to seamen and Marines living abroad 1879–1921 are in PMG 71/5–13.

PIN 71 contains the personal files on over 5,000 disabled ratings and soldiers who served before 1914 (with some who returned to serve in the First World War, perhaps as Royal Fleet Reserve men). The information contained includes medical records, accounts of how injuries were incurred, and the men's own accounts of the incidents, and conduct sheets. These conduct sheets give place of birth, age, names of parents and siblings, religion, physical attributes, marital and parental status. The series is alphabetically arranged: unfortunately it is a selection only, and does not cover all disabled soldiers and sailors of that date, nor does it give any identification other than name. However, it is easy to search in PROCAT by name.

For First World War pensions, see **18c.1.6**.

19.8.4 Naval ratings: pensions and other benefits to widows and orphans

Dependants of ratings killed in action were entitled to one year's pay, known as the Royal Bounty: see **19.2.1.**

The Chatham Chest also paid pensions to the widows of warrant officers, ratings and dockyard workers killed in action or on service: the registers of payment were shared with the pensions to wounded men (ADM 82, described in **19.8.1**). Before the mid nineteenth century, Greenwich Hospital paid no widows' pensions as such, but employed seamen's widows in its infirmary. They may be traceable through the establishment books (ADM 73: see **19.13.3**). Greenwich Hospital also provided a school for children of officers and men, to which orphans had priority of admission (see **19.2.4**).

For ratings serving from about 1880 on, try PIN 71, which contains over 1,000 personal files on the widows of naval ratings and Army other ranks. This is only a selection of such files, but it is alphabetically arranged, and very informative (see **19.8.3**). For some widows' pensions, 1921–1926, see PMG 72/1–2. For First World War pensions, see **18c.1.6**.

19.9 Naval reserve forces

The Navy was backed up in time of need by a pool of expert seamen formed into a formal reserve, and volunteers, in a series of reserve forces. For a catalogue of the many reserve forces, see Rodger, *Naval Records for Genealogists*, Appendix III.

19.9.1 Sea Fencibles, 1798–1810

The Sea Fencibles were a part-time organization of fishermen and boatmen commanded by naval officers, formed for local defence, especially against invasion. Musters and pay lists, 1798–1810, are in ADM 28, together with the appointments of naval officers to the Sea Fencibles.

19.9.2 Royal Naval Reserve, 1859 onwards

The Royal Naval Reserve was established in 1859, as a reserve force of officers and men of deep-sea merchant ships. By 1890 there were 20,000 men in the RNR. In 1911, it was decided that trawlers should be employed in wartime as minesweepers and patrol vessels, so the Royal Naval Reserve Trawler Section was set up, enrolling fishermen. Also in 1911, the Royal Fleet Auxiliaries were established, with RNR officers (until 1921, when they were ranked with other Merchant Navy officers). From 1914 to 1921, a separate organization of the RNR operated on the Shetland Islands – the Shetland Royal Naval Reserve. This was effectively a coast-watching and local defence organization.

Also from 1914 to 1916, a large number of officers and ratings of the RNR served ashore in Flanders, effectively as soldiers, and formed the Royal Naval Division. In 1916, this was actually transferred to the Army as the 63rd (Royal Naval) Division. War diaries of the Royal Naval Division are in ADM 137 until 1916, and then in WO 95.

RNR officers are included in the *Navy List* from 1862. Service records of RNR officers, from 1862 to 1910 (and of honorary officers to 1960), are in ADM 240. They show details of merchant as well as naval service, and are arranged in numerical order of commission. Service records for RNR officers after 1910 are still with the Ministry of Defence. Those for 1910 to 1920 are due to be transferred to the PRO in 2002. Meanwhile, you can access some information from the medal rolls in ADM 171/92–93.

For RNR ratings serving between 1860 and 1913, try BT 164, with indexes in BT 377. The index refers to all ratings who served, but only a selection of service records were kept, so you may be unlucky. The records in BT 164 are volumes and cards. Each page or card represents five years' service, with successive terms indicated by A, B, C, etc. For any one seaman you may therefore need to look in several places.

For RNR ratings who served in the First World War and entered up to c.1921, try BT 377, indexed by BT 377/1–6. The records are in service number order: you can also pick up the service number from the ratings' First World War medal rolls in ADM 171/120–124.

For RNR ratings who entered 1922–1958, records are still with the Ministry of Defence, Royal Naval Records: for men who entered after 1958, records are with HMS *Centurion*: addresses are in **48**.

Long Service medal records are in ADM 171/70–72, covering 1909–1949.

For other records of merchant seamen, see **26**.

19.9.3 Royal Fleet Reserve, 1901 onwards

The Royal Fleet Reserve was composed of ex-naval seamen: the equivalent for officers was the Emergency List. Records of service in the Royal Fleet Reserve, 1914–1918, will be found as further entries on the original service record in ADM 188.

19.9.4 Royal Naval Volunteer Reserve, 1903 onwards, and Mine Clearance Service

The Royal Naval Volunteer Reserve was founded in 1903. It was composed of men of all walks of life – except the merchant seamen and fishermen, who formed the Royal Naval Reserve, and naval short service men, who formed the Royal Fleet Reserve. Records of the Royal Naval Volunteer Reserve, 1914–1918, are in ADM 337.

RNVR officers' records for 1903–1919 are in ADM 337/117–128, accessed by a card index. You will get an old reference: look at the list of ADM 337/117–128 to convert it.

RNVR ratings' records for 1903–1919 are also in ADM 377. A few have indexes, but to find most you have to know the rating's service number. You can get this from the RNVR ratings' medal roll in ADM 171/125–129. The records in ADM 377 are arranged by division, and then by service number. Each division had its own 'distinguishing letter'.

Letter	Division	Volumes	Index
AA	Anti-Aircraft	ADM 337/93–94	ADM 337/92 ADM 188/1155–1177
B or BZ	Bristol Division	ADM 337/1–18	–
C or CZ	Clyde Division	ADM 337/19–32	–
E	Birmingham Electrical Volunteers	ADM 337/95	–
KP, KW, KX	Crystal Palace (entered from Kitchener's Army)	Try the Fleet Air Arm Museum	
L or LZ	London Division	ADM 337–33–48	–
M or MZ	Mersey Division	ADM 337/49–61	–
MB	Motor Boat Reserve	ADM 337/96–99	ADM 188/1155–1177
MC	Mine Clearance Service	ADM 337/101–108	ADM 337/100: see below
R	Royal Naval Division	Try the Fleet Air Arm Museum (see also **19.9.5**)	
PZ	Crystal Palace (entered from civil life or from the Royal Navy)	ADM 337/62–67	–
S or St	Sussex Division	ADM 337/68–69	–
SWS	Shore Wireless Service	Try the Fleet Air Arm Museum	
T or TZ	Tyne Division	ADM 337/70–84	–
WZ	Wales Division	ADM 337/85–91	–
Y	Allocated when a man volunteered, to be replaced by a service number when called up. If only a Y number is found, the implication is that the man was not called up to serve.		

The Fleet Air Arm Museum holds Engagement Papers (the contract). For some divisions, this is all you can expect to find. Other divisions sometimes have gaps in their records. If you cannot find a service record, write to the Fleet Air Arm Museum (address in **48**).

The Mine Clearance Service (MCS) was created at the end of the First World War to clear all sea mines. It was manned by the Royal Navy, but administered by the RNVR. The service records are in ADM 337, in RNVR MC number order (see the Table above). However, the index in ADM 337/100 gives only the man's old Royal Navy service number. In this case the medal roll index is of no help, as members of the Mine Clearance Service did not receive campaign medals for this postwar work. It is therefore very difficult to find an MCS service record unless you know the number from a private source.

RNVR records from 1919–1958 have not yet been transferred to the PRO: contact the Ministry of Defence, Royal Naval Records (address in **48**). In 1958, the RNVR was amalgamated with the RNR.

19.9.5 Royal Naval Division 1914–1918

From 1914 to 1916, a large number of officers and ratings of the RNR and RNVR served ashore in Flanders, effectively as soldiers, as the Royal Naval Division. In 1916, this was actually transferred to the Army as the 63rd (Royal Naval) Division. War diaries of the Royal Naval Division are in ADM 137 until 1916, and then in WO 95.

Service records are in ADM 339, in three alphabetical sequences: ratings who survived; ratings who were killed in action; and officers (both survivors and dead). Names beginning with Mc or Mac are filed at the end of M. For RNVR entrants only, there are engagement papers at the Fleet Air Arm Museum (address in **48**). Some RND officers joined from the Royal Marines: their records do not seem to be in ADM 339. Try looking in ADM 196 (see **20.2–20.3**).

19.10 Women's Royal Naval Service

The Royal Navy was the first of the armed forces to recruit women. The Women's Royal Naval Service (WRNS) was founded in 1916, to release men from acting as cooks, clerks, electricians, signallers, storekeepers, telegraphists and many other shore-based posts. By 1919, over 6,000 women were 'Wrens'. For more detail, see Fletcher, *The WRNS A History of the Women's Royal Naval Service*. Registers of appointment of Short Service Officers are in ADM 318, for 1917–1919. Personal Files for Short Service Officers, 1916–1931, are in ADM 321. Ratings' service records are in ADM 336 for 1918–1919.

19.11 Royal Dockyard employees

The Royal Dockyards were the first great industrial enterprises of the United Kingdom. As well as the great dockyards of Chatham, Deptford, Portsmouth, Plymouth and Sheerness, other naval dockyards were situated all round the world. They were run by civilian employees of the Navy Board, who were naval officers but not sea officers. However, there was considerable movement between the two branches of the service. The commissioners (in charge of the yards) and the masters attendant (in charge of ships afloat) were usually retired sea officers. Dockyard shipwrights, having served their apprenticeship, often became carpenters in the Navy, and might return to be master shipwrights, and in the same way the other master tradesmen and the boatswain were normally recruited from the sea service. The career of any skilled man may therefore have to be traced in the records of both services: naval pensioners often began a second career in the dockyards. A Naval Dockyards Society has recently been established (address for enquiries in **48**). Correspondence from the seventeenth- and eighteenth-century dockyards is being listed in full on PROCAT by volunteers: you may find it well worth trying a search in ADM 106 on PROCAT, as it is full of personal information.

The main source for larger dockyards is the series of Yard Pay Books, 1660–1857 (ADM 42); for minor yards, treated as ships, try the pay books and musters in ADM 32, ADM 36, and ADM 37. In addition, ADM 106 contains some interesting sources, particularly the description books of artificers, 1748–1830 (ADM 106/2975–3005 and 3625); these include physical descriptions of the men in the main English yards. The Chatham Chest paid pensions to the widows of dockyard workers (and others) killed in action or on service: the registers of payment were shared with the pensions to wounded men (ADM 82, described in **19.8.4**). Pensions for dockyard workers (including many ex-seamen) for 1836–1928 are in PMG 25: for earlier records, see ADM 23.

There are other sources for dockyard employees given in the leaflet, *Dockyard Employees*, available at the PRO or on www.pro.gov.uk. This also gives a summary of records relating to individual yards, arranged by place. For dockyard police, see **24.2–24.5**.

For baptisms, marriages and burials, 1826–1946, in the naval dockyards in Bermuda, see ADM 6/434, 436 and 439. The registers at the dockyard church at Sheerness are even more extensive, covering 1688–1960 (ADM 6/429–433 and 438).

If you do find an ancestor who worked in one of the many naval dockyards, you may be interested in the photographs of work in dockyards, 1857–1961, in ADM 195.

19.12 Royal Navy apprentices

Information about dockyard and other naval apprentices may be found among the Admiralty and Secretariat Papers (ADM 1) and the Navy Board Records (ADM 106). In the Admiralty Digest (a subject index in ADM 12, relating to ADM 1 and other series), it is worth checking under the heading 'Apprentices in Dockyards'. Examination results for dockyard and artificer apprentices, from 1876, are among the records of the Civil Service Commission (CSC 10). See also CSC 6 for the regulations on applications for dockyard apprenticeships, 1885–1956. The information for candidates included with these CSC documents can give you a good idea of what the life and expected career pattern was like.

19.13 Naval medical services

Surgeons and their mates were the only medical help available on individual ships, although female nurses worked in naval hospitals and hospital ships from the seventeenth century. Male nurses were later called sick berth staff, and records were kept with the usual ratings' records.

List of ARTICLES recommended (but not obligatory) as an OUTFIT for an ENGINEER STUDENT on joining a TRAINING SCHOOL in one of HER MAJESTY'S DOCKYARDS, with their probable Cost.

	£	s.	d.		£	s.	d.
6 White Shirts - -	1	10	0	Brought forward -	6	17	0
6 Coloured Shirts -	1	4	0	6 Towels -	0	5	0
12 Collars - -	0	8	0	1 Clothes Brush - -	0	3	0
3 Night Shirts - -	0	15	0	1 Sponge -	0	2	6
6 Pairs Merino Socks -	0	9	0	1 Leather Bag -	0	8	0
4 Pairs Cotton or Merino				1 Clothes Bag -	0	5	0
Drawers - -	0	16	0	1 Brush and Comb -	0	5	0
4 Merino Vests -	0	18	0	1 Tooth and 1 Nail Brush	0	1	6
2 Neck Ties -	0	5	0	3 Pairs Boots -	2	5	0
2 Pairs Braces - -	0	4	0	1 Pair Slippers -	0	7	0
6 White Handkerchiefs	0	5	0	2 Pairs Gloves -	0	7	0
6 Coloured do.	0	3	0	1 Waterproof Coat -	1	1	0
Carried forward -	6	17	0		12	7	0

The probable annual expense attending renewals of uniforms and other clothes is estimated to be—

	£	s.	d.
For uniform - - -	9	4	0
Other clothes - -	5	14	6
	14	18	6

Washing personal clothing will cost on an average 1s. 6d. per week.

A subscription of 6d. per week by each Student is made to a "Recreation Fund," which is found to be sufficient to cover all expenses attending out and indoor games, purchasing papers, &c.

A small sum, say 9d. per week, should be included for repairs to clothes, soap, and blacking.

On the whole, a Student's annual expenses, exclusive of the yearly payments mentioned in par. 14, will be about £22 1s. 6d.

Figure 39 This kind of information adds so much to our appreciation of people's daily experiences. (PRO, CSC 6/4)

19.13.1 Naval surgeons

Until 1796, surgeons qualified by examination at the Barber-Surgeons' Company in London, and were then warranted to ships by the Navy Board. There is an incomplete collection of surgeons' passing certificates, c.1700–1800, issued by the Barber-Surgeons, or by examining boards of surgeons at the outports or overseas (ADM 106/2952–2963, arranged alphabetically). There is an index to these at the PRO, giving dates and texts of the certificates, but no references to the documents.

There are several series of service registers for surgeons: the longest covers 1774–1886 (ADM 104/12–29, indexed in ADM 104/11). Separate full pay registers of surgeons run from 1797 to 1858, before merging with the general series (ADM 24: see **19.3.2**). One particularly interesting series of registers of service contains correspondence on the merits of individual officers, 1829–1873 (ADM 104/31–40). Another interesting series of reports on questions of pay, half pay and promotion of surgeons, 1817–1832, includes much personal information about named officers (ADM 105/1–9, with internal indexes). See also the memoranda and reports on surgeons (individually and collectively), 1822–1832, in ADM 195/10–19. For other sources, consult Rodger's book.

There are full pay books of surgeons (and nurses) at Haslar Hospital (near Portsmouth), 1769–1819 (ADM 102/375–397) and at Plymouth Hospital, 1777–1819 (ADM 102/683–700). Other volumes in ADM 102 include the pay lists, often bound up with the musters, of many hospitals and stationary hospital ships in Britain and many other parts of the world; the musters of sea-going hospital ships will be found with the other musters in ADM 36 and ADM 37.

19.13.2 Naval surgeons' logs, 1785–1946

The surgeons' logs or medical journals for naval ships, 1785–1963 (ADM 101) and for convict ships, 1858–1867 (MT 32) are well worth a look: unfortunately, only a selection survives, and logs from 1946 onwards are closed for 75 years. Surgeons on board ship were required to keep a general journal on the health of the ship's company. Such journals contain accounts of the medical or surgical treatment of men, daily sick lists, statistics on diseases and comments on the state of health of the crew: quite often in the eighteenth and nineteenth centuries they include more general information as well. The Navy was always keen to preserve the health of its men and these journals, often written by educated men with acerbic and independent opinions, are usually the most accessible and informative source for the history of a voyage.

19.13.3 Naval female nurses

Greenwich Hospital, in its original form, paid no widows' pensions, but it employed the widows of seamen in its infirmary.

1704–1864	Alphabetical lists of nurses.	ADM 73/87–88
1704–1865	Registers of service. Give name, date of entry and date of and reason for leaving.	ADM 73/83–86
1783–1863	Register of nurses. Give name, age at time of entry, date of entry, where born, husband's forename, husband's date of death and in which service employed, amount of pension, whether husband hurt or wounded and on what service, number of children, and ages at time of entry. (Details of husband and family are not completed for the early entries.)	ADM 73/85
1817–1842	Applications of ratings' widows for admission to Greenwich Hospital as nurses.	ADM 6/329, ADM 6/331

There are also full pay books of nurses at Haslar Hospital, 1769–1819 (ADM 102/375–397) and at Plymouth Hospital, 1777–1819 (ADM 102/683–700). Hospital musters give details of patients, not staff.

During the later nineteenth century the Navy ceased to employ women as nurses, until the establishment of the professional Naval Nursing Sisters in 1883. They were employed first at Haslar (Portsmouth) and Plymouth, from 1897 at Chatham and Malta, and from 1901 at all Royal Naval Hospitals. In 1902 they were renamed as Queen Alexandra's Royal Naval Nursing Service (QARNNS).

From 1884, Head Nursing Sisters were included in the *Navy List*: other nursing officers were included from 1890.

1884–1909	Nursing sisters. Gives name, rank, dates of birth, entry and discharge. Indexed.	ADM 104/43
1890–1908	Annual reports on nursing sisters. For each year staff are listed in order of seniority, with name, age, hospital, dates of service and very brief comments on character and work.	ADM 104/95
1894–1929 [1959]	Nursing sisters. Dates are of appointment – the register includes service and other details up to 1959. Gives name, rank, dates of birth, entry and discharge, next of kin, annual report marks, sick leave, comments of character and ability, training qualifications and medal awards. Indexed.	ADM 104/161
1914–1919	QARNNS Reserves, signed up for wartime service only. Gives civil hospital, naval hospital, service details, brief reports of conduct and ability, recommendations for Royal Red Cross. No personal information given.	ADM 104/162–164

Succession books, listing nursing sisters and wardmasters by hospital and barracks, are available for 1921–1939 (ADM 104/96). Staff are listed in rough date order, name, rank, date and cause of appointment and discharge.

Later records are not in the PRO. Write to the Ministry of Defence, Royal Naval Records (address in **48**).

Naval nurses were eligible for the Royal Red Cross Medal from 1883, and bars, from 1917: see WO 145/1–3.

19.13.4 Naval hospital records

There are extensive muster lists of patients in naval hospitals and stationary hospital ships dating from 1740 to 1880 (ADM 102) covering Antigua, Ascension Island, Bermuda, the Cape of Good Hope, Chatham, Deal, Gibraltar, Halifax in Nova Scotia, Haslar, Jamaica, Madras, Malta, Plymouth, Woolwich, Yarmouth and for many other hospitals and hospital ships as well. There are also several musters of lunatics at Hoxton House, 1755–1818 (ADM 102/415–420) and at

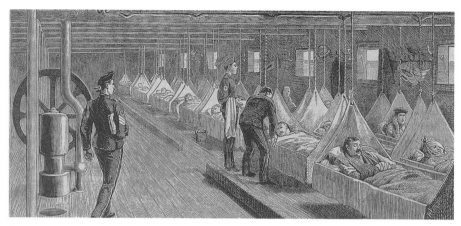

Figure 40 HMS *Euphrates* bringing home wounded troops in 1882 (Mary Evans Picture Library)

Haslar, 1818–1854 (ADM 102/356–373); Yarmouth too was a major hospital for naval lunatics. Reports on the treatment of naval lunatics, 1812–1832, are in ADM 105/28. The musters of sea-going hospital ships will be found with the other musters in ADM 36 and ADM 37.

19.14 Naval medals

Medal rolls do not give detailed information about individuals. Campaign medal rolls for the Navy are in ADM 171. Before 1914 they are arranged by ship, with no name indexes. For 1914–1920, they are in alphabetical order, with separate sequences for the Royal Navy, the Royal Naval Reserve, and the Royal Naval Volunteer Reserve. The award of the medals shown here, and some other, campaign medals are recorded in ADM 171.

1793–1840	Naval General Service Medal (Lists of recipients, 1793–1840, are given in the book by Douglas-Morris)
1840, 1857 and 1900	China Medal
1854	Crimea Medal
1857	Indian Mutiny Medal
1873	Ashanti Medal
1875–1876	Arctic Medal
1899	Queen's South Africa Medal
1901	King's South Africa Medal
1902	Africa General Service Medal
1911	Delhi Durbar Medal
1914–1920	British War Medal and Victory Medal and Stars

Gallantry medals are discussed in detail by Pappalardo. They were first instituted during the Crimean War: others were added later, particularly during the First World War. Some surviving recommendations are in ADM 1 and ADM 116 (look under code 85 in both). Registers of gallantry awards to naval officers during the First World War are also in ADM 171; there is an index available, which gives the dates of entries in the *London Gazette*. Another index gives the dates of entries in the *London Gazette* for most awards to naval personnel from 1942 onwards. The PRO holds a complete set of the *London Gazette*, in the series ZJ 1.

19.15 Finding out more about life in the Navy

Many people, having found details of a naval forebear, want to investigate the records of the ships in which their ancestor served. This really means looking at operational records.

19.15.1 Logs and reports of proceedings, 1669–1967

Naval logs (with the exception of the surgeons' logs) recorded the ship's position and movements, and the weather: they rarely provide personal information on the officers and crew of a particular ship. However, they do provide a reliable record of a ship's voyages.

1669–1852	Captains' logs	ADM 51
1672–1871	Masters' logs	ADM 52, ADM 54
1757–1904	Explorations logs	ADM 55, ADM 51
1799–1967	Ships' logs	ADM 53
1914–1967	Submarines' Logs	ADM 173
	Lieutenants' logs	At the National Maritime Museum

For the Second World War, the logs of ships smaller than cruisers do not appear to have survived, apart from those for 1939 and the early months of 1940.

The logs in the PRO can be found very easily by doing a search in PROCAT using the ship's name and the date range you want (this will also bring up musters and pay books). If you are unsuccessful, try checking variant spellings of a ship's name as the catalogue is not always consistent – you may find references to both the HMS *Weasel* and the HMS *Weazle*, for example. Look in the *Navy List* of a suitable date for variant spellings.

The surgeon's log may give a glimpse of daily life on board ship, from a less official perspective: it is well work looking to see if one exists for a ship that you are interested in. See **19.13.2**.

Another set of records is less easy to find, but may be much more interesting, as they were intended to be (and are) very informative. These are the letters and reports of proceedings from the captain of each ship, reporting back to the Admiralty from all parts of the world. To use them, you have to discover the name of the ship's captain (from documents you have already looked at, or from the *Navy List*). You will not be able to find them on PROCAT, as you find them through original indexes at the PRO.

- For 1698–1839, they are in ADM 1/1435–2738, in a sub-series of Captains' Letters, filed by the initial letter of the captain's name. For a subject index from 1793 onwards, use the indexes in ADM 12, looking under the ship's name and picking out *Captain's Letters* or *R of P*: then go back to the ADM 1 list.
- For 1839–1938, you will need to use the indexes in ADM 12 to find similar letters in ADM 1 (for the First World War, in ADM 137).
- For 1939 on, they may be found in ADM 1 or ADM 199, but there is as yet no ADM 12 to help you.

Once you have learned how to use ADM 12, you will discover that it is a detailed index to Admiralty letters, and can contain references to almost anything. It is certainly worth exploring for officers, and can be for men.

Lieutenants' letters to the Admiralty can also be found the same way, although letters before 1791 were destroyed by enemy action in 1941.

19.15.2 Naval operational records

Operational records are extensive, and can be complicated. There are leaflets available at the PRO and at www.pro.gov.uk giving guidance on naval operational records for 1660–1914, 1914–1918 and 1939–1945. If you are interested in the world wars, try looking in the PRO Library for the two detailed official histories written directly after the wars from the documents, the *History of the Great War* and *History of the Second World War*. Each of these has volumes on the war at sea.

19.16 Naval (war) dead and casualties

There are various collections of material on naval dead (see table on p. 285): see also the records discussed in **19.2**, many of which related to naval dead.

There is a card index of naval officer casualties of the First World War (1914–1919) at the PRO, annotated with details of on which naval memorial they are commemorated, and of next of kin informed of the death. The Commonwealth War Graves Commission includes naval dead from both World Wars in its Debt of Honour Register (see www.cwgc.org and **18c.1.1** for more details). See also the indexes to the registers of naval war deaths, 1914–1921 and 1939–1948, and to naval births, marriages and deaths abroad, 1881–1965, available at the FRC and PRO mentioned in **4.14**. Certificates have to be bought in the usual way.

1742–1782	Names of seamen slain	ADM 106/3017
1787–1809	Dead men's wages: alphabetical list of seamen: no. 4 gives name and ship, no. 5 also gives date of death	ADM 80/4–5
1798–1831	Register of dead men's wages	ADM 80/6–12
1854–1929	Registers and indexes of killed and wounded	ADM 104/14–149
1859–1878	Ratings discharged dead	ADM 154
1893–1950	Index to registers of reports of death	ADM 104/102–108
1900–1941	Registers of reports of deaths	ADM 104/122–126
1903–1933	Naval officers died	ADM 10/16
1915–1929	Index to registers of killed and wounded	ADM 104/140–143
1939–1948	Register of reports of deaths: naval ratings	ADM 104/127–139

Information on men who died in the two world wars can be easily accessed from the Debt of Honour Register on the website of the Commonwealth War Graves Commission (www.cwgc.org). This is accessible from the PRO. You can find here a record of all Navy personnel who died in the First and Second World Wars, with date of death, place of burial, ship and sometimes a mention of parents or wife. If you are looking for a really common name, you may have some problems, as quite often only an initial is given instead of a forename.

19.17 The Royal Navy: bibliography

Lists etc., of personnel
British Biographical Archive (London, 1984)
J Campbell and W Stevenson, *Lives of the British Admirals* (London, 1917)
J Charnock, *Biographia Navalis* (London, 1794–1798)
Dictionary of National Biography (London, 1909 continuing)
K Douglas-Morris, *The Naval General Service Medal, 1793–1840* (Margate, 1982)
N H G Hurst, *Naval Chronicle, 1799–1818: Index to Births, Marriages and Deaths.* (Coulsdon, 1989)
A J Kealy, *Chaplains of the Royal Navy, 1626–1903* (Portsmouth, 1905)
J Marshall, *Royal Naval Biography* (London, 1823–1830)
National Maritime Museum, *Commissioned Sea Officers of the Royal Navy, 1660–1815* (London, 1954 and later)
Navy List (London, 1814 onwards)
W R O'Byrne, *Naval Biographical Dictionary* (London, 1849)
D Steele, *Steele's Navy List* (London, 1782–1817)
D Syrett and R L DiNardo, *The Commissioned Sea Officers of the Royal Navy 1660–1815* (Navy Records Society, 1994)

General works
Calendar of State Papers Domestic, Charles I (London, 1858–1897)
Calendar of State Papers Domestic, Charles II (London, 1860–1947)
Calendar of State Papers Domestic, Commonwealth (London, 1875–1886)

M H Fletcher, *The WRNS A History of the Women's Royal Naval Service* (1989)

History of the Great War (HMSO)

History of the Second World War (HMSO)

B Pappalardo, *Royal Naval Lieutenants: Passing Certificates 1691–1902* (List and Index Society, vol. 290, 2002)

B Pappalardo, *Tracing Your Naval Ancestors* (PRO, 2002)

N A M Rodger, *Naval Records for Genealogists* (PRO, 1988)

N Tracy, *The Naval Chronicle: the contemporary record of the Royal Navy at war. War Reports, Commanding Officers' Gazette Letters of Naval Actions, Narratives taken from foreign sources, Intelligence Reports on the fleets of Europe and of the American Republic, letters from serving Officers on naval strategy, tactics, gunnery, ship design, and professional concerns, and with a variety of original papers on nautical subjects* (London, 1998)

A Trotman, 'The Royal Naval Museum, Portsmouth: Genealogy at the King Alfred Library and Reading Room', *Genealogists' Magazine*, vol. XXIV, pp. 197–199

20

The Royal Marines

◆ ◆ ◆

20.1 History of the Royal Marines

Soldiers formed part of the complements of ships of war from the earliest times, but the first British military unit to be raised specifically for sea service was the Lord Admiral's Regiment, formed in 1664. From 1690 additional Marine Regiments were raised in wartime for sea service, and disbanded at the end of the war, when the soldiers were discharged and the officers went on half pay. Oath rolls exist for the oath of association in support of William III taken by the First and Second Marine Regiments in 1696 (C 213/290–291).

Though intended for and usually employed in the sea service, these early Marine Regiments were part of the Army and were organized like other foot regiments. Parties serving at sea came under naval discipline and were borne on their ships' books (on a separate list) for wages and victuals (see **19.7.1**), but in other respects their administration and records did not differ from those of other foot regiments. Marine Regiments sometimes served ashore as ordinary infantry, while other (non-Marine) infantry regiments contributed soldiers for sea service as necessary.

These Marine Regiments were disbanded for the last time in 1749. At the approach of war again in 1755, a new Corps of Marines was formed under Admiralty authority. This was not part of the Army, and it had no regimental structure, though it continued to use Army ranks and uniform. The 50 companies were divided for administrative and recruiting purposes between three Divisions, with their depots at Portsmouth, Plymouth and Chatham. From 1805 to 1869, there was a fourth Division, based at Woolwich. Both Divisions and companies were purely administrative entities and not fighting formations; officers and other ranks were drafted for sea service without regard to them, and each ship's party of Marines commonly included men of several companies. The Marine depots maintained records similar to those of foot regiments, while Marine detachments at sea were borne on the ships' books as before. Marines sometimes served ashore, particularly as landing parties, when they would be organized into companies and battalions. If serving under military command in such circumstances they came under military discipline, but otherwise they were responsible solely to the Admiralty.

Figure 41 A private of the Royal Marines, 1805 (Royal Marines Museum)

The duties of Marines afloat were, in action to lay down musketry on the enemy's decks; and otherwise to mount sentries and contribute to the unskilled labour of working the ship. From time to time they continued to be supplemented in these roles by infantrymen lent by the Army. Until the twentieth century the duties of the Royal Marines were almost entirely to provide detachments for ships. In 1914, however, a large force of Marines was landed to defend Antwerp, and some subsequently fought on the Western Front. In the 1930s the Marines developed a new role as part of the Mobile Naval Base Defence Organization, and from 1942 they contributed units known as Commandos which operated under Combined Operations Headquarters, and specialized in raids on enemy coasts. After the war this became the principal duty of the corps.

Another category of troops serving afloat were the artillerymen who manned the mortars carried by bomb vessels. Disciplinary and other problems with them led the Admiralty in 1804 to form companies of marine artillery to man the bomb vessels. This led to a formal division in 1859 between the Royal Marine Artillery (with barracks at Eastney, near Portsmouth) and the Royal Marine Light Infantry, which lasted until the two corps were amalgamated in 1923. They were known respectively as the Blue Marines and the Red Marines.

Correspondence and papers on policy matters, including the raising and deployment of marine companies, may be found in several series of records. The In-Letters of the Admiralty include a special section for letters from marine officers 1787–1839 (ADM 1/3246–3357), and the Out-Letters also include a section for letters to, or concerning, marines for the period 1703–1845 (ADM 2/1147–1251).

There is a specialist guide to the PRO's holdings by Thomas, *Records of the Royal Marines*. Other records (usually less formal records, and personal material) are held by the Royal Marines Museum, at Eastney. Their archives contain manuscripts, letters, documents, diaries and administrative material dating back to the eighteenth century, plus a photo, tape and video collection. They also have a library that contains *Navy Lists* from 1783 and *Marine Officer Lists* from 1755, supplemented with *Army Lists*, for tracing the service of any Marine officer. The collection includes biographical, campaign and uniform sections along with various regulations, laws, orders and reports. Sets of professional journals are also available. Of particular interest is the Marines' own magazine, *The Globe and the Laurel*, from 1892 to date, which contains obituaries of officers and other ranks. A card index to officers' obituaries exists, and one is being created for the other ranks. These collections can only be made available for research by appointment. For more information, try the Museum's website (www. royalmarinesmuseum.co.uk) or write to the address in **48**.

20.2 Royal Marines: commissioned officers appointed up to 1925

The scattered nature of Marine forces meant that a considerable number of junior officers was required. Commissions in the Marines, unlike Army commissions, were not sold, but were free appointments. As a result, a large number of Marine officers came from the poorer gentry families of the remoter parts of Ireland and Scotland who could not afford to buy commissions but still sought honourable employment. There was little chance for promotion within the Marines as the number of senior officers needed was so small. Some Marine officers went on to buy further promotion in the Army.

Commissions and appointments for 1703–1713 are recorded in ADM 6/405; for 1755–1814, they are in ADM 6/406. There is no index, and they contain no genealogical information. There are some lists of officers' services, 1690–1740, in ADM 96/1–2. Apart from these, no original service records of officers appointed before 1793 have survived. You can discover the outline of an officer's career from the *Marine Officers Lists*, 1757–1850 (ADM 118/230–336) and 1760–1886 (ADM 192): they are indexed from 1770. You could also use the *Army Lists* from 1740 onwards. The *Navy List* (from 1797) and *Hart's Army List* (from 1840) also include Marine officers. There is a register of commissions issued between 1849 and 1858 in ADM 201/8.

Service records for Marine officers commissioned between 1837 and 1925, with some from 1793 onwards, will be found in ADM 196/58–65, 83 and 97–114. These give full service details and in some cases the name and occupation of the officer's father. For officers appointed up to 1883, use the composite index in ADM 313/110: after that each of the ADM 196 volumes are indexed. There is a separate service register for officers of the Royal Marine Artillery, 1798–1855, in ADM 196/66.

There are some other sources, which may be worth investigation. Pay records in ADM 96 can give some extra information. There are lists of half pay officers for 1789–1793 and 1824–1829 in ADM 6/410–413. The survey of officers conducted in 1822 (as for the Navy: see **19.4.1**) can provide details of age (ADM 6/73–83 and 409). There was a further survey in 1831 (ADM 6/84–85). For 1837, there is an address book for Marine officers on half pay (PMG 73/2). Confidential letters on officers' affairs, 1868–1889, are in ADM 63/27–30; they are indexed. The general administrative papers in ADM 193 and ADM 201 may provide more information on individuals.

Very comprehensive obituary material may be found in *The Times* as well as in *The Globe and the Laurel* (held by the Royal Marines Museum).

All enquiries concerning officers appointed after 1925 should be sent to the Royal Marines, Historical Record Office at the address given in **48**.

20.3 Royal Marines: warrant officers appointed up to 1920

For Woolwich Division, 1812, there is an alphabetical list of warrant officers and ratings, entered for limited service (ADM 6/407).

Dates of entry	Latest date of discharge	
1875–1903	1946	ADM 196/34
1873–1907	1946	ADM 196/35
1904–1912	1923	ADM 196/67
1890–1920	1944	ADM 196/102

There is a name index of Royal Marine warrant officers and references for their records filed with the ADM 196 list. Many warrant officers went on to become commissioned officers: you may need to check the records of commissioned officers as well.

20.4 Royal Marines: other ranks enlisting up to 1925

Records relating to Royal Marines other ranks are abundant. Marines aboard ship (provided that their ship is known) can be found in the ship's muster books and pay lists: see **19.7.1**. There are three main series of records relating to a marine's service (attestation forms, description books, and service registers) and each is arranged by Division. It therefore cuts down the length of your search if you can identify the Division in which your man served. A marine usually stayed in the same Division throughout his career. If you do not know the Division, try the following methods to find it out:

- Look in the card index to the attestation records in ADM 157.
- If you know any of his medal entitlements, look at the campaign medal rolls in ADM 171.
- If you know the name of a ship he served on, and the date, use the *Navy List* (copies are on the open shelves in the Microfilm Reading Room) or Ship's musters (ADM 36–39) to establish the ship's home port. Before 1947 marines

who were to serve on board a ship were drawn from the same RM Division as the home port of the ship.

- If you know his Company number, and a date, consult the table in Appendix 1 of Thomas's *Records of the Royal Marines*. Or you can consult the tables of allocation of Company Numbers to Divisions as set out in the *Lists of Officers of the Royal Marines* in ADM 118/230–336 and ADM 192.
- If your man was a war casualty in the First World War consult ADM 242/7–10. These are documents similar to a war graves roll. For the Second World War see the Royal Marines Museum book *A Register of Royal Marine Deaths, 1939–1945*, available at the PRO.
- If you have an address where he lived, from a birth or marriage certificate, or from the census, you may assume with some certainty that he would have joined the nearest Division to that address. He would have belonged to that Division's 'catchment area'.

The attestation forms, 1790–1925 (ADM 157) were completed at the time of enlistment, but are now filed in order of discharge date (except for those of the Chatham division) up to 1883. They can include details of discharge or death. There is a card index, covering the first 659 pieces of ADM 157, up to 1883.

Each division also kept its own discharge books (ADM 81 and ADM 183–185). For the Woolwich Division there is an alphabetical list of warrant officers and ratings who had entered for limited service, dated 1812 (ADM 6/407).

The description books, c.1750–1940 (ADM 158) consist of several different, though related, types of register, arranged by date of enlistment, and then by first letter of surname. They provide information similar to the Army's description books (see **18b.4.6**); age on enlistment, parish of birth, and a brief physical description. They do not give details of service.

The service registers cover 1842–1936, but are subject to a 75-year closure rule: they are in ADM 159. In 1884, a system of divisional numbers was introduced, with each man having a unique number in his Division: it was applied retrospectively, so each Division has a different starting date for the numbers. Men who had served with the Woolwich Division (disbanded in 1869) were numbered among their new Division, from 1869. If you do not have the service number, order the index for your man's surname in ADM 313. This should give you the service number. If you have not been able to identify his Division, you will have to order each piece within ADM 159 that contains his service number, regardless of Division. However, the information contained in these registers is worth looking for: date and place of birth, trade, religion, date and place of enlistment, physical description, a full record of service, and comments on conduct, promotions, etc. The registers so far available cover some men who served up to the Second World War.

For records of service of men enlisted after 1925, write to the Ministry of Defence, Royal Marines Historical Records Office, at the address given in **48**.

20.5 Royal Marines: records of families

Each Division of the Royal Marines kept its own registers of births, marriages and deaths, and of children and wives borne on the strength. These registers give the Marine's rank, and some information on posting from the Division to a ship or station, under the heading 'disposal'.

Chatham	1830–1913	ADM 183/114–120
Portsmouth (marriages only)	1869–1881	ADM 185/69
Plymouth	1862–1920	ADM 184/43–54
Woolwich (marriages only)	1822–1869	ADM 81/23–25
Royal Marine Artillery	1810–1853 1866–1921	ADM 193 ADM 6/437

20.6 Royal Marines: casualty and pension records

Marines casualties from 1893–1956 are listed alphabetically in ADM 242/7–10, giving name, rank, number, ship's name, date and place of birth, cause of death, where buried and next of kin. Try also the Commonwealth War Graves Commission (see **4.12**). There are also many registers of killed and wounded in ADM 104, covering 1854–1941, although the later ones are closed for 75 years. For more information on other possible sources, see Thomas, *Records of the Royal Marines* or the leaflets available at the PRO or on the PRO website.

Pension records for the Royal Marines and their families are fairly extensive, but in general the records are the same as those for Naval pensions: the Royal Hospital Greenwich was founded to aid both the Navy and the Marines. For more details, see **19.8.2**. There are two alphabetical registers of Marine officers receiving Greenwich pensions, 1862–1908, which give considerable details (ADM 201/22–23).

Pensions to the widows of Marine officers will be found in ADM 196/523 (1712–1831), PMG 16 (1836–1870), PMG 20 (1870–1919), and PMG 72 (1921–1926). The last series, PMG 72, appears to relate to other ranks as well. For pensions to officers' children, 1837–1921, see PMG 18. More information on families may perhaps be found in the registers of powers of attorney, 1800–1899 (PMG 51).

For details of pensions and other help provided to families by the Royal Greenwich Hospital, which catered for the Marines as well as the Navy, see **19.8.2, 19.8.3** and **19.2.4**.

20.7 Royal Marines: wills

There is a collection of Royal Marines' wills and administrations, 1740–1764, in ADM 96/524. Wills were later deposited in the Navy Pay Office by Royal Marines other ranks: see **19.2.2–19.2.3**. There is also a register of probates affecting the payment of pensions, 1836–1915, in PMG 50.

20.8 Royal Marines: medals

Medal records for the Royal Marines are the same as those for the Navy: see **19.14**. Many Marines also received Army gallantry medals. For correspondence on good conduct medals and gratuities, 1849–1884, which includes individual service records, see ADM 201/21.

20.9 The Royal Marines: bibliography

H E Blumberg, *Britain's Sea Soldiers 1914–1919* (Devonport, 1924)

C Field, *Britain's Sea Soldiers* (Liverpool, 1924)

J A Good, *A Register of Royal Marine Deaths, 1914–19* (Royal Marines Historical Society, 1991)

J A Good, *A Register of Royal Marine War Deaths, 1939–1945* (Royal Marines Historical Society, 1991)

A C Hampshire, *The Royal Marines Tercentenary, 1664–1964* (1964)

A J Lowe ed., *Records of the Portsmouth Division of Marines, 1764–1800* (Portsmouth Record Series 7, 1990)

J L Moulton, *The Royal Marines* (London, 1972)

Royal Marines, *The Globe and the Laurel* (1892–)

Royal Marine Museum, *The Royal Marines: a Short Bibliography* (Southsea, [1978])

P C Smith, *Per Mare Per Terram: A History of the Royal Marines* (St Ives, 1974)

C C Stadden and others, *Uniform of the Royal Marines* (Romford, 1997)

G Thomas, *Records of the Royal Marines* (PRO, 1995)

21

The Royal Air Force and earlier air services

◆ ◆ ◆

21.1 History of the air services

The first air service was the Royal Flying Corps, created by royal warrant in 1912, to counter the potential threat of German airships. It was composed of the Military and Naval Wings, the Central Flying School and the Royal Aircraft Factory, and came under the control of the War Office. A brief biography of those RFC/RAF airmen whose service number was between 1 and 1400 (i.e. those men who joined the RFC between 1912 and August 1914), can be found in *A Contemptible Little Flying Corps* by Webb and McInnes. In July 1914, the Naval Wing was detached to become the Royal Naval Air Service, controlled by the Admiralty. The services were reunited as the Royal Air Force on 1 April 1918, by the amalgamation of the Army's Royal Flying Corps and the Navy's Royal Naval Air Service.

The official histories of both the First and Second World Wars, in the PRO Library, give accounts of events. Spencer's *Air Force Records for Family Historians* is a specialist guide to the records, which you can consult for more detail. Leaflets at the PRO and on the PRO website give advice on medals, and on using operational records to track down individuals.

For war dead, see **4.12** on the Commonwealth War Graves Commission. The FRC has indexes to RAF war deaths, 1939–1948, and also to RAF births, marriages and deaths abroad, from 1920: these indexes can also be seen at the PRO. The actual certificates have to be bought from the GRO at Southport. See **4.14**. See also Hobson's *Airmen Died in the Great War*.

The RAF has its own historical website, which is well worth a look at www.raf.mod.uk/history. The RAF Museum at Hendon has photographs, air logbooks and a huge collection of privately-deposited officers' records, as well as planes. Its archive includes a card index of every aircraft that flew in the RAF. The Imperial War Museum at Duxford is another place to see early RAF planes. The addresses are given in **48**.

21.2 Officers in the RFC, RNAS or RAF

Service records of RFC officers who died or were discharged before 1 April 1918 will be found with the usual run of Army officers' records in WO 339 or WO 374, and are subject to the same warnings (see **18c.1.4**). RFC officers still alive at the creation of the RAF took their records with them, and these will now be found filed with their later records in AIR 76.

Royal Naval Air Service registers of officers' service records from July 1914 to March 1918 are in ADM 273, with a card index of names at the PRO. The RNAS registers include confidential reports on the officer's ability, some combat details and brief accident or sickness reports. They should (but don't always) give birth date and next of kin.

Once the RAF was formed, it created its own records of service, rather than using those created by the Admiralty or War Office. These new records, mainly for officers discharged before 1920, are in AIR 76, in alphabetical order.

Medals awarded for First World War service are in WO 329 for the RFC and RAF and in ADM 171 for the RNAS. Disablement pensions and gratuities for the First World War may be found in PMG 42. Pensions paid to the dependants of deceased officers are in PMG 44. See also PMG 43 for supplementary payments to officers and dependants.

Service records after the early 1920s (it is difficult to be exact) are still kept by the Ministry of Defence. The officer or next of kin, or someone else with their formal permission, can ask for brief details by writing to the Ministry of Defence, RAF Innsworth (address in **48**). They also have details about campaign and gallantry medals for the same period, and their file reference can provide a much needed clue in locating recommendations in AIR 2 at the PRO that would otherwise be very difficult to find.

Officers' careers can also be traced in the *Air Force List*, available at the PRO. The *Air Force List* starts in 1918: before that you will need to use the *Army List* or *Navy List*. For 1939–1954 the *Confidential Air List* is kept separately (in AIR 10). Correspondence with officers, recommendations for awards and promotions, confidential reports and combat reports are found in AIR 1: indexes are available. For records of RAF prisoners of war, see AIR 20/2336, and **22.6–22.7**.

21.3 Airmen in the RFC, RNAS or RAF

Records of RFC airmen who were killed or discharged before 1 April 1918 may be found in WO 363 or WO 364 – subject to the usual warnings (see **18c.1.5**). The records of RNAS other ranks are in ADM 188 (see **19.7.3**), and contain information on service up to 31 March 1918.

A muster of all other ranks (in service number order) serving in the RAF on formation can be found in AIR 1/819 and AIR 10/232–237. The muster can provide the man's rate of pay, his trade, the date of his last promotion and whether he was on an open engagement or was serving for the duration of the war only.

Service records of RAF airmen with a service number up to 329000 are in AIR 79, arranged in service number order. Use the index in AIR 78 to find the service number. The service records usually give date and place of birth, physical description, religion, next of kin, wife and children, date of joining, promotions, units served in, award of medals and date of discharge.

However, if a man within this number range (1–329000) went on to see service in the Second World War, his record will not be in AIR 79 as it is still kept by the Ministry of Defence. Details for these men (and of men whose service number was 329001 or higher) can be obtained by the airman, or his next of kin, or someone with their formal permission, from the Ministry of Defence RAF Innsworth (address in **48**).

Medals awarded for First World War service are in WO 329 for the RFC and RAF, and in ADM 171 for the RNAS. Pensions to disabled airmen and gratuities for the First World War may be found in PMG 42.

21.4 Operational records

Operational records of the RFC during the First World War are in AIR 1, AIR 23, AIR 25 and AIR 27–29. Operational records of the RNAS can be found in ADM 1, ADM 116 and ADM 137.

Operations Record Books (AIR 24–29) are the diaries of the RAF and do not contain much personal detail, apart from promotions, transfers and awards. Crashes and casualties incurred during operations are recorded here. For those that happened on non-operational flights, apply to the Ministry of Defence, Air Historical Branch (address in **48**).

21.5 Women's Auxiliary Air Force

The Royal Flying Corps had all-women companies to ease the labour shortage by 1917. The Women's Auxiliary Air Force was founded with the RAF on 1 April

Figure 42 Aerial bombing started in the First World War (H.N.Wilson *The Great War* Vol. 11, PRO Library)

1918. Over the next nine months alone 9,000 women were recruited to work as clerks, fitters, drivers, cooks, armourers, radio operators, parachute packers, balloon operators, flight mechanics, instrument mechanics and pigeon women. Women were divided into those who could only work locally (because of domestic responsibilities) and 'mobiles'. In March 1919, 'mobiles' were sent to France and Germany to replace demobilized airmen. Approximately 500 women served abroad between 1919 and 1920. The WAAF finally disbanded on 1st April 1920, only two years after it had been formed. There is a very interesting website at www.raf.mod.uk/history/wraf, the source of much of this information.

Service records for the Women's Auxiliary Air Force officers are not known to survive. Service records for airwomen, 1918–1920, are in AIR 80, in alphabetical order by blocks of names. There is also an index in AIR 78. The records give name, age, home address, marital status, details of dependants, appointments and promotions, and whether the woman was mobile or not.

The WAAF was reformed on 28th June 1939, and renamed the Women's Royal Air Force on 1st February 1949. Records from 1939 onwards are still kept by RAF Innsworth (address at **48**).

21.6 Royal Air Force Nursing Service

This service began in January 1919: in 1923 it became Princess Mary's Royal Air Force Nursing Service. Service records remain at the Ministry of Defence, RAF Innsworth (address in **48**).

21.7 The Royal Air Force and earlier air services: bibliography

Air Force List (from 1918)
B E Escott, *Women in Air Force blue: the story of women in the Royal Air Force from 1918 to the present day* (Wellingborough, 1989)
C Hobson, *Airmen Died in the Great War* (Hayward, 1995)
W Spencer, *Air Force Records for Family Historians (PRO, 2000)*
J V Webb and I McInnes, *A Contemptible Little Flying* Corps (London, 1989)

22

Prisoners of war

◆ ◆ ◆

22.1   Introduction

Information on prisoners of war is not all that easy to find. A search of PROCAT using the keywords 'prisoners' and 'war' reveals a vast array of documents. However, most of these are about the cost of feeding, clothing and transporting foreign prisoners, or the technicalities of prisoner conventions, rather than about individuals.

22.2 Prisoners of war before 1793

These records mainly relate to the American Revolutionary War, and to wars with France. Other records relating to prisoners of war from these conflicts can also be identified from Andrews, *Guide to the Materials for American History, to 1783, in the Public Record Office of Great Britain*. The few records available relate largely to French or American prisoners in British custody. These include the

- In-Letters of the Admiralty Medical and Prisoners of War Department in ADM 97;
- Correspondence and Miscellaneous Papers in ADM 105, which contain the petitions and complaints of prisoners from 1703;
- State Papers Naval in SP 42.

Lists of American seamen made prisoners of war, and removed from the ports to Shrewsbury in the 1770s, are in SP 42/57.

Records concerning the exchange of British prisoners can be found in ADM 97, WO 1/11 and 13, and WO 34/67 and 170. A list of names of both British and American officers who were prisoners of war was drawn up in 1781 with a view to an exchange. The list gives the name, rank and corps/regiment of British and German officers who were to be exchanged with American officers of the same rank. They can be found in WO 40/2. Reference to this can also be found among Treasury files in T 64/23–24.

22.3 Prisoners of war, 1793–1914

There is a lot of material for the period of the Revolutionary, French and American wars, but it is not easy to access. For Britons in enemy hands, there are lists and accounts of prisoners of war in France and elsewhere, in ADM 103. The agent in charge of each prison transmitted these, and recorded, in a numbered sequence, the names, origins and eventual disposal of all the prisoners under his charge. They mainly cover naval and civilian prisoners. Pay lists for British prisoners of war at Givet, Verdun, Valenciennes, Arras and Bitche, 1806–1807, are in ADM 30/63/12–17.

French army prisoners held in the Low Countries, 1793–1796, were the responsibility of the Commissary of Prisoners. There are lists in AO 11/1–4 and in AO 3/875–877 (officers and NCOs only). The letter books of the Commissary for this period are in AO 16/146–148. All other prisoners, and all prisoners from 1796 whatever their service or nationality, were the responsibility of the Admiralty's Sick and Hurt Board, later called the Transport Board. Miscellaneous reports, prisoners' applications, etc, are in ADM 105/44–66. In-Letters for this period are in ADM 97/98–131. Out-letters are in ADM 98, which also includes Out-Letter books of the Transport Board and Victualling Board concerning prisoners of war. Transport Board minutes relating to prisoners are in ADM 99/92–263 (with an index in ADM 99/264–265), and various accounts are in ADM 100/4–5, and ADM 10/14. The Transport and Sick and Hurt Boards' main series of records, the Registers of Prisoners of War, is in ADM 103. The majority of the Registers consist of the General Entry Books kept by the agents in charge of each depot, prison ship or parole town. They contain many lists of prisoners, usually arranged by nationality or by place of confinement or parole. The agent was in most cases also required to record the circumstances of the prisoners' capture and their eventual disposal. There is no general index to prisoners, although some of the lists in ADM 103 do have integral indexes. A search for references to an individual prisoner may therefore be difficult. However, there is an alphabetical list of American prisoners compiled by the University of Virginia, available at the PRO. This supplements a general register of American prisoners compiled in 1813 in ADM 6/417. Lists of enemy prisoners on parole in Britain were sent to the Home Office, and are in HO 28: they are not indexed.

For the Crimean War from 1853–1855, there is some official material relating to Russian prisoners in British hands in the headquarters papers in WO 28/182 and in naval hospital musters in ADM 102. The records of the Russian Orthodox Church in London in RG 8/180 include lists of Russian prisoners (in Russian) with correspondence in Russian, English and French relating to the distribution of money to them. Britons captured during the Crimean War are listed in the *London Gazette* (available in the PRO as ZJ 1). These lists are incomplete, arranged by regiment, and usually give officers only.

For the South African or Boer War from 1899–1902, there are registers of Boer prisoners, recorded in prisoner number order and arranged by area of confinement (e.g. Natal, Transvaal), in WO 108/303–305 and 368–369. Correspondence about their confinement in Ceylon, St Helena and elsewhere can be found in CO 537/403–409 and 453. Correspondence concerning Dutch, German and French prisoners is in FO 2/824–826. Britons captured by the Boers during the South African War are listed in the *London Gazette* (available in the PRO as ZJ 1). These lists are incomplete, arranged by regiment, and usually give officers only.

22.4 British prisoners of war, 1914–1919

The PRO holds no comprehensive lists of British and Commonwealth prisoners of war. Card indexes to NCOs and other ranks held as prisoners of war were compiled and maintained by the British Red Cross, but they have not survived.

To trace an individual, ask at the Research Enquiries Desk at the PRO for the guide by Bowgen, 'Researching British and Commonwealth Prisoners of War: World War One'. This will give you

- the PRO sources most likely to provide personal details;
- copies of name indexes of British, Irish, Colonial and Indian POWs extracted from WO 161/101;
- references to lists of names of Military and Merchant Navy POWs;
- a list of POW camps in Germany and Enemy territory;
- an indexed map of the main POW camps in Germany and Austria.

Officers were required to provide a report concerning the circumstances behind their capture. These, if they survive, may be found with the officer's service records (see **18c.1.4**, **19.5** or **20.2–20.3**). If you are looking for an officer, ask in the PRO Library for *List of British Officers taken prisoner in the various Theatres of War between August 1914 and November 1918*. The military agents Cox and Co. compiled this in 1919. It has a name index at the back, and is arranged by theatre of war, and then by regiment. The list covers the British Army, Royal Air Force, the Royal Naval Air Service and the Royal Naval Division, and gives the name and rank of the officer, the date when he went missing, where and when he was interned (but not the specific camp/s), and the date of his repatriation. If the officer died while a prisoner, the list gives the date and place of death.

There are no known official or published sources to help discover whether an ordinary serviceman or NCO was made a POW. It should be recorded on their service record (usually giving only dates of capture and release) or the Medal Indexes (see **18c.1.5**, **19.7.3** or **20.4**). Some made narrative reports, described next.

The primary source for personal information are the narrative reports made by officers, medical officers, other ranks, and occasionally merchant seamen and civilians, held in WO 161/95–100 and indexed by WO 161/101. These can include details of unit, home address, when and where captured, wounds suffered, transfer between camps, comments on treatment and conditions and escape attempts.

Both Military and Merchant Navy POWs can also be searched for by name within the card index to Foreign Office correspondence at the PRO. If an entry is found this will usually lead to an FO 383 reference, although it must be stressed that only a small percentage of these records has survived. Other Merchant Navy POW records are contained in MT 9 (code 106), which includes some files indexed by individual name and/or ship. In addition, for Royal Navy, RNAS, RNR and RNVR POWs try searching the ADM 12 registers of correspondence. For the RAF, RFC and RNAS try the Air History Branch indexes at the PRO, which refer to AIR 1.

Records concerning POW camps can also be found. The most comprehensive are the reports held in WO 161/95–100, which can be accessed by using the place and subject indexes in WO 161/101. Individual camps can also be searched for by name in the card index to Foreign Office correspondence, held at the PRO. This contains references to the files of the Prisoners of War and Aliens Department (FO 383: 1915–1919) set up to deal with all matters relating to conditions for prisoners, repatriation and general policy. Each year within the index also has a dedicated POW section arranged by country and subject. Further records relating to POW camps, administration and policy are found in CO 693, with related registers in CO 754 and CO 755. Records of the Committee on the Treatment by the Enemy of British POWs (1914–1919) are in HO 45/10763/270829, and HO 45/10764/270829, with additional policy and administrative material in WO 162/341 (Prisoner of War Information Bureau) and WO 106/45 (Prisoner of War Directorate). War diaries for POW camps can be found in WO 93.

Deaths of prisoners of war and internees occurring in military and non-military hospitals and in enemy and occupied territory were notified to the British authorities by foreign embassies, legations, registration authorities and American authorities in charge of British internees: these certificates may be found in RG 35.

The International Council of the Red Cross in Geneva keeps an incomplete list of POWs and internees of all nationalities for the First World War. Searches are only made in response to written enquiries, and an hourly fee is charged: write to the International Council of the Red Cross (address in **48**).

You may like to read the personal accounts of the last-surviving British prisoners of war, in *Prisoners of the Kaiser*, by Van Emden, for an understanding of their experience.

22.5 Prisoners of war in British hands, 1914–1919

Lists of names of enemy prisoners and internees were routinely forwarded to the Prisoners of War Information Bureau in London, which in turn informed the International Red Cross Headquarters in Geneva. The International Council of the Red Cross in Geneva keeps a list of all known POWs and internees of all nationalities for the First World War. Searches are only made in response to written enquiries, and an hourly fee is charged (address in **48**).

Unfortunately, bombing in 1940 largely destroyed the lists compiled by the Bureau. However, two specimen lists of German subjects interned as POWs in 1915–1916 survive in WO 900/45–46. The list is divided into army, naval and civilian prisoners, and gives the regiment, ship or home address of each prisoner.

The correspondence of the Prisoners of War and Aliens Department of the Foreign Office in FO 383 covers both British and enemy prisoners. A substantial amount of material relating to POWs (British, Allied and enemy) is contained in FO 371. For references to both series, try the Foreign Office card index at the PRO. Try also the Prisoners and Aliens Registers, 1915–1919, arranged by country, in FO 566/1837–1874. However, it has to be said that a large proportion of Foreign Office correspondence has not survived.

Correspondence about enemy merchant seamen taken prisoner is in MT 9 (code 106) and MT 23.

22.6 British and Commonwealth prisoners of war, 1939–1945

The International Council of the Red Cross in Geneva keeps an incomplete list of POWs and internees of all nationalities for the Second World War: searches are only made in response to written enquiries, and an hourly fee is charged (address in **48**).

There are no central lists of British servicemen who were prisoners of war. However, the PRO Library holds alphabetical registers of British and Dominion POWs of all ranks who were held in Germany and German occupied territories, available on the shelves at the PRO. They give details of name, rank and service/army number as well as regiment/corps, prisoner of war number and camp location details. The lists are corrected generally up to 30th March 1945, and are in three volumes:

- *Prisoners of War: British Army 1939–1945*
- *Prisoners of War: Naval and Air Forces of Great Britain and the Empire 1939–1945*
- *Prisoners of War: Armies and other Land Forces of the British Empire 1939–1945*

Figure 43 Soldiers of the British Expeditionary Force captured near Dunkirk, 1940 (PRO, CN 11/9/ 215)

The books were compiled from the lists of POWs in WO 392, and from other sources as well, so that they are more comprehensive than WO 392.

Also at the PRO, ask for Bowgen, 'British Prisoners of War, World War Two'. This provides full document references, dates and descriptions, for

- Reports on Prisoners of War Camps;
- Prisoner of War Lists;
- Prisoner of War escape and evasion reports;
- Miscellaneous reports.

For prisoners of war held by the Japanese, try first the index cards in WO 345, and the registers in WO 367. At the time of writing, WO 345 has been returned to the Ministry of Defence, to help in handling reparation claims, but it is expected back in the PRO shortly. The index cards are some 56,000 pre-printed cards of uncertain provenance. They appear to have been compiled by a central Japanese authority. There has been some degree of Allied assistance in compiling, maintaining, etc. The cards record camp (in Japanese); name; nationality (in English, or English and Japanese); rank (in English, or English and Japanese); place of capture (in English, or English and Japanese); father's name; place of origin; destination of report (assumed to be report of capture, sent to next of kin at address given); 'no', i.e. prisoner's camp number (established by comparison with other records) (may be subject to change due to transfer) (in Japanese). The three registers in WO 367 record the names of some 13,500 allied prisoners of war and civilian internees of British and other nationalities. The registers give minimal information about each prisoner, apparently compiled for the Japanese camp administration although the majority of the information is given in English. The registers refer to camps numbered 1–4 but the identity of these has not been established.

The War Office Registered Files (WO 32 code 91) and the Directorate of Military Operations Collation Files (WO 193/343–359) both contain material on Allied POWs. The Military Headquarters Papers: SHAEF (GI Division) contain files relating to the organization of the Prisoners of War Executive and reports on Allied POWs (WO 219/1402, 1448–1474). The War Diary of MI 9, the division of Military Intelligence which dealt with escaped prisoners of all services and those who evaded capture, is in WO 165/39, and its papers are in WO 208/3242–3566. These include camp histories (some with aerial photographs), escape and liberation reports, and files on MI 9 staff, some of which are subject to extended closure. In addition, the PRO holds over 100 files dispersed among various series on the incident that became known as the 'Great Escape'. Medical reports on conditions in POW camps, with some reports on escapes, are among the Medical Historians' Papers in WO 222/1352–1393. Details of war crimes committed against Allied POWs have mostly been preserved in WO 235, WO 309–311 and TS 26 and among the Control Commission for Germany records in CCG. Aerial photographs of camps are in AIR 40/227–231.

Records concerning RAF and Allied Air Force prisoners will be found in the correspondence of the Air Ministry in AIR 2 code B 89, as well as in the

Unregistered Papers (POWs) in AIR 20 code 89. An alphabetical list of British and Dominion Air Force POWs in German hands in 1944–1945 is in AIR 20/2336. Nominal rolls of prisoners in German camps are in AIR 40/263–281, and AIR 40/1488–1491. Nominal rolls for some Japanese camps are among papers prepared for a history of the RAF services, in AIR 49/383–388, but they are generally disappointing. The roll for Changi is fuller: it is in AIR 40/1899–1906.

A substantial quantity of material concerning British and Dominion POWs, mostly Air Force personnel, can be found in the Headquarters Papers of Bomber Command and in the Air Ministry's Directorate of Intelligence Papers. Location lists and some more aerial photographs of POW camps in Germany, Italy and Occupied Europe, including reports on transfers, are in AIR 14/1235–1240, and similar documentation on German camps occurs in AIR 40/227–231. Reports of escaped RAF personnel, including some nominal lists of reported Air Force POWs, are in AIR 14/353–361; these files deal mainly with aids to escape and conduct in enemy territory. Similar material, with reports on German interrogation methods, is in AIR 14/461–465. Reports of RAF and Dominion Air Force escapers, including lists of POWs in enemy hands, can also be found in AIR 40/1545–1552. Reports on many individual RAF servicemen taken prisoner in occupied Europe, detailing the circumstances of their capture, are in AIR 14/470 and 471. Reports on the condition of British and Dominion POWs in German and Japanese camps towards the end of the war occur in AIR 40/2361 and 2366.

A list of Royal Marines known to have been held in German camps between 1939 and 1945 is to be found in ADM 201/111.

Lists of Royal Navy personnel interned in enemy camps may be found in many of the files in ADM 1 code 79 and ADM 116 code 79, although the exact files are not identifiable from the catalogue.

Diplomatic correspondence with the Red Cross and the Protecting Powers is in FO 916. The reports of these organizations on enemy POW camps and hospitals are in WO 224. Papers dealing with the treatment of British POWs in German hands are in DEFE 2/1126–1128. Colonial Office files on British prisoners and internees in the Far East, and British Colonial prisoners in Europe, occur in CO 980 and CO 537/1220–1221. Correspondence on British merchant seamen taken prisoner is in MT 9 code 106.

The Prisoners of War and Internment Files in the Admiralty and Secretariat Papers (ADM 1 code 79) contain documentation on many aspects of the Royal Navy's involvement with the capture and internment of enemy and Allied POWs, naval and other services.

The *Index to General Correspondence* of the Foreign Office, 1920–1951 (available at the PRO) contains numerous entries relating to POWs, displaced persons and refugees. The bulk of the correspondence that has been preserved (and not all of it has) is in FO 371.

22.7 British and Commonwealth escape, evasion and liberation reports, 1939–1945

Officers and men of the armed forces, and the merchant navy, made these escape and evasion reports, which are an invaluable source of personal information – but only for a small percentage of the 192,000 British and Commonwealth prisoners of war during the Second World War. They usually include service details; when and where captured; home address and civilian occupation. For RAF personnel they also give details of where based, type of aircraft, when, where and how the aircraft was lost, and the presumed fate of the other aircrew.

Every report has a narrative, of variable length, which describes an individual's experiences as an escaper, evader or prisoner of war. In addition, many include appendices which, if they survive, can provide the names and addresses of civilian helpers, nature of help given, and relevant dates; details of the escape method and allied personnel who assisted in an escape; details of the usefulness of officially provided escape aids, which ones were used, and suggested improvements and/or additions. The reports mostly relate to the European, Mediterranean or North Africa theatres of war. There were few successful escapes and evasions in South East Asia.

The reports are in three sequences in WO 208: they are accessed by a card index at the PRO. Make sure you check the user's guide by the card index, as it explains the various references on the cards. Additional escape and evasion reports are also in WO 208 and AIR 40/1545–1552, AIR 14/353–361 and AIR 14/461–465, but are not indexed. Other similar reports are dispersed among various record series. A keyword search in PROCAT may turn something up, but in many cases a report is hidden within a file with an uninformative description.

22.8 Merchant seamen prisoners of war, 1939–1945

There is an extensive collection of records in BT 373, giving the circumstances of capture and the eventual fate of UK and allied Asian merchant seamen captured during the war of 1939–1945. Details of ships captured or lost due to enemy action are in BT 373/1–359, searchable in PROCAT by ship's name. These contain miscellaneous papers relating to the circumstances of loss/capture. There are document pouches for individual seamen in BT 373/360–3716: these are searchable by surname and sometimes by forename as well. Each pouch typically contains the name of the ship lost; a card or form containing circumstantial details (including POW camp, POW number, surname, forenames, date of birth, place of birth, Discharge A number, rank or rating, name of ship, ship's official number, date of loss of ship, next of kin, relationship, address and country of detention); Prisoner of War Branch PC 96 (postal censorship) forms vetting messages to and from family and friends; Envelope RS3 which usually has notes of release from captivity/repatriation written on it where appropriate, containing many of the details from the POW card and additionally a National Service AF Account Number. Some of the pouches may also contain personal letters to and from prisoners of war.

Collective alphabetical listings of prisoners of war (as opposed to individual pouches) are contained in BT 373/3717–3722. For details of prisoners of war who died in captivity in Japan and Germany, try BT 373/3720–3721.

22.9 Prisoners of war in British hands, 1939–1945

Individual prisoners of war in British hands are very difficult to trace. Most of the following records do not mention individuals by name. The best sources for Axis prisoners are local archives, libraries, newspapers and local history groups.

The War Office was responsible for the custody of POWs of all services. There is a card index at the PRO to the limited number of POW camp war diaries in WO 166. Lists of POW camps are among the Military Headquarters Papers: Home Forces, in WO 199/404–409. Lists of enemy POWs temporarily interned in the Tower of London are in WO 94/105

The War Diaries of the Directorate of Prisoners of War are in WO 165/59–71. Registered Papers concerning prisoners both during and after the war are in WO 32 code 91. The Medical Historians' Papers in WO 222 include reports on the health of POWs and on the work of POW hospitals. War diaries of a few hospitals, depots and camps are in WO 177/1833–1855, and of a few more camps in WO 166. Numerous files on individual POW camps in the United Kingdom are among the records of the Prisoners of War Section of the London-based Control Office for Germany and Austria (FO 939).

The War Diary of MI 19, the division of Military Intelligence responsible for the interrogation of enemy POWs, is in WO 165/41. Records of Axis POW interrogations are in WO 208/3582–3662, with additional Combined Services Detailed Interrogation Centre files in WO 208/4363–4367. These files are not indexed. A few interrogation reports on German POWs in 1944 exist in the files of the Control Commission for Germany: Internal Affairs and Communications Division, in FO 1050/169. Interrogation reports on enemy airmen are in AIR 40/2394–2431. Some debriefings of enemy POWs can be found in the files concerning the Prisoners of War Campaign conducted by the Political Warfare Executive of the Foreign Office, in FO 898/320–330.

Correspondence between the British government, the Red Cross and the Protecting Powers, including inspection reports on POW camps, is among the records of the Consular (War) Department of the Foreign Office, in FO 916. In addition, the Home Office Internment (General) Files in HO 215 contain a large amount of material on Home Office involvement with the internment of enemy aliens and POWs. Correspondence between the Home Office and the Prisoners of War Information Bureau (UK) and general correspondence concerning the treatment of interned enemy aliens is in HO 213/494–498. The few surviving records of the PWIB itself are in WO 307.

The Admiralty Prisoners of War and Internees Files (ADM 1 code 79) contain documentation on many aspects of the Royal Navy's involvement with the capture and internment of enemy and Allied POWs, naval and other services. Similar correspondence and papers are to be found in ADM 116 code 79.

For lists of enemy POWs in various colonial territories, see CO 968/33–36. Correspondence about the employment of Italian merchant seamen taken prisoner is in MT 9 code 106.

22.10 Prisoners of war, 1950–1953

There are lists of British and Commonwealth servicemen who were known or believed to be prisoners of war in Korea. Men captured between January 1951 and July 1953 are listed in WO 208/3999. For a list of Commonwealth prisoners of war, compiled in January 1954, see WO 308/54. Correspondence with returned Korean War POWs, and on personnel missing or presumed dead, is in WO 162/208–264, WO 32/19273 and DO 35/5853–5863.

Documents on the formation of the British Repatriated POWs Interrogation Unit can be found in AIR 20 code 89/9168 and WO 162/208–264. The interrogation reports on ex-POWs in WO 208 are closed for 75 years.

22.11 Prisoners of war: bibliography and sources

Unpublished works
A Bowgen, 'Researching British and Commonwealth Prisoners of War: World War One' (2000: available at the PRO Research Enquiries Desk)
'British Prisoners of War, World War Two' (available at the PRO Research Enquiries Desk)

Published works
C M Andrews, *Guide to the Materials for American History, to 1783, in the Public Record Office of Great Britain*, 2 vols. (Washington D.C., 1912–1914)
A Bowgen, 'British Army POWs of the First World War', *Ancestors* no. 6, Feb–March 2002, pp. 34–40
A Crawley, *Escape from Germany* (Stationery Office, 2001)
M R D Foot and J M Langley, *MI 9: Escape and Evasion 1939–1945* (London, 1979)
O Hoare, *Camp 020: MI 5 and the Nazi Spies: the official history of MI5's wartime interrogation* (PRO, 2000)
A Neave, *Saturday at MI 9* (London, 1969)
Prisoners of War: British Army 1939–1945 (Polstead, 1990)
Prisoners of War: Naval and Air Forces of Great Britain and the Empire 1939–1945 (Polstead, 1990)
Prisoners of War: Armies and other Land Forces of the British Empire 1939–1945 (Polstead, 1990)
R Van Emden, *Prisoners of the Kaiser: The Last POWs of the Great War* (Barnsley, 2000)

23

The preventive services and the Coastguard

◆ ◆ ◆

23.1 The preventive services

During the 'long' eighteenth century, three armed preventive services were created, to prevent the smuggling of goods in and out of the country, and the avoidance of customs duty. These were the Revenue Cruisers, the Riding Officers (both dating from 1698) and the Preventive Water Guard, set up in 1809. These three services were part of the Customs, although from 1816 the Admiralty appointed the officers and men of the Revenue Cruisers, and the Riding Officers were often appointed from the Army. The Riding Officers operated in Kent and Sussex. The Revenue Cruisers were largely confined to the Kent, Sussex and East Anglian coasts and the Thames estuary, until the end of the eighteenth century, when they covered the English and Welsh coasts: Scotland had its own fleet.

Confusingly, the Board of Excise also had its own Revenue Cruisers and its own officers called Riding Officers. These covered the entire country, not just the coasts of Kent and Sussex, and were concerned with the collection and evasion of excise duty (a tax on goods made within the country, not imported).

23.2 The preventive forces: service records

For information relating to the (Customs) Riding Officers and the Preventive Water Guard, try the records of the Board of Customs (see **25.2**). For the (Excise) Riding Officers and (Excise) Revenue Cruisers, try the Excise records (see **25.2** again). For the Revenue Cruisers, try both the Admiralty (**19**) and the Customs (**25.2**) records.

A good place to start may be with the published reports made to Parliament about the operation of the various preventive services. There is a CD-ROM index to these in the PRO Library, and the reports can be seen on microfiche in the Microfilm Reading Room. These reports can include information such as name, age, place of birth, date of appointment, etc. Examples include officers and men appointed to the Preventive Boat Service (i.e. the Preventive Water Guard), November 1816–March 1819 (microfiche reference 1819. 20, 141–142). Later reports on the Coastguard can give details of earlier service in the preventive services (see the CD-ROM index). Pension records for c.1818–1825 are in CUST 40/28. See also **23.4**.

Administration of the Revenue Cruisers was split between the Customs and the Admiralty, with the latter appointing the officers and men after 1816; this system continued when the Revenue Cruisers were merged into the Coastguard in 1822. Officers serving in Revenue Cruisers are given in the *Navy List* from 1814. Admiralty appointments to Revenue Cruisers of lieutenants, masters and boatswains for 1816–1831 are in ADM 6/56; for later appointments see **23.4**.

23.3 The Coastguard

The Coastguard was formed in 1822 by the amalgamation of these three services. In 1831 another preventive service, the Coastal Blockade (set up by the Admiralty in 1816) became part of the Coastguard. The four preventive forces employed nearly 6,700 men at the time of amalgamation.

The Board of Customs had overall control of the Coastguard from 1822 until 1856, when the Admiralty was granted control by the Coastguard Service Act. Most members of the Coastguard were in fact ex-Navy men. After 1856, many people from the Bengal Marine entered the Coastguard after the East India Company gave up its navy. The Coastguard as run by the Admiralty consisted of three distinct bodies; the Shore Force, the Permanent Cruiser Force and the Guard Ships, naval ships which lay at major ports to act as headquarters of

Figure 44 The Shore Force of the Coastguard tried to prevent looting at the wreck of the *Lily* of Liverpool, off Cornwall, 1843 (Mary Evans Picture Library)

Coastguard districts. After 1856, the duties of the Coastguard were the defence of the coast, the provision of a reserve for the Navy, and the protection of the revenue against evasion by smuggling: over the next 70 years new responsibilities were added, stressing assistance to shipping, supervision of the foreshore and life-saving. Volunteer Life-Saving Apparatus Companies were set up in the 1860s, attached to each Coastguard Station around the coasts of Britain and Ireland.

The First World War showed that the Coastguard could not act as a reserve for the Navy: instead, the Navy and the Marines had to provide manpower for the Coastguard to maintain adequate coastal defences.

In 1925, the Coastguard's duties were split, into a Naval Signalling Force (run by the Admiralty); a Coast Prevention Force (run by the Customs) and a coast watching force (run by the Board of Trade), which was allowed the name of the Coastguard. Its focus was on saving life, the salvage of wreck and the foreshores. From 1923, responsibility for the Coastguard moved around between departments.

1923–1939	Board of Trade
1939–1940	Ministry of Shipping
1940–1945	Admiralty
1945–1964	Ministry of (War) Transport
1964–1983	Department of Trade

See BT 166/39 for a brief history of the Coastguard (up to 1954), and for a report into the efficiency of the Coastguard, in 1931. Records are widely scattered for the twentieth century. If you want to do a search in the computer catalogue, remember to use the variants 'coast guard' and 'coastguard'.

23.4 The preventive services and the Coastguard: published service records

A good place to start may be with the published reports made to Parliament about the operation of the various preventive services. There is a CD-ROM index to these in the PRO Library, and the reports can be seen on microfiche in the Microfilm Reading Room. These reports can include information such as name, age, place of birth, date of appointment, etc. Examples include officers and men appointed to the Preventive Boat Service (i.e. the Preventive Water Guard), November 1816–March 1819 (microfiche reference 1819. 20, 141–142), and Coastal Blockade men killed in conflicts with Kent and Sussex smugglers, 1821–1825 (microfiche reference 1825. 27, 154). Later reports on the Coastguard can give details of earlier service in the preventive services.

The published Parliamentary Papers on the Coastguard can provide information such as name, age, place of birth, date of appointment, etc., for commanders of Revenue Cruisers in Scotland, 1822–1823; captains and commanders in the Preventive or Coastguard service and Revenue Cruisers on 1 July 1833; and chief (warrant) officers of the Coastguard, with previous service, 1853.

A number of papers printed for Parliament during the nineteenth century contain information about members of the preventive services:

- *A Return of Officers and Men appointed to the Preventive Boat Service between November 1816 and March 1819* (House of Commons Sessional Papers 1819 (569) XVII, 77; provides name, age, place of birth, trade, length of time at sea, salary, other allowances or appointments;
- *Names of Commanders of Revenue Cruisers in Scotland 1822–1823* (House of Commons Sessional Papers 1823 (94) XIV, 293;
- *Names of Men Killed on the Kent and Sussex Coasts in Conflicts between the Coast Blockade and Smugglers 1821–1825* (House of Commons Sessional Papers 1825 (95) VXIII, 385;
- *A Return of Captains and Commanders in the Preventive or Coastguard Service and Revenue Cruisers on 1 July 1833* (House of Commons Sessional Papers 1833 (744) XXIV, 285; provides name, rank, date of appointment, salary and other emoluments;
- *Return of Names, Age, Date of Appointment, Gross Pay and Allowances of all Chief Officers of the Coastguard, with Previous Service* (House of Commons Sessional Papers 1857 XXVII, 253.

Officers serving in Revenue Cruisers (part of the Coastguard since 1822) are given in the *Navy List* from 1814. Admiralty appointments to Revenue Cruisers of lieutenants, masters and boatswains for 1816–1831 are in ADM 6/56; for 1822–1832 they are in ADM 2/1127. Quarterly musters of Coastguard and Revenue Cutters, 1824–1857, are in ADM 119. Men serving on the Revenue Cruisers can also be traced in the ships' Establishment and Record Books, 1816–1879 (ADM 175/24–73). For the establishment of the Revenue Cruisers between 1827 and 1829, try CUST 19/52–61.

Among the Customs records are some other items relating to the Coastguard. Coastguard minute books, 1833–1849, are in CUST 29/40–42; Coastguard statistics are in CUST 38/32–60; and CUST 39/173 contains the salaries and incidents of the Thames Coastguard, 1828–1832. Pension records for c.1818–1825 are in CUST 40/28.

The main nineteenth century personnel records were actually a kind of succession book, recording the officers and ratings serving at the various stations: these can give personal details. They are arranged by place or type of ship, so you need to have some idea of locality: you may be able to get this from the records in the table shown on p. 312. The succession books are in ADM 175/1–26 for 1816–1869, and in ADM 175/27–73 for 1861–1878. Other personnel records do survive, although there is an unexplained gap in the records between 1866 and 1886.

Nominations		Records	Indexes
1819–1866	Nominations of officers and ratings: England Index in ADM 175/97–98	ADM 175/74–80	ADM 175/97–98: 1819–1862 only
1831–1850 1851–1856	Nominations of boatmen	ADM 6/199 ADM 175/101	
1820–1849	Nominations of officers and ratings to stations in Ireland. Indexes give a lot of detail.	ADM 175/74, 81	ADM 175/99–100
1820–1824	Nominations of officers and ratings to stations in Scotland	ADM 175/74	
Service records			
1886–1947	Coastguard officers: indexes	ADM 175/103–107, 109–110	
1900–1923	Coastguard ratings (apparently including Naval and Marine ratings): service record cards – alphabetical	ADM 175/82A–84B	
1919–1923	Naval ratings serving with the Coastguard	ADM 175/85–89	ADM 175/108
1919–1923	Royal Marines serving with the Coastguard	ADM 175/90	
1921–1929	Naval Shore Service Signal Service	ADM 175/111	
Discharge			
1858–1868	Index to discharges	–	ADM 175/102
1919	Reduction of Coastguard 1919: registers of discharges, all self indexed, except 96	ADM 175/91–96	ADM 175/107 for ADM 175/96

During the First World War, many men of the Coastguard qualified for medals: see ADM 171.

You may have some trouble understanding the abbreviations used in Coastguard personnel records: the following are the most common.

- Boatn = Boatman

- Chf Btman; Chief Boatn; Chief Bn = Chief Boatman
- Chf Officer = Chief Officer
- Comd Bn; Comd Btman = Commissioned Boatman
- Permt Extn = Permanent Extraman
- Tempoy Extn = Temporary Extraman

Pensions can be found in the registers in the table shown below. Pensions were normally notified to the Treasury by the Board of Customs (before 1856) or the Admiralty (after 1856). Annual lists of names of those superannuated appear in the Treasury registers under 'Public Offices' (T 2). Only rarely do the papers to which they refer survive among the Treasury Board Papers (T 1). The text of the Customs letters to the Treasury can usually be obtained from the Out-Letter Entry Books: Extra-Departmental (CUST 30); these often give information about a man's career and his grounds for retirement.

1866–1884	Coastguard	ADM 23/17–21
1884–1926	Civil Coastguard	ADM 23/71–75; ADM 23/194–199
1857–1935	Coastguard, Civil pensions	PMG 23
1866–1928	Greenwich pensions for officers	PMG 70

23.5 Coastguard stations and cottages

Some plans of Coastguard stations, officers' houses, cottages, gun batteries, watchrooms and other structures, 1844–1914, are in WORK 30. A schedule of deeds and leases in respect of Coastguard premises in Great Britain in 1857 is in CUST 42/66. References to Coastguard properties may also be traced in the Treasury Board Papers in T 1 and the Admiralty and Secretariat Papers in ADM 1, using registers in T 2 and ADM 12 at the PRO. Information about cottages erected or leased by the Admiralty between 1856 and 1863 can be obtained from a series of Parliamentary Papers (House of Commons, 1860 XLII 275; 1861 XXXVIII 133 and 1863 XXXV 157), which can be seen on microfiche at the PRO: for microfiche references, check the CD-ROM index to Parliamentary Papers in the PRO Library.

A series of registers giving information about repairs to buildings and the supply and replacement of equipment 1828–1857 are in ADM 7/7–39. They are arranged by the name of the Coastguard Station. Papers about the station at Pett, Sussex, 1870–1923, are in WO 55/270.

23.6 The Coastguard: volunteers

The volunteer Life Saving Apparatus Companies, set up in the 1860s, were composed of sets of up to 25 local men. From 1911 they were eligible for the Rocket Life Saving Apparatus Long Service Medal: a register for 1911–1935 is in

BT 167/84. In 1932, the Coast Life Saving Corps of about 6,000 civilians was set up to coordinate the work of the Life Saving Apparatus Companies, plus the Watchers and the Intelligence Section (general volunteers). Annual lists of enrolled volunteers for 1920 to 1937 are in BT167/87–97. Some of them were very elderly, having been volunteer lifesavers since the 1860s. The records can give name, date of birth, date of enrolment, residence and distance from the Coastguard Station. Earlier name lists do not seem to survive: although there are annual reports among the *Parliamentary Papers*, these do not specify names.

23.7 The preventive services and the Coastguard: bibliography

F C Bowen, *His Majesty's Coastguard* (London, 1928)
E Carson, *The Ancient and Rightful Customs* (London, 1972)
N A M Rodger, *Naval Records for Genealogists* (PRO, 1998)
B Scarlett, *Shipminder: The Story of Her Majesty's Coastguard* (London, 1971)
G Smith, *Something to Declare! 1,000 Years of Customs and Excise* (London, 1980)
W Webb, *Coastguard: An Official History of HM Coastguard* (London, 1976)

24
Police forces

◆ ◆ ◆

24.1 Introduction

Police forces in the sense that we now understand the term did not exist until the mid nineteenth century. Before then, the day to day work of policing was carried out by a number of local forces such as watchmen, constables, headboroughs and magistrates. The records they created are almost always held in local record offices. The first modern police force in the UK mainland was the Metropolitan Police Force. Although there were some earlier local experiments, provincial police forces did not begin until after the County Police Act of 1839, and no part of England and Wales could be compelled to provide a police force until the County and Borough Act of 1856. Storch's 'The policeman as domestic missionary' and Emsley's *The English Police* tell more about the social context within which the early police forces acted, and why there was so much opposition to them.

24.2 London

The Metropolitan Police Force was created in 1829. Its jurisdiction was initially defined as an area of about seven miles' radius from Charing Cross (excluding the City of London) but this was extended in 1839 to a 15 miles' radius. In 1835 the Bow Street Horse Patrol was incorporated into the force, followed by the Bow Street Foot Patrol and the Thames Police Office in 1839. The Metropolitan Police also had responsibility for the police of the royal dockyards and military stations at Portsmouth, Chatham, Devonport, Pembroke, Rosyth and Woolwich, from 1860 to 1934. Some records of the Bow Street Horse Patrol are included in MEPO 2/25. An unindexed service register for the Bow Street Foot Patrol, 1821–1829 is in MEPO 4/508. This gives name, place of residence, age, place of birth, height, marital status, number of children, name of recommender, military service and date of appointment, together with date and reason for discharge.

The City of London Police is quite separate from the Metropolitan Police and its records are not held in the PRO. Surviving personnel records are good. They include a complete series of registers listing everyone who has ever served in the force together with personal files on about 95 per cent of City of London police officers. For further information, write to the City of London Police Record Office (address in **48**).

24.3 The Metropolitan Police Force: service records

From the beginning, the Metropolitan Police Force attempted to recruit young men who were well built, physically fit, literate and of good character. Women were not recruited until 1919. Service records of policewomen do not survive.

Many recruits came from outside the metropolitan area, partly because poor living conditions meant that young Londoners often failed to meet the required standards of health but also because there was a prevalent belief that standards of moral fitness were higher in the provinces than in London. There was a high turnover of staff, especially in the very early years of the force.

Full certificate of service records survive only for the period from January 1889–November 1909 (MEPO 4/361–477). They are arranged by warrant number and give a description of the recruit, date of birth, trade, marital status, residence, number of children, name and place of last employer, previous public service, surgeon's certificate, postings to divisions, dates of promotion or demotion, and causes of removal. However there is a wealth of other material that can be used to reconstruct basic personal information about most Metropolitan Police officers except that *no records survive for the period between May 1857 and February 1869*. Annual Police Orders (MEPO 7) can be used to try to trace officers who were pensioned, promoted, dismissed and transferred during the 1857–1869 gap in the records.

In order to gain maximum information you may need to use more than one type of record. The easiest source to use is the alphabetical register of joiners, covering September 1830–April 1857, and July 1878–1933 (MEPO 4/333–338). This normally gives name, rank, warrant number, division and dates of appointment and removal. The earliest volumes also supply the names and addresses of referees. The registers of leavers, March 1889–January 1947 (MEPO 4/339–351), are also relatively easy as each volume is indexed; they too will give name, rank, warrant number, division and dates of appointment and removal.

Other useful sources, each providing name, rank, warrant number, division and dates of appointment and removal, are:

- alphabetical register, 1829–1836 (HO 65/26), which also gives dates of promotion or demotion;
- numerical registers (arranged by warrant number), September 1829–March 1830 (MEPO 4/31–32), which also gives the officer's height and cause of removal from the force;
- attestation ledgers, February 1869–May 1958 (MEPO 4/352–360), which includes signatures of recruit and witnesses; there is a section at the back for police stationed at the royal dockyards and military stations arranged by warrant number;
- returns of death whilst serving, 1829–1889 (MEPO 4/2), with an index (MEPO 4/448), which also gives cause of death.

Annual Police Orders (MEPO 7) can also be used to trace officers who were

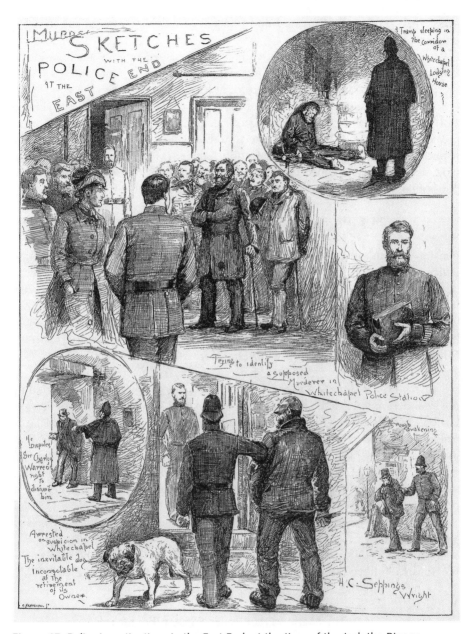

Figure 45 Police investigations in the East End, at the time of the Jack the Ripper murders. (*Illustrated London News* 1888, PRO, ZPER 34/93)

pensioned, promoted, dismissed and transferred, but they are subject to a 50-year closure.

Papers relating to the service of certain distinguished officers are held in the Special Series of correspondence and papers from the Commissioner's Office (MEPO 3/2883–2921); they are closed for at least 75 years.

Some name indexes are available at the PRO. The most extensive is a general alphabetical index of former serving officers, mainly based on information in police orders (MEPO 7) supplemented by the joiners' ledgers, leavers' ledgers, records of service ledgers and attestation ledgers (MEPO 4). There is also an index to officers who joined the Metropolitan Police, 1880–1889 and an index to pensioners who left the force between 1852 and 1889 (see **24.4**).

24.4 The Metropolitan Police Force: pension records

Pension records are an excellent source of family history information. Before the Police Pensions Act was passed in 1890, pensions were awarded on a discretionary basis, but after that date they were granted as of right to officers who had served for 25 years and a modified pension/gratuity was paid to those who were discharged as medically unfit. Pensions and gratuities granted between 1829 and 1859 are mentioned in correspondence and papers (MEPO 5/1–90). Records of pensioners who retired or resigned between 1852 and 1932 are in MEPO 21.

The records in MEPO 21 contain detailed personal information, including physical description, date and place of birth, marital status, and dates of service. Until 1923 they also give details of promotions and postings, intended place of residence after retirement and names of parents and next of kin. After 1923, they include date and place of marriage, together with a physical description of the wife and her date and place of birth. The records are arranged by pension number (which approximates to a chronological order of resignation). Post-1932 pension records are still held by the Metropolitan Police.

A register of pensions to widows of officers killed on duty, 1840–1858 is in MEPO 4/33.

From 1867 to 1894, pensions to members of the Metropolitan Police who were previously employed in the old Admiralty Dockyard Police are included in PMG 25.

24.5 The Metropolitan Police Force: other records

Records relating to complaints and disciplinary actions against Metropolitan Police officers are held in MEPO 3 and HO 287.

There is an unindexed register of local constables sworn to act within the Metropolitan Police district, 1839–1876 (MEPO 4/3–5).

The Metropolitan Police District was divided into several divisions each under the charge of a superintendent: maps of the divisions and their changing boundaries can be found in MEPO 15. Divisional records have not been transferred to the PRO. Incomplete divisional records are held by the

Metropolitan Police Museum, and those of the Thames division are held at the Wapping Police Museum. Neither of these is open to the public, but both will try to answer written enquiries: the addresses are given in **48**.

Other information on the early years of the Metropolitan Police can be found in *Hue and Cry* and the *Police Gazette*, 1828–1845 (HO 75). Records of investigations conducted by the Metropolitan Police are mainly to be found in MEPO 2, MEPO 3 and MEPO 4.

For information concerning gallantry awards to Metropolitan Police officers, see **24.11**.

24.6 Other police forces in England and Wales

The Metropolitan Police Force is the only British police force to be directly controlled by the central government (its chief officer, the Commissioner, reports directly to the Home Office). Its records are therefore held in the PRO. Local government runs other police forces in the UK. Their records are not public records and are not held in the PRO, although our library does hold some published histories of local forces. To find out more about them you should try the appropriate local record office first. It may also be worth contacting the police force itself or the local police museum. Details of a good, but now dated, guide to local police records by Bridgeman and Emsley are given in the Bibliography below.

For the Royal Military Police, see **18d.3**.

For railway police, see **27.3**.

24.7 Ireland

The work of Herlihy has transformed searching for Irish policemen: see his two books, *The Royal Irish Constabulary: a complete alphabetical list of officers and men 1816–1922*, and *The Royal Irish Constabulary: a short history and genealogical guide with a select list of medal awards and casualties*. These are both available at the PRO. See also Brewer's *The Royal Irish Constabulary: an oral history*.

Until 1836, there were a number of local forces of constables in Ireland. Some information about the careers of superannuated constables can be found in *Parliamentary Papers: House of Commons Sessional Papers, 1831–1832*, vol. XXVI, p. 465 (list of superannuations of local Irish forces). The list gives name, period of service, amount granted, and the nature of the injury that was the cause of the superannuation. Copies of *Parliamentary Papers* are readily available at the British Library and good local reference libraries; they are also available on microfiche at the PRO. In 1836, these local groups were united into a single force known as the Irish Constabulary, which was renamed the Royal Irish Constabulary in 1867. The RIC was responsible for the whole of Ireland with the exception of Dublin (policed by the Dublin Metropolitan Police, founded in 1786), and so was disbanded in August 1922, when Ireland gained its independence.

The service records of members of the Royal Irish Constabulary are held in HO 184. The registers are arranged by service number, but there are separate alphabetical indexes. They normally give name, age, height, religious affiliation, native county, trade, marital status, native county of wife (but not her name), date of appointment, counties in which the man served, length of service and date of retirement or death, but no information about parentage. The same series (HO 184) also includes separate registers, with integral indexes, for officers and for members of the auxiliary forces (colloquially known as the Black and Tans) who helped suppress unrest in Ireland in the period immediately before independence. Further information about the activities of the Black and Tans is held in series WO 35.

Pensions and allowances granted to officers, men and staff, and to their widows and children are recorded among the Paymaster General's records (PMG 48), and usually give the recipient's address. This series also includes registers of deceased pensioners (1877–1918) and of awards of pensions made on the disbandment of the force. Files on pension options at the time of disbandment, arranged by county, are held amongst the records of the Colonial Office (CO 904/175–6).

Records relating to appointments to the Irish Revenue Police, 1830–1857, are in CUST 111. This was a force initially under the control of the Board of Excise, but from 1849 controlled by the Board of Inland Revenue, formed to combat the making of malt and distillation of spirit in Ireland in contravention of the Illicit distillation (Ireland) Act of 1831.

24.8 South Africa

The PRO has the original correspondence and registers of In- and Out-Letters of the Colonial Office, relating to the South African Constabulary, 1902–1908 (CO 526, CO 639 and CO 640). A large proportion of this correspondence relates to individuals: however, much of the correspondence that is noted in the registers has in fact been destroyed. The registers have name indexes, and can provide some information even if the correspondence noted has not survived.

Although there are no service records, information on individuals can be found. The general orders give appointments, postings, leave on medical grounds and resignations. There are some pension returns, supplying the name of the widow and place of payment (Britain or South Africa). There are also nominal rolls of various kinds: casualties, men taken on (sometimes supplying the name and address of next of kin), men placed on the married establishment, and men taken off the strength. In addition, individuals are sometimes mentioned in correspondence.

There appears to have been some confusion between the South African Constabulary and the various local armed forces: men who joined the Constabulary sometimes served with other forces (see **18b.10**).

24.9 Palestine

As explained below (**24.10**), personnel records of officers serving overseas do not normally survive amongst the records of the British government. However, service records for the Palestine police (and other Palestine government servants such as dockyard and railway workers) for the period of the British mandate (1920–1948) have been kept in this country, for pension purposes. They are presently held by the Department for International Development, and any individual involved or their next of kin can write to them for further information (address in **48**). Negotiations are taking place to find an archive prepared to hold them closed until the 100th birthday of the individuals concerned. They will not be available to general researchers for some years to come.

Some records relating to medal entitlement for members of the Palestine police are held by the Foreign and Commonwealth Office, Records and Historical Service Unit (address in **48**). These consist of a card index for awards of the Defence Medal, 1939–1945, and rolls for awards of the Defence and General Service medals. The card index entries always include the surname and initial of the first name of the recipient and whether the Defence or General Service Medal was awarded. The entries may also contain further information such as rank and number, full name and address together with file number and the date of issue of medals, but it is extremely unusual for all these details to be present on a single card. The medal rolls are not arranged in alphabetical order, but by rank and list number, so it can be difficult to identify individual entries. They are also fragile. The Records and Historical Services Unit is not open to the public but is prepared to answer written enquiries concerning the issue of medals. However, you should note that the cards cannot be used to prove whether someone was or was not a member of the police force at any time, and that they will not establish length of service of any individual, nor whether there was any entitlement to a pension.

Colonial Office records held in the PRO sometimes contain information about the activities of the Palestine police. For the most part, however, they relate to political aspects of operations, major disturbances (involving large numbers of deaths, or extensive damage to property), and enquiries into corruption. They do not contain material on recruitment, promotion, resignations or routine administrative detail, nor information on day to day work. Details of an excellent, although now dated, guide to records relating to Palestine by Jones are given in the bibliography below.

24.10 Other colonial police forces

As a matter of general principle, you are unlikely to find personnel records for individuals who served in colonial police forces or information about the day to day activities of colonial police forces in the PRO. Nor is it likely that the Foreign and Commonwealth Office or any other government department holds such information for future transfer to the PRO. This is because such forces were administered by the government of the colony concerned, rather than directly by the Colonial Office (later Foreign and Commonwealth Office) in London. Any files created would therefore have been in the possession of the relevant colonial government. They would have remained in that colony even after independence because they would have been essential to the day to day administration of policing in the newly independent country. However, as noted above for South Africa and Palestine, it is possible that some personal information is included in files that were created by the Colonial Office for other purposes. Such information is likely to be incidental to the main purpose of the file and is unlikely therefore either to be indexed or even indicated in the lists. Conducting a search of this kind would require considerable determination, a lot of time, and a willingness to accept that it may not be successful. If you wish to undertake such a search, you would be well advised to consult a good guide to colonial records such as the one by Thurston listed below.

24.11 Police honours and decorations

Although the PRO does hold Home Office files relating to recommendations for the award of the King's Police Medal from its introduction in 1909, all the information of substance in those files appears in Farmery's *Police Gallantry*. Farmery's book also uses information from the *Police Review*, the *Police Chronicle* as well as other sources, and often includes a photograph of the individual concerned. It gives direct references to the Home Office files in HO 45. Awards were notified in the *London Gazette* but entries before 1960 do not include a citation. The PRO holds copies of the London Gazette in series ZJ 1, and there is a copy of Farmery's book in the PRO Library, but as both are published works, copies should be available to you at a good local reference library or via the inter-library loan system.

Records relating to awards of the King's Police Medal to Metropolitan Police officers are:

* 1909–1951 register of Metropolitan Police Officers under consideration for the award, MEPO 22/2;
* 1909–1912 list of awards, MEPO 2/1300.

An indexed register of decorations, honours and awards to Metropolitan Police officers, 1945–1988 is in MEPO 22/1.

24.12 Police forces: bibliography

D Ascoli, *The Queen's Peace: the origins and development of the Metropolitan Police 1829–1979* (London, 1979)
V Bailey, *Policing and punishment in nineteenth century Britain* (London, 1981)
J D Brewer, *The Royal Irish Constabulary: an oral history* (Belfast, 1990)
I Bridgeman and C Emsley, *A guide to the archives of the police forces of England and Wales* (Police History Society, 1989)
C Emsley, *The English Police: a political and social history* (Hemel Hempstead, 1991)
J P Farmery, *Police Gallantry, The King's Police Medal, the King's Police and Fire Service Medal and the Queen's Police Medal for Gallantry 1909–1978* (Periter, Sydney, 1995)

J Herlihy, *The Royal Irish Constabulary: a complete alphabetical list of officers and men 1816–1922* (Dublin, 1999)

J Herlihy, *The Royal Irish Constabulary: a short history and genealogical guide with a select list of medal awards and casualties* (Dublin, 1997)

C J Jeffries, *The colonial police* (London, 1952)

P Jones, *Britain and Palestine* (Oxford, 1979)

S H Palmer, *Police and Protest in England and Ireland, 1780–1850* (Cambridge, 1988)

S Petrow, *Policing morals: the Metropolitan Police and the Home Office, 1870–1914* (Oxford, 1994)

D Philips and R D Storch, *Policing Provincial England 1829–1856: The Politics of Reform* (Leicester, 1999)

Police History Society, *Journal of the Police History Society* (1986 onwards)

Police History Society, *Notes for Family Historians* (Police Historical Memo No. 1, 1987)

A Sherman, *My ancestor was a policeman: how can I find out more about him?* (Society of Genealogists, 2000)

C Steedman, *Policing the Victorian community: the formation of English provincial police forces, 1856–80* (London, 1984)

R D Storch, 'The policeman as domestic missionary: urban discipline and popular culture in northern England, 1850–1880', *Journal of Social History* (Summer 1976)

M B Taylor and V L Wilkinson, *Badges of office: an illustrated guide to the helmets and badges of the British police 1829 to 1989* (Henley-on-Thames, 1989)

A Thurston, *Records of the Colonial Office, Dominions Office, Commonwealth Relations Office and Commonwealth Office* (London, 1995)

R Whitmore, *Victorian and Edwardian Crime and Punishment from Old Photographs* (London, 1978)

25

In the service of the Crown

◆ ◆ ◆

This is a bit of a catch-all chapter, as it covers people formally employed in Crown service (serving the government), people employed by or servicing the Royal Household, people awarded coronation and jubilee medals, and people who served in some of the non-military organizations during the Second World War.

25.1 Civil servants

Many senior civil servants are best sought, not in the records, but in such publications as the *Dictionary of National Biography*, or the *British Biographical Archive*. For 1883–1977, try the PRO Library's holdings of *Kelly's Handbook to the Titled, Landed and Official Classes*, which gives a potted biography. There are a number of official printed sources available at the PRO on the postings of senior civil servants, but they do not provide personal information. The main one is the *British Imperial Calendar*, which runs from 1810 to 1972, when it became the *Civil Service Year Book*. From 1852 there is the *Foreign Office List*, and from 1862 the *Colonial Office List*. Try also Sainty's lists of *Office Holders in Modern Britain* which cover the period 1660–1870. They include officials of the Admiralty, the Board of Trade, the Colonial Office, the Foreign Office, the Home Office, the Navy Board, Royal Commissions of Inquiry, the Secretaries of State, the Treasury, and the Lord Chamberlain's and Lord Steward's Departments of the Royal Household.

Entry to the Civil Service, after 1855, was by competition. Even posts as lowly as lady telegraph learners or post sorters had examination as the means of entry. The Civil Service Commission administered examinations for the Army, Navy and India services (civil, forestry, etc.) as well as for the Civil Service. Surviving records are mostly about the qualifying examinations (CSC 8 and CSC 10), and contain little personal information except clues as to a person's educational and social status, and ability. In these terms, the examination results can be quite interesting, especially when matched up with the regulations in CSC 6. As well as specifying what the candidates were to be examined in, these regulations often give an idea of the nature of the work and of any potential future career. You do need an idea of likely date of entry in order to use them but they are well worth looking at to set people in context.

Individual application papers have been destroyed, though a selection of those of famous or infamous people can be found in CSC 11. The evidences of age submitted by candidates between 1855 and 1880 (which used to be at the PRO) are now kept by the Society of Genealogists (CSC 1).

There are few personal details about civil servants in the public records, and it is quite difficult to trace them. If you know the office or department, it is worth looking through its records to find establishment lists, etc., which may possibly be useful. If you want details of payments of wages and pensions, try looking in E 403 (a huge class with lots of little used material). Colwell's *Dictionary of Genealogical Sources in the Public Record Office* has two pages of references to appointments and payments, which you may find helpful.

To discover where to find the establishment records of a particular office, including defunct offices, use the *PRO Guide* (which will give you ideas) or a keyword search on PROCAT (staff lists, or establishments are useful keywords). As an example of what can be found, MAF 39 will give you:

- staff lists for 1892–1947, with ranks and salaries;
- registers of service 1854–1929;
- lists of those serving in the armed forces in the two world wars;

for the Board of Agriculture (up to 1903), the Board of Agriculture and Fisheries (1903–1919), and the Ministry of Agriculture and Fisheries.

Another possibility, for nineteenth-century departments, would be to explore the *Parliamentary Papers*, which contain annual reports from the various branches of the civil service, and also include many reports on aspects of its work. These may give you details of the work actually done, as well as establishment lists. There is a full set available on microfiche at the PRO: from the indexes it is not clear if some of the returns are statistical, or if they contain personal information of some kind. If you do find useful lists as a result of exploring the *Parliamentary Papers*, please could you inform the staff at the Research Enquiries Desk, so that the information can be shared.

Other possible sources outside the particular department's own records may be among the records of the Treasury (e.g. the Departmental Accounts in T 38) or the pension records of the Paymaster General (PMG 27 and PMG 28). In the indexed pension records in PMG 28, you can find details on people who worked in prisons at home and in the colonies, or in the 'public departments' of England, Scotland and Ireland. The later registers generally give name, office held, age on retirement, length of service, salary, pension, cause of retirement, pension start date, and a reference to the Treasury letter authorizing the pension. Some include annotations, which can provide clues to past or future life – or to death.

For instance, the tragic entry for Magnus Fea Ogilvy shows that on his retirement (for ill-health) at the age of 34 in June 1869, he was the chief clerk of the Scottish Board of Lunacy with a salary of £300 a year. He had served for 11 years 8 months, and was granted an annual pension of £55. In November 1869, a note was added that payment should be made to his mother Mrs Martha

Ogilvy, while he was detained in James Murray's Lunatic Asylum. A further note recorded his early death, in October 1871 (PMG 28/15).

25.2 Customs, Excise and the Inland Revenue

In contrast to other civil servants, there is a fair amount of material for the employees of the separate Boards of Customs and Excise. Customs officers were responsible for collecting duty on imports, and preventing smuggling, and excise men were responsible for collecting taxes levied on home products. For indexed directories of customs officers, excise men and inland revenue officials, 1875–1930, see *Ham's Customs Year Book* and *Ham's Inland Revenue Year Book*, in the PRO Library. Entry was by civil service competition at this period: see the second paragraph of **25.1**.

Warrants for the appointment of Customs officers, 1714–1797, are in C 208, indexed by C 202/267–269. The Customs Board minute books, in CUST 28, contain information on the first and later postings of Customs officers, with details of any praise or censure: they contain no family details, but they can be used to work out the details of a man's career. For Ireland, there are registers of officers' appointments, 1761–1823, in CUST 20/154–159.

For the Customs, there are pay lists and staff lists, arranged by place: in general these give little personal detail, although very occasionally details of marriage might be given.

1671–1922	CUST 39	Staff lists
1673–1689	PRO 30/32/15–29	Quarterly bills of salaries
1675–1813	CUST 18	Quarterly bills of salaries for England and Wales (and Isle of Man from 1810)
1684–1826	CUST 20	Salary and establishment books, Ireland
1714–1829	T 43	Scotland: quarterly returns of staff
1716–1847	T 42	England: quarterly returns of staff
1814–1829	CUST 19	Quarterly bills of salaries for England, Wales, Isle of Man and Scotland (1829 only). Includes revenue cruisers in UK from late 1827

Some family details can be found in the pension records in CUST 39/145–151, which cover 1803 to 1922. For Ireland, there are pension records covering 1785–1851 in CUST 39/161. The most useful for family historians are, as always, the sections relating to widows' pensions, which give details of any children. Applications for pensions can be found in T 1, using the indexes in T 2 and T 108. Other family details may be found among the correspondence of the individual ports ('outports' in the Customs service) with the Customs Board: look among the various CUST series for these.

The Board of Excise was responsible for collecting the payments for internal indirect taxes on consumable goods: in 1849 it was amalgamated with the Board of Stamps and Taxes to form the Board of Inland Revenue, but in 1909 it went back to join with the Customs instead.

Many of the sources for tracing Excise men are similar to the Customs records. There are pay lists for the English Excise, 1705–1835 (T 44) and the Scottish Excise, 1708–1832 (T 45). The Excise Board minute books, 1695–1867 (CUST 47) contain the same kinds of information as those of the Customs Board, as do the Excise pension records, 1856–1922 (CUST 39/157–159). It is always worth having a good poke around in these kinds of records, as extra material can turn up. For example, in 1796 nearly all Excise officers signed local petitions for an increase in their salary. The petitions show the problems they had managing on their pay, give details of the cost of living, and point out the difficulties that arose for their families from being frequently moved from post to post (T 44/38).

However, there are also the Excise Entry Papers, 1820–1870 (CUST 116). There is an alphabetical index to these. The Entry Papers usually consist of two letters, folded together. The first is a letter of recommendation, giving the name of the applicant, his age, place of birth, marital status (but no details of his wife), and a character reference. The second letter is from the Excise officer responsible for the applicant's training: this states whether he is proficient in writing, spelling and arithmetic.

Records relating to the Irish Excise men, 1824–1833, and the Irish Revenue Police, 1830–1857, are in CUST 110 and CUST 111. For later brief details, see *Ham's Customs Year Book* and *Ham's Inland Revenue Year Book*, in the PRO Library.

Another potential source is the archive of the Excise (later Inland Revenue) Life Assurance and Benevolent Fund Society, in IR 92: this was set up in 1845 to grant annuities to the widows and orphans of its members. Its register of members in IR 92/15 can be used to trace a taxman's career, movement round the country and date of birth and death, even if he left no widow or orphan.

25.3 The Royal Household

The responsibilities of the two departments of the Household could be broadly divided between above stairs (Lord Chamberlain's) and below stairs (Lord Steward's). In addition to the Household records described below, there are many other sources for Royal Household servants, such as the accounts in E 101, E 351, LC 9, LS 1, LS 2, LS 3 and T 38.

25.3.1 The Royal Household after 1660: general

There are published lists by Sainty of *Officials of the Royal Household, 1660–1837*, which you should consult first: they are available at the PRO. The Royal Archives hold a comprehensive card index of persons employed in the Lord Chamberlain's and Lord Steward's departments, 1660–1837, compiled from the records of the Lord Chamberlain and the Lord Steward, which are in the

TO THE

Right Hon. the LORDS COMMISSIONERS

OF THE

TREASURY.

◆—◆—◆—◆—◆—◆—◆—◆

The humble Petition of the Supervisors and Officers of Excise in York Collection,

SHEWETH,

THAT your Petitioners have presented a Petition to the following Purport, to the Hon. Board of Excise, stating the Hardships of their Situation, and the Difficulties under which they labour, which Petition has been rejected.

With due Deference and Submission, they humbly beg Leave to observe, That, when their Salaries were augmented, a Reduction was also made in the Number of Officers, so that the Increase of Salary was no additional Charge upon Government; but the Benefit and good Effect arising from that necessary Advance was entirely done away and rendered nugatory, by reviving the System of Removes; a System which, they beg Leave to say, subjects them to such great Inconveniences and Expences, as their Salaries are not equal to difcharge; and which, as far as they are able to judge, can be of no Advantage to the Revenue. Many Officers, from an Inability to support the Expence, are obliged either to do Injustice to their Creditors, or conduct themselves in that Manner which will ultimately prove injurious to the Revenue.

The Hon. Board of Excise have granted a small Sum towards the Expences of such of your Petitioners as were last removed; but it is far from being equivalent to that Purpose. The Loss they experience in Travelling, House-Rent, breaking and damaging Household Furniture, or selling it to a great Disadvantage, extraordinary Board and Lodging, until a House can be procured, Alterations frequently to be made in a fresh House, to suit different Families, and many other Expences which cannot be enumerated, and which amount to a considerable Sum, if the Remove is only to a small Distance.

That from the great Increase in Price of all the Necessaries of Life, within the short Period of three or four Years, their Salaries are not equal to procure them Subsistence, exclusive of other Necessaries, which they presume will appear manifest, upon a slight View of the advanced Price of the following Articles, viz. Corn, Flesh Meat, Butter, Milk, Cheese, Soap, Starch, Candles, Malt, Shoes, Coals, Sugar, &c. which Articles, taken in the aggregate, have increased in Price, upon a moderate Computation, 35l. per Cent. and from the great Increase of the National Debt, the extended Trade of this Kingdom, and the consequent Increase of Paper in Circulation, no Prospect remains to afford them Hope that the Necessaries of Life will be reduced to their former Limits. On this Ground, they humbly presume it will appear evident, that a Salary, which some Years ago was only deemed sufficient for their Subsistence, (exclusive of Removes) must now be very inadequate, and fall far short of a Maintenance for their Families.

To render the Matter still more clear, they beg Leave to refer to the following Statement of a medium Family, consisting of a Man, Wife, and three Children, into which no Articles of Luxury are introduced, nor any Thing inserted, but what is absolutely necessary.

WEEKLY ACCOUNT.		£	s.	d.	YEARLY ACCOUNT.		£	s.	d.
Meal	—	0	7	4	Brought forward		68	0	8
Beef, 10lb. at 7d. per pound	—	0	5	10	Sitting Expences		2	8	0
Tea and Sugar	—	0	2	3	House Rent and Taxes		7	10	0
Candles for House and Surveying	—	0	1	0	Cloathing for five Persons		10	0	0
Salt, Mustard, Pepper, &c.	—	0	0	2	Shoes		3	0	0
Milk	—	0	2	0	Tax and Charity upon Salary		1	17	6
Cheese, 1lb.	—	0	0	7					
Butter, 1lb.	—	0	0	10		Total	92	16	2
Potatoes and Greens	—	0	0	7	Footwalk Salary		65	0	0
Soap, Starch, Blue, and Washing	—	0	1	6					
Baking	—	0	0	3	Footwalk deficient		27	16	2
Beer	—	0	1	6					
Coals	—	0	1	6	Total brought down		92	16	2
Yeast	—	0	0	2	Ride Officer's Salary		60	0	0
Schooling for Children	—	0	1	0					
	Total per Week	1	6	2	Horse-keeping and Tax	Remains	32 16 13		2 0
	Amounting per Annum to	68	0	8					
					Difference of House Rent and other Conveniences, not to be had in a Market Town, to deduct		45 6	16 0	0 0
						Rides deficient	39	16	2

Exclusive of the great Expences of Removes, which cannot be estimated, the Casualties of Sickness and other incidental Expences which Families are subject to, and which amount to a considerable Sum.

From

Figure 46 Petitions for a pay rise, from Excise Officers across the country, give a valuable account of the cost of supporting a family of five in 1796, and of the particular difficulties faced by Excise families. (PRO, T 44/38 no. 30)

PRO, and from other sources elsewhere, and is prepared to answer postal enquiries. The address is in **48**.

Payments relating to salaries and retirement allowances of the royal household and of people on the Civil List, 1834–1929, are in PMG 27, but these are not usually informative.

25.3.1.1 The Lord Chamberlain's Department after 1660

The Lord Chamberlain was broadly responsible for 'upstairs': the chambers, the wardrobe, the office of robes, ceremonies, revels, musicians, chapels, housekeepers, messengers, yeomen of the guard, watermen, physicians, artists, craftsmen and other offices such as Librarian, Latin Secretary, Poet Laureate, Examiner of Plays, and Keeper of Lions at the Tower. A good place to start for 1660–1784 would be the Glencross Index to many of the establishment records in LC 5 (filed with the LC 5 list). This includes the entry books of wills and letters of attorney of household servants, 1750–1784 (LC 5/104–106).

There are records of appointments, 1660–1851 (LC 3/61–71) and 1851–1901 (LC 5/237–241). LC 3/56–60 is a less complete series for various dates between 1685 and 1838. Established servants are named in LC 3/1–23, for various dates between 1641 and 1849. Records of payments, 1516–1782 are in LC 5/11–83.

Officers are not usually named in the Salary, Livery and Pension Books, LC 3/37–52 (1667–1857), except for pensioners, holders of offices about to be discontinued, and widows. LC 3/37 is a book of arrears for 1667–1685, where the names of both salaried and waged servants appear. Servants appointed to the Office of Robes appear in the Letter Books of that office, LC 13/1–5 (1830–1901).

Servants' names are given in respect of various payments and appointments in the Warrant Books of the Treasurer of the Chamber, LC 5/11–26 (1660–1800), the Comptroller, LC 5/27–30 (1754–1781), and the Wardrobe, LC 5/31–83 (1516–1782). LC 5/247 concerns officers and servants, 1864–97. Warrants of Several Sorts, LC 5/248–251 (1820–1866) include some appointments, among payments, general instructions and grants of 'grace and favour' lodgings. Several of these are indexed by the Glencross Index, filed with the LC 5 list.

There is material relating to servants among the Correspondence Books in LC 1, while servants at various royal palaces appear in the Palaces Ledgers, LC 9/367–374 (1806–1846). Messengers' travelling expenses can be found in LC 10/1–9 (1784–1838).

Records about royal mourning may include lists of people receiving mourning clothes. The servants of royal households other than those of the monarch and consort rarely appear, but the records of funerals in LC 2 may list the households of deceased royal persons. The household of the Duke of York in 1827 is listed in LC 2/56. Housemaids are named in connection with mourning in the Bill Books for sundries, LC 11/144–5 (1846–1857).

25.3.1.2 The Lord Steward's Department after 1660

The Lord Steward was responsible for 'downstairs', until 1854, when his office was abolished, and its functions were taken over by the Master of the Royal Household, whose records are not public records, but are held by the Royal Archives. The Lord Steward, and later the Master, had responsibility for the kitchen offices (almonry, ewery, bakery, pastry, confectionery, buttery, spicery, poultry, larder, pantry, wine cellar, scullery), the counting house, the wood and coal yards, the gardens and stables, and a whole host of other offices such as keeper and repairer of the buckets. Warrants of appointments, 1660–1820, are in LS 13/246–267.

The names of servants, including purveyors, extraordinary staff and the higher officers of the stables appear in the Cheque Rolls, LS 13/6–13 (James I–George II). Certificate Books of Admission, LS 13/197–204 (1672–1820) include servants of the Steward's department, stables, chapels, and the Secretaries of State. Special duties and leaves of absence are recorded in LS 13/205–208 (1766–1811).

In the middle ages household servants had been entitled to eat at the board as part of their remuneration. By the seventeenth century the entitlement had often been translated into money payments, or boardwages, the responsibility of the Lord Steward's Department, paid by the Board of Green Cloth. The Kitchen Ledgers, LS 9/60–77 (1660–1729) show these payments to the Steward's staff, staff of the Chamber and Wardrobe, including the Lord Chamberlain himself, the Secretaries of State and chapel staff. Other expenses are recorded, including travelling expenses, pheasant keeping and payments to widows and for burials. Receipt books for wages and allowances, LS 13/154–167 (1761–1816) contain the signatures of many servants for receipt of boardwages and other payments, including 'carpet and cushion money'. These chronological entries are not indexed.

The Creditors also record the payment of boardwages, LS 8 (1641–1854). The Creditors of two minor royal households survive in LS 8/315–316, for Princess Charlotte, 1814–1815, and LS 8/317, for the Prince of Hesse-Homburg, 1818. The households of royal princesses and the Duke of Clarence are mentioned in LS 8/237 (1805). LS 13/321 records pensions for members of Princess Charlotte's household. Stable Creditors, LS 13/210–230 (1761–1781) show creditors and salary bills for the stables, Chamber and chapels. LS 13/295–299 (1815–1834) record allowances in kind, including 'pitchers and platters'. The names, and often the signatures of clerks, housemaids, footmen, laundresses, coachmen and postilions appear among those of servants of all household departments.

Records of the royal gardens, which provided produce for the table appear in LS 10–12 (1796–1854), but staff, other than head gardeners, are rarely named. Garden labourers at Kew, Windsor and Hampton Court, 1834–1835, are named in LS 11/19–20. Gamekeepers are rarely named in the royal household records, although four gamekeepers at Richmond are named in LC 3/23 (1846–1849). There are detailed records relating to the employment of estate staff, such as gamekeepers, park and gatekeepers and fishermen, at Windsor Great Park in the records of the Crown Estate Office, in CRES 4 (1766–1958).

In 1854 the office of Lord Steward was abolished, and its functions were taken over by the Master of the Royal Household, whose records are not public records. Contact the Royal Archives (address in **48**) for more information.

25.3.2 The Household during the Commonwealth

There is a break in the series of Royal Household records for this period, but some bills of the 1650s have been preserved in series of Bills and Vouchers LC 9/377–390 (1622–1843). There are also requests for arrears of payments dated in the 1660s. This series is mostly unsorted.

25.3.3 The Royal Household before 1660

If you are looking for a member of the Royal Household before 1660, you may need specialist advice: a leaflet is available at the PRO and on the PRO's website. For a series of articles on the court, look at Starkey, *The English Court from the Wars of the Roses to the Civil War.*

Try the name indexes to SC 1, Ancient Correspondence, and SC 6, Ancient Petitions, and also to the printed Calendars of Patent Rolls and Close Rolls, for details of patronage. The Exchequer's Various Accounts in E 101 may contain information, but they are not indexed. Names of members of the Royal Household are separately listed for 1523–1696 in the E 179 taxation returns (see **43.1**). For the lower household answerable to the Lord Steward, there is an entry book for 1627–1641, LS 13/251. An index to the members of Charles's household from LC 3/1 (1641) is filed with the list.

The Verge was the area stretching for 12 miles around wherever the Household happened to be, and as the Household was always on the move, the boundaries of the Verge were constantly changing. The Marshal of the Household, who was in charge of discipline of the royal staff, had the right to try crimes which occurred within this area. See E 37 to 1623 and PALA 6 for 1629 to 1849. For further details see Jones, 'The Court of the Verge'.

25.4 Royal warrant holders

Today the Royal Household carefully controls the issue of royal warrants to tradesmen. The grant of such a warrant entitles the holder to use the phrase 'By Appointment', and to display the royal coat of arms. For a general view, see Heald's *By Appointment: 150 Years of the Royal Warrant and its Holders.*

From 1900 lists of royal warrant holders are published annually in the *London Gazette* (ZJ 1 at the PRO). False claims to possession of royal warrants became a prosecutable offence under the Patents Act, 1883, and the Merchandise Marks Act, 1887. The issue of royal warrants to tradesmen was recorded systematically from the 1830s. Warrants to tradesmen supplying ceremonial items (e.g. peruke makers) and to those supplying more personal items (e.g. combs, perfumes and corset stays) to the office of robes, 1830–1901, are in LC 13/1–5. Warrants to tradesmen supplying such items as furnishings, linens and stationery for Queen

Victoria are in LC 5/243–246. Each volume has an internal index. The original bills presented by tradesmen, whether warrant holders or not, are in LC 11.

Before the 1830s, the situation was not so well regulated. Tradesmen's appointments, 1660–1837, appear with the appointment of Household servants in LC 3/61–70. Unfortunately no appointments were recorded between 1767 and 1773. Orders to tradesmen and for court mourning, 1773–1827, are in LC 5/197–199. Suppliers of all kinds of goods are named in the series of Warrant Books LC 5/132–163 (1628–1810). The Accounts (LC 9) and Bill Books (LC 10 and LC 11) may also reveal suppliers of goods to the household between 1600 and 1900. Office of Robes accounts can be found in LC 12 (1860–1901).

The Lord Steward's Department was responsible for the royal kitchens, cellars, stables and gardens. Suppliers to the department were appointed as purveyors. They were often appointed in the place of a previous purveyor, not for a salary or wage, but to enjoy 'rights, profits, privileges and advantages'. Some original warrants to purveyors survive in the series of Original Warrants, LS 13/246–250 (1761–1782). Other tradesmen also received this kind of warrant, e.g. cork cutter, wine chest maker, and cake maker. Copies of these warrants were recorded in the Warrant Books, LS 13/251–267 (1627–1820). From 1674 they are divided into two series, Royal and Steward's. Warrants to purveyors appear in the Steward's series. Groceries, poultry, wines and wax candles are among the goods to be purveyed. Tradesmen's warrants do not appear to have been recorded in the Lord Steward's records after 1820, but there is a volume showing fees for warrants, which includes fees for purveyors' warrants, from 1838–1850 (LS 13/306).

The Kitchen Ledgers LS 9/60–77 (1660–1729) include the names of suppliers of such items as beer, glasses, bottles and toothpicks among other expenses. Suppliers are also named in the Mensils, LS 9/227–290 (1761–1814), monthly lists of the consumption of foodstuffs and wines, and also supplies of coals and brushes.

Orders to tradesmen are recorded in LS 13/134–153 (1763–1851). The tradesmen are not always named, especially in the earlier period, where often only the trade is given, e.g. the Brazier, the China and Glassman. There are orders for food, wine, beer, fuel, lights, china, cutlery, turnery, ironmongery, linen, floorcoverings and stationery. Tradesmen's bills appear in the Accounts Books in LS 2 (1761–1854). The Creditors in LS 8 show amounts owed to various suppliers. LS 8/1–98 (1641–1760) are a single series, while those for 1761–1815 are divided into three series (LS 8/100–270): Kitchen Creditors for foods; Household, for foods, fuel, lights and laundry; Incidental for stationery, hardware and cartage. There are also separate Creditors for Hampton Court Palace for 1795–1799. A new system, where quarterly accounts were arranged according to palaces, recorded the names of goods, suppliers and costs, LS 8/271–314 (1815–1854). Suppliers to the stables appear in the Stables Creditors, LS 13/210–230 (1761–1781).

25.5 Coronation and Jubilee medals, 1935–1977

Lists of people who received the following medals can be found in the PRO Library:

- King's Silver Jubilee Medal 1935
- Coronation Medal 1937
- Coronation Medal 1953
- Queen's Silver Jubilee Medal 1977

For other similar civilian awards, try the *London Gazette* (available in the PRO as ZJ 1).

25.6 The National Fire Service and the Air Raid Precaution Service, Second World War

The PRO does not hold the records of these services, although we do get some queries about them. Please write to the Home Office (address in **48**).

25.7 The Women's Land Army, 1939–1950

The Women's Land Army was set up in June 1939 to help increase the amount of food grown within Britain. By 1941, its numbers had risen to 20,000 and, at its peak in 1943, over 80,000 women were 'Land Girls'. Numbers did not rise after that, as women were needed to make aircraft and were encouraged to take up

Figure 47 My mother's stories of her experiences as a Land Girl bear no similarity to this romantic view of the life! (PRO, INF 2/42)

factory work instead. However, women did continue to join and in fact many served until it was disbanded in 1950.

Women joined the Land Army from all backgrounds, a third coming from London and other large cities. About a quarter were employed in milking and general farm work. Six thousand women worked in the Timber Corps, felling trees and running sawmills. The Women's Land Army had a uniform, but as the Land Army was not a military force, it was not compulsory. Some women lived in hostels but most lived on individual farms. Conditions were often poor and pay was low.

The original service records of the Women's Land Army have not survived. However, the index cards to them have survived, as they were used for pension purposes. The PRO has them on microfiche only in MAF 421, for 1939 to 1945 only. The cards give name, change of name on marriage, address, date of birth, previous occupation, WLA service number and dates of service. Some cards have photographs and remarks on suitability for the service. Watch out when selecting your fiche, as only the first five letters of the start and end surnames are given on the fiche label. The final fiche is a compilation of mis-sorted cards.

The original cards are kept by the Imperial War Museum (address in **48**): if you want to see them, you must give them at least a week's notice as they are stored off site. The MAF 21 reference is not needed, as they are kept in alphabetical order.

25.8 In the service of the Crown: bibliography

British Imperial Calendar (London, 1810–1972)
Colonial Office List (London, annually from 1862)
S Colwell, *Dictionary of Genealogical Sources in the Public Record Office* (London, 1992)
Court & City Register (London, 1742–1808)
Foreign Office List (London, annually from 1852)
E B Fryde ed., *Handbook of British Chronology* (London, 3rd edn, 1986) (Lists monarchs, officers of state, archbishops and bishops, dukes, marquesses and earls, in chronological sequence.)
C J Given-Wilson, *The Royal Household and the King's Affinity: Service, Politics and Finance in England, 1360–1413* (New Haven, Conn., and London, 1986)
Ham's Customs Year Book (annual: PRO Library has 1875–1930)
Ham's Inland Revenue Year Book (annual: PRO Library has 1875–1930)
T Heald, *By Appointment: 150 years of the Royal Warrant and its Holders* (London, 1989)
W R Jones, 'The Court of the Verge', *Journal of British Studies*, vol. X (1970)
Kelly's Handbook to the Titled, Landed and Official Classes (annual: PRO Library has 1883–1977)
Royal Kalendar (London, 1746–1849)
J C Sainty and others, *Office Holders in Modern Britain* (London, 1972–1998). This so far comprises:

I	*Treasury Officials 1660–1870*, J C Sainty, 1972	
II	*Officials of the Secretaries of State 1660–1782*, J C Sainty, 1973	
III	*Officials of the Boards of Trade 1660–1782*, J C Sainty, 1974	
IV	*Admiralty Officials 1660–1870*, J C Sainty, 1975	
V	*Home Office Officials 1782–1870*, J C Sainty, 1975	
VI	*Colonial Office Officials 1794–1870*, J C Sainty, 1976	
VII	*Navy Board Officials 1660–1832*, J M Collinge, 1978	

VIII   *Foreign Office Officials 1782–1870*, J M Collinge, 1979
IX   *Officials of Royal Commissions of Enquiry 1815–1870*, J M Collinge, 1984
X   *Officials of Royal Commissions of Enquiry 1870–1939*, E Harrison, 1995
XI   *Officials of the Royal Household 1660–1837: Department of the Lord Chamberlain and associated offices*, J C Sainty and R O Burcholz, 1997
XII   *Officials of the Royal Household 1660–1837: Department of the Lord Steward and the Master of the Horse*, J C Sainty and R O Burcholz 1998

G Smith, *Something to Declare!: 1000 years of Customs and Excise* (London, 1980)
D Starkey, ed., *The English Court from the Wars of the Roses to the Civil War* (London, 1987)

26

Merchant seamen

◆ ◆ ◆

26.1 Introduction

The Britain of the past was a great maritime nation. Its island status and the widespread nature of its empire meant that merchant shipping was of huge importance, and many more families relied on the sea for a living than is conceivable now.

Records of officers exist from 1845, and are currently available up to approximately 1969. Accessible records of merchant seamen survive in bulk for 1835 to 1857, and again from about 1918 to 1972. Ship-based records also exist and can be used to fill the gaps, but these records are not easy to access, and you do need to know what ship to look for.

The records relating to merchant seamen have been fully examined in two specialist guides: Smith, Watts and Watts, *Records of Merchant Shipping and Seamen*, and Watts and Watts, *My Ancestor was a Merchant Seaman*: try these, if you find you want more detail. The Society of Genealogists has a useful collection on merchant seamen; see Hailey, *Maritime Sources in the Library of the Society of Genealogists*.

26.2 Looking for merchant seamen and officers before 1835

This is not easy. There is a lot of recorded information but most of it is about ships. Before 1835 there are no systematic records of merchant seamen, although some crew lists of merchant vessels do survive from as early as 1747. Before 1835, you have to work out where the path of a seaman crosses with officialdom, to leave a record of some kind. The most likely records relate to trade, taxation, legal disputes and the Royal Navy. Such material, by its very nature, will contain many more references to the masters of ships than to the ordinary seamen who sailed in them. The chances of finding information on a particular sailor are very slim. Make sure you consult one of the two specialist guides on the topic.

There are many wills of merchant seamen from the late seventeenth century to 1857 among the records of the Commissary Court of London (London Division) at the Guildhall Library (address in **48**). The Prerogative Court of Canterbury wills, at the PRO, also include wills of very many seamen who died abroad before 1858: see **6**.

There are indexes of apprentices registered in the merchant fleet from 1824 (BT 150), giving name, age, date and term of indenture and the name of the master. For 1710–1811, there was a general tax on apprenticeship indentures: try looking for references to seamen both as apprentices and as masters in the Apprenticeship Books (IR 1) and their modern indexes (see **28**). For the port of Colchester, there is a register of seamen's indentures covering 1704–1757, and 1804–1844 (BT 167/103). A list of children apprenticed to the sea from Christ's Hospital, 1766, survives in T 64/311. A register of apprentices from all over England, bound to fishermen in the south-east, survives for 1639–1664 (HCA 30/897).

From 1747, the masters or owners of merchant ships had to keep muster rolls for each voyage. These recorded the names of officers and seamen employed on the ship, their usual place of abode, dates of engagement and discharge, and the name of the ship in which they last sailed (BT 98). Unfortunately, there are no indexes. The only surviving rolls from before 1800 came from Shields, Dartmouth, Liverpool and Plymouth. Some strays also survive for Plymouth, 1776–1780 (CUST 66/227) and Scarborough, 1747–1765 (CUST 91/111–112).

Other series that may yield useful information include:

- Surveys of maritime resources made on a parish-by-parish basis, in the 1620s to 1640s; these survive mostly in SP 16;
- Port Books, 1565–1798 (E 190);
- Board of Trade and Naval Officers' Shipping Returns, c.1678–1867;
- High Court of Admiralty, 1519–1943 (HCA 15–20, HCA 24, HCA 27 and HCA 30–31);
- High Court of Delegates, 1536–1866 (DEL 1, DEL 2, DEL 7–11);
- Registers of Protection from being Pressed, 1702–1828 (in ADM 7);
- Registers of Ships' Passes, 1683–1845 (ADM 7/73–164) (these give the destination and duration of voyages);
- Letters of Marque, 1549–1834 (ADM 7/317–332, DEL 2, HCA 25, HCA 26 and PC 5);
- Accounts of the Receiver of Sixpences for the Thames, 1725–1830 (ADM 68/194–219) and the port of Exeter, 1800–1851 (BT 167/38–40);
- Navy Board: Registers of Payments to masters of merchant ships for giving passage home to shipwrecked mariners etc., 1729–1826 (ADM 30/22–25).

You could also try various CO series, BT 6, HO 76, T 1 and T 64.

The Society of Genealogists has copies of the petitions to Trinity House from merchant seamen requesting charitable support, 1787–1854: the originals are at the Guildhall.

26.3 Officers' certificates of competency and service, from 1845: masters, mates and engineers

By an order of 1845, the Board of Trade authorized a system of voluntary examinations of competency for men intending to become masters or mates of foreign-going and home-trade British merchant ships (BT 143/1). Certificates for masters and mates gradually became compulsory and could be obtained by proving long service (service) or by examination (competency); details are to be found, up to 1921, in BT 122–127. From 1862 there are also certificates for engineers (BT 139–142), and from 1883 for skippers and mates of fishing boats (BT 129, BT 130, BT 138). Colonial certificates were entered separately (BT 128, BT 140). All series are well indexed.

The certificate registers give name, place and year of birth, date and place of issue of the certificate, and rank examined or served in. Deaths, injuries and retirements have often been noted. Up to 1888, the registers record details of the ships served in, and this may be followed up in the crew lists, in a similar way to that described above for ordinary seamen. Applications for certificates, for those issued in the UK up to 1928, are preserved at the National Maritime Museum – these often record voyage details prior to the issue of a certificate; later applications are believed not to have survived.

From 1910, a combined index to masters, mates, engineers and skippers and mates of fishing boats was started to replace those formerly kept in registers (BT 122–130 and BT 138–142). The term 'index' for this collection is a slight misnomer in that it is not an index to any other records; in effect it replaced the earlier registers and indexes and became a self-indexing register. It was kept in card form

Figure 48 Officers of the steamship *Norman*, built in Belfast in 1894, photographed at Southampton in 1896. The *Norman* was a Union Line mail ship, on the fast regular run between Southampton and South Africa. (PRO, COPY 1/424A)

covering the period 1910 to approximately 1969, covering home and foreign trade and each card gives name, date and place of birth, certificate number, rating, date of passing and port of examination. The index is available on microfiche as BT 352.

From 1913, voyage details of officers can be found in the registers of seamen: see **26.6** and **26.7**.

26.4 Registration of seamen, 1835–1857

The Merchant Shipping Act 1835 ordered the registration of merchant seamen (with the aim of creating a reserve for manning the Royal Navy in time of war). Registers of seamen, and associated indexes, were created and information was entered in them from crew lists, the filing of which was also required by the same Act (see **26.9**). This form of registration of seamen lasted from 1835 to 1857.

There are three series of Registers of Seamen, which were compiled directly from the crew lists. In addition there is a Register of Seamen's Tickets (1845–1854), which contains personal information, supplied by each seaman on applying for his register ticket, as well as that gleaned from the crew lists. All these registers give the seamen's age and place of birth and contain cross-references to the crew lists (see **26.9**).

The first (BT 120) consists of alphabetically arranged entries, 1835–1836. The second series (BT 112) covers 1835 to 1844: it is organized into two sections, one of which is roughly alphabetical, with the other being separately indexed (BT 119). In 1845 the ticket system, which lasted until October 1853, was introduced; these registers (BT 113) give date and place of birth as well as a physical description. Coastguards and Royal Navy, as well as merchant seamen, were often issued with a register ticket. The registers are arranged in order of ticket number to which there is a name index in BT 114. We know that the index contains references to some ticket numbers for which there is no entry in the ticket registers. The last series (BT 116), which started in 1853 after the ticket system was abolished, lists seamen alphabetically. All these series are seen on microfilm. See also **26.9**, on agreements and crew lists.

26.5 No registration of seamen, 1853–1913

Registration of seamen was abandoned in 1857 and, until its reintroduction in 1913, there is no easy way to discover the career of a merchant seaman, although crew lists do continue to be kept throughout this period. For advice on using ship-based sources, see **26.9** and onwards.

The Royal Naval Reserve, which was established in 1859, was officered and manned by deep sea merchant seamen, and there are some service records: see **19.9.2**. The Modern Records Centre at the University of Warwick has some National Union of Seamen material: the address is given in **48**.

26.6 Registration of seamen, 1913–1941

The Central Indexed Register (sometimes referred to as the Fourth Register of Seamen) was started on index cards in October 1913 and was maintained until 1941. About 1.25 million cards survive in all.

However, there is very little for 1913 to 1920. It seems that CR 1 and CR 2 index cards for these years were destroyed in error in 1969. There is also a special index surviving covering the period 1918–1921 (CR 10 cards in BT 350), so it may be possible to find at least some early records there, or perhaps in the fourth index in BT 364. Another possibility is to look at the seamen's pouches in BT 372, as these can include men who served as far back as 1913, as long as they were still serving in 1941: see **26.7**.

The Register consists of four large card indexes, seen on microfiche.

1. The CR 1 cards, 1921–1941 (BT 349), are arranged alphabetically by surname, and so provide the starting point for a search. They record place and date of birth, discharge number, rating, and a short description of the seaman; a few of these cards also have a photograph of the seaman.
2. The CR 2 cards, 1921–1941 (BT 348), are arranged numerically by discharge number and include a brief record of the ships on which the seaman served (by ship's number) and the dates of his signing on.
3. The CR 10 cards, 1918–1921 (BT 350), form a special index, and, as well as including similar information to the CR 1 cards, bear a photograph of the seaman. This index, made by a 1918 Order under the Defence of the Realm Act, seems to have been intended to record the issue of seamen's identity certificates.
4. The fourth index (BT 364) we think was compiled by extracting cards from the other three indexes, for reasons that are unclear. It is arranged numerically, with the CR 1 card leading, and there are usually three cards (CR 1, CR 2 and CR 10) for each seaman.

The Southampton City Archives now has the original index cards, and are able to provide better copies of the cards and particularly of any photos attached to them (address in **48**).

For information on seamen who were prisoners of war, see **22.4**.

26.7 Registration of officers, seamen and women, 1941–1972, and seamen's pouches 1913–1972

In 1941 the Essential Work (Merchant Navy) Order created a Merchant Navy Reserve Pool, to ensure that men would always be available to man vessels. The government paid officers and seamen to remain in the Reserve Pool when they were ashore. For the first time continuous paid employment (instead of casual employment) was available to all seamen (and women), and comprehensive registration became possible.

All those who had served at sea during the previous five years were required to register and a new Central Register of Seamen (sometimes referred to as the

Fifth Register of Seamen), was established. CR 1 and CR 2 cards of seamen who were still serving in 1941 were removed from the old Central Indexed Register, and placed in the new Central Register of Seamen which was maintained until 1972. There are two series of records: the main registers or docket books, and individual seamen's pouches.

The seamen's pouches are in BT 372, and are easily found. You can do an online search in PROCAT using the surname and BT 372. The date and place of birth is shown in the description, which helps in sorting out people with the same initials. In the pouch were placed records relating to the individual, often including small loose photographs, at the time of discharge. The pouches can contain documents going back to 1913, for those who transferred from the Fourth Register. They have to be seen under special supervision.

Unfortunately, there is no longer a pouch for every seaman or woman. It seems that pouches with discharge numbers below 95000 were destroyed sometime before 1988. In other cases, pouches were not created, or do not survive.

Fortunately, the docket books in BT 382 cover any gap. The main series give place and date of birth, discharge number, rank or rating (with certificate numbers for officers), details of other qualifications, and details of ships served on. This has various abbreviations – F for Foreign, H for Home, and MNRP for Merchant Navy Reserve Pool, i.e. ashore. They are arranged in a number of sub-series, and then alphabetically by surname; the major subseries relate to seamen

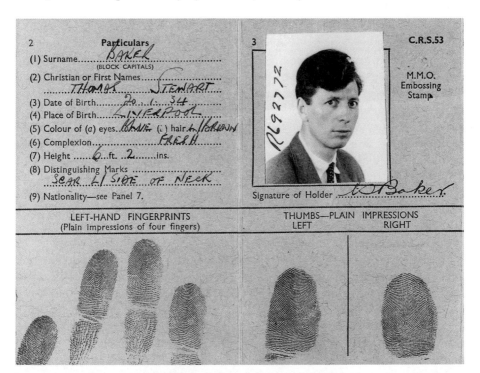

Figure 49 The young Tom Baker, in an earlier career as a merchant seaman, before he took to travelling in a different kind of ship as Dr Who. (PRO, BT 372/2134/103)

mainly of European origin, 1941–1946, and 1946–1972. Although described as 'mainly of European origin' these do include many individuals from British colonies outside Europe, and the date ranges should only be considered as a guide. Separate, smaller sub-series exist for Asiatic Seamen, mainly of Indian origin (1941–1965), Asiatic Seamen, mainly of Indian origin (1966–1972), Seamen of Indian, Chinese and Foreign Nationalities – Unnumbered Series (1941–1972), Allied Prisoners of War and Internees (1941–1945), Service on Royal Navy Ships: Auxiliary War Vessels (T124, T124T, T124X, etc) (1939–1945) and Deaths of Merchant Seamen recorded for pension purposes (1944–1951).

For more on merchant seamen who were prinsoners of war, see **22.8**.

26.8 Registration of officers and seamen, 1973–

The current, Sixth Register, called the 'UK Register', dating from 1973, is kept by the Registry of Shipping and Seamen (address in **48**). In it are recorded details of when the seafarer joined, the granting and renewal of certificates, and any disciplinary matters; voyage details are not given. Information is released only to the individual or, if deceased, the next of kin. Both ordinary seafarers and officers are included in this register, which has a supporting alphabetical index.

26.9 Ship-based sources: using Agreements and Crew Lists, 1835–1857

In 1835 a new system of crew lists and agreements was introduced, by the Merchant Shipping Act 1835: records are in BT 98. Masters of any ships belonging to UK subjects undertaking a foreign voyage, and masters of any British registered ships of 80 tons or more employed in the coastal trade or the fisheries, had to enter into a written agreement with every seaman on conditions of service. On return to the home port, the master of a foreign trade vessel had to deliver a list of the crew and the original agreements to the Registrar General of Shipping and Seamen. Documents for home trade vessels were delivered half-yearly at the end of June or December. Before 1857 these are arranged alphabetically by ships' names within port of registry; from 1857 they are arranged by the ship's official number. To find the official number, use *Lloyds Register of Shipping*, or the *Mercantile Navy List*; there are only incomplete sets of *Lloyds Register* and the *Mercantile Navy List* at the PRO, but there are full sets at the Guildhall Library and National Maritime Museum (addresses in **48**).

The crew lists in BT 98 should provide name, age, place of birth, quality (i.e. rank), previous ship, date and place of joining, and time and date of death or leaving the ship. The crew lists are arranged by the year in which they were handed in. This should be the *end* of the voyage for foreign trade voyages and, for home trade voyages, at the end of June or December of the appropriate year.

If you want to trace an individual seaman, in the crew lists, you must first refer to the appropriate seamen's register (see **26.4**) to get the ship's port of registration and name. Between 1835 and 1844, make a note of the number of the port and the name of the ship given in the register entry (ignore the port rotation number). There is a key to the port numbers in the list for BT 98, and the crew lists are arranged by port of registry of the ship and then by ships' names.

Between 1845 and 1854, you will still need to start with the appropriate seamen's register, but the procedure is more complicated and differs for foreign and home trade. A full explanation is given in Smith, Watts and Watts, *Records of Merchant Shipping and Seamen* or Watts and Watts, *My Ancestor was a Merchant Seaman*. The key feature is that, at this period, ships' names are not given, only the port number and a port rotation number, to which there is no key. Crew lists are organized annually (in BT 98) according to port of registry and ships' names, not port rotation numbers. Also, during this period, it is known that not all details of voyages were actually entered into the registers: those for 1849, 1850 and 1852–1854 appear never to have been entered at all even though the crew lists do survive.

From 1853 to 1857 details of voyages are to be found in the appropriate seamen's register, but now ships' names and port of registry are given so the crew list should be readily located in BT 98 where they are arranged by year, port of registry and ship's name.

After 1857 you can no longer go through the seamen's registers to use the crew lists in BT 98, which thenceforth were arranged each year by ships' official numbers: these numbers can be found by consulting the *Mercantile Navy List* or *Lloyds Register of Shipping*. Since there is no longer an index of seamen indicating which ship they were on, it can take a great deal of hard work and good luck to trace individual seamen through the crew lists.

26.10 Ship-based sources: log books, from 1850

The Mercantile Marine Act of 1850 required masters to keep a ship's Official Log recording illnesses, births and deaths on board, misconduct, desertion and punishment, and a description of each man's conduct. They were to be deposited after each foreign voyage, or half-yearly for home trade ships. They begin to appear amongst the records from 1852 onwards, though many have been destroyed; usually only those recording a birth or death have survived. Except for the period 1902–1919, where there is a separate series (BT 165), they are to be found with the agreements and crew lists in BT 98.

26.11 Current location of agreements, crew lists and log books, from 1861

From 1861 onwards, only a sample of agreements, crew lists and log books (which were generally filed together with the crew lists) are preserved at the PRO. Many have been preserved at other archives. The Registry of Shipping and Seamen (address in **48**) holds all crew lists from 1995 onwards. The PRO holds 10 per cent of all Crew Lists 1861–1938 and 1951–1994; these are to be found in BT 99, BT 100, BT 144 and BT 165. The PRO will be taking all crew lists for the period 1939–1950 and these are in the process of transfer into series BT 99, BT

100, BT 380 and BT 381. The bulk of the records for 1939–1946 are in the process of transfer and are not yet available. Those for 1947–1950 are at the PRO, together with some other miscellaneous categories of vessels for the whole period.

The National Maritime Museum (address in **48**) holds the remaining 90 per cent of crew lists for the years 1861, 1862 and all years ending in a 5 (except 1945). No list is available of these holdings. Those for 1975 and 1985 have not been arranged, and so access to them is restricted. Various county record offices, libraries and other repositories hold some of those crew lists not at the PRO or the National Maritime Museum, for the period 1863–1912. The Maritime History Archive, Memorial University of Newfoundland (address in **48**), took those crew lists not taken by any other institution for the years between 1863 and 1976, and offers a copying and research service, for a fee, of the material held by them. The Maritime History Archive has published guides to their holdings and those of local repositories in the UK; copies of all these are available at the PRO. After 1976 only the 10 per cent sample of agreements and crew lists held by the PRO have been preserved (with the exception of 90 per cent of those for 1975 and 1985 at the National Maritime Museum); the rest of these records, up to 1994, have been destroyed.

26.12 Merchant seamen: apprenticeships, to 1953

There are indexes of apprentices registered in the merchant fleet between 1824 and 1953 (BT 150). The earlier volumes give name, age, date and term of indenture and the name of the master: entries in later volumes include the port where the apprentice signed on and the ship's name. In addition, specimens of copy indentures, taken at five-yearly intervals, are preserved in Apprentices' Indentures, 1845–1950 (BT 151) and the Apprentices' Indentures for Fishing, 1895–1935 (BT 152).

Some later registers do survive amongst the Customs records, e.g. Bideford (1857–1880; CUST 69/224), Fowey (1825–1925; CUST 67/81), Littlehampton (1856–1897; CUST 57/28), Newhaven (1893–1908; CUST 56/89), Ramsgate (1893–1908; CUST 52/112), Scarborough (1884–1894; CUST 91/121), Scilly Isles (1857–1878; CUST 68/185) and Teignmouth (1853–1893; CUST 64/205); it is possible that others may also be found. The collection Crisp's Indentures, preserved at the Society of Genealogists, contains some original indentures of seamen from the north-east of England dated between 1845 and c.1861.

26.13 Merchant seamen: births, marriages and deaths at sea

For births, marriages and deaths at sea, see **4.7–4.11** and **4.14**.

26.14 Medals for gallantry at sea

Records of medals awarded for saving lives at sea, 1839–1882, are in FO 83/769. The Albert Medal was awarded for gallantry at sea: the medal registers, 1866–1913 (BT 97), also include awards to sailors in the Royal Navy until 1891.

Records of other awards for gallantry at sea, 1856–1981, are in BT 261, BT 339 and MT 9 code 6. There is a leaflet available at the PRO and on the PRO website, which gives more details of gallantry medals and honours.

26.15 Merchant seamen: bibliography

N G Cox, 'The Records of the Registrar General of Shipping and Seamen', *Maritime History*, vol. II, pp. 168–188

Index to Crew Lists, Agreements and Official Logs at the Memorial University of Newfoundland, microfiche

Guide to the Agreements and Crew Lists: Series II (BT 99), 1863–1912 (in three volumes) at the Memorial University of Newfoundland

Guide to the Agreements and Crew Lists: Series II (BT 99), 1913–1938 at the Memorial University of Newfoundland

A Guide to the Crew Agreements and Official Logbooks, 1863–1913, held at the County Record Offices of the British Isles, published by the Maritime History Archive, Memorial University of Newfoundland

J Hailey, *Maritime Sources in the Library of the Society of Genealogists* (Society of Genealogists, 1997)

Lloyds Register of Shipping (London, annually from 1764)

K Matthews 'Crew Lists, Agreements and Official Logs of the British Empire 1863–1913, now in possession of the Maritime History Group, Memorial University', *Business History*, vol. XVI, pp. 78–80

Mercantile Navy List (London, annually from 1857)

K Smith, C T Watts and M J Watts, *Records of Merchant Shipping and Seamen* (PRO, 1998)

C T Watts and M J Watts, 'Unravelling Merchant Seamen's Records', *Genealogists' Magazine*, vol. XIX, pp. 313–321

C T Watts and M J Watts, *My Ancestor was a Merchant Seaman* (Society of Genealogists, 2nd edn, 2002 in press)

27

Railway workers

◆ ◆ ◆

27.1 Railway staff records

The records of the nationalized railway companies, together with those of the canal, dock and shipping companies owned by them, were collected by the British Transport Historical Commission, and were formerly housed in London, York and Edinburgh. The Edinburgh collection has now gone to the Scottish Record Office, and the York and London collections have come to the PRO. The core of the collection is formed by the extensive records of the Great Western Railway, but the records of several hundred railway, canal and dock companies have also ended up at the PRO. The PRO has produced a specialist guide, Edwards's *Railway Records*, which gives valuable advice on railway staff records. Other railway company records may be in local record offices. Hawkings's *Railway Ancestors* provides detailed information on the content of record types, along with lists (for each company) of the surviving records which may be useful for family history, and their whereabouts.

Good staff records have survived from relatively few railway companies, and there are no union indexes to the names of employees. You need to know the name of the railway company for which your man worked. Staff records of a kind exist, and those companies whose staff records are in the PRO are listed in **27.4.** Some staff records give only names, wages and positions, others may give a full record of service.

Before ordering these staff records, you may have to sign an undertaking to respect the confidentiality of any personally sensitive information.

The covering dates given in **27.4** and in the lists themselves can be very misleading. For example, the dates given in the list for RAIL 426/14 are 1923–1937: in fact, the documents are history sheets for clerical staff retiring between 1923 and 1937, so the information in them actually goes back into the nineteenth century. Another problem is that covering dates for a staff register often seem improbably long, because the first date was taken to be the earliest date on the first page (usually a birth-date) and the last date the latest date given on the final page (usually a death-date). The actual years that the register covers are often much shorter, but difficult to discover.

27.2 Other sources of information

The Railway Benevolent Institution was a general cross-company body: railwaymen had to subscribe to become eligible for its benefits. Subscribing railway staff or former staff and their families who applied for its aid could be granted money. Its records are in RAIL 1166. The Annual Reports for 1881–1959 mainly consist of lists of supporters, but they do include reports from its orphanage at Derby, often with letters back from grown-up orphans (identified by initials). However, for a wonderful source for railway families try the books of grants for 1888–1919 (but also covering much earlier railway involvement). They detail approved grants, and give information about individual railwaymen, wives and families who were in difficulties through accident, sickness, old age or death. If the grant is to the widow or family, the railwayman himself is not named, but his company and job are given. Each volume has its own index.

Another possible source of information on individuals may be the large collection of railway periodicals. The British Transport Historical Collection Library, which is held at the PRO under code ZPER, has a number of these: ZPER is worth exploring by anyone with an interest in railway history.

Figure 50 The Railway Benevolent Institution depended on donations, subscriptions and fund-raising events – like this one – to support railwaymen and their families when in need. (PRO, RAIL 258/362)

27.3 Railway police

Records for the railway police of the various railway companies do not appear to be amongst the railway staff records in the PRO. Information about the numbers and organization of the railway police c.1900 can be found in RAIL 527/1036. The occasional references to 'Police Department' in the railway staff records relate to signalmen, etc.

27.4 Staff records at the PRO, arranged by name of railway company

Barry Railway Company	1886–1922	RAIL 23/46–60, 64–65
Brecon and Merthyr Tydfil Junction Railway Company	1880–1922	RAIL 65/31–35
Cambrian Railways Company	1898–1944	RAIL 92/142–148
Cardiff Railway Company	1869–1923	RAIL 97/32–44
Chester and Holyhead Railway Company	1862	RAIL 113/53
Cleator and Workington Junction Railway Company	1879–1923	RAIL 119/13
Furness Railway Company	1852–1922	RAIL 214/97–104
Great Central Railway Company	1857–1949	RAIL 226/193–235, 637
Great Eastern Railway Company	1855–1930	RAIL 227/445–490
Great Northern Railway Company	1848–1943	RAIL 236/727–745
Great Western and Midland Railway Companies Joint Committee	1865–1915	RAIL 241/28
Great Western Railway Company	1835–1954	RAIL 264/1–463
Hull and Barnsley Railway Company	1885–1927	RAIL 312/77–81
Hull and Selby Railway Company	1845–1875	RAIL 315/30
Isle of Wight Central Railway Company	1860–1963	RAIL 328/16–18
Lancashire and Yorkshire Railway Company	1853–1941	RAIL 343/827–845
Lancashire, Derbyshire and East Coast Railway Company	1904–1906	RAIL 344/56
Liverpool and Manchester Railway Company	1845	RAIL 371/23
London and Birmingham Railway Company	1833–1847	RAIL 384/284–291
London and North Eastern Railway Company	1920–1942	RAIL 397/1–11
London and North Western and Great Western Railway Companies Joint Committee	1871–1897	RAIL 404/177–180
London and North Western and Midland Railway Companies Joint Committee	1861–1911	RAIL 406/16
London and North Western Railway Company	1831–1927	RAIL 410/1217–1218, 1797–1986
London and South Western Railway Company	1838–1944	RAIL 411/483–537
London Brighton and South Coast Railway Company	1837–1925	RAIL 414/750–796

London Midland and Scottish and London and North Eastern Railway Companies Joint Committee	1891–1938	RAIL 417/16
London Midland and Scottish Railway Company	1923–1946	RAIL 426/1–15
London, Tilbury and Southend Company	1871–1923	RAIL 437/44–57
Manchester, Sheffield and Lincolnshire Railway Company	1847–1926	RAIL 463/177, 210–215
Midland and Great Northern Railways Joint Committee	1879–1893	RAIL 487/115
Midland and South Western Junction Railway Company	1891–1921	RAIL 489/21
Midland Railway Company	1864–1924	RAIL 491/969–1081
Neath and Brecon Railway Company	1903–1921	RAIL 505/13
Newcastle upon Tyne and Carlisle Railway Company	1845–1848	RAIL 509/96
North and South Western Junction Railway Company	1883–1916	RAIL 521/19
North Eastern Railway Company	1843–1957	RAIL 527/1895–1965
North London Railway Company	1854–1920	RAIL 529/130–138
North Staffordshire Railway Company	1847–1923	RAIL 532/58–67
North Sunderland Railway Company	1893–1948	RAIL 533/75–76
North Union Railway Company	1841–1856	RAIL 534/29
Otley and Ilkley Joint Line Committee (Midland and North Eastern Railway Companies)	1865–1901	RAIL 554/24–25
Port Talbot Railway and Docks Company	1883–1918	RAIL 574/13
Rhondda and Swansea Bay Railway Company	1882–1922	RAIL 581/36–37
Rhymney Railway Company	1860–1922	RAIL 583/41–65
Sheffield District Railway Company	1897–1916	RAIL 611/25–26
Shropshire Union Railways and Canal Company	1844–1897	RAIL 623/66–68
Somerset and Dorset Joint Line Committee	1877–1928	RAIL 626/44–53
Somerset and Dorset Railway Company	1863–1877	RAIL 627/6
South Eastern and Chatham Railway Companies Managing Committee	1850–1944	RAIL 633/343–382
South Eastern Railway Company	1845–1944	RAIL 635/302–310
South Wales Railway Company	1844–1864	RAIL 64/45, 47, 52, 55–56
Southern Railway Company	1923–1957	RAIL 651/1–10
Stockton and Darlington Railway Company	1835–1856	RAIL 667/1283–1291
Stratford upon Avon and Midland Junction Railway Company	1873–1923	RAIL 674/11
Taff Vale Railway Company	1890–1924	RAIL 684/94–120
Trent Valley Railway Company	1845–1946	RAIL 699/5
Wirral Railway Company	1884–1926	RAIL 756/10–11
York and North Midland Railway Company	1848,1843–1850	RAIL 770/77–81
York, Newcastle and Berwick Railway Company	1845	RAIL 772/106

27.5 Railway workers: bibliography

Published works

H V Borley, *Chronology of London Railways* (Railway & Canal Historical Society, 1982)

E Carter, *An Historical Geography of the Railways of the British Isles* (Cassel, 1959)

C Edwards, *Railway Records: A Guide to Sources* (PRO, 2001)

F Hardy, 'Railway Records for Family Historians', *Genealogists Magazine*, vol. XXIII, pp. 256–260

D Hawkings, *Railway Ancestors* (1995)

T Richards, *Was Your Grandfather a Railwayman?* (FFHS, 2nd edn, 1989)

Unpublished finding aids

Card index of subjects to British Transport Historical Commission Records

28

Apprentices

◆ ◆ ◆

28.1 Civilian apprenticeships

Apprentices were traditionally bound by indentures to serve their master for the space of seven years: the master was equally bound to teach the apprentice his trade. In the early years of the system, it was policed by the guilds, to which the master had to belong. Later apprenticeships were not necessarily with guild members, but they were still established by means of the legally enforceable indentures. Many disputes about apprenticeship can be found in the Chancery pleadings (see **47b**). Formal indentures involved some trouble and expense. By the eighteenth century apprenticeships were often undertaken without any formal indenture, especially in common trades such as weaving. In many trades it was expected that men would bring up their sons or nephews to the trade. Further, it was ruled that the Statute of Apprentices did not extend to trades which did not exist when it was passed in 1563; this excluded many eighteenth-century industries, most notably the cotton industry. In many areas the Statute was not enforced – for example, in the Yorkshire woollen industry formal apprenticeship hardly existed by the end of the eighteenth century. In 1814, compulsory apprenticeship by indenture was abolished, although apprenticeship continued well into the mid twentieth century.

The training of working people was not usually a matter of public record and the actual indentures of apprenticeship were private documents. If they survive at all they will normally be in private hands. There is the Crisp collection of about 1,500 indentures, from the seventeenth to nineteenth centuries, at the Society of Genealogists. Many records of apprenticeship survive with guild, London livery company (at the Guildhall Library) or parish records. For apprenticeship lists from the Stationers' Company, 1701 to 1800, check the *Biography Database 1680–1830* in the PRO Library. Some local history societies have published apprenticeship registers, often in combination with material extracted from the PRO registers: try a search on 'apprentice' or 'apprenticeship' in the PRO Library catalogue.

Between 1710 and 1804, however, apprenticeship indentures were subject to stamp duty, and payment registers are kept in the PRO. Beware – masters did not have to pay stamp duty for apprentices taken on at the common or public charge of any township or parish, or by or out of any public charity (8 Anne, c.5, s.59). This means that very many apprentices were never subject to the duty: they were therefore not mentioned in the registers. In such cases, local (borough or vestry) or charity records, if they survive, are likely to be the only source of information on individuals. For example, the Foundling Hospital kept apprenticeship registers, now at the London Metropolitan Archives (address in **48**). London livery companies often kept full records of membership, which give places of birth, previous residences and other details. For these, apply to the Guildhall Library.

The apprenticeship stamp duty registers, 1710–1811, are in IR 1, with separate indexes (compiled by the Society of Genealogists). As the tax could be paid up to one year after the completion of the apprenticeship, the records continue until 1811, eight years after the end of the tax in 1804. As a general rule, you may need to search the records of several years' payments in order to find a particular entry, even if you know the date of the indenture. Duty was payable by the master at the rate of 6d for every pound under £50 which he received for taking on the apprentice, and 1s for every £1 above that sum.

These Apprenticeship Books record the names, addresses and trades of the masters, and the names of the apprentices and dates of their indentures. Until 1752 the names of apprentices' parents are given, but rarely after that year. There are indexes of masters' names from 1710 to 1762, and of apprentices' names from 1710 to 1774. These were made on behalf of the Society of Genealogists and copied from their originals in the Guildhall Library, London. Where the stamp duty was paid in London, entries will be found in the 'City' registers in this series; where it was paid elsewhere, entries will be found in the 'Country' registers.

28.2 Military apprenticeships

The PRO has records of the apprenticeships of children from the Royal Naval Asylum, Greenwich, and the Duke of York's Military School, Chelsea: see **19.2.4** and **18a.4.2** respectively. For Royal Navy apprenticeships, see **19.12**. Among the War Office records there is a list of apprentices who enlisted in the Army but had to return to their masters until their indentures expired, 1806 to 1835 (WO 25/2962).

28.3 Merchant seaman apprenticeships, 1824–1953

Under the Merchant Seamen Act of 1823, ships of over 80 tons had to carry apprentices, whose names were to be enrolled with local customs officials. Under the Merchant Seamen Act of 1835 registration of apprentices in London was to be by the Registrar General, to whom also returns of regional registration (still made by local customs officials) were to be submitted quarterly. Compulsory apprenticeship was abolished in 1849, but registers were still maintained of those who were apprenticed after that date. Indexes of apprentices registered in the merchant service between 1824 and 1953 will be found in BT 150, where the earlier volumes give the apprentice's name, age, the date and terms of his indenture, and the name of his master. Later volumes (from BT 150/15) include also the port where he signed on and the name of the ship. Samples of the original indentures, including some for fishing vessels, will be found in BT 151 and BT 152.

28.4 Apprentices: bibliography

Biography Database 1680–1830 (Newcastle, 1998 ongoing)

I Maxted, *The British Book Trades, 1710–1777: an index of Masters' and Apprentices' Records in the Inland Revenue Registers at the PRO, Kew* (Exeter, 1983)

Public Record Office, *Alphabetical Guide to War Office & Other Material* (Lists and Indexes, vol. LIII)

W B Stephens, *Sources for English Local History* (Manchester, 2nd edn, 1981)

University of Warwick, *Trade Union and Related Records* (Coventry, 1988)

29

Lawyers

◆ ◆ ◆

29.1 Lawyers: printed sources

For a specialist guide to finding out about lawyers, see Holborn, *Sources of Biographical Information on Past Lawyers*.

The published *Law Lists*, produced annually from 1775, are the easiest place to start. There is a set running from 1799–1976 in the PRO, and the Guildhall Library also has a good, but incomplete, set, including *Law Lists* for 1787 and 1795. However, they can be difficult to use effectively. Between 1775 and 1789, they contain the names of some men never actually admitted to a court, whereas from 1790 they only give the names of those who had taken out the annual certificate to practise that year. Until 1861 they do not give the date of admission. The entries also give the name of the firm for which the solicitor/attorney worked, together with an indication of its address.

Lists of attorneys and solicitors admitted in 1729 and 1730 were printed for presentation to Parliament: a copy is available at the PRO.

29.2 Judges and serjeants-at-law

The PRO does hold some records of the appointment of judges and of the creation of serjeants-at-law (who had the monopoly of pleading in the court of Common Pleas until 1846, and from whom, for several centuries, the judges were selected). However, these are widely scattered and not very informative. As there is a great deal of biographical information in print on the judges and the serjeants-at-law, you would be well advised to investigate the published sources first: the main ones are listed in **29.8**.

29.3 Barristers

The term barrister is used, in England and Wales, to describe someone admitted to practise in the superior courts and who is entitled to act as an advocate in those courts. Traditionally, barristers have had a higher level of education and also higher social status than solicitors and attorneys (**29.4**). The PRO is not the place to look for records relating to barristers: entry to the profession was and is controlled by the Inns of Court (Lincoln's Inn, Gray's Inn, the Inner Temple and the Middle Temple). The Inns of Court have published many of their records of genealogical interest: see the printed sources listed in **29.8**. For further information, contact the libraries of the particular Inn of Court: the addresses are given in **48**.

However, the PRO does have records of the oaths of allegiance sworn by barristers: the swearing of this oath was required before a barrister could practise in the courts. Signatures to the oath, 1673–1944, are in KB 24, and 1858–1982, in KB 4.

29.4 Solicitors and attorneys: the central courts

The words attorney and solicitor have had a changing meaning, not only over the centuries, but also in different parts of the English speaking world. The word attorney, strictly defined, means a person appointed by another to act in his/her place: often but not necessarily a person who is legally qualified. In the USA and other countries that have a unitary bar, the term attorney-at-law has thus become virtually synonymous with legal practitioner. This was not, and is not, the case in England and Wales. In England and Wales the term was used for lawyers who were admitted to practise in the superior courts of common law and whose function was to deal with the procedural steps of litigation rather than advocacy. They were officers of court and subject to the discipline of the court. Solicitors performed similar procedural functions in courts of equity. Many individuals combined both roles, and in 1873 under the terms of the Judicature Act all solicitors and attorneys became 'Solicitors of the Supreme Court'.

Until 1838, solicitors and attorneys had to be admitted to each of the courts in which they wished to practise. The various central and regional courts regulated the admission of new solicitors and attorneys, and each court kept its own records relating to such admissions. In 1728 an Act of Parliament required attorneys and solicitors to have served five years as clerks under articles before they could be admitted to a court. Then in 1749 a further act required that a statement to the effect that the articles had actually been carried out (an 'affidavit of due execution') should be filed in the court within three months of admission. Articled clerks were effectively apprentices and so it is also sometimes possible to trace them by using the apprenticeship books in IR 1 (see **28.1** for further details).

If you are trying to trace a man who described himself as an attorney, then you should try the records of the common law courts first. Registers and indexes of affidavits of due execution of articles for the King's Bench (formerly in record class IND 1) are now in KB 170. They cover the period 1749–1875. In practice these registers contain most of the details that are in the actual affidavits, so a search of the registers may well be sufficient in itself. The affidavits themselves survive only from about 1775 to 1875 and are in KB 105–107 and KB 109. They usually contain the following details: the name of the clerk, the name, address and occupation of his parent or guardian, the name and address of the master to whom he was bound and the date of the articles and length of the term of the articles. Occasionally they also give the age of the clerk. Similar material for the

[*Corrected to March 1st, 1815.*]

CLARKES'

NEW LAW LIST:

BEING A LIST OF THE

JUDGES AND OFFICERS

OF THE DIFFERENT

Courts of Justice:

COUNSEL,

SPECIAL PLEADERS, CONVEYANCERS;

AND A COMPLETE AND ACCURATE LIST OF

CERTIFICATED ATTORNIES, NOTARIES,

&c.

IN ENGLAND AND WALES,

WITH THE

London Agents to the Country Attornies,

As printed by Permission of the Commissioners of the
Stamp Duties.

TO WHICH ARE ADDED

A TABLE of Sheriffs, and Agents, Lifts of Bankers, Notaries Public, Mail Coaches, Newfpapers, Army	and Navy Agents, Law and Public Offices, Circuits of the Judges, Quarter Seffions, &c.

And a Variety of other Useful Matter

BY SAMUEL HILL, OF THE STAMP OFFICE.

LONDON:

Printed for W. CLARKE and SONS, Law-bookfellers, Portugal-Street,
Lincoln's Inn; and R. PHENEY, Temple Gate.

1815.

[*Price 6s. neatly bound.*]

Figure 51 The *Law List*, like many other annuals, contains much useful information
beyond the obvious contents (*Law List* 1815, PRO Library)

Common Pleas survives from about 1725 (with a few earlier items going back to 1713) to 1838 in CP 5. Registers of articles (formerly in IND 1) are in CP 71, but they are difficult to use as they are arranged by date of admission rather than by name. Fortunately, there is a personal name index to CP 5 filed with the list in the reading rooms. Since many attorneys practised in both the King's Bench and the Common Pleas, and were therefore admitted to both courts, it is always a good idea to start a search by checking the CP 5 index. Registers of affidavits of due execution for the Exchequer of Pleas survive for 1833–1855 only in E 4/3.

The admission rolls or books themselves are likely to be less useful for family history purposes, since they give at most simply a name, date of admission and address. Rolls of attorneys for the King's Bench (formerly in IND 1) are now in KB 172 (1729–1875); those for the Common Pleas are in CP 11 (1730–1750); those for the Exchequer of Pleas (formerly in IND 1) are now in E 4 (1830–1875). Admission books for the Common Pleas (formerly in IND 1) are now in CP 70 (1729–1848) and CP 72 (1740–1853).

Attorneys' admission rolls for Common Pleas are in CP 8 (1838–1860). They record the signatures of attorneys and solicitors who had originally enrolled in other courts, and also give the court to which the individual was originally admitted, together with the date of admission and place of residence both at the time of the original admission and at the time of signing the roll. A contemporary index (formerly in IND 1), covering not only these rolls but others that have not survived, is now in CP 72 (1838–1875). A supplementary admission register (formerly in IND 1) is now in CP 69/1. The admission roll and registers of town and country solicitors, 1832–1883 for the Court of Bankruptcy are in B 2/8–11.

If your man was described as a solicitor then you probably need to look at the records of the equity courts. For Chancery (the main equity court) the main records are the Petty Bag Office Solicitors' Rolls in C 216. These cover 1729–1875. Nominal rolls that partially duplicate the 1729–1858 material are in IND 1/4613–4614. Various affidavits of due execution of clerkship and other admission papers are also in C 216. There are certificates of admission, giving names and dates of admission and addresses in C 203/7 (1730–1787), which sometimes include admissions to the King's Bench, and also in C 217/21, 22, 181–187 (c.1804–1843). Some affidavits of due execution, 1730–1839 are in C 217/23–40, 181–187. Other admission papers are also in C 217/40–54, 182–187. Alphabets of solicitors taking out certificates, 1785–1842, and an address book of attorneys c.1849–1860, are in C 220/11.

Admission papers after 1874 have not survived, but some information can be gained from the indexes to affidavits of due execution in KB 170/13 (formerly in IND 1), IND 1/29729–29733 and indexes to articles of clerkship, 1875–1889, in IND 1/29712–29713.

For the equity side of Exchequer there are Solicitors' Certificate Books in E 108 (1785–1843), Rolls of Books of Solicitors in E 109 (1729–1841) and oath rolls for solicitors and commissioners for oaths (1730–1841) in E 200.

29.5 Solicitors and attorneys: the Palatine and Welsh courts

Affidavits of due execution and registers of affidavits of due execution for attorneys admitted to the courts of the Palatinate of Chester, 1728–1830, together with oath rolls, 1729–1830, are in CHES 36. There is also an admission roll (1697–1728) in CHES 35/3/1 and a further admission roll (1777–1806) for the Chester court of Exchequer in CHES 36/3/7. Affidavits of due execution for those admitted to the courts of the Palatinate of Durham, 1660–1843, are in DURH 9, with admission rolls, 1660–1723 and 1730–1843 in DURH 3, and a register of certificates to practise, 1785–1842, in IND 1/10152. Records of attorneys admitted to the Palatinate courts of Lancaster, 1730–1875, are in PL 23: they include affidavits of due execution, 1749–1814, registers of affidavits, 1749–1823, rolls of attorneys, 1730–1785, an oath roll, 1730–1793, a register of certificates to practise, 1785–1871 and minutes of attorneys' assize dinners, 1790–1805.

Before 1830, solicitors and attorneys practising in the Courts of Great Sessions in Wales were enrolled in the records of those courts. These are now at the National Library of Wales (address in **48**). See Parry, *A Guide to the Records of Great Sessions in Wales*. After 1830, attorneys practising in the assize courts in Wales were allowed to enrol in the courts at Westminster. For attorneys enrolled in the court of Common Pleas, 1830–1844, use the supplementary admission register formerly in IND 1 but now in CP 72; for those enrolled in King's Bench, 1830–1834, see KB 172. This privilege was also extended to attorneys and solicitors working in the courts of the Palatinate of Lancaster and the Palatinate of Durham.

29.6 Solicitors and attorneys: records kept by the Law Society

The Law Society has the records of the Registrar of Attorneys and Solicitors, established in 1843. These include lists of admissions from 1845 onwards, with additional lists of admissions back to about 1790. They also have some registers of articles of clerkship from about 1860 onwards. These records are kept at the Law Society Archives (address in **48**).

29.7 Civil lawyers

For civil lawyers (i.e. those who practised the civil law used in the church courts and the High Court of Admiralty, and the High Court of Delegates), there is a selective index of advocates and proctors attached to the class list for PROB 39. Civil lawyers were also listed in *Law Lists* (**29.1**). There are short biographies of London advocates (the civilian equivalent of barristers) in Squibb's *Doctors' Commons*. The admission of proctors (the civilian equivalent of attorneys) in London – that is, those practising from Doctors' Commons – is recorded in the registers of the Archbishop of Canterbury, at Lambeth Palace Library. Records of civil lawyers who practised in provincial church courts are best sought locally, in diocesan record offices. Some papers relating to the admission of proctors to the High Court of Admiralty are in HCA 30 and warrants relating to their appointments are in HCA 50.

29.8 Lawyers: bibliography

R L Abel, *The Legal Profession in England and Wales* (Oxford, 1988)

J H Baker, *The Order of Serjeants at Law*, Selden Society, Supplementary Series vol. V (London, 1984)

E H W Dunkin, C Jenkins and E A Fry, *Act Books of the Archbishop of Canterbury, 1663–1859* (British Record Society, Index Library, 1929)

E Foss, *A Biographical Dictionary of the Judges of England* (London, 1870)

J A Foster, *Men-at-the-Bar: A Biographical Handlist of the Members of the Various Inns of Court including Her Majesty's Judges etc.* [as at 1885] (London, 1885)

J A Foster, *The Register of Admissions of Gray's Inn, 1521–1889* (London, 1889)

G Holborn, *Sources of Biographical Information on Past Lawyers* (British and Irish Association of Law Librarians, 1999)

J Hutchinson, *A Catalogue of Notable Middle Templars* (London, 1902)

F A Inderwick and R A Roberts, *A Calendar of Inner Temple Records, 1505–1800* (London, 1896–1936)

Law List (London 1775, continuing)

Lincoln's Inn, *Admissions, 1420–1799* (London, 1896)

Lincoln's Inn, *The Black Books, 1422–1914* (London, 1897–1968)

Parliament, *List of Attorneys and Solicitors Admitted in Pursuance of the Late Act for the Better Regulation of Attorneys and Solicitors, 1729–1730* (London, 1729–1731)

G Parry, *A Guide to the Records of Great Sessions in Wales* (Aberystwyth, 1995)

J Sainty, *A List of English Law Officers, King's Counsel and Holders of Patents and Precedence*, Selden Society, Supplementary Series vol. VII (London, 1987)

J Sainty, *The Judges of England 1272–1990: a list of Judges of the Superior Courts*, Selden Society, Supplementary Series vol. X (London, 1993)

G D Squibb, *Doctors' Commons* (Oxford, 1977)

C Trice Martin, *Minutes of Parliament of the Middle Temple, 1501–1703* (London, 1904–1905)

30

Medicine and education

◆ ◆ ◆

30.1 Doctors' records

In general, the PRO is not the place to look for records of doctors except if they were engaged upon government service. Records of doctors in the Army and Navy, however, are quite extensive: see **18d.4** and **19.13.1**. Appointments of medical staff to workhouses can sometimes be traced in MH 9 and MH 12. For a guide to the subject, see Bourne and Chicken, *Records of the medical professions: a practical guide for the family historian.*

The *Medical Directory* lists names and addresses from 1845: the PRO Library has copies from 1895 to 1987. From 1858, all doctors had to be registered, with details published in the annual *Medical Register.* The PRO Library has this from 1915–1973. For the eighteenth century, look at Wallis and Wallis, *Eighteenth Century Medics (Subscriptions, Licences, Apprenticeships),* which lists many thousands of individuals, including physicians, surgeons, apothecaries, dentists and midwives.

The Royal College of Physicians was established in 1518, and holds records on its members. Some records of the Barber-Surgeons' Company are at the Guildhall Library, including registers of naval surgeons 1705–1745. Physicians and surgeons had to have a licence from the bishop, from 1580 to 1775: records of these will be in local record offices, or at Lambeth Palace Library for licences from the Archbishop of Canterbury. The Bishop of London's records of licensing doctors are at the London Metropolitan Archives and the Guildhall Library.

30.2 Civilian nurses' records

The PRO holds few records relating to individual civilian nurses in the nineteenth century. Paid workhouse nurses can sometimes be found among the Registers of Paid Staff in MH 9. Appointments of workhouse matrons and nurses may also be found among the correspondence and papers in MH 12.

Before 1919, the individual nurse training schools kept records: these are often still with the hospital records (see **30.4**). The London Metropolitan Archives holds records of some London training schools, including Guy's Hospital, the Nightingale Training School and the Nightingale collection.

The registration of civilian nurses began in 1921, following the foundation of the General Nursing Council in 1919. From 1921 to 1973, State Registered Nurses were entered on the Register of Nurses (DT 10): the Register included nurses who were currently active, and who may therefore have qualified well before that date. From 1947 to 1973, State Enrolled Nurses were entered on the Roll of Nurses (DT 11). After 1973, information on both registered and enrolled nurses can be found in the Computerised Register and Roll in DT 12 (currently until 1983). The information given in the Registers and Rolls includes name and maiden name, qualifications and training, address, change of name, date of marriage, and date of death.

30.3 Midwives' records

For eighteenth-century midwives, see Wallis and Wallis. There are registration records of midwives from 1872–1888 and 1904 onwards in DV 7, but many of these are unfit for production.

30.4 Hospital records

The PRO and the Wellcome Institute for the History of Medicine have compiled a computerized database of the location in records offices of the records of over 1,000 civilian hospitals in England and Wales. If you are interested in finding the records of a particular hospital you can look at the HOSPREC database at the PRO. Administrative records are normally closed for 30 years, and patients' records are closed for 100 years.

The PRO has some hospital records, such as those of the British Lying-In Hospital, 1749–1868 in RG 8, as well as many field hospital records from wartime.

30.5 Teachers' records

The PRO holds policy papers on teacher training and registration, rather than staff records themselves. Information about staff of individual schools may sometimes be found in the appropriate local record office. For a full discussion, see Morton, *Education and the State*. In the PRO, there are some records of teachers' pensions available for teachers in England 1899–1930 (PMG 68). Other pension records relate to Army schoolmasters and schoolmistresses, 1909–1928 in PMG 33 and PMG 34.

The Society of Genealogists now keeps the registers of the Teachers Registration Council for 1902–1948. They are not open to public inspection, but a search can be made on your behalf. See also *School, University and College registers and histories in the Library of The Society of Genealogists.*

30.6 School and pupil records

If you know which parish a person lived in, it may be worth checking the Victorian and later school records for that parish, both in the PRO and locally.

Figure 52 Milton School, in Kent, must have been an unusually large and progressive school – playing the violin and lute was not part of the normal curriculum. (PRO, COPY 1/160)

You can gain an interesting perspective on an ancestor's early days by looking at school records, although he or she will not be mentioned by name in the PRO records. In the local record office, ask for school logbooks and admission registers: these will name individuals. Some are still held by the schools.

At the PRO, you can find what exists for a particular place by using the place name as a keyword and searching in ED in PROCAT. The most likely series are listed here.

ED 49	Elementary endowed schools (schools with charitable foundations – often very old)	1853–1945	3 days' notice
ED 21	Elementary schools set up or taken over by the state after 1870: includes inspection reports	1870–1945	3 days' notice
ED 27	Secondary endowed schools (schools with charitable foundations – often very old)	1850–1945	3 days' notice
ED 35	Secondary schools set up or taken over by the state	c.1900–1945	3 days' notice
ED 109	Secondary schools: inspectors' reports	c.1900–1945	

For more detailed advice, use Morton, *Education and the State*.

Deeds relating to the foundation of schools, and other charitable foundations, were enrolled in Chancery (C 54) until 1902, and then in the Supreme Court (J 18). There are indexes to these trust deeds, arranged by place, covering 1736 to 1904: although most relate to nonconformist chapels, very many concern schools.

30.7 Medicine and education: bibliography

Published works

B Abel-Smith, *A history of the nursing profession* (London, 1975)

P Allan and M Jolley, eds, *Nursing, midwifery, and health visiting since 1900* (London, 1982)

E Bendall and E Raybould, *A history of the General Nursing Council for England and Wales, 1919–1969* (London, 1969)

J Harvey Bloom and R Rutson Jones, *Medical Practitioners in the Diocese of London, Licensed Under the Act of 3 Henry VIII, c.11: An Annotated List 1529–1725* (Cambridge, 1935)

S Bourne and A H Chicken, *Records of the medical professions: a practical guide for the family historian* (1994)

C Hillam, *Brass Plate and Brazen Impudence: Dental Practice in the Provinces 1755–1855* (Liverpool, 1991)

A Morton, *Education and the State from 1833* (PRO, 1997)

W Munk, *The Roll of the Royal College of Physicians of London, 1518–1825* (London, 1861–1878)

R Porter, *Bodies Politic: Disease, Death and Doctors in Britain, 1650–1900* (London, 2001)

J H Raach, *A Directory of English Country Physicians, 1603–1643* (London, 1962)

School, University and College registers and histories in the Library of The Society of Genealogists (Society of Genealogists, 1996)

C H Talbot and E A Hammond, *The Medical Practitioners of Medieval England: A Biographical Register* (London, 1965)

P J Wallis and R V Wallis, *Eighteenth Century Medics (Subscriptions, Licences, Apprenticeships)* (Newcastle-upon-Tyne, 2nd edn 1988) – lists about 35,000 individuals

Unpublished finding aids

Indexes to trust deeds, by place 1736–1904

31

The poor and the Poor Laws

◆ ◆ ◆

31.1 The Old Poor Law of 1601

Paupers have attracted the active interest of the state since the Elizabethan Poor Laws were codified in 1601. Most pre-1834 records (such as those discussed in this section) will be found in the local county or borough record office as paupers were a charge on their parish of settlement and local taxes were raised for their support.

The various accounts kept by the parish Overseers of the Poor and Church-wardens will usually give the names of people who paid the rates and those who received relief. These would be the key family history records. The parish of settlement was generally the parish of birth although this could change for married women, apprentices or those working in another parish for long periods. It was important for the parish authorities raising and spending these local rates that only those with a right to relief from their particular parish received aid.

People with doubtful settlements were examined by local Justices of the Peace with a view to determining which parish was responsible for them. These written and sworn statements, referred to as examinations, are in effect brief biographies of the poor that may supply concise details of place of birth, marriage, movement across the county (following work) and their recent employment. Many disputes of individual settlements between parishes can be found in the records of Quarter Sessions. The records produced in the course of proving settlement can be very informative for family history. For a brief and lucid guide to the poor relief system, the various Poor Laws, and the idea of settlement, see Herber, *Ancestral Trails*.

There is very little detailed material in the PRO about the operation of the Elizabethan Poor Law and its system of outdoor relief for the deserving poor, and Houses of Correction established for the undeserving poor. See Cole, *An Introduction to Poor Law Documents before 1834* or Fowler, *Using Poor Law Records*.

31.2 The Poor Law Amendment Act (1834). The New Poor Law and the workhouse system

Workhouses to supply indoor relief in as repulsive a way as could be designed (in order to put people off applying for help) were established by the Poor Law Commission under the Poor Law Amendment Act of 1834. The act required parishes to be grouped together into 'poor law unions'. These unions were managed by 'guardians of the poor' who were elected by the ratepayers of the constituent parishes. The guardians then appointed permanent staff to run the union workhouse on a day to day basis. Although the New Poor Laws underwent various changes throughout their existence the Poor Law Unions continued until 1930. You need to know which union your people may have belonged to before you begin your search. To find out in which union a particular parish belonged, see Gibson and Youngs, *Poor Law Union Records: 4 Gazetteer of England and Wales.* The three previous pamphlets in this excellent series give advice on the range of records to be found, and references to documents in local record offices and in the PRO.

For the records created under the New Poor Law you will need to search both local record offices and the PRO. For family history purposes the local material will be of the most use. Where records survive you should expect a wide variety of material for particular Poor Law Unions, including rate books, guardians' minute books, punishment books, admissions and discharge books.

The records of the Poor Law Commission (and later the Poor Law Board and Local Government Board) are held at the PRO under the code MH. They are not particularly easy to use for family history and searches are likely to be lengthy, but could be ultimately very rewarding. MH 12, the main class of correspondence, is known to contain the names of thousands of individuals but will not contain the names of all (or even most) of those claiming poor relief. The records contained in MH 12 begin in 1834 and end around 1900, with most of the twentieth-century material being destroyed by enemy action and fire during the Second World War. There is no name index to these records. They are listed by Poor Law Union and the covering dates of each volume is provided. However, there is no indication as to subject matter covered in these volumes. The correspondence index in MH 15 refers only to correspondence which created a precedent and which the Poor Law Commission would thus have needed reference to in the future. The Assistant Commissioners (and other inspectors) Reports in MH 32 will also provide a great deal of information of the Poor Law Unions under their remit but have only a small number of references to individual relief claimants. Many of the records in MH 12 and MH 32 are in a poor condition.

Local records are easier to use, particularly with Gibson and Youngs to hand.

31.3 Poor Law Union staff

For workhouse staff, 1837–1921, you should consult the registers in MH 9. The registers include information on the wide variety of staff, including workhouse mistresses and masters, nurses and work instructors. The entries are brief and to the point; dates of appointment and salary are given and the date of death is sometimes noted. Personal details of people appointed, up to c.1900, may be found in various forms among the mass of papers in MH 12. The forms often give full name, age, address, details of previous jobs and reasons for appointment to the present post, and salary. Names of wives and number of children are sometimes given, as are details of religion and qualifications. MH 12 can also contain references for applicants, and correspondence on dismissal.

You may find it worth checking the *Index to Parliamentary Papers* on CD-ROM in the PRO Library, to check on returns Poor Law Union officials made to Parliament: these can give personal details. The index refers to microfiches seen in the Microfilm Reading Room.

31.4 The poor and the Poor Laws: bibliography

A Brundage, *The English Poor Law, 1700–1930* (Basingstoke, 2002)

A Cole, *An Introduction to Poor Law Documents before 1834* (FFHS, 1993)

S Fowler, *Using Poor Law Records* (PRO, 2001)

D Fraser, ed., *The New Poor Law in the nineteenth century* (London, 1976)

J S W Gibson, C Rogers and C Webb, *Poor Law Union Records: 1. South-East England and East Anglia* (FFHS, 1993)

J S W Gibson and C Rogers, *Poor Law Union Records: 2. The Midlands and Northern England* (FFHS, 1993)

J S W Gibson and C Rogers, *Poor Law Union Records: 3. South-West England, The Marches and Wales* (FFHS, 1993)

J S W Gibson and F A Youngs, *Poor Law Union Records: 4. Gazetteer of England and Wales* (FFHS, 1993)

M Herber, *Ancestral Trails* (Society of Genealogists, 2000)

L Hollen Lees, *The Solidarities of Strangers: the English Poor Laws and the People, 1700–1948* (Cambridge, 1998)

Index to Parliamentary Papers

J Knott, *Popular opposition to the 1834 Poor Law* (London, 1986)

S Pearl, 'Charities: the forgotten poor relief', *Family Tree Magazine*, May 1991

K D M Snell, *The Annals of the Labouring Poor* (Cambridge, 1985)

W Tate, *The Parish Chest* (Cambridge, 1969)

T Wood, 'Workhouse Ancestors', *Family Tree Magazine*, October and November 1995

32

Lunacy

◆ ◆ ◆

32.1 Introduction

For most of the past, the state has had little interest in the mental health of its subjects, unless they had a sufficient amount of property to require the intervention of the Crown as a feudal lord. Pauper lunatics were dealt with locally.

For a guide for family historians, see Faithfull, *Basic Facts about Lunatics*. For a detailed guide to records on lunacy, read Lappin's thesis, 'Central Government and the supervision of the treatment of lunatics 1800–1913', in the PRO Library. Copies are also available at the Wellcome Institute. For the historical background, try Porter, *A Social History of Madness*.

32.2 Chancery lunatics: royal interest in the property of lunatics and idiots

The custody of the lands and persons of idiots ('natural fools from birth') and lunatics ('sometimes of good and sound memory and understanding and sometimes not') belonged to the Crown. Idiots and lunatics were the responsibility of the Lord Chancellor, although the Court of Wards took this over for 1540–1646: they were sometimes known as the 'Chancery lunatics'. The king was entitled to administer the lands of an idiot during his life, but of the lunatic only during periods of insanity. The lands or possessions were not generally retained in Crown hands, but granted out for the term of the lunacy or idiocy to 'committees' (i.e. those to whose care the lunatic or his estate was committed – possibly the next of kin).

Although the Crown's interest was at first paramount, over time the priority appears to have become the proper administration of the lunatic's estate, an issue often of vital importance to the next of kin. The whole point of getting a person declared of unsound mind by a Chancery inquisition was to take away his or her power of independent legal action in the disposition of property: it had nothing to do with committal to an asylum, which was a separate medical procedure. In many cases the alleged lunatic was already in an asylum when the inquisition took place: the only requirement for committal to an asylum was for two doctors to issue a certificate.

Lunatics and idiots were brought to the Chancellor's attention by relatives; by solicitors, or others, acting as the executors of a will or trustees, where one of the beneficiaries was a supposed lunatic; by the Lunacy Commissioners, fearing that the money of an asylum inmate was being misappropriated; and by creditors of the alleged lunatic, who could claim payment from the Master in Lunacy once their debtor had been declared of unsound mind. All petitioners had to support their request for a commission of inquiry with at least two sworn affidavits supporting their opinion of the state of mind of the supposed lunatic: these affidavits do not generally survive, but the gist is given in the abstract of the petition in C 211. About 1,000 affidavits supporting petitions for a lunacy commission are to be found in C 217/55, dating from 1719 to 1733: they are as yet not listed individually nor indexed.

The Lord Chancellor had first, to find out by ordering commissioners to hold an inquisition into whether a person was of sound mind or not; second, to commit the custody of the lunatic and his estate to suitable persons (called 'committees'); and third, to examine the accounts, etc., of the committees.

Commissions and inquisitions are in Latin until the Interregnum, and between 1660 and 1733; for the Interregnum and from 1733 they are in English. Inquisitions of lunacy produced before 1540 are with the inquisitions post mortem in C 132–142 (see **41.7**). From 1540 to 1648 they are in WARD 7. Inquisitions from about 1648 to 1932 are in C 211 (or in PL 5 for Lancashire). Disputes ('traverses') on the validity of an inquisition may be found in the common law side of Chancery: see **47a.2**. There are few lunacy commissions for England in the twentieth century. The later records, however, do contain copies of inquisitions taken in Ireland, and in some British colonies: the latter are specifically concerned with the mental health of the people, and with getting them transported back to Britain.

Information on the estates and possessions of a lunatic was sent to the Clerk of the Custodies, who granted out the custody of the persons and estates of lunatics and idiots, by the issue of letters patent to the committees. These were not generally enrolled on the patent rolls, but in a separate series of rolls, which unfortunately appear to have been destroyed in the later nineteenth century. However, there is register of bonds by committees, 1817–1904, in J 103. From 1900, registers of bonds given as security by the committees are in J 92. Some bonds given by committees from the eighteenth to twentieth centuries are in J 117.

Accounts were supposed to be submitted annually by the committee to the Chancery Master: these are easy to find (if they survive) by checking C 101, the Chancery Masters' accounts, in the online catalogue or in IND 1/10702. They often give more detail about the tenants than they do about the lunatic, but they can provide some extra information.

The most informative records may be found among the Chancery Masters' reports and exhibits, but there is no guarantee of finding anything. You can pick out lunatics from Chancery litigation, because they are described as *In re Smith, a lunatic*. The reports are in C 38: there are indexes in IND 1, which can be identified from the C 38 list. Some exhibits from cases relating to lunatics will be found in C 103–115: in fact, the whole series C 115 exists because of the lunacy of Frances Scudamore, Duchess of Norfolk. There is an index to exhibits in C 103–114 filed before the C 103 list. Later exhibits will be found in J 90, but these are kept off site and need to be ordered three working days in advance. If you find that exhibits exist, you may have struck lucky. For example, the exhibits in *Re Freeman: a lunatic*, in C 110/164, include extracts from the parish register of St Peter's, Antigua, 1719–1728 and 1752, relating to the lunatic Thomas Freeman's family, several letters from his brother Arthur, and the original letter patent sent out to the family's lawyer committing Freeman to his custody, as well as a further 50 or so papers detailing a legacy of £1,500 by his godfather and namesake to Freeman as an infant, and the difficulty of deciding if it was going to be paid in Antiguan or British currency.

Decrees and orders relating to lunatics should be found in C 33 and J 79 (records from this series need to be ordered three days in advance).

Official visitors' reports on Chancery lunatics, from 1879 (with a 75-year closure) are in LCO 10: they give name, address, age, income and allowance.

32.3 Lunatic asylums

People of means had to make private arrangements for any lunatics in the family. The private madhouses were licensed by the justices of the peace, and were examined by several series of government commissioners. One register of admissions to private asylums outside London, for 1798–1812, is in MH 51/735: it includes the names of 1,788 patients, and is indexed by both lunatics (at the front) and keepers of licensed houses (at the back).

Pauper lunatics were dealt with locally under the poor law, vagrancy law or criminal law, and were therefore likely to end up in workhouses, houses of correction or prisons before the establishment of lunatic asylums in the mid nineteenth century. These records would be kept locally, but at the PRO are returns of insane inmates in workhouses and asylums from 1834 to 1909 (MH 12). These give name, age, type of disability and whether considered dangerous. Unfortunately, they are arranged by county and Poor Law Union, and there are subject indexes only (MH 15). Correspondence with asylum districts in MH 17 may be worth looking at. See **31** on how to identify the Poor Law Union, and on guides to what records exist.

There are also returns of insane prisoners in prisons and houses of correction, submitted in March 1858 (MH 51/90–207).

From the early nineteenth century, justices of the peace were encouraged to build county lunatic asylums to house any pauper lunatics in their county: in 1845, this became compulsory. The 1890 Lunacy Act gave them a wider role, and patients with means began to be admitted. Records of the county asylums are likely to be kept locally, as may those of the private asylums: check the HOSPREC database at the PRO.

Most patient files have been destroyed. A very few survive in MH 85, MH 86 (with 75-year closures) and MH 51/27–77. However, the registers to the patient files survive in MH 94, for various categories of inmates from 1846 to 1960. The register gives name and sex, name of the institution, and dates of admission, discharge or death. A union card index to all patients admitted (possibly from as early as 1774) was destroyed in 1961: apparently it covered over 2.5 million names.

32.4 Naval lunatics

For naval lunatics, see **19.13.4**.

32.5 Lunacy: bibliography

P Faithfull, *Basic Facts about Lunatics in England and Wales for Family Historians* (FFHS, 2002, forthcoming)

J H Lappin, 'Central Government and the supervision of the treatment of lunatics 1800–1913: a guide to sources in the Public Record Office' (unpublished MA thesis, 1995). Available in the PRO Library.

W Parry-Jones, *The trade in lunacy: a study of private madhouses in England in the eighteenth and nineteenth centuries* (London, 1972)

R Porter, *A Social History of Madness* (1989, reissued 1999)

33

The established church

◆ ◆ ◆

33.1 Introduction

Until the break with Rome in 1534, the established religion of England and Wales was (Roman) Catholic. After this (with the brief exception of Mary I's reign 1553–1558), the established religion was that of the Church of England, covering a wide range from high church to low church, Anglo-Catholic to Calvinist.

The PRO is not the obvious place to look for ecclesiastical records: see Owen's book on the records of the established church, and Bourne and Chicken's guide to Anglican records. In fact, the PRO does have considerable holdings on the administration of the church in relation to the state, and particularly on the monasteries, but relatively little of this contains information of interest to family historians.

However, there are some sources in the PRO which can provide information on the clergy and the lay members of the church, before and after the Reformation.

33.2 Anglican clergymen

Descent from pre-Reformation clergy, in theory at any rate, should not be possible, as they were vowed to celibacy: however, the Church of England allowed priests to marry.

Before using any documentary sources, you should consult the following printed works, which should be available in a good reference library (and are in the PRO Library). *Crockford's Clerical Directory*, published annually from 1858, is the place to start, followed by the lists of Oxford and Cambridge *Alumni* [students]. For the higher clergy, down to archdeacons, try the *Fasti Ecclesiae Anglicanae, 1066–1857*; not all dioceses have been covered up to 1857. The PRO Library also holds the

- *Clerical Guide* of 1836, which is almost a snapshot of the state of the national church in 1836;
- *Clergy List* for 1842–1917, which includes some details of the higher clergy of the Anglican church worldwide;

- *Clergy Directory* for 1872–1916 (an annual alphabetical list of beneficed clergy and their positions).

There is a card index of clergy, the Fawcett Index, in the library of the Society of Genealogists.

The ordination records in the appropriate diocesan archives can be a very useful source of genealogical information: they usually include a certified copy of the baptismal entry, or a letter explaining why there was none, details of education, and character references. There were several life insurance companies catering solely for the clergy: the Guildhall Library has a collection of London insurance company records, which can provide a wealth of personal details.

Most PRO documents relating to the appointment of Anglican clergymen to benefices are very formal, and do not include any information of great use to family historians. The bishops' certificates of institutions to benefices, 1544–1912 (E 331) are usually approached through the Institution Books, 1556–1838 (IND 1/17000–17015). These are arranged firstly by county (1556–1660) or diocese (1661–1838), then by place: they give the name of the clergyman instituted to the benefice, the date, and the name of the patron of the benefice. They can be useful for tracing the ecclesiastical career of the clergyman, but they do not provide any personal details. The Composition Books record payments due by the cleric on taking up his benefice, 1535–1795, (IND 1/17016–17028) and refer to the records in E 334.

For the Commonwealth period, the surveys of church livings provide the name of the incumbent, and details of the value of the living as assessed by the parishioners (C 94). Matthews' *Calamy Revised* is a useful source of information about clergy appointed during the Interregnum.

If you are researching someone who was a clergyman in 1801 or 1851, you may like to investigate two series of records composed of returns made by the parish clergy on conditions in their parish. The Acreage Returns of 1801 (HO 67), although intended to provide factual information on the state of agriculture at a village level, can include some very individualistic comments made by the parish priest on his parishioners. The Ecclesiastical Census of 1851 (HO 129), although a survey of places of worship, can also provide an interesting picture of life at the parish level and sometimes personal details on the clergy as well.

33.3 Excommunicates, 1280s–1840s

Excommunication was a punishment imposed by the church for a wide variety of offences, both religious and moral. The PRO holds the requests (technically, known as *significavits* or significations) from the bishops for the 'secular arm' (i.e. the power of the state) to be used against people excommunicated by the church. These significations survive from the 1220s to 1611 (C 85), and again from George II to the 1840s (C 207). It is not clear what has happened to the intervening requests.

The earliest significations usually provide little more than the name of the person excommunicated, but the later ones in C 85 can include reference to occupation, place of residence, father, nature of the offence, etc. About 7,600 significations survive from C 85, and there is a card index to these, first by diocese and then alphabetically by name of the person excommunicated. The documents themselves are in Latin. The significations in C 207 are in English, but have not yet been indexed: as a result, they are less easy to use than the earlier ones.

Significations for the county palatine of Chester were issued by Chester officials, and are in CHES 38. Those for the counties of Flint, Henry VIII to Elizabeth I, and for Pembroke, George II, have been transferred with the rest of WALE 28 to the National Library of Wales.

33.4 Sacrament certificates

From the Test Act of 1672 onwards, various statutes required that office-holders and aliens seeking naturalization should take certain oaths in support of the Crown and against papal supremacy; to afforce these oaths, the swearer was required to take the sacrament of the Lord's Supper according to the Anglican rites. Evidence of this was provided by a certificate completed and signed by the minister and churchwardens of the parish with the signatures of two witnesses appended. The certificates were presented when the oath was sworn, at one of the central courts if within 30 miles of Westminster, and at the Quarter Sessions if further away. As a result, the majority of sacrament certificates in the PRO are from Middlesex, Hertfordshire, Surrey and Kent, within the 30 mile radius of Westminster.

Certificates presented to Chancery, 1673–1778, are in C 224; those presented in the Exchequer, 1700–1827, are in E 196. Certificates presented in King's Bench survive from 1676 and from 1728–1828 (KB 22). Certificates presented in the Cheshire courts, 1673–1768, are in CHES 4: many of them date from the 1715 Jacobite Rising. Sacrament certificates presented to the Quarter Sessions should be in local record offices.

33.5 The established church: bibliography

S Bourne and A H Chicken, *Records of the Church of England: A Practical Guide for the Family Historian* (Maidstone, 1988)

Clergy Directory (1872–1916)

Clergy List (1842–1917)

Clerical Guide (1836)

Crockford's Clerical Directory (Oxford, annually from 1858)

J Foster, *Alumni Oxonienses, 1500–1886* (Oxford, 1891)

J Le Neve and others, *Fasti Ecclesiae Anglicanae* (London, 1716). There is a revised and updated version, covering 1066–1857 (London, 1962 continuing).

F D Logan, *Excommunication and the secular arm in medieval England* (Toronto, 1968)

A G Matthews, *Calamy Revised* (Oxford, 1934)

D M Owen, *The records of the established church in England, excluding parochial records* (British Records Association, 1970)

L F Salzman, 'Sussex excommunicates', *Sussex Archaeological Collections*, vol. LXXXIII, pp. 124–140

J Venn and J A Venn, *Alumni Cantabrigienses, from the Earliest Times to 1900* (Cambridge, 1922–1927)

34

Protestant nonconformists

◆ ◆ ◆

34.1 Nonconformist church records

The PRO holds the majority of nonconformist registers of births or baptisms, marriages, and deaths or burials for the period before 1837, and also a considerable number after that date: these are discussed in **3b.5–7**. However, in some cases, these registers contained other records of the church or chapel as well. The General Register Office, to whom they had been surrendered, adopted the practice of tearing out the other records where this could be done easily, and returning them to the church. To discover their present location, you need to consult a guide to the particular denomination's archives (see **34.5**). In a few cases, the information was spread throughout the volume, and this piece of archival vandalism was not carried out, so that some of the registers discussed in **3b.5–7** still include more general records.

The PRO has published a specialist guide to Nonconformist records, *Protestant Nonconformity and Roman Catholicism*, by Shorney, as well as the useful *Tracing Nonconformist Ancestors* by Gandy.

34.2 Nonconformist chapels and charities

Under the Toleration Act of 1689, Justices of the Peace were made responsible for licensing nonconformist meeting houses: these licences may be found among the Quarter Sessions records in local record offices. From 1736, deeds involving the inalienable transfer of land for charitable purposes had to be enrolled on the Close Rolls (C 54 and, from 1902, J 18). The great majority of these deeds involved the establishment of nonconformist chapels, schools, burial grounds and charities: between 1736 and 1870 over 35,000 deeds were enrolled. There are two indexes to these deeds, both to places: for 1736–1870 there are volume indexes to trust deeds, and for 1870–1904 there are card indexes. In addition, C 54 and J 18 also have annual indexes to their whole contents. These deeds are a very valuable source for local history and for the involvement of individual nonconformists in establishing their chapels and setting up schemes for self improvement.

Figure 53 The Wesleyan Synod, Williton, Somerset, 1896. This was the local governing body for Wesleyan Methodists, composed of ministers and lay-people of the various local circuits and districts. (PRO, COPY 1/424)

34.3 Nonconformists: other records

There are a number of oath or affirmation rolls for nonconformists in the PRO. The Association Oath of 1696, in support of William III, was sworn or affirmed by London and Hampshire dissenters (C 214/9–10), Quakers in Colchester (C 213/473), nonconformist ministers in Cumberland (C 213/60–61) and Baptist ministers in London (C 213/170). There are also affirmation rolls for Quaker attorneys, 1831–1835 (E 3) and 1836–1842 (CP 10).

The Recusant Rolls, 1592–1691 (E 376 and E 377) are annual returns of both Protestant nonconformists and of Catholics, who had property forfeited or who were fined for dissenting from the Church of England.

34.4 Huguenots

Huguenots were French Protestants fleeing from religious persecution from the 1550s onwards, and in large numbers after the Revocation of the Edict of Nantes (which reversed the previous policy of toleration of them) in 1685. It is quite possible, however, for a Huguenot ancestor to appear in England some time after this, as many fled first to Holland or Germany and only later moved to England. The Central Bureau of Genealogy of Holland may be able to assist in these cases. There are often strong family traditions of Huguenot descent, and names with a French flavour are usually a good indication of such a background.

The main Huguenot settlements were in London (notably in Spitalfields and Soho), Norwich, Canterbury, Southampton, Rye, Sandwich, Colchester, Bristol, Plymouth, Thorney and various places in Ireland. In the late seventeenth century, it is estimated that some 45,000 Huguenots settled in Britain. There are no known records of any communities in the Midlands or the North of England, and there is little on settlement in Scotland. It is, naturally, more difficult to trace a family which struck out on its own to a new part of the country where no French church existed, and which used the local parish church for baptisms. Huguenot burial records are rare at all times, and by the nineteenth century almost non-existent, except for the records of deaths of the inmates of the London Huguenot Hospital, which are in the Huguenot Library. The Huguenot Library will, for a fee, undertake a brief search in their archive, which includes pedigrees and records about the administration of funds collected for the relief of the refugees. No personal callers can be seen, so you will need to write (address in **48**).

Huguenot material is also to be found in other areas of settlement: in the Guildhall Library of London, the Cathedral Library at Canterbury, the County Record Office at Norwich and the Southampton City Archives, for instance.

Most of the sources for Huguenot genealogy in the PRO have been published by the Huguenot Society in some form, and are available in the PRO Library. The *Calendars of State Papers* are also useful, as are the various lists in print of aliens resident in England, naturalized, or taking oaths of allegiance (see **12.11** and **15**).

34.5 Protestant nonconformists: bibliography

Published works

R W Ambler, 'Enrolled Trust Deeds – A source for the History of Nineteenth Century Nonconformity', *Archives*, vol. XX (1993), pp. 177–186

G R Breed, *My Ancestors were Baptists* (Society of Genealogists, 1995)

N Currer-Briggs and R Gambier, *Huguenot Ancestry* (Chichester, 1985)

Dr Williams's Trust, *Nonconformist Congregations in Britain* (London, 1973)

M Gandy, *Basic Facts about English Nonconformity for Family Historians* (FFHS, 1998)

M Gandy, *Tracing Nonconformist Ancestors* (PRO, 2001)

N Graham, *The Genealogists' Consolidated Guide to Nonconformist and Foreign Registers in Inner London, 1538–1837* (Birchington, 1980)

R D Gwynn, *Huguenot Heritage: the History and Contribution of the Huguenots in Britain* (London, 1985)

Huguenot Society, *Publications* (1885 continuing)

W Leary, *My Ancestors were Methodists* (Society of Genealogists, 1999)

E H Milligan and M J Thomas, *My Ancestors were Quakers* (Society of Genealogists, 1999)

M Mullett, *Sources for the History of English Non-Conformity 1660–1830* (British Records Association, 1991)

P Palgrave-Moore, *Understanding the History and Records of Nonconformity* (Norwich, 2nd edn, 1989)

A Ruston, *My Ancestors were English Presbyterians/Unitarians* (Society of Genealogists, 1993)

D Shorney, *Protestant Nonconformity and Roman Catholicism: A Guide to Sources in the Public Record Office* (PRO, 1996)

D J Steel, *Sources of Nonconformist Genealogy and Family History* (London, 1973)

E Welch, 'The Early Methodists and their Records', *Journal of the Society of Archivists*, vol. IV, p. 210

R Wiggins, *My Ancestors were in the Salvation Army* (Society of Genealogists, 1997)

Unpublished finding aids

Indexes to trust deeds, 1736–1904

Index to C 54

Index to J 18

35

Roman Catholics and Orthodox Christians

◆ ◆ ◆

35.1 Roman Catholic registers

The registers of Catholic churches are either in the PRO (see **3b.9**) or with the congregation. The relevant diocesan archivist or the Catholic Central Library may be able to assist in tracing them. The *English Catholic Ancestor* aims at acquiring and disseminating information about Catholic families. The Catholic Record Society has published a great deal of useful record material, but does not handle enquiries. Burials of Catholics often took place in the parish churchyard and are therefore recorded in the parish registers. For much fuller information on Catholic genealogy, see the book by Steel and Samuel. For an overview of being a Catholic in England from 1558 to 1778, see Rowlands, *Catholics of Parish and Town*.

The PRO has published a specialist guide to Nonconformist records, *Protestant Nonconformity and Roman Catholicism*, by Shorney, as well as the useful *Tracing Catholic Ancestors* by Gandy.

35.2 Records of persecution of Catholics

In the PRO, records of Catholics are largely the records of their persecution, and the bulk of these accordingly varies with fluctuations in anti-popery. The Recusant Rolls (E 376 and E 377) are annual returns of dissenters (Protestant and Catholic) who had property forfeited or were fined, 1592–1691. However, they are large, mostly in Latin, and difficult to use. It is a good idea to check one of the published editions first, in order to understand the format of the rolls. Entries are arranged by county, and they record convictions, fines, rentals for forfeited lands and details of chattels seized. There are several 'returns of papists' in the State Papers and records of the Privy Council. For example, there is a printed return for 1625–1642 in SP 16/495; and a return for 1708 in SP 34/26. Try also the manuscript indexes to the Privy Council registers in PC 2, under 'Church affairs'. Most Catholics supported the King in the Civil War, so their estates may be referred to in *Calendars of the Committee for Compounding with Delinquents*. There are many inventories of Catholic possessions in the State Papers for the Interregnum (SP 28). From the reign of George I and the Jacobite risings, there are lists of Catholics who forfeited their estates (E 174, KB 18, FEC 1, and FEC 2).

County record offices hold much material on persecutions of Papists. Between 1715 and 1791, Catholics were required to register their estates with the local Clerk of the Peace.

35.3 Oath rolls

There are lists of Catholic solicitors and attorneys for the period 1790–1836 (CP 10), 1791–1813 (C 217/180/5) and 1830–1875 (E 3). The 'Papists' oaths of allegiance, etc., in E 169/79–83 give names and addresses for 1778–1857 (with gaps).

35.4 Records of the Russian Orthodox Church in London

The archive of the Russian Orthodox Church in London (sometimes known as the Orthodox Greco-Russian Church), 1721–1951, is in RG 8/111–304. Most of the archive is in Russian, with some documents in Greek, English, French and German: there is a descriptive list, in English.

The records are of various kinds to do with the organization of the church, and the Russian community in England, including Russian prisoners of war during the Crimean War. There are also registers and other records of baptisms, marriages and deaths as well as communicants and conversions, dating from 1721 to 1927. Some of these relate to Greeks and other non-Russians.

35.5 Roman Catholics and Orthodox Christians: bibliography

D A Bellenger, *English and Welsh priests 1558–1800: a working list* (Bath, 1984)

J Bossy, *The English Catholic Community, 1570–1850* (London, 1975)

Calendar of State Papers, Domestic, Committee for Compounding with Delinquents, 1643–1660 (London, 1889–1893)

Catholic Directory (London, annually from 1837)

Catholic Record Society, *Bibliographical Studies*, vols I–III, changed to *Recusant History*, from vol. IV (Bognor Regis, 1951 to date)

Catholic Record Society, *Publications* (1905, continuing)

The English Catholic Ancestor (Aldershot, 1983–1989; Ealing, 1989 continuing)

M Gandy, *Basic facts about tracing your Catholic ancestry in England* (FFHS, 1998)

M Gandy, *Catholic Family History: A Bibliography* (4 vols, 1996)

M Gandy, *Catholic Missions and Registers* (6 vols, 1993)

M Gandy, *Catholic Parishes in England, Wales and Scotland: An Atlas* (1993)

M Gandy, *Tracing Catholic Ancestors* (PRO, 2001)

R M Gard, *Directory of Catholic archives in the United Kingdom and Eire* (Newcastle upon Tyne, 1984)

M B Rowlands, ed., *Catholics of Parish and Town 1558–1778* (Catholic Record Society Monographs, 1999)

D Shorney, *Protestant Nonconformity and Roman Catholicism: A Guide to Sources in the Public Record Office* (PRO, 1996)

D J Steel and E R Samuel, *Sources for Roman Catholic and Jewish Genealogy and Family History* (London, 1974)

J A Williams, *Sources for Recusant History (1559–1791) in English Official Archives* (1983)

36

Jews

◆ ◆ ◆

36.1 Jewish genealogy

For specific guides to Jewish genealogy see Wenzerul, *A Beginner's guide to Jewish Genealogy in Great Britain*, or Joseph, *My Ancestors were Jewish*, or Steel and Samuel, *Sources for Roman Catholic and Jewish Family History and Genealogy*.

The registers of the London Spanish and Portuguese Synagogue are partly published. The registers of the Ashkenazim contain a high proportion of entries totally in Hebrew before 1840. Some earlier entries are included in the *International Genealogical Index*. Later records are not easily accessible as the congregations concerned hold most. The names and addresses of synagogues throughout the British Isles are, from 1896, in the *Jewish Year Book*.

The London Metropolitan Archives has a large and growing collection of archives on Jewish settlement in London and the UK. The Hartley Library at Southampton University has part of the Anglo-Jewish Archive, which used to be in the Mocatta Library University College, London, but the main genealogical collections, which used to be part of that archive are now at the Society of Genealogists. These are the collections of Sir Thomas Colyer Fergusson, Ronald D'Arcy Hart and A M Hyamson. Addresses are given in **48**.

For Internet searching, try www.jewishgen.org for a major gateway site, based in the US. A UK site, which will take you on to other sites, is www.jgsgb.ort.org.

36.2 The Jewish community in England and Wales

There were Jews in England in the early Middle Ages, but no line of descent has been traced from members of this early community, which was expelled in 1290. For records relating to this early community, see the *PRO Guide*. The Jewish community was re-established in the mid seventeenth century, from which time there has been a steady rate of assimilation into the gentile population.

The immigrants were of two sorts: Sephardim (Portuguese, Spanish and Italian), arriving from 1656 onwards; and Ashkenazim (Central and East European), first coming in the 1680s from Holland and Bohemia. The main influx of Ashkenazim, however, was of Russians and Poles in the last two decades of the nineteenth century (about 120,000 in the period up to 1914).

Figure 54 An eighteenth century Jewish wedding (Engraving, Private Collection/Bridgeman Art Library)

A good place to start is with the State Papers up to 1782, followed by the Home Office papers, in particular: Correspondence, George III–Victoria (HO 42, 43); Out-Letters, 1782–1921 (HO 43, 136, 152); Registered Files, from 1841 (HO 45); and Registered Files, Supplementary (HO 144: some are still under extended closure).

36.3 Colonial Jewish communities

The State Papers, Domestic, also contain numerous references to colonial Jews and similar material may be found in Colonial Office records relating to the American and West Indies colonies, including: Colonial Papers, General Series (CO 1) 1574–1757; America and West Indies, Original Correspondence, etc. (CO 5) 1606–1807; British North America, Original Correspondence (CO 6) 1816–1868; Emigration Registers (CO 327) 1850–1863; Canada, Original Correspondence (CO 42) 1700–1922; and West Indies, Original Correspondence (CO 318) 1624–1949. There are also similar classes for particular West Indies colonies. Selected papers have been published in the *Calendars of State Papers, Colonial* (to 1738). Try also the Privy Council, Unbound Papers (PC 1) 1481–1946; Privy Council Registers (PC 2) 1540–1966; and the Plantation Books (PC 5) 1678–1806.

36.4 Foreign Jewish communities

Material on the condition of Jews in foreign countries is occasionally to be found in the various series of State Papers, Foreign, which are arranged by country. These are continued after 1782 in Foreign Office classes. From 1905 such material will be found in the class of General Correspondence: Political (FO 371), though the parallel classes for Commercial (FO 368), Consular (FO 369), news (FO 395) and Prisoners (FO 383) correspondence may also be useful.

36.5 Jewish immigrants and refugees

For material on Jewish immigration in the 1770s, try SP 37. For immigration of German, Polish and Russian Jews, 1887–1905, try HO 45. Foreign Office classes contain material on the conditions of Jews in Europe and sailings of immigrant ships from the German ports in the late nineteenth century. The Correspondence and Papers of the Commissioner of the Metropolitan Police (MEPO 2) contains material on landing of Jewish immigrants, work of Jewish charities and settlement of immigrant Jews in the East End of London, 1887–1905.

The records of the Jewish Temporary Shelter, at the London Metropolitan Archives, start in 1886. They include files on Jewish immigrants, and give name on arrival, age, town of origin, destination after leaving the Shelter, and trade or profession.

The London Metropolitan Archives also house administrative records of the Jewish Refugees Committee from the 1930s, as well as some personal files on the children who came on the Kindertransport programme. Other personal files on about 400,000 Jewish refugees (including children) are still kept by the Jewish Refugees Committee: these give date and place of birth, nationality, profession, home address, date of arrival, and address in Britain. Access to all of these different records may be restricted: at the Jewish Refugees Committee, for example, to the person on whom the file was kept, or to their proven next of kin if they have died (write first). The Hartley Library at the University of Southampton also holds material on individual refugees: you need to write to them first. All these addresses are in **48**.

For material on immigration of Jews from central Europe into the United Kingdom in the 1930s, try HO 45 again. AST 1/24 contains details on assistance to about 10 Jewish refugees in the 1930s.

36.6 Jewish naturalization

In the eighteenth century, large numbers of Spanish Jews in Jamaica threw off their New Christian identity to become British Jews: Jews in the colonies could get naturalization about 85 years before they could in Britain. For denization and naturalization, look at **12.11–12**. For changes of names see **17**.

36.7 Settlement

By 1800, there may have been 15,000–20,000 Jews in England. Three-quarters of these were in London, with significant communities in Bristol and Exeter. Clearly the census returns of 1841 to 1901 provide the most complete demographic and residential data for the Jewish community as well as making possible analysis of the density of settlement in particular districts – once identification of Jewish families has been made.

36.8 Economic life

Evidence on the distribution of trades among the Jewish community in London and the provinces in the eighteenth and early nineteenth century might be gleaned from the Apprenticeship Books among the records of the Board of Inland Revenue (IR 1) (see Jewish Historical Society, *Transactions*, vol. XXII, for just such a study). Probate records of the Prerogative Court of Canterbury (PROB group) contain wills and related documents of many prominent Jewish families and extracts have been published by the Jewish Historical Society. Further information about the estates of leading Jews may be found in the eighteenth- and nineteenth-century Estate Duty Office Registers (IR 26) which cover local as well as central probates. Files of Jewish companies occur among the various classes of Companies Files of the Board of Trade Companies Office (BT 41, BT 31, BT 34). Rules and activities of Jewish Friendly Societies, Benefit Societies and Loan Societies are reflected in several classes of records of the Registrar of Friendly Societies (FS 1, FS 3, FS 9, FS 15). Another rich source of Jewish economic and financial activities would be on the records of various royal courts of law, not only the records of the common law courts, but more particularly the Chancery Court which dealt with equity cases and mercantile cases and the High Court of Admiralty dealing with maritime and trading disputes. Detailed records of some Jewish businesses from the seventeenth to the nineteenth centuries may be found as exhibits in Chancery, in C 103–114: see the subject index and index to parties held with C 103.

36.9 Trade

The State Papers (SP) and the Colonial Office (CO) and Foreign Office (FO) series also contain material relating to trade between England and the colonies and foreign countries, in which Jewish merchants may have been involved. In the West Indies colonies this was certainly the case. In addition to the series of original correspondence for each colony there are also copies of Acts and Sessional papers of colonial executive councils and legislatures, government gazettes, shipping returns, trade statistics and newspapers. Board of Trade records relating to the colonies include Original Correspondence (CO 388) 1654–1792, Minutes (CO 391) 1675–1782 and Miscellanea (CO 390). Among the State Papers, Foreign, the following are likely to be useful: State Papers, France (SP 78); Holland (SP 84); Germany (Empire) (SP 80); Portugal (SP 89); and

Hamburg and Hanse Towns (SP 82). Further material on colonial and foreign trade will be found in the Treasury Board Papers (T 1) 1557–1920. The Port Books (E 190) 1565–1798 survive for the outports, but not for London.

36.10 Social life

Sources here are too numerous to cover adequately. But, as examples, the following may serve. Poor Law Board and Local Government Board correspondence with local poor law authorities in areas of Jewish settlement may be expected to yield information on local conditions. Indeed the Clerk to the Whitechapel Guardians was in the late 1880s the chief source of such information for both the Home Office and the Metropolitan Police. The records of the Department of Education and its predecessors are likely to throw light upon Jewish schools and Jewish educational problems. Home Office and Prison Commission files reveal the special arrangements made in H.M. Prisons for the conscientious requirements of Jewish prisoners. Finally, a recent accession to the PRO is HO 239, the records of the Jewish Tribunal under the Shops Act 1936 and 1950 which deals with the licensing of Sunday trading by Jewish traders with conscientious objections to trading on the Jewish Sabbath.

36.11 Jewish soldiers

In addition to the usual methods of searching for soldiers, try Adler, *The British Jewry Book of Honour, 1914–1918*. This includes many photographs.

36.12 Jews: bibliography

M Adler, ed., *British Jewry Book of Honour 1914–1918* (London, 1922, reprinted Aldershot, 1997)

D Berger, *The Jewish Victorian: Genealogical Information from the Jewish Newspapers 1871–1881* (Oxford, 1999)

D Cesarani, ed., *The making of modern Anglo-Jewry* (Oxford, 1990)

C Clapsaddle, *Tracing Your Jewish Roots in London* (1988). The addresses given are no longer correct.

Jewish Historical Society of England, *Transactions*

Jewish Year Book (London, annually from 1896)

A Joseph, *My Ancestors were Jewish* (Society of Genealogists, 2002, forthcoming)

J M Ross, 'Naturalization of Jews in England', *Transactions of the Jewish Historical Society*, vol. XXIV (1975)

D J Steel and E R Samuel, *Sources for Roman Catholic and Jewish Family History and Genealogy* (London, 1974)

C Tucker, 'Jewish Marriages and Divorces in England until 1940', *Genealogists' Magazine*, vol. XXIV, pp. 87–93, 139–143.

R Wenzerul, ed., *A Beginner's guide to Jewish Genealogy in Great Britain* (London: The Jewish Genealogical Society of Great Britain, 2000)

37

Coroners' inquests

◆ ◆ ◆

37.1 Introduction

Coroners have been responsible for investigating sudden, unnatural or suspicious deaths, as well as the deaths of people detained in prisons, ever since the twelfth century. Inquests (or inquisitions) are normally held in public and are regularly reported in the press. The survival of coroners' records after 1850 is not good – it is probably easier and more rewarding to search for a newspaper report rather than for the coroner's record. The inquest verdict gives the cause of death: if depositions survive, they are very much fuller. Verdicts were in Latin until 1733, after which English was used. Incidentally, coroners' inquests (or the modern post mortem medical examinations) are not the same as an inquisition post mortem: the latter is concerned with establishing the identity of the heir, not the cause of death (see **41.7**).

Most modern coroners' records are held in local record offices rather than at the PRO. To find out where to look, consult *Coroners' Records in England and Wales*, by Gibson and Rogers. This lists the location of records available, by county, and includes a section on sources in the PRO. It is also a good idea to seek the advice of your local record office or reference librarian as inquests for many counties have been published by local record societies. The bibliography includes only a few of them but these are worth looking at even if you are interested in other counties. They have very good introductions that explain the context of the records and the procedures that created (and kept) them.

If original inquests have not survived, it is sometimes possible to piece basic information (such as the name of the deceased and verdict) together from coroners' bills. These record the coroners' claims for expenses; if they survive at all they will be in local record offices, usually amongst the quarter sessions records. Hunnisett's volume on *Wiltshire Coroners' Bills* will give you a good idea of the quality of information that they can provide.

37.2 Coroners' records in the PRO

The PRO has many coroners' rolls for the late thirteenth to the early fifteenth centuries: they are arranged by county (JUST 2). Most coroners' inquisitions in the PRO are filed with the records of the court of King's Bench. This is because, from 1487, coroners were required to bring their inquests to the judges at the twice-yearly assizes. Those that did not result in a trial for murder or manslaughter were forwarded to the King's Bench, where they were filed with the indictments according to the law term in which they were handed in. There are no indexes. For the period 1485–1675, the inquests are in KB 9; after 1675 they are in KB 11 (for the provincial or 'out-counties') and KB 10 (for the City of London and Middlesex). However, the King's Bench clerks stopped filing inquests in the indictment files after 1733 and the general practice of handing in inquests appears to have declined from the mid seventeenth century and to have stopped on most circuits in about 1750. The exception is the Western circuit (Cornwall, Devon, Dorset, Hampshire, Somerset, and Wiltshire) whose inquests survive, c.1740–1820 in KB 13.

A coroner's inquisition could act as an indictment, so both it and related depositions are often found among assize papers, even if no trial actually took place (see **38**). Such inquisitions do not simply relate to obvious cases of murder. They often also include records of inquests in cases we would now consider to be manslaughter, or accidental deaths. From the thirteenth to seventeenth centuries, inquests taken during proceedings that resulted in the granting of pardons can be found amongst Chancery files in C 260. Copies of the proceedings were often included in the pardons themselves, which, if enrolled, are in C 66.

The Palatinates of Chester and Lancaster have extensive coroners' records. The Chester records also include Flint. Inquests from 1714 to 1851, with a few earlier ones, are in CHES 18: from 1798 to 1891 they are in ASSI 66. For the period of overlap, you will need to look in both series, as the division is an arbitrary one apparently based on some local administrative quirk. Inquests from the Palatinate of Lancaster, 1626–1832, are in PL 26/285–295. For coroners' inquests taken within lands of the Duchy of Lancashire that are outside the county of Lancashire, look at DL 46. This has inquests for certain lands in Middlesex (1817–1884); Surrey (1823–1896); Essex (1821–1822); Halton, in Cheshire (1848–1849); Pontefract, in Yorkshire (1822–1894); and Norfolk (1804–1824, 1853–1875, 1885–1889). There are also very informative depositions about accidental deaths and homicides in PL 27.

Other sources in the PRO relate to the deaths of prisoners. The inquests of prisoners (usually debtors) held in the King's Bench prison, 1747–1750, and 1771–1839 (KB 14), can be informative about previous occupations. There is also a register of deaths of prisoners and of inquests upon them for the Millbank Penitentiary, 1848–1863 (PCOM 2/165). Some deaths fell within the jurisdiction of the High Court of Admiralty (usually those who died on or in the River Thames or who had been prisoners in the custody of the court) and records of inquests therefore survive among the records of that court, in HCA 1.

37.3 Coroners' records outside the PRO

Modern coroners' records do not survive very well. Records of individual inquests (other than treasure trove) created after 1875 may be weeded or destroyed, unless they are of significant public interest. Even if they do survive, inquest records are usually closed for 75 years. They are normally held in the local record office, unless they remain in the custody of the coroner. It is most unlikely that they will be indexed by name. *Coroners' Records in England and Wales*, by Gibson and Rogers, is the essential guide.

37.4 Murder

Records relating to murder victims are normally found by searching trial and associated records, published literature (see **38**) and appeals for mercy (see **39.6**). For much of the nineteenth and twentieth centuries many provincial police forces asked the Metropolitan Police Force to assist them in the investigation of murder, so files relating to provincial murders may survive alongside those of London cases in MEPO 3. There are police registers of murders and of deaths by violence (including the deaths of women by illegal abortion) in the Metropolitan Police area, for 1891–1909, 1912–1917, and 1919–1966. These give the name, address and occupation of the victim, date and place of death, and subsequent charges or convictions (MEPO 20).

37.5 Coroners' inquests: bibliography

J S W Gibson and C Rogers, *Coroners' Records in England and Wales* (FFHS, 1992)

R F Hunnisett, *Calendar of Nottinghamshire Coroners' Inquests, 1485–1558*, Thoroton Society, Record Series, vol. XXV

R F Hunnisett, 'Medieval Coroners' Rolls', *American Journal of Legal History*, vol. III, pp. 95–221, and 324–359

R F Hunnisett, *Sussex Coroners' Inquests, 1485–1558*, Sussex Record Society, vol. LXXIV

R F Hunnisett, *Sussex Coroners' Inquests, 1558–1603* (PRO, 1996)

R F Hunnisett, *Sussex Coroners' Inquests, 1603–1688* (PRO, 1998)

R F Hunnisett, *Wiltshire Coroners' Bills, 1752–1796*, Wiltshire Record Society, vol. XXXVI

38

Criminal trials: courts in England and Wales

◆ ◆ ◆

38.1 Introduction

Are you sure that trial records are what you want? They are not easy to use, and will not necessarily give you good family history information: they do not, for example, normally include transcripts of evidence given in court. For family history purposes, tracing convicts (especially transported ones) is usually easier and more rewarding (see **39, 40**).

The first problem to be overcome is the lack of name indexes. Unless you know when and where your ancestor was tried it will be extremely difficult to track down the trial record. There is no central index of persons tried: some indexes do exist, but they are far from comprehensive. There are indexes to people who were transported (see **40**). Surviving indictments of people who were tried in the sixteenth and seventeenth centuries at the assizes for the Home circuit (Essex, Hertfordshire, Kent, Surrey and Sussex) have been published, and indexed, in the *Calendar of Assize Records*. The names of those who were tried in Kent in 1602 are indexed in *Kent at Law 1602*. There is a name index in the class list for ASSI 45 for those who made sworn statements on the North Eastern circuit between 1613–1800. Finally, the microfiche publication *British Trials 1660–1900* is indexed by defendant, victim and location (see **38.3**).

Even if you know roughly when and where the trial took place, you still need to know what kind of court tried the offence. Until the sixteenth century, many manorial courts exercised jurisdiction in cases of petty theft, affray, drunkenness, and other offences (see **41.2**), but from the sixteenth century onwards jurisdiction over minor crimes increasingly passed to Justices of the Peace (also known as magistrates). Justices of the Peace were (then as now) effectively volunteer amateur judges, who were commissioned by the Crown because of their importance in the local community rather than for their legal expertise. Justices of the Peace were empowered to try some offences without a jury: this was called summary jurisdiction. They could do this either singly or in groups of two or more. Summary courts with more than one justice were usually called petty sessions. The scope of summary jurisdiction has been steadily widened since the late seventeenth century: far more crimes in England and Wales are tried summarily than by full jury trial. Surviving records of summary trials are held in local record offices, but the survival is generally poor until the mid nineteenth century. The justices also met together, usually four times a year, at meetings that became known as quarter sessions. Here, until the late nineteenth century, they transacted administrative business of the kind that would now fall to elected local councils and were also empowered to hear certain criminal cases that were to be determined by a jury. With certain limited exceptions (see **38.4**), quarter sessions and other records created by justices of the peace are usually held in local record offices, rather than at the PRO: see Gibson, *Quarter Sessions Records for Family Historians.*

From the thirteenth century, criminal cases could also be tried before professional judges acting as justices of gaol delivery: pairs of judges literally rode through groups or circuits of counties in order to hold their courts, which became known as the assizes. They took their authority from commissions of gaol delivery and peace, and (from the 1530s) of oyer and terminer. These enabled them to try or 'deliver' anyone who was imprisoned in the county gaol or who was on bail from it, and also to 'hear and determine' certain other cases such as treason, riot, rebellion, coining, murder, burglary, etc. In most parts of England and Wales therefore there were multiple courts able to try criminal cases. Additionally, the King's Bench, which was a central royal court sitting at Westminster, had an overriding jurisdiction over them all. Records of assize courts and of the King's Bench are held in the PRO (see **38.4** and **38.8**).

In some areas of the country the judicial system worked slightly differently. If the case in which you are interested was tried in the City of London, in the ancient county of Middlesex, in Bristol, Wales, or one of the Palatinates of Chester, Durham or Lancaster, read **38.5** and **38.6** below.

It is a fallacy to believe that minor offences were tried in minor courts and that serious offences were tried in the higher courts. Even today there are a number of offences that can be tried with a jury in a county court (the modern equivalent of assizes and quarter sessions) or without a jury in a magistrates court. In the past there was an even greater overlap between the various courts and the kind of cases that they could hear: some offences, such as assault, could be tried at any of the four levels of the court hierarchy. The division of cases between assize courts and sessions was very much a rough and ready one, and depended on convenience and cost as well as on the gravity of the crime. It is possible to generalize only about those crimes for which the penalty was death or transportation.

From at least the sixteenth century, it would have been extremely unusual for capital crimes to be tried anywhere other than assizes (or a court with equivalent power). Anyone who was transported before 1718 or who was transported for 14 years after 1718 must have been tried at assizes (or equivalent). Anyone who was sentenced to transportation for less than 14 years after 1718 could have been tried either at assizes or at quarter sessions. In trying to match the crime to a court, you need to remember that the law kept changing and that some of those changes would influence the kind of trial that could be held. Sheep stealing, for example, was a 'serious' offence in the eighteenth century, normally tried at assizes, but by the middle of the nineteenth century, records of trials for sheep stealing can often be found in quarter sessions or even summary jurisdiction. The reason is simple: the death penalty for sheep stealing was abolished in 1832 with the result that, as far as the law was concerned, it suddenly ceased to be a 'serious' offence.

Scotland has a very different legal system, whose surviving records are in the National Archives of Scotland and local record offices in Scotland.

38.2 Using trial records

The second problem is the nature of the trial records themselves. The nature and quality of the assizes records varies considerably from period to period and from circuit to circuit. Trial records consist of a variety of documents: indictments, witness statements, gaol calendars, recognizances (bonds, usually for bail, but sometimes to testify or prosecute), and minute books. With certain limited exceptions, however, they do not contain transcripts of evidence and will not normally give details of the age of the accused or of his/her family relationships.

The indictments set out the nature of the charge against the accused. As with all formal legal records, until 1733 (with a brief interruption between 1650 and 1660) they are in heavily abbreviated Latin and are written in distinctive legal scripts. Even after 1733 when indictments were written in English and in an ordinary hand, the language used is so convoluted and archaic that it can be difficult to understand exactly what the defendant was being charged with. Indictments were not expressed in clear plain English until 1916. Even more disappointing for the family historian is the fact that although the indictments appear to tell you the occupation and parish of residence of the accused, the information given is fictitious. Men are almost always described as labourers, even if they were skilled artisans. The parish of residence is invariably the place at which the crime was committed. If you are prepared to make a thorough search of the indictment and deposition files then you may be able to find more accurate information from some of the associated documents. By doing just this, Knafla has been able to establish correct occupation and place of residence for 87 per cent of the defendants he studied for *Kent at Law 1602*. But remember that a search of this kind is going to be both time consuming and speculative; it will also require a sound knowledge of trial procedures and records as well as palaeographic skills. If you want to attempt it you will need to do a lot of background reading: the works listed in the bibliography below, especially those by Baker, Beattie and Cockburn, will get you off to a good start.

Pre-trial witness statements may survive either with the indictments or in a separate series (usually described in the PRO as depositions, but often described in local record offices simply as sessions papers). These are in English and in the ordinary hand of the day, but if you are not familiar with early modern handwriting you may find them difficult to read. From about 1830, the deposition files have been heavily weeded, so that only depositions in capital cases, usually murder and riot, tend to survive. From the mid twentieth century, depositions survive for a greater variety of cases. The deposition files (especially more modern ones) may also contain items used as trial exhibits such as

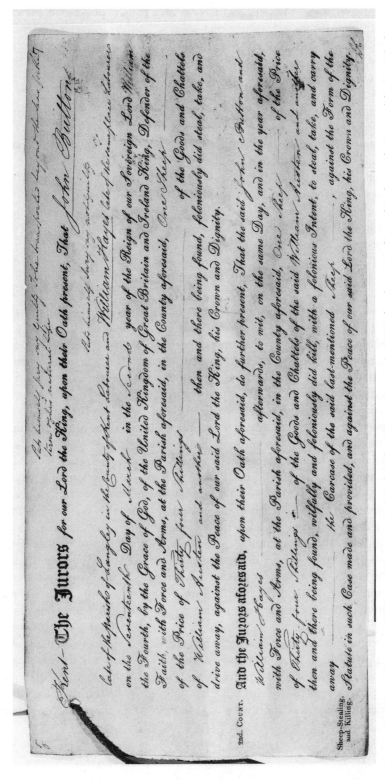

Figure 55 John Button and William Hayes were indicted at the Kent assizes, July 1832, for sheep stealing. This shows the printed form, with the relevant details added. The clerk has used blank spaces to add what happened at the trial. Both Button and Hayes pleaded not guilty ('*puts himself on the country*' – i.e. goes for a jury trial). In Button's case he added '*Jury say Guilty. To be transported beyond the seas for the term of his natural life.*' Hayes was luckier. See also Figure 58. (PRO, ASSI 94/2130)

photographs, maps, appeal papers and in one case even a policeman's pocket book. Some of the exhibits are distressing.

Minute books (usually described by the PRO as crown books or gaol books) may also survive. These usually list the defendants at each session with a brief note of the charges against them and are often annotated with verdicts and sentences. Similar information is contained in sheriffs' assize vouchers (see **38.11**). Trial records are subject to the normal 30-year closure rule; some may be closed for longer periods.

Unofficial transcripts of evidence survive for some early nineteenth-century cases in which convicts petitioned for mercy (see **39.6**). Official transcripts of selected criminal trials of special interest, 1846–1931, are held amongst the records of the Director of Public Prosecutions in DPP 4. The records of the Director of Public Prosecutions also include case papers relating to prosecutions (1889–1992) in DPP 1 and DPP 2, and registers of cases (1884–1956) in DPP 3. Most of these records are closed for 75 years.

38.3 Using other sources

Although the formal trial records might be disappointing, it is worth remembering that even quite ordinary trials attracted a lot of journalistic coverage, which sometimes included transcripts of all or part of the evidence, as well as comments on family or occupational background. If you really want to know what happened at the trial, it is probably better to start with published reports of trials rather than with actual trial records.

Newspaper coverage became common from about 1750. *The Times,* which has been produced since 1786, is available on microfilm at most major reference libraries, as well as at the PRO, and is indexed. Transcripts, confessions, dying statements of those who were hanged and other 'true crime' accounts have been published in pamphlet, magazine and book form from early modern times to the present day. In the early period such publications were sometimes produced as a one-off attempt to break into what was obviously a lucrative market, but local printers sometimes also tried to establish a market of their own by producing a series of pamphlets about local trials. The most famous of these is the *Old Bailey Proceedings* which have been published since at least the 1690s (see below **38.6**). Similar accounts were produced for other parts of the country too: the earliest known copy of the *Surrey Assize Proceedings* dates from 1678 and the series is known to have continued until at least 1780. Surviving pamphlets of this kind can be traced using the British Library's *English Short Title Catalogue* (previously known as the *Eighteenth Century Short Title Catalogue*). A number of these pamphlets have been republished on microfiche by Chadwyck-Healey as *British Trials 1660–1900* together with indexes of defendants, victims and locations; a copy is available at the PRO. To find out more about how to trace printed works on crime, ask for advice at your nearest central reference library or the PRO Library.

38.4 Quarter sessions and assizes

Before the assizes were created the judges were sent to try cases in the counties at irregular intervals on what became known as general eyres. The surviving records of these cases, both civil and criminal, are described in Crook's *Records of the general eyre*; Crook also lists those that have been published. The records are in JUST 1–4: their use requires a high level of skill. Few quarter sessions records for the fourteenth and fifteenth centuries survive. Those that do are in the PRO, mostly in JUST 1; they are listed in Putnam's edition, and many have been published by local record societies. From the sixteenth century onwards, quarter sessions survive in increasing quantities, and they are deposited in local record offices. Gibson's *Quarter Sessions Records* gives details and locations. Ratclif's *Warwick County Records* and Emmison and Gray's *County records* give a very full indication of the nature of the records and the sort of information they contain.

Although a few strays are known to survive in local record offices, assizes records are normally held in the PRO. For the fourteenth and fifteenth centuries they are mostly in JUST 3, with some others in JUST 1, JUST 4 and KB 9. After 1559, they are normally in the many ASSI series, although the survival rate is very patchy. A county checklist is given in **38.7**. If your county is lacking records for the relevant date, you may find it worthwhile (though difficult) to check the returned indictments in KB 9, KB 10 or KB 11. Assizes and Quarter Sessions courts were abolished in 1971.

38.5 Anomalous jurisdictions: Bristol, Wales and the Palatinates of Chester, Durham and Lancaster

In Bristol the right to hear criminal cases was one of the ancient chartered privileges of the Corporation of Bristol. This right was abolished in 1832, after which date assize courts were held for Bristol as for any other county. Surviving trial records before 1832 are held in the local record office; those after 1832 are in the PRO amongst the ASSI classes.

Wales and the palatinates had special jurisdictions serving much the same function as assizes. In Wales, the equivalent jurisdiction was exercised from 1542 to 1830 by the Great Sessions of Wales, whose records are in the National Library of Wales (see Parry for a guide to these records). From 1830 to 1971 the Welsh counties were included among the assizes circuits, so the records are in the ASSI classes at the PRO. Records of the Palatinate of Chester, primarily comprising Cheshire and Flint are held in the PRO under CHES. Those of the Palatinate of Durham covering County Durham and certain areas beyond are in DURH, and the Palatinate of Lancaster, covering Lancashire, in PL. For a county checklist see **38.7**.

38.6 Anomalous jurisdictions: London, the Old Bailey and the Central Criminal Court

Jurisdictions in the London area are even more complex. The area we now know as central London (north of the Thames) was historically part of the county of Middlesex (and its subordinate jurisdiction of Westminster). Those parts of London that had spread south of the Thames were largely in the borough of Southwark. Southwark was normally held to be part of the county of Surrey, although to complicate matters still further, the City of London did occasionally try to claim jurisdiction over parts of it. The City of London was and is a specific administrative area covering approximately one square mile at the heart of modern London. If you are trying to trace the records of a 'London' crime before 1834, it is essential that you first find out whether it took place in the City or in urban Middlesex. You can establish this from the printed *Old Bailey Proceedings*. If your 'London' crime was committed south of the river before 1834, then you need to look at the records of assize courts for the Home circuit.

Until 1834, sessions of oyer and terminer and of gaol delivery for the City of London were held before the lord mayor and the recorder of London at the Old Bailey. Ordinary sessions cases for the City of London were tried at Guildhall. As part of its privileges, the City of London had also acquired rights over its neighbouring county of Middlesex. These included the right to appoint its own sheriffs to the office of sheriff of Middlesex, and control of the county gaol (Newgate) together with the right to deliver the gaol. This meant that the Middlesex sessions of gaol delivery were also held at the Old Bailey. However the Middlesex sessions of oyer and terminer were held alongside the sessions of the peace, before the Middlesex justices at their sessions house in Clerkenwell.

In 1834 the Old Bailey sessions were abolished and replaced with a court that is officially known as the Central Criminal Court (but which in practice is still called the Old Bailey). The geographical jurisdiction of this new court reflected the continuing spread of London and therefore included parts of Essex, Kent and Surrey as well as the City of London and Middlesex. The court's legal jurisdiction was made equivalent to an assize court as it was given oyer and terminer and gaol delivery functions for both the City of London and for Middlesex. Between 1834 and 1844, it was also given the jurisdiction over crimes on the high seas that had previously belonged to the High Court of Admiralty (**38.10**).

The original records of Old Bailey trials before 1834 are not held in the PRO but *either* at the Corporation of London Record Office (City of London cases) *or* at the London Metropolitan Archives (Middlesex cases). The addresses of both are given in **48**. Records of the Old Bailey or Central Criminal Court after 1834 are held in the PRO in CRIM. As a result of the recommendations of the Denning Report, only a two per cent sample of depositions survives.

Trials at the Old Bailey and Central Criminal Court were, and are, particularly well covered by newspapers and other printed sources. Before attempting to use any original trial records you should look for published material. The *Old Bailey Proceedings* were published from the 1690s onwards. These are virtually verbatim reports of the proceedings in court, giving the name of the accused, the charges, the evidence of witnesses, the verdict (often with the prisoner's age if found guilty), and the sentence. The report will also indicate whether the case was a London or a Middlesex one. They are roughly indexed within each volume. Copies of the printed sets are held in many libraries, as well as the PRO in record classes PCOM 1 (1801–1904) and CRIM 10 (1834–1912), but such sets are invariably incomplete. For the period between 1714 and 1834 it would be better to use the microfilm edition, which is also available in many libraries as well as at the PRO. Some additional information, 1815 to 1849, can be found in HO 16 and for 1782 to 1853, in HO 77 (see **38.11**).

The court rooms of the Old Bailey were also used, from about 1660 to 1834, for the trials of individuals accused of offences within the jurisdiction of the High Court of Admiralty. Trial records in these cases if they survive are to be found amongst the various High Court of Admiralty series in the PRO (see **38.10**)

38.7 Assize and similar courts: a county by county checklist of criminal trial records surviving in the PRO, 1559–1971

English assizes, 1559–1971

County	Crown & Gaol Books		Indictments		Depositions		Other
Bedfordshire	1863–76	ASSI 32	1658–98	ASSI 16	1832–76	ASSI 36	ASSI 34, ASSI 38,
	1734–1863	ASSI 33	1693–1850	ASSI 94	1876–1971	ASSI 13	ASSI 39, ASSI 15
	1876–1945	ASSI 11	1851–1971	ASSI 95			
Berkshire	1657–1971	ASSI 2	1650–1971	ASSI 5	1719–1971	ASSI 6	ASSI 4, ASSI 9,
	1847–1951	ASSI 3					ASSI 10, ASSI 93
Buckingham-shire	1863–76	ASSI 32	1642–99	ASSI 16	1832–76	ASSI 36	ASSI 34, ASSI 38,
	1734–1863	ASSI 33	1695–1850	ASSI 94	1876–1971	ASSI 13	ASSI 39, ASSI 15
	1876–1945	ASSI 11	1851–1971	ASSI 95			
Cambridgeshire	1902–43	ASSI 31	1642–99	ASSI 16	1834–1971	ASSI 36	ASSI 34, ASSI 38,
	1863–1971	ASSI 32	1692–1850	ASSI 94			ASSI 39
	1734–1863	ASSI 33	1851–1971	ASSI 95			
Cheshire	1532–1831	CHES 21	1341–1830	CHES 24	1831–1944	ASSI 65	ASSI 59, ASSI 63,
	1341–1659	CHES 24	1831–1945	ASSI 64	1945–71	ASSI 84	ASSI 66, ASSI 67
	1831–1938	ASSI 61	1945–71	ASSI 83			
	1835–83	ASSI 62					
	1945–51	ASSI 79					
Cornwall	1730–1971	ASSI 21	1801–1971	ASSI 25	1861–1971	ASSI 26	ASSI 24, ASSI 30
	1670–1824	ASSI 23			1951–53	ASSI 82	
Cumberland	1714–1873	ASSI 41	1607–1876	ASSI 44	1613–1876	ASSI 45	ASSI 43, ASSI 46,
	1665–1810	ASSI 42	1877–1971	ASSI 51	1877–1971	ASSI 52	ASSI 47, ASSI 93
Derbyshire	1818–1945	ASSI 11	1868–1971	ASSI 12	1862–1971	ASSI 13	ASSI 15
			1662, 67, 87	ASSI 80			
Devon	1746–1971	ASSI 21	1801–1971	ASSI 25	1861–1971	ASSI 26	ASSI 24, ASSI 30
	1670–1824	ASSI 23			1951–53	ASSI 82	

Dorset	1746–1971 1670–1824	ASSI 21 ASSI 23	1801–1971	ASSI 25	1861–1971 1951–53	ASSI 26 ASSI 82	ASSI 24, ASSI 30	
Durham	1770–1876 1753–1858 1858–1944	DURH 15 DURH 16 ASSI 41	1582–1877 1876–1971	DURH 17 ASSI 44	1843–76 1877–1971	DURH 18 ASSI 45	DURH 19, ASSI 46, ASSI 47, ASSI 93	
Essex	1734–1943 1826–1971	ASSI 31 ASSI 32	1559–1688 1689–1850 1851–1971	ASSI 35 ASSI 94 ASSI 95	1825–1971	ASSI 36	ASSI 34, ASSI 38, ASSI 39	
Gloucestershire	1657–1971 1847–1951	ASSI 2 ASSI 3	1662–1971	ASSI 5	1719–1971	ASSI 6	ASSI 4, ASSI 9, ASSI 10, ASSI 93	
Hampshire	1746–1971 1670–1824	ASSI 21 ASSI 23	1801–1971	ASSI 25	1861–1971 1951–53	ASSI 26 ASSI 82	ASSI 24, ASSI 30	
Herefordshire	1657–1971 1847–1951	ASSI 2 ASSI 3	1627–1971	ASSI 5	1719–1971	ASSI 6	ASSI 4, ASSI 9, ASSI 10, ASSI 93	
Hertfordshire	1734–1943 1826–1971	ASSI 31 ASSI 32	1573–1688 1689–1850 1829–1971	ASSI 35 ASSI 94 ASSI 95	1851–1971	ASSI 36	ASSI 34, ASSI 38, ASSI 39	
Huntingdon-shire	1902–43 1863–1971 1734–1863	ASSI 31 ASSI 32 ASSI 33	1643–98 1693–1850 1851–1971	ASSI 16 ASSI 94 ASSI 95	1851–1971	ASSI 36	ASSI 34, ASSI 38, ASSI 39	
Kent	1734–1943 1826–1971	ASSI 31 ASSI 32	1559–1688 1689–1850 1812–1971	ASSI 35 ASSI 94 ASSI 95	1851–1971	ASSI 36	ASSI 34, ASSI 38, ASSI 39	
Lancashire	1524–1843 1686–1877	PL 25 PL 28	1660–1867 1877–1971	PL 26 ASSI 51	1663–1867 1877–1971	PL 27 ASSI 52	PL 28 ASSI 46, ASSI 53, ASSI 93	
Leicestershire	1818–64 1864–75 1876–1945	ASSI 11 ASSI 32 ASSI 11	1653, 56 1864–75 1876–1971	ASSI 80 ASSI 35 ASSI 12	1862 1863–75 1876–1971	ASSI 13 ASSI 36 ASSI 13	ASSI 15, ASSI 34, ASSI 38, ASSI 39	
Lincolnshire	1818–1945	ASSI 11	1868–1971 1652–79	ASSI 12 ASSI 80	1862–1971	ASSI 13	ASSI 15	
London & Middlesex	1834–1949	CRIM 6	1834–1957 1833–1971	CRIM 4 CRIM 5	1839–1971 1923–71	CRIM 1 CRIM 2	CRIM 7, CRIM 8, CRIM 9, CRIM 10, CRIM 11, CRIM 12, CRIM 13	
Monmouth-shire	1657–1971 1847–1951	ASSI 2 ASSI 3	1666–1971	ASSI 5	1719–1971	ASSI 6	ASSI 4, ASSI 9, ASSI 10, ASSI 93	

Norfolk	1902–43	ASSI 31	1606–99	ASSI 16	1817–1971	ASSI 36	ASSI 34,
	1863–1971	ASSI 32	1692–1850	ASSI 94			ASSI 38, ASSI 39
	1734–1863	ASSI 33	1851–1971	ASSI 95			
Northampton shire	1818–64	ASSI 11	1659–60	ASSI 80	1862	ASSI 13	ASSI 15, ASSI 34
	1864–76	ASSI 32	1864–75	ASSI 95	1864–75	ASSI 36	ASSI 38, ASSI 39
	1876–1945	ASSI 11	1876–1971	ASSI 12	1876–1971	ASSI 13	
Northumber land	1714–1944	ASSI 41	1607–1971	ASSI 44	1613–1971	ASSI 45	ASSI 43, ASSI 46,
	1665–1810	ASSI 42					ASSI 47, ASSI 93
Nottingham-shire	1818–1945	ASSI 11	1868–1971	ASSI 12	1862–1971	ASSI 13	ASSI 15
			1663–4, 1682	ASSI 80			
Oxfordshire	1657–1971	ASSI 2	1661–1971	ASSI 5	1719–1971	ASSI 6	ASSI 4, ASSI 9,
	1847–1951	ASSI 3	1688	PRO 30/80			ASSI 10, ASSI 93
Rutland	1818–64	ASSI 11	1667, 85	ASSI 80	1862	ASSI 13	ASSI 15, ASSI 34,
	1864–76	ASSI 32	1864–75	ASSI 95	1864–73	ASSI 36	ASSI 38, ASSI 39
	1876–1945	ASSI 11	1876–1971	ASSI 12	1876–1971	ASSI 13	
Shropshire (Salop)	1657–1971	ASSI 2	1654–1971	ASSI 5	1719–1971	ASSI 6	ASSI 4, ASSI 9,
	1847–1951	ASSI 3					ASSI 10, ASSI 93
Somerset	1730–1971	ASSI 21	1801–1971	ASSI 25	1861–1971	ASSI 26	ASSI 24, ASSI 30
	1670–1824	ASSI 23			1951–53	ASSI 82	
Staffordshire	1657–1971	ASSI 2	1662–1971	ASSI 5	1719–1971	ASSI 6	ASSI 4, ASSI 9,
	1847–1951	ASSI 3	1662	ASSI 80			ASSI 10, ASSI 93
Suffolk	1902–43	ASSI 31	1653–98	ASSI 16	1832–1971	ASSI 36	ASSI 34, ASSI 38,
	1863–1971	ASSI 32	1689–1850	ASSI 94			ASSI 39
	1734–1863	ASSI 33	1851–1971	ASSI 95			
Surrey	1734–1943	ASSI 31	1559–1688	ASSI 35	1820–1971	ASSI 36	ASSI 34, ASSI 38,
	1826–1971	ASSI 32	1689–1850	ASSI 94			ASSI 39
			1851–	ASSI 95			
Sussex	1734–1943	ASSI 31	1559–1688	ASSI 35	1812–1971	ASSI 36	ASSI 34, ASSI 38,
	1826–1971	ASSI 32	1689–1850	ASSI 94			ASSI 39
			1851–1971	ASSI 95			
Warwickshire	1818–1945	ASSI 11	1868–1971	ASSI 12	1862–1971	ASSI 13	ASSI 15
			1652, 88	ASSI 80			
Westmorland	1714–1873	ASSI 41	1607–1876	ASSI 44	1613–1876	ASSI 45	ASSI 43, ASSI 46,
	1718–1810	ASSI 42	1877–1971	ASSI 51	1877–1971	ASSI 52	ASSI 47, ASSI 53,
							ASSI 93

Wiltshire	1746–1971	ASSI 21	1729,	ASSI 25	1861–1971	ASSI 26	ASSI 24, ASSI 30
	1670–1824	ASSI 23	1801–1971		1951–53	ASSI 82	
Worcestershire	1657–1971	ASSI 2	1662–1971	ASSI 5	1719–1971	ASSI 6	ASSI 4, ASSI 9,
	1847–1951	ASSI 3					ASSI 10, ASSI 93
Yorkshire	1718–1863	ASSI 41	1607–1863	ASSI 44	1613–1863	ASSI 45	ASSI 15,
	1658–1811	ASSI 42	1864–76	ASSI 12	1868–76	ASSI 13	ASSI 43, ASSI 46,
	1864–76	ASSI 11	1877–1971	ASSI 51	1877–1971	ASSI 52	ASSI 47,
							ASSI 53, ASSI 93

Figure 56 An admiring view of Dick Turpin, flying from justice up the Great North Road, only to be indicted as John Palmer (alias Richard Turpin) at the York assizes on 1 March 1739, for stealing a mare. He was executed on York racecourse seven weeks later. (Bruce Castle Museum/Mary Evans Picture Library)

Welsh assizes, 1830–1971

(For Welsh assize (great sessions) records before 1830, contact the National Library of Wales, or use Parry, *A Guide to the Records of Great Sessions in Wales.*)

County	Crown & Gaol Books		Indictments		Depositions		Other
Anglesey	1831–1938 1835–83 1945–51	ASSI 61 ASSI 62 ASSI 79	1831–1945 1945–71	ASSI 64 ASSI 83	1831–1944 1945–71	ASSI 65 ASSI 84	ASSI 59, ASSI 63, ASSI 66, ASSI 67
Breconshire	1841–42 1844–1946 1945–51	ASSI 74 ASSI 76 ASSI 79	1834–1945 1945–71	ASSI 71 ASSI 83	1837–1971 1945–71	ASSI 72 ASSI 84	ASSI 73, ASSI 77
Caernarvon-shire	1831–1938 1835–83 1945–51	ASSI 61 ASSI 62 ASSI 79	1831–1945 1945–71	ASSI 64 ASSI 83	1831–1944 1945–71	ASSI 65 ASSI 84	ASSI 59, ASSI 63, ASSI 66, ASSI 67
Cardiganshire	1841–42 1844–1946 1945–51	ASSI 74 ASSI 76 ASSI 79	1834–1945 1945–71	ASSI 71 ASSI 83	1837–1971 1945–71	ASSI 72 ASSI 84	ASSI 73, ASSI 77
Carmarthen-shire	1841–42 1844–1946 1945–51	ASSI 74 ASSI 76 ASSI 79	1834–1945 1945–71	ASSI 71 ASSI 83	1837–1971 1945–71	ASSI 72 ASSI 84	ASSI 73, ASSI 77
Denbighshire	1831–1938 1835–83 1945–51	ASSI 61 ASSI 62 ASSI 79	1831–1945 1945–71	ASSI 64 ASSI 83	1831–1944 1945–71	ASSI 65 ASSI 84	ASSI 59, ASSI 63, ASSI 66, ASSI 67
Flint	1831–1938 1835–83 1945–51	ASSI 61 ASSI 62 ASSI 79	1330–1541 1831–1945 1945–71	CHES 24 ASSI 64 ASSI 83	1831–1944 1945–71	ASSI 65 ASSI 84	ASSI 59, ASSI 63, ASSI 66, ASSI 67
Glamorgan-shire	1841–42 1844–1946 1945–51	ASSI 74 ASSI 76 ASSI 79	1834–1945 1945–71	ASSI 71 ASSI 83	1837–1971 1945–71	ASSI 72 ASSI 84	ASSI 73, ASSI 77
Merionethshire	1831–1938 1835–83 1945–51	ASSI 61 ASSI 62 ASSI 79	1831–1945 1945–71	ASSI 64 ASSI 83	1831–1944 1945–71	ASSI 65 ASSI 84	ASSI 59, ASSI 63, ASSI 66, ASSI 67
Montgomery-shire	1831–1938 1835–83 1945–51	ASSI 61 ASSI 62 ASSI 79	1831–1945 1945–71	ASSI 64 ASSI 83	1831–1944 1945–71	ASSI 65 ASSI 84	ASSI 59, ASSI 63, ASSI 66, ASSI 67
Pembrokeshire	1841–42 1844–1946 1945–51	ASSI 74 ASSI 76 ASSI 79	1834–1945 1945–71	ASSI 71 ASSI 83	1837–1971 1945–71	ASSI 72 ASSI 84	ASSI 73, ASSI 77
Radnor	1841–42 1844–1946 1945–51	ASSI 74 ASSI 76 ASSI 79	1834–1945 1945–71	ASSI 71 ASSI 83	1837–1971 1945–71	ASSI 72 ASSI 84	ASSI 73, ASSI 77

Please note that the covering dates given in the table are meant to give a general indication of survival and that there may be small, unexplained gaps within an otherwise continuous run of records.

38.8 King's Bench

The Court of King's Bench was the highest court of common law in England and Wales until it was absorbed into the High Court in 1875. This section considers only its criminal jurisdiction; for a discussion of the records relating to civil litigation see **47a**. The Court of King's Bench evolved from the Curia Regis and had become an established institution by the thirteenth century. The court was not an itinerant one but since it was attached to the person of the King it necessarily moved with the seat of government. By 1422 the court had settled at Westminster, although the wording of its records still maintained the fiction that it was always held in the presence of the King himself.

The King's Bench gradually developed three separate jurisdictions: original jurisdiction over all criminal matters, supervisory powers over lesser courts, and a local jurisdiction over the county in which it sat (which in practice from 1422 onwards was Middlesex). Like all courts in England and Wales, its formal records were written in heavily abbreviated Latin and in distinctive legal scripts until 1733 (except for a brief period during the Interregnum). Its procedures were elaborate and created complex, inter-connected series of records for which there is no single or obvious point of entry. The indexes and finding aids are inadequate. In short, these are not records that should be attempted by anyone but the most determined of searchers. As with assize and quarter sessions records, records of King's Bench trials do not contain transcripts of evidence and it may be better to start by looking for a newspaper or other published account of the trial that interests you (see **38.3**).

Despite the received wisdom of traditional legal historians who have assumed that use of this court must have been restricted to the rich and influential, the reality is that the court was accessible to almost all ranks of society. Its wide jurisdiction also meant that cases initiated or referred to the King's Bench (few of which were actually tried) covered a wide range of subject matter, from minor assaults, disorderly houses and obstructed highways to riot, attempted rape, and high treason. The records of the King's Bench are a particularly fruitful source of information about Londoners, but cases also came to the court from all over the country. Occasionally, they even came from the colonies as well.

Records of the King's Bench survive from the thirteenth century until its abolition in 1875. Formal and formulaic narratives of both civil and criminal proceedings are given in the plea rolls: KB 26 (1194–1272) and then in KB 27 until 1702. After 1702 entries for criminal business are found on the Crown Rolls (KB 28). Indictment files, arranged by term, are in KB 9 until 1675. Between 1675 and 1845 there are two series of indictments: KB 10 for London and Middlesex and KB 11 for the provincial or out-counties. From 1845 to 1875 there is once again a single series of indictments (KB 12). Indictments in special cases are in KB 8 (**38.9**). For a description of the kind of information that can be gained from indictments see **38.2**. Minute books, known as Crown side rule books, survive from 1589 in KB 21. Occasional witness statements survive in affidavits from the mid seventeenth century, but the survival is particularly good from the eighteenth century onwards (KB 1 and KB 2).

From 1329 the controlment rolls in KB 29 provide references to the entries of criminal business, in KB 27 and KB 28. Some contemporary indexes to indictments exist in IND 1. They are arranged alphabetically by the first letter of the surname of the accused, and then chronologically by term and supply the number of the indictment on the relevant indictment file. There are indexes to London and Middlesex defendants, 1673–1843; to provincial defendants, 1638–1704 and 1765–1843; and to London and Middlesex defendants and some defendants in northern counties, 1682–1699. There is a modern card index to entries on the plea rolls (KB 28), 1844–1859. From 1738, there is also a contemporary listing of the statements in KB 1 in KB 39. The great docket books and modern pye books in IND 1 can also be used as finding aids. Both give information about the way that cases were processed through the courts, but as they are arranged chronologically they are of limited use unless you already have some information about the date of the trial.

38.9 Sedition and high treason

Records of certain treason trials and other special cases were held in the so-called *Baga de Secretis* (KB 8). Unlike the other KB classes, KB 8 is well listed so it is comparatively easy to find cases. Some other records of, or relating to, treason trials, including lists of prisoners and convicts, are in KB 33, PC 1, TS 11 and TS 20; see the PRO leaflet *The Jacobite Risings of 1715 and 1745*. Many of the most celebrated cases in King's Bench are reported in detail in the published *State Trials*. Trials for seditious libel should be traced through the King's Bench records in the normal way (see **38.8**).

38.10 High Court of Admiralty

The criminal jurisdiction of the High Court of Admiralty was established by Act of Parliament in 1535; it lasted until 1834. Commissions of oyer and terminer and of gaol delivery were issued to the Admiral or his deputy authorizing them to try cases of piracy and other crimes committed on the high seas, according to the procedures of common law. Its criminal jurisdiction also included the English havens and the Thames below London Bridge (then the limit of the tidal Thames). Until about 1660 the court usually met at the Guildhall or in Southwark; after 1660 it began also to use the Old Bailey and from 1700 the admiralty sessions were always held there. Published reports of cases are sometimes included in the *Old Bailey Proceedings* (**38.3**). As explained above (see **38.2**), all formal legal records are written in heavily abbreviated Latin and in distinctive legal script until 1733, the information given in indictments is often fictitious, and trial records do not normally include transcripts of evidence.

The main series of criminal records is held in HCA 1, which is well listed but not yet searchable on PROCAT. It covers the period 1537–1834, with a gap between 1539–1574. The files contain a variety of different kinds of document such as lists of prisoners, bails and bonds, and jury panels, as well as indictments and depositions. It also contains material about cases tried by Vice Admiralty Courts in the maritime counties of England (excluding the Cinque Ports) and Wales as well as overseas. An index of persons and ships is available at the PRO; both the list and the index have been published by the List and Index Society (volumes 45 and 46). Criminal examinations for 1607–1609, 1612–1614 and 1661–1674 are in HCA 13/98, 99 and 142. Warrants relating to arrests on ships are in HCA 38 and those relating to executions are in HCA 55. Admiralty Out-Letters concerning the court, 1663–1815, is in ADM 2. Records relating to appeals from colonial admiralty courts are in DEL and PCAP.

The jurisdiction of the High Court of Admiralty passed to the new Central Criminal Court in 1834. In 1844 the judges of assize were allowed to try offences in any county. For the period 1834–1844, therefore, you should look for the records in the CRIM classes and after 1844 in the relevant ASSI classes.

The High Court of Admiralty also had jurisdiction over instance and prize cases; for a fuller description of instance and prize jurisdiction see **47e.1**.

38.11 Criminal trial registers, and other lists of prisoners to be tried, 1758–1892

Most records of criminals and criminal trials are not easy to use, as they are not usually arranged by name. If you have some information, however sketchy, about the date and place of trial then you should try using sheriffs' assize vouchers, the Criminal Registers or the Calendars of Prisoners. Please remember, however, that these sources will only help you to find those who were tried by jury: they will not help for trials held in ordinary magistrates' courts without a jury.

Sheriffs' assize vouchers, 1758–1832, give some information about prisoners to be tried at assizes (they do not include those tried at quarter sessions), including their sentences, the length of time they spent in prison and the costs of maintaining them. They are held in E 370/35–51.

The Criminal Registers are returns from the counties, bound up in alphabetical order of county. They show all persons charged with indictable offences, giving the date and result of the trial, sentence in the case of conviction, and dates of execution for those convicted on capital charges. The registers are in two series: HO 26, which covers Middlesex only, 1791–1849; and HO 27, which covers all England and Wales, 1805–1892 (including Middlesex from 1850). For 1807–1811 only, the Middlesex registers in HO 26 relate only to those tried at the Old Bailey; prisoners tried at the Middlesex and Westminster sessions are listed in HO 27.

Printed Calendars of Prisoners, 1868–1971, are held in HO 140 and also in CRIM 9 (for London, 1855–1949). Some are closed for 75 or 100 years. The calendars list prisoners to be tried at courts of assize and quarter sessions, and for each one gives age and occupation, level of literacy, the name and address

KENT.

A

CALENDAR

OF

PRISONERS FOR TRIAL

AT

THE SUMMER ASSIZES,

TO BE

HOLDEN AT MAIDSTONE,

On MONDAY, the 30th of JULY, 1832,

BEFORE

The Right Honourable CHARLES, LORD TENTERDEN,

Chief Justice of His Majesty's Court of King's Bench,

AND

The Honourable Sir JOHN BAYLEY, Knight,

One of the Barons of His Majesty's Court of Exchequer,

AND OF THE PRISONERS UNDER SENTENCE.

GEORGE DOUGLAS, ESQ. SHERIFF.

PRISONERS UNDER SENTENCE.

No:	Name.	Age.	Offence.	Sentence.	When Convicted.
1	Ann Tonnick,	60	Privately stealing in a shop	Transported for Life	Summer Assizes 1823
2	Susanna Hopson,	70	Stealing a quantity of Lead	Transported Seven Years	Lent Assizes 1828

PRISONERS FOR TRIAL.

No.	Name and Trade, &c.	Age	By whom and when Committed.	Offence.	Sentence, &c.
1	John Vant,	43	Rev. J. Poore, D. D. 1832, March 15	Stealing two lambs, value two pounds, the property of Thomas Young Greet and others, at Halstow	
2	John Williamson,	20			
3	Thomas Chambers, alias Challender, Laborers.	26			
4	John Green. Laborer.	28	T. Day, Esq. 17 Mayor of Maidstone.	Charged on one of the Coroner's Inquisitions, with having at Maidstone, maliciously caused to be taken by Mary Ann Masters, she being then quick with child, a quantity of white arsenic, with intent to procure a mis-carriage.	
5	John Button,	24	J. Jacobson, Esq. 22	Stealing one wether sheep, value thirty-four shillings, the property of William and John Austen, at Langley.	
6	William Hayes, Laborer.	28			

Figure 57 Calendar of prisoners awaiting trial at the Kent Summer 1832 assizes. For Button and Hayes (see Figure 55), it gives the extra detail of the Justice of the Peace who committed them for trial, and the date. John Green was charged on a coroner's inquest, held on the death of Mary Ann Masters: in his case the grand jury (which assessed the indictments) found no case to answer. (PRO, ASSI 94/2130)

of the committing magistrate, details of the alleged offence, verdict and sentence. Like the Criminal Registers they are arranged by county. Printed calendars of this kind were compiled from at least the early nineteenth century, and earlier calendars can sometimes be found in PCOM 2 as well as scattered amongst assizes classes. Copies are also sometimes to be found in local record offices. For the Old Bailey (Central Criminal Court) there are returns of prisoners to be tried, 1815–1849, in HO 16 and printed lists of defendants, 1782–1853, with the results of their trials, in HO 77.

38.12 Criminal trials: bibliography

K R Andrews, *Elizabethan Privateering* (1969)

J H Baker, 'Criminal courts and procedure at common law 1550–1800', in *Crime in England 1550–1800*, ed. J S Cockburn (London, 1977)

J M Beattie, *Crime and the Courts in England 1660–1800* (Oxford, 1986

E Berckman, *Victims of piracy: the admiralty court 1575–1678* (1979)

British Trials 1660–1900 (Chadwyck-Healy, 1990)

M Cale, *Law and society, an introduction to sources for criminal and legal history from 1800* (PRO, 1996)

J S Cockburn, ed., *Calendar of Assize Records, Home Circuit Indictments* (London, 1975–1995; Woodbridge, 1997)

D Crook, *Records of the general eyre* (London 1982)

H Deadman and E Scudder, *An introductory guide to the Corporation of London Record Office* (London, 1994)

F G Emmison and I Gray, *County records (quarter sessions, petty sessions, clerk of the peace and lieutenancy)* (Help for students of history 62, 2nd edn, Historical Association, 1987)

J S W Gibson, *Quarter Sessions Records for Family Historians: a Select List* (FFHS, 1995)

D T Hawkings, *Criminal ancestors, a guide to historical and criminal records in England and Wales,* (Sutton, 1992)

T B Howell and T J Howell, eds, *A complete collection of state trials . . .* (London, 1816–1826)

L A Knafla, *Kent at Law 1602, The county jurisdiction: assizes and sessions of peace* (London, 1994 continuing)

List and Index Society, *High Court of Admiralty, Oyer and Terminer Records (HCA 1), 1535–1834* (1969, vols 45 and 46)

J McDonell, ed., *Reports of State Trials, New Series* (London, 1858–1898, reprinted Abingdon, 1982)

R Paley, *Using Criminal Records* (PRO, 2001)

G Parry, *A Guide to the Records of Great Sessions in Wales* (Aberystwyth, 1995)

B H Putnam, ed., *Proceedings before the Justices of the Peace in the Fourteenth and Fifteenth Centuries* (1938)

S C Ratclif and others, eds, *Warwick County Records* (Warwick, 1935–1964)

G O Sayles, *Select cases in the court of King's Bench under Edward I* (Selden Society, 1936–1971), 7 vols

39

Remanded and convicted prisoners

◆ ◆ ◆

39.1 Introduction

Today, we are accustomed to regard imprisonment as one of the most likely punishments for criminal behaviour. This was not so in the past. Most offences either carried the death penalty (often commuted to transportation) or were punished by a fine and/or whipping. Each county had its own county gaol, which was primarily used to hold prisoners awaiting trial. Many counties also experimented with new prisons where vagrants and later also criminals could be put to work and subjected to disciplines that were intended to reform them. This kind of prison was often called a bridewell or house of correction. However, such initiatives were highly localized and met with varying degrees of success. Most prisons, whether designated as houses of correction or not, were simply used to house prisoners on remand. With certain exceptions (see **39.3**), their records, if they survive, are usually held in the local county record office. For an expert guide, use Paley, *Using Criminal Records*. A good overview to the wide range of records relating to imprisonment is provided by Hawkings's *Criminal Ancestors*, which provides transcripts and facsimiles, not only of material in the PRO but also in local record offices.

39.2 Conviction and sentence

There is no single central index of either prisoners or convicts. From the early nineteenth century (later eighteenth for London and Middlesex) the criminal trial registers and calendars of prisoners (see **38.11**) will help you to find some information about those who were convicted and sentenced after trial by jury. For prisoners convicted earlier than this, you will have to rely on the information you can gain from trial and associated records: the verdict and sentence are usually noted on the indictment and can also be traced through minute books and sheriffs' assize vouchers (see **38**).

As noted above, imprisonment was rarely used as a punishment in its own right until the nineteenth century. Those convicted of crimes were more likely to be sentenced to death, to transportation or to a fine or whipping. Few of those who were sentenced to death actually hanged: most were reprieved, or had their sentences commuted to transportation. Published pamphlet and newspaper literature is the best source for finding out about the lives of those who were hanged (see **38.3**). If you are really determined, you may find additional information about the costs of imprisonment and execution amongst the financial papers of sheriffs in E 370 (1714–1832), T 64 (1745–1785), T 90 (1733–1822) and T 207 (1823–1959). These records may also contain information about the cost of administering whippings.

If your convict was sentenced to transportation (or had a death sentence commuted to transportation), then turn to **40**. If you discover or already know that your convict was sentenced to death or to transportation or was actually transported, you should look at applications for clemency (**39.6**). In fact you should consider looking at these even if your convict received a lesser sentence, as the records created by such applications are often extremely informative, especially about family background and relationships.

Court orders for imprisonment or transfer from one prison to another, with details of the convict's penal history, 1843–1871, are in PCOM 5, with indexes in PCOM 6. They give the name of the convict (and any aliases), age, marital status, trade or occupation, crime, date and place of committal and conviction, sentence, information as to previous convictions and character; name and residence of next of kin, literacy level and religion, together with a physical description. Thereafter you can trace the history and course of the convict's imprisonment via the prison registers (**39.3**).

39.3 Registers of prisoners

Except for a brief period during the nineteenth century, prison records were not collected or retained centrally. Many are still kept by the prisons, or by the authorities that took them over. As a matter of policy, it has been decided that in future prison registers should be deposited in local record offices: essentially this means that most prison registers created after 1878 are more likely to be found in a local record office than in the PRO. Nevertheless the PRO does have various registers, mainly nineteenth century, of some criminal prisons (for debtors' prisons see **46**). These include the prison ships or 'hulks' that were moored in British coastal waters (at Woolwich, Chatham, Sheerness, Portsmouth and Plymouth) to house prisoners (usually, but not always, those awaiting transportation), 1776–1857, as well as some of those that were used in Gibraltar and Bermuda until 1875. Lists of those in prison on the night of a census will be included in the census returns from 1841 (see **2**).

Registers giving details about convicts in prisons and on the hulks are held in PCOM 2 (1770–1951), and registers of prisoners on the hulks, 1802–1849, are in HO 9. The information given is variable but is likely to include physical description (sometimes with a photograph), as well as details of occupation, marital status, aliases and previous character, as well as an indication of discharge or transfer to another prison. Similar registers, also including detailed descriptions of the prisoners, 1838–1875, are in HO 23 and HO 24, while KB 32/23 has a return of convicts in the Millbank Penitentiary in 1826, which gives name, offence, court of conviction, sentence, age, 'bodily state' and behaviour.

The quarterly returns of convicts in prisons and hulks, 1824–1876, in HO 8 can be used to trace details of behaviour, state of health, transfers to other gaols and eventual release. There are quarterly returns relating to the hulks, 1802–1831, in T 38; registers for the *Cumberland* and *Dolphin* hulks 1819–1834, are in ADM 6, and registers for the *Antelope, Coromandel, Dromedary,* and *Weymouth* hulks, 1823–1828 are in HO 7/3. Some registers and returns of prisoners in the hulks are also found in T 1, but the inadequacy of the lists makes searching extremely difficult. Some useful tips are given in Hawkings's *Criminal Ancestors,* which also has a useful (but now slightly dated) list of prison registers held in local record offices.

39.4 Registers of habitual criminals

Transportation to Australia was effectively stopped in 1857, although it was not formally ended until 1867. This meant that prisoners who would previously have been transported were instead kept imprisoned and subsequently released back into the community. In an attempt to dispel some of the anxiety this caused, local prisons were asked to compile registers of 'habitual criminals' – that is, prisoners convicted of any of the many crimes specified by the Habitual Criminals Act 1869, or by the Prevention of Crime Act 1871.

Printed forms were supplied with these registers: these required name and alias, age, description, trade, prison from which released, date of liberation, offence, sentence, term of supervision, intended residence, distinguishing marks

Figure 58 Prisoners admitted to the Pentonville National Penitentiary, July–August 1882. (PRO, PCOM 2/101)

and any previous convictions. In addition photographs were pasted onto the forms. These local registers were supposed to be sent to the central Habitual Criminals Registry, where an alphabetical national register of habitual criminals was compiled, of people thought likely to reoffend: the idea was to distribute the printed national register to police stations. The national register did not include the photographs. The first national register of habitual criminals covered December 1869 to March 1876, and included 12,164 people under 22,115 names, out of a total of 179,601 submitted in the local registers (PCOM 2/404).

The PRO does not have a full set of these national registers, but since they were compiled for local distribution, others may survive elsewhere. The registers in the PRO are to be found in PCOM 2/404 (1869–1876) and in MEPO 6/1–52 (1881–1882, 1889–1940); they are closed for 75 years from the date of creation. The PRO also has the local prison registers of habitual criminals for Birmingham, 1871–1875 (PCOM 2/296–299, 430–434) and Cambridge, 1875–1877 (PCOM 2/300). Other local registers are still in the custody of the prisons and constabularies that took over their responsibilities.

There are similarly informative registers of habitual drunkards, 1903–1914 (MEPO 6/77–88).

39.5 Licences and 'tickets of leave', 1853–1887

The increased use of imprisonment as a punishment naturally led to increased costs for the criminal justice system, both in terms of the maintenance of individual prisoners and in the costs of prison buildings. By 1853, there were considerable anxieties about the expansion in the prison population that would result from the diminishing numbers of convicts being transported to Australia. A system of licences was introduced to prevent this, by allowing convicts of good behaviour to be released before the completion of their sentences. The licences (popularly known as 'tickets of leave') could be revoked in cases of misbehaviour or reoffending.

These registers of licences to be at large give name, physical description, age, marital status, educational level, occupation, details of convictions, conduct whilst in prison, name and address of next of kin, religion and health. They are annotated with details of any subsequent revocation of the licence.

Male convicts	Registers in licence number order	1853–1887	PCOM 3
	Indexes	1853–1881	PCOM 6
Female convicts	Registers in licence number order	1853–1887	PCOM 4
	Indexes	1853–1885	PCOM 6

39.6 Pardons, appeals for mercy and other non-trial records

There were well over 300 offences carrying the death penalty by the end of the eighteenth century. However, only a minority of those sentenced to death were actually hanged. By the later nineteenth century, the death penalty had been removed from all but the most serious of crimes.

Pardons were freely granted, either unconditionally, or (from the 1600s onwards) on condition of transportation. Those sentenced to lesser penalties also applied for pardons. Not unnaturally, those who had influence to call upon, or who were able to claim mitigating factors, were more likely to succeed in having their sentences reduced or commuted. Petitions were based on such things as youth, extreme age, provocation, the existence of dependent relatives who might become a burden to the poor rates, and previous good character. For these reasons, applications for mercy often contain a lot of biographical information and are thus exceptionally useful for family history purposes.

Before 1784, you will need to look at the correspondence of the secretaries of state in the State Papers, Domestic, which continue after 1782 as Home Office General Correspondence (HO 42). Much of the early correspondence of the secretaries of state has been published and should be available to you at a good reference library or by inter-library loan, as well as at the PRO. Records for the reign of Henry VIII have been published as *Letters and Papers . . . of Henry VIII*. For his son, Edward VI and subsequent monarchs, the series is known as the *Calendar of State Papers, Domestic*, and currently extends from 1547 to 1704. Similar records for the period 1760–1772 are published as the *Calendar of Home Office Papers*. Individuals are often not indexed under their names, but under 'Pardons'. For the period 1654–1717, pardons on condition of transportation are entered on the Patent Rolls (C 66) but such enrolments are in Latin, and in any case rarely contain the kind of detail that family historians need.

Separate series of papers relating to applications for mercy start in 1784. The judges' reports in HO 47 (1784–1829) are a particularly rich source of information. They often include virtual transcripts of the trial evidence (sometimes annotated with the judge's opinion of the veracity of witnesses and the credulity of the jurors) together with character references (both for and against the convict) and other personal information. Volunteers are currently working on this series, and the descriptive list will be entered into PROCAT as each volume is finished. Other letters and statements from trial judges, 1816–1840, are in HO 6. They are somewhat formal, but do include recommendations for mercy together with useful supporting information about the convict and his/her crime.

You may also find it worthwhile to look at the Home Office General Correspondence in HO 42 (1782–1820) and Home Office Criminal Papers Old Series, 1849–1871, in HO 12 (approached via the registers in HO 14). Similar papers after 1871 are in HO 45 and HO 144.

Surviving petitions for mercy are in HO 17 (1819–1840) and HO 18 (1839–1854). They are arranged in coded bundles and you will need to use the registers in HO 19 to identify them. The registers are arranged by date of receipt of petition, and give the name of the convict, date and place of trial, offence, code number of the bundle in which the petition was filed and, in most but not all cases, the outcome of the application. Incidentally, the indexes do not start in 1819 but in 1797. There are also petitions in HO 48, HO 49, HO 54 and HO 56, but the lists are inadequate which makes these classes extremely difficult to search.

Formal records of pardons and reprieves are given by the Home Office warrants in HO 13 (1782–1849) and HO 15 (1850–1871). The modern registers of remissions and pardons, 1887–1960 (HO 188) are far more informative, as details of the cases are given and reasons for the decision are given; each volume has its own rough index.

39.7 Executions

Although most records about condemned persons should be traced as if they were ordinary convicts, there are some additional series of records relating specifically to the hanged, mainly in HO 163 (1899–1921), MEPO 3, and PCOM 9. HO 336 contains the complete records of nine condemned prisoners in order to illustrate the kind of information that was kept on such individuals. Background information on the way the death penalty was implemented can be found in PCOM 8, with more discursive contextual discussion in HO 42 and HO 45. There is no comprehensive list either of those executed or of the men who executed them. However, HO 334/1 contains a register of prison burials (1834–1969) which could provide the basis of establishing a list of the executed. Some personal details about executioners can be found in HO 144 and PCOM 8.

39.8 Remanded and convicted prisoners: bibliography

M Cale, *Law and society, an introduction to sources for criminal and legal history from 1800* (PRO, 1996)
Calendar of Home Office Papers (3 vols, London, 1873–1881)
Calendar of State Papers, Domestic (London, 1856–1972)
D T Hawkings, *Bound for Australia* (Phillimore, 1987)
D T Hawkings, *Criminal Ancestors, a guide to historical criminal records in England and Wales* (Sutton, 1992)
W B Johnson, *The English Prison Hulks* (revised edn, Phillimore, 1970)
Letters and papers . . . of Henry VIII (London, 1864–1932)
S McConville, *History of English Prison Administration 1750–1877* (London, 1981)
S McConville, *English Local Prisons, 1860–1900: next only to death* (London, 1995)
R Paley, *Using Criminal Records* (PRO, 2001)
S and B Webb, *English Prisons under Local Government* (reprinted, London, 1963)
R Whitmore, *Victorian and Edwardian Crime and Punishment* (London, 1978)

40

Convicted prisoners transported abroad

◆ ◆ ◆

40.1 Transportation: an introduction

As explained in **39**, the range of punishments open to the authorities for serious criminal offences before the nineteenth century was very limited: it was quite literally a choice between enforcing the death penalty or releasing criminals back into the community. The expansion of Britain's overseas territories added a further possibility. Now convicted criminals could be sentenced to a period of exile, during which they would be removed from his/her previous bad associates, be forced to work productively and thereby learn new habits of industry and self-discipline. At the same time, they would benefit the development of the colonial economy.

Transportation, for the imperial government, was not a question of simply dumping human refuse on the colonies: it was genuinely thought to be effective, efficient and humane. Those who were transported were often quite young: it was after all the young who were most likely to benefit from a new life in a new world, and who were most likely to be fit enough to supply the productive labour that that new world needed. The colonial authorities, not unnaturally, tended to take a more jaundiced view of the benefits of transportation, and bitterly resented it.

After 1615, as a result of an order by the Privy Council, it became increasingly common for a pardon to be offered to convicts who had been sentenced to death, on condition of transportation overseas. In 1718 an Act of Parliament standardized transportation to America at 14 years for those who had been sentenced to death and introduced a new penalty, transportation for seven years – as a sentence in its own right for a range of non-capital offences.

Some 40,000 people had been transported to America when the system came to an abrupt halt in 1776 because of the outbreak of the American Revolution. Prisoners who had been sentenced to transportation had to be held in prison instead. The overcrowding that ensued soon resulted in the creation of floating prisons or 'hulks' (see **39**), but of course they too soon became overcrowded. A solution took over ten years to find, but in 1787 the 'first fleet' set out for Australia to found a penal colony in New South Wales. Transportation to Van Diemen's Land (Tasmania) began in 1803.

Transportation was at its height in the 1830s and was probably already in decline when, as a result of the Penal Servitude Act of 1853, it was removed from all but the most serious offences. In 1857 it was effectively abolished, although the Home Secretary retained the right to impose transportation in specific cases until 1867. It is estimated that over 160,000 people were transported to Australia and Tasmania between 1787 and 1867: in the 1830s 4,000 people were being transported every year.

The National Archives of Ireland have an online database of transportation records, 1791–1868, at www.nationalarchives.ie. Unfortunately, the PRO does not have any such tool as yet. However, we do have a microfiche and CD-ROM index to convicts who arrived in New South Wales and Van Diemen's Land between 1788 and 1842, and to the ships that transported them, provided by the Genealogical Society of Victoria. Many of the records relating to voluntary emigration (see **14**) may also contain details of convicts or ex-convicts. For records of trials resulting in transportation, see **38**. For records of prisons and prison hulks, in which convicts were housed for various periods prior to transportation, see **39**.

40.2 Transportation to America and the West Indies

If you are looking for an individual who may have been transported to America or the West Indies, a good starting point is Coldham's *The Complete Book of Emigrants in Bondage, 1614–1775*, based on records in the PRO as well as in local record offices. A supplementary volume, adding about 3,000 further names, was published in 1992. Coldham lists transported convicts and gives, where known:

- date and place of trial
- occupation
- month of embarkation and landing
- name of ship
- destination

You can move on from this to other published works, since (with the exception of trial records) most of the PRO's original sources relating to transportation in this period have been published. An earlier version of Coldham's research findings, published as *Bonded Passengers to America* (but also covering transportation to the West Indies) includes a readable history of the system and gives a detailed overview of the published sources that are available.

Coldham's books will give you enough to start looking for the trial record. If your convict was transported before 1718 or was transported after 1718 for 14 years, then you should look for the trial amongst the records of assize or assize equivalent courts. If your convict was transported after 1718 for a period of seven years then the trial could have been either at an assize or assize equivalent court, or at quarter sessions (see **38**). Remember that not all those who were sentenced to transportation actually went: perhaps your convict was successful in an application for mercy (see **39.6**). If your convict was involved in a particularly notorious trial then you may find that there are published works available that will save you much time and effort. For example, lists of those transported after the Monmouth rebellion are included in Wigfield's *The Monmouth Rebels 1685*.

The PRO also holds Treasury money books (T 53) which include details of payments by the Treasury to contractors engaged to arrange transportation between 1716 and 1772. Until October 1744 names of all those to be transported from the Home Counties are listed, together with names of ships and their captains. Thereafter only totals for each county are given. Until 1742 the colony of destination is usually recorded. Similar information is given in a broken run of transportation lists, 1747–1772, in T 1.

Colonial Office correspondence with America and the West Indies (CO 5) includes material on all aspects of transportation to the American colonies. Much of the material relevant to transportation amongst the records of the Treasury and of the Colonial Office has been published (**40.5**), and is therefore available at major reference libraries, as well as at the PRO. For other records relating to the American and West Indian colonies which may include details of convicts or ex-convicts, as well as free emigrants, see **14.5**. For records in the United States, see **14.6**.

40.3 Transportation to Australia

As with transportation to America and the West Indies, it is advisable to start your search with published sources. For a general overview of the kind of documents that are available and what sort of information they contain, you will find Hawkings' *Bound for Australia* and *Criminal Ancestors* particularly useful as they provide transcripts and facsimiles of a wide range of records relating to imprisonment and transportation. Readers in Australia should know that microfilm copies of many PRO documents are available in Australia at the National Library in Canberra and at the Mitchell Library in Sydney. The PRO has a microfiche and CD-ROM index to convicts who arrived in New South Wales and Van Diemen's Land between 1788 and 1842, and to the ships that transported them, provided by the Genealogical Society of Victoria.

Most family historians start by searching for the trial records, but as explained in **38**, such records are rarely very informative. Remember that no matter how short the sentence, few people would ever be able to return from Australia and that the voyage was long and dangerous: applications for mercy were commonplace and it is far better to start there than with the formal court record.

In order to get started you will need to have some idea *either* of the date and place of trial, so that you can trace the convict forward, *or* of the date and preferably the ship on which the convict arrived in Australia so that you can trace him or her back. You can find this information in a number of ways. The Convict Transportation Registers, 1787–1867 (HO 11) provide the name of the ship on which the convict sailed as well as the date and place of conviction and the term of the sentence. They are not indexed by name of convict, but if you know the name of the ship and preferably also when it either left England or

Figure 59 Convicts working under armed guard at Chatham dockyard, before being transported, 1828. A hulk can be seen in the background. (Mary Evans Picture Library)

arrived in Australia, it should be relatively easy to find the convict. The names of the convicts on the first fleet which left England in May 1787, reaching Australia in January 1788, are listed by Fidlon and Ryan in *The First Fleeters*. A list of convicts transported on the second fleet of ships, which left in 1789, is in Ryan's *The Second Fleet Convicts*. Censuses or musters were taken periodically in New South Wales and Tasmania between 1788 and 1859. Convicts and former convicts had to identify themselves as such and to supply information about their dates and ships of arrival (see **40.4**). Once you know when and where the convict was sentenced it is comparatively easy to search for an application for clemency (see **39.6**) and/or for the trial record (**38**).

It was possible for wives to accompany their convict husbands, and some wives applied to do so. Their petitions survive for 1819–1844 (PC 1/67–92) and from 1849–1871 (HO 12, identified via the registers in HO 14).

Privy Council correspondence, 1819–1844 (PC 1/67–92) contains additional material about transportation as do the Privy Council registers (PC 2), which also give lists of convicts transported for 14 years or less. Contracts with agents to transport the prisoners, with full lists of ships and convicts, 1842–1867, are in the Treasury Solicitor's Department general series papers (TS 18/460–525 and 1308–1361). Reports on the medical condition of the convicts while at sea may be found in the Admiralty medical journals, 1817–1856 (ADM 101), and in the Admiralty Transport Department surgeon-superintendents' journals, 1858–1867 (MT 32).

40.4 Settlement in Australia

Musters or censuses, primarily but not exclusively concerned with the convict population, were taken periodically in New South Wales and Tasmania between 1788 and 1859 (HO 10). The New South Wales census of 1828 (HO 10/21–27) is the most complete, and is available in a published edition by Sainty and Johnson. It contains the names of more than 35,000 people with details of age, religion, family, place of residence, occupation and stock or land held. Whether each settler came free, or as a convict (or was born in the colony) is recorded; and date of arrival and the name of the ship are given. The musters for New South Wales and Norfolk Island, 1800–1802, for New South Wales, Norfolk Island and Van Diemen's Land, 1811, and for New South Wales in 1822, 1823, 1824, 1825 and 1837 have also been published. Copies of all these works are available at the PRO. Papers relating to convicts in New South Wales and Tasmania (HO 10) contain material about convicts' pardons and tickets of leave from New South Wales and Tasmania, 1835–1859. Home Office records also include some information about deaths of convicts in New South Wales, 1829–1834 (HO 7/2). There are a clutch of conditional pardons for convicts in Western Australia, 1863–1873, scattered in HO 45: try a search on 'Australia AND pardons' in PROCAT to get the references.

Colonial Office records relating to Australia sometimes note individual convicts as well as policy decisions, but they are not easy to search for particular named individuals. There are, however, lists of convicts, together with emigrant settlers, 1801–1821, in New South Wales Original Correspondence (CO 201). Names can also be traced in New South Wales entry books from 1786 (CO 202), and registers from 1849 (CO 360 and CO 369). Records of the superintendent of convicts in New South Wales, 1788–1825, are now held in the State Archives of New South Wales; the PRO holds microfilm copies (CO 207). Some of the lists from these records have been printed in Robson, *The Convict Settlers of Australia*.

For other records which may provide relevant information, see **14.8**.

40.5 Convict transportation: bibliography

C M Andrews, *Guide to the materials for American history to 1793 in the Public Record Office of Great Britain* (Washington, 1912–1914)

C Bateson, *The Convict Ships, 1787–1868* (Glasgow, 2nd edn, 1969)

C J Baxter, *Muster and lists of NSW and Norfolk Island, 1800–1802* (Sydney, 1988)

C J Baxter, *General Musters of NSW, Norfolk Island and Van Diemen's Land, 1811* (Sydney, 1987)

C J Baxter, *General muster and lands and stock muster of NSW, 1822* (Sydney, 1988)

C J Baxter, *General Muster of New South Wales, 1823, 1824, 1825* (Sydney, 1995)

J M Beattie, *Crime and courts in England 1660–1800* (Oxford, 1986)

N G Butlin, C W Cromwell and K L Suthern, *General Return of convicts in NSW 1837* (Sydney, 1987)

Calendar of State Papers, Colonial, America and West Indies, 1574–1738 (London, 1869–1969)

Calendar of Treasury Books, 1660–1718 (London, 1904–1962)

Calendar of Treasury Papers, 1557–1728 (London, 1868–1889)

Calendar of Treasury Books and Papers, 1729–1745 (London, 1898–1903)

P W Coldham, *Bonded Passengers to America, 1615–1775* (Baltimore, 1983)

P W Coldham, 'Felons Transported to America', *Genealogists' Magazine*, vol. 26, pp. 61–65

P W Coldham, *The Complete Book of Emigrants in Bondage, 1614–1775* (Baltimore, 1987, Supplement, 1992)

A R Ekirch, *Bound for America: The Transportation of British Convicts to the Colonies, 1718–1775* (Oxford, 1990)

P G Fidlon and R J Ryan, eds, *The First Fleeters* (Sydney, 1981)

Friends of the East Sussex Record Office, *East Sussex Sentences of Transportation at Quarter Sessions, 1790–1854* (Lewes, 1988)

D T Hawkings, *Bound for Australia* (Chichester, 1987)

D T Hawkings, *Criminal Ancestors, a guide to historical criminal records in England and Wales* (Sutton, revised edn, 1996)

R Hughes, *The Fatal Shore: A History of Transportation of Convicts to Australia, 1781–1868* (London, 1987)

Journals of the Board of Trade and Plantations, 1704–1782 (London, 1920–1938)

R Paley, *Using Criminal Records* (PRO, 2001)

Public Record Office, *Australian Convicts: Sources in the Public Record Office* (Information Leaflet)

L L Robson, *The Convict Settlers of Australia* (Melbourne, 1981)

R J Ryan, *The Second Fleet Convicts* (Sydney, 1982)

M R Sainty and K A Johnson, eds, *New South Wales: Census . . . November 1828* (Sydney, 1980)

W M Wigfield, *The Monmouth Rebels 1685* (Somerset Record Society, 1985)

I Wyatt, ed., *Transportees from Gloucester to Australia, 1783–1842* (Bristol and Gloucester Archaeological Society, 1988)

41

Land ownership and tenancy

◆ ◆ ◆

41.1 Introduction

In England and Wales, records of the ownership and transfer of particular lands are difficult to locate, as there was no national system of registration before the nineteenth century. Registries of deeds were established in the Bedford Level in the fens, in the three Ridings of Yorkshire and in Middlesex early in the eighteenth century; the registry in Middlesex closed in 1940, but those in Yorkshire continued to operate until the 1970s. The Bedford Level register can be seen at the Cambridgeshire Record Office and the Middlesex register at the London Metropolitan Archives; the registers for the North, East and West Ridings of Yorkshire are in the respective county record offices (addresses in **48**).

Although a national Land Registry was established in 1862, registration was voluntary and little used. Compulsory registration on sale was introduced in London in 1899 and now covers all the major conurbations, although some rural areas are still excluded and there are still many unregistered properties in the areas where registration is compulsory. The Land Registry does not normally hold original deeds once property has been registered. General enquiries concerning the registration of a property can be made to the Land Registry (address in **48**), by letter or telephone. Personal visits can be made either to the Land Registry headquarters in Lincoln's Inn Fields, or to the relevant district office.

The PRO holds hundreds of thousands of property-related records; these have come into its custody either because the particular property was at some point in the possession of the Crown or government, or because the property was the subject of litigation and documents were presented as evidence to the courts and never reclaimed; or because documents were enrolled in the records of a court to demonstrate transfer or proof of ownership. However, there is no general index to the plethora of documents available for inspection and searching may be difficult without some idea of when, where and why a conveyance took place. Nevertheless, it is always worth a search in PROCAT, using the place, as more material is added. Some understanding of the varieties of landholding and transfer prevailing at different periods is useful; for instance, records discussed in this chapter may relate to property held by various different types of tenure (e.g. feudal, freehold, leasehold, copyhold) and may reflect transfers by any one of a

Figure 60 Advice for husbandmen, published in the sixteenth century. This was the beginning of a long publication boom in such manuals. (Woodcut, Private Collection/ Bridgeman Art Library)

number of different methods (e.g. royal grant, agreement between parties, surrender and admission).

The records of tithe redemption, enclosures and land valuation, discussed in **42**, also provide information on landowners in a particular place.

41.2 Manorial records

A large proportion of the records of landholding and transfer in the PRO relate to property on manors. The manor is usually defined as a type of estate, in existence before the time of the Norman Conquest, lasting into the twentieth century and in a very few cases to the present day, which came to be characterized by the right of the lord to hold courts exercising jurisdiction of a particular nature over that estate. These courts were responsible for the regulation of local affairs, including landholding, as defined in the customs of the manor.

One of the principal courts was the court leet, held by rights devolved from the Crown, which might also include the right to hold the view of frankpledge, which ensured that all men over the age of twelve were grouped together in bands, called tithing groups, and were mutually responsible for their good behaviour. The court leet had a criminal jurisdiction in the early period, but this was gradually lost, so that it later dealt with minor misdemeanours and such matters as nuisances and obstructions. It was often responsible for the assizes of bread and ale, to maintain standards of quality and quantity in those commodities, as well as the election of officials such as the constable, ale-taster and the head of each tithing group.

The other main court, the court baron, held by the lord of the manor in his own right, supervised primarily all matters to do with the lands and tenures of customary and villein tenants including transfers of property, the regulation of agriculture in the manor and the settlement of disputes (not involving bloodshed) between tenants, as well as choosing the lord's officials, such as the reeve and the beadle. Although the court leet was usually only held twice a year, and the court baron as often as every three weeks, the courts were sometimes held together and in some cases, distinctions in the court rolls between the business of the courts may be blurred.

Tenants might hold land in a manor by one of several types of tenure:

- freehold;
- customaryhold (in villeinage, copyhold, at will), if this existed in the manor;
- leasehold.

Freehold tenants' property was not regulated by the manor courts and therefore, transfers were not recorded there. However, freeholders paid rents, were obliged to attend the court baron, where they might appear as jurors, and made payments on entry into property ('reliefs') and on the death of tenants ('heriots', the 'best beast', or else cash), all of which may be recorded in the court rolls.

Customary tenants' property was entirely regulated by the manor courts and transfers performed and recorded there; customary tenure being either of inheritance or for life or lives. The most prevalent form of customaryhold tenure was copyhold, so-called because tenants held their land 'by copy of court roll' and according to the custom of the manor. Copyhold land was transferred in the ceremony of surrender and admission, usually carried out on behalf of the lord by the steward of the manor in court. In the nineteenth and twentieth centuries, the steward was very often a solicitor and the ceremony might take place in his office, out of court. Firstly, the land was surrendered to the lord of the manor from whom it was held, then regranted and the new tenants admitted. These conveyances of copyhold property were entered on the court rolls and the tenant generally given a copy of the relevant entry as a record. Copyholders were also obliged to attend the lord's court and paid rents; in the early middle ages, they were obliged to perform labour services for the lord, but on most manors, by the sixteenth century, these were converted into money payments. They might also be liable to make cash payments on entry into property ('fines') and heriots on the death of tenants.

In the early modern period, leasehold became more popular and also copyhold tenure was sometimes converted into leasehold. Tenants held leases which ran either for a term of years, or for lives – usually that of the tenant and two others. Rents were payable for leasehold property, often with payments in kind and some obligations, as well as heriots and payments on renewal or granting of a lease. Records of such payments may be found in the court rolls and in some cases, in separate registers of leases. However, lists of tenants by type of tenure, their holdings and rents may often be found in the different types of manorial survey (see **41.4**).

Copyhold tenure could, from the early modern period, be converted to leasehold, as noted above, or freehold ('enfranchised'), but the process of enfranchisement was only addressed by legislation from the mid nineteenth century onwards. Copyhold tenure was finally abolished by the Law of Property Acts, 1922 and 1924, which virtually brought the life of the manor to a close. The PRO holds nineteenth- and twentieth-century files of copyhold enfranchisements in MAF 9 (searchable in PROCAT by place and name) and MAF 20 (searchable only by place). Manorial incidents, the lord's residual financial interest in this newly enfranchised land, including entry fines, reliefs and heriots, were also abolished under the Acts and twentieth-century files relating to compensation for manorial incidents are found in MAF 13 and MAF 27. Further material on these subjects will be found in MAF 48, MAF 76 and MAF 233.

Apart from court rolls, the other main types of record produced by manorial administration were rentals and surveys (see **41.4**) and accounts (see **41.5**), as well as several kinds of subsidiary documents, including estreats, minutes, inquisitions and registers of court attendance. Manorial documents of all kinds are held in the PRO and in many other repositories. The main means of discovering their existence, nature and location is the Manorial Documents Register, held and maintained by the Historic Manuscripts Commission (address in **48**). This register, covering England and Wales, mostly consists of a slip index; however, it is undergoing gradual revision and computerization and updated sections comprising Wales, Yorkshire, Hampshire and the Isle of Wight are now available on the HMC website (www.hmc.gov.uk/mdr); Norfolk is forthcoming. The revised sections include all known manorial documents for that particular area, wherever they are held, including in the PRO. The published and unpublished lists of court rolls, surveys and accounts in the PRO further described below have been thoroughly trawled for manorial material relating to those areas and many original documents have been checked during the course of revision. Some material in the published lists, however, has proved not to be manorial in origin and therefore may not appear in the revised register. Full details of criteria used to distinguish manorial and non-manorial documents may also be found in the website in a section devoted to manorial records in the PRO; the website also contains sections giving full details of the register, information on manorial documents and a comprehensive bibliography on manorial and related subjects, among others.

It may not be easy to discover whether an individual was a manorial tenant or not. A clear pointer would be, for example, if a copy of court roll is found with other deeds among family papers. Without clues such as these, it will be necessary to discover which manor or manors covered the township or parish of residence of an individual and then consult any surviving manorial records speculatively. This may be a time consuming process, unless, of course, the relevant court rolls have been published, such as those for Wakefield in Yorkshire, printed in the Yorkshire Archaeological Society Record Series. It may not be easy to identify the particular manor or manors, as there might have been several manors in one parish or the property of one manor might have been scattered over several parishes. Boundaries of manors are sometimes difficult to reconstruct and boundaries of individual holdings within manors may be impossible to map, even if clearly described in the court rolls. However, if it can be shown that an individual was a tenant of a particular manor and records have survived, then these records may provide an invaluable source of information about him, his property, and possibly some generations of his family, particularly the court rolls.

41.3 Court rolls

Court rolls, which may date from the thirteenth to the twentieth centuries, are the central records of the manor court. They generally either record proceedings as the court was being held, although some written material may have been prepared before the court session, or were drawn up afterwards. To be able to read the documents, it is useful to have a knowledge of old handwriting, as well as a knowledge of Latin, as this is the language of most court rolls from the earliest times until 1733. Although the records are also often highly abbreviated, they make regular use of certain formulaic phrases, which once grasped, can be easily recognized. During the Commonwealth period (1649–1660) and after 1733, court rolls are written in English. For assistance with reading court rolls and other documents, see the section on manorial records in **41.12**, particularly the works by Bass, Haydon, Harrop and Stuart. As the name suggests, court rolls may be found in roll form, possibly containing records of courts held in one manor over a period of years, or of one court held for several manors. Court rolls might also be found on single sheets of parchment, or sometimes in the form of a series of volumes or court books. Although court rolls exist in continuous series covering many years for some manors, this is not the case for the majority of manors, and for some, no records may exist at all. The Manorial Documents Register should be consulted for details of the existence and location of any known surviving court rolls for a particular manor.

If court rolls have survived, they are of great interest to local and family historians for the wealth of detail about the locality which they may contain, but the records of property transactions relating to customary land will probably be of most importance to the genealogist, particularly customary land of inheritance. Much litigation took place in the Exchequer which involved the taking of depositions locally about the varying customs (customary law) of individual manors. If you are interested in a particular manor, it may be worth a PROCAT search in E 134 to see if anything of interest exists: see **47c**.

Deaths of tenants since the last court were reported in the court baron, from

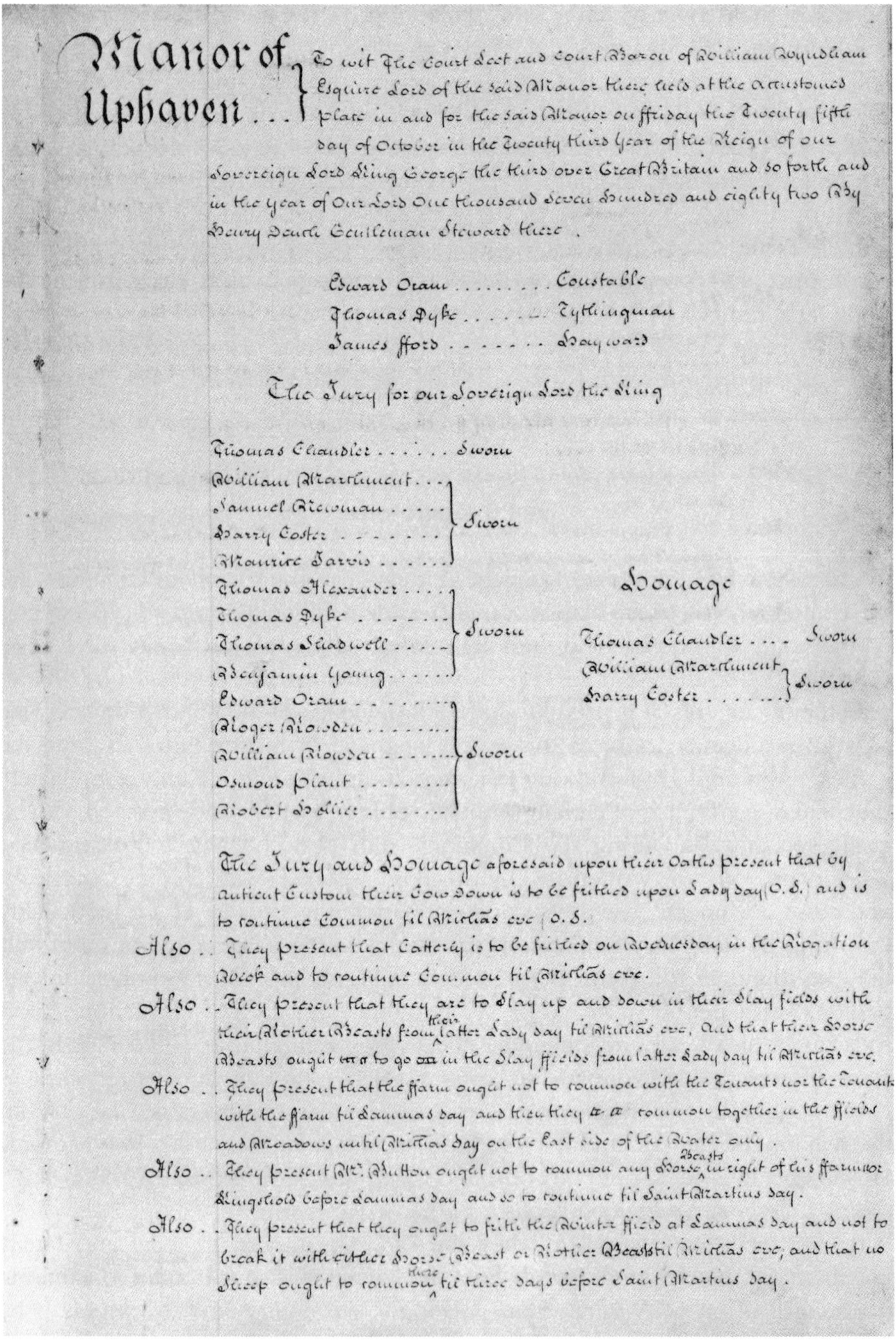

Manor of Uphaven . . . } To wit The Court Leet and Court Baron of William Wyndham Esquire Lord of the said Manor there held at the accustomed place in and for the said Manor on ffriday the Twenty fifth day of October in the Twenty third Year of the Reign of our Sovereign Lord King George the third over Great Britain and so forth and in the year of Our Lord One thousand Seven Hundred and eighty two By Henry Dench Gentleman Steward there .

Edward Oram . . . . Constable
Thomas Dyke . . . . . . Tythingman
James ffford . . . . Hayward

The Jury for our Sovereign Lord the King

Thomas Chandler . . . . Sworn
William Marchment . . . } Sworn
Samuel Newman . . . . }
Harry Coster . . . . }
Maurice Jarvis . . . . . }
Thomas Alexander . . . . } Sworn
Thomas Dyke . . . . }
Thomas Shadwell . . . . }
Benjamin Young . . . . . }
Edward Oram . . . . } Sworn
Roger Blowden . . . . . . }
William Blowden . . . . . }
Osmond Plant . . . . }
Robert Hillier . . . . }

Homage

Thomas Chandler . . . . Sworn
William Marchment } Sworn
Harry Coster . . . . . . }

The Jury and Homage aforesaid upon their Oaths present that by antient Custom their Cow Down is to be frithed upon Lady day (O. S.) and is to continue Common til Michas eve (O. S.

Also . . They present that Catterly is to be frithed on Wednesday in the Rogation Week and to continue Common til Michas eve.

Also . . They present that they are to Hay up and down in their Hay fields with their Mother Beasts from their latter Lady day til Michas eve, and that their Horse Beasts ought to go in the Hay ffields from latter Lady day til Michas eve.

Also . . They present that the ffarm ought not to common with the Tenants nor the Tenants with the ffarm til Lammas day and then they common together in the ffields and Meadows until Michas day on the East side of the Water only .

Also . . They present Mr. Button ought not to common any Horse Beasts in right of his ffarm nor Kingstold before Lammas day and so to continue til Saint Martins day .

Also . . They present that they ought to frith the Winter ffield at Lammas day and not to break it with either Horse Beast or other Beasts til Michas eve, and that no Sheep ought to common there til three days before Saint Martins day .

Figure 61 The manor court book of Uphaven or Upavon, Wiltshire, survives from 1650–1824 and details generations of manorial tenants and the regulation of manorial life. These entries date from Friday 24th October 1800.

They show dates given as regnal years (40 George III) and the adherence of country people to old Lady Day and old Michaelmas in the regulation of the use of common land, nearly 50 years after these dates had shifted (see **1.16**). (PRO, TS 19/4) which a date of death for individual tenants may be inferred. The subsequent admissions of heirs may also be of interest, as the relationship between the former tenant and his heir should be made plain. Various patterns of inheritance were used on manors; according to the custom of the manor, the heir might be the eldest son (primogeniture) or the youngest son (Borough English) or in certain areas of the country such as Kent and parts of Wales, the property might be divided between all the sons or all the daughters, if there were no sons (gavelkind). If the heir was not the son or daughter of a former tenant, but a more distant relation, then this might also be explained. If court rolls do survive in good series, then they may provide a source of information about individuals which may run back to a time before the start of the parish registers and beyond. They may also provide continuity where parish registers contain gaps, especially during the Commonwealth period.

Most of the PRO's holdings of court rolls come from manors which formed part of the Crown lands or were documents used as evidence in legal cases. Apart from those areas included in the online Manorial Documents Register, there are various means of reference to these records. The majority of court rolls in the PRO are found in SC 2 and DL 30; there are over 800 bundles divided between these two series, the first 251 of which are included in a published list containing a place-name index: the *List and Index of Court Rolls* (Lists and Indexes, vol. VI). This list also contains references to a few court rolls in other series. For the rest of the material in SC 2 and DL 30, there are lists for both series, also containing indexes. The 'Union Indexes to Court Rolls', available in the Map Room, gives references to court rolls in a wide variety of other series.

41.4 Rentals and surveys

The second major group of manorial records consists of the various types of manorial survey, containing written details of the manor, including details of property, tenants, their tenure and rents, and in the early period, services. Although there are some twelfth-century surveys, this form of manorial document did not become common until the mid thirteenth century. Among the earliest types of survey are:

- the custumal, a list of tenants with the customs by which they held their property;
- the extent, a list of every item on the manor with its valuation;
- the terrier, a plot-by-plot description of lands;
- the rental, a list of tenants and their rents owed to the lord.

By the sixteenth century, however, some surveys began to consist of three elements: a written description of the boundaries of the manor, a list of the customs and a rental or rent roll. These were made at a special court baron, the court of survey, before commissioners of survey appointed by the lord and a jury of survey, who would answer a detailed list of questions concerning all aspects of the manor. Tenants were expected to attend the court with their record of title, so that the rental could be compiled. The rental will generally list tenants by type of tenure – freehold, leasehold and customaryhold, including copyhold – and may give brief details of the property held by each tenant, including acreage, amount of rent payable, services owed, if any, sometimes including names of former tenants or stating how present tenants came to occupy the property, for example, by inheritance, which may lead to relationships being stated. With leasehold property, the duration of the lease may be given, together with the date of entry. Although this kind of survey became common, other types, such as rentals and rent rolls, continued to be made. During the sixteenth century, the profession of surveyor began to develop and, increasingly, a surveyor may have been employed to make the survey and in some cases a map may also have been produced, accurately measured and drawn to scale, although manorial maps are very rare before 1600.

Surveys were often created as part of the routine of estate management and may have been made on a regular basis; however, they were often made before or after a change in ownership of the manor, or if the manor was the subject of litigation. Surveys may cover an individual manor, or an estate made up of manors; therefore, they may exist as a single sheet of parchment or in a large volume. By the eighteenth century, documents such as rentals may normally be set out in regular columns under clear headings, kept in a series of annual volumes. The early surveys are in Latin, but from the sixteenth century, surveys are often found in English.

Surveys of all kinds are found among manorial records in the PRO and the principal finding-aid for these is the *List of Rentals and Surveys* (Lists and Indexes, vol. XXV) which lists and indexes all relevant documents in DL 29, DL 42–44, E 36, E 142, E 164, E 315, E 317, LR 2, SC 11, SC 12, SP 10–18, and SP 46, including the type of document known as a valor, which could be described as a survey, but was used for financial purposes, being compiled annually from the manorial accounts. Of special interest are the detailed Parliamentary Surveys (E 317) of Crown lands taken in the Commonwealth period (see **41.6**). This volume is supplemented by the *List of Rentals and Surveys: Addenda* (Lists and Indexes, Supplementary Series, vol. XIV), which contains references to documents mostly in SC 12 and E 142, but includes isolated references to documents in C 47/37/8, C 205 and T 1/462. Other examples of surveys may be found scattered throughout the following series: CRES 2, CRES 5, CRES 34, CRES 35, CRES 36, CRES 38, CRES 39, DL 30, DL 32 (including transcripts of Parliamentary Surveys of Duchy lands), LR 9, LR 10, LR 13, LRRO 5, LRRO 11, LRRO 12, LRRO 37 (including duplicate Parliamentary Surveys), LRRO 67, SP 13 and WARD 2. Maps and plans relating to manors may be found in ADM 79, DL 31 and F 17, but mostly in LRRO 1.

Besides court rolls, the series of Chancery Masters' Exhibits (C 103–116 and C 171) and similar classes of the Exchequer (E 140 and E 192) are also worth exploring for surveys and other material. Surveys taken as a result of litigation or for other reasons will also be found in Special Commissions (E 178), which cover the period from the sixteenth century to the nineteenth century and can be identified by consulting the *List of Special Commissions and Returns in the*

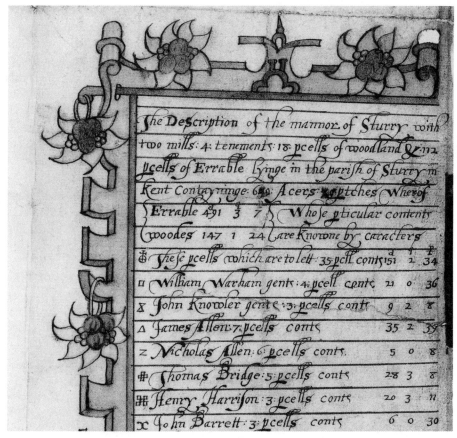

Figure 62 The 1643 map of the manor of Sturry, Kent, includes a key that lists tenants by name. (PRO, LRRO 1/275)

Exchequer (Lists and Indexes, vol. XXXVII). Depositions taken locally concerning the varying customs of individual manors, also in connection with litigation that took place in the Exchequer, are found in E 134: these are searchable online.

41.5 Ministers' and receivers' accounts

The practice of compiling regular and accurate manorial accounts seems to have begun during the early thirteenth century, at a time when the manor was still synonymous with a type of estate, to show an annual reckoning between the lord and his official. These accounts are rare before the middle of that century, but the creation of written accounts quickly became a normal part of estate management and more documents survive from the end of the century. They reflect changing trends in medieval estate management, from the lord's direct running of the demesne through a minister, reeve or bailiff (the terms may vary across the country), to the leasing of demesnes to tenant farmers. The various tiers of estate management are reflected in the accounts of the local officials such as the bailiff or beadle, who presented them to a steward or receiver for a group of manors, who in turn presented accounts to the receiver-general of the entire estate. From the mid to late thirteenth century, they generally relate to groups of manors forming large estates and are found together with household accounts. Surviving examples of early accounts were typically created on estates of the church or of religious houses, compiled by a receiver and show what was agreed by the lord at audit. Later, between roughly the late thirteenth and late fourteenth centuries, the accounts are for one manor, compiled by a local official to be presented at audit, often showing signs of alteration as items were agreed or disallowed. Thirdly, from the late fourteenth century, the accounts change to those of the farmer (lessee) or collector (of rents) and may only consist of summaries of payments.

Medieval accounts were compiled on the basis of the 'charge and discharge' system of accounting and follow a set format; they are likely to include details of cash, and corn and stock of various kinds, containing sections both on the incoming revenue and the outgoing expenses of each item. They therefore predominantly provide detailed information on the type of agriculture being carried out on the manor, rather than any detailed information on tenants. The documents are written in highly formulaic and abbreviated Latin and are not easy for the beginner to use; indeed, they should not be the first port of call for those wishing to discover details of individual manorial tenants. To become familiar with the layout and contents of the documents, look at some published editions in the first place; for instance, those relating to Cuxham in Oxfordshire (see **41.12**).

Accounts in the PRO include accounts of Crown lands, or lands held temporarily by the Crown, and are known as 'ministers' accounts', or 'receivers' accounts', depending on the type of official who created them. For the most part, local officials appear to have delivered their accounts to a receiver-general, who in turn submitted his final account to the Exchequer; as a result, the contents will comprise summaries of payments, rather than detailed sections on crops and livestock. Few original accounts for Crown lands survive after the sixteenth century.

Most surviving accounts held in the PRO are in series SC 6 and DL 29. These are listed in the *List of Original Ministers' Accounts, Part I – Henry III to Richard III* (Lists and Indexes, vol. V), which is supplemented and indexed by the *List of Original Ministers' Accounts: Appendix, Corrigenda, and Index to Part I* (Lists and Indexes, vol. VIII). These are continued in the *List of Original Ministers' Accounts, Part II – Henry VII to Henry VIII* (Lists and Indexes, vol. XXXIV), adding references to material in E 36 and E 315, and in the *List of Ministers' Accounts Edward VI – 18th century and analogous documents* (Lists and Indexes, Supplementary Series No. II), which adds material from LR 12. Further accounts relating to manors can be found in DL 28, LR 5–8 and LRRO 3 and these are described in the relevant class lists. As with surveys, the series of Chancery Masters' Exhibits may contain manorial accounts, particularly C 103–108, C 110, C 111, C 116 and C 171. Although not of manorial origin, other series of possible interest containing accounts for manors temporarily held by the Crown may be found in E 164, E 199, E 364, E 372 and also E 352. Material of interest may also be found in the *List of the Lands of Dissolved Religious Houses* (Lists and Indexes, Supplementary Series No. III, vols 1–7).

For details of other types of manorial record, see the various works in **41.12**. References to material not described above may be found in the standard lists for the Chancery Masters' Exhibits, particularly C 103, C 106, C 110 and C 116; CRES 2 and CRES 5; DL 30; LR 11 (for estreats not included in the 'Union Indexes to Court Rolls'), LR 17; LRRO 11 and LRRO 37 and PEV, which contains records of the Court of the Honour of Peveril, which included jurisdiction over the manor of Worksop.

41.6 Crown lands

Many properties have at some time been in the hands of the Crown. Crown lands lacked a system of overall management until the late medieval period. Although a range of officers emerged to manage royal lands during the twelfth and thirteenth centuries, there was no centralized system of control. By the fifteenth century, however, lands were often placed under the stewardship of a senior noble or brought together under a receiver-general and auditors to provide an endowment for a member of the royal family. At the beginning of Henry VIII's reign, general surveyors of Crown lands were appointed. In 1542, the Court of General Surveyors of the King's Lands was created and given control over all lands falling into Crown hands through attainder, escheat, exchange and forfeiture. The dissolution of the monasteries had also seen the establishment of the Court of Augmentations of Revenues of the Crown in 1536 to manage the revenues of former ecclesiastical and monastic property. In 1547, both these courts were abolished and replaced by the single Court of Augmentations and Revenues. Following the abolition of this court in 1554, Crown officials presented their accounts to the Auditors of the Exchequer (subsequently known as the Auditors of the Land Revenue). The Auditors were abolished only in 1831; their records were transferred to the new Land Revenue Record Office, which amalgamated with the PRO in 1902. Since then, Crown lands have been administered by the Crown Estate Commissioners, under various titles.

If there is any evidence to suggest that a piece of property was in the Crown's hands or that a person was a Crown tenant, it is worth exploring the various codes which contain the bulk of material relating to Crown lands – CRES, LR, LRRO and E, particularly series in the E 300s. There is also FEC, the Forfeited Estates Commission. The court rolls, rentals and surveys, ministers' and receivers' accounts in CRES 5, DL 30, DL 43, LR 3, LRRO 12, SC 2, SC 6, SC 11 and SC 12 are particularly fruitful sources for identifying Crown lands and tenants (see **41.3**, **41.4** and **41.5**).

For 1786–1830, there is the *Crown Lands Return*, of 1831, available in the Map Room. It may be that other, similar, returns to Parliament exist among the Parliamentary Papers, which can be seen on microfiche in the Library. For Wales, for example, there is the *Crown Lands (Wales and Monmouthshire) Return* of 1911 (London, 1912). If it is unclear whether certain lands were part of the Crown estates, there is a useful list of Crown manors as at 1827 in CRES 2/1613, and the Annual Reports of the various bodies administering the Crown lands are in CRES 60 for 1797–1942. From 1914–1961, there is a card index (on open access) to the buyers and lessees of Crown lands; the actual deeds (in LRRO 16) are closed for 100 years. For 1832–1913, there are indexes to buyers, lessees and places in LRRO 64, to deeds now in LRRO 13, LRRO 16, and other series; again the indexes can be seen but documents of more recent date than 100 years ago are also closed.

The Parliamentary Surveys in E 317, recorded in English, can be used to establish the occupation of lands in the mid seventeenth century as well as providing an indication of the size, extent and layout of the buildings themselves. These surveys were taken by virtue of two Acts of 1649 and 1650, which authorized the sale of honours, manors and lands formerly belonging to King Charles I, Queen Henrietta Maria and Prince Charles. The trustees appointed to sell the lands employed local surveyors to conduct surveys of the Crown lands. The registrar's books of particulars (based on the surveys) and contracts for sale are in CRES 39/67–74. Individual particulars and contracts for sales of Crown lands are in E 320. Many of these sales were reversed following the Restoration of Charles II in 1660.

41.7 Inquisitions post mortem, homage and wardship

Before the abolition of feudal tenure in 1660, the death of any holder of land who was thought to have held that land directly from the Crown (called a tenant in chief by knight service), would prompt an inquiry to be held by the escheator of the county involved. The escheator was one of the most important royal officials in the locality and it was his responsibility to maintain the Crown's rights as feudal overlord. When land was deemed to have no owner, for whatever reason, the property reverted to the King as ultimate feudal lord.

Inquisitions post mortem were conducted according to well-established procedures. A local jury would be summoned by the sheriff and had to swear to the identity and extent of the land held by the tenant at the time of his death, by what rents or services they were held, and the name and age of the next heir. If there was no heir, the land escheated (reverted) to the Crown; if the next heir was under age, the Crown claimed rights of wardship and marriage over the lands and the heir until he or she came of age. If the heir was adult, livery of seisin of the lands was granted on performance of homage to the King, and on payment of a reasonable fine or relief. If the heir's age was in doubt, there might have been a separate inquiry to produce proof of age; this inquiry was known as an inquisition *de aetatis probanda*. These proofs often record memories of other notable events to fix the heir's year of birth. Widows also had rights of dower in the lands, which may have continued long after the deaths of their husbands, and there are inquisitions *de assignatio dotis* into this as well. These inquisitions are included with the inquisitions post mortem. The jury's findings were returned to Chancery as an indenture, along with any associated documentation such as the Chancery writ. A duplicate indenture was kept by the escheator. The documents produced by inquisitions post mortem are a very valuable source for both family and local history; however, it must be remembered that not all the information given is reliable.

The inquisitions give details of what lands were held (a separate inquisition was held for each county involved), and by what tenure, and from whom, as well as the date of death, and the name and age of the heir. They are in Latin and follow a standard pattern. Each inquisition starts with the county, the name of the escheator (the official holding the inquest), and a list of the jurors. The name of the deceased and the date of death are given next. Then follows a brief description of each landholding, its value (often underestimated) and the tenure by which it is held. This section may include extracts (in English) from a will or an enfeoffment to use (putting the lands into the hands of trustees, in order to avoid the King's claims to livery and wardship, etc., and also to allow lands to be left to people other than the heir at law). At the end, the next heir is identified, and an age given. If the heir was of age (over 21, or over 14 for an heiress), the actual age given may be an estimate. The next heir is usually one male, or one female, or a number of females; lands were split between daughters (who were treated as having an equal claim if there was no male heir), but not between sons.

The main series consists of those returned into Chancery (C 132–142): unfortunately they are often illegible. Transcripts of some were sent to the Exchequer (E 149–150, E 152) and to the Court of Wards from the reign of Henry VIII (WARD 7), and these are usually in better condition. There are a series of calendars and indexes to inquisitions post mortem (see **41.12**). Inquisitions from the Palatinate of Durham are in DURH 3; for the Palatinate of Chester, in CHES 3; for the duchy of Lancaster in DL 7.

The right to wardship was often sold by the Crown, by no means always to the next of kin; grants of wardship may be found in the Patent Rolls (C 66). The Close Rolls (C 54) contain writs of livery of seisin, while the Fine Rolls (C 60) include grants of wardship and marriage and writs of livery of seisin: see **41.8**.

If the heir was under age and did hold land in chief from the Crown, then it is worth investigating the records of the Court of Wards and Liveries, which operated between 1540 and 1660. The records of most potential value are the legal proceedings in WARD 3, WARD 5, WARD 9 and WARD 13; the Court of Wards used equity procedure (see **47d**), and so the records are full, informative, and in English. The deeds and evidences, in WARD 2, go back as far as the twelfth century; there is a partial index to them in the *Deputy Keeper's Sixth Report*, Appendix II. For more information, consult Bell, *An Introduction to the History and Records of the Court of Wards and Liveries*.

For other legal proceedings about the validity or accuracy of inquisitions post mortem, see the records of the plea side of Chancery. Chancery had a common law jurisdiction over matters affected by the King's prerogative rights, such as royal grants, royal rights over its subjects' lands as discovered through inquisitions post mortem and inquisitions of lunacy, feudal incidents due to the Crown, and division of lands between joint heiresses. Pleadings for Edward I–James I are well-listed, in C 43 and C 44; pleadings for Elizabeth I to Victoria are in C 206. There are remembrance rolls in C 221 and C 222, and writs in C 245.

41.8 Chancery enrolments

The records of Chancery contain many useful references to grants of land and conveyances. Evidence of early grants from the Crown can be traced on the Charter Rolls (C 53). From 1199 to 1216, they are transcribed, with indexes, in *Rotuli Chartarum*, and thereafter to 1516, in the *Calendars of Charter Rolls*. The principal source of grants of land, however, is found on the Patent Rolls (C 66). From 1201 to 1232, they are transcribed with indexes, in *Rotuli Litterarum Patentium* and *Patent Rolls . . . Henry III*; from 1232 to the reign of Elizabeth I, they are calendared, with indexes, in *Calendars of Patent Rolls*, except that from 1509 to 1548 they are calendared in *Letters and Papers . . . of Henry VIII*. Modern calendars of Patent Rolls for 1584 onwards are being published by the List and Index Society and will eventually cover the period to 1603. Contemporary calendars for 1603–1625 have been published by the List and Index Society. There are also contemporary manuscript indexes in C 274, which survive from 1485 (1 Henry VII) to 1946 (10 George VI). They are arranged in letter order of grantees' names; some have indexes. Only those for 17–44 Elizabeth I and 1 Charles I–22 George V are on open access. The remainder must be ordered as original documents using the C 274 list.

The Patent Rolls and Close Rolls were also used to enrol private conveyances. The Close Rolls (C 54) became a popular means of recording private deeds and from 1536, the type of deed known as a 'bargain and sale' was required to be enrolled there or in local records (see also **41.9**). The Patent Rolls record licences to alienate. These were used by individuals holding property by tenure in chief. This could only lawfully be sold with the Crown's permission. Copies of the licences were enrolled on the Patent Rolls (C 66). Using the indexes to the calendars is an easy and sometimes rewarding way of searching for early conveyances. After the printed calendars cease, it is easier to leaf through the Entry Books of Licences and Pardons for Alienation, 1571–1650 (A 4) than to use the contemporary finding aids to the Patent Rolls.

41.9 Deeds

There are many original deeds in the PRO, but it is very difficult to find particular documents. There is no single index, and in many cases, their original context has been lost.

The overwhelming majority of private deeds came into the Crown's possession either when it acquired property through purchase, forfeiture or other forms of escheat, or when the deeds were produced as evidence in lawsuits and were not collected by the litigant afterwards. Most deeds are conveyances and other evidences of title, although various other record types, including wills, bonds and receipts, might also be found. A typical deed will contain the name of the vendor, the purchaser, details of the property concerned, the sum paid for the property and the date on which the transaction was conducted. Latin is the language of most medieval and early modern deeds, with the remainder written in either English or French. Modern deeds are written

Figure 63 Rolled up Patent Rolls, from 1218 to 1221. Patent Rolls, containing copies of Crown grants, are the longest series of records in the PRO. They run from 1201 to the present day. (PRO, C 66/20-24)

in English. In some instances, one or more seals may survive, still attached to the original deed.

The large collections of individual deeds emanating from private or monastic sources are primarily in C 146–149; DL 25–27; DURH 21; E 40–44; E 210–213; E 326–330; LR 14–16; PL 29; WALE 29–31; and WARD 2. Many of these have been calendared or descriptively listed: they are gradually being entered into PROCAT. There is also a card index to deeds in C 146–148. Some series of deeds, DURH 21, E 44, E 330, E 355, LR 16 and WALE 31, have not been listed and access to them is currently restricted.

It remained common practice until the nineteenth century to enrol private deeds in the central courts as a way of recording ownership; certain types of deed continued to be enrolled up to 1925 (see **34.2** for trust deeds). As noted above, the greatest number of deeds was enrolled in the Chancery (C 54); others were enrolled in the Exchequer (E 13, E 159, E 315 and E 368), the Court of Common Pleas (CP 40 before Easter 1583 and 1834–1875 and CP 43, 1583–1834) and the Court of King's Bench (KB 26, KB 27 before 1702 and KB 122, 1702–1875). There are manuscript and typescript indexes and calendars to deeds in C 54, CP 40, CP 43, E 13, E 315, KB 26 and KB 27. Deeds enrolled in E 368 can be traced by referring to IND volumes, which must be ordered as original documents. In the City of London and in many other cities and boroughs, transfers of property were often entered on the rolls of the Court of Husting or other courts, and these records should be sought in the appropriate local record office. Also, in most counties, the type of deed known as the 'bargain and sale' was enrolled in the records of Quarter Sessions from 1536 to the early seventeenth century, and these records will also be found locally, if not in Chancery.

There are many deeds relating to Crown lands amongst the records of the Auditors of Land Revenue and Surveyors General of Woods and Forests (LR), and the Office of Woods, Forests and Land Revenues (LRRO). For deeds in LR 14 and LR 15, refer to the class lists. Deeds in LRRO 13–18, LRRO 20 and LRRO 25 can be traced by using the Registers in LRRO 64. There is also a card index to LRRO 16. For deeds in LRRO 37 refer to the class list. Some of these series of deeds are still closed to public inspection. There are also some deeds amongst the records of the Crown Estate Commissioners (CRES) in CRES 38. Two small collections of deeds relating to Crown lands can be found amongst the records of the Board of Inland Revenue (IR) in IR 10; and the records of the Treasury Solicitor (TS) in TS 21.

In addition, deeds were sometimes used as evidence in lawsuits and their texts can be found on the plea rolls, the pleadings or as separate series of documents amongst the records of the relevant court. Deeds used as evidence in Chancery suits exist in large numbers in C 103–115, C 171 and J 90. Deeds used in suits in the Court of Wards and Liveries are in WARD 2, but the list, such as it is, is very difficult to use.

41.10 Fines and recoveries

Other ways to transfer the ownership of land involved the common law and the King's courts: the most usual, fines and common recoveries, were methods of conveying property by means of fictitious legal actions. Conveyancing by fines (also known as final concords) became increasingly common during the late twelfth century. By 1195, the procedure was well established and fines continued to be used until their abolition in 1833. Until the fourteenth century, fines were made in the Court of Common Pleas, the Court of King's Bench and the general eyre, a periodic visitation of the English counties by royal justices. From the fourteenth century onwards, all feet of fines made in the central common law courts were made in the Court of Common Pleas.

A foot of fine was the bottom copy of a series of three or more copies of a final agreement, or concord, written on a single piece of parchment. A copy was given to each of the parties to the agreement to retain as their own record, while the foot was retained by the court. The contents of the documents tend to follow a set formula. The intended purchaser, as plaintiff, claimed the property from the vendor, as defendant (or deforciant); the property was then transferred by a legally sanctioned agreement. The largest series of Feet of Fines are in CP 25/1 and CP 25/2. Other fines are in CHES 31, for the Palatinate of Chester; DURH 12, for the Palatinate of Durham; and PL 17, for the Palatinate of Lancaster. Fines can be located by using the manuscript indexes of fines and recoveries in IND 1/1–6605 and IND 1/17183–17216 arranged by date. Furthermore, certain manuscript indexes to fines from the reign of Henry VIII onwards (CP 25/2) are available on microfilm. Many fines have also been published, mainly by local record societies: it is best to look first in *Texts and Calendars*, by Mullins, to see if any fines for the relevant shire have been printed (this publication is kept up to date on the HMC website, www.hmc.gov.uk). For medieval feet of fines, see the article by Kissock, which includes a catalogue of those published.

The recovery was a method of transferring property developed in the fifteenth century, which also lasted until its abolition in 1833. It was used to enable entailed estates to be broken up so that they could be disposed of at will rather than descending within a specific family line. Having already agreed terms beforehand, the individual who wished to acquire the entailed lands would bring a fictitious action against the person wishing to dispose of the land, known as the tenant-in-tail. The tenant-in-tail named a third party to warrant the title to him. This individual became known as the common vouchee. He would appear to defend the tenant's title but would subsequently default (i.e. not turn up in court). This was a contempt of court, which allowed the justices to make a judgement against the tenant, thus breaking the entail and enabling the smooth transfer of the property in question. The recovery is a distinctive document, taking the form of a type of copy known as an 'exemplification', written on a large sheet of parchment, worded as a royal writ and sealed with the Great Seal.

The majority of common recoveries are in CP 40 and CP 43. There are additional recoveries for the Palatinate of Chester in CHES 31. Recoveries can be traced by referring to the manuscript indexes of fines and recoveries in IND 1/1–6605 and IND 1/17183–17216.

41.11 Chester, Durham and Lancaster

The palatinates of Chester, Durham, and Lancaster had their own administrations, which paralleled those of the central government and records created by these administrations will be found in PRO series CHES, DURH and PL respectively. Fines and recoveries can be found in CHES 2, CHES 29, CHES 30, CHES 31, CHES 32, DURH 12, DURH 13, PL 15 and PL 17. Deeds can be found in CHES 2, CHES 29, DURH 13, DURH 21, PL 2, PL 14, PL 15 and PL 29. For a description of the nature and format of these types of documents, refer to the relevant subject headings in this chapter.

41.12 Land ownership and tenancy: bibliography

General works
B English, 'Inheritance and Succession in Landed Families 1660–1925', *Genealogists' Magazine*, vol. XXIV, pp. 433–438
M Gandy, *Basic Approach to Latin for Family Historians* (Federation of Family History Societies, 1995)
E Gooder, *Latin for Local History* (2nd edn, London, 1978)
J H Harvey, *Sources for the History of Houses* (British Records Association, 1968)
E C Mullins, *Texts and Calendars: an Analytical Guide to Serial Publications* (London, 2 vols, 1978, 1983). Continues on the HMC website.
A W B Simpson, *A History of the Land Law* (Oxford, 1986)
D Stuart, *Latin for Local and Family Historians: A Beginner's Guide* (London, 1995)

Deeds and Feet of Fines
N W Alcock, *Old Title Deeds* (Chichester, 2001)
J Cornwall, *How to Read Old Title Deeds XVI–XIX Centuries* (Federation of Family History Societies, 2nd edn, 1997)
A A Dibben, *Title Deeds* (Historical Association, 1968)
J Kissock, 'Medieval feet of fines: a study of their uses, with a catalogue of published sources', *Journal of the Society of Archivists*, vol. XXIV (1994), pp. 66–82
F Sheppard and V Belcher, 'The Deed Registries of Yorkshire and Middlesex', *Journal of the Society of Archivists,* vol. VI (1978–1981), pp. 274–286
K T Ward, 'Pre-Registration Title Deeds: The Legal Issues of Ownership, Custody and Abandonment', *Journal of the Society of Archivists*, vol. XVI (1995), pp. 27–39

Manorial records

R Bass, *Manorial Records: 16th–19th centuries.* University of York, Borthwick Institute of Historical Research, Borthwick Wallet 8 (York, 1998)

J Beckett, 'Estate Surveys as a Source for Names', *Genealogists' Magazine*, vol. XXIV (1993), pp. 335–341

J H Bettey, 'Manorial Customs and Widows' Estates', *Archives*, vol. XX (1992), pp. 208–216

M Ellis, *Using Manorial Records* (PRO, revised edn, 1997)

P D A Harvey, *Manorial Records* (Loughborough, revised edn, 1999)

P D A Harvey, ed., *Manorial Records of Cuxham, Oxfordshire c.1200–1359* (London, 1976)

E Haydon and J Harrop, eds, *Widworthy Manorial Court Rolls 1453–1617* (Honiton, 1997)

P B Park, *My Ancestors were Manorial Tenants: How can I find out more about them?* (Society of Genealogists, 2nd edn, 1994)

D Stuart, *Manorial Records* (Chichester, 1992)

A Travers, 'Manorial Documents', *Genealogists' Magazine*, vol. XXI (1983), pp. 1–10

H Watt, *Welsh Manors and their Records* (National Library of Wales, 2000)

Inquisitions post mortem and wardships

H E Bell, *An Introduction to the History and Records of the Court of Wards and Liveries* (Cambridge, 1953)

Calendar of Inquisitions Miscellaneous, Henry III to Henry VII (London, 1916–1968)

Calendar of Inquisitions Post Mortem, Henry III to Henry V, and *Henry VII* (London, 1898–1995)

Calendarium Inquisitionum Post Mortem (Record Commission, 1806–1828)

R F Hunnisett, 'The Reliability of Inquisitions as Historical Evidence', *The Study of Medieval Records*, eds D A Bullough and R L Storey (Oxford, 1971)

J Hurstfield, *The Queen's Wards* (London, 1958)

R E Latham, 'Hints on Interpreting the Public Records: III, Inquisitions Post Mortem', *Amateur Historian*, vol. I (1952–1954), pp. 77–81

List of Inquisitions Post Mortem, Henry V–Richard III; Inquisitions ad quod damnum and miscellaneous inquisitions, Henry VII–Charles I (C138–C142) (List and Index Society, vols 268–269, 1998)

M McGuinness, 'Inquisitions Post Mortem', *Amateur Historian*, vol. VI (1963–1965), pp. 235–242

Chancery enrolments

Rotuli Chartarum (Record Commission, 1837)

Calendar of Charter Rolls (London, 1903–1927)

Calendar of Close Rolls (London, 1892–1963)

Rotuli Litterarum Patentium (Record Commission, 1835)

Patent Rolls . . . Henry III (London, 1901–1903)

Calendar of Patent Rolls, Henry III to Henry VII, and *Edward VI to 1582* (London, 1891–1986)

Letters and Papers of Henry VIII (London, 1864–1932). (This includes a calendar of the Patent Rolls for Henry VIII.)

Crown lands

C D Chandaman, *The English Public Revenue, 1660–1688* (Oxford, 1975)

R Hoyle, *The Estates of the English Crown, 1558–1640* (Cambridge, 1992)

W C Richardson, *History of the Court of Augmentations, 1536–1544* (Baton Rouge, 1961)

B P Wolffe, *The Crown Lands, 1460–1536* (London, 1970)

B P Wolffe, *The Royal Demesne in English History* (London, 1971)

42

Surveys of land and house ownership and tenancy

◆ ◆ ◆

42.1 Introduction

For very many parishes of England and Wales there is either a tithe map and apportionment or an enclosure award and map, which can provide valuable information about land ownership. The tithe maps and apportionments were created in the mid nineteenth century while the enclosure awards and maps relate to a broader time span covering, in the majority of cases, the eighteenth and nineteenth centuries. They give you the opportunity to find out where in a particular parish your ancestors were living, who their neighbours were, what land they owned or occupied, what industries were important locally and a mass of further information. Less well known but equally important are the records of house and land ownership produced by the Valuation Office. This was a survey carried out under the Finance (1909–1910) Act 1910, which has left behind a series of maps and field books which between them provide a detailed record for family and local historians

42.2 Tithe survey records

Tithes were originally a tax of one tenth of all produce paid to the local clergyman by his parishioners. After the Reformation many entitlements to receive tithes came into the hands of laymen. That is to say, the right to collect tithes came to be 'owned' by non-clerics and could be bought and sold on the open market. Disputes about tithes were a major part of the business of the equity side of the Exchequer (see **47c**).

By the nineteenth century there was much popular disenchantment with the system of tithes, and many parishes had local agreements regarding the payment of money in lieu of produce. In 1836, the Tithe Commutation Act set a national framework for all tithes to be fixed as a money payment, which was linked to the changing price of wheat, barley and oats. The maps and apportionments created by Tithe Commissioners set out the names of owners and occupiers for the 75 per cent of parishes and chapelries that were still titheable in the 1830s. These records also provide the name and description of the premises and land (for example 'Farm House and Out Buildings'), as well as providing details of the extent of land and the state of cultivation. Copies of tithe maps and apportionments are held in some county record offices, as well as in the PRO (IR 29, IR 30).

For some areas no tithe maps and apportionments were made. This is because satisfactory arrangements for money payments had already been agreed or an award of land in lieu of tithes had been made during an enclosure. There were also some districts where no apportionment was made, even though tithes for the area were commuted under the Tithe Commutation Act. This was because either the amount involved was negligible, or because the landowners were themselves the tithe owners, and the agreement or award of a gross tithe rentcharge was followed by the redemption or merger of the tithe rentcharges. By this procedure the owners of the land/tithe avoided the need (and expense) of producing a map and apportionment. In these cases the result of the proceedings would still need to be recorded as a formal agreement or instrument of merger (in TITH 3), and there should also be a tithe file (IR 18). Although disappointing for genealogists, these may give valuable information to the regional or local historian.

The easiest way to find out about the existence of and document reference for maps and apportionments for a particular parish is to look at Kain and Oliver's *The Tithe Maps of England and Wales*. This is available in the Map Room: it is arranged by county, and each parish entry starts with a number. A brief description of the map is also given. To get the apportionment add IR 29 to this number: for the map, add IR 30. A search on PROCAT in IR 29 and IR 30 is also possible if the parish name is unique and obvious. Maps for English counties in the alphabetical sequence Bedfordshire–Middlesex are seen on microfiche. The apportionments in IR 29 are seen on microfilm for all counties.

For detailed advice on using tithe maps and apportionments, look at Foot's *Maps For Family History*. It is a good idea to look at Foot before trying to understand an apportionment, because the arrangement of the information is not easy to grasp on film. There is a numerical key at the beginning of each apportionment, in which you look up the plot number found on the tithe map (hundreds across the top, tens and units down the side: at their intersection you will find the page number of the apportionment).

42.3 Enclosure maps and awards

The term enclosure, as applied to land, usually refers to either the fencing in of commons for private and exclusive landownership, or the consolidation of plots of land formerly distributed over the shared open fields into compact blocks, linked together and surrounded by hedges or fences and gates. A useful starting point before embarking on research (for enclosures from c.1730) among the surviving records is Tate's book, *A Domesday of English Enclosure Acts and Awards* and Chapman's *A Guide to Parliamentary Enclosure in Wales*.

Enclosures of common lands, pastures and manorial wastes were made from an early period, sometimes arbitrarily and sometimes by agreement. There is a list at the Map Room Enquiry Desk of references to agreements and awards (and early enclosure by parliamentary act) in the PRO, arranged by county and then parish. However this is by no means comprehensive. It should be recognized that some of the earliest enclosures have left no records, although some will be contained within manorial and estate records, which are usually deposited with the local county record office.

From at least the middle of the sixteenth century it was common to effect enclosures by decree in the equity courts (especially Chancery and Exchequer). There is no full list of enclosures by this means and they are difficult to find with no preliminary information. From the middle of the eighteenth century (there are a small number earlier than this), it became common to effect enclosure by Act of Parliament. These are far easier to trace and to use. The Act would name the larger owners of property who had promoted it. As a result of the enclosure, an award and (in many cases) a map would be drawn up. The award would list the people who were allotted land at enclosure, along with the amounts of land involved. These records can usually be found in the county record offices although others have been listed from several classes in the list referred to earlier. The original Acts are held at the House of Lords Record Office.

The General Inclosure Acts of 1801 and 1836 did not specify where the awards were to be kept. Some were enrolled at Westminster and these are now at the PRO in C 54 or E 13. Where these have been identified they have also been inserted in the list referred to earlier. Others will be found in the county record offices. In 1845 the Enclosure Commission was set up under the Enclosure Act of the same year. The Commission (and its successor departments, the Land Commissioners, the Board of Agriculture, and the Ministry of Agriculture and Fisheries) retained copies of the awards. These awards (which include maps) are now in MAF 1.

Enclosure material varies in the amount of information given. References to individuals are restricted to those who were allotted land: enclosure awards do not list everyone within a particular parish. Where enclosure maps were created (usually from the late eighteenth century onwards) they often cover only that part of the parish or manor affected.

42.4 Valuation Office Surveys, 1910–1913

The survey carried out by the Valuation Office under the Finance (1909–1910) Act 1910 saw a comprehensive mapping and valuation of the country involving a description of each property, its extent, value, owners and tenant. Much of the initial work was done starting from existing Ordnance Survey maps. The PRO has two specialist guides to these records: Root, *Maps for Family History* and Barratt, *Tracing the History of Your House*.

Under the Finance Act of 1910, a tax was attached to the profit of house sales, if part of the profit was judged to have occurred because of the provision of amenities at the public expense. For example, if a park was opened nearby, trees planted in the road, and the road paved, the house price might increase because the site had become more attractive, although the householder had given neither effort nor financial contribution to the improvements.

In order to establish a fixed point from which to measure subsequent increases in value, a huge (and expensive) valuation exercise took place, between 1910 and 1913, the largest since 1086 and Domesday Book. The valuers wrote detailed descriptions and valuations of each house, and details of owners and tenants (but not occupiers), in the Field Books (IR 58). To find the right entry in a field book, you have to use the maps (IR 121/1–135/9) to discover the property number. There is guidance available in the form of a leaflet to use at the PRO: you may need to ask for help as well, as actually finding the right map and the right field book can be quite complicated.

A second set of books, known as Domesday Books, was also made: these included the actual occupiers as well as owners and tenants; these are particularly useful as most people lived in rented accommodation. Most of these Domesday Books are to be found in county record offices, which may also have duplicates of the Record Maps. The PRO has the Domesday Books for the City of London and for Paddington (IR 91).

It should be noted that although the valuation was supposed to include all land, even if exempt from payment, there are gaps in the records. Maps covering Portsmouth and Southampton, and an area around Chichester, were all lost during the Second World War. In addition to this many records for around Chelmsford in Essex and for the whole of Coventry appear to be lost. For large properties and estates, the field books may simply have the phrase 'description filed'. This indicates that the information was entered on a separate document in specially created files. These files are not thought to have survived.

As an exercise in raising money, the whole operation proved to be an expensive failure: it was called off in 1920.

42.5 Surveys of land and house ownership and tenancy: bibliography

N Barratt, *Tracing the History of Your House: A Guide to Sources* (PRO, 2001)
G Beech, 'Maps for Genealogy and Local History', *Genealogists' Magazine*, vol. XXII, pp. 197–202
J. Chapman, *A Guide to Parliamentary Enclosure in Wales* (Cardiff, 1992)
W Foot, *Maps For Family History, A Guide to the Records of Tithe, Valuation Office, and National Farm Surveys of England and Wales, 1836–1943* (PRO, 1994)
J H Harvey, *Sources for the History of Houses* (British Records Association, 1968)
R J P Kain and R R. Oliver, *The Tithe Maps of England and Wales* (Cambridge, 1995)
A Parliamentary Return of Inclosure Awards (House of Commons Sessional Papers, 1904 (50) LXXVIII, 545)
B Short and M Reed, 'An Edwardian Land Survey: The Finance (1909–10) Act records', *Journal of the Society of Archivists,* vol. VIII (1986), pp. 95–103
W E Tate, *A Domesday of English Enclosure Acts and Awards* (Reading, 1978)

43

Taxation

◆ ◆ ◆

43.1 Introduction

Tax records have always been a fruitful source for historians, and many before 1680 have been published by local record societies. This is one obvious case when it is better to go first to the PRO Library to see what is in print, rather than ordering up original documents. For a list of publications by local societies, ask to see Mullins' *Texts and Calendars* which is continued on www.hmc.gov.uk.

Most tax records until the late seventeenth century are in the Subsidy Rolls (E 179). This contains the surviving records of a number of different types of tax that were levied before 1700, the best known of which is the Hearth Tax (see **43.6**). It includes documents relating to scutage (a feudal payment in lieu of knight service), poll taxes, taxes on land, taxes on goods, taxes on aliens, forced loans, an abortive sheep tax in 1549, etc. Overall sums raised by most of these taxes are enrolled in E 359 and E 360. No tax return can be used as a total census of the population – there were always exemptions and evasions. For full details on the taxes themselves, see Jurkowski, Smith and Crook, *Lay Taxes in England and Wales, 1188–1688.* This invaluable book has been produced as part of the large-scale E 179 project run by the University of Cambridge and the PRO. This has been re-examining the lay tax records, and entering details of tax and place covered (*not* personal names) into a database, which is available for public searching at the PRO. So far all English counties except Gloucester, London, Middlesex, Norfolk, Suffolk and Worcester have been entered. The plan is to enter the data into PROCAT as soon as practicable.

Many inquisitions and assessments relating to feudal payments based on land, drawing on E 179 and other classes, are printed in *Feudal Aids*, which is indexed by place-name and personal name and is on open access. The original records are mainly in Latin, some are damaged and the handwriting can be difficult to read but lists of names should become legible with practice.

The current E 179 lists are arranged by (pre-1974) county, for England and Wales, with separate sections for the Cinque Ports; members of the Royal Household (both courtiers and officials) and Divers, Miscellaneous and Unknown counties, that should be consulted by anyone wishing to carry out a complete study of a particular area. There are separate lists for taxes paid by clergy, arranged by diocese – those paid by laymen (i.e. non-clergy) are called lay subsidies. Only those documents described in the lists as including *Names* actually list the names of taxpayers. Within each county, they are arranged by date, using regnal years (e.g. 18 Edward I: these can be converted into a calendar year by using Cheney's *Handbook of Dates*); and then by sub-divisions of the county known as hundreds, or in some areas, wapentakes. To find out the subdivision of the county for the place you are interested in, look at the Gibson guide, or at Lewis's *Topographical Dictionary of England*, or his *Topographical Dictionary of Wales*. These dictionaries are very informative, and give a brief history of each town and most villages. You can also use Youngs' *Guide to the Local Administrative Units of England*. Once the E 179 database becomes available, you will be able to pinpoint tax records for a particular place immediately.

43.2 Lay subsidies of 1290–1332

The earliest type of tax for which the most comprehensive returns survive are the fractional lay subsidies of 1290–1332, a tax on the moveable, personal wealth of individuals, rather than on the land that they owned, which had been levied sporadically throughout the thirteenth century. They were granted by Parliament in Acts which specified what proportion of an individual's wealth was taxable, after agreed exemptions had been made. Exemptions often included equipment necessary to pursue one's occupation, ranging from a knight's armour to a merchant's capital. Apart from in 1301, the grant normally exempted the poorest, e.g. in 1297 those assessed at less than a shilling did not have to pay anything. The heading of the lay subsidy roll will normally state what fraction of assessable property has been granted in tax, ranging from a sixth to a twentieth during this period. If two fractions are given, the higher one normally applies to more 'urban' areas. After 1334, assessment of individuals was replaced by fixed quotas levied on individual townships, based on a fifteenth on most taxpayers and a tenth on those living in boroughs or ancient Crown demesne. Glasscock's *The Lay Subsidy of 1334* lists the places assessed, giving modern Ordnance Survey grid references. Although the 'fifteenth' continued to be levied intermittently until the seventeenth century, it was fossilized at these 1334 rates, although local or national disasters, such as the Black Death, might lead to reductions being granted to particular places. They are more fully described in Beresford's *Lay Subsidies and Poll Taxes*.

43.3 Poll taxes

In 1377, the first poll tax was granted by Parliament, at a flat rate of 4d a head (one shilling for clergy who had a benefice). All men and women were liable – only those under 14 (possibly one third of the population) and those who begged for a living were exempt. It was also granted in 1379 (on those over 16) and 1380 (on those over 15), but at different rates according to status, thus giving details of occupations, although evasion was widespread. Some returns listed in the E 179 class list as being of 1377 (51 Edward III) are mis-dated as the actual documents record payments at different rates and therefore belong to 1379 or

1380, while those also recording occupations probably belong to 1379. For any revisions, see the E 179 database and Fenwick's *Poll Taxes of 1377, 1379 and 1381*. The failure of this unpopular tax led to its abandonment until the seventeenth century when it was intermittently revived in 1641 and on a number of occasions after 1660, although few nominal returns survive of these later poll taxes.

43.4 Subsidies and other taxes after 1522

After 1522, a fresh attempt was made to assess individual wealth, based on income from freehold land, the capital value of moveable goods and income from wages. Not all categories of wealth were taxed in every subsidy and rates varied – of the four collections of the subsidy granted in 1523, the first two (1524 and 1525) levied 1 shilling in the £1 on land, with the same on goods over £20 in value (6d in the £1 on goods under £20) and 4d in the £1 on wages (only on those earning £1 or more), but the third and fourth collections only taxed those with more than £50 in land (1526) or goods (1527). Aliens (foreigners) had to pay double rates. Wages were not taxed separately after 1525 and the threshold for payment on goods varied (£5 after 1553 and reduced to £3 in 1563). The most informative returns are those relating to the grants of 1523 and 1543; later assessments generally represented only a minority of the population. These subsidies are fully described and illustrated in Hoyle's *Tudor Taxation Records* which also covers the 'Military Survey' of 1522 and other sources for forced loans required from wealthier individuals, such as the privy seal letters to contributors of 1588–1589 in E 34/16–40. He argues that values given in assessments are rough estimates rather than precise valuations – 'they describe reputed wealth rather than real wealth'. Under-assessment was endemic. For more on the use of the 1523 lay subsidy returns for economic and local history, see Sheail, *The Regional Distribution of Wealth in England as indicated in the 1524/5 Lay Subsidy Returns.*

Certificates of residence appear in E 115 (mainly from 1558–1625) and were intended to prevent double charging of individuals who resided in more than one county. Each taxpayer was to be assessed at his normal place of residence on all his lands and goods throughout the country. The certificates are indexed alphabetically by personal name.

43.5 Seventeenth century: new taxes

In 1642, a new parliamentary tax, the assessment levied on counties, was imposed and was levied sporadically until c.1680. County commissioners were to assess and enforce payment and records of payments by individuals may survive locally. Returns of sums raised are in E 179. In fact, the mid seventeenth century was a time of great experimentation in tax-raising. Details of many previously undescribed taxes, such as have been discovered by the E 179 Project, are presented in Jurkowski, Smith and Crook, *Lay Taxes in England and Wales, 1188–1688.* See also Gibson and Dell, *The Protestation Returns 1641–42 and other contemporary listings: collection in aid of distressed Protestants in Ireland, subsidies, poll tax, assessments or grants, vow and covenant, solemn league and covenant.*

The list of contributors to the 'Free and Voluntary Present' to Charles II in 1662 provides names and occupations or status of the wealthier members of society. About half the numbers who paid the hearth tax subscribed to the 'Present'. Returns for Surrey have been published.

The parish lists of contributors to the fund for the relief of Protestant refugees for Ireland in 1642 provide a number of names; but survival is patchy (SP 28/191–195, E 179). The Surrey lists are very good and a typescript list and index are available.

43.6 The hearth tax, 1662–1688

The surviving hearth tax returns and assessments of 1662–1674 relate to the levy of two shillings per year on every hearth: as such, they are one of the obvious sources for family, local and social history. The hearth tax actually continued until 1688, but the later records were not returned into the Exchequer, and most do not survive.

The most complete hearth tax records are those for 25 March 1664. Information supplied includes names of householders, sometimes their status, and the number of hearths for which they are chargeable. The number of hearths is a clue to wealth and status. Over seven hearths usually indicates gentry and above; between four and seven hearths, wealthy craftsmen and tradesmen, merchants and yeomen. Between two and three hearths suggests craftsmen, tradesmen, and yeomen; the labouring poor, husbandmen and poor craftsmen usually only had one hearth. There are many gaps in the series of records, partly because of the loss of documentation and there was also widespread evasion of this most unpopular tax. Hearth tax returns for particular areas have been published by many local record societies, and some records are to be found in county record offices, among the quarter sessions records.

The hearth tax consisted of a half-yearly payment of one shilling for each hearth in the occupation of each person whose house was worth more than 20s a year, and who was a local ratepayer of church and poor rates. This actually left out quite large numbers of people, and paupers were not liable at all. Exempt from the tax were charitable institutions with an annual income of less than £100; industrial hearths such as kilns and furnaces (but not smithies and bakeries); people who paid neither church nor poor rate (paupers); and people inhabiting a house worth less than 20s a year who did not have any other property over that value, nor an income of over £100 a year. To prove that you were in the last category, you needed a certificate of exemption from the parish clergyman, churchwardens and overseers of the poor, signed by two JPs. After 1663, the hearth tax returns include lists of those chargeable and not chargeable (exempt), although these may be entered in a block, not necessarily at the end of the parish entry of payers. From 1670, printed exemption forms were used; many are now in E 179/324–351 (listed in the standard set of lists), arranged by county only. They can give you more detail on why someone was exempt, and for the returns which do not include the 'not chargeables' you may need to look at them to get information about poorer inhabitants, or those engaged in industry. Some of these pieces are unlisted and access to them may be restricted. See Seaman

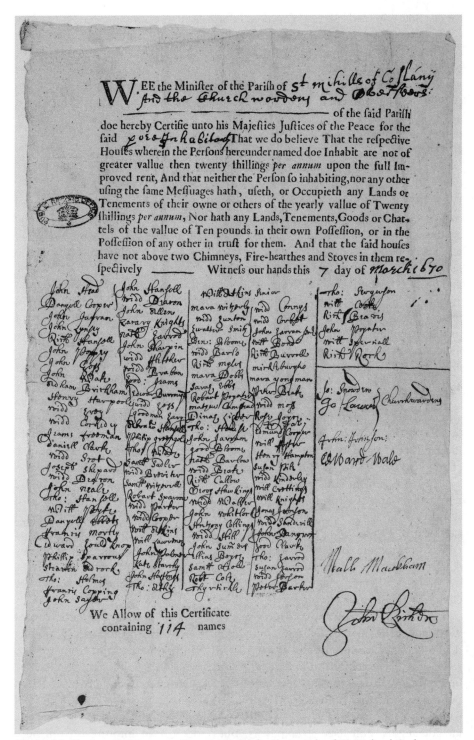

Figure 64 The hearth tax exemption certificate for the parish of St Michael Coslany, Norwich, dated 7 March 1670 (i.e.1669: see **1.16** for dating problems). (PRO, E 179/338)

(under British Records Society) for more information on exemption certificates.

The British Records Society and the Roehampton Institute are running an ongoing project to provide a printed edition of at least one hearth tax return for each county (and ideally one from the 1660s and one from the 1670s). So far, volumes for Kent, Cambridge and Norfolk (exemption certificates) have been published. The introductions to these volumes are worth reading, even if you are looking at another county, as they will give you much help in teasing out the implications of any assessment.

43.7 Land and other taxes from 1689: in local record offices and at the PRO

From 1689 to 1830, there are records of land and assessed taxes in local record offices (which list names) and in the PRO (which do not, in general). The accounting records of the taxes are in the PRO, in E 181–184. They do not list all taxpayers, although defaulters or people whose assessments changed may be listed. Three groups of taxes were administered centrally by the Board of Taxes, and locally by county commissioners. First was the land tax, voted annually from 1692 to 1798, and then made a perpetual charge. Second, the assessed taxes, a group of taxes assessed on the possession or occupation of certain kinds of property, beginning with the window tax in 1696. By 1803, the assessed taxes included taxes on inhabited houses, male servants, carriages, horses for riding and drawing carriages, horses for husbandry, dogs, horse dealers, hair powder and armorial bearings. The third was the income tax, which began in 1799.

Land tax assessments may be found in county record offices: they give owners and occupiers of land. The PRO has what is effectively a national snapshot taken in 1798–1799, in IR 23. This lists all owners of property subject to land tax in England and Wales in 1798–1799, when the land tax became a fixed annual charge and many people purchased exemption from paying. The arrangement is by land tax parish and there is no index of names. The records of these transactions are also useful and may include maps and plans (IR 22, Parish Books of Redemptions. 1799–1953, and IR 24, Registers of Redemption Certificates. 1799–1963). The arrangement is again by parish. See the book by Gibson and others for lists of records in the PRO and elsewhere, arranged by county. There is a useful introduction to using local and PRO land tax records, by Pearl, 'Land tax: yesterday's electoral register'. For a scholarly study, see Ginter, *A Measure of Wealth*.

If you are a keen explorer of records and have a lot of time, the Particulars of Account in E 182 may be the series to investigate. This series comprises supporting documentation to the tax accounts in E 181. The particulars run from 1689 to 1830, and relate to the land tax, the assessed taxes and the income tax. It has an uninformative list giving no descriptions other than county and covering dates, but the introductory note is good. The records do not in general include lists of names, but it can produce the occasional nugget of information. It does not include regular full lists of taxpayers, but it does have information on those whose circumstances and therefore taxes change – including those who died, or who got another horse, etc. Many payments authorized by central government were made at a local level from the tax revenues and not recorded elsewhere (e.g. rewards to informers leading to the arrest of army deserters, or bounties paid to parishes for getting people to enlist in the army). It sometimes has lists of militia volunteers. This is certainly a series ripe for a large-scale listing project. At the moment it is not really suitable to recommend to novice researchers.

For death duties, see **6.2**.

43.8 Taxation: bibliography

M W Beresford, 'Lay Subsidies', *Amateur Historian*, vol. III, pp. 325–328 and vol. IV, pp. 101–109

M W Beresford, *Lay Subsidies and Poll Taxes* (Phillimore, 1963).

M W Beresford, 'Poll Taxes of 1377, 1379 and 1381', *Amateur Historian*, vol. III, pp. 271–278

British Records Society and others:
    Cambridgeshire Hearth Tax Returns, Michaelmas 1664, N Evans and S Rose (2000)
    Kent Hearth Tax: Assessment Lady Day 1664, D Harrington, S Pearson and S Rose (2000)
    Norfolk Hearth Tax Exemption Certificates 1670–1674, P Seaman (2001)

C R Cheney, *Handbook of Dates for Students of English History* (London, 1991)

C C Fenwick, ed., *The Poll Taxes of 1377, 1379 and 1381 Part I Bedfordshire–Leicestershire, Part II Lincolnshire–Westmorland* (British Academy, 1998 and 2001)

Feudal Aids (London, 1899–1920)

J S W Gibson, *Hearth Tax Returns, other later Stuart Tax Lists, and the Association Oath Rolls* (FFHS, 1996)

J S W Gibson and A Dell, *The Protestation Returns 1641–42 and other contemporary listings: collection in aid of distressed Protestants in Ireland, subsidies, poll tax, assessments or grants, vow and covenant, solemn league and covenant* (FFHS, 1995)

J S W Gibson, M Medlycott and D Mills, *Land and Window Tax Assessments, 1690–1950* (FFHS, 1997)

D E Ginter, *A Measure of Wealth: English Land Tax in Historical Analysis* (Montreal, 1992)

R E Glasscock, ed., *The Lay Subsidy of 1334* (British Academy Records of Social and Economic History, new series, II, 1975)

R W Hoyle, *Tudor Taxation Records* (PRO, 1994)

M Jurkowski, C L Smith and D Crook, *Lay Taxes in England and Wales 1188–1688* (PRO, 1998)

S Lewis, *Topographical Dictionary of England* (London, 4th edn, 1840)

S Lewis, *Topographical Dictionary of Wales* (London, 1840)

L M Marshall, 'The Levying of the Hearth Tax; 1662–1668', *English Historical Review*, vol. LI, pp. 628–646

C A F Meekings, *Introduction to the Surrey Hearth Tax, 1664* (Surrey Record Society, vol. XVII)

E L C Mullins *Texts and Calendars* (Royal Historical Society, 2 vols, 1958, 1983: continued on the HMC website, www.hmc.gov.uk)

S Pearl, 'Land tax: yesterday's electoral register', *Family Tree Magazine*, June 1991

K Schurer and T Arkell, *Surveying the people: the interpretation and use of document sources for the study of population in the later 17th century* (Oxford, 1992)

J Sheail, *The Regional Distribution of Wealth in England as indicated in the 1524/5 Lay Subsidy Returns* (List and Index Society, *Special Series,* vols 28 and 29, 1998)

C Webb, *Calendar of the Surrey Portion of the Free and Voluntary Present to Charles II* (West Surrey Family History Society, 1982)

C Webb and East Surrey Family History Society, *Surrey Contributors to the Relief of Protestant Refugees from Ireland, 1642*

F A Youngs Jr., *Guide to the Local Administrative Units of England*, 2 vols (Royal Historical Society, 1980, 1991)

44

Tontines and annuity records

◆ ◆ ◆

44.1 Tontines and annuities

In the late seventeenth and the eighteenth centuries, the government organized several money-raising schemes by selling tontines and annuities. These schemes and the records produced are described by Colwell in *Family Roots*.

There were three English State Tontines, in 1693, 1766 and 1789, and three Irish State Tontines, in 1773, 1775 and 1777. In return for an original investment, participants were guaranteed a yearly income for the life of a living nominee chosen by the investor. People usually nominated their youngest relative. As the nominees died off, the central fund was distributed between fewer and fewer people and the annuity therefore became more valuable as the years passed. There were in all about 15,000 participants. Surviving records often involve proof of identity, or proof of continued existence. The records continue long after the original date of issue: for example, the last surviving nominee of the 1766 Tontine died in 1859. Most of the records are in NDO 1–3. They may give details concerning the marriages, deaths and wills of contributors and nominees. Contributors were usually substantial people. Many were spinsters. The registers have integral indexes.

Records of the British Tontine, 1792–1800, are in C 114/4, 151 and 166–168: these include lists of subscribers.

Annuities were similar to tontines, in that an original investment paid out an annuity for term of life. However, the annuity did not grow as other annuitants died off. Annuities were offered throughout the eighteenth century. Again, the records obviously extend way beyond the date of issue. NDO 1–2 are the main series, but Colwell's *Dictionary of Genealogical Sources in the Public Record Office* includes many other detailed references to tontine and annuity records.

44.2 Tontines and annuity records: bibliography

S Colwell, *Family Roots: Discovering the Past in the Public Record Office* (London, 1991)
S Colwell, *Dictionary of Genealogical Sources in the Public Record Office* (London, 1992)
F Leeson, *A Guide to the Records of the British State Tontines and Life Annuities of the 17th and 18th Centuries* (Shalfleet Manor, 1968)

45

Business records

◆ ◆ ◆

45.1 Companies' registration, from 1844

Until 1844, companies could only be incorporated by Royal Charter or special Act of Parliament. From 1844 onwards, various Companies Acts enabled companies to be formed cheaply and easily. Some information about directors and shareholders of registered companies can be found in the companies' registration records.

For records relating to live companies, and to those that have ceased to function within the last 20 to 30 years, you should contact the Companies Registration Office (www.companieshouse.gov.uk, address in **48**). For a small fee they will produce a microfiche copy, which contains all the required documents relating to any one company.

At the PRO are registration records for dissolved companies from 1844 until about 30 years ago.

For companies registered under the 1846 and 1856 Acts, and dissolved before 1860, look in BT 41. This is searchable online by the name of the company.

For registered companies dissolved after 1860, use BT 31 (searchable online by name of company). Records have been kept for only a sample of companies dissolved after 1860 – a large sample at first, dwindling to 5 per cent for modern records. If you do locate a file for your company, you will find that the file itself has been weeded, so that it only contains certain documents. These include memoranda and articles of association, and lists of shareholders, directors and managers, for the first, last and some intermediate years of the company's operation. These give name, address, occupation, sometimes date of death and very rarely change of name. Between 1918 and 1948 they also give nationality if not British.

Notices of receiverships, liquidations and bankruptcies appear in the *London Gazette*, available at the PRO in ZJ 1.

45.2 A company's own records

The PRO has the records of canal and railway companies nationalized in 1947 (in RAIL: see **27**); other transport undertakings and chartered and commercial companies which have passed into public ownership or whose records have come into public custody; and numerous records of various companies and other commercial undertakings among the exhibits used in litigation in C 103–114 and J 90 (see **47b.11**) and bankruptcy (see **46**). Otherwise, for records of companies themselves, advice may be obtained from the Business Archives Council, or the Business Archives Council of Scotland (addresses in **48**).

45.3 Business records: bibliography

J Armstrong, *Business Documents: their origins, sources and uses in historical research* (London, 1987)

H A L Cockerell and E Green, *The British Insurance Business, 1547–1970* (London, 1976)

D J Jeremy, *Dictionary of Business Biography: Biographical Dictionary of Business Leaders active in Britain in the Period 1860–1980* (London, 1984–1986)

C T Watts and M J Watts, 'Company Records as a source for the Family Historian', *Genealogists' Magazine,* vol. XXI, pp. 44–54.

46

Debtors and bankrupts

◆ ◆ ◆

46.1 Introduction

The court and prison records held in the PRO and locally (see **39** and **47**) include very many references to legal proceedings against insolvent debtors: responsible for their debts but unable to pay them, they remained subject to common law proceedings and indefinite imprisonment, if their creditors so wished. From 1861, insolvent debtors were allowed to apply for bankruptcy.

Bankruptcy was a process whereby a court official declared qualifying debtors bankrupt, took over their property, and distributed it to their creditors in proportion to what they were owed: bankrupts could then usually be discharged from their debts and escape imprisonment. Their annual numbers increased from a few hundreds to many thousands between the eighteenth and twentieth centuries. Partnerships of individuals could also declare themselves bankrupt, but companies were not covered until after 1844.

From 1543 to 1861 debtors who were traders and who owed large sums were usually exempt from the laws relating to debtors and from imprisonment as debtors. They were subject instead to bankruptcy proceedings. Until 1841, the legal status of being a bankrupt was confined to traders owing more than £100 (reduced to £50 in 1842). The legal definition of 'trader' came to embrace all those who made a living by buying and selling and by the late eighteenth century, included all those who bought materials, worked on them and then resold them: in other words, most skilled craftsmen. Farmers were specifically excluded but, nonetheless, do appear in the records. Those who wished to qualify as bankrupts, and thus avoid the awful fate of an insolvent debtor, sometimes gave a false or misleadingly general description of their occupations: *dealer and chapman* was very common.

46.2 Published sources for debtors and bankrupts

Official notices relating to many bankrupts (from 1684) and insolvent debtors (from 1712) in England and Wales, were placed in the *London Gazette* (ZJ 1), which is indexed from 1790: however before about 1830 the notices include some names not found in the records and omit some names which are. Scottish notices were placed in the *Edinburgh Gazette*, although a few are found in the

London Gazette. Details were also published in *Perry's Bankruptcy and Insolvent Weekly Gazette* (later *Perry's Gazette*), from 1827. From 1862 official notices relating to county court proceedings were placed in local newspapers, held by the appropriate local record office or by the British Library Newspaper Library (address in **48**).

These publications rarely give more than debtors' names, addresses and occupations and sometimes those of their creditors, with formal details of conviction and imprisonment, where appropriate.

46.3 What can you expect to find in the records?

In most bankruptcy cases, the records held by the PRO are confined to brief, formal entries in various register series that will establish the fact of bankruptcy but will not provide much background detail. Case files, in B 3 and B 9, survive only for a very small sample. Additional information can sometimes be found in the court records of legal actions against them: see **47**.

From 1842 separate records of bankruptcy proceedings outside the London area were kept by district bankruptcy courts (1842–1869) and by county courts with bankruptcy jurisdiction (from 1861), and these are now held locally.

Throughout, legal issues relating to bankruptcy were heard separately in local and central courts, and especially in Chancery. Bankrupts guilty of fraud, dishonesty or misconduct remained liable to imprisonment. Records relating to Scottish bankruptcies ('sequestrations') are held in the National Archives of Scotland (address in **48**).

Bankruptcy records usually give only the names, addresses and occupations of the debtors and of their creditors, and a formal summary of court proceedings. In some instances, where case papers survive (B 3, B 9, BT 221, BT 226) or where the proceedings were subjected to legal review (B 1, B 7), they may also provide interesting information about the bankrupts' family and business links, trading activities and economic circumstances.

46.4 Insolvent debtors before 1862

Insolvent debtors were held in local prisons, and often spent the rest of their lives there: imprisonment for debt did not stop until 1869. These will be kept in local record offices.

The PRO holds records for the prisons of the central courts, and of the Palace Court. The Palace Court, 1630–1849, was used for the recovery of small debts in the London area (PALA 1–9). Records of the Fleet, King's Bench, Marshalsea and Queen's prisons for debtors, 1685–1862 are in PRIS 1–11, with gaolers' returns of insolvents in certain London prisons, 1862–1869, in B 2. PCOM 2/309 is a register of Lincoln Gaol, 1810–1822, which lists the names of many people imprisoned for debt: other PCOM records may be worth exploration. Try also the returns of imprisoned debtors made to the Court of Bankruptcy, 1862–1869 (B 2/15–32). The periodic passing of Acts for the Relief of Insolvent Debtors allowed for their release, if they applied to a Justice of Peace and submitted a schedule of assets.

Records relating to this process may be with quarter sessions records, held by local county record offices: exceptionally, some for the Palatinate of Chester, 1760–1830, are here in CHES 10. For an overview of debtors' process, read the article by Innes.

In 1813, the Court for the Relief of Insolvent Debtors was established. After 1847, this court also dealt with London bankruptcies under £300. Petitions for the discharge of prisoners for debt in England and Wales, 1813–1862, were registered by this Court (B 6/45–71: indexes in B 8). Petitions by debtors (who were not traders or who were traders owing small amounts) for protection orders against the laws relating to debtors were registered by the Court of Bankruptcy, 1842–1847. After this, they were registered by the Court for the Relief of Insolvent Debtors, 1847–1861 (B 6/88–89, 94–96), and also by local courts of bankruptcy jurisdiction. The Court of Bankruptcy recorded proposals for repayments by insolvent debtors, 1848–1862 (B 6/97–98).

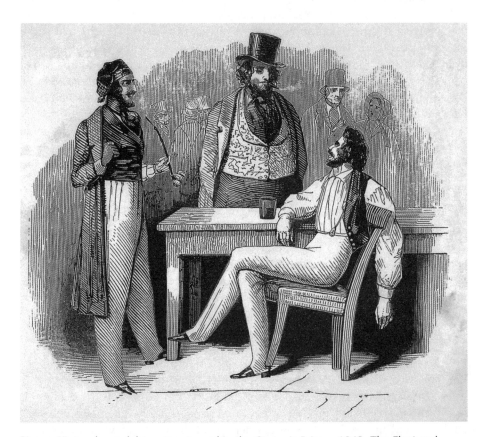

Figure 65 Insolvent debtors imprisoned in the Queen's Prison, 1842. The Fleet and Marshalsea prisons had just been closed, and the King's (or Queen's) Bench Prison renamed the Queen's Prison. It was abolished in 1862. (Mary Evans Picture Library)

46.5 Bankruptcy before 1869

Under the Bankruptcy Act of 1571 (13 Eliz. I c.7) commissioners of bankrupts could be appointed to allow a bankrupt to legally discharge his debts to his creditors by an equitable and independent distribution of his assets, and then begin trading again with his outstanding debts wiped out.

The creditors petitioned the Lord Chancellor for a commission of bankruptcy (a fiat after 1832 when the Court of Bankruptcy was established). Registers of commissions of bankruptcy and fiats issued are in B 4 for the period 1710–1849. Entries vary in detail over this period and may give the address and trade of the bankrupt (not between 1770 and 1797), and the names of either the petitioning creditors or those of the bankrupt's agent or solicitor. Entries that have been underlined or ticked mean that a case file on that particular bankrupt should be found in B 3.

The Commissioners published notices in the *London Gazette* (in ZJ 1) to inform creditors about their proceedings. Such notices are found from 1684 and are indexed from 1790: before 1832, they include many bankruptcies not included in the surviving B series. Bankruptcy notices also appear in *The Times* (held at the PRO on microfilm). The records of these commissions, in the B series, survive from 1710 only, and are incomplete until after 1832 (1821 for London). Earlier commissions of bankruptcy can be found enrolled on the Patent Rolls (C 66–67); conveyances of bankrupts' estates are enrolled on the Close Rolls (C 54) and relevant petitions are sometimes found in the State Papers (SP).

For the period after 1759, look first at the B 3 list which contains a sample (about 5 per cent only) of bankruptcy case files, indexed by personal name (*D.C.* stands for *Dealer and Chapman*). Most files date from after 1780 and before 1842. A further sample of case files after 1832 is in B 9 – after 1869, most relate to the London area. Case files may contain balance sheets submitted by the bankrupt. These are usually very general statements, rather than itemized accounts, and assignees' accounts. If your bankrupt is not listed in B 3 or B 9, you will have to search various register and enrolment series that will normally lead to only brief formal entries. These will confirm the fact of bankruptcy, if it took place, but will not provide much detail. Some case files of proceedings under the Joint Stock Company Acts, 1856–1857, for 1858–1862, are in B 10. C 217 also contains miscellaneous exhibits in a few bankruptcy cases.

46.6 Bankruptcy procedure before 1869

Enrolments of bankruptcy commissions (after 1758) and fiats may be in B 5. After 1849, creditors petitioned for an Adjudication in Bankruptcy, the registers of which (to 1869) are in B 6. The Commissioners took statements from the bankrupt and his creditors about his debts and the creditors would then elect trustees or assignees to value his assets and distribute them as dividends. Full-time Official Assignees, to prevent fraud, were also appointed after 1831 (appointments made 1832–1855 are in B 5) and thereafter assignees had to pay cash from the sale of a bankrupt's estates into the Bank of England – AO 18 contains records of their accounts for the period 1832–1851. Miscellaneous accounts, dating after 1844, are in BT 40.

When sufficient creditors (the proportion varied from three quarters to four fifths, by number and value) were satisfied, they signed a request for a Certificate of Conformity (a statement that the bankrupt had satisfied all the legal requirements). The Commissioners could then issue the certificate which effectively discharged him, although dividends might continue to be paid after that date. From 1849 to 1861, there were three classes of certificate:

I – where the bankrupt was blameless,
II – where some blame could be attributed,
III – where it was entirely the bankrupt's fault.

Indexed Registers of Certificates of Conformity for 1733–1817 and deposited Certificates for 1815–1856 are in B 6. These give the name and address of the bankrupt and the date of the certificate. Enrolled copies of some certificates of conformity, 1710–1846; some assignments of assets to trustees, 1825–1834 and some appointments of trustees, 1832–1855, are in B 5. After 1861, Orders of Discharge were issued instead. Records relating to issues the Commissioners were unable to resolve or appeals in bankruptcy cases are in B 1 and B 7. Actions against individual bankrupts or their assignees may sometimes be found in the records of other courts – Chancery, Exchequer, King's Bench and Common Pleas – many cases coming before the Palace Court (PALA) which dealt with small debt cases in the Westminster area.

46.7 District bankruptcy courts, after 1842

District bankruptcy courts were set up after 1842 to deal with cases outside London, sometimes defined as a 20-mile radius from the centre, and after 1869 (in part from 1847, for sums under £20) their jurisdiction passed to the county courts. After 1842, records relating to bankruptcy cases outside London may be held by county record offices and, after 1869, should normally be held there with the records of county courts, although sometimes 'country' cases were heard in London.

From 1849 until 1869, when the London Court of Bankruptcy was established, the two series of London District and Country District General Docket Books in B 6 show the class of certificate awarded. After 1861 they give instead the date of discharge, name, address and trade of the bankrupt and sometimes the names of petitioning creditors. For London Court cases, 1861–1870, deeds of composition with creditors or of assignment to trustees are summarized in a series of registers in B 6 (indexes in B 8). Registers of Petitions for protection from bankruptcy process in county court cases, from 1854, are in LCO 28.

46.8 Bankruptcy 1869–1884

After 1869, routine imprisonment for debt ceased, other than in cases of fraud or deliberate refusal to pay, and the Court for the Relief of Insolvent Debtors was wound up. Creditors who were owed more than £50 could petition for bankruptcy proceedings. Cases in London were dealt with by the London Court of Bankruptcy, and the records are in the PRO. London was defined as the City and the areas covered by the metropolitan county courts of Bloomsbury, Bow, Brompton, Clerkenwell, Lambeth, Marylebone, Southwark, Shoreditch, Westminster and Whitechapel. Cases outside London were normally heard by the county courts after 1861 (they had some jurisdiction since 1847) although they could be transferred to the London Court by special resolution of the creditors. The appropriate local record office normally holds county court records. Registers of Petitions for protection from bankruptcy process in county court cases, from 1854, are in LCO 28. There is a Register of London bankruptcies for 1873–1874 in BT 40/27 and one for County Court bankruptcies for 1879 in BT 40/46.

After 1883, the London Court of Bankruptcy was incorporated into the Supreme Court as the High Court of Justice in Bankruptcy. It subsequently became responsible for the additional metropolitan county court areas of Barnet, Brentford, Edmonton, Wandsworth, West London and Willesden. Bankruptcy petitions were only to be presented to the High Court if the debtor had resided or carried on business within the London Bankruptcy District for six months, if he was not resident in England or if the petitioning creditor could not identify where he lived. A High Court judge could, however, transfer any bankruptcy case to or from a county court. After 1883, official receivers supervised by the Bankruptcy Department of the Board of Trade took over responsibility for the administration of the bankrupt's estate, once a court had determined the fact of bankruptcy and made a receiving order. Its records therefore cover cases dealt with by both the High Court and the county courts.

The Registers of Petitions for Bankruptcy for 1870–1883, in B 6/184–197, are arranged alphabetically by initial letter of the bankrupt's surname. They cover both London and Country cases but only give a very brief entry with the case number, bankrupt's name, occupation and address. There are also registers of bankrupts, in both the London Bankruptcy Court and the county courts, for 1870–1886 in BT 40. These give dates of orders of discharge. More detail, for cases heard by the London Court of Bankruptcy, is given in the Registers of Creditors' Petitions (B 6/178–183), the best place to begin a search for cases heard in London 1870–1883. They are arranged chronologically and in alphabetical order of the first letter of the bankrupt's surname. They give his name, address and occupation and that of the petitioning creditor(s), details of what formal act of bankruptcy was committed, the date (and place if outside London) of adjudication as a bankrupt; the date of advertisement in the *London Gazette*, the names of any trustees appointed, the amount of any dividend paid, as shillings in the £, and the date when proceedings closed. Indexes to Declarations of Inability to pay (London Court cases only after 1854), which were one means of committing a formal act of bankruptcy, give the date of filing and basic details of the name, address and occupation of the debtor and the name of his solicitor, 1825–1925, are also in B 6.

Official Assignees' accounts, before 1884, are in BT 40.

46.9 Bankruptcy from 1884

After 1884, the Board of Trade supervised the work of the official receivers, who had the status of court officials and, after a receiving order had been made by the court, held meetings of creditors, investigated the circumstances of the bankruptcy and acted as interim administrators of the bankrupt's assets, pending, or in default of, the appointment of a trustee chosen by the creditors. If the bankrupt's assets were likely to be less than £300, the official receiver normally acted as trustee. When the trustee had realized as much of the bankrupt's assets as possible to pay his debts, he could apply for a release, discharging his responsibility.

For the period 1884–1923, Board of Trade registers in BT 293, which are indexed alphabetically by name, should contain entries for all persons served with a petition for bankruptcy, whether the case was heard in London or locally although it should be noted that not all petitions resulted in formal bankruptcy. Each entry should give the name, address and occupation of the debtor; the date of filing of the petition for bankruptcy; the dates of orders in case, including final discharge; the names of any trustees and the rate of dividend paid to the creditors. The incomplete set of Estate Ledgers in BT 294, arranged alphabetically by name, may show how the assets were distributed.

From 1888, registration of Deeds of Arrangement, made privately between debtors and creditors outside normal bankruptcy proceedings, became compulsory and the registers are in BT 39, with some case files in BT 221. These case files, dating from 1879, may also deal with audits and official releases – there is a card index of names for the official release files on open access. Case files of the Official Receiver relating to High Court cases from 1891 are in BT 226, sampled after 1914. The pre-1914 cases are indexed by name in a card index also on open access. Thereafter, the indexes are in BT 293. Most cases are personal bankruptcies, ranging from comedians to stockbrokers.

From 1924, you need to contact the Insolvency Service (www.insolvency. gov.uk or see **48**). They hold docket books, with internal indexes, that continue the kind of information previously found in BT 293 up to 1923.These docket books include the date of the announcement in the *London Gazette*, which can be seen at the PRO in ZJ 1.

46.10 Petitions to the High Court, from 1884

Registers of petitions to the High Court, by or against debtors, chronologically arranged by initial letter of surname from 1884, which record the names, addresses and occupations of the debtors and petitioning creditors, the name and address of the solicitor, and the alleged act of bankruptcy committed, are in B 11. The actual petition will only have survived if there is a case file in B 9 on which it has been filed. Registers of receiving orders from 1887 (orders from 1883 are noted in the B 11 Registers) are in B 12 and give the dates of formal court orders including the receiving order, the order of discharge with a note of any conditions attaching to it, and the date of the trustees' release. Names of trustees may also be given, although not if the official receiver was acting as trustee. For London and High Court bankruptcies after 1869, there is a very small sample (less than 5 per cent) of bankruptcy case files, arranged roughly chronologically by date of filing of petition, in B 9. These files may be one or more substantial volumes – those for A W Carpenter, trading as the Charing Cross Bank, run to 152 volumes.

46.11 Bankruptcy appeals

Before 1875, minutes of appeal cases are in B 7, with entry books of orders in B 1. Thereafter, appeals were directed to the Supreme Court's Court of Appeal (J 15, J 56, J 60, J 69–70). From 1883, appeals in county court cases went to a divisional court of the High Court (J 60, J 74 and J 95). An incomplete series of registers of petitions for protection from process in county court cases, covering the period 1854–1964, is in LCO 28.

46.12 Debtors and bankrupts: bibliography

W Bailey, *List of Bankrupts, Dividends and Certificates, 1772–1793* (London, 1794).
H. Barty-King, *The Worst Poverty: A History of Debt and Debtors* (Alan Sutton, 1991)
Edinburgh Gazette (Edinburgh, 1699 continuing)
J Innes, 'The King's Bench Prison in the later eighteenth century', in eds J Brewer and J Styles, *An Ungovernable People* (London, 1980)
London Gazette (London, 1665 continuing) in ZJ 1
S Marriner, 'English Bankruptcy Records and Statistics before 1850', *Economic History Review*, 2nd series, vol. XXXIII, pp. 351–366
Perry's Bankrupt and Insolvent Weekly Gazette (London, 1827–1881)
Perry's Gazette (London, 1882 continuing)

47

Civil litigation: introduction

◆ ◆ ◆

47.1 Introduction: the law and the courts

The records of civil litigation are so vast, and so complicated to describe, that this chapter has been split:

47   Introduction
47a   Central common law courts
47b   Chancery equity proceedings
47c   Exchequer equity proceedings
47d   Courts of Wards, Star Chamber, Requests, Augmentations and palatine equity
47e   Admiralty, Delegates and Privy Council appeals

Civil litigation (legal disputes between two parties) makes up a large part of the PRO's holdings of legal records, covering disputes about land, property rights, debts, inheritance, trusts, frauds, etc. All the legal records held by the PRO now have excellent introductory notes, filed before the list of each class, which should be consulted for detailed guides to the finding aids.

Records of civil litigation differ according to the kind of law and procedure used by the court in which they were heard. Cases heard in the common law courts were usually known as 'actions' and those in equity courts as 'suits'.

The development of law in medieval England was quite different from that of the rest of Europe. Scotland has a very different legal system, whose surviving records are in the National Archives of Scotland and local record offices in Scotland.

In England, the common law provided a powerful centralized system of justice which was based on principles derived from the common customs of the country, but was essentially unwritten. This law was used by the ancient royal courts of Common Pleas and King's Bench, in the civil actions heard at the assizes, and in the Exchequer of Pleas and the common law side of the Chancery. The remedies offered by the common law did not always meet litigants' needs. It was difficult, for example, to enforce trusts and wills at common law. In cases of breach of contract the common law remedy would ensure the payment of damages, but it could not compel enforcement of the terms of the contract (a remedy that lawyers describe as specific performance). Courts of equity, which developed alongside the common law courts, were able to provide a different kind of remedy, as they were empowered to give judgements according to conscience and justice, rather than according to law. Courts of equity could (and did) order specific performance (but they could not award damages for non-compliance). The two systems of justice co-existed until the nineteenth century when the Common Law Procedure Acts allowed equitable pleas to be considered in common law actions. The old central courts were abolished in 1875, on the creation of the new Supreme Court of Judicature.

Unfortunately for the family historian, surviving common law records relating to civil litigation (although extensive) are extremely difficult to use. They are very formal and are largely composed of standard legal formulae. It requires considerable expertise to understand the meaning that lies behind the formulae and the records rarely contain useful details.

In contrast, the records of the equity courts are full and informative and provide a wonderful source for social, family and local history. However the complexity of the filing procedures of the equity courts and the inadequacy of the available lists and indexes mean that it can be difficult to search for a particular case. This is a problem that will eventually disappear, as more of the equity finding aids become searchable online. The main equity court was the Chancery, where the Chancellor acted as the King's deputy: of lesser, but significant importance was the equity side of the Exchequer. Other courts, such as the Court of Requests (supposedly for poor plaintiffs) and Star Chamber grew out of the King's council, and used procedures based on those of the equity courts.

In addition to these royal courts, there were similar common law and equity courts in the palatinates of Chester, Durham and Lancaster, and in Wales: the records of Welsh courts are now in the National Library of Wales. The duchy of Lancaster (not the same as the palatinate) had its own courts, available to tenants of duchy lands throughout the kingdom.

Three other systems of law also operated in England. Civil law (a branch of Roman law) was used in the High Court of Admiralty and in the High Court of Delegates; ecclesiastical law (another branch of Roman law) was used in the church courts; and customary law, used in the many local courts based on the jurisdiction of the lord rather than the king.

All these legal systems (except for the ecclesiastical and local courts) were brought together in a series of mid nineteenth-century reforms, which resulted, in 1875, in a single Supreme Court of Judicature, with separate Divisions of Chancery, Common Pleas, Exchequer, King's Bench, and Probate, Divorce and Admiralty.

47.2 Civil litigation: bibliography

J H Baker, *An Introduction to English Legal History* (London, 3rd edn, 1990)
W R Cornish and G de N Clark, *Law and Society in England 1750–1950* (London, 1989)
A H Manchester, *A modern legal history of England and Wales, 1750–1950* (London, 1980)

47a

Civil litigation: the central common law courts

◆ ◆ ◆

47a.1 The central common law courts before 1875

Since the creation of the Supreme Court in 1875, we have become accustomed to the idea that legal business is organized on functional lines: that is, one division of the court deals with matters relating to trusts and real estate, another with personal actions, and so on. Before 1875, the division of business was not by type of case but by type of litigant. Thus Exchequer dealt with litigation between those who were Crown debtors, Common Pleas dealt with actions between subjects of the Crown, and King's Bench dealt with actions between Crown and subjects. Civil litigation in the King's Bench was heard on the 'Plea Side' (for information about its criminal jurisdiction, known as 'Crown Side', see **38.8**). Common law actions based on similar subject matter could therefore be heard in any of these courts, so that even if you know that someone was involved in a civil case and what the subject matter was, it will still be difficult to predict the court in which the action took place. Predicting which court a litigant might choose is further complicated by the fact that over the centuries a series of legal fictions were developed which enabled each of the courts to extend its clientele and effectively therefore to poach business from one another. The only exceptions to this are disputes between clergymen and laymen about the right to demand tithes, which were more likely to be heard in the equity side of the Exchequer than in any of the other courts.

These central common law courts were based in Westminster, but it was possible, and indeed usual, for trials to be held locally under a writ known as *nisi prius*. In effect this meant that the cases were heard at the next visit of the circuit judges to hold assize courts, and some records of trials held at *nisi prius* are therefore found amongst the records of the clerks of assize in the ASSI series.

47a.2 The records before 1875

Although much research has been undertaken on the medieval records, the more modern ones have been underused and are still imperfectly understood. The procedures, and hence the records, of the common law courts were extraordinarily complicated, and the task of understanding how they fit together is not helped by the fact that they were heavily, systematically and

Figure 66 The central courts each occupied their own carved-out portion of the great medieval Westminster Hall. It is very hard to imagine them there now. This is the King's Bench, in 1808: the others all had similar medieval relics in odd parts of their fabric. (From R. Ackerman's *Microcosm of London*, aquatint by T. Rowlandson and Pugin. Private Collection/The Stapleton Collection/Bridgeman Art Library)

unsympathetically weeded in the twentieth century. You also need to be aware that, with the exception of a short period during the Interregnum of 1649–1660, all formal legal records were written in abbreviated Latin and in distinctive legal scripts until 1733. Even after that date the use of archaic legal phraseology and of legal fictions mean that it can be difficult to interpret the records accurately. There are as yet no published guides to using these records; the lists are inadequate and there are no modern indexes (although there are a number of contemporary finding aids). Researching common law records is not for the fainthearted and you will have to be exceptionally determined even to attempt it. However, as the article by Watts and Watts shows, determination can occasionally pay handsome dividends.

Since we know that even in the present day most legal actions are compromised or dropped well before any formal legal hearing, the wisest course of action, in theory, would be to attempt to trace cases from the earliest initiation of procedure to the last conceivable entry. However in the current state of knowledge, such an approach is not practical. It is far better, and very much easier, to concentrate on a few major series of records, such as plea rolls, posteas, and judgement books/rolls. Most of these records were not created until the closing stages of cases that were either tried or came very near to being tried, and they will not therefore pick up the many cases that faltered soon after the initial steps of process.

Plea rolls are the formal record of the court's business. They are made up of individual parchment rotuli (a Latin term which literally means 'little rolls') on which are set out, in formulaic language, the nature of the action and an account of the process and final judgement (if any). Those of the King's Bench are in KB 26 (1194–1272), then in KB 27 until 1702, and are continued, for plea side only, in KB 122. These rolls also include the texts of deeds enrolled in the court. Reference to plea side enrolments, 1656–1839, is by means of a contemporary series of dockets now held in IND 1, which give, term by term, alphabetical lists of defendants' names together with the appropriate rotulus numbers in the plea rolls. The practice of filing rotuli on the plea rolls declined after 1760, so much so that by 1841 90 per cent of rotuli went unfiled. For this period therefore, it is essential to use the Entry Books of Judgements, 1699–1875, in KB 168 and J 89, which are arranged chronologically and give the date, county, names of plaintiffs, defendants and attorneys and brief details of the sum in dispute. There are indexes in the same series.

The plea rolls of Common Pleas, 1273–1874, are in CP 40. Between 1583 and 1838 they include personal and mixed actions only, as pleas of land were enrolled separately on the recovery rolls (CP 43). Although there are no indexes, there are a number of contemporary finding aids that can be used to help a search. These include the prothonotaries' docket rolls in CP 60, 1509–1859 (formerly in IND 1). The docket rolls were probably compiled for the collection of fees, but they do give direct references to the rotuli and so can be useful as a means of reference. From the middle of the sixteenth century the termly entries give the county, the names of the attorney, plaintiff and defendant and the kind of entry made. Until 1770 there are three separate series of docket rolls: one for each of the three prothonotaries. In order to check all the entries for a particular term, you have to use all three rolls. There are gaps in each of the three series. No docket rolls survive for the period 1770–1790. From 1791 onwards there is a single series which ends in 1859. Thereafter similar information, 1859–1874, is contained in the Entry Books of Judgements in CP 64. There are also docket books, 1660–1839, in IND 1 which give the rotulus numbers of cases reaching judgement, and various calendars of entries, also in IND 1.

The plea rolls of the Exchequer of Pleas, 1325–1875, are in E 13. The most useful means of reference to them are the docket books of judgements, 1603–1839, which are in E 46 (formerly in IND 1). These are arranged first by legal term, then alphabetically by name of the defendant against whom judgement was given. They usually give the name of the plaintiff, the type of suit (and sum in dispute in cases of debt), the amount of damages awarded and the resolution of the case. Two series of (selective) calendars of the records down to 1820 have been compiled. The first, arranged by date, is in IND 1; the other, arranged alphabetically by persons and places, is in E 48 and is available on open access in the PRO. Repertory rolls, in E 14, can also be used as a means of reference, but the series is very broken, and covers only the periods 1412–1499, 1559–1669 and 1822–1830. Entry books of judgements, 1830–1875, formerly in

IND 1, are now held in E 45. These give the dates of interlocutory and final judgements, but do not give any direct references to the plea rolls.

Chancery also had a common law jurisdiction, called the plea side of Chancery. Its basic jurisdiction covered relations between Crown and subjects on such matters as royal grants, royal rights over its subjects' lands as discovered through inquisitions post mortem and inquisitions of lunacy, feudal incidents due to the Crown, and division of lands between joint heiresses. It also had an increasing role in debt jurisdiction, on actions for recognizances for debt entered in Chancery. Pleadings for Edward I–James I are well-listed and are searchable online, in C 43 and C 44; pleadings for Elizabeth I to Victoria are in C 206. There are remembrance rolls in C 221 and C 222, and writs in C 245.

47a.3 The Supreme Court of Judicature, from 1875

In 1875, the existing superior civil courts were amalgamated into a new Supreme Court, consisting of a High Court of Justice and a Court of Appeal, which was able to apply either common law or the rules of equity as needed. The High Court consisted of five divisions: King's (or Queen's) Bench, Common Pleas, Exchequer, Chancery, and Probate, Divorce and Admiralty. In 1881, the Common Pleas, Exchequer and Queen's Bench Divisions were amalgamated. Theoretically all jurisdiction belongs to all divisions alike, but in practice the exercise of jurisdiction in particular matters is assigned to particular divisions. The Queen's Bench Division deals with actions founded on contract or tort (causing harm or injury to a person without legal justification), and in commercial cases. The Chancery Division deals with actions relating to land, trusts, mortgages, partnerships and bankruptcy. In 1971 the Probate, Divorce and Admiralty Division was renamed the Family Division; its Admiralty business was transferred to the Queen's Bench Division and contentious probate actions were transferred to the Chancery Division.

The records of the High Court are filed by type rather than by case, so it can be extremely difficult and time consuming to trace and assemble all the surviving material for any particular action. You also need to be aware that it is rarely possible to gain detailed information about the cases after 1945. Specimen judgement books are in J 89. The entry books of decrees and orders (J 15) can be useful in tracing cases heard in the Chancery Division; there are contemporary annual indexes to these orders under the name of the first plaintiff in IND 1. If you are tracing a case heard in the Queen's Bench Division you should start with the cause books in J 87 and J 168. Exhibits, which are always a source of fascinating information, are in J 90.

The Appeal Court, which was also created as part of the Supreme Court in 1875, heard civil appeals only until 1966. Its surviving records are in J 83 and J 84 with judgements (1907–1926) in J 70. Such records are rarely informative, since the cases were argued verbally, usually on points of law rather than on new evidence.

47a.4 Civil litigation: the central common law courts: bibliography

J H Baker, *An Introduction to English Legal History* (London, 3rd edn, 1990)

M Cale, *Law and Society: An Introduction to Sources for Criminal and Legal History from 1800* (PRO, 1996)

W R Cornish and G de N Clark, *Law and Society in England 1750–1950* (London, 1989)

A H Manchester, *A modern legal history of England and Wales, 1750–1950* (London, 1980)

C T Watts and M J Watts, 'In the High Court of Justice. . .', *Genealogists' Magazine* vol. 20, pp. 200–6

47b

Civil litigation: Chancery equity proceedings

◆ ◆ ◆

47b.1 Introduction

Over the centuries, the Lord Chancellor or his deputies heard hundreds of thousands of disputes over inheritance and wills, lands, trusts, debts, marriage settlements, apprenticeships, and other parts of the fabric of daily life. People turned to his court of Chancery because it was an equity court, promising a merciful justice not bound by the strict rules of the common law courts. The procedure was quite different, and involved the gathering of written pleadings and evidence. These still exist in such quantity that today the equity records of the court of Chancery are one of the treasures of the PRO, and a major resource for social and economic history. Many family historians have accessed them from the Bernau Index, but it would be fair to say that they have not had the popularity they deserve.

This chapter may appear dry – but the records themselves can be the nearest we get to a window into people's lives for the fourteenth to the late nineteenth centuries. Recently, I helped a novice to Chancery searching to follow up a reference to his rare surname that he had found in PROCAT in one of these Chancery pleadings series. We found a dispute between a man's wife and his long-term mistress (the mother of his children), which explained the circumstances in some detail. Where else could you find out that the mistress had been a servant in the marital house for only two weeks; that the wife dismissed her when she was discovered in bed with the husband; that the husband then set up a separate household with the mistress; and that he came back to the marital home whenever he fancied a fishing holiday?

Most Chancery records are in English: many appear (misleadingly) to be written speech. The initial pleadings are the best known, but behind them is a huge hinterland of investigation (and administration of properties in dispute) by the court. Chancery suits, and the subjects of dispute, have not been easy to research because of the difficulties of the Chancery filing system, and the lack of good catalogues and indexes.

The advent of PROCAT has started to transform searching for the initial stages of a Chancery suit. Already, simple name searches on PROCAT bring up many references to suits in 'C', and many more people are exploring records they had never considered before. In particular, PROCAT has opened up the fifteenth- and early sixteenth-century suits in C 1, which are well catalogued.

After 1558, the various series of initial pleadings are not catalogued in so much detail, but their rather rudimentary finding aids are slowly being added to PROCAT. However, several series of pleadings have no searchable list online. Later stages of the suits are even less visible from the lists, and still require use of contemporary 'indexes' or 'alphabets' available at the PRO only. Subject or place searching is almost impossible, as all reference is by the titles of suits. For an overview of what material it is possible to find, look at Horwitz, *Samples of Chancery Pleadings and Suits: 1627, 1685, 1735 and 1785.*

Part of C 6 was entered into a separate database, funded by the Pilgrim Trust, the Transport History Trust and the Friends of the Public Record Office and the PRO. The database is now available, but the decision has been made to add any further improvements to PROCAT itself, rather than to a separate database.

Many families have stories about money 'in Chancery'. For further information on how to check this out, ask for the leaflet on dormant funds in court from the PRO, or find it on the PRO website (www.pro.gov.uk).

47b.2 Titles of suits

The records of any one equity suit heard in Chancery were not kept together. Instead of being filed by the suit, they were filed by the type of document. This makes it difficult to trace all the documents in a suit, and at each point you will have to search for relevant records. To track a case in Chancery, you must have some idea of the title of the suit.

Suits are sometimes named *In re Bloggs*: these tend to be where the court is acting on behalf of someone incapable of acting for themselves: a minor, or a lunatic perhaps.

However, the usual title (which is all that most series lists give) is something like *Smith v Jones*, after the first named plaintiff and first named defendant. In the online catalogue, searching for the first defendant is easy if the title of the suit is given. It is very time consuming to search by defendant in the paper lists and alphabets.

This short form, *Smith v Jones*, was used even when the parties were Achitophel Smith, Methuselah Brown and the other copyholders of Camberwick Green (all 50 named in the bill) versus Zebediah Jones and the inhabitants of the parish of Trumpton (all 100 named in the bill or answer). This means that Smith v Jones will be found in the various lists and alphabets under S, but not under J. The second plaintiff, Brown, and the others will not be mentioned at all. An exception to this is when archivists have relisted the series to give more historical detail. Even then, 'others' is sometimes used for large numbers of people.

Another problem is that the court could alter the principal plaintiff or defendant, and thus the name of the suit, so Smith v Jones became Brown v Jones. It was not at all unusual for a trial to be opened under one title, and to end with a completely different title, especially if parties had died or married along the way. Consider looking under the names of secondary plaintiffs or defendants, picked up from the documents already consulted. And again, large numbers of suits were just not proceeded with.

47b.3 The five main record categories

The records fall into five main categories:

- Pleadings: statements made by the parties to a case. These bills, answers, replications and rejoinders are collectively known as Chancery Proceedings.
- Evidence: depositions (sworn examinations of persons chosen by the parties), affidavits (voluntary statements on oath) and exhibits brought into court.
- Decrees and orders: in the course of a suit.
- Chancery Masters' reports and accounts: on evidence and subjects remitted for investigation or administration.
- Final decrees – and appeals against them.

Spoken activity before the court is *not* recorded.

47b.4 The pleadings

Anyone wishing to start a suit in Chancery would get a lawyer to draw up a bill of complaint to submit to the Lord Chancellor. This would set out the offences of the defendant. It needed to claim that because of his or her lack of resources and power, or some other factor, the common law courts could not deliver justice. An equitable solution was therefore asked of the Lord Chancellor. The name of the Lord Chancellor can sometimes be the best clue to the date of the bill.

Bills (apart from the earliest ones) are in English, and give the plaintiff's name, occupation, rank and place of abode: the lawyer's name usually appears written by itself in a top corner. The defendant was required to make a similar written answer to all the points raised. The plaintiff could submit a replication, which might in turn produce a rejoinder from the defendant, and so on, until the allegations of the bill had been whittled or 'pleaded' down to a set of agreed points at issue. These were then used for the next stage, the gathering of evidence (see below, **47b.5**).

Chancery clerks filed the proceedings in a complicated system. As a result, you may need to look in several series. Some series have contemporary 'alphabets' of suit titles – very rough indexes – that need to be keyed up with the series list. Advice is available at the PRO. The filing system is described in detail in the 1963 *Guide to the Contents of the Public Record Office* vol. 1, pp. 32–33. Unfortunately, the relevance of this description was lost for years, when the finding aids were subsequently sorted into the 'alphabets'. We hope to be able to insert information into PROCAT soon (probably at header level) about whether the suit was one which continued for years, or which stopped at the initial stage, using the superseded finding aids in OBS 1 as the source.

It is exceptional to find bills and answers filed together under the same reference: carry on looking – but remember that if the dispute was settled out of court, you will find no further record.

All the catalogues, etc., mentioned below can be seen at the PRO, except for the Bernau Index. The Bernau Index is available on microfilm at the LDS Family History Centres and at the Society of Genealogists. It is a vital source, with a few minor drawbacks: it can be difficult to read, it gives obsolete references, and it makes no attempt to standardize variant spellings of the same surname. It rarely gives any additional information (such as address) that allows individuals with common surnames to be identified without recourse to the original documents.

If you use the Bernau Index, *please* copy the Bernau reference in full, as you will otherwise be lacking vital clues when it comes to translating the obsolete references given into modern PRO references. If you have references to translate, ask at the Map Room Enquiry Desk for Sharp's *How to use the Bernau Index*, or use Lawton's articles in *Family Tree Magazine* – but you may still need to ask for advice.

Some series have published catalogues, which can be accessed through public and other libraries as well as at the PRO: see the Bibliography for details.

Pleadings 1558–1714

1558–1649	C 2	Chancery Proceedings: Series I.
		    Several sequences of paper finding aids, including name and place indexes, at the PRO.*
		    Some published catalogues: see Bibliography.
			Not searchable online. Some but not all are included in the Bernau Index.

1558–1660	C 3	Chancery Proceedings: Series II.* Some published catalogues: see Bibliography.	Searchable online for 1st plaintiff, 1st defendant and county.
1570–1714	C 8	Six Clerks Series: Mitford.**	Not searchable online.
1613–1714	C 5	Six Clerks Series: Bridges. Some published catalogues: see Bibliography.	Searchable online for 1st plaintiff, 1st defendant and county.
1620–1714	C 7	Six Clerks Series: Hamilton.**	Not searchable online.
1625–1714	C 6	Six Clerks Series: Collins.**	Not searchable online.
1640–1714	C 10	Six Clerks Series: Whittington. Miscellaneous pleadings are listed at the end of the Whittington volume.**	Searchable online for 1st plaintiff, 1st defendant and county.
1649–1714	C 9	Six Clerks Series: Reynardson. Some published catalogues: see Bibliography.	Searchable online for 1st plaintiff and 1st defendant.

* A miscellaneous set of bills, answers and subsidiary documents, are in C 4. These are in the process of being listed.
** For C 6, C 7, C 8 and C 10, there are indexes to disputed wills (by the name of the testator, not of the plaintiff) available at the PRO, compiled by P W Coldham.

Pleadings after 1714

1715–1758	C 11	Various Six Clerks, Series I. The Bernau Notebooks give (for all parties) surname, forename, occupation and date: available at the PRO and Society of Genealogists.	Searchable online for 1st plaintiff and 1st defendant.
1758–1800	C 12	Various Six Clerks, Series II.	Searchable online for 1st plaintiff and 1st defendant.
1800–1842	C 13	Various Six Clerks, Series III.	Not searchable online.
1842–1852	C 14	Modern Series: Pleadings.	Not searchable online.
1844–1864	C 18	Miscellaneous Pleadings. Contains a very few 17th and 18th century pleadings.	Searchable online for 1st plaintiff and 1st defendant. Gives forename as well.
1853–1860	C 15	Modern Series: Pleadings.	Not searchable online.
1861–1875	C 16	Modern Series: Pleadings.	Not searchable online.
1876 onwards	J 54	Chancery Division: Pleadings, Common Law Orders, etc.	Not searchable online. Index for 1876–1890 only in IND 1/2218–2226.

47b.5 Depositions and affidavits

When the pleadings were finished, and the issues in dispute defined, the court commissioned neutral men of substance to examine an agreed list of people (deponents), and report back in writing (in English, with commissions and some small amount of material in Latin before 1733). Both sides drew up separate lists of numbered questions, called interrogatories, to be put to the deponents under oath. The answers, called depositions, provide more information about the case and often about the parties involved in the dispute. They also give the deponent's name, place of abode, age and occupation, at the head of his or her deposition. Affidavits were voluntary statements made upon oath during the progress of a suit. Indexes at the PRO are to the title of the suit, not to the person giving the deposition or affidavit. For indexes to these people, try the Bernau Index at the Society of Genealogists.

The depositions fall into two groups: town depositions taken in London, and country depositions taken elsewhere, usually before local worthies commissioned by Chancery to do so.

Figure 67 It can sometimes take almost as long to research a Chancery suit as it did to sue one: the difference is now that the profit (knowledge) is all yours, instead of accruing solely to the lawyers. (Richard Carstone 'In Chancery', illustration by Phiz to Charles Dickens' *Bleak House*/Mary Evans Picture Library)

Town depositions

1534–1853	C 24	Mostly listed by term: use IND 1/16759 and IND 1/9115–9121.	C 24/2450–2508 are searchable on line. Deponents indexed in Bernau Index
1854–1880 March	C 15, C 16, J 54	Filed in the same series as the pleadings.	
1880 April–1925	J 17	See Country depositions	

Country depositions

1558–1649	C 21	Searchable online for 1st plaintiff and 1st defendant. Deponents indexed in Bernau Index.
1649–1714	C 22	Searchable online for 1st plaintiff and 1st defendant. Deponents indexed in Bernau Index for C 22/1–75, and for all cases where the plaintiff's name began with A: about 8 per cent of the total.
1715–1880 March	C 11, C 12, C 13, C 14	Filed in the same series as (but not necessarily with) the pleadings. Make sure you have picked up all references. Depositions are usually found further on in the index volumes than the pleadings: on PROCAT they will have a higher reference number. Unfortunately, details of type of document have not been included in PROCAT, although they may be included reasonably soon at header level.
1880 April–1925	J 17	Town *and* Country depositions. Use IND 1/16748–16752.

If you cannot find the interrogatories, try the annual bundles of Detached Interrogatories, 1598–1852, in C 25. In addition, there are the Sealed, or Unpublished Depositions, taken for use in contingencies which never arose. These are in C 23, but they are not listed.

Affidavits

1611–1800	C 31, C 41	Indexes in IND 1/14545–14567. Entry marked with a cross: the original affidavit is in C 31. No cross: try the copies in C 41, for 1615–1747 only.
1801–1875	C 31	Indexes in IND 1/14575–14684. The name listed after the plaintiff and defendant is that of the solicitor, initiating the affidavit.
1876 onwards	J 4	There are indexes in IND 1: check the IND 1 list at the PRO.

Further (i.e. different) affidavits are known to be in the Chancery Masters' Documents in C 117–125. You may need to take advice at the PRO on accessing these, as they currently have peculiar references.

47b.6 Decrees and orders in the course of a suit

Any orders made during the course of a case, and the final judgement, are recorded in the Entry Books of Decrees and Orders. These also give the date for the recording of the depositions and affidavits, the hearing and the final decree. Decrees and orders before 1733 may be in Latin.

1544–1875	C 33	Accessed by contemporary annual indexes at the PRO. No indexes for 1544–1546.
1876–1954	J 15	Accessed by contemporary annual indexes at the PRO.
1955–1966	–	Destroyed.

The Entry Books are in two sequences known as 'A' and 'B'. Until Trinity term 1629, both 'A' and 'B' books list suits (by plaintiff v defendant) from A to Z. From 1629, entries for plaintiffs A–K are in the 'A' books, and entries for plaintiffs L–Z are in the 'B' books. In 1932 the 'A' and 'B' books were amalgamated.

The annual indexes (which are nearly all on the open shelves) reflect the A and B arrangement. Although annual, they start their year from the Michaelmas term. This means the dates on the spines are out by one year for the other three law terms. For example, the index listed as 1849 covers Michaelmas 1849 and Hilary, Easter and Trinity terms 1850. From 1860 each index covers a calendar year, not a 'legal' year. The reference found in the index has to be matched up to the C 33 or J 15 series list: make sure the IND volume number matches as well, to ensure that you have the right year.

Sometimes, of course, the case did not proceed after the bill and answer had been filed and thus no orders will be found.

Abbreviations found in the decrees and orders

acco^tt accountant	*exor* executor	*mre* matter
affd affidavit	*fur^r* further	*Ora^r* Orator (plaintiff)
Appo^t appointment	*hrinbef^e* hereinbefore	*Ors* others
Bequed bequeathed	*hrs* heirs	*ppr* paper
Co^l Counsel	*incon* or *inion* injunction	*rev^r* revivor
Cot Court	*indre* indenture	*suppl* supplement
Conson consideration	*L C* Lord Chancellor	*testor* testator
declon declaration	*M R* Master of the Rolls	*tree(s)* trustee(s)
Excepons Exceptions	*Mr* Master	*w^o* widow

47b.7 Involvement of the Chancery Masters

In many Chancery suits, the judge referred matters for investigation or action to one or more of the Chancery Masters in Ordinary. The Masters investigated the evidence (including depositions, affidavits and exhibits), administered the estates that were in Chancery care during the (often very lengthy) course of a suit, and reported to the court.

47b.8 Masters' reports and certificates

The Master's report back to the court often formed the basis for the court's final decrees. The Masters also sometimes acted as arbitrators, and the reports are therefore full of arbitrations and awards of various sorts. Until 1842, the reports include dealings with the infant and lunatic wards of court. The draft reports were submitted to both parties who were allowed to review the reports and to submit their response in the way of 'exceptions'. Longer reports can include detailed material taken from the pleadings and other papers being examined by the Master, and can provide a very useful summary or overview of a case. The Masters also returned short certificates into court, for example, authorizing the delivery of money. Masters were also responsible for assessing costs. From 1842 taxing masters did this instead. In 1852 the Masters' other functions were transferred to the judges. The judges then started referring many matters to their chief clerks (who soon took on the title of Master). The clerks' and taxing masters' reports were filed in the same series as the earlier Masters' reports. To find specific reports and certificates, you will need to use the contemporary 'indexes' in IND 1 at the PRO.

1544–1605	C 38	Reports: main series	No indexes
1606–1759	C 38	Reports: main series	IND 1/1878–2028
1760–1800	C 38	Reports: main series	IND 1/10700/1–41
1801–1875	C 38	Reports: main series	IND 1/14919–14993
1756–1859	C 39	Oversize documents	No indexes
1756–1859	C 40	Exceptions to the reports: appeals by either party	1836–1840 only: IND 1/30785–1/30786
1875–1962	J 57	Reports: main series	IND 1: many sequences

47b.9 Masters' documents

These may contain the affidavits, examinations of witnesses, estate accounts, wills and other documents on which the Masters founded their reports, together with the drafts of reports. As such, they can be a treasure chest of information – but they are not always easy to find.

You will need to know the name of the Master dealing with the suit. The various C series are named for the last Master to occupy the office on its abolition in 1852. Look at the succession lists of Masters filed with the C 103 list, at the PRO only, to see where the papers of your Master will be. There are contemporary indexes to these records, available at the PRO only, but currently no lists. The indexes are not always reliable.

Master Blunt	C 124	IND 1/6616
Master Brougham	C 117	IND 1/6625
Master Farrar	C 122	IND 1/6624
Master Horne	C 118	IND 1/6620 to IND 1/6621
Master Humphrey	C 123	IND 1/6618
Master Kindersley	C 126	IND 1/6622
Master Lynch (no separate collection)	C 123; C 124	IND 1/6618, IND 1/6616
Master Richards	C 121	IND 1/6626 to IND 1/6627
Master Rose	C 119	IND 1/6619
Master Senior	C 125	IND 1/6623
Master Tinney	C 120	IND 1/6617

Similar documents after 1852

Master Romer's Miscellaneous Books	1850–1911	J 23
Master Romer's Papers	1860–1890	J 24
Master Satow's Miscellaneous Books	1855–1899	J 26
Master Satow's Papers	1850–1900	J 27
Master Fox's Miscellaneous Books	1828–1895	J 29
Master Fox's Papers	1870–1910	J 30
Master Watkin Williams' Miscellaneous Books	1850–1909	J 32
Master Watkin Williams' Papers	1850–1900	J 33
Master Hulbert's Miscellaneous Books	1850–1903	J 35
Master White's Miscellaneous Books	1850–1903	J 36
Master Ridsdale's Miscellaneous Books	1855–1907	J 37
Master Ridsdale's Papers	1850–1938	J 38
Master Keen's Papers	1850–1910	J 40
Master Jobson's Miscellaneous Books	1850–1900	J 42
Master Jobson's Papers	1850–1910	J 43

Master Chandler's Miscellaneous Books	1847–1877	J 45
Master Chandler's Papers	1850–1890	J 46
Master Mosse's Papers	1852–1917	J 63
Master Hawkins' Pedigrees	1849–1925	J 64
Master Hulbert's Pedigrees	1849–1926	J 66
Master Newman's Pedigrees	1893–1931	J 67
Pedigrees (Various Masters)	1852–1977	J 68

As yet there is no succession list for these later Masters to show where records of a particular Master will be found.

47b.10 Accounts of disputed estates

The Masters had to receive annual accounts of the estates they administered while the ownership was in dispute in Chancery, or while the owner was a ward of the court, from trustees to whom the care of the estate had been remitted. The accounts are a very underused source, but need to be listed better to be accessible for local or business history.

The accounts for c.1750–c.1850 are in C 101 which is searchable online by the names of the parties: unfortunately no dates are given. For accounts after 1852, see the various J series noted in the table above. These are less easy to search online. Another useful source, searchable online, are the receivers' accounts in C 30, covering 1859–1901.

Other records of estates administered by Chancery are still held by the Supreme Court of Justice.

47b.11 Masters' exhibits

Exhibits are private papers brought into court as part of litigation: most were reclaimed at the end of a suit, but some were not. The minority that remained unclaimed now forms the PRO's lucky dip – a major collection of sources for social, economic and business history, as well as family papers.

The Chancery Masters' exhibits range in date from the twelfth to the nineteenth century; although the cases they come from are mostly eighteenth and nineteenth century. They were handed on from each of the 12 Masters to his successor, and the collections are named after the last Master to hold them before the abolition of the office.

The subject range is that of life itself – you can find papers relating to dentists; privateers; lunatics; the Great Fire of London; alum works; loyalist troops in America; West Indian plantations; the diamond trade; the newspaper trade; monastic records; and estate papers galore. The classes also include major collections relating to the Royal African Company, the Million Bank and the religious houses of Llanthony by Gloucester, Reading, Repton and Sudbury.

The lists are all searchable online, but their quality is patchy. Some descriptions are good, others ludicrously brief. You are likely to get one or more boxes of papers, sometimes in their original order and with the schedule (a list drawn up on their deposit with the Master still attached).

In theory, if the exhibits exist you should be able to match them up with the relevant case. This is not easy, as many of the pleadings are unindexed. The Master's documents, reports, accounts, etc. (C 117–129) are also in theory a source to move onto, if you can work out which Master was involved. Use the various lists of Masters attached to the C 103 paper list to find out who was the last holder of that Mastership, and whose name was therefore given to the surviving records inherited from his predecessors. See the introductory notes to each of C 103–114 for advice on this.

1085–1842	Duchess of Norfolk Deeds	C 115
1180–1857	Master Humphrey	C 109
1200–1853	Master Richards	C 106
1200–1856	Master Tinney	C 104
1200–1857	Master Brougham	C 111
1200–1859	Master Blunt	C 103
1220–1847	Master Farrar	C 108
1235–1837	Master Kindersley	C 113
1250–1851	Master Senior	C 107
1270–1857	Master Rose	C 112
1295–1808	Court Rolls (extracted from the other C series)	C 116
1306–1853	Master Horne	C 110
1350–c.1850	Six Clerks' Office	C 171
1481–1829	Master Lynch	C 105
1566–1841	Unknown Masters	C 114
1700–1918	Chancery Masters' Exhibits. These need to be ordered three days in advance.	J 90

47b.12 Final decrees, arbitrations, and appeals

Decrees (and orders) could be enrolled in the Decree Rolls, at an extra cost. Any appeal against such enrolled decrees or orders would have to be made to the House of Lords: try the House of Lords Record Office (address in **48**). As a result, very few decrees were enrolled, as it made a case more difficult to reopen. After 1875, the only decrees enrolled related to railway schemes and orders of other courts.

| 1534–1903 | C 78 Decree Rolls | IND 1/16950–16961B |
| 1534–1903 | C 79 Supplementary Series | IND 1/16960B |

There is a place-name index for enrolled decrees, Henry VIII to George III, in IND 1/16960A. Work undertaken to calendar the rolls in C 78 is described in Beresford, 'The decree rolls of Chancery as a source for economic history 1547–c.1700'. Parts of this series have been calendared and indexed as a result of projects undertaken by Beresford (1974–76) and Hoyle (1992). As a result, there is a detailed list and index of C 78/1–130, while for C 78/131–750 there is a detailed list with no index. After this, every fifth roll was listed, covering C 78/755–1250. These rolls appear to cover about 1534 to about 1700, but the enrolling system was not by date, so it is difficult to be sure if they include all decrees of that period. The List and Index Society have published these calendars. As yet, they have not been put on PROCAT. There are also a number of contemporary indexes, arranged in alphabetical order by the first letter of the name of the parties in the dispute.

If final decrees were not enrolled, they will be found in the Decree and Order Books (see **47b.6**). *Not* enrolling had advantages in some cases, as appeals were made back to the Lord Chancellor, and cases could be reopened more easily.

Appeals against unenrolled decrees (and orders) are among the Petitions. These also include 'ordinary' petitions, for example for winding up associations or for the appointment of new trustees to administer an estate.

| 1774–1875 | C 36 Ordinary and Appeal Petitions | IND 1/15029–15047 |
| 1876–1925 | J 53 Chancery Division Petitions | IND 1/15048, IND 1/15049, IND 1/15050, IND 1/15051 and IND 1/15282 |

Many suits were ended by arbitrations, mediations, compositions and awards of various sorts, made by commissioners appointed by Chancery. Quite frequently these were the Chancery Masters.

1544–1844	C 38 Reports on arbitrations by Masters	See 2.4
1544–1694	C 33 Awards enrolled	See 2.3
1694–1844	C 42 Awards not enrolled	No indexes

47b.13 Cause Books, 1842–1880: an integrated record

For 1842–April 1880 only, Cause Books survive in C 32. These bring together for convenience all references to decrees and orders, reports and certificates made during the course of a case, together with the names of all the parties to it and their solicitors and the dates of all their appearances. Indexes for 1860 to 1880 are in IND 1/16727–16747.

Cause Books from April 1880 onwards were destroyed on the recommendations of the Denning Committee on Legal Records, leaving no primary means of access to the records after 1880. Specimens only are preserved in J 89 for April–December 1880, 1890, 1900, 1910, 1920, 1930 and 1940.

47b.14 Civil litigation: Chancery equity proceedings: bibliography

M W Beresford, 'The decree rolls of Chancery as a source for economic history 1547–c.1700', *Economic History Review*, 2nd series, 32 (1979), pp. 1–10.
Calendar of Chancery Decree Rolls (C 78/1–14) List and Index Society, vol. 160, 1979
Calendar of Chancery: Decree Rolls (C 78/15–45), List and Index Society, vol. 198, 1983
Calendar of Chancery Decree Rolls (C 78/46–85) List and Index Society, vol. 253, 1994
Calendar of Chancery Decree Rolls (C 78/86–130) List and Index Society, vol. 254, 1994
P W Coldham, 'Genealogical Resources in Chancery Records', *Genealogists' Magazine*, vol. XIX, pp. 345–347 and vol. XX, pp. 257–260
D Gerhold, *Courts of Equity – A Guide to Chancery and other Legal Records* (Pinhorn, 1994)
H Horwitz, *Chancery Equity Records and Proceedings 1600–1800* (PRO, 1998)
H Horwitz, *Samples of Chancery Pleadings and Suits: 1627, 1685, 1735 and 1785* (List and Index Society, vol. 257, 1995)
W J Jones, *The Elizabethan Court of Chancery* (Oxford, 1967)
G V Sanders, *Orders of the Court of Chancery* (1845)
Public Record Office, *Guide to the Contents of the Public Record Office* (HMSO, 1963)
H Sharp, *How to Use the Bernau Index* (Society of Genealogists, 1996)

Published finding aids

The level of detail given in these published catalogues is not always included in the online catalogue.

C 2 • 1558–1603, *Calendar of Proceedings in Chancery in the Reign of Queen Elizabeth I*, ed. J Caley and J Bayler (London, Record Commission, 1827–1832)

• 1603–1624, *Index of Chancery Proceedings, James I*, A–K only, PRO Lists and Indexes, vol. XLVII (1922) *Index of Chancery Proceedings, 1603–1625*, A–L only, ed. R Topham, *The Genealogist*, n.s. vols IV, VI–IX (1887, 1889–1892)

• 1625–1649, *Calendar of Chancery Proceedings, Bills and Answers filed in the reign of Charles I*, vols 1–3, ed. W P W Phillimore, vol. 4, ed. E A Fry (British Record Society Index Library, 1903–1904)

C 3 *Index of Chancery Proceedings*, PRO Lists and Indexes
• 1558–1579, vol. VII (1896)

• 1579–1621, vol. XXIV (1908)

• 1621–1660, vol. XXX (1909)

C 5 *Index of Chancery Proceedings, Bridges' Division, 1613–1714*, PRO Lists and Indexes

- A–C, vol. XXXIX (1913)
- D–H, vol. XLII (1914)
- I–Q, vol. XLIV (1915)
- R–Z, vol. XLV (1917)

C 9   *Index of Chancery Proceedings, Reynardson's Division, 1649–1714,* ed. E A Fry
      (British Record Society, Index Library, 1903–1904)

Many local record societies have published catalogues of Chancery Proceedings
for their own county. For a list of local record society publications, see Mullins,
Texts and Calendars (continued on www.hmc.gov.uk). Most are available in the
PRO Library.

47c

Civil litigation: Exchequer equity proceedings

◆ ◆ ◆

47c.1 Introduction

Many people will access the Exchequer equity records in the first place by discovering an interesting description with the reference starting E 134, in the course of a keyword search on PROCAT. What is this court? What are these records, recently described by Milhous and Hume as an astonishingly rich potential source?

In the mid sixteenth century, the Exchequer developed an equity jurisdiction, which ran alongside the ancient common law Exchequer of Pleas. Its business included disputes over titles of land, manorial rights, tithes, mineral rights, ex-monastic land, debts, wills, etc. – anything where the plaintiff could allege (usually fictitiously) that the Crown had some kind of revenue interest in getting the matter sorted out. In effect, any suit that could be brought in Chancery could equally well be brought in the Exchequer. For decades the court provided a quicker forum than Chancery. As more people realized this, and started using the Exchequer court, so its advantages disappeared and the court became overburdened. In 1841, the Exchequer lost its equity side, and its outstanding business was transferred to the court of Chancery. The PRO publishes a specialist guide to these records: Horwitz, *Exchequer Equity Records and Proceedings 1649–1841.*

If you start investigating Exchequer equity proceedings with an interesting E 134 reference, you will find on looking at the document that you are in the middle of a case. This is because the depositions in E 134 are the only Exchequer equity records to be listed in any detail, giving plaintiffs, defendants and subjects in dispute. Most descriptions up to early 1772 have been incorporated into PROCAT: most of those from Easter 1772 to 1841 are currently awaiting entry.

Using E 134 for an initial search can be an easy way into exploring the records, but remember that E 134 only includes depositions taken in the country, and the catalogue does not include the names of the deponents. If depositions were taken in London only, or if the case did not involve depositions, you will have to try tracing the case from other series of records. These have not been listed at anything like the same level of detail, and need to be accessed by contemporary 'indexes' available only at the PRO. There is no union index of names. Few of the contemporary indexes are in strict alphabetical order.

47c.2 Working through a case

Documents relating to cases heard in the Exchequer fall into many different categories, pleadings, evidence, and court decisions and opinions, each filed separately. Almost all are in English. In general, Exchequer cases are easier to follow through than Chancery ones, as the Exchequer clerks developed a rational filing system early, and stuck to it.

If you suspect that an equity dispute was heard in the Exchequer, try a keyword search (using variant spellings) in E 134, or look in the manuscript calendar of E 134. If nothing turns up this way but you know the case was heard in the Exchequer, then look at the pleadings (see **47c.3**) and proceed logically through the case. The most important documents are the pleadings, the depositions, and the decree, if any.

For named people. If nothing turns up from a keyword search in E 134, then a speculative search can be difficult. The Bill Books, which are the original filing registers for the pleadings, are sub-divided by county and are not alphabetically arranged, although the full names of the plaintiffs and defendants are given. Many defendants are recorded in the appearance books (E 107): these are arranged by date, but are not indexed. However, the Bernau Index (at the Society of Genealogists) indexes deponents and defendants in Exchequer Depositions (E 134) but may not be complete. A list of deponents 1559–1695 is available at the PRO and at the Society of Genealogists, but is not indexed.

For places/subjects. Try a keyword search restricted to E 134. You may also wish to look through the paper versions at the PRO, which are arranged in three sequences, by county and also by date up to 1772 and then in manuscript calendars by date until 1841. Read through the Bill Books for the county at the PRO, to find any pleadings which did not produce depositions in E 134. The Board of Celtic Studies has published details of cases relating to Wales before 1625.

Some commissions in the series of Special Commissions (E 178), which are arranged by county in a chronological sequence, also relate to equity disputes. The list is descriptive, and searchable online. To find the title of the suit (if any) you will have to read the commission itself (in Latin until 1733) or look for an endorsement or other annotation on the return. The exhibits (E 140) and exhibits in Clerks' Papers (E 219) may also be worth checking.

47c.3 Pleadings

Pleadings were statements made by the parties to a suit: these bills, answers, replications and rejoinders are collectively known, for short, as bills and answers.

A bill of complaint submitted by the plaintiff initiated a suit, by setting out the case against the defendant. It conventionally included a statement that the parties were 'Debtors and accountants to his/her Majesty'. This was to imply that if the wrong was not righted the revenues of the Crown would be affected, either directly, or indirectly, because the plaintiff would then be less able to pay his own debts or dues to the Crown. There is a possibility that fairly lowly tenants of Crown manors were likely to use this court, but in many cases the status as a Crown debtor was fictional.

The bills and answers usually give much circumstantial detail. In addition to the plaintiffs' and defendants' names, the pleadings give their occupation, rank, and address. When brought by the Attorney General the bill was known as an 'Information'.

The defendant replied to the bill with his answer; the plaintiff might respond with a replication, and the defendant with a rejoinder, and so on. A purely legal objection given by way of reply was called a demurrer. Because both bills and answers are *ex parte*, each party setting out his case at length, and in the most favourable light, they may include a wealth of background detail: but may not necessarily be true or accurate representations of the facts.

Bills, answers, etc., in each suit were strung together in a single file, and given a reference number, which is entered on the top left hand corner of the bill. The bills and answers are in two series as shown here.

| c.1485–c.1558 | E 111 | Early Bills and Answers | Most of these are *not* Exchequer documents but strays from the records of other courts, such as the Court of Requests. Searchable online. |
| c.1558–1841 | E 112 | Bills and Answers | These are arranged by reign, subdivided by county. Not searchable online. To find individual pleadings, you
 • order up the Bill Books described below;
 • get a suit number and county;
 • key this up in the E 112 list to find the modern number of the portfolio;
 • use the suit number to find the right papers in the portfolio. |

Bill Books (Elizabeth I–Victoria)

These are the original, and still the best, means of access to the bills in E 112. They still serve as the main 'index'. The Exchequer clerks entered the bills under different sections for each county. They are indexed by plaintiff, and give the full names of the parties. Before 1700, and sometimes after, they give the subject. Entries up to 1733 are usually in Latin – but as you are looking for names this is not usually a problem. Some of the very early ones are faded, and need to be seen under ultraviolet light.

- Bedford, Buckingham, Cambridge, Cheshire, Cornwall, Cumberland, Devon, Essex, Hampshire, Hereford, Hertford, Huntingdon, Kent, Lancashire, Lincoln, Middlesex and all Welsh counties

Elizabeth I	1558–1603	IND 1/16820
James I	1603–1625	IND 1/16822
Charles I	1625–1649	IND 1/16824
Commonwealth	1649–1660	IND 1/16826
Charles II	1660–1674	IND 1/16828
	1669–1685	IND 1/16830
James II	1685–1688	IND 1/16832
William and Mary	1688–1694	IND 1/16834
William III	1694–1702	IND 1/16836
Anne	1702–1714	IND 1/16836
George I	1714–1727	IND 1/16838
George II	1727–1760	IND 1/16840
George III	1760–1801	IND 1/16842
	1776–1820	IND 1/16844
	1779–1820	IND 1/16846
George IV	1820–1830	IND 1/16848
William IV	1830–1837	IND 1/16850
Victoria	1837–1841	IND 1/16852

- Berkshire, Derby, Dorset, Durham, Leicester, Monmouth, Norfolk, Northampton, Northumberland, Nottingham, Oxford, Rutland, Shropshire, Somerset, Stafford, Suffolk, Surrey, Sussex, Warwick, Westmorland, Wiltshire, Worcester, York

Elizabeth I	1558–1603	IND 1/16821
James I	1603–1625	IND 1/16823
Charles I	1625–1649	IND 1/16825
Commonwealth	1649–1660	IND 1/16827
Charles II	1660–1674	IND 1/16829

	1669–1685	IND 1/16831
James II	1685–1688	IND 1/16833
William and Mary	1688–1694	IND 1/16835
William III	1694–1702	IND 1/16837
Anne	1702–1714	IND 1/16837
George I	1714–1727	IND 1/16839
George II	1727–1760	IND 1/16841
George III	1760–1801	IND 1/16843
	1776–1820	IND 1/16845
	1779–1820	IND 1/16847
George IV	1820–1830	IND 1/16849
William IV	1830–1837	IND 1/16851
Victoria	1837–1841	IND 1/16853

There are two manuscript indexes available at the PRO. One indexes plaintiffs and defendants for James I–Victoria: Miscellaneous Bundles, referring to the bundles of miscellaneous material grouped at the end of each reign in E 112. The other is a calendar of Elizabethan cases in E 112, for the counties Bedford–Kent. This gives a brief description of the subject of the suit: it is arranged by name of plaintiff, with defendants' names cross-referred.

Replications and rejoinders, the responses to the bill and answer, are often found with the bills and answers in E 112 before c.1700. However, there are others in E 193. Before 1700 the replications and rejoinders in E 193 appear to be strays from E 112. Those dated before 1660 add details on the alleged facts of the case. After that date, they are formulaic, and add nothing material to our knowledge of the case. They are listed by date.

The appearance in court of the defendant, whether in person or, as was usual, by his attorney, was noted in the appearance books (E 107). Before 1815 the books record the names of defendants both in cases on the Memoranda Rolls (E 159) as *Per Rec*; and in equity disputes as *Per Bill Anglican* or, where the Attorney-General was the plaintiff, as *Per Informac*. The early books sometimes enter subsequent proceedings under the first entry. Since the defendant's name is given first, the order of the parties should be reversed to obtain the title of the suit, if this is not already known.

47c.4 Evidence: depositions, surveys, affidavits and exhibits

Evidence took the form of affidavits (statements on oath); depositions (examinations of witnesses on lists of questions filed in advance by the parties); surveys (enquiries conducted by commissioners acting on instructions from the Exchequer); and exhibits.

Depositions

When the pleadings were finished, and no more counter-replies remained to be filed, the court commissioned certain persons to examine witnesses. Both sides drew up a list of simple questions, called interrogatories, to be put to the witnesses. Each question was given a number, and was subject to vetting by the court. The answers to these questions, called depositions, provide information about the case, and often about the parties involved in the dispute, which may not be included in the pleadings. The answers can be fully understood only by reference to the numbered questions of the interrogatories; and separate sets of depositions were taken to answer each party's interrogatories. The deponent's

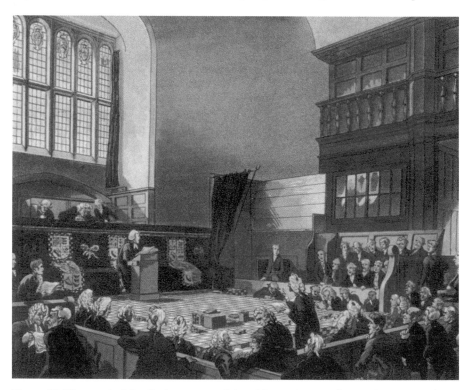

Figure 68 The court of the Exchequer proclaimed its origins as a financial institution by the chequered cloth in the centre of the court, on which accounts had been calculated with counters since at least 1118. When roman numbers were in common use, such a device was essential. All plaintiffs had to allege that the Crown had a financial interest in the outcome of their search for justice – although this was not necessarily true. (Aquatint by J Stadler after T. Rowlandson and Pugin. Reproduced by permission of the Palace of Westminster)

name, address, age and occupation are set out at the head of his deposition.

The depositions fall into two groups: depositions taken before the barons of the Exchequer at Westminster, and depositions taken in the country by commissioners appointed by the court. In a few cases, especially those in which the Crown had an interest, the court appointed commissioners to conduct an inquiry into the facts of the case such as, for example, the boundaries of a manor. The parties might themselves request such a survey after filing an affidavit (E 103). The records are arranged in the series shown here.

E 133	1558–1841	Depositions before the Barons [in London]	Searchable online for plaintiff or defendant: no dates. These are listed in three groups. • alphabetically by plaintiff, excluding Crown cases; • Crown cases listed alphabetically by defendant; • cases in which the plaintiff is not known, plus miscellanea. For 1558–1603, there is a manuscript calendar, giving date, parties, and subject.
E 134	1558–1841	Depositions taken by Commission [in the country]	Easily searchable online by name, place or subject up to 1772: later descriptions have not yet gone into PROCAT, although we hope to do them soon. These are listed in some detail in calendars, which give the names of the parties, the date, and the nature of the dispute.
E 103	1774–1841	Affidavits	In a minority of cases involving misunderstanding or malpractice, deponents could swear an affidavit in the Exchequer, sometimes giving additional details about themselves as well as about the case.

The Bernau Index at the Society of Genealogists includes many deponents and defendants, although the coverage may not be complete. Deponents are also listed in a county arrangement 1559–1695 in a typescript list, of which copies are in the PRO and at the Society of Genealogists. The PRO copy is not indexed, but the Bernau Index includes references to this list.

Commissions and surveys

Commissions of enquiry, c.1558–1841, in both equity and revenue causes are in E 178: they are searchable online. The return of executed commissions (and depositions) into the Exchequer is recorded in E 221.

There are also Commission Books, which record the issue of commissions, writs, etc., in both revenue and equity proceedings. They therefore include commissions to take the answers of defendants, or the depositions of witnesses, although the majority of entries relate to revenue proceedings on the Memoranda Rolls (E 159) rather than equity disputes.

1578–84	E 165/43
1624–30	E 165/44
1725–45	E 165/45. Gives the names of the commissioners, identifying those appointed at the suggestion of the plaintiff and of the defendant.
1725–1842	E 204

Affidavits

These are sworn statements made before the court or, in the country, before commissioners of oaths. Most are procedural, and many relate to the service of process, especially of the subpoena intended to secure the appearance in court of the defendant. They are usually in common form, but some add considerable circumstantial detail; others enlarge on the status of individual deponents, on the evidence, or the circumstances of the case. Affidavits in equity causes and in revenue cases enrolled on the Memoranda Rolls (E 159) are filed in the same bundles. There are three series, shown here.

E 207	1558–1774	Bille: contain much other procedural matter. Date list only, no index.
E 103	1774–1841	Date list only: the later indexes relate solely to revenue proceedings.
E 218	1695–1822	Date list only, no index.

Exhibits

Documents produced in court as supporting evidence, but not subsequently reclaimed by the parties. With the transfer of outstanding business to the Chancery in 1841 one of the Exchequer clerks became a Chancery Master. Exhibits in Exchequer cases can therefore found in the series shown here.

E 140	1319–1842	Exhibits. Listed alphabetically by parties where known, but without indication of date or subject matter. Some exhibits are described in more detail in OBS 1/752: this list has to be keyed with the modern list.
E 219	17th–19th century	Exchequer Office, Clerks' Papers. Includes exhibits. Descriptive list, searchable on PROCAT. Card index of plaintiffs where known.

C 106	13th–19th century	Chancery Masters' Exhibits, Master Richards. Most are exhibits in Chancery actions, but the series includes Exchequer cases also (although the list does not identify them as such). Descriptive list, searchable on PROCAT.
C 121	c.1600–c.1900	Chancery Masters' Documents, Master Richards. Most relate to Chancery actions, but the series also includes Exchequer cases.

Clerks' papers

Much of the work in Exchequer equity cases was done by the clerks of the King's Remembrancer's Office. The clerks' papers in E 219 include correspondence, office copies, exhibits, briefs, drafts produced for each stage of the suit, and bills of costs, as well as papers relating to the working of the Exchequer Office itself.

47c.5 Court decisions and other formal records

Court decisions are recorded in several overlapping series of decree and order books, and in reports by the officers of the court.

Decrees and Orders

At each stage of a dispute, an order of the court was required to move on to the next stage. Orders therefore appointed days for hearing, authorized the issue of commissions and the like, and, on occasion, made interim settlements. Most orders ran 'of course' and were little more than formalities; a few add substantially to our knowledge of the case. The first notice of an order was a brief entry in the Minute Books (E 161); orders were then written out in full (Original Orders, E 128, E 131) and registered (E 123–125, E 127). The final judgement was called a decree. Many cases were either withdrawn or settled out of court before they reached this stage, so that the court would reach no conclusion.

The first notice of a decree was an entry in the Exchequer Chamber Minute Books (E 162). These, with the clerks' papers (E 219), are the only records which give any indication as to what actually happened in court, as distinct from the decisions of the court. Like the orders, decrees were first written out in full (E 128, E 130) and then registered (E 123–124, E 126). Some drafts and copies of both decrees and orders are in the Clerks' papers (E 219). A full description of the interrelationship of the several series is given in the introduction to the E 123 list. The series overlap, and entries relating to any one case may be found in more than one series.

You could also try Martin, *Index to Repertories, Books of Orders, and Decrees, and other Records in the Court of Exchequer*, which is a place-name index for the earlier records. The references have to be keyed to modern lists.

Reports and Certificates

At any stage in the dispute the written pleadings, interrogatories, etc., might be referred for comment to the officers of the court. Many surviving reports represent a fairly late stage in the proceedings, dealing with funds in court or the taxation of costs. A few contain very detailed accounts of the disposition of estates. Reports and Certificates (1648–1841) are in E 194.

Funds in Court

The Court could order that disputed monies should be paid into court, to be held in trust pending settlement of the dispute in question. Where the quarrel was over the estate of a deceased person, the court sometimes ordered the sale or realization of the profits of that estate. Monies paid into court were frequently invested in consolidated stock: that is, in the Bank of England. Initially administered by the King's Remembrancer or his deputy, those funds were, from 1820, administered by the Accountant General of the Court. Account Books of Funds in Court (1675–1841) are in E 217. E 217/1–6, which are indexed, are detailed accounts under the titles of the suits. Other volumes in the series are chronologically arranged, and the entries brief. They contain many entries unrelated to equity proceedings: see the introduction to the list.

Many of the Equity Petitions (1627–1841) in E 185 were made after the filing of the decree, and relate either to the taxation of costs or the payment of funds into or out of court. Petitions earlier than 1800 are mostly for admission to sue *in forma pauperis*.

47c.6 Civil litigation: Exchequer equity proceedings: bibliography

W. H. Bryson, *The Equity Side of the Exchequer* (Cambridge, 1975).

D B Fowler, *The Practice of the Court of the Exchequer* (2 vols, London, 1795). A manual produced by a working officer of the court, and much the best guide, at least to eighteenth-century procedure.

H Horwitz, *Exchequer Equity Records and Proceedings 1649–1841* (PRO, 2001)

E G Jones, *Exchequer Proceedings (Equity) Concerning Wales. Henry VIII–Elizabeth* (Cardiff, University of Wales, Board of Celtic Studies, *History and Law* series, 1939)

T I Jeffreys Jones, *Exchequer Proceedings Concerning Wales in Tempore James I* (Cardiff, University of Wales, Board of Celtic Studies, *History and Law* series, 1955)

G Lawton, 'Using Bernau's Index', *Family Tree Magazine*, vol. VIII, 1991–2 (3 parts)

A Martin, *Index to Various Repertories, Books of Orders, and Decrees and other Records preserved in the Court of Exchequer* (London, 1819). Selective index to places mentioned in decrees and orders, memoranda rolls, etc.

J Milhous and R D Hume, 'Eighteenth Century Equity Lawsuits in the Court of Exchequer as a Source for Historical Research', *Historical Research*, vol. 70, no. 172, pp. 231–246, 1997

H Sharp, *How to use the Bernau Index* (Society of Genealogists, 1996)

T Trowles, 'Eighteenth-century Exchequer records as a genealogical source', *Genealogists' Magazine* vol. 25, pp. 93–8

47d

Civil litigation: Courts of Wards, Star Chamber, Requests, Augmentations and palatine equity

◆ ◆ ◆

47d.1 Bill procedure courts

All these courts used English bill procedure very similar to that used by the equity sides of Chancery and Exchequer: for a description of that procedure, look at **47b**. For Court of Wards suits using bill procedure, see **41.7**.

47d.2 The Court of Star Chamber, 1485–1641

Star Chamber (named after the room in the Palace of Westminster in which it met) was effectively the King's Council sitting as a tribunal to enforce law and order. It became a separate court of law after 1485. Its business expanded significantly throughout the sixteenth century, but its success brought enmity from practitioners in the traditional common law courts and it was abolished in 1641. Although cases brought to Star Chamber were described as if they were about offences against public order, many of them were actually private disputes about property rights. The Court used procedures like those of the equity courts, so the main series of records are in English.

The case papers or proceedings are well listed in the paper lists (except for STAC 5) – in some cases, not all the information has been transferred onto PROCAT. However, most cases can be searched for on PROCAT, even if subject or place searches are not fully reliable yet.

For STAC 8 (James I), Barnes has produced three volumes of indexes, indexing parties, places, offence, and counties in considerable detail, using a numeric code system which is explained in each volume. Copies are available at the PRO. These indexes are quite difficult to get used to, but very helpful for local history, or for the history of offences, as well as for people searching for particular parties. You will need to read the introductory material, explaining the codes used, and you have to identify which index and which column to look in.

The records of Star Chamber do not survive in entirety. There are large numbers of proceedings, but no decree or order books survive. You can find out a great deal of detail about a case, but with little chance of discovering its final outcome. Barnes has argued that every Star Chamber case in which at least one

Assigned to	Actual date range	Series	Finding aids	Searchable in PROCAT by name subject and place?

Henry VII	1485–1509	STAC 1	Listed in the standard list set, giving plaintiffs, defendants, subject and county (with appendices for stray and newly listed documents).
			    Name index in *Lists and Indexes Supplementary Series IV*.
			    Included in the Bernau Index at the Society of Genealogists.
				Yes

Henry VIII	c.1450–1625	STAC 2	As above	Yes
Edward VI	Hen VII–Eliz I	STAC 3	As above	Yes
Mary	Hen VII–Eliz I	STAC 4	As above	Yes
Elizabeth I	1558–1601	STAC 5	Listed in an eighteenth century 4-volume manuscript list, in several sequences of letter bundles, by first plaintiff's surname. Name index in *Lists and Indexes Supplementary Series IV*.	By name of plaintiff and defendant only
		STAC 7	Manuscript list giving parties, subject and county.	Yes
James I	1601–1625	STAC 8	Listed as above: indexed by the Barnes Index.	Not all in as yet, although most plaintiffs and defendants are in
Charles I	1625–1641	STAC 9	Listed as above: cases begun under James I will be in STAC 8.	Yes

defendant was convicted resulted in a fine, and that notes of these fines were recorded on the Exchequer Memoranda Rolls in E 159. Another old computer print-out at the PRO lists these for 1596–1641. The series E 101 and E 137 also contain some accounts of fines.

A list of cases relating to Wales is in Edwards, *A Catalogue of Star Chamber Proceedings Relating to Wales*. It is also worth exploring the publications of local record societies, as they have published many cases. For more information, try Guy's handbook on Star Chamber and Barnes' article.

47d.3 The Court of Requests, 1483–1642

The Court of Requests was an offshoot of the King's Council, intended to provide easy access by poor men and women to royal justice and equity. It was established in 1483, when the Chancery official responsible for sorting petitions from the poor became clerk of the council of requests. A cheap and simple procedure attracted many suitors (not all of them poor, but particularly including women). The Court used procedures like those of the equity courts, so the main series of records are in English. The records of the court cease in 1642. Its privy seal was removed during the Civil War. Although the court was never formally abolished, much of its caseload eventually passed to local small claims courts. The types of case heard included title to property, annuities, matters of villeinage, watercourses, highways, wilful escape, forgery, perjury, forfeitures to the King by recognizance and dower, jointure and marriage contracts.

Requests records are not searchable on PROCAT as yet. In addition, watch out when ordering from REQ 2: you currently have to check the paper list in the Standard Set in order to get the reference exactly right. (You need to put in the bundle number with its range of items – e.g. REQ 2/1/1–129 – to order any one case in that range.)

Figure 69 A typical bill or petition, as submitted to an English bill procedure court, from the time of Henry VIII. Later ones were very much larger – so large that they can be physically difficult to read. (PRO, REQ 2/12/229)

Monarch	Date range	Bundles in REQ 2	Finding aids
Henry VII–Henry VIII	1485–1547	1–13	Listed in *List and Index, XXI, Proceedings in the Court of Requests* (gives parties, subject and place): 1–40 also listed with a little more detail, and some dates, in the lists marked 'Hunt's series'. Indexed in *List and Index Supplementary, VII, vol. 1.* Included in the Bernau Index at the Society of Genealogists.
Edward VI	1547–1553	14–19	As above
Mary I	1553–1558	20–25	As above
Elizabeth I	1558–1603	26–136	As above
		137–156	Listed in the manuscript 'Atkin's Calendar', and indexed in *List and Index Supplementary, VII, vol. 1.*
		157–294	Listed in a further unnamed manuscript list, and indexed by person, subject and location in: bundles 157–203 in *List and Index Supplementary, VII, vol. 2.* bundles 204–294 in *List and Index Supplementary, VII, vol. 3.*
		369–386	None
James I	1603–1625	295–311	Listed in a further unnamed manuscript list, and indexed by person, subject and location in *List and Index Supplementary, VII, vol. 4.*
		387–424	Bundles 387–409 are listed in a further unnamed manuscript list, indexed by person, subject and location in *List and Index Supplementary, VII, vol. 4.*
		425–485	None
Charles I	1625–1649	486–806	None
?	various dates	807–829	None

Unlike the Star Chamber, the judicial and administrative records (in English and Latin) of the Court of Requests have survived fairly well: most are in REQ 1, but there may be some unsuspected material in REQ 2/369–386. REQ 1 includes:

		REQ 1/	
Order and decree books	Hen VII–Chas I	1–38, 209	orders, decrees, final judgements and, before 1520, appearances
Order books	Eliz I–Chas I	39–103	draft orders, decrees and memoranda
Appearance books	Hen VIII–Chas I	104–117	records of appearance by defendants, usually by attorney
Contemporary indexes to affidavits	1637–1641	118, 150	incomplete
Affidavit books	1591–1641	119–149	signed affidavits (by servers) that process, especially writs of summons, had been served
Note books	1594–1642	151–170	outline records of the progress of suits
Process books	1567–1642	171–197	recording the issue of writs of privy seal, attachments for arrest, appointment of commissions, injunctions, and orders for appearances
Witness books	Eliz I–Chas I	198–206	
Register of replications	1632–1636	207	
Commission book	1603–1619	208	recording return dates of depositions by commission

For a general overview, see Leadam, *Select Cases in the Court of Requests.*

47d.4 Court of Augmentations, 1536–1554

The Court of Augmentations was founded in 1536, to deal with the transfer of land to the Crown when the monasteries were dissolved. Most historians consider the court to be an administrative court, and it was certainly involved in a huge amount of administration. However, it was also a court of law, using English bill procedure, to settle disputes relating to the land and other rights claimed by monastic tenants, pensioners, founding families, local communities, debtors and creditors, and so on.

Records of the legal proceedings are scattered among several series. None are searchable on PROCAT as yet.

	Date	Series	Finding aid	Indexes
Pleadings (and some depositions)	1536–1554	E 321 E 315/19–23	MS list filed as: <refers to E 321 vol. 1>,<refers to E 321 vol. 2>, <refers to E 315 vol. 1>. Gives plaintiff, defendant, subject and county.	Place index to all three lists, filed as <refers to E 315 vol. 2>
Depositions	1536–1554	E 315/ 108–134	MS list filed as: <refers to E 315 vol. 1>. Gives plaintiff, defendant, subject and county.	
Decrees and orders	1536–1553	E 315 /91–105	MS list filed as: <refers to E 315 vol. 5> <refers to E 315 vol. 7>	Indexes at: <refers to E 315 vol. 6> <refers to E 315 vol. 8>

The court of Augmentations was absorbed into the Exchequer in 1554. There are many later suits relating to the lands of the monasteries in the Exchequer equity proceedings (see **47c**).

47d.5 The palatine equity courts of Chester, Durham, Lancaster and the Duchy of Lancaster

The record keeping practices of these courts were very similar to those of the central equity courts. None of them is searchable on PROCAT as yet.

Palatinate of Chester: Exchequer equity court
The local equity jurisdiction of the Chester equity court, known as the Exchequer, lasted from the fifteenth century to 1830.

Pleadings in cases relating to real property (i.e. land)	Henry VIII–1830	CHES 15
Pleadings in cases relating to debts and personal property	1559–1762	CHES 16
Depositions	Elizabeth I	CHES 12
Affidavits, exhibits and other miscellaneous papers	Henry III– Charles II; 1501–1830	CHES 11; CHES 9
Decrees and orders	1559–1790	CHES 13
Entry books of decrees and orders	1562–1830	CHES 14

Palatinate of Durham: Chancery equity court
The local equity jurisdiction of the Chancery of Durham lasted from the fifteenth

Pleadings	1576–1840	DURH 2
Interrogatories and depositions	1557–1804	DURH 7
Affidavits, exhibits and other miscellaneous papers	1657–1812	DURH 1
Decrees and orders	1633–1958	DURH 4
	1613–1778	DURH 5
Decrees and orders: drafts	1749–1829	DURH 6

century to 1971.

Palatinate of Lancaster: Chancery equity court
The local equity jurisdiction of the Chancery of the County Palatine of Lancaster

Pleadings: bills	1485–1853	PL 6
Pleadings: answers	1474–1858	PL 7
Pleadings: replications	1601–1856	PL 8
Depositions	1581–1854	PL 10
Affidavits, exhibits and other miscellaneous papers	1610–1678, 1793–1836; 1795–1860	PL 9; PL 12
Reports and certificates	1813–1849	PL 30
Decrees and orders: entry books	1524–1848	PL 11

lasted from the fifteenth century to 1971.

Duchy of Lancaster: Duchy Chamber equity court
The equity court of the Duchy of Lancaster, known as the Duchy Chamber, started in the fourteenth century and still exists in theory. The Duchy of Lancaster is not the same as the county: the Duchy holds lands in many other parts of the country, and its tenants were able to use its court centred on the Savoy, in London.

Pleadings	1485–1835 1558–1818 1502–1853	DL 1 DL 3 DL 49
Draft injunctions	1614–1794	DL 8
Depositions	Henry VII–1818	DL 3, DL 4

Depositions (sealed)	1695–1739	DL 48
Affidavits, exhibits and other miscellaneous papers	1502–1853; 1560–1857	DL 49; DL 9
Decrees and orders: entry books	1472–1872	DL 5
Decrees and orders: drafts	Henry VIII–1810	DL 6

47d.6 Civil litigation: Courts of Star Chamber, Requests, Augmentations and palatine equity: bibliography

J H Baker, *An Introduction to English Legal History* (London, 3rd edn, 1990)

T G Barnes, 'The archives and archival problems of the Elizabethan and early Stuart Star Chamber', *Journal of the Society of Archivists*, II (1963)

C G Bayne and W H Dunham, *Select cases in the council of Henry VII* (Selden Society, 1958)

I Edwards, *A Catalogue of Star Chamber Proceedings Relating to Wales* (Cardiff, University of Wales, Board of Celtic Studies, *History and Law* series, 1929)

K Emsley and C M Fraser, *The courts of the County Palatine of Durham* (Durham County Local History Society, 1984)

J A Guy, *The court of Star Chamber and its records to the reign of Elizabeth I,* (HMSO, 1984)

G Lawton, 'Using Bernau's Index', *Family Tree Magazine,* vol. VIII, 1991–2 (3 parts)

I S Leadam, *Select cases in the Court of Requests* (Selden Society, 1898)

I S Leadam, *Select cases . . . in Star Chamber* (Selden Society, 1903)

E A Lewis and J Conway Davies, *Records of the Court of Augmentations relating to Wales and Monmouthshire* (Cardiff, University of Wales, Board of Celtic Studies, *History and Law* series, 1954)

H Sharp, *How to use the Bernau Index* (Society of Genealogists, 1996)

R Somerville, 'The palatinate courts in Lancaster', *Law and law makers in British History, papers presented to the Edinburgh Legal History Conference 1979* (Royal Historical Society Studies in History Series, XXII)

47e

Civil litigation: Admiralty, Delegates and Privy Council appeals

◆ ◆ ◆

47e.1 The High Court of Admiralty

This court was a civil law court, generally applying Roman or 'civil' international law. Civil disputes (concerning commercial disputes, wages, salvage and damage to ships or cargoes) were normally heard in the High Court of Admiralty (which also had a common law criminal jurisdiction, see **38.10**). The civil business of the High Court of Admiralty was conducted from c.1660 in a separate Instance Court. The records of the Instance jurisdiction are extensive, but like other legal records they can be difficult to use. The records most likely to interest family and social historians are the examinations and answers in HCA 13 (1531–1768), and the Instance papers in HCA 15–19 (1586–1874). The examinations and answers are in English and contain detailed accounts of evidence tendered by witnesses; they also include information about the witness's name, age, address, occupation and age. Instance papers contain a variety of papers including affidavits, allegations, answers, decrees, petitions and exhibits. If you know the name of your ancestor's ship, the indexes to ships' names in HCA 56 (1772–1946) can be useful.

47e.2 The High Court of Delegates

The High Court of Delegates was established during the reign of Henry VIII to hear appeals from the ecclesiastical courts which, before the break with Rome, would have been made to the Pope: as such it used canon law. It also had appellate jurisdiction from the Instance court of the High Court of Admiralty, the Court of Chivalry and the courts of the chancellors of Oxford and Cambridge Universities. Every appeal necessitated the appointment of a special commission under the great seal directed to judges delegate appointed by the Lord Chancellor. Its records are in DEL, and its lists are searchable online. The Court was abolished in 1833.

47e.3 The Judicial Committee of the Privy Council

The Privy Council devolved its judicial authority to a committee in 1833. It took over the old High Court of Delegates jurisdiction in matrimonial, ecclesiastical and maritime appeals until 1858 (1879 for maritime cases). Its records are listed under PCAP, and are largely searchable online.

The PRO does not hold records of the Judicial Committee's criminal or modern civil appeal jurisdiction as the court of appeal for colonial or ex-colonial jurisdictions. These are still kept by the Judicial Committee, and an appointment is needed to see them (address in **48**).

47e.4 Civil litigation: Admiralty, Delegates and Privy Council appeals: bibliography

J H Baker, *An Introduction to English Legal History* (London, 3rd edn, 1990)
G I O Duncan, *The High Court of Delegates,* (Cambridge, 1971)
P A Howell, *The Judicial Committee of the Privy Council, 1833–1876, its origins, structure, and development* (Cambridge, 1979)
R G Marsden, *Select pleas in the Court of Admiralty* (Selden Society, 1897)
M J Prichard and D E C Yale, *Hale and Fleetwood on Admiralty Jurisdiction* (Selden Society, 1992)

48

Useful addresses

◆ ◆ ◆

Army *see* Ministry of Defence

Army Medical Services Museum, Keogh Barracks, Ash Vale, Aldershot GU12 5RQ; tel: 01252 340212; internet: www.army.mod.uk/medical/ams_museum

Association of Genealogists and Researchers in Archives, 29 Badgers Close, Horsham, West Sussex, RH12 5RU; internet: www.agra.org.uk

Association of Scottish Genealogists and Record Agents, 51/3 Mortonhall Road, Edinburgh EH9 2HN; internet: www.asgra.co.uk

Bedfordshire Record Office, County Hall, Bedford MK42 9AP; tel: 01234 228833 ext 2833

Black Cultural Archives, 378 Coldharbour Lane, London SW9 8LF; tel: 020 7738 4591

Borthwick Institute of Historical Research, St Anthony's Hall, Peasholme Green, York YO1 7PW; tel: 01904 642315; internet: www.york.ac.uk/inst/bihr

British Association for Cemeteries in South Asia, 76½ Chartfield Avenue, London SW15 6HQ; internet: http://members.ozemail.com.au/~clday/bacsa.htm

British in India Museum, 1 Newtown Street, Colne, Lancashire BB8 0JJ; tel: 01282 870215

British Library, 96 Euston Road, London NW1 2DB; tel: 020 7412 7677; internet: www.bl.uk

British Library Newspaper Library, Colindale Avenue, London NW9 5HE; tel: 020 7412 7353; internet: www.bl.uk/collections/newspaper/overview.html

British Library, Oriental and India Office Collections, 96 Euston Rd, London NW1 2DP; tel: 020 7412 7873; internet: www.bl.uk/collections/oriental/

British Red Cross, British Red Cross Museum and Archives, 9 Grosvenor Crescent, London, SW1X 7EJ; tel: 020 7201 5153; internet: www.redcross.org.uk

Business Archives Council, 101 Whitechapel High Street, London E1 7RE; tel: 020 7247 0024; internet: www.archives.gla.ac.uk/bac/

Business Archives Council of Scotland, University of Glasgow, Glasgow G12 8QQ; internet: www.archives.gla.ac.uk/bacs

Cambridgeshire Record Office, Shire Hall, Cambridge CB3 0AP

Canterbury Cathedral Library, The Precincts, Canterbury CT1 2EG

Carmarthenshire Archives Service, County Hall, Carmarthen, Dyfed SA31 1JP; tel: 01267 224184; internet: www.llgc.org.uk/cac/cac0028.htm

Catholic Central Library, Lancing Street, London NW1 1ND; tel: 020 7383 4333; internet: www.catholic-library.org.uk

Channel Islands Family History Society, PO Box 507, St Helier, Jersey JE4 5TN; internet: http://user.itl.net/~glen/AbouttheChannelIslandsFHS.html

Chaplain General of the Army, Trenchard Lines, Upavon, Wilts, SN9 6BE; internet: www.armychaplains.com

Chaplain of the Fleet, Room 203, Victory Buildings, HM Naval Base, Portsmouth, PO1 3LS

Chatham Historic Dockyard, Chatham, Kent ME4 4TZ; internet: www.worldnavalbase.org.uk

Child Migrants Trust, 28A Musters Road, West Bridgford, Nottingham NG2 7PL; internet: www.nottscc.gov.uk/child_migrants

City of London Police Record Office, 26 Old Jewry, London EC2R 8DJ

College of Arms, Queen Victoria Street, London EC4V 4BT; internet: www.college-of-arms.gov.uk

Commonwealth War Graves Commission, Information Office, 2 Marlow Road, Maidenhead, Berks SL6 7DX; tel: 01628 634221; internet: www.cwgc.org

Companies Registration Office, Crown Way, Maindy, Cardiff CF4 3UZ; tel: 0870 3333636; internet: www.companieshouse.gov.uk

Corporation of London Record Office, PO Box 270, Guildhall, London EC2P 2EJ; tel: 020 7332 1251; internet: www.cityoflondon.gov.uk

Department for International Development, Overseas Pension Department, Abercrombie House, Eaglesham Road, East Kilbride G75 8EA; internet: www.dfid.gov.uk

East Riding of Yorkshire Archives Service, County Hall, Beverley, HU17 9BA; tel: 01482 392788; internet: www.eastriding.gov.uk/learning/archives/

Family Records Centre, 1 Myddelton St, London EC1R 1UW; tel: 020 8392 5300; internet: www.familyrecords.gov.uk/frc.htm

Federation of Family History Societies, Administrator, PO Box 2425, Coventry CV5 6YX; tel: 07041 492032; internet: www.ffhs.org.uk/

Fleet Air Arm Museum, Records & Research Centre, Box D6, RNAS Yeovilton, nr Ilchester, Somerset, BA22 8HT; tel: 01935 840565; internet: www.fleetairarm.com/

Foreign and Commonwealth Office, Records and Historical Service Unit, Hanslope Park, Hanslope, Milton Keynes MK19 7BH

Friends House Library, Euston Road, London NW1 2BJ; tel: 020 7388 1977; internet: www.quaker.org.uk/library

Friends of the PRO, Public Record Office, Kew, Richmond, Surrey TW9 4DU; tel: 020 8876 3444 ext. 2226; internet: www.pro.gov.uk/yourpro/friends.htm

Genealogical Society of South Africa, Suite 143, Postnet, X2600, Houghton 2041, Republic of South Africa; internet: www.rootsweb.com/~zafgssa/Eng/

Genealogical Society of Utah, 50 East North Temple, Salt Lake City, Utah 84150, USA; internet: www.lds.org www.familysearch.org

Genealogical Society of Utah, British Isles Family History Service Centre, 185 Penns Lane, Sutton Coldfield, West Midlands B76 8JU; tel: 08700 102051

General Register Office of England and Wales
- Adoptions Section, Trafalgar Rd, Southport PR8 2HH; tel: 0151 471 4313
- Certificate enquiries, PO Box 2, Southport, Merseyside PR8 2JD; tel: 0870 243 7788
- Family Records Centre, 1 Myddelton St, London EC1R 1UW; tel: 020 8392 5300
- *Traceline*, PO Box 106, Southport PR8 2WA; tel: 0151 471 4811 (Mon-Fri 9:00-4:30); fax: 01704 563354
- Corrections and Re-Registration, Room D209, Smedley Hydro, Trafalgar Road, Birkdale, Southport, PR8 2HH; tel: 0151 471 4806; internet: www.statistics.gov.uk/

General Register Office of Ireland, 8–11 Lombard Street, Dublin 2, Republic of Ireland; tel: 00 35 31 635 4000; internet: www.groireland.ie

General Register Office of Northern Ireland, Oxford House, 49–55 Chichester Street, Belfast BT1 4HL; tel: 028 9025 2000; internet: www.groni.gov.uk

General Register Office of Scotland, New Register House, Edinburgh EH1 3YT; tel: 0131 334 0380; internet: www.open.gov.uk/gros/groshome.htm

General Registry (Isle of Man), Finch Rd, Douglas, Isle of Man; tel: 01629 673358; internet: www.gov.im/infocentre/faqs/FAQ21.HTML

Gray's Inn Library, 5 South Square, Gray's Inn, London WC1R 5EU; internet: www.graysinn.org.uk

Greffe, Royal Court House, St Peter Port, Guernsey GY1 2PB; tel: 01481 725277

Guards Regimental Headquarters, The Coldstream/Grenadier/Irish/Scots/Welsh Guards (deleta as appropriate), Wellington Barracks, Birdcage Walk, London SW1E 6HQ

Guild of One Name Studies, Box G, c/o 14 Charterhouse Buildings, Goswell Road, London EC1M 7BA; internet: www.one-name.org/

Guildhall Library, Aldermanbury, London EC2P 2EJ; tel: 020 7332 1863; internet: www.ihr.sas.ac.uk/gh/

Hartley Library, Special Collections, University of Southampton, Highfield, Southampton SO17 1BJ; tel: 023 8059 2721; internet: www.archives.lib.soton.ac.uk/guide

Historic Manuscripts Commission, Quality House, Quality Court, Chancery Lane, London WC2A 1HP; tel: 020 7242 1198; internet: www.hmc.gov.uk

HMS *Belfast,* Symons Wharf, Vine Lane, Tooley Street, London SE1 2JH; internet: www.iwm.org.uk/belfast

HMS *Centurion see* Ministry of Defence

HMS *Victory,* HM Naval Base, Portsmouth, Hampshire PO1 3PZ; internet: www.hms-victory.com

Home Office, Departmental Record Officer, 50 Queen Anne's Gate, London, SW1H 9AT; internet: www.homeoffice.gov.uk

House of Lords Record Office, House of Lords, London SW1A 0PW; tel: 020 7219 5316; internet: www.parliament.the-stationery-office.co.uk/pa/genlinfo.htm

Huguenot Library, University College, Gower Street, London WC1E 6BT; tel: 020 7697 7094; internet: www.ucl.ac.uk/Library/huguenot.htm

Immigration and Nationality Department, Nationality Office, B4 Division, India Buildings, Water Street, Liverpool L2 0QN; tel: 0151 2375200; internet: www.ind.homeoffice.gov.uk

Imperial War Museum, Department of Documents, Lambeth Road London SE1 6HZ; tel: 020 7416 5221; internet: www.iwm.org.uk/

Imperial War Museum, Duxford, Cambridgeshire CB2 4QR; internet: www.iwm.org.uk/duxford

India Office Library and Records *see* British Library, Oriental and India Office Collections

Inner Temple Library, Inner Temple, London EC4Y 7DA; internet: www.innertemplelibrary.org.uk

Insolvency Service, Bankruptcy Public Search Room, 2nd Floor, West Wing, 45-46 Stephenson Street, Birmingham B2 4UP; tel: 0121 698 4000; internet: www.insolvency.gov.uk

Institute of Heraldic and Genealogical Studies, 79-82 Northgate, Canterbury, Kent CT1 1BA; tel: 01227 768664; internet: www.ihgs.ac.uk/

International Council of the Red Cross, Archives Division, 19 Avenue de la Paix, CH–1202 Geneva, Switzerland; internet: www.icrc.org

International Society for British Genealogy and Family History, PO Box 3115, Salt Lake City, Utah 84110–3115, USA

Irish Genealogical Research Society, 82 Eaton Square, London SW1W 9AJ; internet: www.igrsoc.org

Island Archive Service, 29 Victoria Road, St Peter Port, Guernsey GY1 1HU; tel: 01481 724512; internet: http://user.itl.net/~glen/archgsy.html

Jersey Archive, Clarence Road, St Helier, Jersey JE2 4JY; internet: www.jerseyheritagetrust.org

Judicial Committee of the Privy Council, Privy Council Office, Downing Street, London SW1A 0PW; tel: 020–7270-0483/0485/0487; internet: www.privy-council.org.uk/judicial-committee/

Kingston University, Centre for Local History Studies, Penrhyn Road, Kingston upon Thames, Surrey KT1 2EE; internet: http://humansciences.king.ac.uk/humanities/history/local/project.htm

Lambeth Palace Library, Lambeth Palace Road, London SE1 7JU; tel: 020 7928 6222; internet: www.lambethpalacelibrary.org

Land Registry, Lincoln's Inn Fields, London WC2A 3PH; tel: 020 7917 8888; internet: www.landreg.gov.uk

Law Society Archives, Ipsley Court, Berrington Close, Redditch, Worcestershire; tel: 020 7242 1222; internet: www.lawsoc.org.uk

Library of Congress, Washington DC 20540, USA; internet: www.loc.gov

Lincoln's Inn Library, Lincoln's Inn, London WC2A 3TN; internet: www.lincolnsinn.org.uk

List and Index Society, Public Record Office, Kew, Richmond, Surrey, TW9 4DU

London Metropolitan Archives, 40 Northampton Road, London EC1R 0HB; internet: www.cityoflondon.gov.uk

Manorial Documents Register, Historic Manuscripts Commission, Quality House, Quality Court, Chancery Lane, London WC2A 1HP; tel: 020 7242 1198; internet: www.hmc.gov.uk/mdr

Manx National Heritage Library, Manx Museum, Kingswood Grove, Douglas, Isle of Man IM1 3LY; tel: 01624 648000; internet: www.gov.im/mnh

Maritime History Archive, Memorial University of Newfoundland, Memorial University of Newfoundland, St John's Newfoundland, Canada A1C 5S7; internet: www.mun.ca/mha

Metropolitan Police Archives, New Scotland Yard, Victoria St, London SW1 0BG; internet: www.met.police.uk/

Metropolitan Police Museum, c/o Room 1334, New Scotland Yard, Victoria Street, London SW1 0BG

Middle Temple Library, Middle Temple Lane, London EC4Y 98T; internet: www.middletemple.org.uk

Ministry of Defence Service Records
Army
[For personnel records after early 1920s]

Army Personnel Records, CS(R)2b, Bourne Avenue, Hayes, Middlesex, UB3 1RF; internet: www.army.mod.uk/contacts/divisions/records.htm

Military graves outside the World Wars
PS4(CAS)(A), Bourne Avenue, Hayes, Middlesex, UB3 1RF

Polish Service
[For personnel records, 1939–1945]

Polish Service Personnel Records, CS(R)2e, Bourne Avenue, Hayes, Middlesex, UB3 1RF

Royal Air Force
[For casualties on non-operational flights]

Air Historical Branch, Building 266, Royal Air Force, Bentley Priory, Stanmore, Middlesex HA7 3HH

[For personnel records after early 1920s]

RAF Personnel Management Agency, *[For officers]* PMA(CS)2a(2)a or *[For airmen]* PMA(CS)2a(2)b, RAF Innsworth, Gloucester GL3 1EZ

[For medal claims]
RAF Personnel Management Agency, Sec 1c, Building 248A, RAF Innsworth, Gloucester GL3 1EZ

Royal Marines
[For Marines enlisted or commissioned during or after 1930]
Royal Marines, Historical Record Office, HMS *Centurion*, Grange Road, Gosport, Hampshire PO13 9XA; tel: 023 9282 2351

Royal Navy
[For other ranks who enlisted between 1924 and 2 September 1939]
[For officers commissioned between 1916 and 1950, who are dead or retired aged 60+]
Royal Naval Records, DR2A Navy Search, Bourne Avenue, Hayes, Middlesex, UB3 1RF
[For other ranks enlisted from 3 September 1939 onwards] Naval Pay and Pensions, HMS *Centurion* Grange Road, Gosport, Hampshire PO13 9XA
[For commissioned officers still serving, or retired under 60]
Naval Secretary, Victory Building, HM Naval Base, Portsmouth, Hampshire, PO1 3LS
[For medal claims]
Medals Section, HMS *Centurion*, Grange Road, Gosport, Hampshire PO13 9XA

Mitchell Library in Sydney, State Library of New South Wales, Macquarie St, Sydney NSW 2000, Australia; internet: www.slnsw.gov.au
Mocatta Library, University College, Gower Street, London WC1E 6BT; internet: www.ucl.ac.uk/Library/jewish.htm
Modern Records Centre, University of Warwick, Library, Coventry CV4 7AL; tel: 024 7652 4219; internet: http://modernrecords.warwick.ac.uk/

National Archives of Australia, PO Box 7425, Canberra Mail Centre, ACT Australia 2610; tel: (00) 61 2 6212 3600; internet: www.naa.gov.au
National Archives of Canada, 395 Wellington St, Ottawa, Ontario K1A 0N3, Canada; tel: 00 1 613 995 5138; internet: www.archives.ca
National Archives of Ireland, Bishop St, Dublin 8, Ireland; tel: 00 35 31 407 2300; internet: www.nationalarchives.ie
National Archives of Scotland, HM General Register House, Edinburgh EH1 3YY; tel: 0131 535 1314; internet: www.nas.gov.uk
National Archives of South Africa, Private Bag X236, Pretoria 0001, South Africa; internet: www.national.archives.gov.za
National Army Museum, Department of Records, Royal Hospital Rd, London SW3 4HT; tel: 020 7730 0717; internet: www.national-army-museum.ac.uk
National Genealogical Society, 4527 17th St North, Arlington, Virginia 22207–2399, USA; internet: www.ngsgenealogy.org
National Library of Australia, Parkes Place, Canberra, ACT 2600, Australia; internet: www.nla.gov.au

National Library of Scotland, George IV Bridge, Edinburgh EH1 1EW; tel: 0131 226 4531; internet: www.nls.uk

National Library of Wales, Aberystwyth, Dyfed SY23 3BU; tel: 01970 623816; internet: www.llgc.org.uk

National Maritime Museum, Romney Road, London SE10 9NF; tel: 020 8858 4422; internet: www.nmm.ac.uk

National Register of Archives, Historic Manuscripts Commission, Quality House, Quality Court, Chancery Lane, London WC2A 1HP; tel: 020 7242 1198; internet: www.hmc.gov.uk/nra

National Register of Archives (Scotland), West Register House, Charlotte Square, Edinburgh EH2 4DF; tel: 0131 535 1314

Naval Dockyards Society, c/o 44 Lindley Avenue, Southsea, Hampshire PO4 9NV; internet: www.hants.gov.uk/navaldockyard

Norfolk Record Office, Gildengate House, Anglia Square, Upper Green Lane, Norwich NR3 1AX; tel: 01603 761349; internet: http://archives.norfolk.gov.uk/

North Yorkshire County Record Office, County Hall, Northallerton, DL7 8AF; tel: 01609 777585; internet: www.northyorks.gov.uk/education

Portsmouth Historic Dockyard, Flagship Portsmouth Trust, Building 1/7, Porter's Lodge, College Road, HM Naval Base, Portsmouth PO1 3LJ; tel: 023 9286 1512; internet: www.flagship.org.uk/welcome.html

Priaulx Library, Candie, St Peter Port, Guernsey GY1 1UG; tel: 01481 721998; internet: www.gov.gg/priaulx/

Principal Registry of the Family Division, Decree Absolute Section, First Avenue House, 42–49 High Holborn, London WC1V 6NP

Principal Registry of the Family Division, Probate Searchroom, First Avenue House, 42–49 High Holborn, London WC1V 6NP; internet: www.courtservice. gov.uk/fandl/prob_guidance.htm

Public Record Office, Kew, Richmond, Surrey TW9 4DU; tel: 020 8392 5200; internet: www.pro.gov.uk

Public Record Office of Northern Ireland (PRONI), 66 Balmoral Avenue, Belfast BT9 6NY; tel: 01232 251318; internet: http://proni.nics.gov.uk/

RAF Innsworth see Ministry of Defence

RAF Museum, Department of Aviation Records (Archives), Hendon Aerodrome, London NW9 5LL; tel: 020 8205 2266; internet: www.rafmuseum.org.uk

Registry of Deeds, King's Inn, Henrietta St, Dublin 1, Republic of Ireland; tel: 00 35 31 670 7500; internet: www.irlgov.ie/landreg

Registry of Shipping and Seamen, PO Box 165, Cardiff CF4 5JA; tel: 029 2074 7333

Royal Archives, Windsor Castle, Windsor, Berkshire SL4 1NJ; tel: 01753 831118 ext.260

Royal Courts of Justice, (for recent changes of name), Room 81, Strand, London WC2A 2LL; tel: 020 7947 6528

Royal Hospital Chelsea, Museum Curator, Royal Hospital Road, London SW3 47R

Royal Marines Museum, Eastney, Southsea, Hampshire PO4 9PX; tel: 023 9281 9385; internet: www.royalmarinesmuseum.co.uk

Royal Marines *see* Ministry of Defence

Royal Military Police, Roussillon Barracks, Chichester, Sussex PO19 4BL; tel: 01243 786311 ext. 237; internet: www.rhqrmp.freeserve.co.uk

Royal Naval Museum, HM Naval Base, Portsmouth, Hampshire PO1 3NH; tel: 023 9272 7577; internet: www.royalnavalmuseum.org

Royal Navy *see* Ministry of Defence

Royal Patriotic Fund, 40 Queen Anne's Gate, London SW1H 9AP

Scots Ancestry Research Society, 8 York Road, Edinburgh EH5 3EH; internet: *www.royalmile.com/scotsancestry*

Scottish Genealogy Society, 15 Victoria Terrace, Edinburgh EH1 2JL; internet: *www.sol.co.uk/scotgensoc*

Société Guernesiase, Family History Section, PO Box 314, Candie, St Peter Port, Guernsey GY1 3TG; internet: www.societe.gov.gg

Sociét´ Jersiase, Lord Coutanche Library, 7 Pier Rd, St Helier, Jersey JE2 4XW; tel: 01534 730538; internet: www.societe-jersiaise.org

Society of Genealogists, 14 Charterhouse Buildings, Goswell Road, London EC1M 7BA; tel: 020 7251 8799; internet: www.sog.org.uk

Southampton City Archives, South Block, Civic Centre, Southampton, SO14 7LY; tel: 023 8083 2251; internet: www.southampton.gov.uk/education/libraries/arch.htm

State Records New South Wales, PO Box R625, Royal Exchange NSW 1225, Australia; internet: www.records.nsw.gov.au/

Superintendent Registrar of Jersey, 10 Royal Square, St Helier, Jersey JE2 4WA; tel: 01534 502335

Thomas Coram Foundation, 40 Brunswick Square, London WC1N 1AZ

Wapping Police Museum, 98 Wapping High Street, London E1

Wellcome Library for the History and Understanding of Medicine, Wellcome Building (2nd floor) 183 Euston Road, London NW1 2BE; tel: 020 7611 8582; internet: http://library.wellcome.ac.uk/

West Yorkshire Archives Service, Registry of Deeds, Newstead Rd, Wakefield WF1 2DE; tel: 01924 305980; internet: www.archives.wyjs.org.uk/wrrd1.htm

York Probate Sub-registry, Postal Searches and Copies Department, Duncombe Place, York, YO1 7EA; tel: 01904 624210; internet: www.courtservice.gov.uk/wills_probate/prob_guidance.htm

Index

◆ ◆ ◆

Figure 70 All human life is here ... (*Illustrated London News* 1851, PRO, ZPER 34/18)